12.95

KT-489-550

CAMBRIDGE TEXTBOOKS IN LINGUISTICS

General Editors: B. COMRIE, C. J. FILLMORE, R. LASS, D. LIGHTFOOT, J. LYONS, P. H. MATTHEWS, R. POSNER, S. ROMAINE, N. V. SMITH, N. VINCENT

Andrew Linn
Cambridge 1990

HISTORICAL LINGUISTICS

In this series:

P. H. MATTHEWS *Morphology*
B. COMRIE *Aspect*
R. KEMPSON *Semantics*
J. ALLWOOD, L.-G. ANDERSON, O. DAHL (eds.) *Logic in Linguistics*
D. B. FRY *The Physics of Speech*
R. A. HUDSON *Sociolinguistics*
J. K. CHAMBERS and P. TRUDGILL *Dialectology*
A. J. ELLIOT *Child Language*
P. H. MATTHEWS *Syntax*
L. BAUER *English Word-formation*
S. C. LEVINSON *Pragmatics*
G. BROWN and G. YULE *Discourse Analysis*
R. HUDDLESTON *Introduction to the Grammar of English*
R. LASS *Phonology*
B. COMRIE *Tense*
W. KLEIN *Second Language Acquisition*
A. CRUTTENDEN *Intonation*
A. J. WOODS, P. FLETCHER and A. HUGHES *Statistics in Language Studies*
D. A. CRUSE *Lexical Semantics*
F. R. PALMER *Mood and Modality*
A. RADFORD *Transformational Grammar*

HISTORICAL LINGUISTICS

THEODORA BYNON
READER IN HISTORICAL LINGUISTICS
UNIVERSITY OF LONDON

The right of the University of Cambridge to print and sell all manner of books was granted by Henry VIII in 1534. The University has printed and published continuously since 1584.

CAMBRIDGE UNIVERSITY PRESS
CAMBRIDGE
NEW YORK PORT CHESTER
MELBOURNE SYDNEY

Published by the Press Syndicate of the University of Cambridge
The Pitt Building, Trumpington Street, Cambridge CB2 1RP
40 West 20th Street, New York, NY 10011, USA
10 Stamford Road, Oakleigh, Melbourne 3166, Australia

First published 1977
Reprinted with corrections 1978
Reprinted 1979
Reprinted with corrections and additional bibliography 1983
Reprinted 1985, 1986, 1990

Printed in Great Britain at The Bath Press, Avon

Library of Congress catalogue card number: 76-62588

ISBN 0 521 21582 x hard covers
ISBN 0 521 29188 7 paperback

CONTENTS

Key to symbols used ix *Preface* x

	Introduction	1
	Part One: Models of language development	
1	The neogrammarian model	17
1	*Basic issues*	17
1.1	*Synchronic irregularity*	17
1.2	*Cross-language similarity*	21
2	*The Indo-European languages*	22
3	*The neogrammarians*	23
4	*Sound change: the regularity principle*	24
5	*Analogy*	32
5.1	*Analogical change*	35
5.2	*Analogical creation*	40
6	*The interdependence of sound change and analogy*	43
7	*Phonological reconstruction ('the comparative method')*	45
7.1	*Correspondence series and protosegments*	46
7.2	*Diachronic rules: form and order*	53
8	*Morphological and syntactic reconstruction*	57
8.1	*Morphology*	58
8.2	*Syntax*	60
9	*Lexical reconstruction*	61
10	*Relatedness of languages (genealogical, or genetic, relationship)*	63
10.1	*The family tree model*	63
10.2	*Protolanguages*	70
2	The structuralist model of language evolution	76
1	*Paradigmatic aspects of phonological change*	77
1.1	*Structure*	77
1.1.1	*Phonological segments*	77
1.1.2	*Phonological features*	80

1.2 *Function* 86
2 *Traces of past phonological change remaining in morphological structure: internal reconstruction* 89
3 *Changes affecting grammatical categories and their exponents* 99
4 *Limitations of structuralist methods applied to diachrony* 104

3 The transformational-generative model of language evolution 108
1 *Phonological change* 110
1.1 *Innovation* 114
1.2 *Systematic restructuring: formal conditions* 122
1.2.1 *Rule simplification* 123
1.2.2 *Rule reordering* 126
1.2.3 *Reduction in rule input (lexical simplification)* 131
1.3 *Systematic restructuring: output conditions* 132
1.3.1 *Reordering which results in increased paradigmatic uniformity* 132
1.3.2 *The form of lexical entries* 133
1.3.3 *Phonotactic constraints* 135
1.3.4 *The motivation of systematic restructuring* 136
1.4 *Synchronic and diachronic grammars* 140
2 *Syntactic change* 145
2.1 *Changes in the syntax of the noun phrase* 147
2.1.1 *Changes in the transformational rule system* 149
2.1.2 *Changes in deep structure* 154
2.2 *Changes in the syntax of the verb phrase* 159
2.3 *Changes in the syntactic properties of lexical items* 167

Part Two: Language contact 171

4 The neogrammarian postulates and dialect geography 173
1 *The domain of a sound change* 173
2 *Lexical replacement: the failure of the 'phonetic etymologies'* 183
3 *Do dialect boundaries exist?* 190
4 *The wave theory* 192
5 *Mutual intelligibility* 196
6 *The social dimension* 196

5 The social motivation of language change 198
1 *The social stratification of language: the evaluation of linguistic variables* 198
2 *The synchronic reflection of historical change* 204
3 *The mechanism of language change* 213

6 Contact between languages 216
1 *Lexical borrowing* 217
1.1 *Loan-words* 217
1.2 *Loan translations (calques)* 232
1.3 *Semantic extension (semantic calques)* 237
1.4 *The structural effects of lexical borrowing* 239
2 *Grammatical borrowing* 239
2.1 *Bilingualism and interference between languages* 239
2.2 *Linguistic areas* 244
2.2.1 *The Balkan linguistic area* 246
2.2.2 *Europe as a linguistic area* 248
2.3 *Restrictions on borrowing* 253
3 *Pidgin and creole languages* 256

7 Language and prehistory 262
1 *Classification and language history* 262
1.1 *Typology and language history* 262
1.2 *Glottochronology (or lexicostatistics)* 266
2 *Linguistic reconstruction and prehistory* 272
2.1 *The evidence of toponymy* 273
2.2 *The evidence of the protolexicon* 278

Further reading 281

References 283

Additional bibliography 295

Index 304

KEY TO SYMBOLS USED

The system of transcription adopted is essentially that of the International Phonetic Alphabet; note however that for the palatal semivowel the symbol [y] has been used rather than IPA [j] and for the rounded high front vowel the symbol [ü] has been substituted for IPA [y].

/ /	encloses an (autonomous) phonemic transcription except in chapter 3 where it marks a systematic phonemic notation
[ ]	encloses a phonetic transcription (systematic phonetic in chapter 3)
:	marks length; thus [a:] is 'long a'
~	'alternates with'
≠	'contrasts with'
#	word boundary
ø	zero morph
→	'is rewritten as' (that is to say 'becomes' in synchronic description)
>	'becomes' in historical linguistics
<	'comes from' in historical linguistics
*	marks a reconstructed earlier form
**	marks a non-attested ungrammatical form in synchronic description
C	any consonant
V	any vowel
S	sentence
NP	noun phrase
VP	verb phrase
PrepP	prepositional phrase
Pron	pronoun
Dem	demonstrative
Aux	auxiliary
Q	question
WH	marks the constituent which is questioned

PREFACE

Although language change has now been studied systematically for a period of one hundred years and somewhat less systematically for a good deal longer than that, there is still a considerable amount of disagreement about its nature and motivation. I have for this reason made no attempt at presenting a theoretically unified account but have rather thought it more useful to describe in chronological sequence the three major models that have been proposed in order to account for the phenomena of language change, that is to say the neogrammarian, the structuralist, and the transformational-generative models. It is my hope that this approach, by making explicit the major points of difference which separate these three schools of thought and allowing the reader to assess their respective merits and weaknesses, may perhaps go some small way towards closing the gap which has arisen between traditional comparative philology and modern theoretical linguistics.

I owe a lasting debt of gratitude to my late teacher Hans Krahe who first introduced me to the rigours of neogrammarian methodology. I am equally indebted to both colleagues and students at the School of Oriental and African Studies for exposing me to the no less rigorous methods of structuralism and transformational grammar and for giving me the opportunity of discussing problems of linguistic comparison outside the Indo-European field. R. H. Robins and Eugénie Henderson in particular were kind enough to read through an earlier version of Part I and to make valuable suggestions. I am also most grateful to W. S. Allen for his extremely helpful criticism and comment on the manuscript as a whole while it was still in draft. And lastly, the script would never have reached its final form without my husband's untiring encouragement and readiness to discuss the problems both of historical linguistics and of English grammar.

London, March 1977 Th.B.

Introduction

Historical linguistics seeks to investigate and describe the way in which languages change or maintain their structure during the course of time; its domain therefore is language in its *diachronic* aspect. Descriptive linguistics on the other hand totally disregards time as a relevant factor in its investigations and attributes to the data a uniform status of simultaneity; its concern is therefore language in its *synchronic* aspect. It will thus be seen that it is not simply the greater or lesser extension in time of the data being investigated which constitutes the fundamental difference between synchronic and diachronic analysis, but rather the linguist's attitude towards the time dimension itself.[1]

Justification for the claim to independent status of synchronic description derives essentially from the observation that the speakers for whom a particular language serves as a means of communication are in general quite unaware of its historical dimension. If, then, the linguist is to create a model of the code which the members of a speech

[1] De Saussure is usually credited with having been the first to make explicit this distinction in his *Cours*, published posthumously in 1916 (de Saussure 1964: 114ff.). He saw the history of a language as a succession of synchronic states, each a complete system *où tout se tient* and therefore definable only in terms of the relationships existing between its various opposing elements. Change on the other hand he saw as applying not directly to the system as a whole but only to individual elements of it, and this in a completely unmotivated and fortuitous fashion. As a result, although each individual change will bring about a new synchronic system capable of description in structuralist terms, there is no such meaningful relationship between successive language states and language change is therefore not amenable to description *in terms of the systems*. De Saussure's position with regard to language change was challenged at the First International Congress of Linguists in 1928 when, in a resolution put forward by among others Trubetzkoy and Jakobson, it was claimed that the diachronic aspect of language is just as amenable to structuralist methods as its synchronic aspect and that every change must be treated as a function of the system as a whole (see Jakobson 1972a: 122).

community share and through which they communicate with one another, this must surely be equally independent of all historical considerations.

But that language does in fact change during the course of time soon becomes evident when documents written in the same language but at different periods in time are subjected to examination. And, once allowance has been made for those orthographic and stylistic conventions which are characteristic of languages in their written form, it may fairly be assumed that such texts are representative samples of the spoken language as it was when they were committed to writing, structured in accordance with the synchronic rules then operating. This means that it is possible to abstract the grammatical structure of the language of each period from the documents and in this way a series of synchronic grammars may be set up and compared. The differences in their successive structures may then be interpreted as reflecting the historical development of the language. In this sense diachronic linguistics may be said to be secondary to synchronic linguistics, since the historical linguist deduces the changes that a language has undergone from the comparison of successive synchronic grammars.

We should beware, however, of confusing the image which must result from such a method with the linguistic reality. The representation of the evolution of a language as consisting in a succession of discrete states is no more a true reflection of the situation than is the representation of a circle by a number of straight lines connecting successive points around its circumference. For, however large a number of such points are taken the resulting figure will never be a genuine circle and, in the same way, however many language states are considered over a given period their succession will never provide a true picture of the unbroken *continuity* of a language in time. It is thus due to the limitations of our methodology that we are faced with the rather absurd situation that language evolution, although observable retrospectively in its *results*, appears to totally elude observation as a *process* while it is actually taking place. We shall see that there are two reasons why this should be so, one relating to certain theoretical assumptions which underlie synchronic analysis and the other to the manner in which language itself is transmitted. Let us consider these in turn.

The first factor which obscures the process of historical change is the fact that the synchronic analysis of a language always requires a certain degree of idealization of the data. For it should not be forgotten that when a linguist makes statements about 'a language', be it in relation to its synchronic structure or to its historical development, this is an abstraction from the observable reality, which can never be more than that of individuals employing speech as a vehicle of communication. And this reality as actually observed is never one of complete homogeneity. There will always be found to be differences between speakers dependent upon geographical location and social class, and there are always variations in the speech of the individual speaker dependent upon the formality of the occasion. These differences do not of course prevent communication, although it is true to say that the wider the range of individuals, localities and classes with which a speaker is confronted, the more likely is it that he will experience some difficulty in understanding everything that is said. Correspondingly, the wider the spectrum in social and geographic terms that the linguist attempts to embrace in his analysis, the greater the degree of abstraction that he must operate in order to maintain homogeneity in his data. This he will achieve in practice by eliminating from his account all individual, local and class-related variations, justifying their omission by pointing to the fact that communication is possible in spite of them and that they are not representative of the speech habits of the community as a whole. Depending upon his theoretical outlook, the linguist will therefore either restrict his analysis to a specific language sample (such as the slow careful speech of an educated speaker) and thus exclude from consideration a whole range of alternative speech patterns actually present in the community, or he will claim that his description is of *langue* (or *competence*) and thus only indirectly related to *parole* (or *performance*) to which speech variation within the community properly belongs. Different schools of thought will thus express the convention in different ways, so that for a structuralist 'descriptive procedure establishes the fiction that the various utterances to be dealt with have no temporal or spatial or social order' (Hockett) while for a generative grammarian 'a grammar of a language purports to be a description of the ideal speaker-hearer's competence', the ideal speaker-hearer being lodged in 'a completely homogeneous speech-community' (Chomsky 1965:4,3). But we shall see that, by representing something which is inherently endowed with variation as if it were of uniform structure, such conventional simplification of the data has the effect of excluding from the analysis precisely those aspects of linguistic structure which appear to be most closely connected with the promotion of language change. For there is good evidence to suggest that synchronic variation in the speech of a community is precisely the vehicle by means of which language change progresses, the favouring or disfavouring (and thus the survival or elimination) of competing variants being governed by social pressures. The rigidly uniform structures of conventional synchronic description simply do not capture these aspects of linguistic reality.

If the degree of idealization that has gone into the description of a present language state may be checked against the spoken language, in the case of a dead language or of an earlier stage of a living one accessible only through the intermediary of written documents, such verification is of course impossible. In their case we can only guess at the distance separating the form of the language of the texts from the underlying reality. Furthermore, the language of such written texts is as a rule already the product of a considerable amount of formalization so that the linguist is obliged to work with rather uniform data which will inevitably lead to an equally uniform synchronic description. The degree of idealization required in order to achieve descriptive regularity will in fact in such cases usually be smaller than that required in the case of living languages, simply because regularity has already been largely imposed by the constraints characteristic of written style. It will thus be seen that, while synchronic description can within the limits of its own theoretical framework provide a record of the *results* of language change, the investigation of the actual change *process* will require both different data and different methods.

After this brief discussion of the part played by certain theoretical assumptions of synchronic description in concealing all direct evidence of the process of language change, we will now turn to the second factor which prevents this process from being readily accessible to observation, namely the way in which a language is perpetuated. A language only exists through the intermediary of the human beings who speak it and, since the life-spans of these are of limited duration, it must be learned afresh by each new generation of speakers if continuity is to be maintained. It has been suggested that this constantly repeated process of acquisition by young children is likely to be an important factor in language change and we will therefore examine it briefly, although it is still poorly understood in many of its details. It is clear that, while the particular language that a child will acquire is determined by its linguistic environment – it will in fact learn the language of the community in which it grows up – every child is born with an innate predisposition towards language learning. The actual process whereby language is acquired is, however, only indirectly accessible to investigation. All that can be directly observed is the model, constituted by the speech of the people around it, and the child's own output. From these it can be deduced that, by subjecting the utterances that it hears to analysis, the child constructs its own grammar. Of the form of this grammar we are however largely ignorant and this is a serious drawback since it is precisely at this stage in transmission that inherited structures are likely to be given a new interpretation differing from that of the previous generation. Glimpses of the child's analysis of the language may, however, be had when it produces incorrect forms. The use of *goed* for *went* would thus imply 'knowledge' both of the category of past tense and of its basic marker but 'ignorance' of the exceptional status of the verb *to go*. Personal innovations of this kind will as a rule quickly disappear from the child's speech under pressure from its environment. It is, however, important to note that certain changes that have actually taken place in languages are essentially of the same nature, for instance the replacement of the older form *holp* by *helped* as the past tense of the verb *to help* in English. On the other hand transformational grammar has shown that the same output may be achieved by means of different grammars, so that even if a child's linguistic output does not observably differ from that of its models, this does not necessarily imply that their grammars are identical (cf. Halle 1962).

It would be a convenient solution if language change could be interpreted simply as the direct result of 'imperfect learning' on the part of children. Such cannot, however, be considered to be the direct cause since it fails to take account of the fact that language change has both persistence and direction. In a less immediate way, however, the assumption may contain some part of truth since the child's emerging grammar, which is after all built on limited data, may well rely more heavily on certain structures of the model, those of higher frequency for instance, than others. This necessarily selective attitude towards the model might account for the fact that, by its persistent and directional nature, language change operates as if its target had in some way been laid down in advance. That adults themselves behave in accordance with certain limited overt targets, at least where careful speech is concerned, is a well-attested fact. Members of a specific group will for instance make a conscious effort to avoid such things as 'dropping one's *h*-s', using *aint* for *isn't*, or confusing *us* and *we*. This shows that at all ages people can, and in fact often do, modify their speech habits in conformity with social pressures from within the community.

We have seen that, because it is embedded in variation patterns current within the community, the process of language change lies for the most part outside the individual speaker's awareness; preoccupied with the social significance of alternative forms, he is largely unaware of their correlation with time. Furthermore the maintenance of communication between speakers of different generations imposes a degree of constraint on the rate at which change can take place. His awareness of language change is likely then to be only of an indirect nature, based on what experience he may have of completed change observable from the comparison of documents from earlier periods with the contemporary system with which he is familiar. The historical linguist is in essentially the same situation with regard to his sources. While the present state is the only one which can provide him with full information on all the phenomena, including the embedding of linguistic variation in the social structure of the community, it is only by comparison via written records of different stages of a language that he can obtain an idea of the nature of diachronic rules. It can, in fact, be said that there is an optimal time-lapse of say four or five centuries which is most favourable for the systematic study of change. This is so because on the one hand the differences between successive language states are then sufficiently large to allow the statement in the form of rules of completed changes and on the other continuity is not at stake – one is clearly still dealing with 'the same language'.

It follows from the foregoing considerations that a two-fold strategy for the investigation of language change is necessary: firstly we must study its results as abstracted from the grammatical descriptions of successive language states and, as we shall see later, of related languages; and secondly we must investigate the actual process of change as an ongoing phenomenon through the methods of sociolinguistic analysis. The first of these approaches will occupy us in the first part of this book, which will be concerned essentially with the systematic analysis of completed change, that is to say the nature of diachronic rules. With the insight thus gained we will then turn to the question of the connection between language change and social and geographical space, which will include contact both between varieties of a single language and between totally different languages. It is this second, sociolinguistic, approach to language change which will be the subject-matter of the second part of the book.

We may gain a first impression of the sort of thing that we can expect with regard to language change by looking at a few examples from languages which have been written over long stretches of time, since here we have series of datable documents whose succession may be taken to reflect the way in which these languages have changed. A convenient text to take for this purpose is the Lord's Prayer, since it is the text which in the history of mankind has probably been most widely recorded.[1] It will provide us with samples of the English language as it was at the time of Shakespeare, of Chaucer, and of King Aelfric. Although on looking at these the present-day English reader may not recognize or know how to pronounce all the words they contain, he is nevertheless likely to experience a certain sense of familiarity with the language in which they are written. There will, on the other hand, be no such feeling of recognition in the case, for example, of those written in Hungarian or Welsh. This sense of familiarity clearly has to do with the fact that he can readily identify certain segments (formatives, words, phrases) with their counterparts in present-day English.

The Lord's Prayer[2]

Authorized version (1611)

Our father which art in heauen, hallowed be thy name. Thy kyngdome come. Thy will be done in earth, as it is in heauen. Giue vs this day our daily bread. And forgiue vs our debts, as we

[1] In spite of its obvious convenience, an objection to this text as a source of syntactic information regarding the earlier stages of a language is the fact that, being the translation of a highly prestigious document, the translators may sometimes have attempted to adhere so closely to the structure of the original that they have forced the translation into a 'foreign' mould. This, for instance, could be the explanation of the treatment of *heaven* as a plural in certain of the earlier versions.

[2] The various English versions, as well as the Old High German one, are taken from Kaiser (1961); the Modern German and Welsh versions are those given in Lockwood (1972), a work which contains nearly a hundred examples of the Lord's Prayer, almost all in Indo-European languages. For the Hungarian text, taken from the Károli Bible, and for its morph-by-morph translation, I am indebted to P. A. Sherwood of the School of Slavonic and East European Studies, University of London.

forgiue our debters. And lead vs not into temptation, but deliuer vs from euill.

Wycliff's version (*late fourteenth century*)

Oure fadir þat art in heuenes, halwid be þi name; þi reume or kyngdom come to þe. Be þi wille don in herþe as it is doun in heuene. Ȝeue to vs to-day oure eche dayes bred. And forȝeue to vs oure dettis, þat is oure synnys, as we forȝeuen tu oure dettouris, þat is to men þat han synned in vs. And lede vs not in-to temptacion, but delyuere vs from euyl.

Old English (*West Saxon, ca. 1000*)

Fæder ure þu þe eart on heofonum, si þin nama gehalgod; to-becume þin rice; gewurþe þin willa on eorðan swa swa on heofonum; urne gedæghwamlican hlaf syle us to dæg; and forgyf us ure gyltas, swa swa we forgyfað urum gyltendum; and ne gelæd þu us on costnunge, ac alys us of yfele.

Modern German

Unser Vater in dem Himmel. Dein Name werde geheiligt. Dein Reich komme. Dein Wille geschehe auf Erden wie im Himmel. Unser täglich Brot gib uns heute. Und vergib uns unsere Schulden, wie wir unsern Schuldigern vergeben. Und führe uns nicht in Versuchung, sondern erlöse uns von dem Übel.

Old High German (*East Frankish, Tatian's version, ca. 830*)

Fater unser thu thar bist in himile, si giheilagot thin namo, queme thin rihhi, si thin uuillo, so her in himile ist so si her in erdu; unsar brot tagalihhaz gib uns hiutu, inti furlaz uns unsara sculdi, so uuir furlazemes unsaren sculdigon; inti ni gileitest unsih in costunga, uzouh arlosi unsih fon ubile.

Welsh (*standard version, sixteenth century*)

Ein tad, yr hwn wyt yn y nefoedd: sancteiddier dy enw.
Our father, that who art in the heavens, be-hallowed thy name.
Deled dy deyrnas. Gwneler dy ewyllys, megis yn y nef,
Come thy kingdom. Be-done thy will, as in the heaven

felly ar y ddaear hefyd. Dyro i ni heddiw ein bara beunyddiol.
so on the earth also. Give to us today our bread daily.
A maddau i ni ein dyledion, fel y maddeuwn ninnau i'n dyledwyr.
And forgive to us our debts, as forgive we to our debtors.
Ac nac arwain ni i brofedigaeth, eithr gwared ni rhag drwg.
And not lead us into temptation, but save us from evil.

Hungarian

Mi Atyánk, ki vagy a mennyekben, szenteltessék meg a te
Our father-our, who art the heavens-in, hallowed-be the thy
neved; jöjjön el a te országod; legyen meg a te akaratod,
name-thy; come the thy kingdom-thy; be the thy will-thy,
mint a mennyben ugy a földön is. A mi mindennapi
just-as the heavens-in so the earth-on also. The our every-day
kenyerünket add meg nekünk ma. És bocsásd meg a mi vétkeinket,
bread-our give to us today. And forgive the our sins-ours,
miképen mi is megbocsátunk azoknak, a kik ellenünk
in the way we also forgive those-to who against-us
vétkeztek; és ne vígy minket kísértetbe, de szabadíts meg
have-sinned; and not lead us temptation-into, but set-free
minket a gonosztól.
us the evil(-person)-from.

These samples are of course not extensive enough to allow us to make a proper analysis of the language of each period, but even without analysis we may note a certain continuity in the lexicon evident in such items as *father*, *heaven*, *name*, *come*, *earth*. We can on the other hand also see that certain syntactic rules, even in the authorized version still in use today, are not the same as those of present-day English. Thus the relative pronoun *which*, reserved in current English for non-humans as opposed to *who* which is reserved for humans, is used in the authorized version to refer to God, and in the earliest version the relative clause is introduced altogether differently by means of the personal pronoun *þu* 'thou' followed by a relative particle since lost, *þe*. But the historical linguist has to do more than merely register isolated similarities and differences, he must show in a systematic way how the rules in the language have changed. Thus, although the native speaker is able to feel the connection in a subjective way, the objective justification for associating the various English versions in spite of their numerous differences, that is to say for claiming that they all belong historically speaking to 'the same language', is the fact that *systematic relations* can be established between the grammars of successive stages. This means that the grammar of present-day English is in principle derivable by means of a series of rules from that of the English of Shakespeare's day, Shakespeare's from Chaucer's, and Chaucer's from Aelfric's.

If we now compare the languages in which the two German versions of the Lord's Prayer are written we will arrive at the same conclusion as for the languages of the English versions, namely that systematic relations hold between them and that they also therefore belong historically speaking to 'the same language'. If on the other hand we compare say present-day English and German, it will be found that although there are still a number of obvious resemblances, the relationship between their structures cannot be expressed directly in the form of rules of the type which link the various stages of English or of German. The historical linguist is, however, able to show that there is continuity between present-day English on the one hand and present-day German on the other, but that the link is not a direct one but must be made through the intermediary of an earlier common system underlying both. Diachronic rules of the type with which we are already familiar can then be set up to link that earlier common stage with each of the languages separately. Thus both languages can be shown to have developed from a common source, but along different paths or – to borrow a term from Hoenigswald (1973) – 'channels of transmission', the English of Aelfric's, Chaucer's and Shakespeare's times constituting one channel, the German of Tatian's, Wolfram's and Luther's periods the other. Because of their evolution from a single common ancestor, English and German are said to be *related* languages, and we ascribe their present-day similarities to their common origin, their differences to the fact that they have reached the present through different channels of transmission.

Welsh and English (or for that matter Welsh and German) are also related languages, although casual inspection of our text would hardly convey that impression. This is because they are much more distantly related than are English and German, that is to say they are separated from their common ancestor by a much greater time-depth and therefore by a correspondingly larger number of diachronic rules. The common ancestor of English and German, in fact, is merely an intermediate stage in an overall development which may be represented diagrammatically as follows:

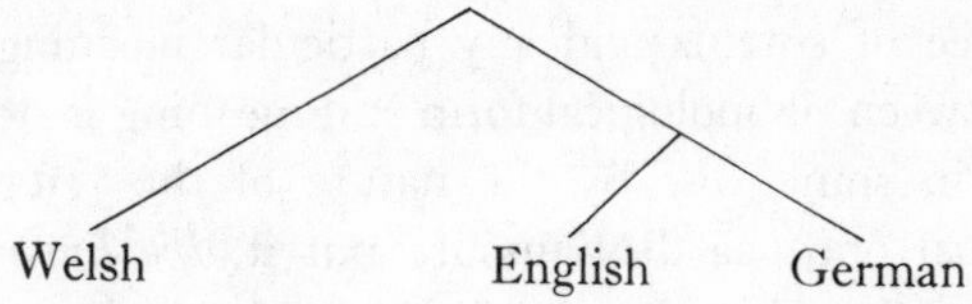

The example of Welsh shows that relatedness cannot necessarily be discovered by simple inspection. On a purely subjective basis Welsh certainly looks about as different from English as does Hungarian, and yet Welsh can be shown to be related to English while, at least in the present state of our knowledge, Hungarian cannot. Hungarian is in fact one of the few languages of Europe which do not belong to the Indo-European language family, being a member of the Finno-Ugric family of languages and related to Finnish. Whether or not the two language families are in fact themselves ultimately related cannot at present be ascertained by the methods of historical linguistics.

The theoretical justification for considering certain languages to be related, that is to say reflexes of a single parent language, rests on two observations: on the one hand there are certain inherent restrictions on the nature of the steps which can take place in language change and on the other the relationship between form and meaning in language is, in the vast majority of cases, an arbitrary one. A language may therefore be thought of as a sign system in which specific sound sequences represent specific meanings but in which, onomatopoeia and sound symbolism apart,[1] there is no necessary connection between any

[1] In all languages, of course, the arbitrariness principle is marginally violated by the presence of onomatopoeic and sound symbolic forms, in which the relationship between phonological form and meaning is to some extent motivated. Onomatopoeic forms imitate real sounds, typical examples being the name of the *cuckoo* (English *cuckoo*, German *Kuckuck*, French *coucou*, etc.) or the term used to describe the crowing of a cock (English *cock-a-doodle-doo*, German *kikeriki*, French *cocorico*), all from their actual cries. Forms such as these are, however, sufficiently restricted to well-defined semantic fields for them not to invalidate the arbitrariness principle and it should be noted that, even in their case, there is considerable latitude between the model and its linguistic codification. Sound symbolism, on the other hand, is a much less tangible phenomenon, being motivated not so much by direct imitation of an extra-linguistic acoustic model as by association with the sounds of lexical items or of parts of lexical items already existing in the language. Associative fields are thus built up of the type *flip, flap, flop, flick* etc. in English, the members of which are often found on investigation to be innovations of the post Middle English period (Marchand 1960: 313–55). Sound symbolism may of course be treated simply as a special case of onomatopoeia in which the

particular sequence of sounds and any particular meaning. In other words the link between phonological form and meaning is not a natural one, determined in some way by the nature of the referent, but a purely conventional one – as de Saussure put it, *the linguistic sign is arbitrary*.[1] Granted that this is so, each language can be seen to be a unique system of rules which, by relating forms to meanings, enables communication within a society. Continuity of communication depends on the system being handed on to each following generation by a process of language learning, and it is obvious that severe constraints must be imposed on the degree of deviation from the model which is permissible at each stage if communication between generations is not to be impaired. This is in turn reflected in the observation that the differences between successive language states, even over time-spans of several centuries, are relatively small and that related languages which are separated from their common ancestor by a comparable time-depth are still recognizably similar.

It is these two facts, that the relationship between form and meaning in language is an arbitrary one and that languages can only change through a succession of restricted steps, that gave significance to certain discoveries that were made by linguists some two hundred years ago when the Sanskrit language of Ancient India became for the first time fully accessible to European scholarship. Despite differences in geographical location and in the cultural content expressed through them, Sanskrit, Greek and Latin were found to exhibit such remarkable similarities in the phonological form of corresponding morphs and in the rules which govern the combination of these that descent from a common ancestor was clearly the only possible hypothesis that could account for them. In the first example we will compare paradigms of the past (or imperfect) tense of the verb 'to carry' in Greek and in Sanskrit. For greater clarity each verb form has been segmented into morphs on the basis of the synchronic grammar, although justification

model is linguistic rather than natural; and, because of the lexical basis of its associations, these are even more language-specific than in the case of simple onomatopoeia.

1 De Saussure 1964: Part 1, chapters 1 and 2. Benveniste (1966: 49–55) draws attention to the fact that there is a certain amount of confusion in de Saussure's description between 'meaning' (*signifié*, concept) on the one hand and referent (the object named) on the other. This old problem of the relationship between form and meaning in language – whether it be a natural or a conventional one – was widely debated in Antiquity and forms for instance the topic of Plato's *Kratylus* (Robins 1967: 18).

for this segmentation cannot be gone into here. The morphs in both languages are, from left to right: (i) past tense marker (or augment); (ii) root; (iii) thematic vowel, a functionally marginal morph which alternates with zero in certain other verbs and which could for our present purposes just as well be considered as forming a part of the personal ending; (iv) personal ending (the digraph *ph* in Greek represents a voiceless aspirated plosive /pʰ/, contrasting with /p/ and /b/; Sanskrit *bh* represents a voiced aspirated bilabial plosive /bʰ/ contrasting with /b/, /p/ and /pʰ/):

Greek		Sanskrit
é-pher-o-n	1. singular	á-bhar-a-m
é-pher-e-s	2. singular	á-bhar-a-s
é-pher-e	3. singular	á-bhar-a-t
e-phér-o-mes (West Greek)	1. plural	á-bhar-ā-ma
e-phér-e-te	2. plural	á-bhar-a-ta
é-pher-o-n	3. plural	á-bhar-a-n

The morphs, which correspond in both languages in order of occurrence as well as in grammatical function, can be seen to correspond also in phonological form provided that the following rules to relate them are set up:

Sanskrit /a/ corresponds to Greek /e,o/
Sanskrit /bʰ/ corresponds to Greek /pʰ/
Sanskrit /-m/ corresponds to Greek /-n/
Sanskrit /-t/ corresponds to Greek -ø

These rules leave unaccounted for only the ending of the first person plural (which does raise a certain number of problems) and the position of the accent in Greek (which is however predictable by a general rule, so that the difference from the Sanskrit is not significant). Now the likelihood of finding in any two languages such correspondence in form, function and arrangement of such a series of morphs as the result of pure chance is infinitesimally small.

As a second example, let us compare some of the case forms of the words meaning 'family, kind' in Greek, Latin and Sanskrit (the cases are labelled after the fashion of traditional grammar; *j* in Sanskrit stands for a voiced palatal plosive /ɟ/):

	Greek	Latin	Sanskrit
nominative-accusative	génos	genus	jánas

genitive	géneos (dialectal)	generis	jánasas
locative	génei ('dative')	genere ('ablative')	jánasi

It will be seen that the Greek and Latin forms present problems of segmentation when compared with more regular paradigms such as Greek ***néktar*** 'nectar', ***néktaros***, ***néktari*** and Latin ***nomen*** 'name', ***nominis***, ***nomine***. Only the Sanskrit forms do not present similar problems. However if we assume that Greek has dropped intervocalic /s/ and that Latin has replaced intervocalic /s/ by /r/ and final /i/ by /e/, a hypothetical stem **genos* ∼ **genes-* (the star indicating that the forms are not attested) may be postulated as a sort of common denominator. If the vowel correspondences are taken to be the same as in the previous example, only the Latin genitive ending remains unaccounted for. This device brings irregular paradigms of Greek and Latin into line with the more regular ones of ***néktar*** and ***nomen*** and at the same time reduces to a unitary paradigm the disparate forms of the three languages. The paradigm underlying all three might then be represented as nominative-accusative **genos*, genitive **genes-es* (*-os*), locative **genes-i*. Note also that the alternation /e/ versus /o/ of the second vowel is not unlike that of the thematic vowel in the previous paradigm.

Justification for the 'reconstruction' method illustrated above and for interpreting the unattested constructs marked with a star as forms of an actual earlier linguistic state preceding the three languages, cannot be given at this point. It will however be seen that the concept of 'correspondence' presupposes the existence of such constructs and of the rules that link the grammars of related languages. Why such hypothetical constructs may be claimed to represent the forms of an earlier language state will be discussed in chapter 1.

PART ONE

Models of language development

In order to describe the way in which a language has developed over a given stretch of time we require a theoretical framework (or *model*) within which the facts may be stated and explained. Ideally such a model should be capable of accounting for all the changes which have taken place in the language by reducing them to a systematically integrated set of rules. Any particular phenomenon will then be considered as 'explained' if we can state it in terms of these rules. All three chapters which follow will deal with the same subject-matter, namely the observable phenomena of language change; they will, however, differ in the way in which they describe these phenomena and in how they integrate them into an explanatory system. This diversity of treatment raises the obvious question of whether the mere restatement of some particular regularity in different theoretical terms is in itself any advance on previous knowledge. However, different models are bound to result in different questions being asked of the data and this in turn can lead not only to better explanations of already known facts but also to the discovery of new ones.

In this first, systematic, section of the book the emphasis will be on the linear development of language through time. The fact that contact between societies results in mutual influence will for the time being be disregarded, so that loan-words and areal features once adopted will be treated as forming an integral part of the language. We will thus for the moment assume that languages are of homogeneous structure and are isolated from one another in space; the questions of the origin and integrating process of loans will be dealt with separately in Part Two.

The three models chosen for description will be taken in chronological order. The neogrammarian model was the earliest, and still constitutes the essential foundation upon which both the structuralist (or 'taxonomic') and the transformational-generative models were erected, these constituting no more than elaborations and modifications of it. They do, however, by adopting different theoretical positions with regard to a number of issues, present alternative hypotheses concerning the nature of language change.

I
The neogrammarian model

1 **Basic issues**

We have said that a theoretical model if it is to be considered adequate must be capable both of describing and accounting for the observed phenomena. Which phenomena are in fact selected for attention by the linguist at any particular period will depend upon prevailing attitudes towards the subject and towards scientific investigation in general. Two main issues dominated the early course of historical linguistics, namely synchronic irregularity within individual languages and the nature of the resemblances existing between related languages. As we shall see, the two questions are in fact intimately connected.

1.1 *Synchronic irregularity*

One problem which obviously requires explanation in a language is its so-called irregular forms, and it could even be said that the more irregular the form the greater the need for it to be explained. Regular past tense forms like ***grabbed*** /græbd/ or ***hoped*** /houpt/ may perhaps be taken for granted, but why should ***to keep*** have a past tense ***kept*** /kept/ or ***to bleed*** /bli:d/ a past tense ***bled*** /bled/? We describe these last two forms as irregular because they do not follow the productive rule for forming the past tense in English which, depending upon the nature of the final segment of the verbal base, suffixes one of the alternants /-d, -t, -id/. We say that this rule is 'productive' because if native speakers of English are asked to form the past tense of some real or hypothetical English verb that they have never heard before they will without hesitation produce a form in compliance with it. Past tense formation thus consists in the affixation of an alveolar plosive, the selection of the precise alternant being automatic (that is to say, it is entirely conditioned by the phonological environment). What makes /kept/ and /bled/ exceptional is that in both their cases past tense formation entails some alteration of the verb base itself. Both verbs replace the vowel /i:/ of the base by /e/, but whereas in the case of /kept/ the vowel alternation is merely additional to suffixation of the past tense marker, it in itself constitutes the marker in the case of /bled/. Neither of these patterns is productive in Modern English, the verbs which follow them forming closed classes which can be defined only by listing. The historical linguist can however show that in an earlier stage of the English language the rules which produced the forms ancestral to *kept* and *bled* were just as regular in terms of the grammar then operating as are those producing *hoped* and *grabbed* today and that it is only as the result of phonological changes that have taken place subsequently that the morphological structure has become obscured. Thus in Old English (or Anglo-Saxon, as it is sometimes also called) weak verbs of the class to which these two verbs belonged formed their past tense by suffixing *-ede* or *-de*/*-te* to the verb base, the choice of the alternant being phonologically conditioned.[1] In the case in question the forms were *cēpte* and *blēdde*, formed from the bases *cēp-* and *blēd-* (infinitives *cēpan*, *blēdan*). The present-day past tense forms are the result of a whole series of subsequent phonological changes which have operated on the Old English forms: first all long vowels were shortened before sequences of two consonants, then unstressed *-e* in final position was dropped, and lastly all word-final long consonants were shortened. The current forms of the present tense stems on the other hand are the result of a change in the quality of long vowels when not followed by two consonants, so that *ē* (but not *e*) was raised to /i:/ to give the present-day alternation in the stem vowel.

It is on the basis of cases such as these that it has been claimed that if a grammar is to go beyond the mere statement of individual facts (such as lists of alternants and of the stems that take them) and is to *explain* these facts, it must necessarily be a historical grammar in which irregular forms are shown to be 'motivated' by reference to rules operative in earlier periods of the language.[2] Irregular forms are thus

[1] Verbs of the first weak class, to which our examples belong, took *-ede* after short syllables and, depending upon the preceding segment, *-de* or *-te* after long syllables (that is to say those containing either a long vowel or a final consonant cluster). For the weak verbs taken as a whole, however, the choice of the past tense alternant was already in Old English only partly determined phonologically (Campbell 1959: 321ff.).

[2] In view of its relevance to present-day discussions, Hermann Paul's famous passage is perhaps worth quoting in full: 'It remains for me to

not forms which are not reducible to any sort of rule but simply forms which do not comply with currently productive rules.

This view is dependent upon the assumption that, at any given stage in the history of a language and for any particular grammatical category, there is one basic mechanism or set of mechanisms relating

briefly justify why I have chosen the title "Principles of the *History* of Language". It has been said in criticism of this that a historical analysis is not the only possible scientific analysis of language. This I must reject. What some consider to constitute a non-historical and yet scientific analysis of language is in fact no more than an incomplete historical one – incomplete partly due to the fault of the analyst and partly due to the fault of the data. As soon as one goes beyond the mere statement of individual facts and attempts to comprehend the connection [between them], that is to say to understand the phenomena, one enters the realm of history although perhaps unconsciously. A scientific analysis of language is indeed by no means only possible when we have at our disposal different stages in the development of one and the same language but also when the available data occur simultaneously. The situation is most favourable when several related languages or dialects are known to us. The task of science is then not simply to state what correspondences exist between them but, in so far as that is possible, to reconstruct from the attested data the non-attested basic forms and meanings. But in this process the comparative analysis becomes a historical one. And even when only a particular stage of development of a single dialect is available scientific analysis is still to some degree possible. But how? When for instance one compares the various meanings of a word, one attempts to establish which of them is the basic meaning or to which lost meaning they point. However, once one establishes a basic meaning from which the others are derived one is making a historical statement. Or if one compares related forms and derives them from a common basic form, once again one is making a historical observation. Thus, unless one is prepared to enter the realm of history, it is quite unjustifiable to claim that related forms are derived from a common source. Or again we may state that [within a single language] there is phonological alternation between related forms and words. But if one wishes to explain this one is necessarily led to conclude that it is the after-effect of a sound change, that is to say of a historical process. If one attempts to characterise the so-called "inner form" of language, as this term is used by Humboldt and Steinthal, one can only do so by tracing the origins of expressions and their basic meanings. And so I cannot conceive how one could with any hope of success think about a language without discovering at least to some extent how it came to be as it is. The only aspect then which might conceivably remain as suitable for non-historic investigation might be general considerations regarding individual usages of language, that is to say the behaviour of the individual speaker relative to general usage, which would include language acquisition. That, however, precisely these considerations are to be intimately connected with the analysis of the historical development of language will emerge in the course of the following pages' (Paul 1970: 20–2).

form and function. That this ideal of a simple relationship between form and function for each grammatical category has at least some degree of validity may be inferred from the existence of such 'incorrect' forms as *goed* (for *went*) and *gooses* (for *geese*) produced by young children and more importantly from certain historical changes which have had the effect of creating like forms for like function and which, because of this underlying one-to-one principle, are called *analogical* formations (see p. 34ff.). For example in Middle English *helpen* 'to help' was a so-called 'strong' verb which formed its past tense *holp* by vowel change (like *to get* : *got* and *to tread* : *trod* in Modern English). This form has, however, not survived and today we have in its place the regular *helped*, created by analogy. Very many regular past tense forms in Modern English can in fact be shown to be the result of such analogical realignment with later productive rules while the opposite change, whereby a weak verb becomes strong, is very rare indeed. This whole question will be taken up again in the section on analogical change (see chapter 1, section 5.1).

Alternations of this sort may take us very far back into the history of the language. In the case of weak past tense forms such as *kept* and *bled* we had to go back as far as the grammar of Old English in order to find the productive rules which accounted for them, and in the case of the strong verbs we have to go back even further. In fact it is only by going back to the ancestor of the Indo-European (chapter 1, section 2) languages that we can show that the vowel alternation between present and past tenses was originally the same in what are now *sing* : *sang*, *drive* : *drove*, *bid* : *bade*, *steal* : *stole*, *see* : *saw*, and *get* : *got*, and that the present diversity is the result of both phonological and analogical changes that have taken place subsequently. In Ancient Greek for instance the relationship was still fairly transparent. Thus in the verbs 'to let' (present *'leip-o* : perfect *'le-loip-a*) and 'to see' (present *'derk-omai* : perfect *'de-dork-a*) a vowel /e/ in the present tense was opposed to an /o/ in the perfect. On the basis of the Greek pattern of alternation and of additional evidence from other Indo-European languages it can be shown that in the parent language from which the Indo-European languages have descended the verb had an /e/ in the present tense and an /o/ in the perfect tense (which corresponds to the English past tense). We will not at this point concern ourselves with the details; what matters is that in the case of the strong verbs the irregularity in the relationship between present and past tense forms in English can be reduced to regularity only by reference to the grammar of the earliest stage of the Indo-European languages. The time-depth existing between the grammar in which these forms were regular and the grammar of Modern English in which they are 'irregular' is thus very considerable indeed, probably something in the region of 5,000 years.

1.2 *Cross-language similarity*

The explanation of synchronic irregularity is thus one of the reasons for which the systematic study of earlier language states is carried out and the nature of the changes that a language has undergone in the past is investigated. Another powerful motive is the desire to explain why related languages have similar, although not identical,

TABLE 1

	English	German
1 'ten'	*ten* /ten/	*zehn* /tse:n/
2 'to, at'	*to* /tu/	*zu* /tsu/
3 'wart'	*wart* /wɔ:t/	*Warze* /ˈva:rtsə/
4 'plant'	*plant* /plɑ:nt/	*Pflanze* /ˈpflantsə/
5 'net'	*net* /net/	*Netz* /nets/
6 'to sit'	*sit* /sit/	*sitzen* /ˈzitsən/
7 'stone'	*stone* /stoun/	*Stein* /ʃtain/
8 'still'	*still* /stil/	*still* /ʃtil/
9 '(the) best'	*best* /best/	(*das*) *Beste* /ˈbestə/
10 'trough'	*trough* (trɔf/	*Trog* /tro:k/
11 'true'	*true* /tru:/	*treu* /troü/ ('faithful')
12 'winter'	*winter* /wintə/	*Winter* /ˈvintər/
13 'bitter'	*bitter* /ˈbitə/	*bitter* /ˈbitər/
14 'water'	*water* /ˈwɔ:tə/	*Wasser* /ˈvasər/
15 'better'	*better* /ˈbetə/	*besser* /ˈbesər/
16 'to eat'	*eat* /i:t/	*essen* /ˈesən/
17 'to hate'	*hate* /heit/	*hassen* /ˈhasən/
18 'what'	*what* /hwɔt/	*was* /va:s/
19 'that'	*that* /ðæt/	*das* /da:s/
20 comparative suffix	*-er* /-ə/	*-er* /-ər/
21 superlative suffix	*-est* /-(i)st/	-(*e*)*ste* /-(ə)stə/
22 past tense marker (of weak verbs)	-(*e*)*d* /-d, -t, -id/	-(*e*)*t*- /-ət-, -t-/

forms and how the differences between such similar forms have arisen. Compare, for instance, the set of lexical items and grammatical formatives in English and German in Table 1.

Comparison of the two sets of forms elicits two observations. Firstly, it is apparent that in view of the fundamentally arbitrary nature of the connection between form and meaning in language, corresponding English and German forms are far too alike for this to be the result of pure chance. The arbitrariness principle, in other words, clearly demands a *historical* link between the two sets. In the second place it can be seen that corresponding items differ in their phonological form in a systematic way (e.g. /tu/ : /tsu/, /ten/ : /tse:n/, etc.). The difference is however not a simple one in the sense that where English has say a /t/ German always has a /ts/; rather we must state the rule as being that where English has a /t/ no sound other than /ts/, /s/ or /t/ is found in German. And what is more important is that this regularity is not confined to the items contained in the list but holds in principle (certain loan-words apart, see chapter 6) throughout both languages. Our historical hypothesis will ascribe the similarities between the two languages to the fact that both have evolved from a single earlier parent language and their differences to the split-up of that earlier language into two branches which then underwent separate development. As we shall see in detail below (p. 49ff.), it is in fact possible to show that a /t/ of the common earlier language state was retained in English but became /ts/, /s/ or /t/ in German depending upon the phonetic environment. Since this change affecting /t/ was rule-governed, the resulting German forms stand in a systematic formal relationship to their English counterparts. And, since the same principle applies to language change generally, it may be stated that related languages resemble each other in a systematic way.

This fact that both synchronic irregularity and cross-language resemblances can only be explained by reference to earlier language states and to the systematic nature of language change is the topic to which we shall now turn.

2 The Indo-European languages

The systematic study of language evolution and the setting up of hypotheses regarding the nature of language change was to prove particularly fruitful in the field of the Indo-European languages (see table p. 68f.), largely because of the nature of the material available for investigation. In the first place this family comprises a number of fairly closely related groups of living languages such as Germanic (English, Dutch, Frisian, German, Swedish, Danish, Norwegian, Icelandic), Romance (French, Provençal, Spanish, Catalan, Portuguese, Italian, Sardinian, Rhaeto-Romansh, Romanian), Slavonic (or Slavic) (Russian, Ukrainian, Polish, Czech, Serbo-Croatian, Bulgarian), and Indo-Iranian (Hindi-Urdu, Panjabi, Gujarati, Marathi, Sinhalese etc. forming the Indic branch, and Persian, Pashto, Kurdish etc. forming the Iranian branch). In addition to this wealth of present-day material there exist for practically every one of these groups, as well as for isolated members of the family such as Greek, written documents going back over many centuries – in the case of Indo-Iranian and Greek well into the second millennium B.C. – so that the investigation of their historical development is possible over an unbroken period of two to four millennia. In the second place there are very ancient records of at least some Indo-European languages, mainly of Vedic Sanskrit, Mycenaean Greek and Hittite, which show that by the second millennium B.C. these languages were already very considerably differentiated, making it possible to reconstruct forms of even earlier date by the comparison of attested divergent forms. Thus Indo-European historical linguistics as a whole spans a time-depth of at least five millennia. If, then, general principles are to be postulated with regard to the nature of language development, the Indo-European languages represent a most suitable field of inquiry and a very important testing ground for hypotheses. It is thus perhaps not surprising that theoretical claims regarding the nature and regularity of language development have come principally from scholars working in this field.

3 The neogrammarians

It is the so-called neogrammarians, a group of Indo-Europeanists working at or in association with the University of Leipzig during the last decades of the nineteenth century, who are credited with putting historical linguistics onto a scientific footing for the first time because they explicitly formulated the methodological principles and theoretical postulates which guided their work and put them to practical test. By the 1860s and '70s the bulk of the Indo-European languages were sufficiently well known and had been studied for long enough for the existing knowledge about them and the hypotheses accounting for their individual histories to be integrated into 'an outline comparative grammar of the Indo-European languages'.[1] The neogrammarians were thus primarily engaged in the practical task of making a comprehensive and orderly statement of the body of knowledge which had by then been assembled, and it is against this background that their theoretical claims about the nature of language change in general must be seen.

The general position from which the neogrammarians approached their subject was the assumption that language change must have order and thus be amenable to systematic investigation. They based their expectation that language development is rule-governed on certain universal aspects of language itself, namely its use by human beings for purposes of communication, the uniform way in which it is transmitted from one generation to another, its production by means of a common articulatory apparatus, etc. Since language is essentially a human activity it was argued, guiding principles for the study of its evolution should be sought within the general rules that govern human behaviour.[2]

In order to account systematically for the phenomena of language change the neogrammarians found it necessary to postulate two fundamental principles governing the development of language through time, namely *sound change* and *analogy*. Sound change deals with processes operating at the phonological level while analogy deals with those at the grammatical (morphological and syntactic) level. The approach thus presupposes a 'dual articulation' of language (Martinet 1964:22), with the phonological and the grammatical levels structured independently of each other and each exhibiting different kinds of regularity.

4 Sound change: the regularity principle

At the phonological level, the neogrammarians claimed,

1 *Grundriss der vergleichenden Grammatik der indogermanischen Sprachen* (by K. Brugmann and B. Delbrück, Strassburg, 1886–1900).

2 See Osthoff and Brugmann 1878; this article is often referred to as 'the neogrammarian manifesto'; see also Delbrück 1919, Paul 1970, Jankowski 1972. The views expressed by the neogrammarians were new by comparison with what had gone before; only a few years earlier Schleicher had claimed that languages were natural organisms with 'lives' of their own, comprising a period of evolutionary progress followed by a period of decay. He considered them to be organisms in their own right on the grounds that the rules of their development were apparently independent of the will of man. Something of this attitude lingered on in the thinking of at least some neogrammarians who claimed sound change to be completely *mechanical*, that is outside the consciousness of the speaker, and thus purely a matter of physiology; only analogy was to be considered a psychological matter (cf. Osthoff 1878a: 13).

language change is governed by the principle of *the regularity of sound change*. This states quite generally that the conditions which govern sound change are purely phonetic ones. Applied to specific changes in particular languages this means that (a) the direction in which a sound changes is the same for all the members of the speech community in question (unless a division into two dialects is in progress), and (b) that all the words in which the sound undergoing the change occurs in the same phonetic environment are affected by the change in the same way (Osthoff and Brugmann 1878). Restated in modern phonemic terms, (b) says that phonological change proceeds through the intermediary of positionally defined allophones, position in turn being stated within the framework of 'the word' as the basic linguistic unit.[1]

In the following discussion we have to a limited extent anticipated structuralism. Instead of talking about 'sounds', as would have been historically speaking more accurate, I have anachronistically introduced the distinction between allophones and phonemes which was made only later by phoneme theory. Such overinterpretation can, I think, be justified since neogrammarian phonology was, insofar as the syntagmatic aspect is concerned, implicitly phonemic. The neogrammarians share with the proponents of so-called taxonomic linguistics the claim that the phonological level is autonomous and independent of grammatical structure – or, to put it more precisely, that phonological rules can be formulated which make no reference to morphology, syntax and semantics.

The rules which govern sound change are thus (1) exclusively phonological since they are independent of the morphological, syntactic and semantic function of the word to whose segments they apply; (2) 'exceptionless', that is to say that all the data which fall within the scope of a rule have to be accounted for and if any data should violate the rule and not be explainable by reference to some other linguistic principle the rule is invalidated. We shall see that the scope of a rule

[1] The 'word' was, it seems, taken for granted as the linguistic unit *par excellence*: on the one hand it was a phonological unit consisting of sounds, on the other it was a lexical unit the different forms of which were described in the morphology and from which sentences were formed. With the emphasis on written languages of the past, segmentation into words probably followed the native scholarly traditions in the languages concerned. Discrepancies between morphologically defined and phonologically defined words were resolved by having a class of enclitics. This will be dealt with again in chapter 3 when the issue of the autonomous or non-autonomous nature of phonology is discussed.

includes not only its input but also the limits of its applicability in terms of time and space. In practice this rigorous demand for a systematic search for the reasons underlying apparent exceptions led to spectacular progress in the Indo-European field, fully justifying the theoretical position adopted. The principle of regularity was generally accepted, as a working hypothesis at least, even by those who objected to the way in which it was formulated.[1] Only such rigour of method made it in fact possible to isolate certain principles other than sound change as determining language change, the most important being analogy and borrowing (see below, section 5 and chapter 6).

As a first example of a sound change we will take the case of *umlaut*, that is to say the fronting of back vowels in certain environments in a number of Germanic languages. Table 2 contains the base, comparative

TABLE 2

Old High German	Middle High German	Modern German
hōh	hōch	hoch /ho:x/
hōhiro	hœ̄here	höher /ˈhö:ər/
hōhisto	hœ̄heste	höchste /ˈhö:kstə/
hōho	hōhe	hoch /ho:x/
scōni	schœ̄ne	schön /ʃö:n/
scōniro	schœ̄nere	schöner /ˈʃö:nər/
scōnisto	schœ̄neste	schönste /ˈʃö:nstə/
scōno ('properly')	schōne	schon /ʃo:n/ ('already')

and superlative of the adjectives 'high' and 'beautiful' together with the corresponding adverbs in three successive stages of the German language: Old High German (approximately 800–1100), Middle High German (1100–1500), and Modern German (after 1500). (For the earlier stages of the language we have only given the orthographic forms since they are for all practical purposes phonemic; for Modern German a phonemic transcription is given in addition.)

It will be seen that in Old High German all forms contain the vowel

[1] Schuchardt (1885, Vennemann and Wilbur 1972) objected to the concept of 'exception' on the grounds that it was a mere surface assessment of the phenomena and demanded a deeper analysis of the relationship between sound change and analogy.

/o:/ whereas in Middle High German and Modern German there is a contrast between the back vowel /o:/ and the rounded front vowel /ö:/ (cf., for instance, the Modern German minimal pair /'ho:ər/ 'a high one' versus /'hö:ər/ 'higher'). In some forms, then, Old High German /o:/ has remained /o:/ while in others it has been fronted to /ö:/. The conditions under which the fronting must have occurred can be readily seen from the Old High German data, namely whenever an /i/ occurs in the following syllable. From this we can assume that in Old High German /o:/ had both back and front allophones depending upon the phonetic environment: [o:] before vowels other than /i/, [ö:] before an /i/ of the following syllable although when precisely the fronted allophones developed cannot be inferred from the data. The fronting must, however, have been an innovation in some earlier stage of the language as can be seen from a comparison with Gothic, the oldest attested member of the Germanic family. The Middle High German forms differ from the Old High German ones not only in having separate orthographic symbols, *ō* and *œ̄*, to represent back and front vowels but also in that the vowels of the following syllables are no longer distinct, a uniform *e* replacing both *o* and *i* of the previous stage. This means that, owing to the neutralization of the opposition between these latter unstressed vowels, the conditioning factor which had determined the distribution of [o:] and [ö:] at the earlier stage is no longer present. The result is that [o:] and [ö:] now occur in identical environments and therefore contrast. At this point only can it be said that /o:/ and /ö:/ have become independent phonemes, and at this point also they are represented by distinct orthographic symbols (Twaddell 1957). The Modern German forms have simply lost certain of the unstressed final vowels.

This fronting rule, or umlaut, in fact affected all back vowels including /a/ and /a:/ and is the chief source of a great deal of morphological variation in Modern German (*gut* /gu:t/ 'good' : *Güte* /'gü:tə/ 'goodness', *Gast* /gast/ 'guest' : *Gäste* /'gestə/ 'guests', etc.). The frequent though not regular association of umlaut in Modern German with certain grammatical categories, such as for instance plural or third person, is thus secondary and simply the consequence of the former presence of an *i* vowel in the syllable which followed the back vowel. It is in this sense that the statement that sound change operates with 'blind necessity' (Osthoff) must be understood: it operates irrespective of the grammatical consequences. It should also be noted that in

Modern German the umlaut rule is no longer productive and the sequence back vowel followed by high front vowel in the next syllable is phonologically quite in order (cf. *gastlich* 'hospitable', *rosig* 'rosy', *ruhig* 'calm', etc.). The validity of the rule was thus restricted to a specific period.

As a second example of sound change we will take the development of Vulgar Latin[1] initial /k/ in French. Whether initial /k/ became French /s/ or /ʃ/ or whether it remained /k/ was determined by the nature of the following sound. (For the purposes of this limited exercise we will ignore the differences between Vulgar Latin and Classical Latin.)

TABLE 3

	Latin	French
1 'side'	costa /ˈkosta/	côte /kot/
2 'body'	corpus /ˈkorpus/	corps /kɔr/
3 'key'	clavis /ˈkla:vis/	clef /kle/
4 'cross'	crux /kruks/	croix /krwa/
5 'to sing'	cantare /kanˈta:re/	chanter /ʃãte/
6 'dear'	carus /ˈka:rus/	cher /ʃɛr/
7 'wax'	cera /ˈke:ra/	cire /sir/
8 'a hundred'	centum /ˈkentum/	cent /sã/
9 'community'	civitas /ˈki:vita:s/	cité /site/

It can be seen that (Vulgar) Latin /k/ when it was situated before a back vowel or a consonant has resulted in French in [k], when before /a/ in [ʃ], and when before any other front vowel in [s]. These reflexes are, however, phonemes in their own right in French since they can be shown to contrast in identical environments: *côte* /kot/ 'side' : *chaud* /ʃo/ 'hot' : *sauter* /sote/ 'to jump'; *cité* /site/ 'city' : *qui* /ki/ 'who' : *chiffre* /ʃifr/ 'number'. Some of the reasons for this development may be

[1] We will use the term 'Vulgar Latin' rather loosely to refer to that spoken language, very close to but not identical with Classical Latin, from which the Romance languages are assumed to have evolved. Strictly speaking the ancestor of the Romance languages is Proto-Romance, which is 'reconstructed' from a comparison of the Romance languages (see p. 23). For our present purposes we will, however, treat Classical Latin *as if* it were in fact the ancestor of the Romance languages.

illustrated from these examples. French /k/, /ʃ/ and /s/ are no longer in complementary distribution because of subsequent changes which included the passage of the sequence /a/ plus /l/ to the back vowel /o/ (*calidus* 'warm' becoming *chaud* /ʃo/) so that [ʃ] now also occurs before a back vowel. Furthermore, the labiovelar /k^w/ of Latin has resulted in French [k] (*quis* 'who' becoming *qui* /ki/), so that this now also occurs before vowels other than back vowels. The [s] from Latin /k/ on the other hand has fallen together with the [s] from Latin /s/, which occurred before certain consonants and before any kind of vowel (*septem* 'seven' becoming *sept* /sɛt/, *saltare* 'to jump' becoming *sauter* /sote/), resulting in a contrast between /s/ and /k/ before front vowels.

Reviewing what has happened in both the German and French examples, it may be said that these so-called *conditioned changes* operating in specific phonetic environments all constitute a partial assimilation of successive segments in the spoken chain, for the fronting of back vowels in the environment of a high front vowel, the various palatalizations of /k/ in the environment of high and low front vowels, and the 'weakening' to the point of loss of unstressed final vowels may all be described in this way. It must, however, be remembered that we have stated the changes in phonemic terms, so that by saying that Old High German /'sko:ni/ has become Modern German /ʃö:n/ we do not rule out the possibility of the pronunciation ['skö:ni] in Old High German times; on the contrary, its existence at least at a period prior to the neutralization of unstressed vowels is to be assumed from the later development. The important point is the phonological status of [ö:]. While in Old High German [ö:] was merely an allophone of /o:/, in Modern German it constitutes a separate phoneme in its own right. There are, of course, certain very close associations of /o:/ and /ö:/ at the *morphological* level in Modern German (see p. 140f.). In the case of the French reflexes of Latin /k/ on the other hand, the palatalized reflexes /s/ and /ʃ/ are associated with /k/ in a much more marginal fashion. Phonologically speaking changes of this kind are all instances of phonemic *split*, that is to say the splitting off of allophones from phonemes. Our examples show that split operates in two quite different ways: either an allophone may split off from one phoneme and join another (as in the case of French [s] from Vulgar Latin /k/), or what were merely conditioned allophones of a single phoneme may become independent phonemes when a contrast in the phonetic environment which had maintained their complementary distribution collapses (as in the case of French /ʃ/, after /a/ plus /l/ had resulted in back vowel, or in the case of umlaut, after unstressed /i/ and /o/ had become /e/). The term *primary split* has been used by structuralists for the former phenomenon, *secondary split* or *phonologization* for the latter (Hoenigswald 1960:77; Jakobson 1972a; see below p. 77ff.).

One far-reaching effect of conditioned sound change is the creation of morpheme alternants. The morphological consequences of umlaut in German, as has already been mentioned, play a prominent part in inflection and derivation. In English, the back vowels of which also underwent umlaut, the resulting rounded front vowels have subsequently become unrounded, merging with the old unrounded vowels and sharing their later developments (/i:/ becoming /ai/ and /u:/ becoming /au/). As a result of these further changes *mice* /mais/ (Old English *mȳs*, from *mūs* by umlaut) now rhymes with *ice* (Old English *īs*), and *king* (Old English *kyning*, from a reconstructed earlier form *kuning*) rhymes with *ring* (Old English *hring*). Traces of umlaut in English morphology are, however, rarer than in German because many of the older forms have been replaced. The more important survivals include *foot* : *feet*, *goose* : *geese*, *mouse* : *mice*, *louse* : *lice* in the inflectional morphology, and *blood* : *bleed*, *food* : *feed*, *stank* : *stench* in the derivational morphology. In this latter category the synchronic link between base and derivative has often been further severed through semantic change; thus, while German *Tag* 'day' and *täglich* 'daily' are well integrated in a morpho-semantic relationship, in cases like *Grund* 'ground' and *gründlich* 'thorough', or *Punkt* 'point' and *pünktlich* 'punctual, punctilious', a semantic connection is no longer felt by the native speaker so that *pünktlich* and *gründlich* are just as isolated lexically as *grün* 'green' and *Tür* 'door' which lack related forms with back vowels altogether.

Unconditioned change, in contrast to conditioned change which is what we have been discussing so far, is not dependent upon phonological environment but affects all the allophones of a phoneme. The change from Vulgar Latin /u/ to French /ü/ is a case in point. Looked at in isolation, we have here no more than a change in the phonetic realization of a phoneme. In fact, however, the change introduces a new *type* of sound, a rounded front vowel, into the phonological system and thus forms part of its overall reorganization (Haudricourt and Juilland 1949:100–4). This latter aspect will not however be pursued at this point since it presupposes methods of structural linguistics which were not fully available to the neogrammarians (see chapter 2).

The type of unconditioned phonological change *par excellence* is the falling together, or merger, of two phonemes into one. If all the allophones of two phonemes merge there is no way of discovering retrospectively whether in any particular word the resulting phoneme derives from one rather than the other of the source phonemes: merger is thus described as being *irreversible*. For instance, in German the Middle High German diphthongs /ei/, /ou/ and /öü/ merged with the long vowels /i:/, /u:/ and /ü:/ respectively, to give /ai/, /au/ and /oü/:

Middle High German

'willow'	'pasture'	'mouse'	'smoke'	'people'	'joy'
/ˈvi:de/	/ˈveide/	/mu:s/	/roux/	/ˈlü:te/	/ˈfröüde/

Modern German

/ˈvaidə/	/ˈvaidə/	/maus/	/raux/	/ˈloütə/	/ˈfroüdə/
Weide	*Weide*	*Maus*	*Rauch*	*Leute*	*Freude*

Basing ourselves upon Modern German alone there is absolutely no way of telling whether, in any particular word, the source of /ai/ was /ei/ or /i:/, of /au/ was /ou/ or /u:/, of /oü/ was /öü/ or /ü:/. Only a knowledge of Middle High German or comparative evidence from a dialect which has not undergone the merger will allow one to sort them out. However, if only certain allophones of a phoneme have merged with those of another, as in the Romance case cited above where the allophones of /k/ before high front vowel merged with /s/, and if the conditioning environments remain intact, some clues remain as to the earlier situation. In that case it can at least be stated that any /s/ which is *not* followed by a high front vowel does *not* derive from /k/. In the environment of a high front vowel the original situation is, however, just as irrecoverable as in the German example.

As a result of merger, what were originally distinct forms may become homophonous, for instance Modern German /ˈvaidə/ which means both 'willow' (from /ˈvi:de/) and 'pasture' (from /ˈveide/), /laip/ which means 'body' (from /li:p/) and 'loaf' (from /leip/). Although Standard German orthography sometimes makes a distinction (*Leib* 'body' but *Laib* 'loaf') this is not always so (cf. *Weide*, both 'willow' and 'pasture'). Such cases of homophony are perhaps even more frequent in English: /mi:t/ *meat* (Old English *mete*) and *to meet* (Old English *mētan*); /ri:d/ *reed* (Old English *hrēod*) and *to read* (Old English *rǣdan*), etc.

5 Analogy

The fundamental neogrammarian contention that phonological change is strictly independent of structure at the higher levels carries with it the corollary that phonological and grammatical structure may get out of step with one another during the course of time. This means that the rules which link phonological and grammatical structure may require readjustment and redefinition for each new language state.

As an example of the consequence of phonological change on grammatical structure we may take the case of the merger which affected the vowels in final unstressed syllables in English to give a single unstressed vowel, represented in the spelling by an *e*. This change, coupled with the loss of final *-n* and *-m* in these same syllables,[1] had the effect among others of reducing the six different forms of the Old English paradigm of nouns of the class to which *stān* 'stone' belongs to three (see Table 4).

TABLE 4

	Old English		expected forms after phonological changes	Middle English	
sg.	nom.acc.	stān	stān	common	stōne
	dat.	stāne	stāne		
	gen.	stānes	stānes	gen.	stōnes
pl.	nom.acc.	stānas	stānes		
	dat.	stānum	stāne	common	stōnes
	gen.	stāna	stāne		

Subsequently the *-e* was lost, although it is often retained and has even been generalized in spelling. As a result Middle English had only two phonologically distinct forms, *stone* and *stones*, and the only morphologically marked forms were the genitive singular in *-s* and the formally

[1] According to Baugh (1965: 190ff.) the development *-um* > *-an* > *-en* > *e* was the result of sound change; Mossé (1959: 71) on the other hand attributes it to analogy, which would explain adverbial forms like *seldom* and *whilom* as relics. Bazell has however noted (1975: 102) that, in specific texts at least, *-on* and *-um* occur side by side with a characteristic distribution, *-on* being found in *pluralia tantum* and in the adverb *hwilon*, *-um* elsewhere. From the fact that the former group were not only the first to lose *-um* but also the last to retain it, he deduces that the change of *-um* to *-on* was not irreversible: under certain conditions *-um* could in fact be restored analogically.

identical plural, which had been extended from the nominative-accusative to the whole plural. As a result the Middle English system had in fact only two cases, 'common' and 'genitive'.

On the other hand English now had, for the first time in its historical development, a separate exponent of 'plural', for in Old English the exponents of this category were conflated with and inseparable from those of case (that is, only 'nominative singular', 'nominative plural', 'dative singular', 'dative plural' etc. were represented by formally identifiable units, there being no partial phonological similarity between the corresponding case forms of singular and plural). Of course 'plural' was not a new category syntactically speaking since verbal concord had all along depended on the number (singular or plural) of the subject of the sentence, it is only the direct representation of plural in the morphology which was new. This may have been the result of the easy segmentability of such plurals as *stones* into *stone* plus *-s*; at any rate whatever the ultimate underlying cause, there can be no doubt that the restructured paradigm of this class of noun acted as a model in the subsequent reshaping of the entire noun system.

We will illustrate this reshaping process from just one class of noun, namely that of the type *sorg* 'sorrow', *rōd* 'cross', *wund* 'wound', whose inflection in Old English was as follows:

singular: nominative *sorg*, genitive-dative-accusative *sorge*
plural: nominative-accusative-genitive *sorga*, dative *sorgum*

It can easily be seen that in nouns of this declension the reduction of unstressed final syllables would have had the effect of completely obliterating all case and number distinctions. In Modern English, however, words of this type have genitive and plural forms in *-s*, just as *stone* does. The only difference is that in words of the *stone* class the forms in *-s* are justified in the sense that they are the continuation of forms ending in *-s* which belonged to the paradigm of this word in earlier stages of the language, whereas the ancestral forms of *sorrow* and *wound* never had forms in *-s* in their paradigm. The presence of *-s* in these must then be the result of a transfer to their paradigms of the *-s* morphs from the *stone* class on the basis of a synchronic segmentation: base (that is, in practice, the common case singular) plus *-(e)s*. The relationship between the paradigm of the class which served as model and that of the class which was attracted may be expressed in the form of the equation: *stone* : *stones* = *wound* : *x*, where *x* is *wounds* rather than *wound*, the form that would be expected as the result of regular sound change. Such an equation is the traditional framework for the description of *analogical change*. It does not, of course, imply that the lexical item *stone* itself constituted the direct model for the lexical items *wound* and *sorrow*; all of these are merely convenient representatives of their classes. What makes analogical changes especially interesting is that through them we learn something of the morphological segmentation and functional interpretation of the forms at the time when the change was taking place. Thus in our example the analogical spread of the -(*e*)*s* as a plural marker clearly presupposes the collapse of the old case system and the productiveness of the rule which interprets plural as base plus -(*e*)*s*.

In neogrammarian theory analogy and phonological change are the two basic components of language change. In contrast however with phonological change, which operates independently of grammatical and semantic structure, analogy is concerned precisely with the relationship between phonological structure and grammatical structure. It is in fact the very mechanism which, either by modifying existing linguistic forms or by creating new ones, brings back into alignment phonological forms and grammatical function after the relationship between these has been disrupted by sound change. We may thus distinguish two types of analogical formation,[1] *analogical change* and *analogical creation*. Thus, while analogical change effects the realignment of exponents in relation to some grammatical or semantic category and amounts to no more than a redistribution of its exponents, analogical creation produces new forms by extending an existing correlation of form and function beyond its original domain. Underlying both types of process we

[1] This is an attempt to render Delbrück's term *Analogiebildung* (1919: 181), that is the diachronic aspect of analogy which covers both analogical change and analogical creation. In the neogrammarian manifesto (Osthoff and Brugmann 1878) *Analogie* is used to cover both the synchronic concept of analogy current in Antiquity and both its diachronic aspects. In Greek philosophy there were two opposing views regarding the relationship between form and meaning in language: (1) that it was governed by analogy (i.e. by orderliness and regularity) and (2) that it was governed by anomaly (i.e. by the absence of such regularity). 'The regularities looked for by the analogists were those of formal paradigms wherein words of the same grammatical status had the same morphological terminations and accentual structure, and those involving the relations between form and meaning, whereby words that were comparable morphologically could be expected to bear comparable, "analogical", meanings, and vice versa' (Robins 1967: 20).

must assume the association by the speaker of specific linguistic functions with specific sets of forms.

5.1 *Analogical change*

As will be seen from the above example, for an analogical change to take place two conditions must be met. Firstly it presupposes the functional identity in respect of some particular grammatical or semantic category (plural, agent noun, dative, etc.) of markers which are formally quite different, and secondly it presupposes that the structure of the form which acts as the model be morphologically 'transparent' for the native speaker – which is of course always the case with forms that result from productive rules. The change will then consist in the replacement of the less or no longer transparent form by a new functionally equivalent one whose structure will mirror that of the model. This means that the morphological segmentation of the model will be transferred to the new form, so that the morph representing the shared category in the model becomes one of its segments with the remainder either being treated as the base or a new base being created on the pattern of the model. Thus, for example, when the plural marker -(*e*)*s* was carried over from the *stone* class to the *wound* class, it was suffixed to the only surviving form of that paradigm, which was reinterpreted as the base. Again, in the case of the large number of strong verbs which went over to the weak conjugation (see p. 20), earlier past tense forms such as *holp* were replaced by new regular ones of the type *helped*, again on the basis of an analysis of 'past' into base (in practice identical with the present tense stem) plus alveolar plosive, the selection of the alternant being automatic.

In fact, as the result of analogical change of this type, over half the surviving verbs which were originally strong have gone over to the weak conjugation since the Old English period (Baugh 1965: 195ff.). The process can be shown to have been a gradual one, with weak forms first developing and being used alongside the strong ones over a period and eventually supplanting them. In only a few cases (*knew*, not *knowed*, etc.) have the strong forms survived. New strong formations are by comparison extremely rare although they do exist: for example *to wear* : *wore*, *to spit* : *spat*, *to stick* : *stuck*, *to fling* : *flung*, *to dig* : *dug*, *to string* : *strung*, and regionally in American English *to dive* : *dove* (Baugh 1965: 197), all of which follow the patterns of common originally strong verbs. It should perhaps be added in this context that analogical change operated not only between the strong and weak conjugations but also within the class of strong verbs itself, so that the surviving strong verbs have seldom retained the exact forms which might be expected on purely phonological grounds from a comparison with the corresponding Old English forms. It should also be noted that parallel changes have taken place in all the Germanic languages and it has in fact been claimed that the grammars of these have still not fully readjusted morphologically to the phonological changes of the early Germanic period.

The first result of these analogical changes on the morphology of the noun and of the verb was merely to effect a redistribution of the morphs representing specific grammatical morphemes, leading to a decrease in the *incidence* (that is to say the frequency of occurrence) of irregular morphs but very little reduction in the actual overall number of allomorphs representing these morphemes. Thus, although the genitive in *-s* has been generalized to all English nouns[1] and has no longer a zero morph as one of its alternants, the plural in *-s* still alternates with zero, *-n* and vowel change in a few cases (*sheep*, *oxen*, *women*, etc.), so that all irregular allomorphs have not been entirely eliminated. The same applies in the case of the past tense forms of the verb. There still remain a large number of strong verbs, so that the total number of alternants of the past tense morpheme has probably remained relatively stable. The changes have thus not substantially reduced the number of *rules* required for plural and past tense formation although they have greatly increased the frequency of the regular alternants. The second, and far more decisive, effect of these analogical changes was on the *lexicon*, for here they brought about a substantial reduction in the number of stems exhibiting allomorphy. Thus all the lexical items which went over to the regular pattern automatically lost their irregular alternants and each came to be represented by a single morph throughout its paradigm. In the case of plural formation the nouns which do not take the *-s* suffix are very few (*feet*, *teeth*, *geese*, *mice*, *lice*, *men*, *women*, *oxen*, *children*, *brethren*, *sheep*) while with the verbs the irregular alternants still play quite a prominent role (about 80 in current use). We see that there are thus two facets to analogical change: on the one hand it may have a regularizing effect on the *grammar* by eliminating irregular

1 There are a few collocations which are sometimes claimed to be unacceptable, *the table's legs* for instance; but other speakers will happily accept *one of the dining room table's legs is loose*.

grammatical alternants or at least decreasing their frequency of occurrence, on the other it reduces the total number of irregular *lexical items* in the language.

One can, however, also look at analogical change from the viewpoint of its effect on *morphological alternation*, that is to say on the number and shape of the allomorphs (or alternants) of individual morphemes in inflectional paradigms and derivational patterns (/kiːp/ ~ /kep-/ in *keep* : *kept*, /guːt/ ~ /güːt-/ in *gut* 'good' : *Güte* 'goodness'). Examined in this way all the cases of analogical change discussed so far may be interpreted as instances of analogical *levelling* since they have had the effect of eliminating, or at least reducing, alternation. Thus since its transition to the weak conjugation the verb *to help* has now only a single alternant /help/ whereas previously it had two, which can be represented as /help/ and /h-lp/. Clearly such cases of elimination of alternation in the lexicon have a regularizing effect on the language since verbs which have gone over to the weak conjugation no longer need listing for separate treatment with regard to past tense formation. The same is true with regard to the plural morpheme of nouns. The replacement of *kine* by *cows* has again both increased the incidence of the regular plural morph and eliminated an alternant from the lexicon. Sometimes alternation is not completely eliminated but only reduced, that is the alternants become more alike without however reaching identity. Thus in Early Modern German the word for 'wheel' had the alternants /raːd-/ and /rat/ while in current German these are /raːd-/ and /raːt/ (see p. 90f.).

Analogical change may also, however, increase alternation, in which case one speaks of the analogical *extension* of an alternation beyond its original domain. This is, as a rule, the rarer change of the two. A familiar example is the spread of the so-called 'intrusive *r*' in certain varieties of present-day British English. From lexical items in which there is an alternation between word-final vowel and vowel plus *r* before vowel (for example *hear* /hiə/ ~ *hearing* /hiəriŋ/, *roar* /rɔə/ ~ *roaring* /rɔːriŋ/, *car* /kaː/ ~ *car of* /kaː-r-əv/), the /r/ has spread to others which previously did not partake in the alternation (for example *saw* /sɔː/ ~ *saw it* /sɔː-r-it/, *law* /lɔː/ ~ *law of* /lɔː-r-əv/), thus creating alternants with /r/ in the case of words which historically never had an /r/. Another example is the analogical spread in German of the plural marker *-er* accompanied by umlaut of the base from a small nuclear class in which the *-er* was inherited, to a very large number of neuter nouns the plurals of which were identical with their singulars. Thus, on the model of certain old forms such as *Kalb* 'calf' : *Kälber* 'calves', *Lamm* 'lamb' : *Lämmer* 'lambs', innumerable umlauted plurals in *-er* have been created for such neuter nouns (*Wort* 'word' : *Wörter*, *Buch* 'book' : *Bücher*, *Kraut* 'herb' : *Kräuter* etc.) and even for a small number of masculine nouns (*Mann* 'man' : *Männer*, *Wald* 'forest': *Wälder*, etc.). It will be seen that the affixation of *-er* is always accompanied by redundant umlaut of the stem vowel so that the alternation non-umlauted : umlauted stem has in fact been extended beyond its original domain to lexical items which previously did not have it. This has resulted in an increase in uniformity in so far as plural formation is concerned but also an increase in the frequency of alternation in the lexicon. It might of course be argued that alternation in lexical items has been only slightly increased since many of these nouns already possessed an umlauted alternant for derivational purposes (for example formation of the diminutive, or of an adjective in *-lich* or *-ig*). But whereas it is completely predictable in the case of the plural in *-er*, in the derivational processes the occurrence of umlaut is unpredictable: *Wort* 'word', *Wörtchen* 'little word', *wörtlich* 'literal', but *Holz* 'wood', *Hölzchen* 'little piece of wood', *holzig* 'woody', *Haus* 'house' , *häuslich* 'domestic', *Gast* 'guest' , *gastlich* 'hospitable', *Beruf* 'profession' , *beruflich* 'professional', etc. Since plural formation automatically entails alternation while none of the derivational processes necessarily does, it is more economical to treat each morphological process as having its own alternation rule rather than attempt to give an overall rule for each lexical base. The extension of morphologically redundant alternation is not easy to explain in terms of structural economy. It has however repeatedly been observed, and even tentatively elevated to the status of a principle, that a form which is more fully characterized morphologically tends to be favoured at the expense of one which is less fully characterized (Kuryłowicz 1966).

The fact that we have restricted this discussion largely to inflectional morphology is not without significance. For, although it is true that analogical changes do also occur in derivational morphology they are usually on a rather limited scale. One reason for this lies in the fact that allomorphy is as a rule less clearly defined in derivational morphology, but analogical change presupposes that some specific semantic category be represented by two or more competing exponents. Certain agent nouns in *-er* in German are a case in point. This type has spread at the expense of an older type, the members of which had become formally unrecognizable as a class as a result of phonological change. The agent noun *Bäcker* 'baker', for instance, can be shown to have replaced an earlier form (which still survives dialectally) *Beck*. On the analogy of word pairs like *fischen* 'to fish' : *Fischer* 'fisher', *graben* 'to dig' : *Gräber* 'digger', *Bäcker* was formed from the verb *backen* 'to bake'. In a parallel way *Trinker* 'drinker', *Geber* 'giver', *Helfer* 'helper' replaced the older functionally equivalent forms *trinko*, *gebo*, *helfo* of Old High German. As a result of this remodelling process and of the continued productivity of the *-er* suffix, agent nouns which are not formed with this suffix are now rare in German.

Reasons for the fact that analogical changes occur less frequently in derivational than in inflectional morphology must in fact be sought in general differences between the two sectors. Thus, while the syntactic rules of a language may demand that for instance every noun and verb inflect for a specific number of grammatical categories, no comparable constraints exist regarding derivational rules – whether a particular derivative will actually occur in the language or not is usually quite unpredictable so that normally all derived forms have to be listed in the lexicon. Furthermore, while the grammatical categories operative in the syntactic rules tend to form relatively small closed classes, the semantic categories involved in the derivation of new lexical items are generally rather numerous, each one often involving only a limited number of bases. To this must be added the fact that, within any given derivational set characterized by a particular formal pattern, the semantic relationship between base and derivative is not in all cases identical. In short, because of their primarily lexical role and their limited participation in syntax, the derivational rules are much less subject to analogical change than the inflectional ones. In fact the two components appear to operate quite independently of one another so that it often occurs that an inherited alternation survives between base and derivative while it is eliminated in the inflectional paradigm. For instance in German /tsuxt/ *Zucht* 'breeding' /x/ before consonant alternates with zero between vowels, as in /'tsi:ən/ *ziehen* 'to breed', but in the inflectional paradigm of *ziehen* the alternation has been levelled: 1. singular /tsi:ə/, 2. /tsi:st/, 3. /tsi:t/ and not */tsixt/, as would be expected before the following consonant. This derivational pattern of nouns in *-t* is, of course, no longer productive.

5.2 *Analogical creation*

While analogical change is the fundamental mechanism whereby the morphological rules in a language are updated, analogical creation is that by means of which the lexical and conceptual resources are renewed. It is a fact that practically all lexical innovation which is not the result of borrowing (see chapter 6) is 'motivated', that is to say formed by rule from existing morphs. The derivation of English adjectives in /-əbl/ (*-able*, *-ible*) may serve to illustrate the way in which such a productive rule may arise. Middle English borrowed from French words like *measurable*, *reasonable*, *acceptable*, *agreeable*, *comfortable*, *profitable*; since their bases without the suffix were also borrowed, either as nouns (*measure*, *reason*) or as verbs (*accept*, *agree*) or as both (*comfort*, *profit*), *-able* could be abstracted as a morph with the function 'fit for . . ., fit for . . . ing, fit to be . . . ed' (Marchand 1960:174ff.). The pattern was to become extremely productive in English, so that adjectives in *-able* are now freely derivable, especially from verbs (*eatable*, *drinkable*, *machine washable*, etc.). It has been suggested that one of the main reasons for the popularity of this pattern is no doubt the fact that it does not entail morphological alternation in the base. More modern examples of analogical creation are the terms for such recently introduced items on the menu as *beefburger*, *cheeseburger*, *eggburger*, *baconburger*, and even simply *burger*, all resulting from a new segmentation and semantic reinterpretation of *hamburger* (in fact from *Hamburg*, and not from *ham*!), and new creations such as *townscape*, *seascape*, *beachscape*, *moonscape*, on the model of the long-established *landscape*.

The distinction between analogical change and analogical creation is in a sense marginal, belonging typically to a corpus-based approach to language in which all attested forms must be analysed and accounted for. If, however, language is considered from its creative aspect which operates with rules in a speaker's competence, the division loses much of its meaning since the same rules which generate existing forms can easily also create new ones. In other words, in a rule-based model of language analogical creation can readily be accounted for, either by reference to existing synchronic rules or to potential rules in the language. New creations like *moonscape* are immediately understood because they are based on a latent rule needed to account for *landscape*.

The cases of analogical formation so far discussed have involved morphologically complex words, and there can be no doubt that inflectional and derivational morphology represent the area of grammar in which the effects of the analogical principle are most readily observable. The extension of patterns beyond their original domain is, however, also well attested in syntax. Let us take as an example the verb *lehren* 'to teach' in German. In the older language this required two accusatives (*einen etwas lehren* 'to teach someone something'), but in present-day German the person affected by the action may just as well appear in the dative (*einem etwas lehren* 'to teach to someone something'), presumably on the analogy of the very large number of 'three place verbs' which have a personal dative object (*einem etwas erzählen/zeigen/geben*, etc., 'to tell/show/give to someone something') (Behaghel 1923:700f.). Another example is provided by the steady decrease in genitive objects; one still says in Standard German *der Toten gedenken* 'to remember (of) the dead', *einer Sache bedürfen* 'to be in need of something', with the object in the genitive, but such verbs are rare and many other verbs which formerly required a genitive object have replaced it with an accusative (*etwas vergessen/begehren/entbehren/geniessen* 'to forget/desire/lack/enjoy something') (Behaghel 1923:574ff.).[1]

It is more difficult, because of lack of documented evidence, to decide whether one is justified in postulating a similar extension of patterns at a very early stage in the history of Indo-European. It has in fact been suggested that the requirement in the Indo-European languages that all active sentences have an overt subject could be the result of the generalization to inanimate subjects of an actor–action construction with an animate noun in subject position so that, on the analogy of sentences like *the farmer is ploughing*, such formations as

[1] The present syntactic status of the various case forms is revealed when the sentences are put into the passive. In the case of *lehren* the noun phrase in the accusative marking the person affected by the action becomes, as one would expect, the grammatical subject in the passive sentence showing number concord with the verb (*sie wurden die englische Sprache gelehrt* 'they were taught the English language'), whereas a noun phrase in the dative cannot be converted into a subject (*ihnen wurde die englische Sprache gelehrt,* in which clearly *die englische Sprache* is the subject). In the case of genitive objects (e.g. *wir gedachten der Toten* 'we remembered the dead') the only possible passive is *der Toten wurde gedacht* in which the subject is the impersonal *es* 'it' as in the case of other verbs which do not take an object in the accusative (*es wurde der Toten gedacht* is like *es wurde gesungen* '(people) sang, there was singing'). In those cases, however, in which a genitive has been replaced historically by an accusative, the passive is no different from that of any transitive verb (*die Toten wurden vergessen* 'the dead were forgotten', like *die Toten wurden begraben* 'the dead were buried').

the cherry is ripening, *the beam broke*, *work stopped*, came to be created (Weisgerber 1963:233–55).

We will not pursue this question of analogical formations in syntax further. One could argue that it is only natural to expect analogical developments to dominate in those areas of the grammar where constructions are essentially generated by rule rather than reproduced unanalysed, and syntax is an obvious case in point. It is, on the other hand, equally plain that analogical formations constitute only the surface phenomena while it is the functional reinterpretation of inherited patterns which represents the underlying change (see p. 101f.).

Whether or not the principle of analogy may extend beyond morphologically complex forms as discussed so far is a question that should at least be asked. We have in mind certain morphologically simple forms which share both phonological segments and semantic features, for instance in English words such as *slip*, *slide*, *slime*, *slush*, *slop*; *bump*, *thump*, *clump*, *stump*, in German verbs like *knacken*, *knarren*, *knarschen*, *knirschen*, *knurren*, *knastern*, *knistern*, *knattern* all referring to noises (Bloomfield 1933:245, Paul 1970:177ff.). Practically all of these are lexical innovations, and it must be assumed that their formation is the result of sound symbolic associations of various kinds (initial clusters, rhyme) which are ultimately based on inherited words. The forms are clearly not analysable at the grammatical level. Their sound symbolism is on the other hand not simply dependent on 'natural' associations but clearly depends to some degree on language-specific formal-semantic associations. A second area in which analogical change may affect morphologically simple forms is in sets of words whose sole connecting link is a semantic one, for instance such closely knit semantic fields as those involving numerals and kinship terms. Interestingly it would appear that as a rule only those forms which are separated by a single semantic feature are involved. Thus, in the case of numerals, it is only adjacent numbers and in the case of kinship terms items such as 'brother' and 'sister', but not 'brother' and 'mother' which influence one another formally. Examples would be Latin *novem* 'nine', which has a final *-m* instead of the expected *-n* on the analogy of *decem* 'ten' or Greek *hoktṓ* and *optṓ* which are found dialectally in addition to the expected *oktṓ* 'eight', presumably on the analogy of *heptá* 'seven' (Winter 1969).

Finally a word should be said about the forms which most persistently resist analogical change – in English for instance nouns like *tooth*, *foot*, *mouse*, *man*, *woman*, and verbs like *to be*, *go*, *eat*, *drink*, *will*, *can*, *do*, etc. All these may be said to be members of so-called *basic vocabulary* which would appear to be the sector of language least influenced by cultural change (see chapter 6). Perhaps their stability and resistance to change is due to their very high frequency of occurrence in discourse and to the fact that their forms are therefore acquired by the child at an early stage before the respective grammatical rules have been acquired.[1] All that may be predicted in their case is what would be their likely form were they to undergo analogical change, although there is no means of predicting whether or not such change will in fact ever occur. At the opposite end of the spectrum rare irregular forms may also survive as archaisms in, for instance, poetic or religious registers but not in everyday speech (e.g. *beseech* : *besought*, *thou* : *thine*, *beloved*, *brethren*, etc.).

6 The interdependence of sound change and analogy

After looking at sound change and analogical formation separately we may now examine their essential interrelationship as seen by the neogrammarians in their theory of language development. It will be remembered that we interpreted the two types of diachronic process, sound change and analogical formation, as reflecting the division of linguistic structure into two distinct levels, that of phonology and that of grammar.[2] Thus, while both processes may on the surface bring about the addition, the replacement or the loss of phonological segments both in the spoken chain and in the phonological system,[3]

1 There appear to be three successive stages: (1) the acquisition of individual past tense forms of verbs; (2) the acquisition of a past tense rule, with 'wrong' generalizations (*goed*, etc.); (3) the adult system (King 1969a: 75, after S. Ervin Tripp).

2 The distinction at the time would appear to have been rather between the *physiological* mechanism of sound change, apparently beyond the influence of the human will, and *psychologically* motivated analogical processes (cf. Krahe 1970: 13; Paul 1970: 215f.; Best 1973: 30). Explicit statements regarding the relationship between the two principles were not, however, always made.

3 Analogical change may add new members to a phonological system. A somewhat artificial example is that of the /ɛ:/ (spelled *ä* or *äh*) of Standard German, which is only found in words which have (or were thought by the grammarians to have had) an allomorph with /a:/ (*Mägen*, plural of *Magen* 'stomach'; *Läden*, plural of *Laden* 'shop'; *Nähe* 'nearness', from *nah* 'near'; cf. however *blähen* 'to swell', *Ähre* 'ear of corn', without any such alternant; note that *ä* alternating orthographically with *a* represent-

analogical formation affects phonemes and phoneme sequences only in their role as elements of grammatical structure, whereas phonological change affects them irrespective of their grammatical function. The difference in the nature of the two processes is reflected in the difference between the kinds of rule at the two levels. Phonological rules are regular in the sense that they operate automatically on any input which meets their terms of reference irrespective of the consequences that this may have on grammatical structure. Analogical changes, on the other hand, are totally dependent on the grammatical structure and, even when the rule is clearly statable, whether or not it will be applied in any particular case cannot be predicted – it is only possible to state with reference to a particular analogical change what *would* be the consequences were it to take place. This complementary relationship between the two processes means that grammatical structures rendered opaque, or under the threat of being rendered opaque, by sound change are likely to be 'repaired' by analogical change. Hermann Paul even went so far as to claim that there is no sound change which has not caused at least one subsequent analogical development (1970:202). It is significant that such analogical readjustments always take the form of changes affecting the exponents of specific grammatical or semantic categories (dative, aorist, agent noun, etc.).

It is frequent for an analogical change to give the appearance of suspending or cancelling a sound change in a specific *grammatical* environment. One such instance is that of the 'retention' or perhaps rather the 'restoration' of /s/ in Greek when this had been lost in intervocalic position, as for example in the genitive *géneos* (from *génos* 'kind') when compared with the corresponding forms in Sanskrit (*jánasas*) and Latin (*generis*, with *-r-* from earlier *-s-*). For in spite of this phonological change, in the aorist of vowel-final verbs in Greek the tense marker /s/ is present even though it stands in intervocalic position (*lū́-ō* 'to loosen', aorist *é-lū-s-a*; *tīmá-ō* 'to esteem', aorist *e-tī́mē-s-a*). The

ing short /a/ is a mere spelling convention based on the same principle but does not stand for a separate phoneme; phonemically it represents the same phoneme /e/ as does the spelling *e*). A perhaps more natural example is the case of the development by analogy of a second rounded front vowel in a Swiss German dialect (Moulton 1962); in this dialect the umlauted forms corresponding to bases with both /o/ and /ɔ/ were originally identical (/ö/), with no difference in vowel height, but later a new phoneme /ɔ̈/ was created analogically so that now /o/ alternates with /ö/ and /ɔ/ with /ɔ̈/; see below, p. 128.

retention of the /s/ in the aorist of these verbs is ascribed to the influence of plosive-final verbs like *trép-ō* 'to turn', aorist *é-trep-s-a*; *deík-nū-mi* 'to point', aorist *é-deik-s-a*, in which the /s/ would not have been affected by the phonological change because it was not in intervocalic position. The terms 'retention' and 'restoration' of course describe the phenomena in terms of our rule-based model of description; in the speech community there was presumably co-existence of forms with and without the /s/ until eventually the former was generalized. We shall see the importance of cases of this kind when we come to discuss the attack made on the neogrammarian position by the transformational-generative school (see chapter 3).

7 Phonological reconstruction ('the comparative method')

We have so far limited our discussion of language change and the principles which govern it to documented cases. The fundamental importance of the neogrammarian model lies, however, in the postulate that the same principles which can be verified in documented language history must also be assumed to apply in the case of linguistic pre-history.[1] This generalization makes it possible to explain the partial similarity of the linguistic systems of related languages as resulting from the fact that each represents the continuation, by way of a different channel of transmission, of a single 'initial' linguistic system. And, since related languages have preserved and modified inherited forms and rules in different ways, systematic comparison should allow the recovery of the original system from which they all derive. It is in fact the historical linguist's task to attempt to reconstruct this initial system and to show how the descendant languages have reached their present form. In so far as the Indo-European languages are concerned, Proto-

[1] This claim may appear self-evident today, but it was a major break-through at the time (Osthoff and Brugmann 1878). In fact only a few years prior to the neogrammarian manifesto Schleicher, Steinthal and others had divided the development of every language or language family into two basic periods, a period of evolutionary development and a period of decay. Thus the more primitive, or archaic, a language, the richer, more spontaneous and more plentiful its 'organic' structure whereas intellectual activity, culture and civilization destroyed that structure. On this basis Schleicher directly linked the decay of the morphological structure of English with the success of the English people in world history (1869: 35). In the Indo-European family the peak was supposedly reached in the earliest stages of the individual languages, after which there was a continuing process of decay.

Indo-European, their hypothetical ancestor, represents the system from which all their grammars are, ideally, derivable by rule and it is the ultimate resort to which the synchronic irregularities of any individual Indo-European language can be traced.

Despite the fact that sound change and analogical formation have equal theoretical status in the neogrammarian model of language evolution, there can be no doubt that, of the two, phonological change plays the more important role. The principal reason for this is that analogical formation can account for only a part of the diachronic phenomena at the grammatical level whereas the rules of sound change cover *all* developments at the phonological level. For it must be remembered that analogical formation is essentially restricted to morphologically complex forms whereas the simple lexical morphs, because of the arbitrary nature of the linguistic sign, are restructured only by the phonological rules of the language. It is through these latter, therefore, that historical connections between languages can be most reliably established. The neogrammarian manifesto in fact recommends resort to analogical hypotheses 'only when the sound laws fail' (Osthoff and Brugmann 1878). Clearly, we are here no longer talking about theoretical principles but about practical procedures. Such discovery procedures are, however, important since the historical linguist has no data at his disposal other than the forms and rules of individual languages. It is only by the systematic comparison of these that he can achieve his objective, which is to produce a body of hypothetical protostructures together with rules by means of which the grammars of these languages can be derived from them. In this section we will illustrate the kind of argument which guides procedures and decisions but will not make any attempt to formalize them. Their ultimate justification lies in the fact that the rules arrived at under their guidance relate and explain all the data in the most economical way.

7.1 *Correspondence series and protosegments*

As an illustration of phonological reconstruction let us take an example from the field of Germanic. With very few exceptions, all of which can be accounted for, lexical items containing an /a:/ in Old English have Modern English equivalents with /ou/ (for example *stān* : *stone*, *āc* : *oak*, *hlāf* : *loaf*). This correlation is the result of a sound change whereby Old English /a:/ regularly developed into /ou/ in Modern English. There is, however, also a regular relationship between Old English /a:/ and Old High German /ei/ (cf. the corresponding Old High German forms *stein* 'stone', *eih* 'oak', *leib* 'loaf') and, because Old English and Old High German were contemporary languages, this obviously cannot be explained in the same way. The regular *correspondence* between Old High German /ei/ and Old English /a:/ can, however, be accounted for using the concept of the regularity of sound change if we postulate that the *common ancestor* of both English and German had a phonological segment which, through regular sound change, became on the one hand Old English /a:/ and on the other Old High German /ei/. For reasons both of phonetic plausibility and descriptive economy this segment is traditionally represented by /ai/ and, in order to indicate that it is not actually attested but merely postulated, we mark it with an asterisk: */ai/. The development would thus have been:

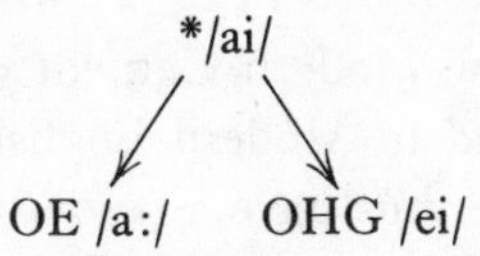

Of course a *reconstruction* such as this must also be as fully compatible as possible with all the other data we possess, such as the reconstructed phonological system as a whole and the rules which govern its previous evolution and further developments. As a general principle we will set up that segment which fulfils all these conditions in the most economical and the most phonetically plausible way.

All that has happened in the above example is that the phoneme of the protolanguage has evolved differently in its phonetic realization in each of the two languages, but in spite of this divergence there is still one-to-one correspondence between its reflexes in *cognates* (that is to say in words which are the direct continuation in the two languages of a single lexical item in the protolanguage). But we have seen that a phonetic change affecting a phoneme may sometimes result in its merger with another phoneme so that the opposition which existed between them in the system is lost (see p. 31). In order to show the way in which such a merger may be reconstructed, we will first follow the developments undergone by Old High German /ei/ and Old English /a:/ as recoverable from the actual documentary evidence and then see how far it would have been possible to reconstruct these developments in the absence of all documentation. From historical records we know that Old English /a:/ became Modern English /ou/ and Old High German /ei/ became Modern German /ai/, and these changes are reflected in their regular correspondence in a long series of Modern English and Modern German words (e.g. *stone* : *Stein*, *loaf* : *Laib*, *home* : *Heim*, etc.). It will however be remembered that Modern German /ai/ also has a second source, namely Old High German /i:/ (see p. 31). The series of developments may be summarized as follows:

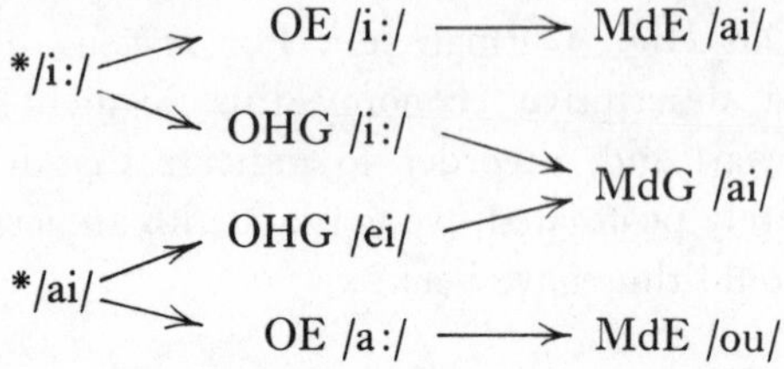

It will be seen that those Modern German words in which /ai/ comes from /i:/ will correspond to Modern English words not with an /ou/ but with an /ai/ and we thus have a second series of words, in which Modern English /ai/ corresponds to Modern German /ai/ (e.g. *ice* : *Eis*, *tide* : *Zeit*, *my/mine* : *mein*, etc.). In other words, those German /ai/s which come from /i:/ correspond to English /ai/ while those which come from /ei/ correspond to English /ou/. This means that even if we did not have the evidence of the historical developments in German we would still be able to recover them from a comparison with English. For, since English has not undergone a parallel merger, the distribution of the two different sources of /ai/ in the Modern German words can be seen from the distribution of /ai/ and /ou/ in their cognates in Modern English. For this to be possible, however, it must first be shown that it is English which has retained the original distribution of the segments and that German has innovated. We must start from the basic assumption that each set of English–German correspondences reflects a single segment in the protolanguage and that, provided no change has affected its phonetic environment, the distribution of the present-day reflexes continues that of the protolanguage. We may thus expect contrastive distribution (that is to say, occurrence in the same environments) of the reflexes of different protophonemes, but complementary distribution (that is to say, in mutually exclusive environments) of the reflexes of allophones of a single protosegment. Now in the case which we are considering the evidence in the descendant languages is conflicting:

in English /ai/ and /ou/ contrast whereas in German there is only /ai/ occupying their combined distribution. Which language has, then, retained the old situation and which has innovated? If we were to assume that it was English which had undergone innovation and that originally the distribution of the two protosegments was complementary, this would imply that all the various environments in which /ai/ and /ou/ now contrast must be secondary, that is the result of sound changes affecting the phonological environment. In view of the very large number of minimal pairs and the great variety of environments involved (cf. *toe* : *tie*, *loaf* : *life*, *loam* : *lime*, *loan* : *line*, *moan* : *mine*, *rope* : *ripe*, *rode* : *ride*, *boat* : *bite*, *pope* : *pipe*, *drove* : *drive*, etc.), this is quite impossible. The occurrence of split on such a scale and producing such diversity is simply unthinkable and an assumption infinitely more complex than the alternative one, namely that English has retained an originally contrastive distribution while German has merged the contrasting phonemes into one. It is this latter solution which we will then adopt. The next step is again the selection of suitable symbols to represent the protophonemes in such a way that the assumed subsequent sound changes are at the same time both minimal and phonetically plausible – a step which has, of course, been anticipated at the outset of our description.

After the above reconstruction of a merger we will now consider the reconstruction of a split. For this we will use the data already given in our discussion of cross-language similarity. If we turn then to the table of English and German pairs of words listed on p. 21 it will be seen that all the English forms contain a member of the /t/ phoneme while the German forms have between them three phonemes, /ts/, /t/, and /s/, corresponding to the English /t/. There are thus three correspondence sets:

(A) /t/ : /ts/ (Nos. 1–6)
(B) /t/ : /t/ (Nos. 7–13)
(C) /t/ : /s/ (Nos. 14–19)

If we examine the phonological environments in which each of these correspondence sets occurs, we will find that they are almost in complementary distribution:

(A) occurs initially before vowel (1, 2), medially after /r/ and /n/ (3, 4); it also occurs finally (5) and perhaps medially under unclear conditions (6), but note however that in (5) it contrasts with (C) in (18, 19), and that in (6) it contrasts with (C) in (16, 17).

(B) occurs in an obstruent cluster, English /st/ : German /ʃt/ initially (7, 8) and /st/ : /st/ medially (9); German /ʃt/ and /st/ are therefore in complementary distribution. It also occurs initially before /r/ (10, 11) and, under unclear conditions, medially in (12, 13). Note however that in (12) it contrasts with (A) in (4), and in (13) it contrasts with (C) in (14, 15).
(C) occurs medially between vowels (14, 15), perhaps also medially in (16, 17), and in final position in (18, 19). In all these positions, however, it contrasts with (A) and (B) (see 5, 6, 13).

The corpus on which these observations are based is of course minimal, but it has been deliberately chosen to be representative of the observable distributional regularities. Starting from the fact of the near-complementary distribution of the three correspondence sets, it is naturally tempting to assume that this reflects an originally complementary distribution of the protosounds underlying them. In that case a reasonable hypothesis would be that English has preserved the older situation and that each of the German reflexes continues one positionally defined allophone of a */t/ phoneme of the common ancestor. This, however, would require that the few instances in which the correspondence sets contrast be shown to be secondary, that is to say the result of phonological changes in the environment subsequent to the protolanguage. Let us therefore consider them in turn.

Judged from the present situation in English and German, items (13) 'bitter' and (15) 'better' appear to indicate identical environments and would thus block the reconstruction of a */t/ for both. We have however seen in (10, 11) that German has /t/ in the environment of a following /r/. This fact provides a possible clue to the resolution of the problem posed by (12, 13). Let us assume that these also originally contained the sequence */tr/ and that this sequence was only later interrupted by a vowel whereas (14, 15) contained a vowel from the start. In this case */t/ in (12, 13) and (14, 15) would originally have been in complementary distribution. If we now compare the environments of /t/ in the corresponding forms of the earliest recorded Germanic language, Gothic, we find the forms *baitrs* 'bitter' and *batiza* 'better'. Ignoring the difference in vowel grade between Gothic *baitrs* and English and German *bitter*, and given that Gothic /z/ regularly corresponds to /r/ in English and German – easily demonstrable from other data – we can now see from the Gothic evidence that the essential difference between the two series of cognates must reside in the earlier presence of a vowel after the /t/ of (15) but not after that of (13). We may thus postulate an original contrast */-tr-/ : */-tVr-/ not only for the pair *bitter* : *better* but also for *winter* : *water*. After the loss of the endings corresponding to Gothic *-s*/*-a* had made the */r/ of */-tr-/ word-final a vowel must have been inserted between it and the */t/, thus eliminating the original difference of environment.

We now turn to the problem of (6) as compared with (16, 17). Here the reflex of the */t/ appears in final position in the English examples but in medial position in the German ones and the first matter to be resolved is which of the languages reflects the environment in the protolanguage. It is obvious that either English must have lost the infinitive ending or German have added it, and the historical evidence of Old English with its infinitive forms *sittan*, *etan*, *hatian* shows that it is the former which has taken place. The correspondence /t/ : /s/ of (16, 17) is therefore the 'regular' one of (C) as in (14, 15). But this still leaves (6) unaccounted for and we are now faced with the situation that correspondence sets (A) and (C) would appear to have existed in identical environments, that is medially between vowels. We must therefore posit some difference in the environments which has subsequently been lost. Now we can see that the /t/ : /ts/ correspondence in (6) is the same as that of (A) in (3, 4) in which the conditioning environmental factor was that of a preceding consonant. If then a preceding consonant could be shown to have been lost in (6) the problem would be resolved. A clue to the solution is given by the Old English spellings *sittan* 'to sit' as opposed to *etan* 'to eat'; the double *t* would thus appear to represent a long /tt/ counting as a cluster and we may therefore posit a protosegment */tt/ for (6), a supposition which can in fact be confirmed from other evidence. A similar assumption resolves the apparent conflict between (5) and (18, 19), the protoform of (5) again being assumed to have had a long */tt/. This also is in fact verifiable independently.

Having thus established the complementary distribution of the three correspondence sets (A), (B), and (C), we can now see that each of these must represent a different positional allophone of */t/ in the protolanguage. In order to arrive at the situation in present-day German we must assume not only subsequent phonetic changes affecting these but also changes in their environments resulting in an alteration of their phonological status. The following phonetic developments must have taken place: (1) affrication of */t/ in initial position before vowel (1, 2) and medially after */n/, */r/ or in gemination provided that the group is followed by vowel or pause (3–6); (2) assibilation (that is, the passage to fricative) of */t/ medially between vowels (14–17) and in absolute final position (18, 19); (3) retention of plosion in the clusters */st/ and */tr/ (7–13). At the phonological level we have already seen how [ts] and [s] came to contrast medially and finally as the result of the passage of geminate */tt/ to [ts] and of single */t/ to [s], and how [t] and [s] came to contrast medially due to the insertion of a vowel between /t/ and final /r/. There are in addition, of course, other sources of [t] and [s] in Modern German, with the result that [t], [ts], and [s] now contrast in a great variety of environments. In present-day English */t/ is reflected in the single phoneme /t/. However, as a result of the loss of the contrast between geminate */tt/ and single */t/ and the loss of certain unstressed endings, as well as the insertion as in German of a vowel between /t/ and final /r/, the distributional properties of /t/ differ to some extent from those of */t/ in the protolanguage.

Looking back over these two examples, one of the reconstruction of a merger and one of the reconstruction of a split, it will be seen that the technique employed closely parallels that of synchronic phonemic analysis. Just as in phonemic analysis phonetically similar phones in complementary distribution are subsumed under a single phoneme, so correspondence sets in complementary distribution are subsumed under a single segment (or protophoneme) of the protolanguage. And it is of course the distributional regularities of the protolanguage which are decisive since they determine the phonological status in it of the segment in question.

The term 'reconstruction' for the analytic operations that we have been performing is perhaps somewhat unfortunate since it is liable to lead to a misunderstanding of the nature of what we are doing. Its use stems from a time when it was believed that the methods of historical linguistics did in fact recover the actual linguistic reality of the past. It is harmless enough, however, provided that we see it as no more than a convenient technical term, for the extent of the gap between construct and reality becomes plain enough when we consider the theoretical basis of our operations. In the first place it must be remembered that the segments with which we operate are phonemes which are themselves already abstractions having no existence outside the phones that represent them. Secondly, we are interpreting directly as sound changes phonological correspondences between cognate forms and are behaving as if the postulated diachronic rules were identical with the historical events which are assumed to underlie them. Thirdly we are, on the basis of the general validity of the regularity principle, choosing the phonetic characteristics of the protosegments in such a way that their reflexes in the descendant languages may be derived from them in the most economical and most phonetically plausible fashion. This means that we simply postulate the minimal possible number of protosegments and such sound changes as do not contradict anything we know about the general processes of phonetic change. Taken together, all these methodological assumptions are bound to add up to a considerable degree of idealization.

7.2 *Diachronic rules: form and order*

The sound changes that we postulate on the basis of phonological correspondences are, like the protosegments, part of the reconstruction process. Ideally, in both their form and their sequence, they are to be considered as representing historical changes which must have taken place in real space and real time. In documented language history successive language states are linked by rules in such a way that the output of each set of rules represents a new state which serves as input to the next set of rules. In most instances, however, owing to the deficiencies of spelling, direct evidence of the actual changes that have taken place and of the new systems that have resulted is lacking. We are then dependent solely on internal evidence. And for prehistoric change it is only the internal evidence that can establish rule order in any case and where such evidence is lacking the changes must be treated as if they had been simultaneous. Limitations on possible rule order are imposed by the formal structure of the data and by the fact that rules have limited validity in time, as well as by the principle of economy of statement. The following example will illustrate the method of reconstruction on the basis of internal evidence as well as its limitations. Note that, although it is taken from a case of documented language history and even though the changes occurred quite recently (within the last seven hundred years), a relative chronology cannot be arrived at from the spelling conventions of the documents and thus relies on internal evidence alone. Let us compare the following Middle High German and Modern German forms:

	'body'	'my'	'loaf'	'stone'	'dear'	'song'
MHG	/li:p/	/mi:n/	/leip/	/stein/	/liep/	/liet/
MdG	/laip/	/main/	/laip/	/ʃtain/	/li:p/	/li:t/

We need at least three diachronic rules in order to arrive at the Modern German forms:

(1) monophthongization (/ie/ > /i:/)
(2) diphthongization (/i:/ > /ai/)
(3) lowering: (/ei/ > /ai/)

Let us apply these rules in the above order and note the output of each:

MHG	/li:p/	/mi:n/	/leip/	/stein/	/liep/	/liet/
(1)					li:p	li:t
(2)	laip	main			**laip	**lait
(3)			laip	stain		
MdG	/laip/	/main/	/laip/	/ʃtain/	**laip	**lait

Clearly, 'dear' and 'song' should not have been put through rule (2) since this produces incorrect forms (indicated by a double asterisk). On the other hand the regularity principle requires that if at a particular language stage there is a rule affecting /i:/ then all /i:/s must be subject to it. By changing the order of application of the rules, however, we are able to avoid the problem:

MHG	/li:p/	/mi:n/	/leip/	/stein/	/liep/	/liet/
(2)	laip	main				
(1)					li:p	li:t
(3)			laip	stain		
MdG	/laip/	/main/	/laip/	/ʃtain/	/li:p/	/li:t/

This new ordering produces the correct forms and is therefore an adequate solution to the problem. We can also see that the rule which changes /ei/ to /ai/ is independent of the monophthongization rule and it does not matter whether it precedes or follows it. The same observation applies in the case of the diphthongization rule – whether we apply (3) before (2), or (2) before (3), we get the same result:

(3)			laip	stain
(2)	laip	main		

or:

(2)	laip	main		
(3)			laip	stain

We could also, however, have obtained the same result by formulating the diphthongization rule differently, namely as (2′) /i:/ > /ei/ and by applying (3) subsequently:

(2′)	leip	mein		
(3)	laip	main	laip	stain

Apart from demonstrating the sometimes imperfect correlation between rules and actual historical changes, alternative formulations of this kind throw light on the relationship between rule form and rule order which, it can be seen, are not independent of one another. By dividing up the development /i:/ > /ai/ into successive changes, first /i:/ > /ei/ and then /ei/ > /ai/, we impose an order on rules which, in the alternative formulation /i:/ > /ai/ and /ei/ > /ai/, are unordered. The model itself would not appear to favour one solution rather than the other. Explicit discussion of theoretical alternatives of this kind is not to be found in the neogrammarian literature, probably because such a case would not have been treated in isolation from the historical development in neighbouring closely related dialects and indeed, if we examine the situation in the Modern German dialects as a whole, we do in fact find arguments favouring the last solution at the expense of the others. Thus, although the diphthongization of the high vowels has affected a large number of adjacent dialects, the merger of its outcome with the old diphthongs is by no means universal and is thus better treated as a separate change. We are here merely concerned, however, with the structure and properties of the model and with noting the interdependence of rule form and rule order.

If we now return to the question of reconstruction but this time in a context of language prehistory, we find that the same considerations apply, with the additional requirement, however, that a protosegment must be chosen from which the postulated changes may be assumed to have started. Clearly the form of the diachronic rules to be set up will depend on this choice, but the order of the diachronic rules will again be determined on internal grounds. An example from the reconstruction of Proto-Indo-European will serve to illustrate the principles involved. Let us compare the initial consonant of the following cognates, in which the digraphs *qu*, *hw* represent unit phonemes, and attempt to reconstruct its source in the protolanguage:

	Latin	Old English	Greek	Sanskrit	
(1)	-que		-te	-ca	'and' (enclitic)
(2)	quis		tis	(-cid)	'who' ('whatever')
(3)	quod	hwæt		(-kas)	'what' ('who')
(4)		hwæþer	poteros	kataras	'which of the two'

The fact that in both Latin and Old English the initial consonant is uniform in all attested forms suggests that we are probably dealing with a case of phonemic split. Looking at the reflexes in the other two languages we may then ask: what sound is most likely to have become a dental plosive before a front vowel but a labial plosive before a back vowel in the Greek forms and is at the same time reflected in the Sanskrit forms as a palatal and as a velar, presumably depending on the environment? Traditional historical linguistics reconstructs a labiovelar $*/k^w/$ as the most economical solution to account for all the facts. In order to give the correct forms in the derived languages, this labiovelar would have to have remained unchanged in Latin, to have become a fricative in English, and to have become a dental plosive before front vowel and a labial plosive before back vowel in Greek. These are all changes which present no particular difficulty. In the case of Sanskrit, however, the situation is clearly more complicated. Here it can be seen that the original labiovelar, apart from becoming delabialized, has in certain cases also become a palatal. A clue to the conditioning factor responsible for the distribution of /k/ and /c/ is to be found in the vowels of the Latin and Greek cognates. For, where these have a front vowel (*i*, *e*) Sanskrit has palatalization and where these have a back vowel (*o*) it does not. But how, then, can we account for the fact that (1), (3) and (4) have identical vowels and yet only the first two have undergone palatalization? Clearly a vowel change is involved and the relative ordering of this and of the palatalization of the consonant is vital. Thus, if on the basis of the Latin and Greek vowels, we reconstruct */e/ for (1) and */i/ for (2) in the protolanguage, we can then say that these front vowels must have been responsible for the palatalization of *[k] to [c] in Sanskrit; for (3) and (4) on the other hand, we can reconstruct the back vowel */o/ which would have had no effect on the neighbouring consonant. Subsequently the */e/ and */o/ must have merged in Sanskrit to become /a/ and this merger in their environments has caused [k] and [c], which had up till then been positionally conditioned allophones, to become fully contrasting phonemes. Thus, although Sanskrit has not preserved the contrast between */e/ and */o/, its postulated former presence in the language is the only way in which the distribution of /c/ and /k/ can be accounted for. The developments in Sanskrit must thus have taken place in the following order:

(I) $*/k^w/ > /k/$

(II) [k] > [c] before front vowel

(III) $\left.\begin{matrix} */e/ \\ */o/ \end{matrix}\right\} > /a/$ (resulting in $/k/ \neq /c/$)

Initial construct, rule form and rule order are thus closely interdependent. The phonology of the protolanguage, together with the sets of ordered rules by which the linguistic systems of the descendant languages are derived from it, form just as much an integrated whole, *un système où tout se tient*, as does the synchronic description of a language. In a previous example, for instance, we postulated an */ai/ as the source of both Old High German /ei/ and Old English /a:/ on grounds of descriptive economy, both reflexes being derivable from it by simple phonological rules. But it should be noted that this solution also fits in with the wider rules which link Germanic to the other Indo-European languages, the */ai/ in question being derived from Proto-Indo-European */oi/ parallel to */a/ from */o/. And such phonological reconstruction in turn makes transparent morphological alternation patterns which in Germanic languages had become synchronically opaque. Thus the alternation of */e/ and */o/ is basic to the morphology of the Indo-European languages, for example Greek /ei/ : /oi/ : /i/ in present *leíp-ō* 'to leave' : perfect *lé-loip-a* : aorist *é-lip-on*. This same alternation, as the result of the phonological changes */ei/ > */i:/ and */oi/ > */ai/ which took place between Proto-Indo-European and Proto-Germanic and */ai/ > /a:/ between Proto-Germanic and Old English, has become thoroughly obscured in English (Old English *rīdan* : *rād* : *riden*, Modern English *ride* : *rode* : *ridden*). But, although its reflexes /ai/ : /ou/ : /i/ in the grammar of Modern English are synchronically quite opaque, reconstruction is able to explain them and to show that their irregularity is secondary, the result of earlier phonological change.

8 Morphological and syntactic reconstruction

We have so far confined ourselves to reconstruction at the phonological level. On purely theoretical grounds one might expect the methods of phonological reconstruction to be matched by independent methods of morphological and syntactic reconstruction justified by theoretical principles comparable to that of the regularity of sound change at the phonological level. There are, however, no such principles in neogrammarian theory, nor for that matter in any subsequent model (cf. however chapters 2, 3 and 7). Grammatical structure is in principle reconstructed via the phonological shapes of words which are, just as in synchronic analysis, segmented at the morphological level and gathered into inflectional paradigms and derivational sets. Syntactic patterns are then established on the basis of the distribution of morphologically characterized classes of forms in sentences. Of course analogical processes are bound to play an important role in this part of the grammar but they depend upon existing syntactic structures rather than create new ones. For the Indo-European languages, especially in their most ancient phases, reconstruction on this basis has proved a fairly successful method since syntactic relationships are basically signalled by the morphological forms of lexemes in sentences. The reconstructed morphological and syntactic systems are thus based on the prior reconstruction of the nominal, pronominal and verbal paradigms and the syntactic distribution of their members. It should perhaps be noted in passing that, no doubt because of the unique role it plays, the American structuralist textbooks restrict the use of the term 'the comparative method' to phonological reconstruction.

8.1 *Morphology*

The establishment by means of phonological reconstruction of the full range of inflectional forms of a lexeme is necessary for the reconstruction of the morphology. We have in fact seen in an example from the history of English (see p. 32f.) that mere phonological change may, by affecting the forms of markers and exponents of categories, result in the functional reinterpretation of inherited forms. This obviously has to be taken account of in reconstruction, and the forms reconstructed for the protolanguage may require a morphological analysis which differs fundamentally from that of later stages. New grammatical categories and classes may thus have to be postulated in order to account for the range (or 'scatter') of reconstructed forms of a lexeme, and it is through the distribution of the exponents of such categories and classes that syntactic patterns are established.

Example 1: Archaic Chinese pronouns

The principle is perhaps best illustrated through an example from the prehistory of Chinese. This case is particularly striking since it implies the presence of inflection for case for a stage in the history of the language preceding the earliest written records, thus suggesting that the isolating character of Chinese was associated only with a particular phase of its history (see p. 265). Karlgren's analysis (1949:72ff.) is based on the functional interpretation of the scatter in the oldest surviving texts of pronominal forms. Although pairs of these were apparently in free variation, from a quantitative analysis he was able to conclude that, in the period immediately preceding these texts, there must have been a syntactically determined distribution of the form pairs based on an opposition between a subject-adnominal function and an object function. On the basis of his evidence he postulated the following distribution of forms:

person	nominative-genitive	dative-accusative
1.	wu	wo
2.	ju	erh
3.	ch'i (genitive)	chih

When the protoforms of these were reconstructed on the basis of the phonological rules established for Chinese, he obtained:

person	nominative-genitive	dative-accusative
1.	*ng-o	*ng-â
2.	*ńi̯-o	*ńi̯-a
3.	*g'-i̯əg (genitive)	*tʸ-i̯əg

The values of the phonetic symbols need not concern us here nor the fact that they have since been somewhat modified (it is after all a common experience that protolanguages change rather rapidly at the hands of scholars!). What matters is that the reconstructed forms are morphologically segmentable and recurrent stretches can be associated with grammatical functions: case suffices *-o* and *-a* for first and second person, case prefixes for third person. From this Karlgren concludes that in Archaic Chinese pronouns inflected for case, and he goes even further and suggests that, since pronominal inflection presupposes nominal inflection, Archaic Chinese must have possessed case also as a category of the noun (see, however, Graham 1969 for a different interpretation).

Example 2: the Proto-Indo-European case system

Eight cases have been reconstructed for Proto-Indo-European, their reconstruction being based principally on the earliest recorded stages of those Indo-European languages which have preserved a fairly full case system (notably Vedic Sanskrit and the Baltic and Slavonic languages). The individual morphemes of the case system of the protolanguage are arrived at through the reconstruction of allomorphs the reflexes of which have like syntactic distribution in the individual languages and exhibit regular sound correspondences between themselves. The case systems of those Indo-European languages which have a smaller number of cases, such as the Germanic languages, are derived from the protosystem by a process of: (1) predicting from the reconstructed protosystem, on the basis of the phonological rules, expected morph shapes and seeing which of these do in fact exist; (2) matching these to the exponents of specific syntactic functions, such as object of transitive verbs, etc. The reconstruction of the Proto-Indo-European accusative singular, for instance, is straightforward since what the synchronic grammars of most Indo-European languages call 'accusative' constitutes its direct continuation in both form and function. Thus the accusative allomorphs *-m*, *-em* and ø of Latin (types *mensa-m* from *mensa* 'table', *homin-em* from *homo*~*homin-* 'man', and *genus* from *genus* 'kind') have corresponding forms in other Indo-European languages and can be subsumed under two protomorphs in complementary distribution, *-*m* (incl. ('syllabic' *m*) and *-ø. In all the Indo-European languages which have retained it, the accusative marks the direct object of transitive verbs, and the goal and extension in time or space of actions (*epistulam scribere* 'to write a letter', *Romam ire* 'to go to Rome', *triduum manere* 'to stay for three days') so that the nature of the original function raises no serious problems. The situation is more complex for certain of the other cases. The 'dative' of the early Germanic languages, for instance, unites the functions of the Proto-Indo-European dative, instrumental and locative and even partially of the ablative, whereas formally it continues Proto-Indo-European dative, instrumental and locative forms. Thus, with some slight oversimplification, we have the following development from Proto-Indo-European to Modern German:

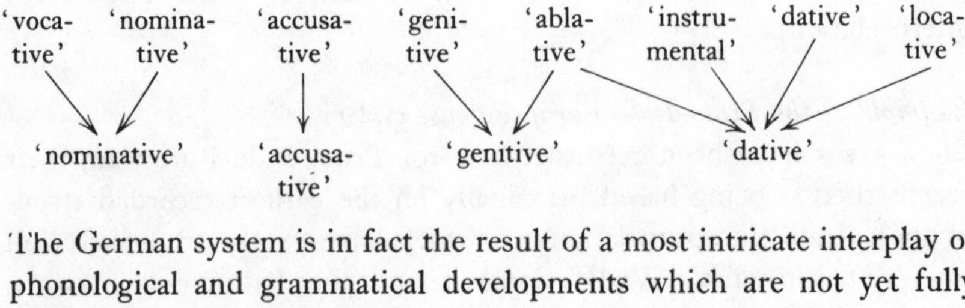

The German system is in fact the result of a most intricate interplay of phonological and grammatical developments which are not yet fully understood in all their details.

8.2 *Syntax*

It is not only at the level of morphology that such functional reanalysis of inherited forms may take place, this may also happen in the case of syntactic structures. It has for instance been claimed that the conjunction *that* in English constructions of the type *I saw that he was asleep*, as well as in equivalent ones in Vulgar Latin (*quod*) and German (*dass*) is the result of 'wrong' syntactic segmentation by the native speaker of a construction which was originally *I saw that. He was asleep* (cf. Modern English *He was asleep. I saw that*). It has been suggested that in the same way the so-called periphrastic tenses of the verb in several western European languages had a parallel origin in the reinterpretation of constructions such as Vulgar Latin *arborem fici habebat quidam plantatam in vinea sua* (Luke 13.6) 'someone had (i.e. possessed) a fig tree [which was] planted in his vineyard'. Here 'planted in his vineyard' is an embedded participial clause acting as an attribute of 'fig tree'; the noun and participle agree in case and gender and the verb of the main clause is 'have'. In the Romance languages this construction must subsequently have been reinterpreted so that the participle came to be treated as the main verb and 'have' as an auxiliary within the same clause, the syntactic complexity of the construction being no longer felt because of the identity of the nominal constituent 'fig tree' in both. The sequence 'had planted' was then taken to contrast paradigmatically with 'has planted', etc., leading to a complete restructuring of the tense system in early Romance, whence the construction is assumed to have later spread into the Germanic languages (Lockwood 1968: 115; see below, chapter 6).

New syntactic patterns may also arise through the reinterpretation of individual words in specific contexts. Thus German *weil* 'because' and English *since* and *while* used with non-temporal meaning must be the result of the reinterpretation of originally temporal conjunctions. In contexts like *He wears only black since his mother died* a 'causal' interpretation of *since* is readily understandable whereas the origin of the 'adversary' meaning of *while* (*While you may of course be right, nevertheless* . . .) is probably to be traced to sentences of the type *While the rich were feasting the poor were starving*.

9 Lexical reconstruction

The context-determined semantic interpretation of forms is in no way restricted to syntax, for it may also be said to constitute a basic mechanism for semantic change at the lexical level (Leumann 1927). The English word *church* today refers not only to the building and to the institution but also to the act of church-going, and we may presume that it is due to the reinterpretation of sentences like *she returned from church* that constructions of the type *after church* eventually became possible. In the same way words may develop or lose pejorative or noble connotations, and what was originally a metaphoric use may become the normal meaning so that, for instance, French *arriver* has totally lost its original associations with water transport ('to come to shore'). Such reinterpretations depend on the fact that there is an element of discontinuity between encoding by the speaker and decoding by the hearer, and utterances may thus be given grammatical and semantic interpretations by the hearer (including the language learner) which did not form part of the speaker's intent. Since, however, the hearer's interpretation is based on the linguistic context it is systematic in the sense that it is conditioned by lexical and syntactic structure.

In lexical reconstruction it is, however, phonological form which plays the key role because here again we have the regularity of sound change as a systematic criterion. If two words in related languages show regular sound correspondences and their semantic differences can be explained by postulating plausible semantic changes from an assumed earlier underlying meaning, an etymological connection will be postulated between the two. The *etymology* of a word is thus its formal and semantic history traced back in time until an earlier grammar, or the grammar of a donor language if it is a loan-word, is reached, the productive rules of which can fully account for it. English *murder* and German *Mord* 'murder' can for instance be traced back respectively to Proto-Indo-European **mrtró-* and **mrtó-*, both nominals derived from the root **mr-* 'to die' (e.g. Latin *mori* 'to die', *mors*, *mort-* 'death'). The etymons (or ancestral forms) of *Mord* and *murder* thus originally meant 'death', but the semantic development in Germanic has led to their much more specific modern meaning of 'the premeditated and unlawful killing of a fellow human being'.

The establishment of an etymological connection between words of different languages or language states thus demands that the sound correspondences be regular and that the semantic developments be plausible. If we try to make explicit what is understood by 'plausible' we may say that the semantic development should have parallels in documented language history or that it should be reducible to generally attested semantic associations. Thus the passage from the meaning 'death' to that of 'murder' may be described as the addition of a number of semantic features (+human victim, +unlawful, +intentional, perhaps +violent, etc.) a type of change which also links such pairs of cognates as German *sterben* 'to die' and English *to starve* 'to suffer almost to the point of death from hunger or (dialectally) cold', German *riechen* 'to smell' and English *to reek*, German *schmecken* 'to taste' and English *to smack of*, German *schmerzen* 'to be painful' and English *to smart*, which implies a particular stinging variety of pain. Like Latin *mors* the German words have a generalized unmarked meaning whereas their English cognates, like *murder*, are all in some way marked. Similarly in the Swabian dialect of German the semantic equivalents of Standard German *gehen* 'to walk', *laufen* 'to run' and *springen* 'to jump' are respectively *laufen*, *springen* and *hopfen*; thus *laufen* has lost the feature +fast and become the normal unmarked term for 'to walk', *springen* is no longer marked for height above the surface but rather for speed, and *hopfen* has come in to take its place with the meaning 'to jump'. Changes of this kind can therefore readily be treated systematically in terms of semantic features.

It must not, on the other hand, be forgotten that the lexicon is the part of a language which has the most direct links with the spiritual and material culture of its speakers and that semantic developments may only be comprehensible by reference to the cultural background. One would probably hesitate to propose an etymological link between English *dish* (meaning both the vessel and its contents) and German *Tisch*, which is the general word for 'table', were it not for Tacitus's report on the eating habits of the Teutons where he describes food as being served to each person individually on 'a wooden plate having its own support' (*Germania* 22). The parallel investigation of *words and things* (*mots et choses*, *Wörter und Sachen*) has thus become a most fruitful branch of research, the importance of which for the possible reconstruction of the natural environment and material culture of prehistoric societies will be discussed in chapter 7.

10 Relatedness of languages (genealogical, or genetic, relationship)

10.1 *The family tree model*

There is one further aspect of the neogrammarian model which requires discussion, namely the process whereby a single initial system develops into a number of independent systems – we must, in other words, account for the coming into existence of new languages.

We have said that languages are related when they have developed from a common ancestor, and the rules whereby they are derived from the protolanguage represent the changes that each has undergone during the intervening period. Now let us consider the case of two related languages: these will by definition share the early rules and differ only in those rules which have been added more recently. The most extreme situation would be the one in which all the rules were identical except for a single 'uppermost' rule possessed by only one of the languages. This would mean that their linguistic systems would be identical except for the effects of this one extra rule. Such a situation might be found in closely related dialects. In general terms, the larger the number of such unshared changes the less closely related will be the two systems. Closeness of relatedness can therefore be seen to depend on the number of rules held in common. This however assumes that shared rules are only the result of joint development and cannot arise independently in two systems after they have separated. In point of fact, for shared rules to have significance in this respect account must be taken of both their nature and their relative position in the system. It is natural enough for the same limited phonological changes, such as assimilations and dissimilations, or for analogical changes which have the effect of 'tidying up' the grammatical rules, to occur independently in two languages. But what about for example certain rules shared by English and German? Consider: (1) the change of the Proto-Indo-European voiceless plosives into fricatives, the devoicing of voiced plosives, and the de-aspiration of aspirated plosives (all aspects of 'Grimm's Law', cf. p. 83ff.); (2) the change of */o/ to */a/; (3) the shift of word stress onto the first syllable and the ensuing weakening of unstressed syllables; (4) the development of a weak past tense by means of suffixation of a dental (or alveolar) plosive. Such fundamental *innovations* could not possibly arise independently in the linguistic systems of two different languages. They must be assigned to a period of common development for English and German preceding their more recent independent development, for shared changes presuppose close communication between speakers whereas independent changes on the contrary presuppose absence of communication. Put in other words, we must postulate for English and German a period of joint development as a single language followed by a split into separate languages each characterized by its independent innovations. The reduction in the number of languages as one moves backwards in time thus follows from the principle of shared innovations as indicators of common development and it is the range and relative chronology of these which determine the structure of the family tree. Thus the above-mentioned shared and unshared rules of English and German produce the following relationship:

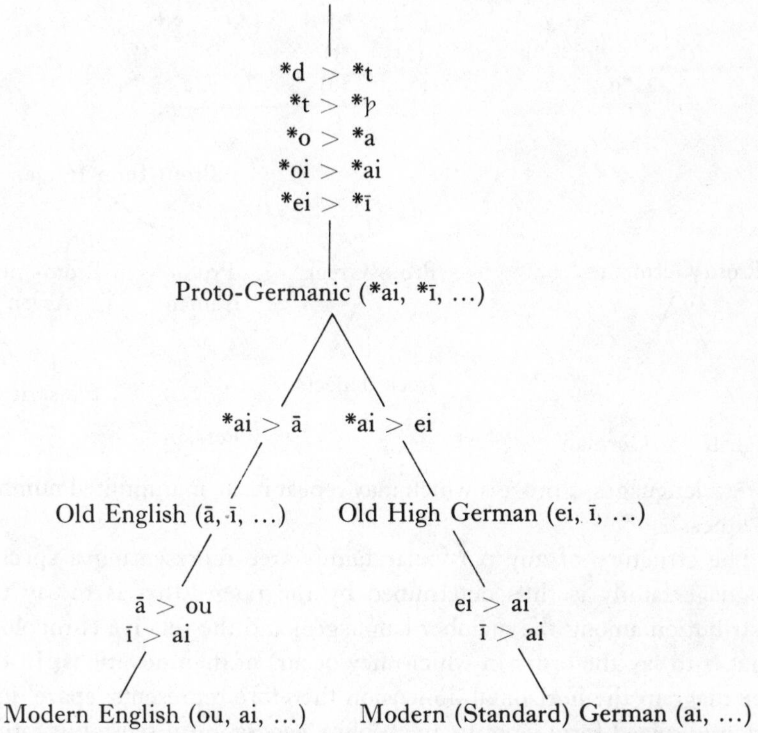

If we carry the principle of the tree diagram backwards in the direction of Proto-Indo-European we find the same pattern repeating itself, the occurrence of mutually exclusive innovations implying the split up of the original speech community and loss of contact between the ancestors of the descendant languages. Thus, limiting ourselves to innovations that we have already discussed, the relationship between the Germanic, Greek and Indo-Iranian language groups gives the tree on p. 66.

Once there has been loss of contact, be it through physical displacement or political division, independent development in the now isolated sectors will gradually result in loss of mutual intelligibility and the rise

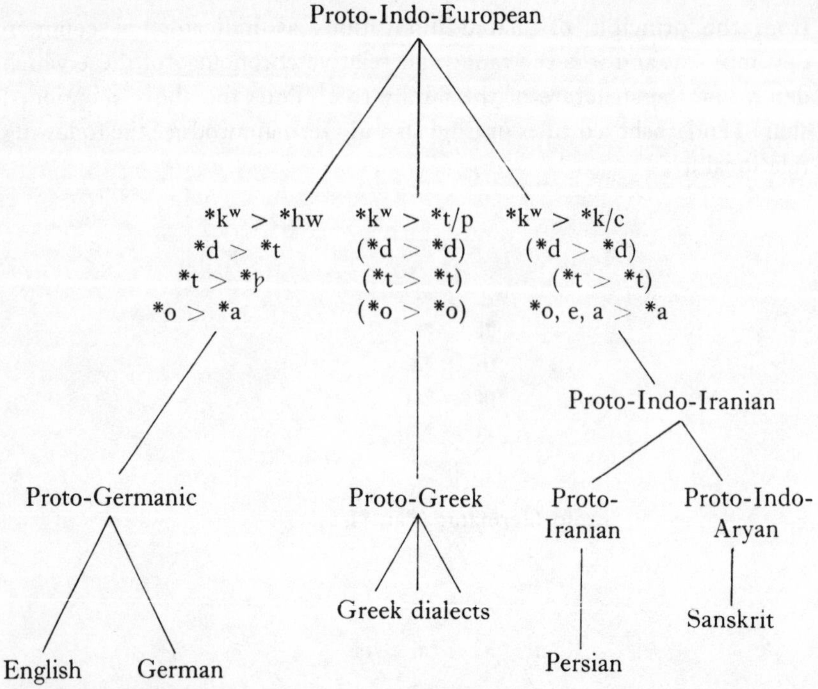

of new languages, a process which may repeat itself an unlimited number of times.

The structure of any particular family tree representing a specific language family is thus determined by the range (that is to say the distribution among the member languages) and the relative chronology (that is to say the order in which they occur) of its innovations. In the tree diagram the horizontal dimension therefore represents 'space' in a much idealized form – not in an absolute geographical sense but rather in terms of contact or absence of contact between speech communities – whereas the vertical dimension represents time. The branches of the tree then represent channels of transmission, that is the paths along which innovations have been transmitted, and whenever a branch divides into two or more this implies the splitting up of a speech community indicated by the fact that subsequent innovations are no longer shared. It will be seen that the length of the path between any two languages expressed in terms of the number of intervening branchings will be an indication of their degree of relatedness. The structure of the tree also shows whether two linguistic systems represent stages in the development of a single language or constitute rather two related languages with a common ancestor. Which of these is the case is a question which depends purely upon internal evidence, namely whether one of the linguistic systems can be derived directly by rule from the other or whether their linkage demands a third system underlying both. The family tree thus represents the *historical continuity* between members of a language family, the unbroken chain of successive grammars linking the ancestor with each of the descendant languages. One such chain for instance connects Proto-Indo-European with English, another with Sanskrit. Translated into the sociolinguistic reality, such a chain of transmission implies an unbroken succession of speakers all freely communicating with one another and considering themselves to be speakers of 'the same language'.

It must never be forgotten, however, that the family tree model merely summarizes the present state of our knowledge with regard to the attested members of a language family and their hypothetical relationships to one another. To what extent it reflects the true historical reality is impossible to say since it is based on only those languages which have survived into the present or of which we possess written records. But many of the Indo-European languages, for instance, must have died out and of these we are naturally not able to take any account so that the picture provided by the model is bound to be to some extent distorted. But although our methodology is not capable of recovering the totality of historical developments we must nevertheless operate *as if* the tree represented the reality, the role of historical linguistics as a scientific discipline being limited to accounting for all the available data in terms of the simplest adequate hypothesis.

We must further remember that the tree model takes no account of the fact that identical changes may occur in more than one of its branches after they have become separated. Thus, if a language divides into two branches and each of these then undergoes separate innovations, implying that their speakers have ceased to form a single speech community, and if at a later date both undergo an identical change, this does not necessarily mean that they have become a single speech community again. The fact is that, quite apart from the possibility of identical changes occurring independently in two places as the result of pure chance, when languages are in close geographical proximity they often undergo identical or similar changes as the result of innovations spreading across language boundaries. But this wavelike spread of innovations in real time and real (that is, geographical) space,

	2000 B.C.	1000 B.C.	B.C. / A.D.	1000 A.D.
Albanian				Albanian
Greek	Mycenaean Greek	Homeric Greek Classical Greek	Koine	Greek
Anatolian	Hittite/ Luwian/ Palaic/ Hieroglyphic Hittite/			
Tocharian			Tocharian A/ Tocharian B/	
Indo-Iranian — Indic (Indo-Aryan)	Vedic Sanskrit	Classical Sanskrit Prakrit Pali		Hindi, Urdu Panjabi Gujarati Bengali Assamese Sindhi Sinhalese
Indo-Iranian — Iranian		Avestan/ Old Persian	Pahlavi Sogdian/ Khotanese/	Persian Kurdish Pashto Balochi Ossetic
Armenian			Classical Armenian	Armenian

	2000 B.C.	1000 B.C.	B.C. A.D.	1000 A.D.
Slavonic			Old Church Slavonic	Bulgarian Serbo-Croat Czech Polish Russian
Baltic				Lithuanian Latvian Old Prussian/
Germanic			Gothic Old Norse	Islandic Norwegian Swedish Danish
			Old English	English Dutch
			Old High German	German
Celtic			Continental Celtic/ Old Irish	Irish Gaelic Welsh Breton Cornish/
Italic		Latin		French Spanish Catalan Portuguese Italian Rhaeto-Romance Romanian
		Oscan/ Umbrian/		

which is merely a special form of borrowing, applies equally to related and unrelated languages in contact. It will occupy us in Part Two. It should be sufficient at this point to note that we do not describe two languages as having undergone *the same change* if they are known to have been widely separated geographically or if the changes did not occur roughly at the same moment in time.

Ideally this section should conclude with a tree showing the relationship between all the historically attested Indo-European languages. In practice, however, if we try to set these out in the form of a tree this can often only be done at the expense of imposing on certain of them a false relationship of ancestor and descendant. This is because the actual material with which the linguist has to operate does not consist of neatly parallel samples equally representative of all branches and all periods but is rather the product of chance preservation or other non-linguistic factors. Thus the written documents to which we give the names Old Persian and Pahlavi, although closely related and belonging to successive periods of time, do not strictly represent two successive grammars along a single channel of transmission. Although therefore the direct ancestor of Pahlavi must be closer to Old Persian than to any other language of which we have actual records, the attempt to force them into a direct relationship within the family tree model can only result in a distortion of the reality. We will therefore content ourselves in the chart (on pages 68 and 69) with bringing together loosely according to branches and periods the main languages of the Indo-European family for which actual material survives, and reserve the family tree model for the display of rules relating successive systems, whether attested or reconstructed (note: a stroke after the name of a language indicates that it was the last surviving member of its branch).

10.2 *Protolanguages*

Justification of the neogrammarian model of language development resides primarily in the explanatory power which the protosystem of a language-family has with regard to the similarities which exist between its members. As Franz Bopp put it (1833–54:v): 'It does not matter that there exist surface differences at certain points in the grammars; all that matters is that these differences have been brought about by general laws and that we can trace the lost paths along which a language has developed from an earlier form. The differences cease to be differences as soon as the laws have been established.'

A protolanguage is no more than a theoretical construct designed to link by means of rules the systems of historically related languages in the most economical way. It thus summarizes the present state of our knowledge regarding the systematic relationships of the grammars of the related languages.[1] Whether it is as close to the linguistic reality it presupposes as is for instance a grammar of the English language to the present spoken reality is hard to say. When dealing with past language states it is possible to assess the distance between construct and reality only in cases where we possess documentary evidence regarding the ancestor or a near ancestor, such as is provided by Latin in the case of the Romance languages (Hall 1950) or Sanskrit in that of Indo-Aryan (Pattanayak 1966). A comparison between the linguistic systems of Classical Latin and reconstructed Proto-Romance for example should, ideally, provide a valid test of the adequacy of reconstruction. In reality the issue is complicated by a sociolinguistic factor, namely the fact that there is evidence of a considerable gap between the highly standardized literary language of the documents and the spoken language of the people. And since it is after all the latter which is assumed to have been the source of the Romance languages this means that each time there is a difference between the attested classical language and reconstructed Proto-Romance it must first be decided whether it is to be ascribed to the sociolinguistic gap between the two varieties of Latin or to the limitations of the methods of linguistic reconstruction. Test cases of this type are not only important as empirical justification of our reconstruction methods, they also give us an idea of the *speed* at which change can take place and thus the degree of differentiation between descendants that is achievable in a given period of time.

Another opportunity for assessing the adequacy of the constructs of historical linguistics may arise when, subsequent to reconstruction, samples of past linguistic states emerge in the form of inscriptions or other written documents unearthed by chance or as the result of systematic excavation. Such documents require in the first place that the

[1] The parallels between this diachronic model and the transformational-generative model of synchronic description are obvious: both operate with an underlying system which is a pure construct and directly observable surface systems which are derived from the underlying system by unidirectional rules. In historical linguistics the underlying system is characterized by its precedence in time, in transformational-generative linguistics by its precedence in the generative process. In both, however, it has explanatory power with regard to the directly accessible structures (cf. Meillet 1937 chapter 1; Ardener 1971).

language in which each is written be situated if possible within a known family of languages. If it can be related to a specific known family, then, in order to determine its exact position within that family, evidence must be sought of the completion of specific diachronic changes. A case in point is the runic inscription on a gold horn found near Gallehus to the south of Denmark and which has been dated to about A.D. 400. It reads: *ek hlewagastiR holtijaR horna tawido* 'I HlewagastiR HoltijaR made (the) horn' (Düwel 1968:28). There can be no doubt that the language of the inscription is Germanic, for the personal name HlewagastiR for instance can be analysed into two stems, *hlewa-* from Proto-Indo-European **klewo-* 'fame' (cf. Greek *kléos*, Sanskrit *śrávas*) and *gastiR* from Proto-Indo-European **ghostis* 'stranger' (cf. Latin *hostis* 'enemy'), and both of these are derivable from their well-established source lexemes by means of the rules that characterize the Germanic languages (*k > h and *gh > g form part of the Germanic Consonant Shift and *o > a is another typical Germanic development). In preserving the *i* vowel before the final consonant the language of the inscription appears more archaic, and thus closer to Proto-Germanic, than any documented state of a Germanic language (cf. Gothic *gasts*, Old Norse *gestr*, Old High German *gast*, all from Proto-Germanic **gastiz* 'guest'). The language of the inscription would thus appear to belong to a very early form of a Germanic dialect little different from Proto-Germanic itself. The sample thus fits very well into the picture that had already been formed of the evolution of the Germanic languages.

Another example of the vindication of the comparative method may be taken from the early history of Greek. It will be remembered that traditional historical linguistics reconstructed a labiovelar */k^w/ for the correspondence set Latin /k^w/ : Sanskrit /k/ and /c/ : Greek /t/ and /p/ (see above p. 55). This reconstruction predated the decipherment of Linear B, which was to make accessible the earliest documents known so far in the Greek language. In these documents orthographic symbols distinct from those representing /p/ and /t/ were used in just those circumstances in which Classical (Attic) Greek has either /t/ or /p/ depending on the phonetic environment. This shows that the postulated labiovelar, or its reflex, must have survived well into Greek.

Such examples of the *power of prediction* of the historical method provide a useful means of assessing the degree to which it reflects objective reality and its consequent value as a scientific tool.

The fact that we reconstruct protosystems must not on the other hand lead us to assume that our reconstructions are either definitive or complete. We will consider these two aspects in turn. Reconstructions are not once and for all discoveries which will retain their validity indefinitely but, like any analysis, are always open to revision as the result of theoretical advances or the acquisition of new data. Our views regarding Proto-Indo-European for instance have changed substantially during the past fifty years, largely due to the discovery of Hittite and its close relatives, the texts of which now constitute the oldest written documents in any Indo-European language. The systematic distance between Hittite of the second millennium B.C. and Proto-Indo-European as reconstructed by the neogrammarians proved to be much greater than could readily be accounted for by language change in the period of time available, and this had led to the rethinking of certain basic assumptions regarding the nature of the prehistoric changes within the Indo-European family. In particular it is now being asked whether certain close agreements between Greek and Sanskrit which were thought to be cases of joint inheritance from the protolanguage may not, at least in part, be the result of independent developments in each.

To turn to our second point regarding the degree of completeness of reconstructed grammars, even if we were able to state confidently what a synchronic grammar ought theoretically to contain we should still ask what areas of a language are in fact, even under the most favourable conditions, accessible to reconstruction. It would be fair to say that we might hope to reconstruct with some degree of confidence the phonological system and the more central aspects of inflectional and derivational morphology and of syntax together with a limited core lexicon, but there are other areas of the language of which we would be bound to remain in almost total ignorance. Some idea of the extent of the problem may perhaps be gained from the following example. August Schleicher's pioneer reconstruction of Proto-Indo-European culminated in 1868 with his publishing a fable composed in the reconstructed language. His attempt was met with ridicule. But 'why?' we may ask. Is it not reasonable to expect of the grammar of a language that we should be able to construct by means of it grammatical sentences? Let us therefore examine some of the problems raised by such a reconstructed text. The fable reads: 'A sheep, shorn of its wool, saw some horses, one moving a heavy cart, another carrying a big load, a third carrying a man at speed. The sheep said to the horses: "It pains me to see man driving horses!" The horses said: "Listen sheep, it pains us to see that man the master makes the wool of the sheep into a warm garment for himself and the sheep no longer has any wool!" On hearing that the sheep ran off into the fields' (Hirt–Arntz 1939:114). There can be little doubt concerning the reconstruction of such lexical items as 'sheep', 'horse', 'wool', and the fact that our starred forms of today differ slightly from Schleicher's is no serious obstacle. There are also no basic problems regarding the formation of the third person singular perfect of the verb 'to see', and the present participles of 'to move' and 'to carry'. There are, however, other more basic problems such as the choice of what tense should be used, what should be the construction for a complement (sheep saw horse carrying load), and what should be the form of a relative pronoun (should one for instance follow the pattern of Latin and certain other languages which use the interrogative pronoun for this purpose, or should one postulate a distinct relative pronoun as in Sanskrit?). And, more seriously, how is one to decide what lexical items collocate in such constructions – in other words, can selectional restrictions be established for a protolanguage? And what determines the choice of specific lexical items? Thus the word selected by Schleicher for 'man' derives from the word meaning 'earth', suggesting a 'non-divine' rather than a 'non-female' meaning, 'it pains me' is rendered as 'the heart narrows itself for me' in imitation of a Greek construction (cf. Iliad 6, 523–4 *tò d'emon kē̃r ákhnutai en thūmō̃*, 14, 38–9 *ákhnuto dé sphi thūmòs enì stēthessin*). In short, there are clearly many aspects of the reconstruction which are extremely tenuous, and it is easy to condemn Schleicher's attempt as imprudent and for failing to distinguish between *langue* and *parole*. But even if we agree that reconstruction must confine itself to *langue*, what kind of rules does this choice imply? Provided, however, that basic problems such as these be kept in mind a reconstruction like that attempted by Schleicher would appear to be a useful and perfectly legitimate exercise.

To conclude, the description of the neogrammarian model which we have given in the preceding pages necessarily contains a certain element of personal interpretation. This it would be difficult to avoid since in the neogrammarian literature criteria are more often implicit in the solution of specific problems than explicitly stated. Moreover, the systematic presentation of comparative grammar was on the whole deductive, starting from the hypothetical structure of the protolanguage and then stating the rules by which the forms of the historical languages could be derived from it. Such a presentation naturally resulted in the begging of many questions. What matters, however, is that the principles underlying the rules they set up to account for the prehistoric development of particular languages can be tested in documented language history and that the earlier structures postulated on the basis of these rules have explanatory power[1] with regard to the irregular forms of later language states, the structure of synchronically unmotivated forms being shown to conform to the synchronic rules of earlier grammars. In fact, were it not for relics of earlier grammars surviving as synchronic anomalies in the descendant languages, the writing of the comparative grammar of a language family would be impossible. And conversely, it may be said that the best indication that a language belongs to a given family is the fact that it retains, as synchronic irregularities, remnants of the productive rules of earlier grammars of that language family.

Admittedly the preoccupation of historical linguists with synchronically irregular forms has often in the past led to the total neglect of synchronic structure, more recent language states being seen merely in the light of the earlier states from which they had evolved rather than being subjected to independent analysis. It is this aspect in particular which has been corrected in the structuralist approach to historical linguistics, which is the subject we will be considering in the next chapter.

[1] Of course synchronic grammar also claims explanatory power for its analyses, since it makes explicit the structural relations between contemporary forms. However, at the phonological level at least, this appears to be possible only at the expense of considerable complication of the rules and of a certain arbitrariness in underlying forms (see, where English is concerned, Chomsky and Halle 1968). The protoforms and diachronic rules of historical linguistics on the other hand are at least based on and generalized from fully documented cases in which both the source and the derived system are open to inspection, so that arbitrariness is reduced to a minimum.

2

The structuralist model of language evolution

Although the neogrammarian framework still remains the basis of historical linguistics, various aspects of it have undergone modification since its inception a hundred years ago. The first major development in linguistics which was to challenge the neogrammarian position was the application of structuralist principles to the analysis of language. The structuralist approach, the origin of which is usually traced to the Swiss linguist Ferdinand de Saussure, was developed in Europe principally by the members of the Prague school and in America by the Bloomfieldians (Robins 1967:198ff.) and varieties of it, under the label 'taxonomic linguistics', still constitute the major alternative to transformational-generative linguistics. For the structuralist a language is to be seen as an integrated whole, *un système où tout se tient*, that is to say a system in which each unit is defined by its place in the overall network of oppositions. This applies equally to all languages, including related ones and even the successive states of one and the same language.

The realization that each language has its own independent structure, a fact which had not been explicitly stated by the neogrammarians, demanded a new attitude towards historical linguistics. With the insight provided by this new structuralist approach neogrammarian 'atomism', the tracing through successive language states of individual sound segments and of grammatical or lexical forms without any attempt to make explicit at each stage their status in the synchronic system, was no longer acceptable. Historical linguistics now turned rather to the effect of change on linguistic structure, that is to say the rise of new systems. In examining the results of this new approach, since structural linguistics postulates that language is structured independently at the different levels of analysis, we will consider phonological change and grammatical change separately.

1 Paradigmatic aspects of phonological change

Like synchronic phonological structure, phonological change (or diachronic phonology) is described by structuralists in terms of the phoneme. We already showed in the previous chapter how through the rules of sound change words or morphs of a later language state can be derived from those of an earlier one. We also said that the same rules can be used to derive the phonological *system* of the later state from that of the earlier one. It is this paradigmatic aspect of phonological change which we will now examine. Neogrammarian preoccupation with the syntagmatic aspect, that is to say with the conditioning factors of change and the shrinkage or 'decay' of individual word forms, had obscured the fact that each language state none the less has its own system of functionally distinctive sound segments or phonemes. It is the rise of new phonological systems as the result of individual changes which will now be considered.

1.1 *Structure*

1.1.1 Phonological segments

We will examine the paradigmatic aspect of phonological change under the headings of inventory, distribution and incidence.

Firstly, phonological change may affect the *phoneme inventory*, causing either an increase or a decrease in the overall number of phonemes. Again we anticipated in the previous chapter these two basic possibilities, showing that an increase in the number of phonemes results from the split of a single phoneme into two or more independent phonemes and a decrease results from the unconditioned merger of two or more phonemes into a single one. It will be remembered, however, that not all splits and mergers have such an immediate effect upon the system. In the case of split, this is only true for what Hoenigswald (1960:91ff.) calls *secondary split* and Jakobson (1972a) *phonologization*, that is to say when allophones have become phonemes as the result of a merger of the conditioning factors which had caused their phonetic differentiation in the first place. We gave as an example the split of the back vowel /o:/ into /o:/ and /ö:/ in German through umlaut (see p. 26ff.). In the case of merger, *dephonologization* of an opposition only takes place when the allophones of two phonemes merge in all environments. The two situations may be represented schematically (following Hoenigswald 1960:76) as:

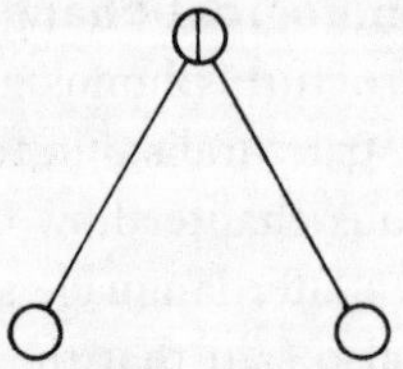

secondary split

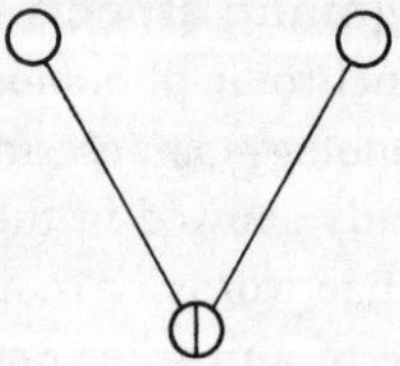

unconditioned merger

Both these cases must be distinguished from *primary split* in which conditioned allophones separate off from one phoneme and merge with another without the overall inventory being affected (Hoenigswald 1960:77, 91ff.). This situation may be represented as:

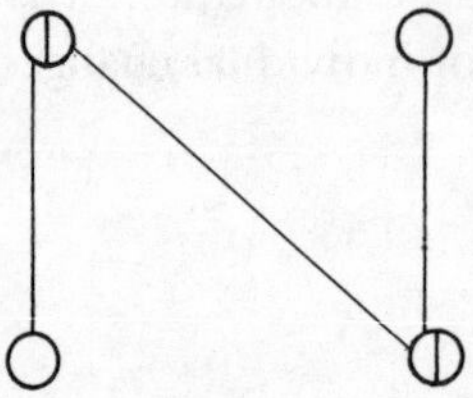

primary split

A case in point is the umlaut of /a/ in Old High German. Unlike the umlauted variant of /o:/, the umlauted variant of /a/ did not develop into an independent phoneme but simply merged with the /e/ phoneme:

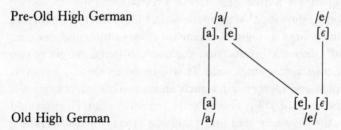

Pre-Old High German	/a/	/e/
	[a], [e]	[ɛ]
	[a]	[e], [ɛ]
Old High German	/a/	/e/

Although this change left the overall inventory unaffected, it altered the *distribution* of both /a/ and /e/. Before it took place /a/ could occur with any vowel in the following syllable and /e/ only with non-*i* vowels in that position (this was because at an earlier period when there was an /i/, /i:/ or /y/ in the following syllable, /e/ had merged with /i/). After the change /a/ only occurred before non-*i* vowels whereas /e/ occurred with any vowel in the following syllable (Twaddell 1957; King 1969a: 92ff.).

The same change also altered the *incidence* of /a/ and /e/, that is to say their distribution in lexical and grammatical items throughout the language. This can be seen from a comparison of individual lexemes at the Pre-Old High German (I), Old High German (II) and Modern German (III) stages. (The reconstructed forms are supported by comparative evidence. The grapheme -ʒʒ- represents a fricative different from /s/ which only later merged with it. It can be seen that the orthographic forms correctly reflect the phonology of Old High German, assigning the 'new' [e] to the /e/ phoneme[1]. In Modern German *ä* is merely an orthographic variant of *e*):

	'water'	'guest'	'guests'	'better'	'fur'	'to eat'
I	*waʒʒar	*gast	*gastiz	*baʒʒiro	*fel	*eʒʒan
II	waʒʒar	gast	gesti	beʒʒiro	fel	eʒʒan
III	/vasər/	/gast/	/gestə/	/besər/	/fel/	/esən/
	Wasser	*Gast*	*Gäste*	*besser*	*Fell*	*essen*

It will be seen from the case of 'guest' that the so-called 'different forms of the same word' have also been affected, that is to say the members of the paradigm of a single lexical item, if the conditioning factor was present in some of the forms and absent in others. The result is a morphological alternation involving /a/ and /e/ which has survived into Modern German.

[1] This is a good example of the problems surrounding the relationship between phonological segments and their orthographic representation, since two opposing interpretations of the same data are available, Twaddell's (1957) in terms of autonomous phonemes and King's (1969a: 92ff.) in terms of systematic phonemes. Neither of these, however, comprises a full phonetic and phonological interpretation of the orthographic system of Old High German. A comprehensive account would have to take into consideration *all* the potential sources of information which could throw light on the phonetic and phonological values of orthographic segments. These sources are summarized in Allen (1974: vii): (1) statements by contemporary . . . grammarians and other writers; (2) word-play of various kinds, contemporary etymologies, and onomatopoeia; (3) representations of forms of the language state in question in other languages; (4) subsequent developments, including the present-day descendant, of the language; (5) spelling conventions and variants; (6) the internal structure of the language itself. In order to see how these various types of evidence are weighed against one another so as to produce the most coherent picture synchronically and diachronically, one should turn to analyses of specific past language states which deal with this problem (see, for instance, Allen 1965 for the phonetics and phonology of Latin; Allen 1974 for Ancient Greek; Campbell 1959, Mossé 1955 and 1959, and Chomsky and Halle 1968: Part III, for earlier stages of English).

1.1.2 Phonological features

We have so far regarded phonological change as being simply the replacement of complete segements (phonemes or allophones) by other complete segments and a phonological system simply as a list or inventory of phonemes. Phonological change can, however, be described more adequately in terms of a framework which relates the internal structure of the individual phonemes to the structure of the phonological system as a whole. The concept of *phonological space*, based upon the componential analysis of phonemes into bundles of distinctive features, is such a framework (Trubetzkoy 1967; Martinet 1952, 1955; cf. King 1969a: 193ff.). Phonological systems can then be represented within this framework by allocating to each phoneme a specific area within the total space covered by the system. In for instance a five-vowel system in which /a/ is the only low vowel, the allophonic scatter of /a/ reaches right across from a back to a front articulation whereas in a system with two low vowels, /æ/ and /ɑ/, the allophonic scatter of /æ/ is confined to the front and that of /ɑ/ to the back area. The feature specification of /a/ will differ in a corresponding manner from that of /æ/ and /ɑ/; for, while all three are low vowels, *low* is the only distinctive feature of /a/ whereas /æ/ is both *low* and *front* and /ɑ/ is *low* and *back*. Because of such regularities it has become the custom to lay out vowel systems in the form of a triangle or a trapezium, the vertical dimension representing tongue-height and the horizontal dimension the front-back axis of the mouth. That this is not merely 'paper phonetics' but does correspond to the actual phonetic reality has been amply demonstrated. For instance Moulton (1962) has shown for a Swiss dialect area that if both /æ/ and /ɔ/ are present /a/ has central allophones, but where there is no /æ/ the allophones of /a/ cover the front area as well. Labov found a similar situation with regard to the relationship between the long vowels /eh/, /oh/ and /ah/ in New York City, where speakers for whom /eh/ is higher than /oh/ have relatively front allophones of /ah/, whereas speakers for whom /oh/ is higher than /eh/ have an /ah/ articulated further back (Weinreich–Labov–Herzog 1968: 172ff.). In languages with minimal vowel systems such as the Caucasian language Abaza, the allophonic scatter is correspondingly wide (Allen 1964a: 115).

When we turn to the consonants the dimensions of phonological space used in their description are both more numerous and less directly related to real space. For whereas the majority of vowels can be adequately defined in terms simply of tongue position the description of the consonants involves not only place of articulation (labial, dental, etc.) but also manner of articulation (plosion, continuance, etc.) and other attendant features (voice, nasality, etc.) (cf. Trubetzkoy 1967:59ff.). It is true that as individual features these were not new, but in structuralist phonology feature analysis was for the first time used systematically as part of an explicit phonological theory. Since phonological change affects both the production and the perception of speech, it is clear that the articulatory based framework outlined above in Prague school terms must be matched by a parallel acoustically based one (cf. Jakobson and Halle 1956). The two systems are however not readily convertible and their correlation raises problems which lie outside the scope of the present discussion. We will therefore confine ourselves to articulatory features.

In terms of the concept of phonological space phonological change is viewed as change in the feature specification of phonemes. The minimum change will be that of a single feature, either in the structure of a single segment or of a series of segments defined by one or more shared features. In either case the distinctive feature framework makes it possible to state precisely and economically the effect of a change on the membership and/or internal structure of the system as a whole, and this is especially so in the case of so-called sound shifts affecting whole series of sounds in a parallel way. We will illustrate the principle from some well established cases.

One of the changes which affected French (as well as certain dialects of northern Italy) was the fronting of Vulgar Latin /u/ to /ü/ and the raising of /o/ to /u/ (Haudricourt and Juilland 1949:100ff.; see below, chapter 6) so that, while the earlier system had four back vowels (/a/, /ɔ/, /o/, /u/), the later system had only three (/a/, /o/, /u/) plus a 'new' rounded front vowel /ü/. This meant that rounding, which had up till then merely been a redundant feature of high back vowels, now became a distinctive feature opposing /ü/ to /i/. Thus, while the internal structure of the system was radically changed, the total number of segments was unaffected. A parallel development took place in Ancient Greek in which the Attic /u:/ inherited from Proto-Indo-European became fronted to /ü:/ while the old /o:/ was raised to /u:/ (Allen 1974:72.; cf. Haudricourt and Juilland 1949:110f.), as for example in Greek *thȳmós* [t^hü:ˈmos] 'courage' compared with Latin *fūmus* 'smoke'.

An even more extensive restructuring of the vowel system occurred in the history of English. In the so-called Great Vowel Shift which occurred in Early Modern English all long vowels were raised by one degree (or unit) of tongue height and the high vowels /i:/ and /u:/ were diphthongized. The shift may be represented as follows (Chomsky and Halle 1968:187 and ch. 6; Anderson 1973:138ff.; Lass 1976:ch. 2):

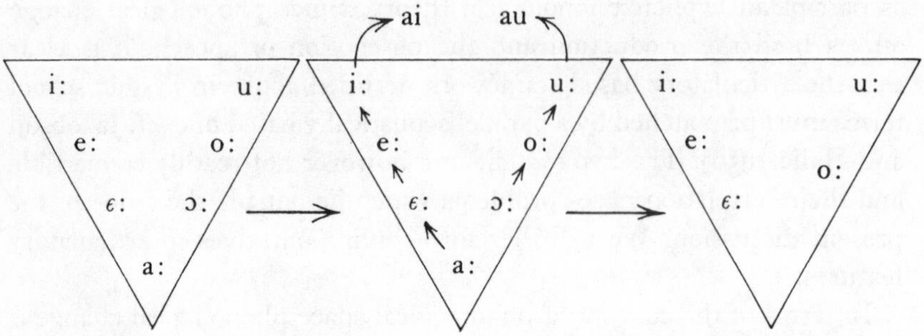

Pre-shift long vowel system

Post-shift long vowel system

It will be noted that the pre-shift situation is still to a large extent reflected in English spelling, which has remained extremely conservative (cf., for example, *divine* /di'vain/, *keep* /ki:p/). Vowel alternations, such as those in *keep* /ki:p/ : *kept* /kept/, *divine* /di'vain/ : *divinity* /di'viniti/, become much more transparent when seen in terms of the older system where the only opposition was one of length.

In each of the above examples a structuralist will seek to interpret the individual changes as part of a single internal modification of the phonological system and look for motivation for the sequence of events in the structure of the system itself. Yet, even within this framework, alternative analyses are often possible and new ones continue to be proposed for particular cases. Such analyses of sound shifts may be grouped into two broad classes, which have been labelled *push-chains* and *drag-chains* (*chaînes de propulsion*, *chaînes de traction:* Martinet 1952; 1955:59f.), according to the nature of the internal motivation which is assumed to link their various phases.

Thus, for example, a drag-chain interpretation of the Attic shift described above would assume that the fronting of /u:/ to /ü:/ was the initial event which made it possible for the high back position thus left vacant to be filled again by the raising of /o:/ to /u:/. The changes which took place in French would be described in a parallel fashion.

$/d^h/ \rightarrow /d/ \neq /\theta/ \neq /\eth/$. However, all voiceless fricatives (including, of course, /θ/) subsequently became voiced in those environments specified by Verner's Law, thus causing the merger in these environments of the reflexes of Pre-Germanic /t/ and $/d^h/$ (see, for example, the cases of 'father' and 'middle' above). At this stage the fricatives /θ/ and /ð/ would jointly have been opposed to a single dental plosive, comprising the old voiced plosive /d/ and those allophones of the old voiceless plosive /t/ which in obstruent clusters had not passed to fricatives (see (1) above). The voiced plosives now lost their distinctive voicing, retaining plosion as the feature which set them apart from the fricatives: $/d/ \neq /\theta/ \neq /\eth/ \rightarrow /t/ \neq /\theta/ \neq /\eth/$. This development in turn made it possible for the voiced fricatives (/ð/) to develop plosive allophones in an increasing number of contexts, the feature voice sufficing to mark them off both from the voiceless plosives and from the voiceless fricatives: $/t/ \neq /\theta/ \neq /\eth/ \rightarrow /t/ \neq /\theta/ \neq /\eth \sim d/$. The new distinctive features of the system are thus voice and continuance and it was the replacement of aspiration by continuance which was the change that ultimately led to the reorganization of the system as a whole.

A push-chain type interpretation of Grimm's Law on the other hand would make use of the pressure of threatening mergers as a conditioning factor of change. Leaving context-sensitive developments aside, the initiating impulse would have been the impending loss by the voiced aspirated plosives of their distinctive aspiration ($/d^h/$ becoming /d/, etc.). This threat of merger with the corresponding unaspirated plosives would have caused these to react by pushing in the direction of the voiceless plosives, and these latter would in turn have avoided merger by moving right outside the plosive system and developing into fricatives. The phases, which would necessarily have had to take place simultaneously, would have been: $/d^h/ > /d/$ [d, ð], $/d/ > /t/$, $/t/ > /\theta/$.[1]

1 According to King (1969b) the push-chain model implies the *gradual* acquisition or loss of a feature, so that there is increasing erosion of the distinctiveness of the phoneme or phoneme series. This interpretation is, however, based on the assumption that the rules which express the phonological differences between two successive language states also directly reflect the linguistic behaviour of their speakers. We shall see later (chapter 5) that this assumption is not confirmed by empirical evidence and that the correlation between the behaviour of speakers and the form of a retrospective rule summing up developments over centuries is much more complex. Instead of assuming *gradual* phonetic transition between the old pronunciation and the new it would, for instance, seem

All the analyses discussed above are characterized by an attempt to impose some kind of internal coherence on the events. They all depend upon the assumption that a phonological system reacts to change as a structural whole and therefore in a systematic way, and all assume that such changes as do take place are conditioned or constrained by the structure of the phonological system. The analyses do, however, differ in the *internal motivation* postulated for particular sequences of events which, in the case of the push-chain model, takes account not merely of the *structure* but also of the *function* of the phonological system. We shall now examine these functionalist arguments more closely together with the claims they make regarding the nature of language change.

1.2 *Function*

We have said that in a drag-chain analysis the phases of a shift occur in chronological sequence and that, while the subsequent phases of the shift are made possible by the previous ones, they neither are their necessary consequence nor is their form determined by them. In a push-chain analysis on the other hand, which depends entirely on the avoidance of mergers, the individual phases are necessarily strictly simultaneous and totally interdependent. This is because the model takes into account not only the structure but also the *function* of phonological systems, that is to say their role in communication. Functionalists in fact claim that change does not occur irrespective of the needs of communication (Martinet 1952; 1955:54ff.). Indeed, looked at from the viewpoint of the maintenance of communication between the different generations of speakers in a community, phonological change is potentially destructive and constraints would appear necessary both in order to limit the degree of change affecting individual sounds over a given period of time and to preserve the phonological oppositions within the system.

The first of these requirements, namely that changes in the realization of particular sounds must be small enough for speakers using both the old and the new realizations still to be able to recognize lexical items, is self-evident. This is why it is usual for change to proceed in small steps which involve the alteration of only one feature at a time,

more realistic to postulate the simultaneous presence within the speech community of both pronunciations with the possibility that either might eventually be generally adopted. A push-chain interpretation, in other words, need not necessarily imply that phonological change be gradual.

such as /a/ becoming /æ/ or /t/ becoming /θ/, and not /a/ becoming /f/ or /t/ becoming /m/. (Certain apparent 'exceptions', such as the change of /kʷ/ to /t/ before front vowel and to /p/ before back vowel in Greek, or of apical to uvular /r/ in French and German, have a straightforward analys is in acoustic rather than articulatory terms; cf. C. Chomsky 1954 on the perception of stop consonants in English).

The second requirement is much more controversial. It depends upon the argument that the merger of phonemes is bound to lead to some measure of homophony in lexical and grammatical forms and is therefore to be avoided (Martinet 1955:26f.). The chances of a merger occurring should thus depend in some measure on the *functional load* (*yield*, *burden*) which the phonological opposition in question carries in the language as a whole. If this is high, so that the opposition keeps distinct 'hundreds of most frequent and useful words' (Martinet 1975:147), merger should not occur whereas resistance should be less in the case of an opposition of low functional yield where the damage would be minimal. Since this is essentially a testable issue, we should first examine the evidence that has been brought forward in justification of the claim that functional load is relevant to phonological change.

Functional load is in the first instance a synchronic concept employed in Prague School phonology for the assessment of quantitative differences in the distribution of phonemic oppositions. The further claim that the weight of a minimal opposition should determine its diachronic stability is a hypothetical extension of the original concept. Its empirical verification is, however, laden with problems. Firstly, there is the question of the linguistic context within which the functional load of a contrast which either was lost, or would have been lost, as the result of a particular merger is to be measured. Should it be phonological environment in running texts? or minimally distinct word pairs in the lexicon? Secondly, should functional load be quantified in terms of phonemes, (allo-)phones or features? (Hockett 1966). Actual investigations, rather than the discussion of principles, are rare and inconclusive (Meyerstein 1970:chapter 1). One such study was undertaken by King (1967), who measured the frequencies in sample texts of minimally distinct phoneme pairs known to have undergone mergers. When the functional load of their oppositions was compared to that of oppositions which had not undergone merger, no significant difference emerged and the investigation proved inconclusive if not positively negative. A further problem is that the functional load hypothesis is unable to account for the existence of far-reaching merger processes in a great variety of languages which did in fact result in large numbers of homonyms and yet were not prevented from taking place. No progress at all seems to have been made in this direction. In neither area in fact has subsequent research lent much support to the original hypothesis.

Perhaps one might go further and say that, in view of the fact that 'destructive' merger processes on the one hand and 'therapeutic' processes *outside the phonological level* which 'repair' the unacceptable results of phonological change on the other are in fact well attested in the form of analogical change and lexical replacement, it may be altogether inappropriate to look for a motivation of phonological change which is based on the structural status of phonological units. We shall return to this question in chapters 4 and 5. For the present we will simply note that other factors than the merely cognitive one of differentiating lexical items influence the choice of speech sounds, in particular certain sociolinguistic pressures.

It would thus appear that push-chain analyses rest on considerably weaker theoretical foundations than do drag-chain analyses. In the case of the latter it has repeatedly been found that positions in phonological space which had become vacant as the result of a sound change were subsequently reoccupied in the course of a redistribution of the segments. Although the principles which govern such redistribution are not fully understood, certain regularities have been observed with regard to the structure of phonological systems. Trubetzkoy, for instance, when he compared the vowel systems of some two hundred languages, was struck by the symmetrical and equidistant distribution of the segments. This and similar observations led to the positing of certain ideal properties of phonological systems. An optimal phonological system will thus be one which, with the minimal number of distinctive features, obtains the maximum number of distinctive segments. The close-knit paradigmatic structure of such a system will even maintain phonemic oppositions of low functional load when they are differentiated by a feature which serves to distinguish elsewhere in the system oppositions of high functional load. Thus, if English /θ/ and /ð/ were to merge the number of homophonous forms that would result would be minimal. Their merger would not, however, entail any saving in the overall feature inventory since voice also serves to distinguish a large number of pairs (/t/ ≠ /d/, /p/ ≠ /b/, /s/ ≠ /z/, etc.) vital to the English lexicon, and it is this fact which would account for their continued differentiation in spite of the low functional load carried by their opposition.

Martinet however has given a number of, on the face of it, sound arguments showing that such a structurally ideal system is not necessarily viable at the physiological level and that an adequate phonological theory must take account of both structural and physiological factors, and has attempted to integrate these considerations into a coherent theoretical framework designed to explain certain properties of phonological change (Martinet 1955:94–152; cf. Sieberer 1958 for the historical background). According to Martinet phonological change is governed by two opposing forces, the requirements of communication on the one hand and human inertia on the other. While the former is reflected in the symmetrical structure of the phonological system, the latter manifests itself in two ways: in the form of assimilation processes and general 'decay' of words, and in the form of certain physiological limitations on speech perception and production. These limitations include such facts as the observation that a larger number of front vowels than back vowels and of oral vowels than nasalized vowels can be distinguished by the human ear, and that the allophones of labial, dental and velar plosives are physically quite different in spite of their being functionally parallel (cf. C. Chomsky 1954). If these and other purely physiological limitations are relevant factors in human inertia, the phonological evolution of a language may be seen as a continual effort to maintain a state of balance between inertia on the one hand and communicative needs on the other. That is, essentially, what Martinet understands by the 'economy' (*économie*) of phonological change. The theory contains, plainly, a certain element of speculation. Martinet does not, however, claim that such internal motivation is the only cause of phonological change nor that the unambiguous representation of messages is the sole function of speech.

2 Traces of past phonological change remaining in morphological structure: internal reconstruction

Although at the time when it takes place sound change is phonologically conditioned it may subsequently manifest itself in the form of *synchronic morphological alternation*. We have already seen a number of examples of this. The alternations *Gast*~*Gäst-* in German and *blood*~*bleed* in English, for instance, are the result of the phonological change known as umlaut, and that between /s/ and /r/ in the paradigm of Latin nominative *genus* 'kind', genitive *generis*, is the result of a sound change which resulted in intervocalic */s/ becoming /r/. We get such morphological alternations when the phonological factor which originally conditioned a sound change was present in at least one member of a paradigm or derivational set and absent from at least one other member. Since some alternations at least are the result of past sound change (see below), we may ask ourselves whether such changes might not be reconstructable solely on the basis of an examination of the present morphological structure. The reconstruction of diachronic phonological rules on the sole evidence of synchronic morphological alternation is known as *internal reconstruction*. Although it is by no means an invention of structuralist linguistics we will discuss it at this point because only the techniques of descriptive linguistics allow the explicit statement of its underlying principles.

The following examples of internal reconstruction are all taken from languages the historical development of which is known so that the results of the method can be checked against the documentary or comparative evidence and we can thus obtain some idea of its effectiveness as a tool.

In procedural terms the method of internal reconstruction is to start from a specific morphological alternation and to attempt to deduce from it the past phonological changes which were its cause together with their conditioning factors.[1] Let us compare for example the following pair of words from German in which the nominative-accusative singular forms are homophonous but the remaining forms in the paradigms are different: /ra:t/ 'counsel' and /ra:t/ 'wheel', identical in the nominative-accusative singular whereas their respective genitives are /ˈra:təs/ 'of the counsel' and /ˈra:dəs/ 'of the wheel'. Thus, while /ra:t/ 'counsel' has the same stem throughout, 'wheel' has an alternation /ra:t/ ~ /ra:d-/. This is in fact a regular pattern where words ending in an obstruent (that is, a plosive or a fricative) are concerned, some of these showing no alternation and others having a regular alternation between voiceless and voiced final consonant of the stem (for example, /bunt/ 'multi-coloured' but /bunt/ ~ /bund-/ 'league', /za:t/ 'seed' but /ba:t/ ~ /ba:d-/ 'bath', /ʃluk/ 'sip' but /ʃlu:k/ ~ /ʃlu:g-/ past tense of *schlagen* 'to beat', etc.). Thus, while there are plenty of cases of alternating stems and of

[1] Hoenigswald (1960: chapter 10) gives a typology of phonological changes together with their chances of recovery by means of internal reconstruction.

non-alternating stems ending in a voiceless obstruent, there are no examples of stems with voiced final obstruent throughout. This situation may be accounted for by reference to a general phonological constraint in German which prohibits the occurrence of voiced obstruents in word-final position and thus makes it possible to formulate the alternation rule. Where there is alternation the alternant with voiced obstruent occurs before a vowel-initial ending whereas the alternant with voiceless obstruent occurs before consonant-initial suffix and word-finally. Instead of stating the distribution of the allomorphs statically in this way we may also state it dynamically, in terms of a base form subjected to certain morphological processes. These two models are known respectively as 'item and arrangement' and 'item and process' (Matthews 1974: chapters 5 and 7). In an item and process type description of the German word for 'wheel', we would have to make RA:D the base form since this permits the prediction of /ra:t/ by the rule which devoices obstruents in word-final position (and before consonant-initial suffix). Had we chosen RA:T as the base form no such prediction would have been possible, since both /'ra:dəs/ and /'ra:təs/ occur. If now it were to be assumed that this morphological alternation rule and the phonological rule barring voiced word-final obstruents were the synchronic reflexes of a past phonological change, we could postulate that an earlier phoneme /d/ split into [t] word-finally and [d] elsewhere, the [t] then merging with the existing /t/ phoneme. This primary phonemic split (see p. 78f.) is confirmed by comparative evidence as well as being reflected in earlier spelling. Thus Middle High German wrote *rat* 'wheel' but *rades* 'of the wheel', *tac* 'day' but *tages* 'of the day' whereas Old High German had *rad*, *rades*, *tag*, *tages* (in which the spelling can be shown to have been phonemic and not morphophonemic). Modern German orthography on the other hand uses a morphophonemic notation and consistently writes a voiced consonant in alternating stems (*Rad*, *Rades* 'wheel') and a voiceless consonant in non-alternating stems (*Rat*, *Rates* 'counsel').

In this example the internal reconstruction of the earlier forms was a fairly simple matter, since the absence of word-final voiced obstruents constitutes part of the synchronic phonology of Modern German. As a result the alternation of voiced and voiceless obstruents is automatic, that is it is completely predictable by general phonological rule. It should be noted, however, that there is no compelling reason for assuming that this particular phonological constraint is *necessarily* the result of an innovatory phonological change. Its phonetic basis and the automatic nature of its operation might equally well have made it an integral part of the phonological structure of the language throughout its history. This is because it is the reflection of a widespread speech phenomenon, namely the anticipation of sentence-final and constituent-final pause. Another example of what might be termed a 'natural' constraint is the assimilation affecting root-final voiced plosives in Latin to the voiceless initial consonant of a following suffix (cf. for example *captus* 'caught' from *capio* but also *scriptus* 'written' from *scribo*). This productive morphophonemic rule is not the result of an innovatory sound change but of a phonotactic constraint which has formed part of successive grammars of the language ever since Proto-Indo-European and there is no reason to assume that consonant clusters comprising segments which differ in voicing need have existed at any time in the past (we shall return to this question in chapter 3).

As a second example of internal reconstruction let us take the alternation /s/ ~ /r/ in Latin as found in nominative *honōs* 'honour', genitive *honōris*, etc. (the alternative nominative *honor* is the result of analogical levelling). With the exception of the nominative singular, *honōs* inflects like *dator* 'giver': genitive *honōris* like *datōris*, accusative *honōrem* like *datōrem*, etc. We have thus side by side paradigms in which /s/ alternates with /r/ and others with /r/ throughout. There are however no corresponding paradigms with /s/ throughout. This fact determines our choice of base forms: HONO:S 'honour', but DATO:R 'giver' (the vowel becoming short when in final syllable), for we may then derive /honor/ from the base form by means of a rule which changes /s/ to /r/ in all the case forms other than the nominative singular. However, if this synchronic rule was the result of a sound change its conditioning factor must have been a phonological one and, since all the case endings are in fact vowel-initial, intervocalic position would be a fair guess. We may therefore postulate a phonological change of /s/ to /r/ inter-vocalically, the medial allophones of /s/ merging with /r/. Our hypothesis is confirmed by comparative evidence from the other Indo-European languages and by the direct evidence of the Latin grammarians (who recorded that *meliosem* and *lases* were the earlier forms of *meliorem* 'better' and *lares* 'household gods') and by the fact that the long-established family name *Papisius* was changed to *Papirius* in the fourth century B.C. (Allen 1965:35).

This Latin example differs from the German one in that the change

[s] to [r] has not left any direct trace in the synchronic phonological structure of Latin. There are in fact many words with intervocalic /s/, for instance *ēsus* 'eaten', *cāsus* 'fallen', etc. Such intervocalic *s*'s are not, however, due to the survival of an older /s/ which somehow escaped the change to /r/, but have a different source. Thus *ēsus*, the past participle of *edō* 'to eat', is from **ēd-tus* via **ēssus* and it must be assumed that the reduction of *-*ss*- to -*s*- postdates the change of /s/ to /r/, otherwise the /s/ from /ss/ should also have become /r/ (see Allen 1965:35 for the relative chronology). The occurrence of intervocalic /s/ in the synchronic structure of Latin deprives us of any direct synchronic evidence of the phonological factor which determined the alternation in paradigms of the type *honos*, *honoris*, and this fact makes our internal reconstruction correspondingly less cogent than in the German example. The Latin example has however brought out another aspect of internal reconstruction: if *honos* had not survived, the alternation having been completely levelled, the phonological change would no longer have been recoverable by means of internal reconstruction. Of course in the present instance it could in fact have been recovered on the basis of other surviving evidence, namely the etymologically connected adjective *honestus* 'honest'. We shall return to this point in chapter 3.

Alternations of the type /waif/ *wife* ~ /waivz/ *wives*, /mauθ/ *mouth* ~ /mauðz/ *mouths*, /haus/ *house* ~ /hauziz/ *houses* in English ought on the face of it to lend themselves ideally to internal reconstruction. They form a small closed class within the basic vocabulary opposed to the great majority of nouns, for which the stem consonants are constant even in the case of fricatives (cf. *cuff* /kʌf/ plural /kʌfs/, *love* /lʌv/ plural /lʌvz/, etc.). Our inability so far to find an effective solution is no doubt due to the fact that a whole series of rules are involved, the ordering of which is crucial. The first step in attempting to solve this case by means of internal reconstruction might consist in establishing synchronically base forms for the lexical items in question, together with a rule which will account for the alternation between voiced and voiceless fricative in base-final position. An item and process synchronic analysis, which postulates base forms like /waiF/, /mauΘ/, /hauS/, is however not very helpful since the morphophonemes F, Θ, S are merely symbols for the alternations *f*/*v*, *θ*/*ð* *s*/*z*. Morphophonemic spellings of this kind, while useful synchronic devices for symbolizing alternating stems (as opposed to /kʌf/ and /lʌv/ where there is no such alternation), are clearly uneconomical diachronically if they demand that a third segment be postulated as the source of the alternants (i.e. a source of F in addition to /f/ and /v/, etc.). We also saw in the previous examples, as well as in our discussion of phonological change, that morphological alternation caused by phonological change is invariably the result of phonemic *split*. Since in our present case the phonemes involved differ by only a single feature, namely voice, it would seem reasonable to postulate that they result from the split of a single phoneme and this must imply either the voicing of a voiceless fricative or the devoicing of a voiced one. The former is a widely attested phenomenon, especially in intervocalic position, and the latter is not uncommon word-finally. One possible synchronic argument in favour of selecting the voiceless fricative as the base form is the fact that voicing does often appear to be associated with derivation in English, for example *a mouth* /mauθ/ but *to mouth* /mauð/, *a house* /haus/ but *to house* /hauz/, etc. Provided that we assume derivation to have been effected at the earlier stage by means of suffixation, these derived forms with voiced fricatives match the plural forms of the lexical items in question, which also have the alternant with the voiced fricative before the plural suffix while the voiceless fricative occurs in the singular, which is the unmarked form morphologically. The next step would then be the synchronic one of establishing a base form for the plural morpheme, whose alternants are /-z/, /-s/, and /-iz/. Various alternative analyses are possible. Theoretically one could choose any one of the alternants as the base form (Z, S or IZ) or postulate a base form IS (see Miner 1975), and there is little reason for favouring any one solution rather than any other. Depending on which solution is chosen, the alternation rules would be formulated somewhat differently. All solutions however require an assimilation rule (making stem-final and suffix consonant agree in voice) and a rule which either deletes or inserts an /i/, together with a statement regarding their ordering. These synchronic rules, once established and correctly ordered, could then be interpreted as representing the sound changes that led to the alternation and the base forms as the earlier shapes of the morphemes in question. In practice, however, this apparently simple task comes up against a number of problems, mainly perhaps due to the fact that the voicing assimilation rule, which states that in English consonants in clusters must agree with regard to voicing, is not of the normal innovatory kind which has limited validity in time and can thus be ordered relative to other phonological rules. Rather it belongs to a class of rules, sometimes labelled 'floating' or 'permanent', which remain productive over long periods of time and govern basic phonological constraints in languages (we shall return to this point in chapter 3). However, even if the rules and the earlier morph shapes had been established successfully, we should still have to explain why a large number of lexical items like *cuff* and *love* which, on the basis of their phonological form, would appear to qualify as input, should not have been affected by these rules. Three possibilities come to mind why they should have escaped their action. They could be lexical innovations which at the time of the phonological changes did not yet form part of the language, or their phonological structure might have been different at that time so that the rules were not applicable to them, or their present forms could be the result of analogical levelling. What is important is that a theory which claims the independence of phonological change from grammatical or semantic structure *must* account for all exceptions to the phonological rules that it postulates. This is especially difficult in our present case since clues from synchronic *phonological* structure are entirely missing, distributionally voiced and voiceless fricatives occurring in identical positions (initially, medially and finally). Of course we have deliberately ignored in the above exercise the evidence of earlier attested stages of English and of comparison with other Germanic languages.

The difficulties experienced in attempting to recover the conditioning factor which caused this alternation bring out another essential difference between a synchronic item and process analysis and internal reconstruction. While the environments which specify the alternation in the synchronic analysis may be either phonological or grammatical, the conditioning factors of the corresponding diachronic rules must necessarily be phonological ones, for morphophonemic alternation is the result of phonemic split, that is to say of a conditioned sound change. This difference constitutes one of the hazards of internal reconstruction for, should the phonological factors which determined a split be subsequently lost or the analogical redistribution of morphs obscure the phonological regularities, it is no longer possible to reconstruct the phonological factor correctly. It might for instance reasonably be supposed on general phonetic grounds that umlaut in German was originally conditioned by the presence of a front vowel in the syllable following the back vowel undergoing the alternation and this hypothesis would even appear to draw synchronic confirmation from such pairs as *rot* 'red' : *rötlich* 'reddish', where the second item has in fact an *i*-containing suffix compared with *roter* 'a red one' which has not. But there are unfortunately other pairs, such as *Gast* 'guest' : *gastlich* 'hospitable', which lack the umlaut in spite of the presence of the *-lich* suffix. Should one nevertheless maintain the original hypothesis in the face of such examples? In this case, however, we know that their irregularity arises from the fact that the formation of adjectives in *-lich* remained productive long after the umlaut rule had ceased to operate.

Of course there is no such problem in the case of *automatic* alternations determined by synchronically valid phonological rules, such as that which precludes voiced obstruents in word-final position in German or that governing voicing assimilation in English. But these, as we have seen, raise another problem, for such alternations *need* not be the result of a sound change, since regularities of this kind may perfectly well constitute permanent phonological characteristics of particular languages.

The recovery of the earlier situation by means of internal reconstruction may, as we have seen, be made impossible by subsequent analogical developments. Thus had the alternation /f/ ~ /v/ in English either been analogically extended to all fricative-final words or analogically levelled, it would no longer be possible to reconstruct the earlier situation.

We have so far not considered the question of what kinds of alternation are amenable to the method of internal reconstruction. Obviously suppletive alternants of the type *go* : *went* in English would not be seriously considered as candidates, since an alternation *go* ~ *wen*(*d*)- is unlikely to be the result of sound change in view of the large number of phonological differences involved. But what about paradigms such as *bring* : *brought*? An alternation /briŋ/ ~ /brɔː/ (the latter selecting the /t/ and not the /d/ allomorph of the past tense) is very likely to be the result of sound change, but is there in fact any chance of recovering, using only the methods of internal reconstruction, the rules which produced it? The selection of the voiceless past tense alternant would suggest the loss of a voiceless base-final segment, but could one get any closer to the actual protoform **branxta*? The same problem arises in the case of such apparently simple examples of alternation as *sing* : *sang*. Since the vowel alternation could have been caused by sound change presumably we are to postulate that it was. But what conditioning factor could have caused the original vowel to split in the first place and which direction did the change take? The fact that synchronically in the case of the weak verbs we must consider the present stem as the base and derive the past tense form from it by means of affixation might suggest the same direction of derivation in the case of the strong verbs, and would imply a change of /i/ to /æ/ rather than the reverse. We do in fact know on comparative grounds that in this particular case the alternation is inherited from Proto-Indo-European (*/e/ ~ */o/) but even at that level positive clues as to the conditioning factor are not available. It would thus seem that recoverability depends on the time-depth which separates the original phonological change from the synchronic state on the basis of which it is to be reconstructed. One might, it is true, consider the possibility that ablaut may have been an original feature and not the result of conditioned phonological change. One would then, however, have to explain why the alternation between */e/ and */o/ in Proto-Indo-European was invariably accompanied by suffixation and why those forms which shared one or other of these vowels do not appear to have also shared any corresponding grammatical or lexical feature.

All the examples discussed so far relate to alternation *within* the paradigmatic scatter of forms belonging to the same lexical item and we have not so far considered any cases of alternation *between* structurally and functionally parallel paradigms of different lexical items.[1] The pattern of perfect tense formation in Sanskrit will serve as an illustration. The relevant rules may be abstracted from the following examples (verbal roots in first column, followed by perfect stem in second):

tan-	tatan-	'to stretch'	kar-	cakar-	'to make'
darś-	dadarś-	'to see'	gam-	jagam-	'to go'
pat-	papat-	'to fly'			
vakṣ-	vavakṣ-	'to increase'			
sad-	sasad-	'to sit'			

The regular forms on the left suggest the setting up of a rule which derives the perfect stem by the prefixation to the root of a morph consisting in a repetition of the root-initial consonant followed by a

[1] An example of this type of internal reconstruction is Gelb's (1969) *sequential reconstruction*, which operates on the assumption that inflectional morphemes, and therefore the morphs that represent them, occur within the word in absolutely fixed order. In the case of Proto-Semitic this leads to interesting discrepancies between the results of internal and comparative reconstruction.

vowel, apparently that of the root, /a/. From the examples in the right hand column it will however be seen that in the case of velar-initial roots the initial of the reduplicated syllable is a palatal. If we make the assumption that the pattern of perfect tense formation was originally identical for all verbs, we may postulate that velars have been palatalized in the prefix. But we know that palatalization is normally conditioned by the presence of a front vowel. If we consider this in combination with the fact that Sanskrit has a conspicuously unbalanced vowel system, opposing five long vowels (/a:/, /e:/, /i:/, /o:/, /u:/) to only three short ones (/a/, /i/, /u/), it is reasonable to suppose that the vowel of the reduplication syllable (though not that of the root) is likely to have been a front vowel, presumably an */e/ which was later to become an /a/. This front vowel would then have palatalized velar consonants before happening to become identical with the root vowel, a classic case of secondary split: (1) [k] > [c] and [g] > [j] before */e/, (2) */e/ > /a/, with [c] and [j] becoming independent phonemes as soon as */e/ and /a/ (or the source of this latter) had merged.

The canonical form of the perfect tense would thus have been the root, whose vowel must have been other than a front vowel, say */a/ or */o/, preceded by a prefix consisting of the root-initial consonant plus a front vowel, say */e/. These two distinct vowels, that of the prefix and that of the root, must then have merged to give /a/. Note that a conditioning factor for the merger cannot be postulated; considering the vast range of possible verbal roots in Sanskrit, the change must have taken place in all environments. We must therefore assume a context-free change, the */e/ merging with the */a/ or */o/ in all environments (we know from comparative evidence that the root vowel was in fact */o/ and not */a/, but this is immaterial to the argument).

This example demonstrates that context-free rules *may* be reconstructed internally and that internal reconstruction *need* not be restricted to context-sensitive rules. But reconstructions based solely on pattern congruity are necessarily less cogent than those based on alternation. Clearly one must consider the question of just how far the principle of one form one function should be carried. The extreme would be to consider any sort of alternation, whether within a paradigm or between functionally parallel paradigms, to be the result of sound change. But this would impose a degree of regularity on the linguistic structures of earlier language states which, unless confirmed by comparative evidence, would by comparison with living languages hardly seem realistic.

3 Changes affecting grammatical categories and their exponents

We have seen that the application of structuralist theory to the problems of phonological change has allowed these to be stated and resolved with a degree of explicitness which was not possible using the older neogrammarian methods. We shall now see to what extent structuralist methodology has also brought about a better understanding of change at the level of morphology.

Morphological change may perhaps best be approached through an examination of its effect on grammatical categories and their exponents. When, for each language state, morphologically complex words are segmented and the grammatical segments are assigned to specific grammatical categories, it becomes apparent that language change may alter both the morphemic division of words and the relation between segments and categories. Furthermore the system of categories may itself undergo change in the course of time. The traditional grammatical categories of person, tense, mood, voice, gender, number and case are elements of structure which embody a covariation of form and function. Old English, for instance, had retained the three-term gender system of Proto-Indo-European, nouns falling into the classes masculine, feminine and neuter each with its own specific inflectional endings; the class of the noun in turn determined the endings of syntactically dependent adjectives and pronouns. In Modern English on the other hand gender has completely disappeared as a category of the noun, and formal survivals of grammatical gender in the personal pronouns (*he*, *she*, *it*) are now determined entirely by the natural gender of the referent. German has preserved the older system almost intact, so that *ein grüner Baum* 'a green tree' (masculine) is referred to as *er* 'he' whereas *eine grüne Wiese* 'a green meadow' is referred to as *sie* 'she' and *ein grünes Blatt* 'a green leaf' as *es* 'it'. When natural gender and grammatical gender are in conflict (*ein junges Mädchen* (neuter) 'a young girl'), both *es* and *sie* are possible. In predicative function, however, adjectives no longer inflect for gender (*der Baum ist grün*; *die Wiese ist grün*; *das Blatt ist grün*).

We will first consider some cases of change in morphological segmentation. Modern English *apron* comes, through Middle English *napron*, from Old French *naperon*, diminutive of *nape* '(table) cloth'. The absence of the initial *n-* in the Modern English form is the result of resegmentation, the *n* having been interpreted as belonging to the article.

In the same way Modern English *adder* comes from Old English *nǣdre* (cf. German *Natter*). In cases such as these we may speak of etymologically 'wrong' word division. The same principle also applies within words. Thus Modern English *pea* comes, through Early Modern English *pease*, from Middle English *pese*, a singular mass noun with collective meaning and a plural *pesen*. The *-s-* was thus originally part of the stem. In Modern English, however, the *-s* became reallocated to the plural morpheme, this analysis being encouraged both by the formal identity of the *-s* with one of the regular alternants of that morpheme and by the syntactic possibility of mass words being formally either singular or plural (cf. *oats*, but *wheat*). We thus now have an etymologically 'wrong' singular form *pea*.

Forms which originally were morphologically complex may cease to be synchronically segmentable at all. Such is the case of the forms of the verb 'to be' in many Indo-European languages, basically because the morphological class to which it belonged in Proto-Indo-European did not survive as a class in the languages concerned. Compare for instance the present-tense paradigm of the verb 'to be' in Gothic with the same paradigm in Proto-Indo-European. The first and second persons plural have undergone restructuring, but all the singular forms and the third person plural are the direct reflexes of the Proto-Indo-European forms:

Proto-Indo-European		Gothic
*es-mi	sg. 1	im
*esi < *es-si	2	is
*es-ti	3	ist
*s-mes	pl. 1	(sijum)
*s-the	2	(sijuþ)
*s-enti	3	sind

While in Proto-Indo-European both the alternation (**es-* ~ **s-*) in the root and the inflectional endings (**-mi*, **-si*, **-ti*, etc.) are well integrated into the verbal system of the language, no segmentation of the Gothic forms will relate them to the regular verbal paradigms in that language. With the exception of the second and third person plural, which had been restructured on the model of the past tense paradigm, the verb is simply 'irregular' and any synchronic analysis is totally arbitrary. In other Germanic languages the paradigm was restructured in a variety of ways, nowhere however achieving integration into the regular verbal system. In Modern Polish and Modern Persian on the other hand the forms of the verb 'to be' are (with the exception of the third person plural in Polish) morphologically analysable and relatable to other verbal paradigms, but this is totally the result of restructuring (Watkins 1962:93–6):

Polish		Persian
jest-em	sg. 1	hast-am
jest-eś	2	hast-i
jest	3	hast
jest-eśmy	pl. 1	hast-im
jest-eście	2	hast-id
są	3	hast-and

In Polish only the third persons singular and plural are direct reflexes of the Proto-Indo-European forms. The other forms of the paradigm have been built on the third person singular form as if it were the basic stem and for which, instead of the 'correct' segmentation *jes-t* (< **es-ti*), we must presuppose a reanalysis *jest-ø*, with a zero suffix. A parallel change must have occurred in Persian, where the third person singular *hast* is again inherited but must also have been reanalysed as *hast-ø* at some stage. In both cases this reanalysis has achieved the integration of the verb into the productive conjugational system of the language, so that the inflectional endings of the other persons (except for the third plural in Polish) are those found in other verbal paradigms.

In order to explain these and parallel changes in other languages the principle has been advanced that of the three grammatical persons – speaker, addressee and person or thing talked about – it is the last (the so-called third person) that is to be considered as the semantically unmarked member of the group, the person that is neither speaker nor addressee. And, it is suggested, it is because of this absence of markedness at the functional level that it has often been reinterpreted as being unmarked at the formal level also thus coming to form the basis of a new paradigm (Watkins 1962:90ff., 1969 passim; Kuryłowicz 1964:148ff.). We have here, then, an example of the restructuring of a paradigm on the basis of the *functional* reinterpretation of forms, a renewal of connection between inherited forms and the basic speech situation (speaker, addressee and topic). This is the kind of explanatory principle which is required in order to account for that component of morphological change which is not ascribable to phonological change.

Exercises of this kind show that prior morphological analysis is indispensable to phonological reconstruction. For, while phonological reconstruction can test whether a given form could possibly be the direct formal descendant of an older form, the decision whether it should in fact be interpreted as such must depend upon grammatical arguments, that is to say a functional analysis. For it must not be forgotten that the development of a morphological system in time is the result of a constant interplay between phonological change and restructuring at the grammatical level.

As another example of this interplay, let us consider the development of the *-s*-stems in Germanic. In the Proto-Indo-European paradigm which underlies the paradigms of Sanskrit *jánas*, Greek *génos* and Latin *genus* 'kind, family' (cf. p. 13f.), each form may be analysed into three grammatical segments: root **gen-*, derivational suffix **-es* ~ **-os* ~ **-əs*, and inflectional ending jointly representing case and number (**-ø*, **-os*, **-i*, etc.). In Germanic this paradigm survived for instance in certain dialects of Old English and in Old High German in the inflection of a few nouns ('lamb', 'calf', etc.), the derivational suffix being reflected where it survived by *(u)r* in Old English, by *ir* in Old High German:

Proto-Indo-European		Old English	Old High German
sg. nom.acc.	*gen-os-ø	lemb	lamb
gen.	*gen-es-os	lombur	
loc.	*gen-es-i	lombur (dat.)	
pl. nom.acc.	*gen-es-ā	lombur	lembir
gen.	*gen-es-ōm	lombra	lembiro
instr.	*gen-es-mis	lombrum (dat.)	lembirum

The Old English forms could, from a purely descriptive point of view, have been open to alternative analyses since the *r*-element, found only in this small class, might have been treated either as part of the stem or of the inflectional ending. It appears, on the other hand, most unlikely that synchronically the *r*-element would still have been interpreted as an independent segment representing a third morpheme since the *r* is absent from the nominative-accusative singular form which is as a rule identical with the stem (the unmarked form). At a later stage nouns of this class came to be inflected: sg.nom.acc. *lomb*, gen. *lombes*, pl.nom.acc. *lomb*, gen. *lomba*, dat. *lombum*, like the main class of neuters (type *barn* 'child') and the synchronic analysis which permits this development most readily is the one which takes the *r*-element as forming part of the inflectional suffix, so that the change would simply have consisted in the replacement of the irregular case endings by the regular ones (*lomb-a* instead of *lomb-ra*, etc.), the phonologically conditioned alternation of the stem vowel being levelled in a final step.

If we accept that the above analysis is a true reflection of the situation as it was in Old English, then the most important change which the paradigm had undergone since Proto-Indo-European was a reduction from three to two in the number of segments of its forms. This was brought about in the first place by a series of phonological changes. First the final syllables, which were unstressed, were either reduced or lost through regular sound change. This resulted in the loss of the inflectional endings throughout the singular and in the nominative-accusative plural, and in the loss of the derivational suffix in the nominative-accusative singular while elsewhere it became *-ur/-r-*. The truncated forms must then have been reanalysed functionally, with the result that the reflex of what was originally a derivational suffix became interpreted as an inflectional ending, or part of an inflectional ending, its absence in the nominative-accusative singular giving rise to a new stem *lemb* ~ *lomb-*.

In Old High German on the other hand the *r*-less nominative-accusative singular form was generalized throughout the singular so that it became possible to reinterpret *-ir* (corresponding to Old English *-ur*) as a plural marker. It did, in fact, become a convenient means of formally marking the plural of neuter nouns, many of which had lost an overt marker, and in this function became extremely productive, spreading far beyond its original domain (the small *s*-stem class) to neuter nouns of all classes (*Kind* 'child' pl. *Kinder*, *Wort* 'word' pl. *Wörter*, *Haus* 'house' pl. *Häuser*, *Buch* 'book' pl. *Bücher*, etc., and even to a few masculine nouns: *Mann* 'man' pl. *Männer*, *Wald* 'wood' pl. *Wälder*, etc.). Clearly, in this case there was not a direct development at the grammatical level of a derivational suffix into an inflectional one. The basic change was phonological, the truncation of the word forms through sound change, and only subsequently could there be integration of the resulting forms into the morphological system through morphological reanalysis.

Although there remain areas of morphological change which are still incompletely understood, our examples have shown that there are at least two basic factors the interplay of which determines change at the grammatical level: phonological change on the one hand and functional reanalysis of inherited forms on the other. Fundamental to such reanalysis is the rerelating of grammatical forms to the basic grammatical categories. As for these categories themselves, some are potentially expendable (gender, case when morphologically defined) while others appear to be obligatory universals (person, perhaps number; see Kiparsky 1972). In the development of many Indo-European languages at least there has been both a reduction in the number of terms within certain categories and a reduction in the number of the categories themselves (Kuryłowicz 1964; 1974). The dual, for instance, is no longer overtly marked anywhere and grammatical gender was variously lost (English, Persian) or reduced (to two terms, masculine and feminine in French, animate and neuter in Hittite).

Analyses such as the above, of course, depend on a morphological definition of 'category'. Only then can it for instance be said that Modern French has lost the category of case since its nouns no longer vary in form according to their syntactic function. If, however, 'case' is semantically defined, one can say that case relations are expressed in Modern French *analytically* by means of prepositional phrases whereas in Latin they were expressed *synthetically* through internal modification of the word form. It is interesting to note in this context that the French prepositions *de* and *à*, which mark the purely syntactic relations of 'genitive' and 'dative', also mark in other contexts spatial relationships ('from' and 'to/at') just as *of(f)* and *to* do in English and *von* in German. Their Latin etymons *de* and *ad* on the other hand designated spatial relationships only. Just how widespread a phenomenon is this tendency for markers of spatial relationships to provide the means of renewing the exponents of indispensable syntactic categories has not been explored. Ideally our syntactic theory should be able to predict those grammatical distinctions for which overt marking is indispensable and those for which it is not, as well as what possible means are available for the replacement of exponents should these be eliminated through sound change. In fact we know very little about developments of this type and are almost totally confined to the retrospective appraisal of attested changes.

4 Limitations of structuralist methods applied to diachrony

We have seen that, by systematically distinguishing between morpheme and morph on the one hand and phoneme, allophone and morphophoneme on the other, the structuralists were able to make explicit in a way that had not previously been possible differences between successive language states. That diachronic work was largely concentrated at the phonological and morphological levels was in keeping with the parallel preoccupations of linguists on the synchronic side. The lack of an adequate syntactic theory, a repeatedly heard criticism of structuralism, as well as its almost total neglect of semantics, clearly had repercussions on the diachronic side. It is possible that a more adequate syntactic theory might have produced a better explanation of morphological change by providing a framework within which the function of the grammatical categories could be situated, but structuralist syntactic theory was too limited in its scope for such an undertaking. We shall return to this question in chapter 3, within the framework of transformational syntax. In the area of semantics the only specifically structuralist contribution on the diachronic side was certain work on lexical change which, through the employment of the concept of the semantic field, was able to demonstrate the systematic interdependence of lexical changes affecting items within one and the same field (Trier 1931; cf. Ullmann 1962: chapters 8 and 9).

Structuralist theory however also raised a certain number of problems. In particular the rigorous attitude adopted regarding the interdependence of structures within a language – *un système où tout se tient* – had the effect of making the process of change something of a mystery. For, if every element is dependent on every other element in a system, how is change possible at all? And on what basis is one to identify specific sounds and forms of different systems as being diachronically 'the same'? (see Allen 1953). To this was added a methodological problem, the requirement that for it to be 'scientific' each step in a structuralist analysis should be explicitly stated and justified by reference to observable facts. In other words, it was not the final analysis that had to be justified but rather the discovery procedures which had led up to it. The methodological problems raised by this requirement become perhaps most apparent in the attempts that were made to establish rigorous procedures for linguistic reconstruction. In spite of the fact that the arguments employed are no longer acceptable, we will briefly examine this problem of procedures. For, in the first place, it highlights the structural distance which often separates related languages, a fact which had not previously been brought out so clearly, and secondly it shows how necessary it is that new thought be given to the nature of the diachronic rules linking synchronic systems.

Linguistic reconstruction starts from the synchronic description of individual languages assumed to be related and seeks to establish their relatedness by interpreting structures and classes within them as reflexes of the structures and classes of the earlier linguistic system from which they are presumed to derive. If, however, each language is considered to be a system the units of which are definable solely on the basis of their mutual relationships, according to what criterion are items from within different languages to be accepted as 'comparable' for the purpose of reconstruction? There is obviously here a clash between the requirements of linguistic reconstruction, which demands that elements of different languages be interpreted as 'the same' (that is to say as putative continuations of a single proto-item) and the principle of the incommensurability of linguistic systems which precludes the equation of individual items from within different systems. The obvious means of resolving such a discrepancy would surely have been for the structuralists to set up diachronic rules to account for changes in the structural status of the units thereby linking the common proto-language and the language states which figure in the comparison. However, in British linguistics at least, *synchronic* justification was sought for the equation of items by historical linguists in their reconstruction procedures. The reason given was that historical linguistics should be considered, from the point of view of procedure, as being only one particular type of comparative linguistics defined simply as the simultaneous analysis of more than one language (Ellis 1966). The only peculiarity of historical as opposed to synchronic comparison (or 'contrastive analysis') would then lie in the fact that its comparable units are equated at all levels of analysis simultaneously whereas in synchronic comparison equation is confined to individual levels of analysis, that is to say that phonological systems, case systems, tense systems, etc. are compared separately from one another (Palmer 1958).

Thus, for instance, English *better* and German *besser* may be related (1) phonologically through recurrent sound correspondences, (2) grammatically as each consisting of two morphs (/bet-/ an allomorph of *good* followed by the comparative suffix /-ə/ in English, /bes-/ an allomorph of *gut* followed by the comparative suffix /-(ə)r/ in German), and (3) semantically, both filling equivalent slots in the lexicon. With the exception of borrowing (see chapter 6), such simultaneous agreement between forms at the phonological, grammatical and lexical levels is never found in unrelated languages and would thus effectively serve to differentiate historical comparison from synchronic comparison.

This works perfectly well for examples such as the above where there happens to be isomorphism of the compared structures. But the historical linguist must also be able to handle cases like English *starve* 'to suffer severe hunger' and German *sterben* 'to die', English *tide* 'periodic ebb and flood of the sea' and German *Zeit* 'time', as potentially comparable items despite their semantic differences. From the purely synchronic point of view such equations are rightly rejected as unjustifiable and, since historical comparison does in fact make them, the only possible course was felt to be the exclusion of historical linguistics from 'scientific' linguistics (Allen 1953; Ellis 1966)! In retrospect it is easy to see that this particular *impasse* was largely of the structuralists' own making, the result of their seeking to justify their analytic procedures rather than the final analyses. There is no *a priori* reason why the acceptance of items as 'comparable' for the purposes of linguistic reconstruction should be governed by the same requirement of exact structural equivalence as is demanded in contrastive analysis. Were structural equivalence a necessary condition, this would imply that related languages either undergo no change in structure whatsoever after split or that they undergo identical changes, both of which are contrary to observable reality. We have nevertheless included the discussion of these methodological limitations in order to see to what extent they may be overcome within a different theoretical framework.

3
The transformational-generative model of language evolution

We shall discuss in this chapter the description and interpretation of language change within the framework of transformational-generative theory. It could be objected that, in the present fluid state of historical work in terms of the transformational model, any attempt at a synthesis is premature and can only serve to perpetuate obsolescent or outdated hypotheses. We think, however, that this objection is outweighed by the consideration that the transformational framework has become the major centre of theoretical rethinking in historical linguistics and that the issues raised by the alternative analyses which it proposes cannot be ignored. We shall concentrate on two basic questions, namely the representation of phonological change within the framework of a non-autonomous phonology (that is to say, a phonology the rules of which take account of structure at the grammatical level), and the representation of syntactic change in terms of deep structure and transformational rules. The examples discussed will include a number of changes for which we have already given traditional analyses so that the comparison of the solutions provided by the different models to the same problems may give some idea of their relative descriptive adequacy and explanatory power.

We shall take as our basis the so-called standard theory of transformational-generative grammar, as outlined in Chomsky's 'Aspects' (Chomsky 1965; Chomsky and Halle 1968; cf. King 1969a: chapter 2). When this model is compared with the taxonomic approach, the following of its features would appear to be those most relevant to our discussion:

(1) It claims that an adequate linguistic description of a language must take account of linguistic *creativity*, that is to say of the fact that native speakers are able to produce and to understand sentences which they have never heard before. This means that the linguist has to devise a model of the native speaker's 'knowledge' of his language (his *com-*

petence) which underlies his actual output (his *performance*). Such a grammar is said to be *generative* in the sense that it is capable of 'generating' all the well-formed sentences of the language and no ill-formed ones.

(2) A transformational grammar consists essentially of three components, syntax, phonology and semantics. Of these only the syntactic component is generative while the other two are said to be *interpretive*, that is to say they operate on structures previously generated by the syntax.

(3) The syntactic component generates the syntactic structure of sentences in two stages. Firstly, the *phrase structure rules* and the *lexicon*, which together form the *base* of the syntactic component, generate its *deep structure*, that is to say essentially its constituent structure (logical subject, etc.) in the form in which the sentence is semantically interpreted. Secondly, the *transformational rules* convert this abstract underlying structure into a *surface structure* which, after the application of the phonological rules, is a close approximation to the spoken form of the sentence. It is a basic contention of transformational grammarians that the deep and surface structures of any sentence are quite distinct and that transformational rules are required in order to relate the two. When it leaves the syntactic component, the sentence is represented as a string of *formatives*. These comprise lexical elements in their 'dictionary form' (or *underlying representations*) and grammatical elements such as 'plural' or 'past'.

(4) The phonological rules then derive from the underlying forms the alternants appropriate to the context and combine these to give the *phonetic representation* of the sentence. The phonological rules of a transformational grammar thus include both the morphophonemics and the phonotactics of a taxonomic grammar; there is no separate morphological component.

(5) The semantic rules produce a semantic reading of the sentence by combining an interpretation of the deep structure's constituent structure and of the structure of the lexical elements.

(6) In the standard theory with which we are here concerned, at least certain of the phonological and of the transformational rules are *extrinsically ordered* (that is to say, their order within their components is distinctive and must be specified).

Transformational grammar is concerned primarily not with the output of a grammar but with the rules which produce that output. It follows that if the language changes this is the result of change in the grammar – not as such a new concept, of course, but a point worth stressing in view of structuralist preoccupation with forms rather than rules. We will discuss change in the phonological and syntactic components in turn.

1 Phonological change

Before discussing the representation of phonological change in terms of the transformational-generative model we must briefly recall the main characteristics of generative phonology (for an outline see Schane 1973). As we have already remarked, generative phonology is non-autonomous so that it in fact includes the morphophonemics of a taxonomic grammar. Its phonological segments are represented as matrices of distinctive features and these, unlike the distinctive features of structuralist phonology which represent the minimal phonological contrasts within a particular language, are claimed to constitute a 'universal phonetic framework' within which may be accommodated all phonetic distinctions which may be relevant to any language and of which a particular language makes use of only a selection. Feature values are of two kinds, absolute (plus or minus) and relative (more or less, expressed in quantitative terms). The relative values are designed to take account of phonetic differences in the realization of segments in different languages and we shall not be concerned with them here. The conversion of the underlying representation into the surface form is effected by means of the phonological rules, which operate on the absolute feature values of the systematic phonemes (changing plus to minus, minus to plus, etc.). This highly formalized theory of generative phonology is claimed to be capable of making significant generalizations both about the structure of particular languages and about that of language in general, and this both in the synchronic and diachronic dimensions.

The distinction made in generative phonology between underlying (or systematic phonemic) representations and surface (or systematic phonetic) representations is perhaps best illustrated by means of an example. As we saw in the previous chapter, Standard German *Rad* 'wheel' is homophonous with *Rat* 'counsel'. In the nominative and accusative singular both have the systematic phonetic form [ra:t][1]

[1] In this chapter square brackets are used to enclose systematic phonetic representations and obliques to enclose underlying representations consisting of systematic phonemes (corresponding to morphophonemes in

while elsewhere in their paradigms the two words differ (['ra:dəs] 'of the wheel' as opposed to ['ra:təs] 'of the counsel', etc.). However, provided that 'wheel' is represented in the underlying structure as /ra:d/, its superficial phonetic forms are predictable by means of a synchronic phonological rule which devoices underlying voiced obstruents when word-final. This rule is represented by the formula:

$$[+\text{obstruent}] \rightarrow [-\text{voiced}] / \_\_ \#$$ [1]

Rat 'counsel' is, on the other hand, represented as /ra:t/.

The only levels of representation which have systematic status are thus the systematic phonemic and the systematic phonetic levels. There is therefore theoretically no place for the traditional autonomous phoneme. (In practice, generative analyses are often insufficiently detailed so that a systematic phonetic representation and an autonomous phonemic one are frequently identical in substance.) Perhaps we should recall at this point the argument, based on the criterion of simplicity of description, which led to the abandonment of autonomous phonemes as a systematic level of representation in generative phonology. It was in fact claimed that a significant generalization may be missed if the conversion of underlying into surface representations has to go through an autonomous phonemic level. A key case in the argument is the following (Schane 1971:517 following Halle). Russian has a phonological (in taxonomic terms, morphophonemic) rule according to which, in certain combinations, a word-final obstruent agrees in voicing with a following obstruent. Thus underlying /mok bi/ is realized as [mog bɨ], /žeč bi/ as [žej̆ bɨ], etc. However, while the contrasts between [k] and [g], [p] and [b], [t] and [d], are phonemic in taxonomic terms that between [č] and [j̆] is merely phonetic, the two being environmentally conditioned allophones. The simplest description is thus in terms of a voicing assimilation rule which simply ignores the phonemic status of the segments. It is however worth noting that this argument against having an autonomous phonemic level situated between the morphophonemic and the phonetic levels is based on a rule typical of certain

taxonomic terms). Although, as we shall see, the former are in practice often identical with taxonomic phonemic notations, their different status must constantly be borne in mind.

1 In the formula the input to the rule is shown on the left of the arrow and the output on the right; the arrow indicates 'replace by'; the slot marked by the underline following the oblique indicates the position relative to the environment in which the rule operates (in this instance, before final word boundary).

phonotactic constraints which appear to remain productive over very long periods of time. We shall be returning to this point.

In the interests of generality of statement and of descriptive economy, generative phonology employs a modification of the Prague school concept of *markedness* which is still being discussed in its detailed implications (Chomsky and Halle 1968:402ff.; Vennemann 1972a; Chen 1973). According to this theory, phonological segments may be specified not merely as either 'plus' or 'minus' a specific feature but alternatively as 'marked' or 'unmarked' for it. In spite of certain difficulties in its application, the underlying principle is clear enough. Its purpose is to ensure that the more common feature combinations are represented in the theory as structurally simpler and therefore 'more natural' while the rarer combinations, which are claimed to be more costly in terms of the technical apparatus required for their description, are represented as 'less natural'. For instance, it is claimed that in the majority of the languages of the world back vowels (with the possible exception of the low vowel [ɑ]) are in general rounded whereas front vowels are unrounded. Rounded back vowels and unrounded front vowels should thus be considered to be the 'normal' or *unmarked* situation, and therefore feature values for rounding do not have to be explicitly specified in the feature matrix, which is thus simplified. Marking for rounding will thus be predictable on the basis of the plus or minus value of the feature of backness. Languages which, on the other hand, do have a contrast between rounded and unrounded front and back vowels will require the specification of both backness and rounding for their segments so that their vowels are more complex in feature terms and constitute the *marked* situation. Markedness conventions will of course apply not only to the characterization of individual segments but also to sequences of segments and, as we shall see, to the form and ordering of rules.

The abandonment of an autonomous phonology has repercussions for diachrony. Thus transformational grammar claims, against the traditional view, that phonological change may take place in any environment specified by the grammar, no matter whether it be phonological ('phonetic' in terms of generative phonology) or grammatical (surface syntactic). Transformational grammar criticized the traditional position chiefly on two grounds: firstly, that its autonomous phonology was only apparently independent of grammatical structure, and secondly that it used the term 'analogy' 'very misleadingly to refer to cases of perfectly regular phonological change in which part of the conditioning environment involves surface constituent structure' (Postal 1968:265). With regard to the first point, it was claimed that, by using *words* as the framework within which to describe phonological change, autonomous phonology did in fact make use of grammatical information since words are *grammatical* units. To this the traditionalists could reply that words are also *phonological* units, and that we have at word level the maximum congruence of phonological and grammatical structure. What in fact the transformationalists fail to see is that in traditional theory it is only the word as *a segmental unit* which is relevant in phonological change, while grammatical information proper (such as word class membership, syntactic function, tense, gender etc.) plays no part at all. The second point, the role of grammatical environments as conditioning factors of phonological change, carries more weight. Let us first be clear about the precise issue involved. This is not whether or not grammatical factors may play a part in phonological change, a fact which no one is going to dispute, but whether they should be treated on a par with phonological factors as conditioning phonological change. Traditional historical linguistics would say that the transformational-generative argument fails to make the linguistically significant generalization that, in contrast to phonological factors, grammatical factors typically play a *negative* role in specifying the domain of a phonological change by stating the environment which *prevents* it. (A typical example is the one already discussed of the loss of intervocalic *[s] in Greek *except* when it marks the aorist of vowel-final verbs. The traditional view is that the loss of *[s] intervocalically was a sound change whereas the retention of the *[s] in spite of the rule and within the domain of a specific grammatical category was a matter of analogical change.) The question of grammatical environments will be taken up later (see p. 128ff.).

We shall now examine the way in which transformational-generative theory deals with phonological change. As in the case of the previous models, we may take as our starting-point the assumption that phonological change may be abstracted from a comparison of the successive synchronic grammars of a language. In a linguistic model which operates with a set of underlying representations and ordered series of phonological rules generating the appropriate surface forms from these, successive synchronic grammars may potentially differ from one another in their rule inventories, in the forms and ordering of their rules and in the forms of the underlying representations of corresponding lexical items.

1.1 *Innovation*

According to Halle (1962) the basic type of sound change, namely innovatory change, is reflected in the transformational model by the addition of a new phonological rule at the end of the phonological component. The addition of the new rule has the effect of systematically modifying the phonetic representations generated by the grammar so that they differ from those generated by the previous grammar in which the rule is lacking. The difference in output must obviously be small enough not to disrupt communication between possessors of the old and the new grammars. This type of change may typically be attributed to the adult speaker, who is capable of modifying his speech in limited ways. The output of this modified grammar will then serve as data for the language learner of the following generation who, it is claimed, has as a child the innate capability of constructing from the data to which he is exposed the 'optimal' or simplest possible grammar. This means that the added rule will be retained in the grammar of the next generation only if a simpler grammar cannot be constructed which will generate the same output. If, however, this is possible the grammar will be restructured[1] so as to account for the same output more simply. Broadly speaking, the new rule will remain as a rule in the grammar of the following generation if it results in morphological alternation, otherwise its effects will be absorbed into the lexicon causing restructuring of the relevant underlying representations. The model thus claims: (1) that the grammar of a language may undergo lexical restructuring as the consequence of innovatory sound change, (2) that such restructuring typically occurs during the course of the transmission of the language from one generation to the next, and that (3) it constitutes a simplification of the grammar. As we have seen, simplification is itself defined within the theory and consists essentially in a reduction in the apparatus required for description.

The following example will serve to illustrate rule addition and subsequent lexical restructuring (King 1969a:80f.). Let us suppose

[1] This term has been used in various ways. We will use it to mean any modification of the structure of the grammar (rules *and* underlying representations) while King for instance restricts its use to modification of the structure of underlying representations.

that in a particular variety of English, words like *witch*, *weather*, etc. are pronounced with [w] whereas words like *which*, *whether*, etc. are pronounced with [ʍ] (a voiceless labiovelar fricative). Since the distribution of the two different sounds cannot be accounted for by rule, it must be included in the underlying representations. Now let us suppose that at some later stage speakers pronounce both word sets alike with [w] – for instance in order to conform to a prestige form of the language. This change in pronunciation will be represented in the grammar by the addition of a rule which modifies the feature specification of /ʍ/ so that it matches that of /w/. If now the child acquiring the language hears only the new pronunciation, there is nothing to indicate to him that words with initial [w] might belong to two different lexical sets, so that there is no reason for him to have in his grammar an underlying /ʍ/; as a result in his grammar the lexical items of both sets will now simply have underlying /w/. The addition of a rule in one generation has thus led to the restructuring of underlying representations and the elimination of the added rule in the following generation, and this clearly represents a simplification of the rule system.

Now let us compare this case with an example with which we are already familiar, namely that of the addition of the devoicing rule to the grammar of early Middle High German:

$$[+\text{obstruent}] \rightarrow [-\text{voiced}] / \_\_\_ \#$$

This rule, which changes +voiced into −voiced in the case of obstruents occurring word-finally, had the effect of creating from /veg/ 'way', /tag/ 'day' alternants like [vek] ~ [veg-], [tak] ~ [tag-]. If we look ahead to subsequent grammars of German we can see that the alternation between voiced and voiceless obstruent has in fact remained in many varieties of the language, for example in Standard German (cf. [veːk] ~ ['veːgəs], etc.), so that the underlying forms still have a voiced obstruent. No simpler grammar can be set up in order to account for the data, for it is only in a small number of lexical items, namely those which do not show alternation, that the addition of the devoicing rule subsequently caused a change in the underlying representations. Thus while 'way' is still represented as /veːg/ the adverb [vek] 'away', which is etymologically connected with the noun, is now represented as /vek/ since, having no alternant with voiced obstruent and being no longer semantically associated with the noun, it has become indistinguishable synchronically from words with underlying voiceless obstruent such as /tsvek/ 'purpose'. (The difference in vowel length between noun and adverb requires a further rule which we will here ignore; see King (1969a: 52f.) for a considerably oversimplified statement of the facts). In this case, then, a rule which was first added to the grammar some 800 years ago is still productive today and has resulted in practically no lexical restructuring.

Further examples of rule addition and its effect on the structure of subsequent grammars are given by Kiparsky (1971: 3ff.) and by King (1969a: 39ff.). Kiparsky's account contains an interpretation of Grimm's Law in generative terms which shows how the rule additions are traceable through a number of intermediate grammars until they eventually lead to new underlying representations. His interpretation closely parallels our drag-chain interpretation of the shift (see p. 83ff.), without however including Verner's Law. The first step, namely the aspiration of voiceless plosives except after obstruent, is a context-sensitive rule which leads to alternation. Thus in the past participles of verbs, the marker *-to-* remains the underlying form but in all environments except after obstruent it becomes *-*t^h*o-*. The second step turns all aspirated plosives, that is both the voiced and the voiceless series, into continuants irrespective of environment. Since the voiceless aspirates also became continuants, the alternation rule has to be reformulated so as to specify alternation between a plosive and a continuant (*-to-* ∼ *-θo-*). The third step devoices the old voiced plosives in all environments. At this point the effects of steps (2) and (3) are transferred to the underlying representations, which undergo restructuring. This requires, again, reformulation of the alternation which is now specified by what is technically a new rule. The effect of Grimm's Law is thus the restructuring of all the underlying representations to give them their typically Germanic form and a corresponding reformulation, to take account of restructured underlying representations, of the alternation produced by the first step of the shift. Since the reformulation of the alternation does not formally constitute a simplification of an existing rule, it must be considered a 'new' rule – which is rather unsatisfactory since it means that new rules can be introduced into grammars by means other than rule addition. From the point of view of *function*, however, the 'old' and 'new' formulations of the alternation are of course the same and traditional historical linguistics would in fact consider them to be 'the same rule'.

All the sound changes that we have discussed in the previous two chapters (Grimm's Law, the Great Vowel Shift, Umlaut, etc.) are examples of new rules being added to the grammars of English or German or to still earlier grammars before the two languages had separated. Some of these rules have remained in the grammars (such as the Great Vowel Shift in English, Umlaut in German) while others have resulted in restructuring (Grimm's Law, the High German Consonant Shift). In Modern English, for example, *to keep* is still represented by the underlying form /ke:p/ as in Middle English, whence the surface form [ki:p] is derived by means of a synchronic rule which is identical with the Great Vowel Shift rule and [kep-] in *kept* by a rule which shortens long vowels in specific environments and which, as we shall see, also reflects an innovatory sound change (see p. 124). Similarly, *divine* is still represented by the underlying form /di'vi:n/, whence [di'vain] is generated by the same vowel shift rule and the short [i] in *divinity* by the same vowel shortening rule. It is claimed that these more abstract analyses are *simpler* than analyses which postulate underlying forms closer to the surface forms (Chomsky and Halle 1968:187ff.).

We are now in a position to see a fundamental difference between the neogrammarian and taxonomic models on the one hand and the transformational model on the other. While in the former every sound change has an immediate effect upon the phonological form of lexical entries, the addition of a phonological rule in the transformational model does not. Change in underlying representations may follow rule addition as part of the process of restructuring but is not directly brought about by rule addition and need not in fact take place at all. The form of lexical entries thus changes more slowly in the transformational model. This is of course a result of the fact that generative phonology is non-autonomous.

We shall now examine more closely the question of just where in the phonological component a new rule may be added. If we consider that the phonological rules span the whole range from the most abstract output of the syntactic component right through to the level of phonetic representation, this is obviously an important question. As opposed to taxonomic phonology, which holds that sound change can only be conditioned by phonological environments, generative theory at first attempted to broaden the range of sound change by claiming that it could also be morphophonemically conditioned, that is to say that rule addition could operate directly on the underlying lexical representations (Halle 1962:68ff.). Let it however be noted from the outset that the present position is that new rules may be added at one point only, namely at the end of the phonological rules – strictly speaking, at the end of the rules which change absolute feature values and before the 'low-level'[1] rules which assign quantified values. This view, that phonological change in the form of rule addition merely modifies the output of the phonological component and constitutes a rather low-level change, is however a fairly recent development (Kiparsky 1972; King 1973). The importance of the earlier argument that phonological change had access to underlying representations was that, if these latter were involved in change they must in some sense have existed in the minds of speakers at the time of the change and must therefore have empirical validity. It was this possible empirical justification of the abstract notations of generative phonology which gave the discussion about rule insertion, that is the addition of a new rule 'high up' in the phonological component, its theoretical importance.

In order to illustrate the arguments for and against rule insertion as a possible phonological change, we will consider a long-standing problem in the historical phonology of Latin (Allen 1965:68f.; Kiparksy 1971a: 17ff.; King 1969a:43ff., 1973; Collinge 1975). Certain past participles (such as *lēctus*, *rēctus*, *āctus*, from the verbs *legō* 'to collect', *regō* 'to rule', *agō* 'to do') have long vowels while others (for instance *factus* and *iactus* from *faciō* 'to make', *iaciō* 'to throw') have short vowels. Lachmann advanced the hypothesis that the long vowel in the former group was due to the fact that the stems of these ended in a voiced obstruent whereas the stems of the members of the other group did not. He therefore postulated a rule which lengthened the vowel of roots ending in a voiced obstruent when this was followed by a suffix starting with a voiceless obstruent.

Lachmann's Law was restated in terms of generative phonology as:

$$V \rightarrow \left[+\text{long}\right] / \underline{\qquad} \begin{bmatrix}+\text{obstruent}\\ +\text{voiced}\end{bmatrix} \begin{bmatrix}+\text{obstruent}\\ -\text{voiced}\end{bmatrix} \qquad (1)$$

Clearly a further rule was required which would devoice a voiced obstruent when followed by a voiceless obstruent:

[1] The rather counter-intuitional convention is that the surface structure is situated 'below' the deep structure. If therefore a rule is described as 'low-level' this implies that it is close to the surface whereas a rule described as 'high up' in the rule system will be at a relatively deep level!

$$\begin{bmatrix}+\text{obstruent}\end{bmatrix} \rightarrow \begin{bmatrix}-\text{voiced}\end{bmatrix} \Big/ \underline{\quad\quad} \begin{bmatrix}+\text{obstruent}\\ -\text{voiced}\end{bmatrix} \qquad (2)$$

The correct Latin forms are in fact generated if these two rules are applied in the above order. Diachronically, however, the long vowel in these participles is known to be an innovation of Latin whereas the devoicing of a voiced obstruent before a voiceless obstruent has formed part of the successive grammars of the Italic branch ever since Proto-Indo-European. One would thus expect rule (1), the Latin innovation, to have been added to the grammar in real time after rule (2). In fact, however, rule (1) must be applied before rule (2) because it depends for its operation on information (namely whether the root-final obstruent is voiced or not) which rule (2) obliterates. Apparently the only way in which both the true historical rule order could be maintained and the correct Latin forms generated would then be for rule (1) to have entered the grammar of Latin later than rule (2) and yet to have been placed in the rule system so as to precede it in the ordering of the rules. This would mean that rule (1) would have to operate directly on the underlying representations /leg-tu-/, /reg-tu-/, etc. It was on the basis of such examples as this restatement of Lachmann's Law that the concept of rule insertion as a possible sound change was postulated.

If the device of rule insertion is to be rejected it must be demonstrated that analyses which make use of it are either unnecessary or inadequate. In the present instance it can be shown that Lachmann's interpretation of the facts simply does not stand up to examination. In the first place his 'law' has far too many exceptions (Allen 1965:69). Secondly, although it is formulated in phonetic terms it appears to be restricted to the past participles of verbs and their derivatives whereas other suffixes which are phonetically parallel do not have the same effect. And finally, in those verbs which do have the long vowel in the past participle it is not only this participle but also the perfect stem which has it (*lēg-ī*, *rēg-ī*, etc.) and in this latter the lengthening of the root vowel could not possibly have been conditioned by an obstruent sequence since there is no such sequence in the perfect. On the contrary in this class of verb it is the lengthening of the root vowel which serves as the unique marker of the perfect stem so that we have a minimal opposition between present *leg-* and perfect *lēg-*, present *reg-* and perfect *rēg-*, etc. (verbs like *fac-i-ō* 'to make', *iac-i-ō* 'to throw', etc. have a present stem marked by an *i*-suffix and thus belong to a different type). And, since the passive of the perfect tense is formed by means of the past participle, it is reasonable to assume that the long vowel of the active *lēg-ī* (the functionally unmarked form) has been carried over analogically into the corresponding passive *lēctus sum* (functionally the marked form). Although this analysis (Watkins 1970) also leaves some exceptions unaccounted for it does constitute a rather more adequate account of the facts and Lachmann's Law should therefore be abandoned (Strunk 1976).

The reanalysis of other putative cases of rule insertion (King 1973) has finally led to the conclusion that it cannot be justified as a possible type of sound change, so that rule addition at the end of the phonological component remains the only acceptable kind of rule addition.[1] As a consequence it is now held that the systematic phonemic level is not involved in, and underlying representations are not accessible to, rule addition. And, since generative phonology has rejected autonomous phonemes as a systematic level of representation, this leaves as the only possible domain of innovatory phonological change the level of systematic phonetic representation. This whole question of rule insertion forms in fact part of a much wider controversy which appears to be resulting in a move away from the excessively abstract phonological analyses originally postulated by the transformational model and which has brought the traditional and transformationalist positions considerably closer together (see Kiparsky 1968c, 1972; King 1973).

The discussion surrounding Lachmann's Law brings out another point to which we shall be returning (see p. 135f.). It would in fact appear that ordering anomalies of this kind are liable to arise whenever a certain *kind* of phonological rule is involved. In our case the rule involved is the assimilation rule (2) which made successive obstruents agree in voice. Now this is precisely the sort of 'low-level' rule which we have already mentioned as being likely to remain productive over long stretches of the history of a language. This was so for Latin where, in any new stem which ended in a voiced obstruent, this was devoiced before a productive suffix with initial voiceless obstruent. As we have seen (p. 94), a similar rule applies today in English, the only difference being that the assimilation operates in the opposite direction. Thus, in the past tense of any new verb or the plural of any new noun, the

[1] King's reanalyses have been challenged by Hogg (1976), although this does not affect the principle that rule insertion is inadmissible.

obstruent of the suffix automatically agrees in voicing with the final segment of the stem (['sputniks], ['haidʒækt]). In other words, although the voicing assimilation rule is in both cases old it is nevertheless still an actively productive rule and its permanence or near-permanence in the language singles it out from ordinary phonological innovations which, even if they result in morphological alternation for a period, are eventually absorbed into the underlying representations. Long-term low-level rules of this kind have been labelled 'permanent', or 'floating' (Chafe 1968; Bennett 1967), rules. The fact that they always come at the end of the phonological rules means that any output of earlier rules which fits their description will be processed by them. Apart from various kinds of assimilation, certain dissimilatory processes (such as the de-aspiration of the first item in a sequence of aspirated plosives, so-called 'Grassmann's Law' in Greek and Sanskrit, or Dahl's Law in Bantu) fall into this class. So do certain restrictions on sequences of segments of one and the same class (vowel, consonant; see below, p. 135f.). To treat widespread phonotactic constraints of this type as being on a par with the highly individual short-term rules which are the norm in innovatory sound change is bound to create problems. It was precisely the demand for descriptive economy with regard to rules of this kind that was to lead to the abandonment of autonomous phonemes in generative phonology.

To sum up, the ordinary innovatory sound changes of traditional historical linguistics are represented in the transformational model as the addition of new phonological rules situated at the end of the phonological component and operating on the systematic phonetic representations. The addition of such a rule may lead to subsequent restructuring if a simpler rule system is capable of producing an identical output. This restructuring process consists in the transfer of the effect of the added rule to the underlying representations in the lexicon. We have seen that the essential difference between the representation of sound change in traditional terms and in the transformational model lies in the rapidity with which lexical items are restructured as a result of sound change. Whereas in the former model lexical representations are restructured immediately, in the transformational model it can be a very much slower process. In both models, however, the primary effect of sound change is the restructuring of the phonological form of lexical entries. In the following section we shall be considering other aspects of restructuring.

1.2 *Systematic restructuring: formal conditions*

We have so far been dealing with differences in the structure of successive grammars which are the direct consequence of rule addition. We have seen that such restructuring of the grammar takes place after rule addition whenever the added rule can be absorbed into the underlying representations, thus simplifying the rule component without changing the output of the grammar. We shall now turn to types of restructuring which, unlike the above, appear to occur independently of rule addition. This new type operates by altering the rule system (including the range of application of rules) and, in contrast with the previous type, *does* result in a different output. Since it is claimed that this type of restructuring is motivated by *the internal structure of the rule system* we shall refer to it as *systematic restructuring*. Like restructuring following rule addition, it is claimed that systematic restructuring also results in a simpler grammar and may thus have the same motivation, namely the simplification or 'optimization' of the grammar by the language learner. In this latter case, however, the language learner goes beyond his model and creates actual differences in output. Since we found that rule addition corresponds to traditional sound change, it might be expected that systematic restructuring would in turn correlate with the traditional concept of analogical change. This is in fact to a considerable extent the case. It must however always be borne in mind that the two concepts depend upon very different governing principles. Thus while, broadly speaking, systematic restructuring claims to lead to a simpler *grammar*, analogical change claims to lead to more regular structures in the *output*. We shall also see that the two concepts do not necessarily cover the same phenomena for, while the changes dealt with overlap to a large extent, they do not always correspond exactly. The following discussion is based on Kiparsky's initial interpretation of systematic restructuring as grammar simplification and as constituting the transformational counter-part of analogical change (Kiparsky 1968a, 1971a: chapter 2) and on his later reappraisal of the principles underlying systematic restructuring (Kiparsky 1972). This substantial reorientation had become necessary because it was found that not all cases of systematic restructuring can in fact qualify as simplifications of the grammar so that such restructuring would in fact appear to be conditioned not so much by the structure of the grammar as by the structure of the output. Before discussing what conditions it, we will first consider the main types of systematic restructuring which have been proposed; these are rule simplification, rule reordering, and lexical entry simplification. We shall examine to what extent these (1) constitute simplifications of the grammar, and (2) correlate with types of traditional analogical change.

1.2.1 Rule simplification

If a phonological rule becomes simpler in the course of time, provided that this does not result in increased complication elsewhere it will contribute to the greater simplicity of the grammar. Simplification itself is defined by generative theory in terms of the notational conventions employed in phonological description, conventions which are claimed to make significant generalizations about phonological structure. Thus a rule is considered to have been simplified if the technical apparatus required to represent it has been reduced. Since in historical linguistics we compare the rules of *successive* grammars of a language, it must first be decided which rules in these successive grammars correspond (that is to say, are diachronically 'the same'). As the criterion for making this decision Kiparsky (1968a:172ff.) adopted the same convention which in generative theory determines that two adjacently ordered rules in a synchronic grammar must be collapsed into a single rule, namely that they are structurally similar. As a result of this, different types of rule simplification may be distinguished depending upon which part of a rule is simplified. The basic distinction is between whether the simplification affects the *structural analysis* part (which comprises the input X and the environment Z in the formula: $X \rightarrow Y/Z$) or the *structural change* part (Y in the same formula). According to Kiparsky's initial hypothesis, simplification of the structural analysis part would correspond to the traditional concept of analogical extension, simplification of the structural change part to that of analogical levelling.

Taking the former claim first, since the *structural analysis* part of a rule comprises both the input and the conditioning factor, it can easily be seen that the simplification of either would extend the domain of the rule, that is make it of wider application. If, for instance, we suppose that the umlaut rule fronting back vowels in German were to have applied only to the high back vowels [u] and [u:] it would have had the form:

$$\begin{bmatrix} \text{V} \\ +\text{high} \end{bmatrix} \rightarrow \begin{bmatrix} -\text{back} \end{bmatrix} / \underline{\quad\quad} \ldots$$

And if we compare this hypothetical umlaut rule with the umlaut rule of Modern German (which affects all back vowels and the input to which is therefore simply 'V'; see however below, p. 142) we can see that the more *restricted* alternation does in fact require a formally more complex rule whereas that embracing a natural class of sounds, namely all back vowels, requires a simpler rule. Since the umlaut rule is a morphophonemic rule in Modern German which requires grammatical information for its operation, the assumed simplification of the input would indeed correspond to the analogical extension of the alternation in question. Exactly the same considerations would apply in the case of the environment part of the rule.

Let us now examine one of Kiparsky's actual examples of the simplification of the structural analysis part of a rule. The synchronic grammar of Old English contained a rule which shortened any long vowel which occurred either before three or more consonants or in the third syllable before the end of a word provided in this latter case that the vowel in question was both stressed and followed by a sequence of two consonants. This rule, which produced a number of morphologically heterogeneous alternations (for example those ultimately resulting in Modern English *good* (< *gōd*) but *gospel* (<*godspell*), *blood* (<*blōd*) but *bless*) (<*bledsian*, via **blǭdsian* by umlaut and unrounding) would be written:

$$V \rightarrow \left[-\text{long}\right] / \underline{\quad\quad} CC\begin{Bmatrix} C \\ ..V..V \end{Bmatrix}$$

Now the grammar of Middle English had a formally very similar rule which differed from the Old English one only in the presence of one rather than two consonants immediately following the oblique:

$$V \rightarrow \left[-\text{long}\right] / \underline{\quad\quad} C\begin{Bmatrix} C \\ ..V..V \end{Bmatrix}$$

In other words, in Middle English one of the consonants was lost from the environment part of the rule, thereby considerably widening its scope. In contrast to the Old English rule the impact of which on the morphological structure was very limited, the Middle English rule had a decisive effect on the inflectional and derivational morphology of English, producing such alternations as *keep*~*kep*(*t*), *five*~*fif*(*teen*), *holy*~*holi*(*day*), *south*~*south*(*ern*), etc. However, in spite of the close *formal* similarity between the Old English and Middle English rules, traditional historical linguistics would hardly consider this to be a case of *analogical* extension. Firstly, the alternating forms created by the Old English rule would appear to be far too few in number for them to constitute a likely model for the extension of the rule, and secondly in terms of the roles they play in the morphological structure of the respective language states, the Old English and Middle English rules have nothing in common. The tradition would rather consider this to be a purely phonetically motivated extension or generalization of a sound change[1] and not an *analogical* extension.

If we turn now to the simplification of the *structural change* part of a rule, we have said that according to Kiparsky this corresponds to traditional analogical levelling. In its most extreme form this kind of simplification would comprise not merely the reduction but the deletion of the entire section following the arrow, which would of course result in the elimination of the alternation and thus correspond to *loss* of the entire rule. And, since the rule is a morphophonemic one, that is to say that it is *grammatically* relevant, simplification of the structural change part of it would indeed correlate with traditional analogical levelling. Thus the rule which devoices word-final voiced obstruents in Standard German has no counterpart in certain present-day varieties of Yiddish (King 1969a:46f., following Weinreich) and words such as *tog* 'day', *lid* 'song', have a voiced obstruent throughout their paradigms. However, unlike the noun /veg/ 'way' which belongs to this class, the etymologically related adverb [a'vek] 'away' *has* undergone devoicing. The devoicing rule must therefore have been present in earlier grammars of the Yiddish dialects in question and have been subsequently lost, for only in this way can one explain why the adverb has a voiceless obstruent whereas the noun from which it derives has the voiced one. At the time when the devoicing rule was lost from the grammar the adverb must already have become dissociated from the noun so that it did not participate in the generalization of the

[1] Since neighbouring dialects have often what may be considered more general, or less general, forms of one and the same rule it has been claimed that generalization is an essential feature in the transmission of rules across time and space. On the strength of this King (1969a: 92) has even gone so far as to surmise that the High German Consonant Shift must have spread from north to south, which is not supported by empirical evidence (see chapter 4 for opposite arguments, and Vennemann (1972a) for an alternative analysis). In any case, traditional historical linguistics would consider rule generalization to be part of innovatory *sound* change and not of *analogical* change.

underlying form. It can thus be seen that the discovery of rule loss depends upon the survival of such relic forms in the language. From the point of view of the grammar the loss of the rule of course represents a considerable simplification of the rule system.

While the traditional counterpart of rule loss is total analogical levelling, the mere simplification of the structural change part of a rule will correspond to partial levelling, that is to say to an increase in the formal similarity between alternants without their becoming identical (see Kiparsky (1968a) for possible examples). If we were to accept the Yiddish example as typical it would appear that transformational grammar, unlike traditional historical linguistics, is capable of predicting the *direction* of analogical levelling, since the loss of a rule will necessarily result in the generalization of the underlying form. We shall however see that this correlation between rule loss and the direction in which levelling takes place is, in spite of claims to the contrary, by no means a general principle.

In summary it may be stated that rule simplification does appear to correlate with *analogical* change unless the simplification is strictly motivated phonetically. In this latter case rule simplification would correspond to the generalization of a *sound* change.

1.2.2 Rule reordering

In traditional historical theory differences in the ordering of identical or near-identical rules in neighbouring dialects are ascribed to the wave-like spread of innovatory changes across geographical space having reached the dialects at different times and therefore at different points in their historical development (see chapter 4). In the transformational model differences in rule order between dialects may also however be interpreted as being the result of *rule reordering* in one of them, and it is this claim that we will now examine. For, unlike traditional historical linguistics, transformational grammar allows for the possibility of the rules of any language or dialect being reordered during the course of its historical development. This rule reordering is regarded as one of the types of systematic restructuring motivated by the resulting simplification of the grammar. If, however, the reordering of rules is to be claimed as a case of grammar simplification it must be shown that its direction is predictable.

Kiparsky attempted to establish the principles governing reordering

How to pay for your books from Heffers

Customers in the United Kingdom

Cheques: Cheques should be payable to W. Heffer & Sons Ltd. and sent to P.O. Box 33, Cambridge, England CB2 1TX.

Bank Giro: Payment may be made through any bank to Barclays Bank plc, Bene't Street, Cambridge CB2 3PZ, to our account number 30466581.

Post Office Giro: Payment may be made at your local post office crediting our giro account number 252 8053

Customers Overseas

In the Countries listed below you may pay to our bank accounts **in your own currency;** please quote your Heffer account number and the numbers of the invoices you are paying.

Australia A.N.Z. Banking Group Ltd, Pitt & Hunter Streets, Sydney, N.S.W. 2001.
Account No. 43-31130

Canada: Royal Bank of Canada, 20 King Street West, Toronto, Ont. M5H 1C4
Account No. 309.805.0.

Denmark: Copenhagen Handelsbank A/S, 2 Holmens Kanal, DK-1091 Copenhagen K.
Account No. 4001 286730

France: Barclays Bank S.A. 33 Rue du 4 Septembre, 75002 Paris.
Account No. 17501 020205 02 00 01 71

Germany: Deutsche Bank A.G., Rossmarkt 18.D-6000 Frankfurt (Main) 1.
Account No. 73/3436.

Holland: Amsterdam-Rotterdam Bank N.V., Leidseplein 25, 1005 EJ. Amsterdam.
Convertible Account No. 46.75.31.641.
or Postgiro (Nederland) Account No. 3903241.

Italy: Banca Commerciale Italiana, Piazza della Scala 6, 20121 Milan.
Estero Lire Account No. 970615/01/19.

Japan: Payments in Japanese Free Yen (not Domestic Yen) at the counter of an authorised foreign exchange bank for the credit of Fuji Bank Ltd., Otemachi I-Chome, Chiyodo-Ku, Tokyo.
Savings Account No. 501886.

Spain: Banco Central;, S.A., Division Internacional, Calle Serrano 38, Madrid 1.
Pesetas Convertibles Account No. 41003987.

Switzerland: Schweizerische Bankgesellschaft, 45 Bahnhofstrasse, Zurich.
Account No. 383.780.01.

USA: Please send your U.S. dollar check made payable to;
W. Heffer & Sons Ltd. to P.O. Box 33, Cambridge, England CB2 1TX

OR By international giro transfer, where available, quoting:
British Postal Giro account (CCP) No. 252 8053.

OR From any country send a bank draft, money order, UNESCO coupons or cheque in sterling or US dollars to us in Cambridge, quoting your Heffer account number.

Or Ask any bank in the country to make payment to our account number 30466581 at Barclays Bank plc, Bene't Street, Cambridge CB2 3PZ, through Barclays Bank International Ltd, Luton Branch, P.O. Box 22, 28 George Street, Luton, England LU1 2HW, and to quote your Heffer account number, **Payments must be made 'FREE OF ALL CHARGES TO BENEFICIARY'.**

Customer Copy

Invoice 226122

heffers:

W. Heffer & Sons Ltd. Booksellers
20 Trinity Street, Cambridge,
England CB2 3NG
Telephone: (0223) 358351
VAT Reg. No. 213 4152 13

J81274 ACCOUNT No.

ANDREW LINN ESQ

CUSTOMER

HEFFERS BOOKSELLERS
CAMBRIDGE

Department	Assistant
E1	LS.

Invoice Date & Tax Point		
16	2	91

	£	p
Customer's order number and/or date of order Cost of books including postage, packing and insurance		
Historical Linguistics	12	95
	12	95

VAT is not chargeable because books are zero-rated

Please keep this invoice to check against your monthly statement. Payment is due in the month following receipt of the books

For payment arrangements see overleaf.

H11

by extending the concept of *markedness* to cover rule order. He thus postulated that the normal unmarked functional relationship between adjacent rules the ordering of which is crucial, is such that the first rule creates forms which act as input to the second rule. It could then be reasonably expected that the functional relationship of rules which did not follow this principle might be 'optimized' by reordering. Two possibilities were envisaged. If, on the one hand, the first rule changes forms to which the second rule should apply in such a way as to make them unfit as input to it, this order (termed by Kiparsky *bleeding order*, because the first rule deprives or 'bleeds' the second of input) is reversed so as to minimize 'bleeding'. If on the other hand the first rule turns forms which could not have served as input to the second rule into forms which could, this would maximize the *feeding relationship* between the two rules. Both reordering principles would thus have in common that they shift rules into their 'natural' order so that each rule will be maximally utilized in the grammar by having as large an input as possible. The reordering of rules would thus always take place from the marked to the unmarked order. We will consider in detail only one type of reordering, namely that which minimizes bleeding.

The first example concerns a number of phonological rules specifying alternations involving the back vowel /o/ in neighbouring dialects of north-eastern Switzerland (Kiparsky 1968a: 178f., with references). In the dialects of both Schaffhausen and Kesswil old [o] had been lowered to [ɔ] in the environment of a dental, palatal, or *r*. As a result [o] and [ɔ] are essentially in complementary distribution (thus *hɔrn* 'horn', *bɔdə* 'floor', *pɔʃt* 'post' but *holts* 'wood', *xopf* 'head', *bogə* 'bow'). However, while in the Schaffhausen dialect the plural of *bogə* is *bögə* and that of *bɔdə* is *bödə*, in the dialect of Kesswil the corresponding plural forms are *bögə* and *bɔ̈də*. As will be seen from the following derivations, the forms within each dialect can be related synchronically by means of two identical rules, namely umlaut (which fronts the back vowel in specific environments of which 'plural' is one), and the lowering of /o/ to [ɔ] before dental, or *r*.[1] The only difference between the two dialects is the order of application of the two rules.

[1] In fact both rules are incomplete as they stand. The umlaut rule lacks specification of the conditioning factor which however, for the present purpose, may simply be said to include 'plural'; the lowering rule lacks the full feature specification, which is however irrelevant for the present purpose.

$$\text{Umlaut: } V \rightarrow \begin{bmatrix} -\text{back} \end{bmatrix} \Big/ \underline{\qquad} \ \ldots$$

$$\text{Lowering: } \begin{bmatrix} V \\ -\text{high} \\ +\text{back} \end{bmatrix} \rightarrow \begin{bmatrix} +\text{low} \end{bmatrix} \Big/ \underline{\qquad} \begin{bmatrix} +\text{consonantal} \\ +\text{coronal} \\ \ldots \end{bmatrix}$$

Underlying form:	/bogə/	/bogə+plural/	/bodə/	/bodə+plural/
Schaffhausen:				
(1) Umlaut:		bögə		bödə
(2) Lowering:			bɔdə	
Phonetic form:	[bogə]	[bögə]	[bɔdə]	[bödə]
Kesswil:				
(1) Lowering:			bɔdə	bɔdə
(2) Umlaut:		bögə		bɔ̈də
Phonetic form:	[bogə]	[bögə]	[bɔdə]	[bɔ̈də]

A historical interpretation of this synchronic situation must take into account one additional fact, namely that a small number of isolated umlauted forms in Kesswil have [ö] and not [ɔ̈] in spite of being followed by a dental or palatal (e.g. *plötsli* 'biscuit(s)', *fröʃʃ* 'frog'). If the rules had been added to the grammar of Kesswil in their present order, these forms would remain unexplained. It can however readily be seen that the phonological structure of these forms conforms to the rule order of Schaffhausen. Excluding borrowing, the only way of accounting for them is to assume that at an earlier period Kesswil had the two rules in the same order as Schaffhausen, with umlaut preceding lowering, and that it subsequently reversed their order. This would explain why the forms *fröʃʃ* and *plötsli*, having no back vowel alternants, were not affected by the restructuring. We may thus assume that the rules of the Schaffhausen dialect have retained the old rule order whereas those of Kesswil have undergone reordering.

At this point we should pause to consider just how such reordering could have come about. We may here recall a criticism of the traditional position by transformationalists, namely that it fails to admit the existence of perfectly regular phonological changes which simply happen to be conditioned by grammatical rather than purely phonological environments. Now it is true that the present example would appear to qualify as a grammatically conditioned phonological change. One could postulate the addition to the grammar of Kesswil of a rule turning those [ö]s which alternate with [ɔ] into [ɔ̈] so that as a result the alternation between [ɔ] and [ɔ̈] exactly parallels that between [o] and [ö], [u] and [ü].[1] In terms of this interpretation rule reordering would in fact also depend on rule addition, the only difference being that the new rule would in this case have a grammatical rather than a phonological environment and thus differ from the restructuring process following rule addition described above (section 1.1). There is however a difficulty associated with this interpretation. For, while the kind of innovatory rule addition discussed in the earlier section constitutes a spontaneous innovatory change quite independent of structural relationships within the language and is in this sense totally unmotivated, the present assumed kind of rule addition in a grammatical environment is not unmotivated structurally and is in fact foreseeable as a possible change given the particular structural relationships in the language in question. Traditional historical linguistics would say that this type of grammatically determined rule addition brings about more regular structures in the output, the transformational model would say that it creates a systematic simplification of the grammar. In other words, while it is perfectly true that rule reordering may be represented as the addition of a grammatically conditioned phonological rule to the grammar, it would appear simpler to motivate the restructuring process directly without going first through a stage of rule addition, for clearly this kind of rule addition would be constrained in an entirely different way from the rule addition which reflects innovatory sound change the constraints on which are purely phonetic. Furthermore, while innovatory changes can often be seen to have spread across contiguous areas of geographical space over a given period of time rule

[1] The developments in Kesswil, and parallel ones elsewhere in Switzerland, are interesting also from the point of view of traditional historical linguistics. According to Moulton (1968) we have here the creation of a new phoneme not as the result of ordinary phonemic split but by morphophonemic analogy: /o/ ~ /ö/ = /ɔ/ ~ /x/, where x = /ɔ̈/. However, the words which now have /ɔ̈/ would presumably have had an /ö/ before, so that the development would in fact be the result of a phonemic split but in a grammatical environment. Of course it may be said that from the point of view of the analogical change the creation of the new phoneme was incidental. One could perfectly well imagine an /ɔ̈/ already existing in the language but having a different incidence, so that the particular analogical change would simply have increased its incidence. We mention below a similar case of the creation of a new phoneme when, in certain German dialects, the synchronic umlaut of /a/ passed from /e/ to /æ/ (see p. 142). The parallel distinction in Standard German orthography between *ä* and *e* is, however, merely graphic.

reordering, being internally motivated, may occur quite independently in languages. On the basis of arguments such as these (see Kiparsky 1971a:29 and passim) it would appear simpler to postulate that rule reordering is independent of previous rule addition. This would in turn seem to imply that there is no need to postulate the addition of a grammatically conditioned phonological rule as a possible phonological change (see p. 113 above). It seems more reasonable therefore to opt for rule reordering unmotivated by prior rule addition as the simpler means of accounting for the facts.

To return to our example, a comparison of the derivations for the dialects of Schaffhausen and Kesswil reveals that in Kesswil, as a result of reordering, the umlaut rule no longer bleeds the lowering rule and the lowering rule has indeed increased its input. The effect of this reordering on the output of the grammar is that [ɔ] now behaves in parallel fashion to [o] and, like [o], alternates with its front vowel in a perfectly regular fashion. In traditional terms we would here have a case of analogical levelling, since the formation of the plural of nouns with [ɔ] is now just as regular as that of those with [o] (and the other back vowels). But, as Hooper in particular (1976: ch. 6) has shown there is no internal justification in Kesswil for postulating an underlying /o/ in words like [bɔdə] since the phonetic representation of these has exclusively [ɔ] and [ɔ̈]. This must surely mean that the addition of the lowering rule caused a restructuring in the underlying representations from /bodə/ to /bɔdə/. Kiparsky's analysis can thus be maintained only within the framework of a phonological theory which does not effectively constrain the 'distance' between the systematic phonemic and the systematic phonetic representations.

As a second example of reordering to minimize bleeding, we shall consider the interaction of voicing and raising in Canadian English (Halle 1962; Chambers 1973; Hudson 1979). The words *writer* and *rider* for instance are by some speakers both realized as [raydər] and by others are [rəydər] and [raydər] respectively. It is assumed that both types of realization, which we shall refer to as 'dialects' A and B, share two phonological rules: the voicing of /t/ to [d] in intervocalic position, and the raising of the vocalic onset of the diphthong /ay/ to give [əy] before voiceless consonant. As the following derivations show, in dialect A the voicing rule bleeds the raising rule whereas in B the raising rule would seem to have increased its input as a result of reordering:

	write	*writer*	*ride*	*rider*
Underlying form:	/rayt/	/rayt-ər/	/rayd/	/rayd-ər/
A: (1) Voicing		raydər		
(2) Raising:	rəyt			
Phonetic form:	[rəyt]	[raydər]	[rayd]	[raydər]
B: (1) Raising:	rəyt	rəytər		
(2) Voicing:		rəydər		
Phonetic form:	[rəyt]	[rəydər]	[rayd]	[raydər]

It will be seen that dialect B has levelled the vowel alternation between the verb *write* and its agent noun *writer*, this latter having the same raised vowel as the base form *write*. The attempt to interpret this analogical levelling, however, as the result of rule reordering faces exactly the same difficulties as were encountered in the example from Kesswil. Here also the loss of the alternation in dialect B would have to be reflected in the analysis as a restructuring of the underlying representation (to give /rəyt/) and again this has been omitted in favour of a more abstract analysis which appears to be guided rather by the attractive, though unsupported, claim that closely related dialects differ in their rule systems but not in their underlying representations.

The other type of rule reordering according to Kiparsky is that which reorders two adjacent rules in such a way that their feeding relationship is maximized. This type of reordering was claimed to correspond to traditional analogical extension. The analyses put forward in favour of this claim by Kiparsky (1968a) have not however gained wide acceptance and, even if one takes account of the fact that analogical extension is much rarer than analogical levelling, it must still cause concern that further examples in support of the claim have not been produced.

1.2.3 Reduction in rule input (lexical simplification)

The input to an alternation rule may be curtailed by certain lexical items to which the rule applied ceasing to be marked as being subject to it. Thus the verb *to help*, of which the past tense was formerly *holp*, no longer undergoes vowel alternation in Modern English and therefore is no longer marked for this particular rule. This simplifies the lexical entry and decreases the input to the rule without however deleting the rule itself, which is still required in the case of other verbs like *to get*. As we have seen in chapter 1, such quantitative changes do not affect the rule system as such but merely decrease the input to specific rules, the domains of which are registered in the lexicon.

1.3 *Systematic restructuring: output conditions*

The justification for subsuming the somewhat heterogeneous changes discussed in the previous section (1.2) under a single heading was the purely formal one that they were claimed to bring about a simplification in the rule system. The examples given also seemed to imply that such simplification, except in the case of phonetically motivated changes, represents within the framework of the transformational model the counterpart of analogical change within that of the traditional models. The following discussion will, however, show that neither of these assumptions is in fact tenable in spite of the fact that there exists a core of cases which permit both interpretations. We shall examine examples of restructuring in which the solutions proposed within the two models cannot be reconciled. These areas of conflict are of particular theoretical interest since they allow one to compare the empirical adequacy and explanatory power of the concept of simplification on the one hand and of analogy on the other. Since the publication of King's work in 1969, it has been amply shown that not all cases which the traditional models ascribe to analogical change and which would intuitively be regarded as examples of simplification do in fact qualify as grammar simplification in the transformational model. Simplification is thus, we shall see, not sufficiently comprehensive as a principle to account for this aspect of language change. We shall consider three areas of difficulty, illustrating each with an example. The changes that we will discuss have in common the quality that they appear to be motivated by the structure of the output of the grammar rather than by the structure of the grammar itself. In fact in all three cases the changes appear to have been conditioned by quite specific properties of *surface* structure.

1.3.1 Reordering which results in increased paradigmatic uniformity

In the first place there are instances of rule reordering which, while corresponding to traditional analogical levelling, do not comply with Kiparsky's ordering principles and thus do not qualify as simplifications of the grammar (Kiparsky 1971a, 1972; King 1973). Although some of these cases may themselves require reanalysis (see, for example, Hogg 1976), they do constitute a body of fact which cannot be accounted for in terms of grammar simplification.

According to King (1973:555), two rules: (1) the devoicing of fricatives in word-final position and (2) the vocalization of the voiced velar fricative /g/ after front vowel to the palatal glide [y], underwent reordering in the course of the history of Old English. Thus at an earlier stage of the language the word for 'day' had the following nominative and genitive forms in the singular.

	day	*day's*
Underlying form:	/dæg/	/dæges/
(1) Devoicing:	dæx	
(2) Vocalization:		dæyes
Phonetic form:	[dæx]	[dæyes]

Later on, however, after reordering, these were:

(1) Vocalization:	dæy	dæyes
(2) Devoicing		
Phonetic form:	[dæy]	[dæyes]

The devoicing rule applies vacuously here but is required elsewhere in the language. It can be seen that both before and after reordering the rules stood in a relationship of mutual bleeding, either the devoicing rule taking potential input away from the vocalization rule or vice versa, but at no point did both rules apply successively to any one underlying form. Their reordering cannot therefore be said to constitute a simplification of the grammar. But traditional historical linguistics would certainly consider this to be an example of analogical levelling, namely the generalization of the allomorph [dæy] throughout the singular (the plural had a back vowel, as in [dagas] 'days', and thus no vocalization). Other cases can be found which follow the same principle, namely the elimination of 'useless' morphological alternation from the paradigm. Thus, while reordering remains as a possible kind of systematic restructuring, it would appear to be motivated not by the structure of the grammar but by that of the output.

1.3.2 The form of lexical entries

As we have seen, instead of being eliminated an alternation rule may come to operate on a smaller body of underlying forms and this again will result in an increase in the number of regular surface structures. The analogical replacement of the nominative singular in *-ōs* by *-or* in Latin nouns of the type *honōs*, *honōris* is a case in point (see above, p. 92f. and Kiparsky 1972). The alternation was not lost altogether from the grammar of Latin since it is still required for masculine and feminine monosyllables such as *flōs*, *flōris* 'flower' and for neuters such as *genus*, *generis* 'kind'. In nouns like *honōs*, however, the alternation was lost and one would expect this fact to be reflected in a twofold simplification of the lexical entry, namely elimination of marking for the rule which governs the alternation of [s] and [r] and restructuring of the underlying form so as to match the surface forms, which now have [r] throughout the paradigm. (It will be noted that in this instance, unlike what happened in the case of /veg/ discussed above, the loss of the rule for this class of items resulted in the generalization of the derived alternant and not of the underlying form.) This solution is, however, excluded by transformational grammar because of the existence alongside nouns of the type *honor* of adjectives in *-tus* (*honestus* 'honest', *arbustus* 'wooded' alongside *arbor* 'tree', *angustus* 'tight' alongside *angor* 'constriction', etc.). Transformationalists claim that these adjectives, despite unpredictable differences in the vowel of the second syllable, are synchronically derived from their respective nouns and that this derivational process still requires an underlying form with /s/ since words like *dator* 'giver', which never had an alternant with [s], do not have corresponding adjectives. Thus, in spite of the fact that the *inflectional paradigm* of 'honour' has [r] throughout, it is still considered necessary to retain an underlying /s/ in order to accommodate patterns of *derivational morphology*. And clearly if *honor* were to be selected as the underlying form the derivation of *honestus* would be infinitely more complex. However, the retention of what is from the point of view of the inflectional morphology an unduly abstract underlying form means that the grammar is not in fact simplified and the actual regularization of the paradigm of *honor* is not reflected anywhere in the transformational description of Latin.

We see here an essential difference between transformational-generative and taxonomic analysis. In the taxonomic model morphophonemic rules are formulated in terms of the morphology of a language and relate to particular grammatical categories and lexical classes. They thus always operate in a specific morphological environment and are differentiated from the purely phonological rules which state phonotactic constraints irrespective of grammatical considerations (for example the fact that in English, as well as in many other languages, the segments of a consonant cluster must agree with regard to voicing, or that German cannot have voiced obstruents in word-final position). Transformational grammar on the other hand formulates alternations only at the phonological level and without regard to individual grammatical categories. Traditional historical linguistics can thus readily accommodate the loss of an alternation affecting only the inflectional morphology, the derivational morphology remaining unchanged.

1.3.3 Phonotactic constraints

So far we have discussed two cases in which phonological change has produced greater paradigmatic regularity in the output. We have seen, however, that these changes do not qualify as examples of simplification in terms of the formal definition of that concept. A parallel problem arises in the case of adjacent rules which are functionally alike in that they have an identical effect on the output. Unlike adjacent rules which are formally similar (p. 123) these may not, however, be collapsed. Thus Kisseberth (1970) reports that in the Amerindian language Yawelmani a number of formally dissimilar rules all 'conspire' to prevent the occurrence of sequences of three consonants in phonetic representation. One such rule breaks up a CCC sequence (or a CC sequence before word boundary) by inserting a vowel:

$$\text{Ø} \rightarrow \text{V} / \text{C}\_\_\text{C}\begin{Bmatrix}\text{C}\\ \#\end{Bmatrix}$$

while another deletes a vowel between two consonants if the second consonant is followed by a vowel:

$$\text{V} \rightarrow \text{Ø} / \text{VC}\_\_\text{CV}.$$

Kissebert claims that such rule conspiracies should, because of their functional unity, have formal status in the grammar.

In a similar way Shibatani (1973) has postulated that the systematic phonetic representation must have its own well-formedness conditions, and Kiparsky (1972) has stressed the essentially negative and substantive character of such constraints. Traditional phonology would handle regularities of this kind in the phonotactics, and we have repeatedly drawn attention to the generality and productivity of phonetically motivated alternations (cf. 'automatic alternations', p. 91ff. and 'floating rules', p. 120 above) by comparison with alternations whose domain must in all instances be stated in the lexicon.

1.3.4 The motivation of systematic restructuring

Looking back over the cases discussed in this section (1.3), since none of them qualifies as a simplification of the grammar, the only remaining factor common to all appears to be the resultant regularity in surface structure. Since, however, the cases which do qualify as grammar simplifications (section 1.2) also result in more regular surface structures, the overriding principle governing systematic restructuring would appear to be the increased regularity in the representation of functional relationships in surface structure, that is to say it is the structure of the output rather than that of the grammar itself which matters. These output conditions can however only be stated if a number of fundamental distinctions which generative phonology had dismissed as irrelevant are reintroduced. The most basic distinction is that between what the tradition would term grammatical conditions as opposed to phonological conditions, the former having to do with phonological form in relation to morphological function and the latter to do with phonological form in relation to phonetic factors. This necessarily demands a division of the phonological rules into those which serve morphological ends and those which serve phonetic ends (cf. Kiparsky 1972; Vennemann 1972b). When discussing rule simplification we in fact saw that it was only the simplification of grammatically motivated rules which corresponds to traditional analogical change and that the simplification of phonetically motivated rules corresponds rather to the generalization of a sound change. The output regularities produced by the two types are correspondingly different. The simplification of a grammatically motivated rule (e.g. umlaut, p. 123, 140f.) creates uniformity either within paradigms or between functionally parallel paradigms, whereas the simplification of a phonologically conditioned rule (e.g. vowel lengthening, p. 124) often creates or increases morphological complexity in quite accidental and unsystematic ways (as for example the case with vowel lengthening). Rule loss again corresponds to analogical levelling only if the rule is a morphophonemic one, and the equating of reordering types with types of analogical change is dependent upon the nature of their motivation.

It has further been shown (Kiparsky 1972) that within morphologically conditioned changes the traditional distinction made between inflectional and derivational processes must be maintained, since systematic restructuring may well be confined to the inflectional morphology and leave the derivational morphology unchanged, as we have seen was the case with Latin *honor*. Kiparsky has also drawn attention to the fact that systematic restructuring may include the conservation, in defiance of a given phonetically motivated rule, of a segment if it serves as marker of a specific grammatical category (for example the phonological rule governing the loss of intervocalic [s] in Greek which was suspended precisely in those cases where the [s] served as the exponent of 'aorist'). In other words morphological regularity may be achieved by *blocking* phonetically motivated rules in specific grammatical environments. All this is well in line with traditional views.

The existence of rule conspiracies serving to maintain specific patterns of phonetic structure may be explained in terms of transformational grammarians' failure to make another distinction made by traditional structural linguistics, namely that between morphophonemic rules and phonotactic rules. The former, it will be remembered, are grammatically motivated and reflect previous innovatory sound changes while the latter are purely phonetically motivated and reflect the so-called permanent rules (voicing assimilation in consonant clusters, etc.) which are likely to persist in successive grammars over long periods in time. These surface co-occurrence restrictions complicate the phonological rules of a generative analysis unless they are permitted to be built into the rule system in such a way that the application of a certain rule depends not merely on the structure of the input form but also on that of the anticipated output. In other words, certain phonological rules can be stated more simply if they are able to 'look forward' to the output and see whether it conforms to the constraint or not. For instance the environment part of the rule which deletes a vowel between two consonants in Kisseberth's example (p. 135) may simply be written as: /C__C if the rule includes the instruction 'unless a CCC cluster results'.

Sometimes rules must also, however, have to be able to 'look backward' to the derivational history of the forms which qualify as input to them. This is for instance necessary in the case of certain varieties of American English where a word-final alveolar plosive is dropped *except when it represents the sole marker of past tense*; thus, although the past of *to keep* is [kep], that of *to heap* is not **[hi:p] but [hi:pt] (Kiparsky 1972 following Labov).

Neither the type of regularity which requires 'looking forward' nor that which requires 'looking backward' can at present be formulated within the framework of generative phonology. This indicates that surface well-formedness must be formulated not only in relation to phonetic but also to morphological factors, and re-emphasizes the relevance of surface structure to language change. The basic principle governing systematic restructuring must clearly be sought in the transparency of surface structure with regard to the underlying functional relationships, the ideal being a simple direct correlation between the two – which tallies well with the traditional interpretation of analogical change. As Kiparsky has pointed out, this principle appears to be closely connected not only with the requirements of language acquisition but also with those of speech perception and production, all of which demand that underlying relationships be unambiguously expressed in surface structure. It would thus appear that the motivation of phonological changes depends rather on performance-related targets, such as the transparency of the surface structure generated by the grammar, than on purely formal considerations in terms of grammar simplification. In other words *performance* has assumed new significance in phonology, as it has in syntax (see below, p. 158).

The following example serves to illustrate the important role of surface structure in language change (Hale 1973:414ff.; cf. Kiparsky 1971b). In Maori, a Polynesian language, the passive forms of verbs retain a base-final consonant which was deleted by a 'pre-Polynesian' rule from the unsuffixed verb stem wherever it was word-final. Thus:

Verb	Passive	
awhi	awhitia	'to embrace'
hopu	hopukia	'to catch'
aru	arumia	'to follow'
tohu	tohuŋia	'to point out'
mau	mauria	'to carry'
wero	werohia	'to stab'
patu	patua	'to strike, kill'
kite	kitea	'to see, find'

The simplest synchronic analysis of the above forms would be that the rule which deleted the word-final consonants is retained in the synchronic grammar of Maori. The underlying form of 'to embrace' would thus be /awhit/, that of 'to catch' /hopuk/, etc. and the passive formative would be [ia] after consonant, [a] after vowel. This would be the most economical way of predicting the correct consonant of the passive forms. The surface form of the non-passive verb would then be obtained by applying the deletion rule, which is in turn motivated by a phonotactic constraint according to which only vowels are permitted word-finally.

In terms of simplicity of description this analysis is preferable to the alternative one which posits base forms identical with the surface verb stems and a variety of passive markers (*-tia*, *-kia*, etc.) the distribution of which would have to be stated in the lexicon. Interestingly, however, it is this latter less simple solution which appears to be the correct one. According to Hale new verbs in the language (derivations from nouns and verbs as well as loan-words) regularly take the passive marker *-tia*. This means that, of the various competing passive markers, only *-tia* is productive and that for native speakers the verb base is identical with the surface form of the verb. It also suggests that a reinterpretation of passive must have taken place in Maori and that the consonant deletion rule is no longer synchronically motivated. This reanalysis means that a phonotactic constraint which originally operated only in surface structure has been extended to the more abstract underlying forms. We shall find a parallel development in syntactic change (see below, p. 157f.).

In view of the more recent findings outlined in section 1.3, a revival of the concept of analogy within generative grammar may perhaps be predicted, especially if the mechanistic view of analogy as a rag-bag of exceptions to sound laws is replaced by the fuller interpretation which sees it as a creative principle in language. More than a century ago Hermann Paul pointed out that one does not do full justice to analogy if one accepts it only where it causes actual changes in usage (that is performance). We think that its rejuvenating effect on the representation of functional relationships in surface structure should be quite compatible with a generative approach (see, for example, Wagner 1969a for a formulation). After all, there is 'naturalness' not only in the phonetic aspect of phonological rules but also in their functional aspect, the ideal target being a simple transparent relationship between underlying function and surface representation. Thus, in spite of the superficial observation that all phonological rules delete, add or modify phonological segments, the 'naturalness' of rule addition relates exclusively to phonetic criteria whereas the 'naturalness' of systematic restructuring relates exclusively to morphological factors (cf. Vennemann 1972b for a similar division based on Schuchardt).

1.4 *Synchronic and diachronic grammars*

It remains for us to see how newly added phonological rules are progressively assimilated into the synchronic grammars of subsequent language states. We shall consider first *rule form*. We have already seen that there may be differences between the form in which a rule is first added to a grammar and its later synchronic reflex. Thus, while this latter may well depend on grammatical factors, it can none the less be shown that when first added all new rules are strictly phonetically conditioned – a fact which is easily verifiable for all the innovatory phonological rules discussed so far (chapters 1–3). Subsequently, however, a rule may become 'grammaticalized', its operation depending on non-phonetic factors. Thus the umlaut rule in Modern German now specifies grammatically determined alternation, whereas the devoicing rule may still be formulated in purely phonetic terms irrespective of grammatical structure.

The devoicing rule does of course figure in grammatical relationships (e.g. *Rad* [raːt] 'wheel' versus *Rades* ['raːdəs]; *er schlug* [ʃluːk] 'he hit' versus *wir schlugen* ['ʃluːgən] 'we hit'), but it can be formulated irrespective of such grammatical relationships ('only voiceless obstruents can occur word-finally'). All the morphophonemic rules follow from this overall phonotactic constraint, so that whenever an underlying voiced obstruent comes to stand in word-final position it is automatically devoiced.

The umlaut rule on the other hand is quite different. Although it too was added as a purely phonetically conditioned rule (dependent on the presence of an *i* vowel or corresponding glide in the following syllable), its operation in Modern German is no longer phonetically conditioned (cf. for example *gastlich* 'hospitable' which lacks umlaut despite the presence of an *i* vowel in the second syllable and *Kühe* 'cows' which has umlaut in spite of the absence of such a vowel). In fact the conditions under which umlauted vowels occur in Modern German are extremely complex. Firstly there are a number of inflectional and derivational suffixes which always produce umlaut, for example the *-e* of the past subjunctive (*er käme* 'he would come' versus *er kam* 'he came'), the *-er* plural marker (*Hölzer*, plural of *Holz* 'wood'), the *-e* suffix which derives abstract nouns from adjectives (*Güte* 'goodness' from *gut* 'good'), and as a rule the diminutive suffixes *-chen* and *-lein* (*Büchlein* from *Buch* 'book', *Blümchen* from *Blume* 'flower'). Secondly there exist a variety of inflectional and derivational suffixes which cause umlaut in the case of certain lexical bases but not of others, for example the suffixes of the second and third person singular present of strong verbs (*er schläft* 'he sleeps' from *schlafen*, but *er ruft* 'he calls' from *rufen*), the plural marker *-e* of masculine and feminine nouns (*Wölfe*, plural of *Wolf* 'wolf', but *Hunde*, plural of *Hund* 'dog'), the agent suffix *-er* (*Bäcker* 'baker' from *backen* 'to bake', but *Maler* 'painter' from *malen* 'to paint'), the suffix *-lich* which derives adjectives from nouns (*stündlich* 'hourly' from *Stunde* 'hour', but *amtlich* 'official' from *Amt* 'official post'), etc. One can thus say that in Modern German the umlaut rule has been 'grammaticalized' but the conditions of its operation are far from straightforward. For we have seen that one and the same (functionally defined) suffix may produce umlaut with regard to some lexical bases but not others, and this quite unpredictably. It is however equally true that one and the same lexical base may behave differently with regard to different suffixes, so that the occurrence of umlaut cannot be predicted on the basis of the lexical class either (cf. for example *Schlaf* 'sleep', *schlafen* 'to sleep', *Schläfer* 'sleeper', *schläfrig* 'sleepy', but *Glas* 'glass', *Glaser* 'glazier', *gläsern* 'of glass', *glasig* 'glassy', *verglasen* 'to glaze', etc.). And finally it must be noted that not all forms with a rounded front vowel have back vowel alternants, which raises the question of whether their underlying forms in the lexicon should in fact be represented as containing a back vowel (e.g. *grün* 'green', *hören* 'to hear').

The occurrence of umlaut is thus predictable neither for a particular lexical base nor for a particular grammatical category or derivational pattern. In view of the extreme complexity of any formulation of umlaut (see Wurzel 1970: 105–69) and its functional redundancy in the majority of contexts, one may in fact wonder whether it is a synchronic rule at all or whether it is just the non-functional debris of an earlier language state complicating almost every morphological process? These remarks on umlaut should suffice to show that the formulation of conditioning factors may be considerably more complicated in the case of synchronic rules than in that of diachronic rules.

We will now turn from the environmental part to the remainder of the umlaut rule. King and Kiparsky have repeatedly pointed out that in many German dialects (as well as in the orthographic representation but not the phonology of Standard German) the *synchronic* umlaut of /a/ is [ä] and not [e]. This means that in these dialects the umlaut rule has become simplified during the course of time. When it was first added it had the form:

$$\begin{bmatrix} \text{V} \\ \langle -\text{long} \rangle \end{bmatrix} \rightarrow \begin{bmatrix} -\text{back} \\ \langle -\text{low} \rangle \end{bmatrix} \Big/ \text{C}^1 \underline{\qquad} \begin{bmatrix} -\text{consonantal} \\ +\text{high} \\ -\text{back} \end{bmatrix}$$

(that is, back vowels are fronted and short [a] is simultaneously raised to [e] before one or more consonants followed by an *i*-vowel or *y*-glide). Its simplified synchronic form in the dialects in question is (ignoring environment): V → [-back]. As a result there is no longer a difference in vowel height between /a/ and its umlaut, and /a/ behaves exactly like the other back vowels:

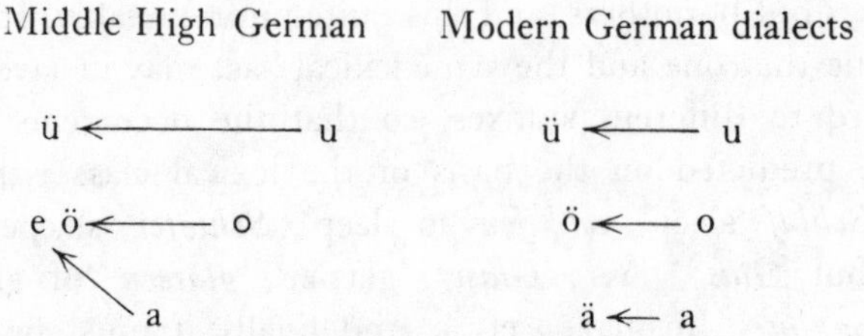

The situation in both contemporary Standard German and in the majority of dialects is, however, complicated by the fact that in addition to the back vowels the diphthong [aw] also takes part in the umlaut alternation, its umlauted form being [oẅ] (that is to say a diphthong consisting of a half-closed back vowel followed by a rounded front glide, the semivowel counterpart of [ü]). Now if the above form of the umlaut rule were retained and were extended to include glides, the umlaut form of [aw] would come out as [äẅ] which is phonetically incorrect; furthermore, and more disturbingly, the diphthong [ay], which does not in fact take part in umlaut alternation, would also be assigned an umlauted alternant [äy]. Without entering into a discussion of the various possible generative formulations of the synchronic umlaut rule (see Wurzel 1970: 105ff.) it is obvious that, if one takes the position that umlaut is to be retained as a phonetically 'natural' and unitary process, the only way to do so is to postulate more abstract underlying representations for [ay] and [aw]. Wurzel suggests /ey/ and /ow/, which correspond to surface forms of an earlier language state (see p. 31). These representations readily permit the application of the umlaut rule, which correctly leaves /ey/ untouched and turns /ow/ into [öẅ] and, by means of two further rules, the first elements of

/ey/ and /ow/ are then raised to [a] and the [ö] of [öẅ] is subjected to a dissimilation rule turning it into a back vowel to give [oẅ]. This solution is formally elegant, but the question is whether the difference between the underlying and surface representations of the diphthongs is synchronically justified. If one demands that an underlying representation must correspond to the phonetic form when there are no alternants (cf. Kiparsky 1968c), /ey/ and /ow/ must be considered too abstract since their surface forms both have a low vowel [a].

The historical reasons which lie behind the generativists' difficulties in describing the synchronic situation with regard to umlaut are clear enough. It will be recalled that umlaut was a phonological innovation of around A.D. 700 and that it was followed in the twelfth century by diphthongization which turned the long high vowels [i:], [u:] and [ü:] into the diphthongs [ey], [ow] and [öẅ], the two former being subsequently lowered to [ay] and [aw] and the latter dissimilated to [oẅ] in Standard German. However, while umlaut was a context-sensitive development leading to alternation, diphthongization and lowering (which operated irrespective of environment) were not and did not result in alternation. One would therefore have expected them to cause restructuring in underlying representations. We have, however, seen that if restructuring is postulated the formulation of a simple phonetically natural synchronic umlaut rule is not possible for Modern German. Generative grammarians therefore hold that the grammar of Modern German still retains at least raising[1] as a synchronic rule and this results in an exaggerated distance between systematic phonemic and systematic phonetic representations.

A traditional historical linguist would not, however, expect to find that a synchronic morphophonemic rule resulting from rule addition at some considerable distance in the past and preceding further phonological changes affecting only some segments would necessarily still have a phonetically natural synchronic reflex. In other words the phonetic naturalness a rule possessed when first added would only continue to apply to its subsequent synchronic reflexes if intervening changes did

[1] Analyses have been suggested which retain diphthongization also as a synchronic rule, taking /i:/ and /u:/ as the underlying representations of [ay] and [aw]. This means that surface [i:] and [u:] would have to have different underlying representations despite their consistent realization as [i:] and [u:], which would hardly seem defensible (see Wurzel 1970 for detail and references).

not affect the segments on which it operated. Generative grammarians however claim that not only diachronic but also synchronic phonological rules must be phonetically natural and this inescapably obliges them to postulate highly abstract underlying segments which, not surprisingly, approximate to the surface segments of the language state before the sound change occurred. In this way restructuring in underlying representations is decelerated in the generative model except in the case of so-called 'relic' forms (such as Yiddish /a'vek/ 'away', Kesswil *plötsli* 'biscuit') the underlying representations of which were restructured.

These relic forms in the lexicon are, however, of fundamental importance to the historical linguist since their structure often reflects newly added rules in their original form and order while the rule system itself has been subjected to restructuring. In the past tense forms *was* and *were* of the verb 'to be', for instance, the consonantal alternation in final position (the *r* is still pronounced regionally and is in any case everywhere present morphophonemically) is all that has survived of Verner's Law in the inflectional morphology of the verb. In traditional terms we would say that all verbs originally subjected to the alternation have either been lost or analogically levelled with the exception of the verb 'to be' which, as an item of basic vocabulary, has escaped remodelling and survives in Modern English as an irregularity. Similarly in Yiddish the adverb /a'vek/ 'away' (but *not* the noun /veg/ 'way') retains evidence of the devoicing rule, lost from the grammar of the modern language. The best clues regarding earlier rules are thus obtained from formally and semantically similar items in the lexicon which have become synchronically separated as a result of restructuring in the rule system. In other words, evidence regarding earlier grammatical rules is to be found in the lexical rather than in the rule part of the grammar and only in the total absence of restructuring will a subsequent synchronic rule system reflect the original form and order of the phonological rules that were added during the course of its history.

We have attempted to show that the generative interpretation of phonological change has undergone substantial revision since the publication of King's synthesis in 1969. In particular we have seen that innovatory sound change (rule addition) must be considered much more a surface phenomenon than was previously assumed to be the case and that systematic restructuring is best seen in terms of the output generated by the grammar rather than of the internal structure of the grammar itself. These developments have brought about a considerable *rapprochement* with traditional views and have led to renewed interest in performance as the area in which language change is likely to originate. For, although language change may be represented as change in competence (that is to say in the internal structure of the grammar), its motivation must probably be sought outside the grammar in performance. It would appear, in other words, that the grammar must undergo constant revision in order to keep it in line with innovations in performance. We shall return to this point in Part Two after discussing syntactic change as seen in terms of the transformational-generative model.

2 Syntactic change

Transformational grammarians reproach the structuralists with having failed to develop an adequate theory of syntactic description and with contenting themselves instead with mere statements of the distribution of morphologically defined forms and the direct semantic interpretation of these distribution patterns. Transformational grammar claims that, by concentrating on surface phenomena of this kind, taxonomic linguistics failed to recognize more fundamental regularities which underlie the level of surface structure. They maintain that these regularities can only be captured by means of a grammar which systematically distinguishes between the deep and surface structures of sentences and employs transformational rules to relate the two. Like traditional grammar, the transformational model thus seeks to relate such structures as active and passive sentences, statements and questions, infinitive and *that* complements, but in contrast to traditional grammar it attempts to do so explicitly. The similarity between, for instance, an active sentence and its passive counterpart would be reflected in their identical constituents in deep structure, the only difference between them being the presence or absence of a passive marker. Both would thus have identical deep subject and object, but in the passive sentence the underlying object is transformed into the surface subject and the underlying subject into the surface agent. As explained earlier, this conversion of deep structure into surface structure is effected by means of transformational rules, while the deep structure itself is generated by means of phrase structure rules.

Syntactic change is thus interpreted in the transformational-generative model as change in the syntactic rules which generate the sentences of a language and may be divided into change in the transformational rules and change in the phrase structure rules. Since, however, the role of the phrase structure rules is to define the basic constituents of sentences and their syntactic functions, they are inherently less language-specific than the transformational rules (the sentences of most languages can probably be described in terms of noun phrases functioning as subject, object, etc.), and it is therefore to be expected that deep structures will in general be more stable through time than surface structures. The great majority of the changes affecting a language are thus likely to occur in the transformational rules, which we shall see are subject to the same processes of addition, simplification and reordering that we have already seen in the case of the phonological rules. The transformational model does however postulate some changes in deep structure and this raises a problem. For, whereas changes in surface structure are more or less accessible to observation, changes in deep structure are not and therefore cannot be directly verified. The question thus arises as to the circumstances under which change in deep structure is to be postulated and this demands an evaluation procedure which can effectively decide between competing analyses. The criterion normally applied is that of descriptive economy, a change in deep structure being postulated whenever the surface structure of a given language state can be derived more simply from a new deep structure than from that postulated for the previous language state. In practice the simplicity criterion does however raise problems since ideally whole grammars and not merely subsets of rules should be compared; alternative synchronic analyses are therefore often possible and this will lead in turn to competing analyses of the historical developments. As a result, in spite of certain undoubted advantages of the transformational model, it does introduce a certain element of arbitrariness into the analysis of language change.

We shall begin our discussion of syntactic change by reexamining the traditional grammatical categories in terms of transformational grammar. In taxonomic grammar, which operates exclusively with surface structures, the grammatical categories are considered to belong to those parts of speech which carry their exponents. Transformational grammar establishes their status solely on the basis of syntactic evidence and any sector of the syntactic component – phrase structure rules, lexicon, transformational rules – may in fact introduce a grammatical

Schleicher, August (1866) Compendium der vergleichenden Grammatik der indogermanischen Sprachen. Weimar — 1877 tr. Herbert Bendall A Compendium of the Comparative Grammar of the Indo-European, Sanskrit, Greek + Latin languages

claimed that the diachronic stability of a
ch sector of the syntactic component it

ion of change in the system of grammatical
eview both their syntactic functions and
ce structure. We shall look first at those
ated with noun phrases, namely gender,
Of these the first three are traditionally
tegories whereas the latter is traditionally
of the verb (see chapter 2 and Lyons

tax of the noun phrase

lish number is represented in the surface
and the verb (*the boy sings*, *the boys sing*).
from traditional grammar, the verb merely
n phrase with regard to number, which is
selected by the verb. Number must therefore be considered as basically a category of the noun phrase and more precisely of the noun which forms the nucleus of the noun phrase. In transformational grammar number is selected in the deep structure and its representation in the surface structure depends on the language in question. In English, German and French for instance, singular is usually unmarked in the noun phrase while plural is marked. However, while English normally marks only the noun for plural (with the addition of *these* and *those*), German and French mark every constituent of a noun phrase for number (its exponent being to some extent fused with those of case and gender). Thus we have English *the little children* (singular *the little child*), German *die kleinen Kinder* (singular *das kleine Kind*), French *les petits enfants*, the *-s* of the adjective being audible in liaison, [le pti-z-ãfã] (singular *le petit enfant*). Thus, although number is introduced at the level of the phrase structure rules, its surface realization is the result of transformational rules the domains of which may differ, even between closely related languages and between successive language states. That number is selected in the phrase structure and is thus relevant to semantic interpretation has been held to account for its survival in a variety of languages which have lost either gender or case or both.

Case. In contrast to number, case (in the traditional sense of an inflectional category)[1] belongs to surface structure and marks the surface syntactic functions of nominal constituents (thus, for example, the subject of a passive sentence is assigned 'nominative' and not 'accusative' markers in spite of the fact that it is the object in the deep structure). In Modern English, with the exception of the genitive in *s* which is perhaps best interpreted as a variant of (*of* + noun phrase), overt case marking is restricted to personal pronouns (*he* : *him*, etc.) and to the interrogative/relative pronoun *who* : *whom*. Old English, however, also distinguished case in nouns, adjectives and demonstratives, a situation very close to that of Modern German. Old English also resembled German in that case was a means of marking the syntactic function of noun phrases, either on its own or in conjunction with a preposition.[2]

Gender. Whereas number is introduced by the phrase structure rules and case by the transformational rules, gender is a category of the noun which has to be specified in the lexicon. In languages like Latin, French and German, every noun is marked for gender and this used also to be the case in Old English. Again, depending upon the language, some or all of the constituents of a noun phrase agree with the head noun with regard to gender (German *ein guter Wein* (masculine) 'a good wine', *eine gute Bowle* (feminine) 'a good punch', *ein gutes Bier* (neuter) 'a good beer'). Modern English has lost grammatical gender from the grammar, the selection of the pronouns *he*, *she*, *it*, etc. being determined by the specification of the referent in terms of animateness and sex. In many inflected languages the declension class of a noun must be noted in the lexicon along with gender; thus, in order to generate the correct paradigm forms, Latin *fruct-* 'fruit' must be marked not only as masculine but also as fourth declension (*u*-stem).

Person. In the surface structure of earlier stages of the Indo-European languages, the only obligatory[3] marker of person was in the morphological form of the verb (Latin *venio* 'I come', *venit* 'he comes', etc.). In certain modern Indo-European languages such as German it is on the contrary marked in both the subject pronoun and the verb (*ich*

[1] And not in the sense of a deep structure universal (Fillmore 1968).

[2] Strictly speaking, the case governed by a preposition would also depend on semantic properties of the verb, as in German *in die Stadt* (accusative) *gehen* 'to go into the town' but *in der Stadt* (dative) *wohnen* 'to live in the town'. Modern English makes the distinction by means of the preposition.

[3] *Ego venio* etc. would be emphatic.

komme 'I come', *er kommt* 'he comes', etc.), while in Modern English for instance it is indicated only in the preceding noun phrase (*I came, he came*)[1]. Despite the various ways of representing it in the surface structure, however, person is considered in transformational grammar to be a category of nouns, specifying their referents in speech situations as either that of 'speaker', 'addressee', or 'topic'.

2.1.1 Changes in the transformational rule system

After this brief survey of the diverse ways in which the nominal categories are interpreted syntactically and represented in the surface structures of a number of Indo-European languages, we shall see how transformational grammar has dealt with specific historical developments in the syntax of the noun phrase in English (Traugott 1969, 1972a,b).

In the transformational grammar of Old English the structure of a noun phrase (NP) is stated in the phrase structure rules as consisting of an optional demonstrative or article (Dem) plus a noun (N):

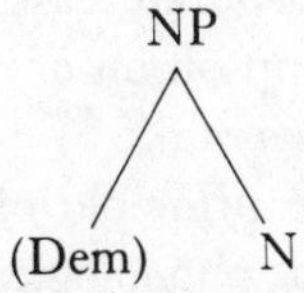

In a particular Old English sentence the combination of phrase structure rules, lexicon and transformational rules specify for the noun a feature matrix:

N [α number]
[β gender]
[γ case]

where α stands for the value singular or plural, β for masculine, feminine or neuter, and γ for nominative, accusative, etc.; the feature combination will be converted into segmental form by the phonological rules.

The feature values of the noun are assigned to the demonstrative or article by means of a transformational rule:

1 In the present tense the *-s* represents not only third person but also singular.

$$\text{Dem} \Longrightarrow \begin{bmatrix} \alpha \text{ number} \\ \beta \text{ gender} \\ \gamma \text{ case} \end{bmatrix} \Big/ \underline{\qquad} \begin{bmatrix} +\text{Noun} \\ \alpha \text{ number} \\ \beta \text{ gender} \\ \gamma \text{ case} \end{bmatrix}$$

The same feature values will also have to be transferred to any adjective, whether attributive (derived transformationally from a restrictive relative clause) or predicative (cf. the corresponding situation in Modern French: *les bonnes idées* 'the good ideas' and *les idées sont bonnes* 'the ideas are good').

It can be seen even from this very sketchy account that the grammar of the noun phrase has undergone considerable simplification between the Old English and Modern English stages. The transformational rule which assigned the number, gender and case features of the head noun to demonstratives and adjectives has been lost (with the exception of number agreement in the case of *this* and *that*), grammatical gender has totally disappeared from the grammar and, if we disregard possessive -*s* which, as mentioned above, has an alternative expression in the form of a prepositional phrase with *of*, the fairly elaborate case system of Old English has been reduced to a two-term opposition of nominative versus non-nominative operating only in the pronoun.

All these developments agree well with the principle of grammar simplification discussed above in relation to phonological change. At the same time they raise the question of how such substantial simplification in morphological structure could have taken place without resulting in structural ambiguity. Clearly the changes described above should not be considered in isolation from other developments, in particular the increasing importance of word order (that is to say the relative position of constituents within the sentence) as a marker of syntactic function. The loss of case distinctions in the grammar and the increasingly fixed position of nominal constituents in sentences has been recognized at least since Sapir (1921: chapter 7) as a long-term tendency ('drift') in English. This tendency is even being carried to the pronouns in which the attachment of a case marker is becoming increasingly dependent on position. Thus, once the interrogative pronoun has become separated from the preposition which governs it and is placed in sentence-initial position, it tends to lose its case-marker. Compare the following sentences:

(a) To whom could she speak?
(b) Whom could she speak to?
(c) Who could she speak to?

In the grammar of Modern English all three sentences are semantically identical, (a) and (b) belonging to more formal registers than (c). Historically of course we know that (a) is an older construction than (b) and (c). As Klima (1964) has shown, the developments from (a) to (c) may be represented in the transformational model as rule reordering within the system of transformational rules. The deep structure of all three sentences may be represented by the following tree (where S stands for sentence, NP for noun phrase, VP for verb phrase, PrepP for prepositional phrase, Aux for auxiliary[1], and Pron for pronoun; Q indicates that S is a question and WH marks the target of the question):

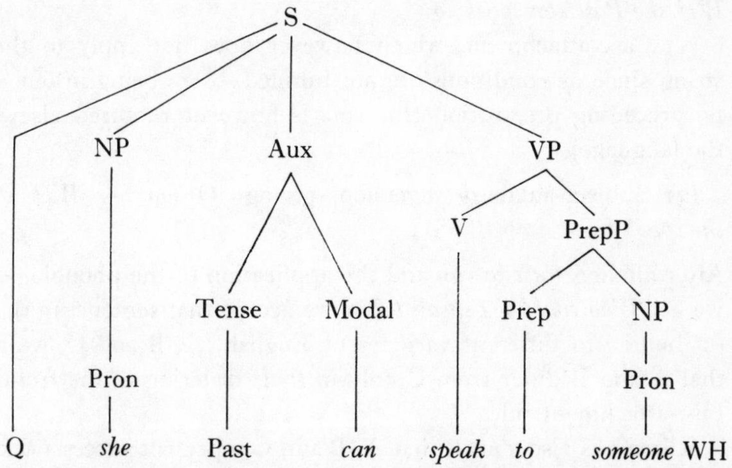

Leaving aside certain details, a series of three transformational rules are required in order to derive the surface structures (a), (b) and (c) from the above deep structure. (a) is derived by means of the following rules:

(1) A case-attachment rule, which assigns non-nominative to the pronoun which, together with the preposition, constitutes the prepositional phrase. This generates: *Q she Past can speak to someone WH CASE*.

[1] For justification of 'Aux' as a constituent distinct from VP see below, p. 161.

(2) A topicalization rule which fronts the constituent carrying WH; if we front the whole prepositional phrase this gives: *Q to someone WH CASE she Past can speak* (see below for alternative possibility).

(3) A question formation rule[1] which inverts subject and auxiliary to give: *Q to someone WH CASE Past can she speak.* After affixing *Past* to *can* and application of a series of phonological rules (including the conversion of Q into question intonation represented by *?*), this gives: *To whom could she speak?*

Sentence (b) is derived by the same set of rules, the only difference being that rule (2) is applied only to the pronoun and not to the whole prepositional phrase.

Sentence (c) is again generated by the same rules but applied in a different order:

(2) Fronting of the noun-phrase containing WH to give: *Q someone WH she Past can speak to*

(1) Case-attachment, which however does not apply to the above string since its conditions are not fulfilled, there being in our example no preceding preposition (the rule is however required elsewhere in the language).

(3) Subject-auxiliary inversion, giving: *Q someone WH Past can she speak to.*

After affixing *Past* to *can* and the application of the phonological rules we get *Who could she speak to?* If we accept that sentences (a), (b) and (c) belong to different varieties of English, A, B and C, we may say that A and B differ from C only in their ordering of the fronting and case-attachment rules.

Klima has also shown that A, B and C represent successive stages in the historical development of English, the most formal variety A being the oldest one. It may then be assumed that in C there has been a reordering of the rules. The effect of this reordering is that, whereas in A and B case-attachment is independent of position, in C fronting of the noun phrase prevents the subsequent application of the case-attachment rule so that case-attachment has in fact become dependent on position.

It will be seen that these developments do not follow Kiparsky's principles of rule reordering based on grammar simplification since

[1] Perhaps question formation should in fact precede the other two rules, but this is not immediately relevant here.

after reordering the fronting rule does in fact 'bleed' the case-attachment rule by robbing it of potential input. It would appear rather that the motivation of the reordering was in order to bring *who*-questions at the surface level into line with other WH-questions (*which*, *when*, etc.) and with declarative sentences, which typically have an initial constituent unmarked for case whereas forms which are marked for case occur typically after a verb or after a preposition (*I saw him*, *I gave it to him*).

It will be noted that, although *who* is in the position preceding the verb and is unmarked for case, it is nevertheless not the surface subject. This possibility is however restricted to questions. In declarative sentences the noun phrase preceding the verb is the subject unless it is marked as not being so. In the following example on the other hand the fronted pronoun has taken on the function of surface subject. The developments in English are best seen if contrasted with the situation in German where the corresponding changes did not take place. Compare the following active sentences comprising subject, direct object and indirect object in each of the languages with their corresponding passive sentences.

(1) Someone gave him a book
(2) A book was given (to) him by someone
(3) He was given a book by someone

(1′) Jemand gab ihm ein Buch
(2′) Ein Buch wurde ihm von jemand gegeben
(3′) Ihm wurde von jemand ein Buch gegeben

In both languages the direct object of the active sentence (1,1′) 'becomes' the subject of the passive sentence (2,2′). Sentences (3) and (3′) are not however parallel for, whereas English has what appears to be a second type of passivization in which the deep structure indirect object becomes the subject of the passive sentence (3), in German it does not become the surface subject, which remains 'the book'. In German the surface structures of (2′) and (3′) are thus identical except for topicalization, the indirect object merely being fronted without however becoming the subject. If we take it that German has preserved the older situation, we can see that in English fronting has, as in the case of *who* above, been accompanied by loss of the case-marking so that *Him was given a book* became *He was given a book*, with change in the syntactic status of the fronted constituent. Preverbal position was thus reinterpreted as marking subject function, as can be seen from the verbal concord (*he was given*, *they were given*).[1]

We have seen that of the nominal categories only person and number have survived in English, gender having completely disappeared and case remaining only in a very reduced form in the pronoun. The traditional explanation given for the loss of these categories is that it is the result of phonological change having affected the inflectional endings which carried the exponents of the categories (see Vennemann 1975 for discussion and references). This does not however account for the fact that, despite the 'decay' of the inflectional endings it is only gender and to some extent case which have been permitted to lapse, person and number having survived and even been attributed new overt markers in surface structure in the form of obligatory subject pronouns and the generalization of the *-s* suffix. Transformationalists would claim that person and number were retained because of their place in the syntactic hierarchy, both being selected in the phrase structure rules and thus contributing to semantic interpretation, whereas case is only introduced in the transformational rules and gender is brought in from the lexicon. In any case it may be said that there does appear to be syntactic motivation for changes of this kind independent of phonological change.

2.1.2 Changes in deep structure

We have seen that in English the syntactic functions previously performed by case endings have increasingly been taken over by word order. Thus in Modern English the basic syntactic functions are indicated by the relative position of constituents within the sentence, the rule being that the surface subject precedes the verb while the surface object follows it. Transformational grammar assumes for English this same ordering of syntactic functions in deep structure. The deep structure of English sentences thus has the general form subject plus predicate:

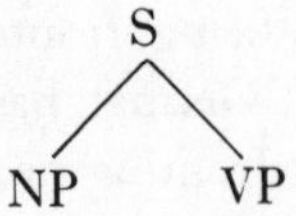

[1] Danish, which like English distinguishes only two case forms for pronouns, behaves in a parallel way: *Jeg fik opgivet forkert adresse* 'I was given a wrong address' (active: *De opgav mig forkert adresse*).

the deep structure subject being defined as the noun phrase which is immediately dominated by S and which precedes the verb phrase. The verb phrase itself consists, in the case of a transitive clause, of the verb and an object noun phrase:

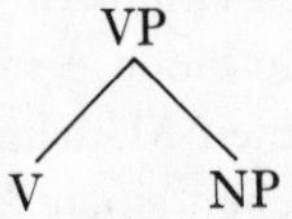

with the object noun phrase following the verb and dominated by VP. This gives the constituents NP–V–NP for a transitive clause, and this constituent order is retained in the surface structure of the great majority of sentences in English. Sentences not marked by a specific intonation pattern indicating emphasis or contrast which differ from this order in surface structure do so systematically and can readily be accounted for by rule. They are either yes/no questions such as *Has John come?* or, as we have seen, questions containing question-words, such as *Who(m) did John see? When did John come?* In the latter type the constituent which is queried (that is, to which WH is attached) may be fronted irrespective of its syntactic status, and in the former the finite verb form is regularly in initial position. The other major exception is formed by sentences with a specific set of initial adverbs, mostly of negative meaning, such as *hardly*, *scarcely*, etc. (No sooner had we arrived . . ., Never will I allow . . .). These examples should suffice to show that in Modern English the surface structure of sentences can be economically derived from the above deep structure.

The same deep structure would however be quite unsuitable for Old English in which, as in Modern German, *any one* but *only one* constituent may precede the verb, the subject being simply one of the possible occupants of this position. How then are the main constituents in Old English to be represented in the deep structure? One possible solution would be to assign deep case functions to nominal constituents, implying that order is not part of deep structure (Traugott 1972; Wagner 1969b). The alternative solution, which postulates constituent order as an essential property of deep structure, has a number of competing variants (Haiman 1974:37–49), which is hardly surprising in view of the complexity of the facts which have to be accounted for. The sequence of the constituents in the surface structure of Old English was fairly free, the only constraint being that the finite verb must occupy second place. Since this situation resembles very closely that of Modern German we shall use German examples in order to illustrate the point. The following four sentences differ from one another merely with regard to topicalization:

(1) Eine alte Frau gab einem kleinen Mädchen einen Apfel
(2) Einem kleinen Mädchen gab eine alte Frau einen Apfel
(3) Einen Apfel gab eine alte Frau einem kleinen Mädchen[1]
(4) Es gab eine alte Frau einem kleinen Mädchen einen Apfel

all meaning 'An old woman gave a little girl an apple'. The verb remains in second position also when an adverbial occupies the first position, and in this case the subject must immediately follow the verb:

(5) Vor Zeiten gab eine alte Frau einem kleinen Mädchen einen Apfel 'A long time ago . . .'

If constituent order is considered to be a feature of syntactic deep structure, transformational grammar must derive all these different surface representations from a single deep order. Using descriptive economy as the criterion permitting a choice between alternative solutions, Haiman (1974) argued that the deep structure order in Old English, as in German, must have been verb–subject–object (VSO), from which all the appropriate surface structures may then be derived by means of only two rules. These are: (1) a rule which topicalizes any single constituent by moving it to the left of the verb and (2) a rule which, when no such fronting takes place, inserts the semantically empty 'it' before the verb, producing the word order 'it'-verb-subject-object of sentence (4) in which all the information is 'new' (which is, that is to say, a discourse-initial sentence). These two rules must be applied in the above order if ungrammatical sentences (such as ***Eine alte Frau gab* es *einem kleinen Mädchen einen Apfel*) are to be avoided.

We may therefore assume that the underlying constituent order for Old English (as for Modern German) was VSO and we have already seen that for Modern English it is, on the same basis of descriptive economy, SVO.[2] How can this change in deep order be accounted for?

1 Acceptability is considerably increased if *Apfel* is modified (e.g. *Einen schönen roten runden Apfel* . . . 'a beautiful red round apple . . .') or if the initial noun phrase is definite (*Den Apfel* . . . 'the apple . . .').

2 *Pace* McCawley 1970.

It may be suspected that in this process the two above-mentioned rules played a decisive role since they had the effect of generating *surface* structures with the verb in second position and this is precisely the Modern English constituent order in the vast majority of sentences.

The surface structure of Modern English declarative sentences differs from that of its counterparts in Old English essentially in two respects. The first difference is that while in Old English any single constituent could be fronted so as to precede the verb, in Modern English the only one which can occur in this position is the surface subject. The second difference is that in Old English sentences in which the adverb had been fronted this was followed by the verb and then the subject whereas in Modern English the order is adverb–subject–verb. These differences may be assumed to have arisen as a result of increasing restrictions having been placed on the application of the fronting rule until finally only the subject could be fronted. An intermediate stage in this process is represented by Early Modern English in which when the adverb was fronted the verb still remained in second position (*Then spake John*). This pattern has survived into Modern English for a small set of adverbs like *never*, *scarcely*, etc. (*Hardly had he recovered* . . .) and in poetic style (*Sweetly sang the maiden* . . .). At this intermediate stage the situation is already most economically described by postulating that the subject preceded the verb in deep structure and that in adverb-initial sentences an inversion rule operated which inverted subject and verb. It can be seen that the only development needed between this situation and the situation in contemporary English for adverb-initial sentences is the loss of the inversion rule so that now both adverb and subject are situated before the verb (*Then John spoke*).

According to Haiman the fundamental change which took place between Old English and Modern English consisted in the gradual movement from the surface towards the deep structure of the constraint that the verb must occupy the second position in a sentence. Significantly however none of the rules which are claimed to have 'conspired' to bring about this development – fronting, 'it'-insertion, subject-verb inversion – applies explicitly to the verb. Taken as a group, however, they may be said to behave *as if* they had been expressly set up for the purpose of moving the verb into second position. The initial motivation for the whole restructuring process would thus appear to have been the emergence of this verb-second constraint in surface structure, and this is in turn it seems closely linked with the creation of obligatory subject pronouns. The final outcome is that every English sentence now has an overt constituent which precedes the verb and functions as subject, a situation best represented by a new deep structure SVO.

The rule conspiracy postulated by Haiman in order to account for the rise of SVO order in the deep structure of English sentences has, as will have been noted, close parallels in certain types of phonological development (see p. 135f.). While phonological targets can however be accounted for in terms of constraints on highly marked phonetic structures, no parallel motivation for syntactic targets has so far been proposed. It would seem likely, however, that any such motivation will have to be sought in factors relevant to the perception and production of speech, that is to say in the requirements of performance, and that the shifting of the target into the deeper levels of structure is a secondary development (cf. the progression of CV structure in Maori from the surface into the deeper levels of structure described above, p. 138f.).

The dependence of syntactic structure on factors relating to speech perception and production may be seen for instance from an examination of relative clauses in English. It is a well-known fact that in English relative pronouns may be deleted under certain circumstances but not others (*The pie I ate was old* is perfectly possible but ***I ate the pie was old* is not). Bever and Langendoen (1972) have argued that such deletion is directly controlled by a 'perceptual strategy' through which utterances are interpreted, the deletion of a relative pronoun being blocked if the resulting sentence would turn out structurally opaque and thus be an impediment to communication. The rule is that a sequence of sentence-initial noun phrase followed by finite verb (NP–V) is interpreted, unless specifically marked otherwise, as the subject and verb of a main clause while a finite verb followed by a noun phrase (V–NP) is, if not marked otherwise, interpreted as the verb and object of a main clause. The relative pronoun can accordingly not be deleted in a relative clause which begins with the shared noun phrase followed by the finite verb and which modifies a noun phrase preceding its verb or which is an object to its verb. For example: *The man* [*the man wants to see the boss*] *is waiting downstairs* ⇒ ***The man wants to see the boss is waiting downstairs*; *The secretary discouraged the man* [*the man wanted to see the boss*] ⇒ ***The secretary discouraged the man wanted to see the boss.*

2.2 *Changes in the syntax of the verb phrase*

Of the grammatical categories associated with the verb, we shall consider only those which are immediately relevant to our discussion of historical changes involving the verb phrase, that is to say tense, aspect and mood.

Tense and aspect. In a transformational grammar tense and aspect are, like number, introduced in the phrase structure rules and are variously represented in surface structure. In the surface structure of English, tense ('present' and 'past') is marked in the main verb when there is no auxiliary (which includes modal) verb, otherwise it is attached to the first auxiliary. The aspects of English ('continuous' and 'perfect') are represented in the surface structure by *be* plus verb plus *-ing* and *have* plus verb plus *-ed* respectively. In the classical Indo-European languages the markers of the categories of tense and aspect are located in the morphology of the verb, the so-called 'tenses' of Latin, Greek and Sanskrit reflecting partly oppositions of tense and partly of aspect.

Mood. The classical Indo-European languages have in their surface structures a number of verbal paradigms representing different values within the category of mood. Thus Latin opposes 'indicative', 'subjunctive' and 'imperative'; Greek has in addition to these three an 'optative'; Sanskrit also distinguishes an 'injunctive', which is the unmarked form of the verb with regard not only to mood but also to tense. In all these languages the choice of mood is partly 'free' (that is, independently selected in the phrase structure rules) and partly syntactically determined (for instance by certain conjunctions or 'verbs of thinking' etc. when it is introduced transformationally). In certain modern Indo-European languages like English and German the inflectionally marked subjunctive is becoming increasingly rare, often being replaced by the indicative or by a periphrastic construction (e.g. English *I wish* (*that*) *I was rich* for *I wish* (*that*) *I were rich*; German *er sagte, er kommt* (indicative) or *er sagte, er würde kommen* (periphrastic) for *er sagte, er komme/käme* (subjunctive) 'he said that he would come').

Perhaps the most important development with regard to the verb phrase in English has been the gradual growth of the 'auxiliary' constituent. We shall briefy consider two developments which were contributory to this growth, namely the creation of the class of modal verbs and the rise of *do*-support. According to an analysis proposed by Lightfoot (1974), the syntax of verbs such as *will*, *can*, *may*, etc. has substantially changed between Old English and Modern English. In Old English the ancestors of the modern modal verbs had all the formal properties of full verbs. Syntactically they could take either an object noun phrase (e.g. *hwæt* in *Hwæt cunnon þas þine geferan?* 'What can these your companions (do)?') or a sentential complement (*Hwæt þær foregange . . . we ne cunnon* 'What there went before . . . we can not (i.e. we know not)'). In Modern English on the other hand modals constitute a special subclass of the verb and, as Lightfoot has convincingly shown, are to be allocated to the 'auxiliary' constituent, always co-occurring with a main verb in the same sentence. Thus, with a good deal of over-simplification, the situation at the two stages may be represented as follows:

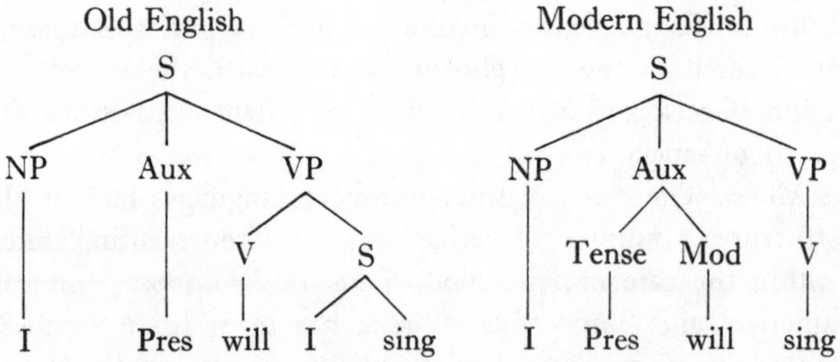

The quite substantial restructuring in the grammar of English appears to have come about as the result of a number of changes. Firstly severe restrictions were placed on the type of construction in which these verbs could participate. Thus, from Early Modern English onwards, they could no longer take an object noun phrase and the subject of the complement sentence became identical with that of the matrix sentence containing the modal verb. Secondly the infinitive marker *to* failed to spread to the complements of these verbs (*I want to go* but not ***I can to go*). Thirdly, because of the loss of a number of verbs from it, the class became co-extensive with the so-called preterito-presents (that is to say verbs whose present tense is formally a past tense) and thus did not show subject–verb concord in the present tense. Finally their past tense forms, perhaps aided by their irregular formation, retained a strong modal dimension which makes them unlike the past of ordinary verbs. For instance *might* and *could* are not simply *may* and *can* plus Past. All these accumulated peculiarities would appear to have facilitated reanalysis so that, instead of the modal verbs being treated as full verbs exceptional in a whole series of points, it became simpler to separate them off completely from the main verbs and to consider them part of the auxiliary constituent. For after all they share with the auxiliary verbs proper *have* and *be* the property that they rather than the main verb undergo inversion with the subject in interrogative sentences and thus do not require *do*-support; similarly the negation marker is placed directly after them, again without *do*-support. They thus attracted into the auxiliary constituent not only the marker of tense but also the indicators of negated and interrogative sentences and, because of their semantic properties, became increasingly used in order to mark modal differences.

The other development that we will briefly consider is the rise of *do*-support (Hausmann 1974; Traugott 1972a, b). Only one of the uses of *do* as a 'dummy' verb in Modern English is in fact inherited from Old English, namely when, in a sequence of two identical verb phrases the second is deleted except for its tense marker which is attached to the dummy verb *do*. Thus *John took a train to London and Mary took a train to London* is reduced to *John took a train to London and Mary did too* in which, of the second instance of the verb phrase, only the tense marker remains. In Old English this was the only way in which *do* was used as a dummy verb, whereas in Modern English *do* must also be inserted as the bearer of tense in interrogative and negated sentences if an auxiliary verb is not present. As a result of this it is only in positive declarative sentences without an auxiliary verb that the tense marker is now attached to the main verb.

In the transformational grammar of Modern English *do* is automatically inserted by a transformational rule whenever, prior to the tense attachment transformation, the tense element is not contiguous with a verb, whether main or auxiliary, in the string. The order of the verbal constituents is determined in the deep structure as Auxiliary (consisting of tense marker and, optionally, modal verb) and Verb, although this order may be subsequently modified by transformational rules operating prior to the tense attachment rule. Thus in a positive declarative sentence such as *John drinks cider* the sequence tense marker–verb is not affected by any transformation intervening before tense attachment, and the tense attachment rule ('affix hopping') simply moves the tense marker from the left to the right of the verb; the phonological rules subsequently convert *drink* + Present into *drinks:*

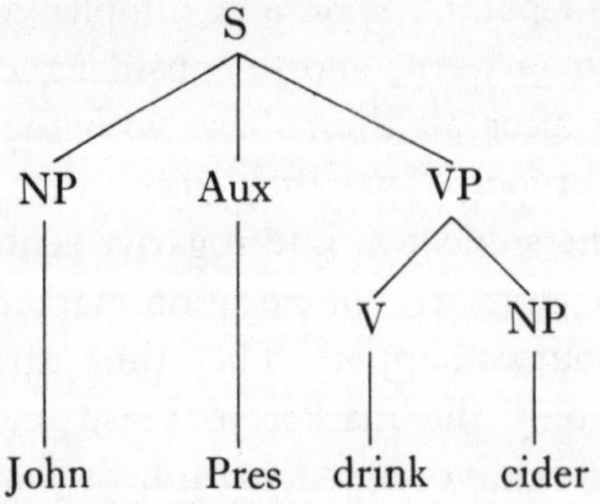

In the derivation of an interrogative sentence on the other hand the subject intervenes between the tense marker and the verb, thereby triggering off *do*-insertion. The deep structure, somewhat oversimplified, of *What do you drink?* is:

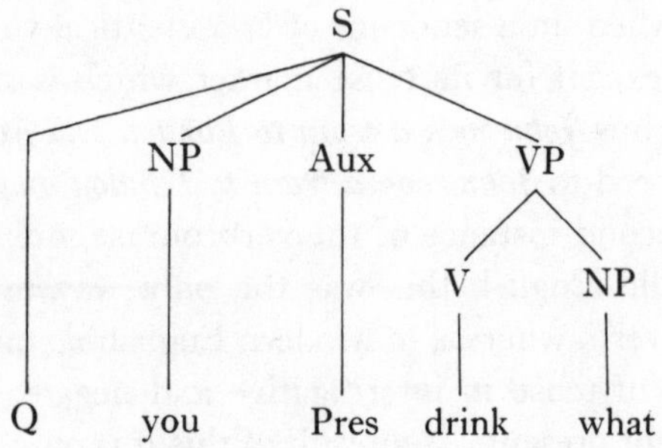

After undergoing question formation (inversion), this produces *Pres you drink what?* The tense marker being separated from the verb, *do*-insertion is required before tense attachment giving *Do you drink what?* and, after fronting of the question word, *What do you drink?*

In Old English on the other hand, *do*-insertion does not take place in questions (*Hwæt drincst þū?*, as in Modern German *Was trinkst du?*). If we postulate the same underlying structure as for Modern English,[1] we must in order to generate the correct surface structure assume that in Old English tense attachment preceded question formation. Thus, again somewhat oversimplified, the deep structure would be: *Þū Pres drinc hwæt?* which, after tense attachment, gives *Þū drincst hwæt?* and, after inversion and fronting of the question-word, *Hwæt drincst þū?*

The difference between the form of questions in Old English and Modern English thus resides in the ordering of the tense attachment and inversion rules and in the obligatory presence of *do*-support in

[1] Ignoring the more appropriate deep order VSO suggested by Haiman.

Modern English. We said above that in Old English *do*-insertion only occurred in the case of identical verb phrase deletion, that is to say when there was no verb present to carry the tense marker of the deleted verb phrase. At a subsequent stage tense could however be attached optionally to *do* rather than to the verb, apparently without denoting emphasis (*She did call after hym ryght pyteously*, Caxton). Finally in Modern English *do*-insertion came to be determined solely by the non-contiguity of tense marker and verb. Thus, although there were also differences in the conditions of the *do*-insertion transformation, one of the principal mechanisms which brought about the difference in structure between Old and Modern English was once again rule reordering.

We have seen that in conjoined sentences identical verb phrases may be deleted in English, leaving only the tense marker of the second verb phrase attached to the dummy verb *do*. In fact any shared constituent is deletable in the second of a pair of conjoined sentences, the only condition apparently being that the constituent in question must have word status. Thus the deep structure of *John ate cheese and Mary sausage* would be:

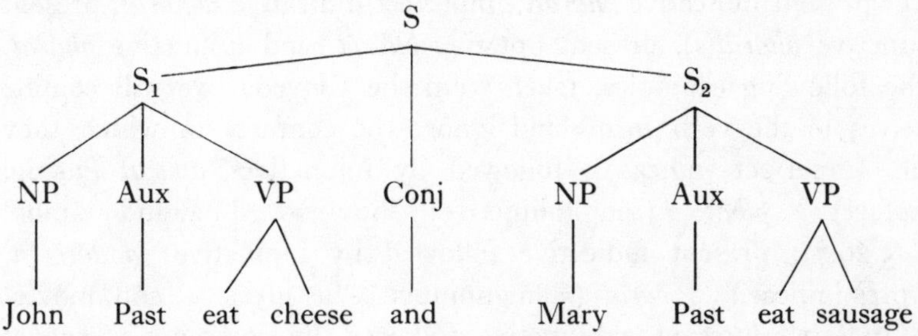

The shared deep structure constituents are deleted transformationally in the second sentence by a conjunction reduction rule. This rule is not, however, applicable to what Chomsky (1965:170f.) calls syntactic features, that is to say categories which are not represented by independent units in surface structure.[1] For example, in Modern German and English: *Hans stieg aus und Grete stieg ein* is reducible to *Hans stieg aus und Grete ein*[2] 'Hans got out and Grete in', but *Hans zerlegte und Grete belegte* cannot be reduced to ***Hans zer- und Grete belegte* 'Hans carved and Grete spread'; in the same way *John was dancing and Mary*

[1] And are thus incapable of carrying stress?

[2] In dependent clauses the deletability is more doubtful: *Weil Hans aus- und Grete einstieg, Als Hans aus- und Grete eingestiegen war* (?).

was singing may be reduced to *John was dancing and Mary singing*, but not to ***John was dancing and Mary sing*, nor can *John danced and sang* be reduced to ***John danced and sing*.

As the last example shows, tense is thus among the categories that have to be expressed twice in conjoined English sentences. Kiparsky (1968b) has shown on the other hand that a large number of anomalies concerning tense sequence in early Greek and Sanskrit can be resolved if one postulates that in the earliest stages of the Indo-European languages there existed a conjunction reduction rule which, in conjoined sentences with identical tense values in deep structure, deleted the surface exponent of tense in the second sentence. The same rule would have applied in the case of mood but in a more limited way. As a result of this rule tense, and to some extent mood, would only have needed to be expressed once in a complex sentence of this type. The earliest situation would have been that found in Vedic Sanskrit, where in these circumstances the second verb appears in the 'injunctive', the formally and semantically unmarked form of the verb. For instance the verb *bhar-* 'to carry' has the following forms in the third person singular active: present indicative *bhárati*, imperfect indicative *ábharat*, present subjunctive *bhárāt*(*i*), present optative *bhárēt*, and injunctive *bhárat*. In the following examples, taken from the Rigveda, we will confine ourselves to the verb forms and ignore the contexts in which they occur. Imperfect indicative followed by injunctive: *apacat* (3.sing. imperfect) . . . *pibat* (3.sing.injunctive) 'he cooked . . . and drank' (RV 5.29.7); present indicative followed by injunctive: *dadāti* (3. sing.pres.indicat.) . . . *carat* (3.sing.injunct.) 'he gives . . . and moves' (RV 10.80.1); present subjunctive followed by injunctive: *śr̥ṇavas* (2.sing.pres.subj.) . . . *dhāt* (3.sing.injunct.) 'you may hear . . . and he may give' (RV 6.40.4).

The so-called unaugmented past tense forms of Homeric Greek may be interpreted in a parallel way as resulting from conjunction reduction, for example in the sequence *élipen* (3.sing.aorist) . . . . *leĩpe* (3.sing.unaugmented imperfect) of the following quotation: *Atreùs dè thnēískōn élipen polúarni Thuéstēi, autàr ho aũte Thuést' Agamémnoni leĩpe phorẽnai* 'Atreus dying left [the sceptre] to Thyestes of the rich flocks, and Thyestes in turn left it to Agamemnon to carry' (Il. 2: 106f.). Kiparsky has shown that the postulation of such a conjunction reduction rule goes a long way towards explaining the apparently arbitrary distribution of augmented and unaugmented forms in Homer.

At a later stage, represented by Classical Greek, Old Norse and Old Irish, there is no longer a morphologically distinct form of the verb unmarked for tense and it is the present tense forms which take over this function. Examples from Classical Greek are: imperfect followed by present: *Háma dè tē̃i hēmérāi tē̃i pólei prosékeito* (3.sing.imperf.) *kaì haireĩ* (3.sing.pres.) 'at daybreak he attacked the city and took it' (Thuc. 7:29); aorist followed by present: *élabon* (3.pl.aorist) *dè kaì tò phroúrion kaì toùs phúlakas ekbállousin* (3.pl.pres.) 'they captured the fort and drove out the garrison' (Thuc. 8:84).

It seems likely that it was from the use of the present tense in this way that the so-called historical present of certain modern Indo-European languages developed. Thus, in a third stage, represented for instance by English and German, a present tense with past tense function is now used as a stylistic device. It is, however, no longer confined to conjoined sentences nor is it introduced transformationally but it is independently selected in deep structure.

Kiparsky considers that there are two possible ways in which the syntactic differences which exist between the oldest stages of the Indo-European languages and present-day languages like Modern English may be interpreted, namely that it must be either the form of the conjunction reduction rule which has changed or the syntactic status of tense and mood which has changed. It is the second of these analyses that he considers to be the correct one, postulating constituent status for both tense and mood in the earliest stages. In corroboration of this choice he adduces two syntactic arguments both of which are in fact confined to tense. Firstly, he points out that tense could have predicative function at the earlier stages and the tense component could thus be asserted, queried or negated; for example *épeithen* (1.sing.imperf.) *autoùs kaì hoùs épeisa* (1.sing.aorist) 'I [attempted to] persuade them and those whom I did persuade . . .' (Xen., Cyr. 5:5,22). In English this apparently is only possible in the case of independent elements, not of suffixes; for example *He* (*has*) *refused and continues to refuse/still refuses*, but not ***He refused and refuses*. Secondly, an adverbial referring to the past could in the earliest stages be followed by the present tense and this may represent a still earlier syntactic rule; for example *aieì gàr tò páros* (adverb) *ge theoì phaìnontai* (present) *enargeis* 'always in the past the gods appeared in visible form' (Od. 7:201). This would suggest that in the earliest stages of the Indo-European languages two successive indicators of 'past' could not occur within the same sentence, just as in English two successive general adverbs referring to the past cannot co-occur (**Formerly earlier ...). On the basis of this, one might feel, somewhat tenuous evidence which is, furthermore, confined only to tense, Kiparsky concludes that the syntactic status of tense and mood must have undergone modification in the later stages of the Indo-European languages, the conjunction reduction rule remaining unchanged.

We have seen the close connection which exists between the surface representation of constituents and their eligibility for reduction in conjoined sentences in Modern English and German. It would therefore seem reasonable to ask whether the postulated different syntactic status of tense and mood in the earlier stages of the Indo-European languages were not reflected in a corresponding difference in representation in surface structure. If, for instance, it could be shown that in Proto-Indo-European and in the earliest stages of the descendant languages the markers of tense and mood had word status, this would suggest that the postulated change in the syntactic status of the categories must have been the result of the change of their surface markers from free to bound forms. There does in fact appear to be some corroborative evidence for such a change in the morphological form at least of the markers of the past and present (although not the future) tenses, for both the Proto-Indo-European augment **é* which characterized past tense forms and the **i* which characterized the 'primary' endings of the present tense have long been believed by historical linguists to have been independent words. The same cannot however be said for the markers of future, subjunctive and optative which, although separable morphemic elements in surface structure, did not have the status of independent words.

The most disturbing aspect of Kiparsky's analysis is that it presupposes for Proto-Indo-European and the earlier stages of its descendant languages a degree of discrepancy between the syntactic status (constituent v. feature) of the categories of tense and mood and the morphological status (free v. bound) of their markers. Thus the conjunction reduction rule in Proto-Indo-European would appear to operate for tense and mood irrespective of the morphological status of their markers whereas in modern Indo-European languages it is governed by the morphological status of these, which is a purely surface matter. Admittedly Proto-Indo-European was considerably more agglutinative than the modern Indo-European languages in question, at least in so far as the markers of tense and mood are concerned, but even in typically agglutinative languages like Turkish, conjunction reduction is constrained in the same way (that is to say, it is dependent on the markers having word status) as in English and German. Kiparsky is at pains to stress that his arguments in favour of the change in syntactic status of the categories, rather than a change in the rule, are entirely syntactic ones and do not require corroboration from surface structure. But why then should surface structure be so much more relevant to the operation of the rule today? And clearly in the majority of cases, which concern sequences of underlying past tenses, there is corroboration from surface structure also at the earlier stages.

Perhaps, more than any other transformational analysis of syntactic change, Kiparsky's paper highlights both the methodological advantages of the model and some of its weaknesses. The essential advantage of his analysis over a taxonomic one is that it interposes a set of syntactic rules between morphological forms and their semantic interpretation which make it possible for him to explain the syntactic distribution of certain surface forms which had hitherto frustrated traditional analysis. Transformational analysis may, however, lead to the setting up of what appear to be excessively abstract deep structures. Especially when we consider the close link which exists in the modern languages between the deletability of a form and its representation in surface structure, it seems reasonable to expect that a similar situation would have applied in the earlier language stages, conjunction reduction being confined to past and present tense.

2.3 *Changes in the syntactic properties of lexical items*

Syntactic information which is specific to individual lexical items is given in the lexicon (which, together with the phrase structure rules, forms the syntactic base). Thus, for instance, the fact that a specific verb may take a sentence as either its subject or object (that is, take a sentential complement) forms part of that verb's entry as does the type of complement construction taken (*I hoped that he would come* and not ***I hoped him to come*, *I wanted him to come* and not ***I wanted that he would come*).

In Latin complements may have the form of accusative with infinitive, *ut* with subjunctive, or *quod* with indicative (rare in Classical but common in Vulgar Latin). Which of these constructions applies depends on the verb in question so that verbs of saying and thinking, for instance, take the accusative with infinitive construction:

Dico Marcum esse consulem 'I say that Marcus is consul'
Dico me esse consulem 'I say that I am consul'

Verbs of wishing and wanting on the other hand may either take accusative with infinitive or *ut* with subjunctive, the two constructions being in free variation (although the latter is rarer):

Volo Marcum esse consulem *Volo ut Marcus sit consul*	'I want Marcus to be consul'
Volo me esse consulem *Volo ut sim consul*	'I want to be consul'

When the noun phrase is identical in both matrix and embedded sentence, it may be deleted in the embedded sentence in the case of a verb of wishing, but not of a verb of saying:

Volo me esse consulem *Volo esse consul*	'I want to be consul'
Dico me esse consulem ***Dico esse consul*	'I say I am consul'

('accusative' being deleted along with the noun phrase).

Turning to the diachronic aspect, a comparison of complementation in Latin and Spanish led Robin Lakoff (1968) to the conclusion that the only changes that had occurred were in the lexical redundancy rules which specify the complement construction for any given verb class, but that the classes themselves and the syntactic form of complements had remained unchanged. Interestingly however, while in Latin the choice of complement construction was entirely determined by the class membership of the verb, in Spanish it depends in addition on the presence of an identical noun phrase in matrix and complement sentence. Thus, for example, verbs of wishing and wanting must take either an infinitive or *que* with subjunctive, the choice no longer being optional as it was in Latin:

Quiero que Juan vaya a Madrid 'I want Juan to go to Madrid'
***Quiero que vaya a Madrid* 'I want to go to Madrid'
Quiero ir a Madrid 'I want to go to Madrid'
***Quiero (a) Juan ir a Madrid* 'I want Juan to go to Madrid'

Verbs of saying and thinking on the other hand can take *que* with indicative in all instances and, if the noun phrase is identical in embedded sentence and matrix, they may also as an alternative take the infinitive construction but in this case the noun phrase of the embedded sentence must be deleted:

Yo digo que Juan ha venido 'I say that Juan has come'
Yo digo que yo he venido
Yo digo haber venido } 'I say that I have come'
** *Yo digo yo haber venido*
** *Yo digo (a) Juan haber venido* 'I say that Juan has come'

It will be seen that all that appears to have happened between Latin and Spanish is some redistribution of complement constructions in relation to (semantically defined) verb classes. With the exception of the lexical replacement of the introductory conjunction (*que* in place of Latin *ut*), the constructions themselves have not changed nor have the constraints governing the deletion of identical noun phrases. These merely apply to different verb classes in Latin and Spanish.

We have in this section examined a number of analyses of syntactic change in which successive grammars were described as differing by the presence or absence and by the form and order of particular syntactic rules. These rules were subdivided into phrase structure rules (governing the deep structure of sentences), transformational rules (relating these to the surface structure), and lexical redundancy rules (specifying which syntactic rules apply to individual lexical items), and we have seen examples of change in all three of these sectors. Although we have found that operating with syntactic rules rather than with surface forms and their distribution has certain definite advantages in describing syntactic change, it has also become apparent that the introduction of a division into deep and surface structures raises a number of problems, not only because the allocation of particular phenomena to one or other sector is to some extent arbitrary, but also because there is no way in which specific changes claimed to have taken place in deep structure can be directly verified from an examination of successive surface structures. As at the phonological level, however, the model does reveal the extent to which underlying structures and transformational rules set up in order to describe particular language states in purely synchronic terms depend upon the surface structures of previous language states and the changes which these have undergone during the course of the period separating them in time.

PART TWO

Language contact

We have seen that the changes undergone by 'the same language' over a given period of time can be extracted from a comparison of its successive states, the states chosen for this purpose being in practice separated from one another by gaps of at least several hundred years. The past states of the language subjected to comparative analysis may be either attested in written documents or the products of reconstruction based on the comparison of related languages or dialects. We have also seen that the diachronic concepts of 'the same language' and of 'related languages' are capable of formal definition. In the same way, the 'change' undergone by a language may be defined as the sum total of the unidirectional rules which must be set up in order to account for the differences between its successive states, or between a reconstructed ancestor and each of its descendants. We have, however, so far said nothing about the actual *mechanism* of language change, and in order to deal with this aspect we must now turn from the examination of *grammars* to the behaviour of individual *speakers*. We have chosen this order deliberately, for unless we are first familiar with the formal properties of diachronic rules we will be in no position to recognize and interpret the phenomena of change as it actually takes place, that is to say as it is reflected in the behaviour of the individual members of a speech community. What remains for us to do now, therefore, is to see how the rules of language change relate to the sociolinguistic present.

The first thing that we shall find is that the change mechanism cannot be comprehended if we continue to maintain the fiction that language is uniform throughout a speech community. In fact we shall see that the sociolinguistic present is characterized by the co-existence of different varieties of the same language and even of totally different languages in close geographical and cultural proximity, and we shall consider the influence on language change of such contact situations. In chapter 4 we will examine contact between language varieties whose differences can be related to geographical space, in chapter 5 language varieties in relation to social space, and in chapter 6 contact between totally different languages. The fundamental point at issue in all these situations is the fact that a speaker's competence may, dependent upon purely environmental circumstances, comprise more than a single language variety or even a single language. If therefore we assume that each speaker's linguistic activities extend over a certain range which may be defined in social and geographical terms, we may in turn use this range to define his communicative competence as the amount of linguistic heterogeneity which is part of his experience and lies within his powers of perception and interpretation, though not necessarily of active manipulation. In other words, we will be dealing with various degrees of *bilingualism* and with the effects it has on language change, defining bilingualism as the co-existence within a single speaker's competence of more than a single grammar.

4

The neogrammarian postulates and dialect geography

1 The domain of a sound change

We shall start our examination of the sociolinguistic aspects of language change by considering just how a sound change taking place in the time dimension is reflected in geographical and political space. This requires that we return to the neogrammarian manifesto and the definition given in it of sound change. A sound change, it was claimed, always affects an entire speech community in a uniform manner. The only exception to this is when the dialect is undergoing a split, in which case the change will affect only a part of the community and leave the remaining part unaffected. Here too, however, each of the two new speech communities which result from the split will behave as a whole and react in a uniform manner. This being so, the domain of a sound change in space should be open to empirical investigation; all that is required is that we observe where the individual forms affected by it actually occur and, on plotting these on a map, we should expect to find a time–space correlation which could be represented as follows:

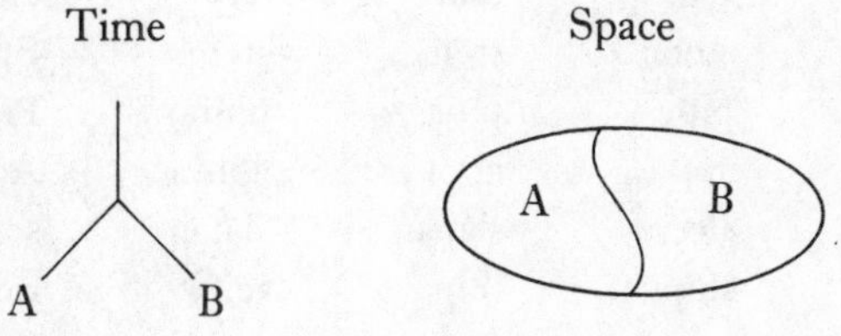

On our dialect map the fact that, for example, dialect B has undergone an innovatory change which is not shared by dialect A will be reflected in a geographical line (or *isogloss*) separating the area of dialect A from that of dialect B.

The year in which the neogrammarian regularity postulate first appeared in print is generally taken as 1876, and in that same year the hypothesis was actually put to the test in the field by a young scholar who was working on the consonants of West Germanic. Georg Wenker set out to establish the precise geographical boundary between High and Low German, a most prominent dialectal division which is the result of a number of changes, the most important of these being the so-called Second or High German Consonant Shift. Participation in this shift, the date of which is usually taken as somewhere around A.D. 500, was the the central feature which was to separate off the High German dialects in the south from the Low German dialects in the north, which were unaffected by the change. The consonantism of Low German thus still agrees basically with that of Dutch and English, whereas that of High German has undergone innovatory change. The following table shows the essential sound correspondences between High German (represented here by Old High German and Standard German) and Low German (represented by Old Low German). Facts not immediately relevant to the discussion have been ignored; see King 1969a: 190ff.; Vennemann 1972a; see also p. 21 above; z = [ts], ph = [pf], ȝȝ = [s], (h)h, ch = [x]).

West Germanic	Modern English	Old Low German	Old High German	Standard German
*t	two	twē	zwei	zwei
	heart	herta	herza	Herz
	eat	etan	eȝȝan	essen
	water	watar	waȝȝar	Wasser
	that	that	daȝ	das
	stone	stēn	stein	Stein
*p	pipe	pīpa	phīfa	Pfeife
	apple	appul	aphul	Apfel
	sleep	slāpan	slāfan	schlafen
	ship	scip	scif	Schiff
	'play'	spil	spil	Spiel
*k	break	brekan	brehhan	brechen
	I	ik	ih	ich
	shine	skīnan	skīnan	scheinen

The phonemic correspondences may be summarized as follows:

Low German (unshifted)	High German (shifted)		
	After Germanic fricative (i.e. */s/, */f/, */h/)	Initially; after consonant other than Germanic fricative; in gemination	Medially between vowels; finally
/t/	/t/	/ts/	/s/
/p/	/p/	/pf/	/f/
/k/	/k/	[k], [kx], [x] dialectally	/x/

Wenker's aim was to establish the precise location of the boundary separating High from Low German by carrying out an investigation along the critical border area to see whether the dialect spoken in each locality had undergone the shift or not. Since it was not a practical proposition to attempt to write a comprehensive grammar of each local dialect within the area under investigation, Wenker devised a language sample containing all the features that he knew to be, or suspected to be, relevant to the inquiry. He thus compressed into 40 (later 42) reasonably natural sentences as many words containing the crucial sounds as possible, each sound appearing in all relevant environments. This language sample, when translated into a local dialect, could thus form the basis of both a descriptive and a historical grammar with particular regard to the phonology. Typical examples of Wenker's sentences, in which the diagnostic words are readily recognizable, are: 'The good old man fell with his horse into the cold water', 'He always eats eggs without salt and pepper'. These sentences, spelt in Standard German orthography, were sent to every school in the boundary area separating High from Low German (initially only in the Düsseldorf district but later in a wider area comprising some 1,500 localities; at a still later date the survey was extended to cover the entire German-speaking area, thus taking into account a total of nearly 50,000 localities).[1] The schoolteachers to whom the questionnaire was sent were asked to translate the sentences into the local dialect, using the normal German alphabet for

[1] *Sprachatlas der Rheinprovinz nördlich der Mosel, sowie des Kreises Siegen*, unpublished manuscript 1878; *Sprachatlas von Nord- und Mitteldeutschland*: first instalment of six maps combining thirty features published in 1881, the remainder unpublished; *Deutscher Sprachatlas*, directed by F. Wrede (1926ff.).

this purpose, and to return the result to Wenker who then plotted the variant forms of each lexical item on a map.

The project did not yield the results expected. Instead of the different isoglosses which represented the items in the sample forming a single line neatly dividing Germany into north and south, they were often found to be separated from one another by quite substantial distances. True, the isogloss which resulted from each individual word did divide an unbroken southern area having the shifted form from an equally unbroken northern area having the unshifted form but, taken together, the isoglosses for all the words did not combine to make a single bundle. At first sight they in fact appeared to confirm the oft repeated claim that 'every word has its own history'. However, when the maps of all the isoglosses were compared, a more orderly pattern did eventually emerge (map after Frings 1957: 86).

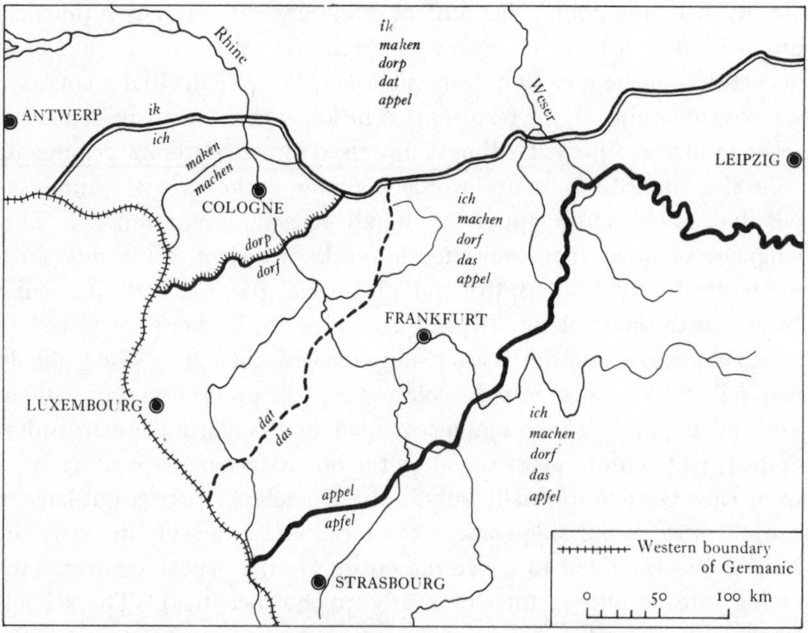

Map 1

It in fact became clear that there *is* a level at which the step-like scatter (see Map 1) of the lines is systematic, namely when account is taken *both* of the position of the sound in the word and of its point of articulation. Thus affrication in word initial position reaches further north in the case of /t/ (coinciding with the *maken/machen* line on our map), lies further to the south for /p/ (coinciding roughly with the *appel/apfel* line) and is so far south for /k/ that it in fact lies right outside the area covered by our map. In intervocalic position on the other hand the shift from plosive to fricative for all three points of articulation (dental, labial and velar) reaches the *maken/machen* line. We thus see that in the case of the allophones which underwent affrication we have a step-by-step progression depending on the point of articulation whereas in the case of the allophones which became fricatives there is a much more uniform picture. Whatever the precise phonetic reasons which lay behind the shift may have been, it can be seen that the distribution in geographical space of the resultant isoglosses clearly conforms to a regular pattern and it is only *within* the zones thus defined that we find certain lexical items 'ahead' of others in the shift.

Taking the few words which furnished the isoglosses in our map as broadly representative of the phonology of their dialects, we obtain the following series of stages connecting Low German in the north and High German in the south:

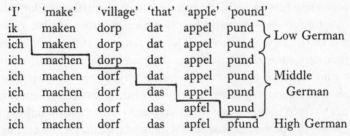

'I'	'make'	'village'	'that'	'apple'	'pound'	
ik	maken	dorp	dat	appel	pund	Low German
ich	maken	dorp	dat	appel	pund	
ich	machen	dorp	dat	appel	pund	Middle German
ich	machen	dorf	dat	appel	pund	
ich	machen	dorf	das	appel	pund	
ich	machen	dorf	das	apfel	pund	
ich	machen	dorf	das	apfel	pfund	High German

Of course if we wished to conduct a thorough examination of the distribution of shifted and non-shifted forms in a particular dialect, we would have to go beyond the information contained in Wenker's language sample and turn to the individual dialect grammars which have been written since his time. A more detailed study reveals, for instance, a phonologically determined distribution of shifted and non-shifted reflexes at Wermelskirchen in the west and Neu-Golm in the east, both close to the *maken/machen* line. In both places we find in intervocalic position fricative (characteristic of High German) after short vowel but plosive (characteristic of Low German) after a long vowel. In the following examples from Wermelskirchen, we give the local form in phonetic brackets, the corresponding Standard German form and an English gloss: [wesən] *wissen* 'to know', [nos] *Nuss* 'nut', [ʃlösəl]

Schlüssel 'key', [ɔfə] *offen* 'open', [brɛçən] *brechen* 'to break', all with short vowel; but [ʃmi:tən] *schmeissen* 'to throw', [bru:kən] *brauchen* 'to use', [li:k] *Leiche* 'dead body', [ri:pə] *reif* 'ripe' etc., all with long vowel. This leads to a morphophonemic alternation in verbs between 1.sing.pres. [ʃmi:t], 1.3. pl. pret. [ʃmesən], and past participle [yəʃmesən] (Schirmunski 1962: 287f.).

What do Wenker's and subsequent investigators' findings tell us about the progress of the consonant shift? It would appear that the step-like scatter or gradation of the isoglosses in geographical space represents the progress of the shift in time, that is to say successive phases in the spread of a phonological innovation. It is also clear that the major steps are phonologically determined but that individual lexical items within the phonologically defined groups are affected one by one in no visibly definable order. In the next chapter we shall see evidence from sociolinguistic studies which supports this interpretation of the way in which a sound change operates. The picture of the progress of sound change which emerges from the dialect maps and grammars is thus very different from the traditional concept (cf., for example, Hockett 1958: 441ff.) according to which the pronunciation of a positional allophone changes in a uniform manner and by phonetically imperceptible steps from the old to the new realization. The evidence of the maps suggests, rather than any such gradual drift in the pronunciation affecting the relevant segments of all the lexemes concurrently, a step-by-step *spread through the lexicon* so that, at any given moment, a particular lexical item either has the old or the new pronunciation. This at least would appear to be the only hypothesis consistent with, and explanatory of, all the facts. The process consists then, as we shall see in the next chapter, in the gradual gaining of the new pronunciation over the old one while both coexist within the community. Of course once a sound change has been completed, that is to say has affected all eligible items in the lexicon, the resulting situation is, as far as appearances are concerned, exactly the same *as if* the change had been simultaneous and uniform for all of them and corresponds in the grammar to the straightforward addition of a phonological rule.

The Second Consonant Shift has reached completion only in the High German dialects of the south, so that the so-called Middle German dialects situated between the *appel/apfel* and *maken/machen* lines, are characterized precisely by the different degree to which they have participated in the shift. This raises the question of just why a particular isogloss should be located precisely where it is. The problem concerns especially those lines in the west of the area in the neighbourhood of the Rhine, for it is these which show the widest discrepancies. Research has in fact established that these lines, which together form the so-called Rhenish Fan (cf. Bloomfield 1933: chapter 19), coincide with certain political boundaries of the fourteenth to sixteenth centuries when the German area was divided into innumerable small independent states. Even the limited evidence of these particular lines would thus appear to confirm a measure of correlation between linguistically and politically defined territories. Isoglosses thus tend to run between, and not within, political territories, and the linguistic situation which results survives subsequent political change.

Turning to the question of its date of commencement, its duration and the direction of its spread, King interprets the shift as a case of rule generalization and argues that, since it has only reached completion in the High German dialects of the south, it must therefore have spread southwards from the north (1969a: 92). It is in fact a claim of transformationalist historical linguistics that rules tend to become more general in their application as they spread through time and space. Traditional dialectology on the other hand would rather expect an innovation to lose some of its impact the further it spread from its point of origin (cf. Hall 1946; Dauzat 1922 passim). This latter view would appear to receive support from the fact that Low German has in the past consistently lost ground to High German, especially in the towns. There is also a certain amount of evidence for a northward movement of at least some of the isoglosses in historical times, although this now appears to be rather less conclusive than it was thought to be some twenty years ago. The evidence in question results from a comparison of dialect features preserved in Old High German manuscripts of known place of origin with the present distribution of these same features in the modern dialects. Provided that it is accepted that the scribal conventions in fact constitute a true reflection of local speech at the period when the manuscripts were written, the location of the isoglosses of the Consonant Shift can be reconstituted at least in broad outline for the eighth century A.D. On the basis of the evidence obtained in this way it was at first thought that all the isoglosses north of the *appel/apfel* line had at that time been situated further to the south than the positions they occupy in Wenker's Atlas (Frings 1957). The recent discovery of additional early manuscripts in the dialect of the Cologne area has, however, somewhat altered the situation (Schützeichel 1973) and it would now appear more likely that only the *dat/das*, *up/uf* and *dorp/dorf* lines have undergone any detectable northward movement since that period, the other isoglosses having maintained their positions. The argument, which involves the somewhat delicate problem of the relationship between the spoken and the written forms of a language at a particular point in time and space, is probably not yet over, but it is safe to say that some of the isoglosses have certainly undergone a northward movement in historical times whereas the *appel/apfel* line appears to have been in its present position bordering on High German ever since the period of the earliest documents. For the High German dialects of the south the shift is well attested from the same period, the only subsequent change being a retreat southward of the line representing the affrication of initial /k/ from a position near the present *appel/apfel* isogloss (Wagner 1927). In all other respects the situation appears to have remained unchanged since the earliest period for which there is documentary evidence.

We must, then, assume that the linguistic fragmentation of the Middle German area is the result of the gradual northward spread of the Consonant Shift, its individual phases being represented by the step-like scatter of the lines forming the Rhenish Fan. Their distribution implies that the shift rule must have gradually widened its scope within each dialect, the process having almost reached completion in the southernmost regions of Middle German. We have seen that the distribution within the lexicon of shifted and non-shifted forms is, in the great majority of cases, phonologically determined; there are, however, a certain number of 'exceptions'. In fact every Middle German dialect has a number of forms with Low German consonantism which are interpreted as survivals of the earlier situation.[1] Conversely the Low German

[1] Words with Low German consonantism, whether they are to be interpreted as 'relics' of an earlier situation (Schirmunski 1962: 278ff.) or simply as loan-words (Schützeichel 1973), are well attested in, for instance, the dialect of the Cologne area and elsewhere in Middle German. These refer to everyday objects and frequently lack a cognate form in High German; cf. with unshifted /t/: *taken* 'corner behind the stove', *timp* 'tip, edge' (High German *Zipfel*), *tö:t* 'can', *gat* 'hole', *rut* 'window pane'; with unshifted /k/: *we:k* 'wick', *bro:k* 'trousers' (English *breeches*), *ki:ken* 'chick', etc. (Schirmunski 1962: 278ff.). The situation found in the extreme west has exact parallels in the east, for instance in Berlin. There exist, in addition, a number of apparent relic words which are all unstressed monosyllables: *dat* 'that', *wat* 'what', *op* 'up', *le:t* 'let', *mo:t*

dialects of the north all have some words with High German consonantism, which are clearly loans. It is these loan-words from High German, referring typically to objects of trade,[1] which would appear to constitute the first wedge driven into the local system from outside. For, once a number of such 'market words' exist in High German form alongside their Low German cognates, the social significance of the formal differences between the members of the two sets is likely to be felt by speakers. And, as we shall see in the next chapter, the social evaluation of such systematic relationships between competing forms is the first step towards a change which will ultimately manifest itself as an added rule.

This process is well documented from French dialect studies. Thus, for instance, in Normandy Proto-Romance */k/ before */a/ is represented by /k/ except in a number of such 'market words', which have Standard French /ʃ/ instead. In Map 2 the isogloss for 'cat', separating /ka/ in the north from /ʃa/ in the south, shows the regular distribution of /k/ and /ʃ/ from */k/ before */a/ in the local dialects. The other isoglosses represent various degrees of penetration by imported words into the local system. It will be seen that the Standard French form for 'champ' has made inroads into the /k/ area in the south and east; that of 'chandeleur' has occupied the whole area except for a small isolated patch in the north-east; 'chandelle' has replaced the local form everywhere except in the south-west; 'chanson' has replaced the local form with /k/

'must' (the High German counterparts being *das, was, auf, lassen, müssen*). In this case the explanation as to why the consonants appear to have missed the shift is not quite the same; either they may be considered to be on a par with the loan-words and thus not to have taken part in the shift or they may be considered to form a special subset within the shift rule because they normally occur in unstressed positions in sentences (Höfler 1957: 288–95).

1 We are adopting the traditional view that the *maken/machen* line forms the boundary between High (including Middle) and Low German. Examples of words in Low German with High German consonantism are 'salt', 'pepper', 'newspaper', etc.; the referent is in all cases an object of trade, implying contact beyond the immediate local level. The proportion of such words decreases as one travels north. Curiously there are also in Low German a number of monosyllabic words which might constitute the reverse phenomenon of *dat, wat*, etc. in Middle German (see above) in the sense that they may be interpreted as forerunners of the shift. These are the dative-accusative forms of the personal pronouns: *mich, dich, sich, euch*, and *och* 'also' (Standard German *auch*). Höfler (1957: 295–312) ascribes their formal peculiarities again to their unstressed position in sentences while Schirmunski (1962: 285f.) considers them to be genuine loans from High German.

everywhere with the exception of two large areas, one in the east and the other in the west; and finally the standard form for 'chaîne' has invaded not only the south and east but also the Norman Islands and most of the Cotentin peninsula (von Wartburg 1962: 22).

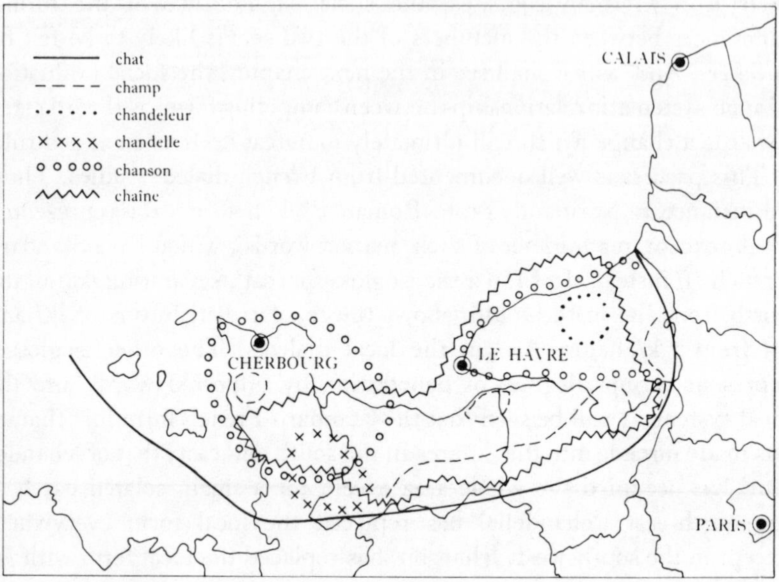

Map 2

Although we do not know how nor exactly where the Second Consonant Shift started, we have seen some of the evidence for its northward *spread* into Frankish territory from the High German dialects (Alemannic and Bavarian) of the south. It is generally supposed that this spread is to be associated with the conquest and subsequent incorporation into the Frankish Empire of the Alemannic territory. The decisive battle was fought in A.D. 496 and, from the study of place-names, it seems fairly certain that at that time the boundary between Frankish and Alemannic lay roughly where the most southerly of the isoglosses, the *appel/apfel* line, now runs. We may thus interpret the isoglosses on our present dialect maps to the north of this line as evidence of the progressive conversion to High German of the Frankish dialects. The location of certain of these isoglosses coincides, as we have already seen, with various political boundaries of the late Middle Ages after the collapse of the Frankish Empire. From the linguistic point of view such boundaries represent weak links in communication, and thus constitute barriers to the spread of innovations whereas within a particular political territory, where circulation is relatively unrestricted, a certain uniformity will be reached during the course of time. It has in fact been found that past political boundaries may survive for several hundred years in the form of isoglosses while, conversely, it takes some fifty years for a new political boundary to become linguistically significant (Schirmunski 1962: 131ff.). The location of the present lines thus reflects to a large degree the political divisions of the area as they were some five hundred years ago.

We will not pursue further the question of dialect boundaries at this point. The intention of this section was to analyse in some detail and on the basis of the available historical and dialectological evidence the spread of a phonological change in time and space. We shall now look at the problem of lexical change, concerning which the Linguistic Atlas of France has brought to light much valuable information.

2 Lexical replacement: the failure of the 'phonetic etymologies'

Our discussion of linguistic geography has so far brought out the value of dialect maps in reconstructing the historical grammar of a language. Without the evidence of the living dialects the interpretation in phonetic and phonological terms of the spelling conventions of the older texts would be well nigh impossible. More importantly, we have seen that from the present distribution of forms in geographical space conclusions may be drawn regarding past linguistic developments. The original aims of the French dialectologists were essentially the same as those of their German colleagues, namely 'to reconstitute the history of words, inflections and syntactic patterns on the basis of the distribution of the present forms and types' (Dauzat 1922: 27). Like their German colleagues, they too started with the regularity postulate of the neogrammarians as the basis of their method. However, partly due to sociopolitical differences in the historical backgrounds of the two regions studied and partly as a result of the nature of particular problems which arose during the course of the work, the French inquiry was to turn towards the resolution of problems and to bring to light facts rather different in nature from those of the German survey.[1]

[1] There is a striking contrast between the political fragmentation of the German-speaking area and the relative unity over several centuries of the

Jules Gilliéron, in the preparation of his Linguistic Atlas of France (1902–12), rejected Wenker's 'postal' method of inquiry in favour of one based on direct field-work. This necessitated the restriction of the investigation to a very much smaller number of localities (639, compared with the 50,000 of the German Atlas). The on-the-spot enquiry was conducted by a certain Edmond Edmont, a simple man who lacked any formal linguistic knowledge but who had considerable natural talents. Gilliéron trained him in the exact observation and notation of phonetic detail but considered his lack of linguistic training an advantage since it would ensure that the data he collected would not be influenced by any preconceived ideas about the outcome of the inquiry. Edmont was simply supplied with a questionnaire, the original questions of which have unfortunately not been preserved but which can be largely reconstituted from the maps of the Atlas, asked to fill it up for each locality visited and to post it back to Gilliéron before going on to the next. Like Wenker's sentences, the questions were designed to elicit samples of the phonology, morphology, syntax and lexicon for each locality. The inclusion of questions designed to elicit all the regional forms for a specific meaning, regardless of whether these were cognates or not, was an innovation which was to have important consequences.

Gilliéron's interpretation of the maps which resulted from Edmont's field-work proceeded roughly along the following lines. First, by comparing the modern local forms with their source forms in Proto-Romance (in practice, usually Latin), he established the phonological rules for the dialect of a given locality. On the basis of these rules he would then check for each individual form whether or not it was in fact the one expected from the application of the local rules. If the attested form differed from the expected one, he would then set about trying to explain why this was so. Put in such discovery-procedure terms, the argument appears of course as thoroughly circular, but it was based on the simplest of hypotheses, namely that the only change which had taken place between the Proto-Romance and the modern local form was

northern half of France under the dominant influence of Paris. The other basic difference between the two is, of course, the fact that in the case of the Romance languages the ancestor was, for practical purposes at least, known and the question dialectologists asked themselves was essentially 'How did Latin become French?' whereas in the case of German they were from the start concerned rather with answering the question 'What was the language like from which the Modern German languages and dialects came?'

a phonological one. This simple relationship between the two forms he referred to as 'a phonetic etymology'. In practice, however, he often found that this hypothesis of a simple direct phonological relationship was not sufficient to account for all the data. Either he would find a totally unrelated lexical item or what was clearly a cognate form but which did not comply with the phonological rules he had set up for the local dialect. He therefore set out, by a careful examination of the maps, to try to account for the replacement of the expected forms. Gilliéron maintained that the distribution of forms in geographical space could not be the result of mere chance and that it was up to the linguist to discover the principle which had caused the discrepancies. His neo-grammarian predecessors had, he claimed, 'noticed in the evolution of a language only what the articulatory organs produce while neglecting what goes on in the brain, by analysing only those aspects of language which destroy it while leaving to others the task of examining what reconstitutes it' (1919: 67).

The maps showed him first of all that local dialects do not exist in a state of isolation from one another. Thus developments which were incomprehensible on the basis of the local rules often became transparent when reference was made to the neighbouring dialects. Phonological forms which were in conflict with the local phonological rules were often, for instance, found to be identical with those of neighbouring localities where they were perfectly justified. This he attributed to dialect borrowing, a principle with which we are already familiar.

Secondly, in the case of a phonemic merger in the local dialect, hyper-correct forms were often found to have developed under the influence of a more prestigious dialect which had not undergone the merger. For example in certain dialects */kl/ and */fl/ had merged to /xl/. This development did not however take place in Standard French, which retained both sequences. Subsequently, under the influence of the standard language, local /xl/ was often 'restored' to its supposedly original form /kl/ with the effect that what had originally been *fl*-initial words now also had /kl/. This 'popular' restoration is explainable, the model being the very large group of *kl*-initial words like *clou* /klu/ 'nail', *clef* /kle/ 'key', etc. which so outnumbered words like *fléau* /fleo/ 'flail' that these were submerged. Thus *fléau* was found to turn up locally as *kla* or *klo*, *flamme* 'flame' as *clambe*, etc. French dialectologists refer to this process as *régression*, whereas we would describe it rather as hyper-correction. Hypercorrections of this type are of course well known from the speech of individuals, but here they were demonstrated also to play a role in *langue*. They could only be explained, however, if account were also taken of surrounding dialects.

The third, and most far-reaching, of Gilliéron's discoveries was that of the importance of homonymic clash (*collision homonymique*) as a factor in lexical replacement. He found that when, on the basis of the phonological rules, two forms must have become homophonous in a dialect, one or other of them, sometimes even both, were likely to be replaced by an entirely new lexical form. The interesting point is that homophony is not always unacceptable, leading to lexical change. It is only if the homophonous forms are capable of occurring *in identical contexts* so that confusion will result that lexical replacement takes place. We thus have a paradigmatic relationship between lexical items in the same semantic field as a conditioning factor of change and the change itself will consist in one of the competing lexical items giving way and being replaced by

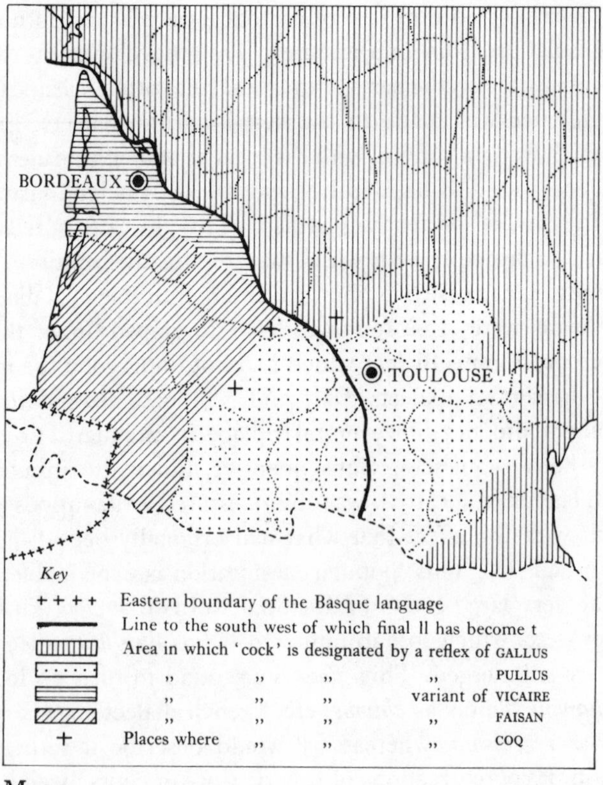

Map 3

a new one in order that a formal opposition be maintained. This whole process Gilliéron refers to as 'a therapeutic change', since it maintains the language in functioning order. It is in this area that French dialectology has perhaps made the most interesting contribution, and we may recall at this point a theoretical question which was raised when we were discussing the interrelationship between the levels of analysis in the structuralist model (see p. 87f.). It would in fact appear that the findings of the French dialectologists lend support to Hermann Paul's claim that phonological change is in itself *never* therapeutic and that, when it causes 'damage' in a language, it is mechanisms which lie *outside* the phonological level, namely analogical change and lexical replacement, which come into operation to restore the situation.

We will take as an example of Gilliéron's discoveries what is perhaps the best known case of homonymic clash, namely that which occurred between the words for 'cat' and 'cock' in Gascony. Our map shows that there are five different lexical items for 'cock' in the various dialects of the region studied (Dauzat 1922: 67). Four of the terms can be seen to cover continuous areas while a fifth, that of the standard language, is attested only in three isolated localities:

(1) GALLUS, reflexes of Latin *gallus* 'cock', in a vast area of the north and east and continuing into neighbouring Spain;

(2) PULLUS, reflexes of Latin *pullus* 'young animal' and later 'young cock', in a central area of the south;

(3) FAISAN, words for 'pheasant', to the west of PULLUS in Gascony;

(4) VICAIRE, words for 'curate', to the north of FAISAN in Gascony;

(5) COQ, from Late Latin *coccus* 'cock', which has become the Standard French word and is found in three isolated localities in the region where GALLUS, PULLUS and VICAIRE come together.

Of these forms, *gallus* was the normal Latin word for 'cock', *pullus* referred to a 'young cock', and *coccus* was a later Latin form; *faisan* and *vicaire* on the other hand are obviously not primary words for 'cock' at all but some kind of lexical substitute which, judging from the distribution of surrounding forms on the map, may be assumed to have replaced either PULLUS or GALLUS. That it is the latter term which they are likely to have replaced is suggested by two arguments. Firstly, a feminine GALLINA 'hen' occurs sporadically in the same area which strongly suggests the previous presence of a masculine GALLUS.

Gilliéron's second argument relates to the phonological form of the words. He approached the problem by asking what the regular reflexes of Latin *pullus* and *gallus* would have been in this particular area and here he discovered the clue to the whole situation. For he found that, due to a phonological rule which changed *-ll* once it had become word-final to *-t* (as in Latin *collum* 'neck' > *cot*), *pullus* would regularly give **put* and *gallus* **gat*. But the form *gat* does occur in the area, being the word for 'cat' coming just as regularly from Latin *cattus*. Thus, on the basis of the sound laws, the following development would have taken place:

cattus 'cat' → **gat* 'cat, cock' ← *gallus* 'cock'

And, since both 'cat' and 'cock' are common domestic animals belonging to the same semantic field, such homonymy would be intolerable. Thus *gat* has survived with the meaning 'cat' while **gat* 'cock' has been replaced.

The phonological isogloss which separates the area to the south-west where the sound change operated from that to the north-east where it did not, is represented on the map by a heavy black line. It can be seen that this isogloss runs exactly along the line separating the area to the north-east in which GALLUS survived from that in the south-west where it was replaced by FAISAN and VICAIRE, that is to say the replacement has occurred in precisely that geographical area in which *-ll* became *-t*. It can also be seen that the line runs right through the middle of the PULLUS area, which suggests that the replacement of GALLUS by PULLUS was independent of the phonological development *-ll* > *-t*. From this Gilliéron deduced that, at the time when *-ll* changed to *-t*, GALLUS must already have been replaced by PULLUS – an interesting chronological observation reached solely from a detailed examination of the map. The replacement of a semantically unmarked term like GALLUS 'cock' by a marked one like PULLUS 'young cock' is a not uncommon development, and that PULLUS is an innovation originating within the GALLUS area is also suggested by its location (the GALLUS area, as has already been noted, continues into Spain). Finally, the fact that the standard form COQ came to be used here and there in the neighbourhood where the three main areas come together is explained as being possibly a result of the conflict between the three rival forms causing impairment of communication. The mesh of localities covered by the Atlas is not, however, sufficiently close to verify this.

It remains to explain why *gat* should have survived with the meaning of 'cat' rather than that of 'cock'. Gilliéron supposed that this was because GALLUS was formally isolated in the language and thus more vulnerable, its feminine having become phonologically removed from it by a change of intervocalic *-ll-* to *-r-* to give *garina*. Thus, while masc. *cattus* : fem. *catta* gave *gat* : *gata*, masc. *gallus* : fem. *gallina* resulted in *gat* : *garina*. In the case of 'cat' there is, in addition to the feminine, a rich family of derived words (the counterparts of Standard French *chatière* 'hole for cat in door', *chaton* 'catkin, kitten', *chatterie* 'coaxing', *chattemite* 'sycophant') whereas no such derivational set exists in the case of 'cock'. All these events have been summed up, in the somewhat anthropomorphic language of the time, in the statement that, 'in Gascony the cat killed the cock' (Dauzat 1922: 66)!

From among the many other well-documented examples of homonymic clash investigated by the French, we will mention only two (Dauzat 1922: 64–72, 104–8). MULGERE 'to milk' was retained in the south but replaced by TRAIRE 'to pull' in the north where it would have become homophonous with MOUDRE, coming from Latin *molere*, 'to grind'. Geographically, the reflexes of *mulgere* stop exactly at the line beyond which they would have become identical with those of *molere*. Latin *claudere* 'to close' gave CLORE. This word is now almost completely replaced by FERMER which, it would appear, originally denoted a different kind of closing. Some forms of the inflectional paradigm of CLORE have in fact survived, especially the past participle *clos* 'closed', but significantly the imperfect (**je clouais* etc.) and the plural of the present (**nous clouons* etc.) have not because these would be homophonous with the corresponding forms of *clouer* 'to nail', a new verb in French derived from the noun *clou* 'nail' and possessing a full paradigm. This means that CLORE survives as an archaism with a very defective paradigm, verbs being as a rule more resistant to wholesale replacement because of the large scatter of forms they possess compared to nouns.

In order to establish facts of this kind it can be seen it is not sufficient to examine the development of individual dialects in isolation, only their *ensemble* can reveal replacement patterns like those described above. It can also be seen that it is essential that lexical and phonological developments be examined together. It should however be stressed that, despite pronouncements to the contrary, the interpreters of the French Atlas by no means abandoned the neogrammarian regularity principle. It in fact remained the indispensable foundation of their work, but they found that it was *insufficient* to account for the full range of phenomena in language change. In particular their closer investigation of the erosive effects of phonological change on the system of lexical oppositions was to lead to a better understanding of how such oppositions may be maintained or reconstituted by means of therapeutic lexical replacement.

3 Do dialect boundaries exist?

As a result of his work on the French linguistic atlas Gilliéron came eventually to the view that no single Romance dialect could be said to constitute in itself an internally consistent development of Latin. Only the *ensemble*, the totality of all the dialects, can be said to do this, since it is only within such a framework that individual deviations can be stated and explained (1919: 118). In fact Romance dialectologists have always tended to deny the existence of dialects altogether, dialect boundaries being held to be subjective in nature since it is the linguist who selects the particular one, or ones, which he considers to be most significant from the mass of conflicting isoglosses. But why should any one phonological feature be given more importance than any other? And what relative weight is to be attributed to phonological as opposed to grammatical or lexical isoglosses? We shall return to this question again. What will concern us now is rather the effect of this position on the subject. Since all that is capable of objective statement is the position of the boundaries of individual words, Gilliéron and his school were led to the conclusion that, if the linguist's operations are to be truly scientific, the study of the history of dialects must be replaced by that of the history of individual words (Gilliéron, quoted from Schirmunski 1962: 94). Justification for such an 'atomistic' approach lay in the fact that it is individual linguistic phenomena rather than dialects as wholes which can be shown to cover continuous areas on maps and to have sharp borders, and this is undoubtedly one of the most striking findings of dialect geography. As we have seen, breaks in the areal continuity of an isogloss can be accounted for by careful interpretation of the map, separate islands sharing some particular feature being explicable as having preserved an older form (Map 2) or as having borrowed independently from some common source, for instance the standard language (see Map 3). The examination of maps can thus, at least to some extent, permit the reconstruction of language history. This observation was carried to its extreme by the neolinguistic (or space linguistic) school of Bartoli and his followers in Italy who, initially at least, claimed that it constituted an independent alternative to neogrammarian methods and that a diachronic perspective could be established solely on the basis of map interpretation (Hall 1946; Vidos 1968: 99ff.).

An obvious effect of the apparently random pattern of distribution which results from the relative independence of individual isoglosses must be that the speakers of any particular locality will be capable of understanding the speech of their immediate neighbours more readily than that of speakers from further afield. Due to the gradual cumulation of intervening isoglosses, ease of communication will fall off in direct proportion to geographical distance and there will be no clear-cut barrier which could be taken as constituting a dialect boundary. In a general sort of way, and in a non-urban setting in particular, this may well be true, but is the picture in fact quite so simple as is suggested by the very widely spaced mesh of the French Atlas? Do the isoglosses in fact form so regular and random a pattern, or can one detect irregularities in the density of their distribution which will result for instance in areas of more or less rapid fall-off in ease of communication? German dialectologists in particular have preoccupied themselves with this problem. Perhaps the greater degree of political fragmentation of the German-speaking area in the past and the much denser network of localities covered by the German Atlas may have contributed to the fact that they have been able to show that the density and location of isoglosses is not a completely random matter and that one can differentiate 'core' areas, relatively free of internal isoglosses, from 'transitional' areas which surround and separate the core areas. It is only in these latter that isoglosses are concentrated and tend to cross one another, fragmenting the area in all possible ways. Core areas are located around cultural centres, whereas transitional areas lie within the sphere of influence of several such centres. Thus the fact that there are no sharp boundaries must not be taken as supporting the claim that there are no dialects. One should think rather in terms of political and cultural centres imposing a unified cultural and linguistic pattern on the surrounding area and of intervening areas subjected to influences coming from several directions. The close correlation which exists between linguistic and non-linguistic factors can further be shown when the linguistic isoglosses are compared with those indicating the structure of farm-houses, of traditional costume, of agricultural implements, etc. As a result of establishing correlations of this kind, German dialectology arrived at the concept that language areas are in fact culture areas (*Sprachlandschaften sind Kulturlandschaften*) and are the result of radiation from cultural centres. In areas situated between such cultural centres there will naturally be conflicting loyalties on the part of speakers and this is reflected in the varying density and non-uniform distribution of their isoglosses.

This does not, of course, imply that innovations cannot spread beyond individual core areas into neighbouring ones. An example of an innovation which had a wide cross-territorial spread is the diphthongization of long high vowels in German (see p. 54). By examining written documents from all the major cultural and administrative centres for this feature, Wagner (1927: 37f.) followed its spread right across the German-speaking area and beyond. He found that in a period of about four hundred years (twelfth to sixteenth centuries) it spread over the whole area between Austria and the Dutch border and in the next hundred years even reached Holland and England.

4 The wave theory

A theoretical model which postulates the spread of linguistic innovations from a centre over the surrounding territory – much as a stone thrown into still water produces progressively wider and fainter ripples around its point of impact – was first proposed by Johannes Schmidt in a book on the interrelationships of the Indo-European languages (Schmidt 1872) and has come to be known as *the wave theory*. It is designed to account for the fact that, when related languages are compared, a certain correlation is generally to be found between geographical distance and linguistic distance, at least in so far as specific features are concerned. A number of different possible situations must be envisaged.

(1) The ideal case is one in which, in an 'undisturbed' linguistic territory, that is to say one in which there have been no massive influxes of immigrants nor assimilations of pre-existing communities, there arises a new political and cultural centre. If innovations from this new centre now spread over only a part of the original territory while the rest of the territory remains under the influence of the pre-existing centre, we will witness the development of isoglosses between the two adjacent territories which will eventually lead to loss of mutual intelligibility and thus to two different languages. In this case the wave model

simply provides a plausible explanation of one way in which linguistic *divergence*, representable in the family tree by a node, may come about. The two languages which result will clearly be more closely related to each other than either of them will be to any third language.

(2) The wave model seeks, however, to account not only for such cases of divergent development but also for the diffusion of features across a number of languages after they have separated. Let us imagine a situation which is the opposite of the one previously described. There are two related but linguistically distinct dialects which are geographically adjacent and whose territories have become united under the influence of some political force with a single administrative and cultural centre. We may now witness the *elimination* of specific isoglosses which previously served to differentiate the two dialects through the spread of features from one dialect area over the territory of the other, accompanied perhaps by a similar process in the opposite direction (so-called *dialect levelling*). The spread of the consonant shift from High German into Middle German after the incorporation of the Alemannic territory into the Frankish Empire was a case in point. Common innovations may also arise which will serve to split both previous dialect areas jointly from adjacent areas which do not undergo the innovations. Thus, through the elimination of internal isoglosses and the creation of new ones around the perimeter of the now joint area, what were originally distinct dialects may become more and more alike. The degree of such convergence will clearly depend both upon the length of time during which they previously underwent separate development as well as the length of time during which they were subsequently subjected to the influence of a common centre. This kind of dialect levelling is observable wherever a standard language gains increasing influence over local and regional dialects, as well as in cases of colonization where settlers from various dialect areas come together to create new communities (see, for example, Gilbert (1971) regarding Texas German). Experience shows, however, that the outcome of such convergence is by no means complete uniformity.

(3) The diffusion of common features is not restricted to related dialects but may be found in any group of languages in close contact, whether these be related or not. We shall return to the question of unrelated languages in contact in chapter 6 and for the moment will confine ourselves to *related languages*. The difference between related languages and related dialects is of course only one of degree. In the case

of languages, however, since their independent divergent development is correspondingly greater, features diffused across them are likely to be more marginal in relation to the individual linguistic systems and their impact correspondingly weaker.

The relationship between divergence and diffusion requires some further comment. As we have seen (p. 63ff.) the family tree, by situating linguistic innovations within an ideal framework of time and space, constitutes a model of the continuity of language through time. It represents the *relative chronology* of the changes which characterize the evolution of a language, but it does not attempt to situate any particular innovation in *real time* and *real space*, nor does it explain why a particular innovation took place when and where it did. The wave model on the other hand represents the spread of linguistic innovations through geographical space irrespective of the relationship of the languages affected, the overlapping and criss-crossing of different isoglosses representing a very real aspect of linguistic evolution which proceeds by individual features. Only by relating the isoglosses in question to the family tree of the languages concerned can it be decided whether a particular isogloss represents the retention of an inherited feature, a shared innovation, or a feature which is the result of diffusion across the branches of a tree after the languages had lost contact (see Southworth 1964 for attempts at graphical representation). This latter kind of diffusion is conventionally represented in the family tree as separate innovations, for it is not difficult to see that were the branches of the tree to be rejoined merely for the purpose of recording a joint change this would imply that the languages concerned had become totally identical again.

The fact that it is sometimes difficult to decide whether particular prehistoric isoglosses are to be considered the result of divergence or of diffusion has nothing to do with the adequacy of either model. Such problems are likely to arise whenever there is insufficient evidence for the setting up of a relative chronology. We shall see in a later chapter (p. 223f.) that it is not always possible to distinguish between common inheritance and borrowing on internal evidence. If the formal criteria are not available, conflicting interpretations may be possible. Let us consider a typical example.

German *Gast* 'guest', Latin *hostis* 'enemy' (earlier 'stranger'), and Russian *gost'* (in which *t'* represents a palatalized dental) 'guest' show the regular phonological correspondences for words of Proto-Indo-

European origin. *Gast* has cognates throughout the Germanic branch, *gost'* has cognates elsewhere in Slavonic, and *hostis* has at least indirect reflexes in Romance (for example French *hôte* from **hosti-potis*). On the basis of the phonological rules for the three languages concerned we may thus reconstruct a Proto-Indo-European form **ghostis* and assign to it the meaning 'stranger' (attested in Old Latin and Gothic) from which can easily be derived the meanings 'guest' and 'enemy'. We may then make the perfectly legitimate assumption that the other Indo-European languages have simply lost this particular lexical item. However, rather than consider it to be the result of shared inheritance in the three branches of the family, we might equally well suppose it to be an innovation. It could hardly however be a *shared* innovation since there is insufficient justification for postulating a common Italic-Germanic-Slavonic branch of the family. On the other hand, since there is ample evidence that these three branches were in close geographical and cultural contact since prehistoric times, the fact that they share this word might be the result of diffusion between them. On purely formal grounds borrowing from Latin into Germanic or vice versa is perfectly conceivable but it would be necessary for such borrowing to have taken place at a very early date indeed, before certain typically Germanic and Latin innovations had taken place (that is when it took place the form would have still had to have been **ghostis*). Borrowing from Germanic into Slavonic at the **ghostis* stage, or later when the Germanic form had become **gastiz*, are also possibilities. On semantic grounds, since the meaning 'guest' appears to have developed within Germanic, the meaning of the Slavonic words could best be accounted for by borrowing from Germanic. Between Latin and Germanic priorities cannot be established since both require an earlier meaning 'stranger'. And of course the initial centre of the diffusion could equally well have been right outside the languages concerned. In this example, therefore, the data are compatible either with an analysis which postulates common inheritance of the word or with one which postulates its diffusion across neighbouring languages in prehistoric times subsequent to separation of the branches. We can exclude however the third possibility of joint innovation before separation of the three branches, since this would involve having to justify their split from a single branch by showing that the isoglosses which link the three branches precede branch-specific changes and such evidence is difficult to produce (see Krahe 1954: 71ff.).

5 Mutual intelligibility

We have so far avoided any attempt at attributing relative weighting to different kinds of isogloss in so far as mutual intelligibility is concerned. It is however perfectly legitimate to ask ourselves whether it is phonological, grammatical or lexical isoglosses which are most disruptive to communication. Little experimental work has so far been done in this field. Levels of mutual intelligibility are usually assessed in the field by playing to speakers of closely related languages and dialects recorded samples of the languages concerned and by measuring the degree of comprehension in some standardized way, for example by asking specific questions concerning the content of the samples or by having these retold in the speaker's own language. Experiments designed to relate degrees of mutual intelligibility obtained in this way to the phonological, grammatical and lexical systems of the languages have been attempted. In the course of the Language Survey of Ethiopia, for a group of related languages the results of mutual intelligibility tests were compared with the percentage of shared basic vocabulary and the frequency of putatively cognate grammatical and lexical morphs in running texts. A close covariance was found to exist between these three factors and the geographical proximity of the languages tested. Geographical distance was measured by map distance between sociocultural centres (Bender 1974, 1975). These tests would appear to show that all levels of linguistic analysis are equally relevant to mutual intelligibility.

6 The social dimension

We will now briefly return to a consideration of the stages which we postulated for the progression of the High German Consonant Shift (p. 180f.). It will be remembered that we interpreted the data as indicating that, as a result of the growing number of loan-words of High German origin, the Consonant Shift rule progressively widened its scope within the grammars of the individual dialects. But why, we may ask, when dialects are brought into contact, should one of these impose its features on the other rather than vice versa? This is a matter which does not depend in any way on the internal structures of the languages concerned and we must turn for an answer to factors external to language itself, namely that for sociocultural reasons the speech of one group had greater *prestige* than that of the other. The missing dimension in our analysis is therefore the social one.

Critics have indeed drawn attention to the fact that the great linguistic atlases operate on the assumption that the speech of any given locality is monolithic and uniform. But in interviews for the French Atlas, which were conducted by the field-worker in Standard French, did the informant always reply in the local dialect or sometimes in a regional variety of the standard language? (Dauzat 1922: 148). In any community some speakers at least will be capable of varying their speech according to circumstances, using perhaps the local dialect when talking among themselves but a more widely acceptable variety of the language when talking to strangers or for official purposes. Such linguistic differences are often institutionalized, a 'high' variety of the language being used for more formal occasions and a 'low' variety used locally and in the home and, as in the case of Arabic, Greek and Swiss German (Ferguson 1959), there may be very considerable differences between the two codes. But outside such 'diglossic' communities the distinction may be much more fluid. To return to the German situation, we know that the conversion of Low German into High German, which is still an ongoing process, has operated chiefly through the cities. In these the communities have always been much more mixed, especially in the eastern areas whose population is largely the result of colonization from the south and west which took place in the Middle Ages. Berlin for instance lies within a loop formed by the main isoglosses which bulge out to enclose the city within the High German area. We know that its speech has been High German since the sixteenth century, though again with some characteristic Low German relics. For Wittenberg Luther reported a local man's speech as being Low German but he himself spoke High German, at least in his after-dinner speeches. The educated people in the towns in Low German territory have been speaking (or at least have been capable of speaking) High German for centuries and today, as the result of the fact that general education is conducted in High German everyone is bilingual. It is clear that the association of social prestige with a specific language variety and the bilingualism of at least a sector of the community must be an important factor in the spread of features belonging to one variety of a language to others. This social dimension is the element missing so far from our discussion of the change process, and we shall turn to it in the next chapter.

5
The social motivation of language change

1 The social stratification of language: the evaluation of linguistic variables

What is perhaps the most important contribution towards an understanding of the actual mechanism of language change has come from the detailed sociolinguistic investigation of living speech communities. The examination of the linguistic behaviour of the individual speaker within his community has proved to be of the greatest relevance to diachronic linguistics but, before we can appreciate its full significance, we must first return to what is in fact a synchronic problem, namely that of the relationship between the linguist's description of a language and the actual data upon which his description is based. As we already pointed out in the Introduction (p. 2ff.), any conventional description of a language presupposes a certain degree of abstraction or idealization of the data. Thus a description which aims at representing the linguistic competence of 'an ideal speaker-hearer in a perfectly homogeneous speech community' will achieve descriptive uniformity by relegating to performance all variation which is cognitively irrelevant. A corpus-based description on the other hand, which selects as its data what is considered to be a representative speech sample (for example the careful colloquial style of an educated speaker), achieves descriptive uniformity by ignoring those aspects of the language which are outside the corpus and by treating as free variants functionally equivalent forms within the corpus. Both models, then, clearly disregard a great deal of overt linguistic *variation* in the actual speech habits of the members of the community. Until relatively recently such variation had never been systematically studied, partly due to the fact that there was no established methodology by which to do it and partly because it was simply considered to be without importance. We shall however see that it is precisely this variation within a speech community which provides the key to the mechanism of language change. By acting as a living vehicle or medium for the retraction and promotion of competing forms, which will show themselves in retrospect as members of the successive grammars of the language, it makes change possible. This does not mean that all linguistic variation is necessarily associated with ongoing change but simply that any change which does take place assumes the presence of linguistic variation. Before, therefore, we can turn to an examination of the change process itself we must first look at the methods employed in the analysis of synchronic linguistic variation.

Sociolinguistic research has established the fact that certain differences in the speech of the members of a community can be correlated in a systematic way with specific social factors. The first large-scale study which was able to show such correlation was undertaken in New York City in the early sixties by William Labov. He had the advantage of being able to base his linguistic survey of the Lower East Side of Manhattan (Labov 1966) on the results of a sociological survey which had previously been carried out in the area. By the interviewing of a random sample, this survey had grouped the population of some 100,000 individuals into a number of socio-economic classes on the basis of three criteria: (1) the occupation of the bread-winner, (2) the education of the informant, and (3) the income of the family. Labov in turn selected from among the informants of that survey a sample for linguistic interview, imposing only one further condition, namely that all should have been born in New York City. His eighty-one principal informants were subjected to a carefully prepared linguistic interview based on a questionnaire the aim of which was to determine the social distribution of a number of specific linguistic features.

Fortunately, and as it turned out significantly, not all aspects of a language are subject to variation at any one time. Thus, in New York City, both variations between socially determined groups and inconsistencies within the speech of individuals were found to be limited to particular areas of the linguistic system. One such area at the phonological level is that of the vowel in words like *bad*, *half*, *dance* etc., for which pronunciations with [ɪːᵊ] (the vowel of *beard*), [ɛːᵊ] (the vowel of *bared*) and [æː] can all be heard. This means that [ɪːᵊ] and [æː] are sometimes found to contrast ([bɪːᵊd] *beard* ≠ [bæːd] *bad*) and sometimes to occur in free variation ([bɪːᵊd], [bæːd] *bad*), making a conventional phonemic analysis impossible. Similarly the pronunciation of words like *car*, *four*, *board* etc. would sometimes have an *r*-glide and sometimes not, making it again impossible to include the presence and absence of consonantal constriction within a single phonemic analysis. Theoretically of course in both these cases the different pronunciations might be assigned to different phonemic systems, implying the co-existence in New York speech of two independent systems in one of which *beard*, *bared*, *bad* have different vowels (/ih/, /eh/, /æh/) and in the other all three have an identical vowel. Similarly, in the case of *car*, *four*, *board*, etc., in the one system /r/ would have word-final and preconsonantal allophones and in the other it would be restricted to prevocalic position. Such an analysis would however fail to account satisfactorily for the fact that no single speaker adheres consistently to either system.

Labov was able to show that the distribution of these variant pronunciations is not a completely random matter and that such variations are in fact rule-governed. He found that (1) there is a systematic correlation between the linguistic behaviour of a speaker and his social status (measured in socio-economic terms), and (2) that inconsistencies in the speech of one individual (which had previously given rise to the view that in New York not even the idiolect was amenable to systematic description) are dependent on the speech style (or 'register') employed. As a theoretical framework within which the patterns of variation could be stated, Labov postulated for the whole community a single phonological system characterized by a certain number of variable units. Each segment of the phonological system which was found to be subject to variant realizations was considered to form a *phonological variable* and its different realizations were made the object of inquiry. Thus an '(r)-variable' was set up to represent the variation in the pronunciation of words like *car*, *four*, *board*, and an (eh)-variable for that in *bad*, *dance*, *half*. It was then the task of the survey to determine the rule which governed the variation pattern in each case. This kind of phonological analysis is of course incompatible with traditional phonemics and Labov presupposes, like generative phonologists, a systematic distinction between an underlying and a surface representation. The theoretical bases of the two approaches are however quite different for, whereas generative phonology justifies a systematic phoneme on the basis of morphological alternation ([kɑ:] # *car* ≠ ['kɑ:-r-ænd] *car and*), socio-linguistic analysis postulates a phonological variable on the basis of phonological variation within the community. In each model, however, the realizations of an underlying unit are governed by a phonological rule.

We will consider in detail the rule governing (r). Labov found that, although it was impossible to predict whether or not any individual speaker would use a glide in any particular word and on any specific occasion, it was possible to state the class of words within which *r*-glides *could* occur and to predict the overall frequency of *r*-glides in a person's speech. With very few exceptions, the class of (r)-words was found to consist of those lexical items which in other varieties of American English are regularly pronounced with an [r] and which in the standard orthography, by reference to an earlier pronunciation, are spelt with an *r*. For the purpose of assessing the overall frequency of *r*-glides, an (r)-score was obtained for each informant by attributing a numerical value of 1 to each occurrence of an *r*-glide and the value 0 to its absence in a position in which its occurrence would have been possible. The percentage of (r = 1) realizations was then plotted against the informant's position in the social scale (six socio-economic classes being distinguished, ranging from 0: 'lower class' to 9: 'upper middle class') on a graph designed to show the relationship between actual, as opposed to potential, glide realizations as a function of class. Labov repeated this operation for each of five speech situations, namely (A) 'casual speech'

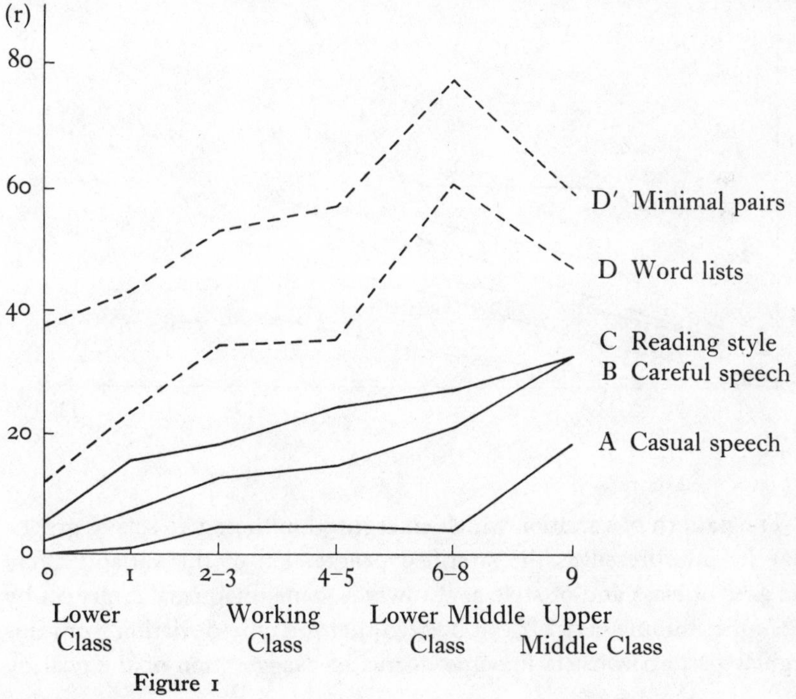

Figure 1

(elicited by asking the informant whether he had ever been in a situation in which his life was in danger, the informant's emotional involvement in the event supposedly making him forget that he was being interviewed for linguistic purposes); (B) 'formal style', the normal free style used in a tape-recorded interview; (C) 'reading style', in which the informant read aloud material handed to him; (D) the reading of word lists, more formal than (C); (D′) the reading of minimal word pairs, most formal of all. When the graphs resulting from all these tests were combined it was clearly visible that the frequency of (r = 1) realizations (that is, pronunciations of (r) as a constricted glide) was directly dependent on the social class of the speaker and the speech style that he was employing (Figure 1: Labov 1966: 240).

Labov also plotted the *r*-score against style for each of the six social classes, as shown in Figure 2 (Labov 1966: 240).

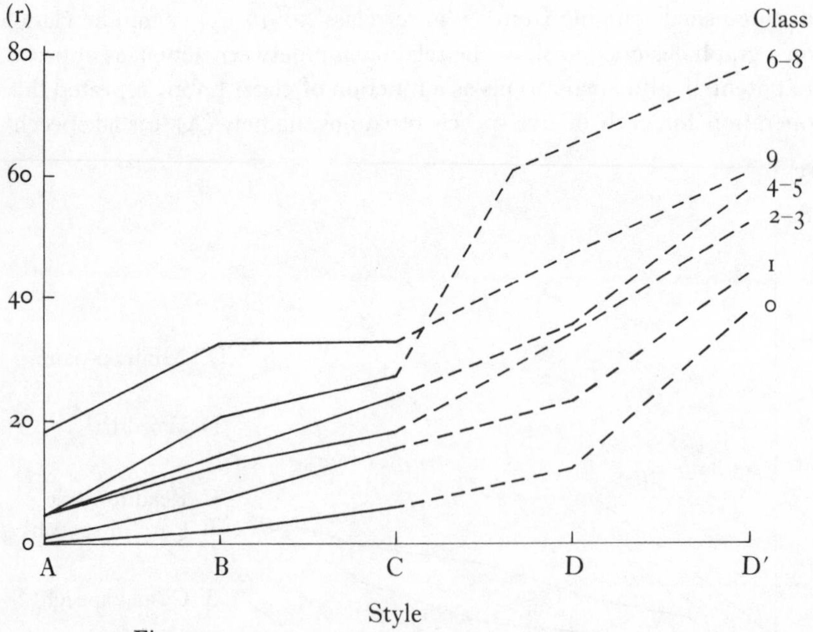

Figure 2

The pattern of variation which emerges from these two sets of graphs may be interpreted as the stratified progression of the variable along the axes of class and of style as if towards some imaginary target set by the upper middle class. It can be seen that the only deviation from this regular pattern consists in some degree of exaggeration of the goal by the lower middle class informants in the two most formal styles (D and D′), reflected in peaks in the minimal pair and word list lines in Figure 1 and in the crossing of the upper middle class line by the lower middle class line in Figure 2. We shall come back to the significance of this phenomenon at a later stage; for the moment we shall simply note it as a deviation and observe that, in all other respects, the pattern is both regular and directional.

We have chosen the (r)-variable for detailed examination because of its simplicity. Some of the other variables examined by Labov – such as the case of (eh) already mentioned, or that of (oh) in words like *lost*, *caught*, *all* where there is variation ranging from [ʊːᵊ] to [ɒ, a] – are more complicated since their realizations are not just dependent on class and style but also on the realization of other variables in the vowel system. However, the rules governing their variation, although not the actual distribution pattern across classes and styles, proved to be quite as regular as those for (r).

Labov supplemented the performance tests described so far by evaluation tests which were of two kinds: (1) evaluation by the informant of the speech of others and (2) evaluation of the informant's own speech by himself. In order to evaluate the speech of others, tape recordings of selected passages containing different shades of realization of the variables and read by what appeared to be different speakers, although it was in fact the same 'bilingual' speaker, were played to the informant and he was asked to assess the job prospects of the 'different' readers. These so-called 'matched guise tests' showed that evaluation of the speech of others followed the same scale of values as the performance tests and was in fact even more regular, in spite of the fact that informants, when questioned about the criteria they were using, were unable to identify the linguistic basis of their assessment. In the self-evaluation tests informants were asked to select from among several current pronunciations of diagnostic words the one they would themselves normally use. It is interesting that the results of this test were very different from the informant's actual performance, reflecting his feelings of what his pronunciation *should* be rather than what it actually was. It was also noted that speakers who themselves used a stigmatized feature (for instance pronunciations like [bɪːᵊd] for *bad*) were most sensitive to the occurrence of that feature in the speech of others. In the case of the (r)-variable the tests showed that its realization as a glide constituted a prestige feature for speakers of all classes between the ages of 18 and 40 and that persons who themselves pronounced *guard* and *god* alike, even in the minimal pairs test, would still claim that they used an (r = 1) pronunciation in the former. This shows clearly that sensitivity to (r) goes beyond the classes who actually use an (r = 1) pronunciation.

Labov's investigations showed that, in spite of substantial differences in the speech of social groups there is a uniform system of values or norms which has validity for the community as a whole, that is to say alternative pronunciations are given social values which are shared by all members of the society.[1] Thus the New Yorker who pronounces an *r*-glide in postvocalic position has better job prospects in the society because speakers of all classes feel (*r* = 1) to be a prestige feature, although they are not necessarily consciously aware of doing so. The synchronic rule governing the (r) variable may thus be expressed by the formula:

$$(\mathrm{r}) \rightarrow n\,[\mathrm{r}] \;/\; \underline{\quad} \begin{Bmatrix} \mathrm{C} \\ \# \end{Bmatrix};\; n\,[\mathrm{r}] = \mathrm{f}\,(\text{class, style})$$

which states that (r) is realized as a glide in preconsonantal and final positions with the frequency *n*, where *n* is a function (f) of class and style.

2 The synchronic reflection of historical change

After considering these purely synchronic aspects of linguistic variation, we must now introduce the diachronic dimension by asking whether such variables as were revealed by Labov's investigations are constant factors in a language or whether they reflect change in progress. Now if, in the sort of situation we have been describing, it could be shown that a particular variable were restricted to the younger speakers in the community, or that the younger speakers were socially sensitive to its occurrence whereas their elders were not, such difference in behaviour according to age group might reasonably be assumed to represent a change in progress. It must be realized, however, that such generation differences do not *necessarily* reflect a process of historical

1 Labov's observations have been substantiated in principle in a number of subsequent studies, for British English for example by Trudgill who investigated the social differentiation in the Norwich dialect of such variables as the third person singular marker in verbs (the presence versus the absence of *-s*), the *-ing* suffix (pronunciation with [n] or [ŋ]), intervocalic *t* ([t] versus glottal stop in words like *butter*), and initial *h-* ([h] versus 'dropped *h*' in words like *house*) (Trudgill 1974b, 1974a: chapter 2).

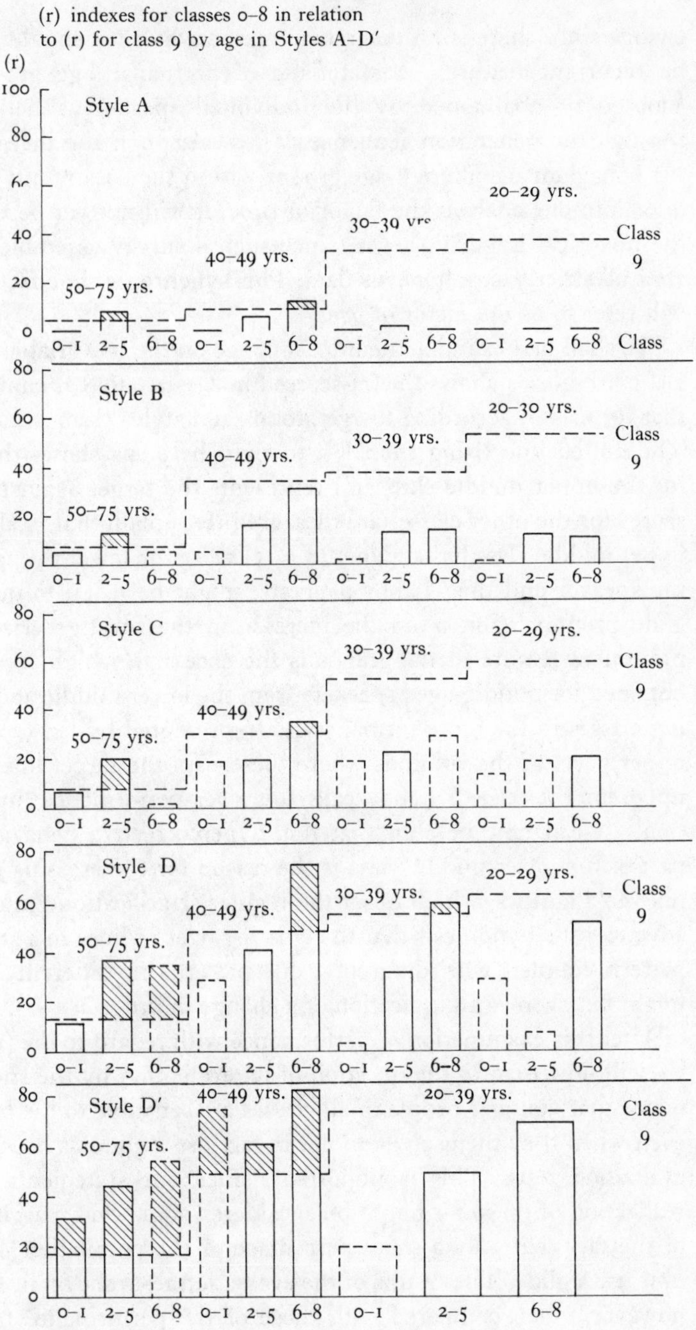
(r) indexes for classes 0–8 in relation
to (r) for class 9 by age in Styles A–D′
(r)
Style A
Style B
Style C
Style D
Style D′
50–75 yrs.
40–49 yrs.
30–39 yrs.
20–29 yrs.
20–30 yrs.
20–39 yrs.
Class 9
Class
0–1
2–5
6–8

Figure 3

change since there is no theoretical reason why they should not simply be recurrent features characteristic of particular age groups, to be adopted or abandoned by the individual speaker as he progressed through the generation sequence. Thus, although the investigation of the behaviour of different age groups within the community will introduce into our analysis the factor of time, it will not yet be *real* time in the historical linguist's sense, since such a survey assembles what are after all strictly simultaneous data. This synchronic time factor then we will refer to as the factor of *age*.

We shall first examine the impact of age on the (r) variable studied by Labov. Figure 3 shows the (r)-scores for classes 0 to 8 as compared with that for class 9 according to age groups and styles (Labov 1966: 344f.). The dotted line rising from left to right by steps shows the (r)-score for the upper middle class and represents the target against which the scores for the other classes are measured. It is plain that in all styles the upper middle class has a higher (r = 1) score the lower the age group of the speaker and this, Labov suggests, might be taken to indicate that glide pronunciation is on the increase in the prestige class. Another prominent feature in the graphs is the excessively high (r = 1) scores obtained for middle-aged speakers from the lower middle and the working classes in the more formal styles (represented by the cross-hatched upper parts of the columns where these pass the target line set by the upper middle class). Labov calls this over-performance 'hypercorrection'. It can now be seen that this hypercorrective behaviour on the part of the lower middle class is the reason for the crossing over of the lines in Figure 2, which upset the regular stratification pattern. Labov advances the hypothesis that the crossing over of lines in a stratification pattern coupled with different value patterns in different age groups might be taken as an indication of a change in progress.

After this examination of performance with regard to the (r)-variable, we will now turn to the question of its evaluation by the speaker. Evidence that younger people of all classes are sensitive to the (r)-variable, even when they themselves do not in fact use a glide, is brought out by evaluation tests. This is important, since our statements about the realization of (r) so far might be considered somewhat marginal in view of the fact that only a small percentage of the population does in fact ever use a glide. The results of the evaluation tests shown in Figure (4b) however, when compared with those of the performance tests shown in (3) and (4a), demonstrate that quite irrespective of their own speech younger speakers react uniformly to the (r)-variable. Thus speakers of all classes below the age of forty will rate the same speaker higher on the job scale when he pronounces [r] than when he does not (Labov 1973: 263f.). This means that *age* must be added to the factors which determine

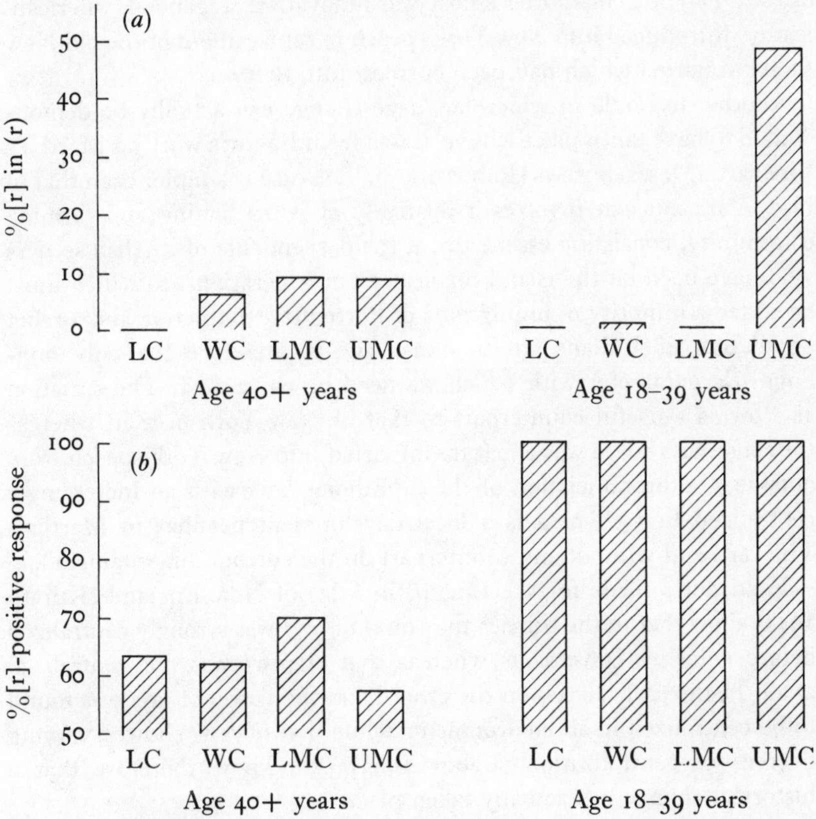

Figure 4

the occurrence of an *r*-glide in the speech of New York City and the rule governing the (r)-variable must be modified to read:

$$(r) \longrightarrow n[r] \; / \; \underline{\qquad} \begin{Bmatrix} C \\ \# \end{Bmatrix}; \; n[r] = f \text{ (class, style, age)}$$

Confirmation of the diachronic hypotheses set up by Labov on the basis of the observed correlation between linguistic variation and age group must be sought outside his survey, which is purely synchronic in nature.[1] In the case of the (r)-variable such evidence does in fact exist.

1 This work is too recent for follow-up studies aimed at testing the actual

Both the Linguistic Atlas of New England (Kurath 1941) and a number of earlier monographs confirm that forty years ago New York speech was, with the exception of an occasional postvocalic glide in the speech of the uppermost class, entirely [r]-less. It would thus appear that the use of an *r*-glide constitutes a post-war innovation, a 'general American' feature introduced into New York speech in replacement of the old New England norms which had been current until then.

Another example in which language change can actually be demonstrated to have taken place will be drawn from Labov's work on Martha's Vineyard, Massachusetts (Labov 1963). The case is simpler than that of New York since it involves a relatively classless fishing and farming community, consisting essentially of the descendants of English settlers who have been on the island for nearly ten generations, to which must be added a minority of immigrants of Portuguese extraction and a relict population of Indians. In this case age is therefore the only non-linguistic parameter with which we need be concerned. The situation also forms a useful counterpart to that of New York in that, whereas the sensitivity to (r) was a feature imported into New York speech from outside, the pronunciation of the diphthong /aw/ with an increasingly centralized first element is a local development peculiar to Martha's Vineyard and without any counterpart on the surrounding mainland.

Field notes made for the Linguistic Atlas of New England (Kurath 1941) show that in the thirties the vowel of /ay/ was strongly centralized before voiceless consonants whereas that of /aw/ was not centralized at all. In the early sixties on the other hand the vowel of /ay/ was found to be centralized in all environments while that of /aw/ showed varying degrees of centralization (Labov 1963). We know therefore that a historical change has actually taken place.

progress of the changes in real time to have been possible. There is, however, one well known case in which the same informants were interviewed a second time after a period of about thirty years. This is Gauchat's (1905) study of the phonetic unity of the speech of Charmey, a small town in the Swiss Alps, which was followed up a generation later by Hermann (1929). During the course of his interviews Gauchat had found certain linguistic differences in the community which could be correlated with differences of age. Hermann found Gauchat's predictions regarding these variables confirmed in so far as the speech of the younger generation was concerned but also found that, of the speakers who had been young at the time of Gauchat's interview and who were now adults, some had modified their realization of the crucial variables further in the direction of the change whereas others had gone back to a more conservative position (cf. Weinreich–Labov–Herzog 1968: 171).

In order to investigate this situation Labov set up an (aw)-variable and studied its realization as a function of both non-linguistic and linguistic structure. His investigations revealed that the transition from the earlier stage in which (aw) showed no sign of centralization to the more recent situation in which it is very strongly centralized in certain positions, especially in the speech of the younger and middle-aged members of the old established settler families, is reflected in the distribution of the various realizations of (aw) according to age group. On the evidence of acoustic analyses Labov divided the phonetic continuum between an uncentralized onset of the diphthong on the one hand and a fully centralized one on the other into four discrete zones, to which he attributed the following numerical values:

(aw = 0) [aʊ] not centralized
(aw = 1) [a^{+}ʊ] ↓
(aw = 2) [ɐʊ]
(aw = 3) [əʊ] fully centralized

If for each lexical item in the test which contains an (aw) the informant's realization of this is assigned a value according to this scale, the extremes being 0 for no centralization and 3 for full centralization, the (aw)-index of a speaker may be calculated. Figure 5 shows the actual distribution of (aw)-values according to age for a number of speakers (Labov 1972a: 274).

The informants ranged in age from over 90 to 31 (column 1). Figure 5a represents the conflated scores of the four informants that were interviewed for the Linguistic Atlas of New England (LANE) in 1933. The average age of these was 65 at the time of their interview which means that, had they been still living in 1963, their ages would have matched that of Labov's oldest informant (5b). In the graphs in column 2 the horizontal axis shows the degree of centralization of (aw) and the vertical axis the number of lexical items for each of the four values. The relative frequency of each of these values for each age group can thus be readily seen. The lexical items used in the questionnaire were divided on a phonological basis into two sets: in the set represented in the graphs by a solid line (aw) is followed by a voiceless obstruent (*house*, *out*, *mouth*, etc.) and in that represented by a broken line it is followed by some other consonant or by pause (*town*, *found*, *now*, *how*, etc.). The absolute number of lexical items for each set is given in the third column, the upper line of figures representing words with (aw) before voiceless

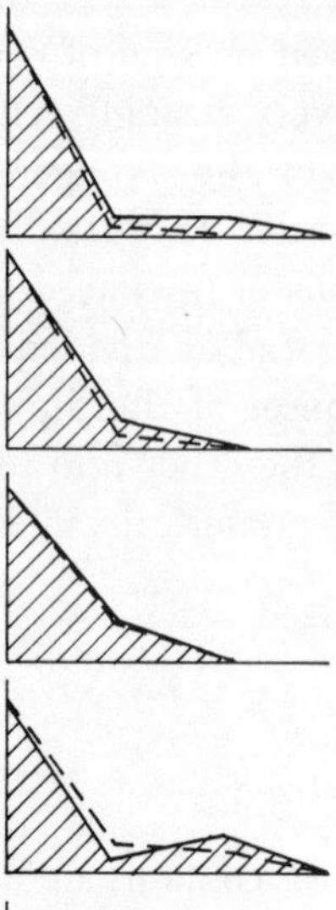

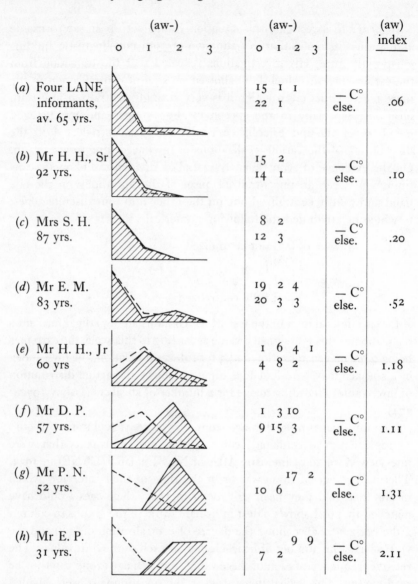

Speaker	(aw-) 0	1	2	3		(aw) index
(*a*) Four LANE informants, av. 65 yrs.	15	1	1		— C°	
	22	1			else.	.06
(*b*) Mr H. H., Sr 92 yrs.	15	2			— C°	
	14	1			else.	.10
(*c*) Mrs S. H. 87 yrs.	8	2			— C°	
	12	3			else.	.20
(*d*) Mr E. M. 83 yrs.	19	2	4		— C°	
	20	3	3		else.	.52
(*e*) Mr H. H., Jr 60 yrs	1	6	4	1	— C°	
	4	8	2		else.	1.18
(*f*) Mr D. P. 57 yrs.	1	3	10		— C°	
	9	15	3		else.	1.11
(*g*) Mr P. N. 52 yrs.			17	2	— C°	
	10	6			else.	1.31
(*h*) Mr E. P. 31 yrs.			9	9	— C°	
	7	2			else.	2.11

Figure 5

obstruent and the lower line the remainder. Finally the right-hand column gives the (aw)-index for each individual speaker.

The graphs show a definite increase in centralization with decreasing age. They also show that centralization is progressively associated with the presence of a following voiceless obstruent, so that in the case of the youngest speakers the distribution of centralized and non-centralized values of (aw) is phonologically determined, centralized allophones occurring before voiceless obstruent and non-centralized ones elsewhere. The situation might in its simplest form be represented by the rule:

$$\begin{bmatrix} +\text{voc} \end{bmatrix} \rightarrow n \begin{bmatrix} -\text{low} \end{bmatrix} \Big/ \underline{\quad\quad} \begin{bmatrix} -\text{cons} \\ +\text{back} \end{bmatrix}; \; n \begin{bmatrix} -\text{low} \end{bmatrix} = \text{f (age)}$$

which merely states that centralization of the vowel onset is a function of age. The rule in this form does not, however, take account of any phonetic conditioning factors and in particular it does not bring out the fact that centralization is becoming increasingly associated with the voicelessness of the following obstruent. A more detailed formulation, in which variable elements are enclosed in angled brackets and their ordering represents their relative weight in implementing the rule, would thus be (Labov 1972d: 123):

$$[+\text{voc}] \longrightarrow \langle -\text{low} \rangle / \underline{\quad} \begin{bmatrix} -\text{cons} \\ +\text{back} \end{bmatrix} \langle +\text{obs} \langle +\text{tense} \langle -\text{cont} \langle +\text{segment} \rangle,$$

the degree *n* of implementation of the rule still being a function of age. This form of the rule embodies the information that of the variable features the obstruent nature of the following consonant is most decisive in producing centralization of the vowel, after that the absence of voicing (represented by [+tense]), next the fact that the segment is not a continuant, next that the diphthong is followed by a segment and not by pause. For younger speakers on the other hand the distribution of centralized and non-centralized values is entirely determined by a single property of the following consonant, namely absence of voice, and the rule is now mandatory. This means it no longer contains any variable elements and has become a categorical rule:

$$[+\text{voc}] \longrightarrow [-\text{low}] / \underline{\quad} \begin{bmatrix} -\text{cons} \\ +\text{back} \end{bmatrix} \begin{bmatrix} +\text{cons} \\ +\text{tense} \end{bmatrix}$$

It can thus be seen that there are two kinds of factor, one non-linguistic and the other linguistic, which govern centralization, namely the informant's age and the phonetic environment of the diphthong. The centralization process of (aw) in fact appears to be following that already taken in the local dialect by (ay). When the interviews for the

Linguistic Atlas were carried out in the thirties centralization of (ay) was noticeable and the phonetic conditions were very similar to those which now determine the variants of (aw); (ay) is now, however, centralized in all positions, so that the presence of a voiceless obstruent was only a transitional conditioning factor in the change process. It appears possible that (aw) will follow the same pattern as (ay) and finally end up centralized in all positions, although such an eventual outcome cannot of course be predicted with certainty.

Sociolinguistically, centralization may be said to correlate with status as a Vineyarder, that is to say with the speaker's sense of local identification with the island in the face of immigration and social pressures from the mainland. It can be shown to have originated with the old-established families but has, in the case of (ay) at least, been taken over also by the Indian and Portuguese inhabitants and has become generally identified with local loyalties.

In the above example, although the change has not altered the structure of the phonological system and although its effect on the two diphthongs concerned is not strictly in phase, these can be shown to be developing in a parallel way. This tendency towards the maintenance of structural symmetry is even more apparent in the case of the development of the long vowels in New York City. We shall see that both (eh) and (oh) are at present in the process of developing very high values ([ɪ:ᵊ], [ʊ:ᵊ] in the casual speech of younger speakers (p. 214f.); this is however accompanied by hypercorrection to a low vowel ([æ:], [ɔ:]) in the more formal styles of the lower middle and upper working classes and by extreme sensitivity to [ɪ:ᵊ] and [ʊ:ᵊ] as stigmatized features in evaluation tests. As in the case of (ay) and (aw) in Martha's Vineyard, both variables can thus be shown to be developing in phonetically parallel ways although, here again, the changes are not simultaneous, (eh) being ahead of (oh). This fact may be taken account of if we say that (oh) is not only a function of class, style, and age but also of (eh). The values for two further variables on the other hand, namely (ah) in *heart*, *hard*, *father* and (ay) in *side*, *my*, appear to depend entirely on the values for (eh) and (oh). The development of all the long vowels may thus be considered to be interdependent in the following way: the realization of (eh) is a function of style, class and age; that of (oh) of style, class, age and (eh); that of (ah) a function of (oh); that of (ay) of both (ah) and (oh) (Weinreich–Labov–Herzog 1968: 172f.). We may interpret this as empirical support for the principle of symmetry and maximum distance between phonemes which was postulated in chapter 2 as governing phonological space.

3 The mechanism of language change

We have seen that the transition between successive language states is achieved by way of intermediate states characterized by the complex but systematic distribution within the speech community of 'old' and 'new' forms; we have also seen that this distribution is governed by variable rules which operate under the joint constraint of both linguistic and non-linguistic factors the forms and relative weightings of which differ from group to group within the community. Of the non-linguistic factors, age is obviously the most important for the historical linguist since its presence in a variable rule indicates that the variation pattern in question is likely to represent a change in progress. Thus, although in retrospect a completed change will give the appearance of a simple categorical rule having been added to the grammar of the language, we see that the process whereby this is actually brought about is the social evaluation by the speakers of the realizations of a linguistic variable within a community. What is relevant to change is thus not the linguistic function of a structural unit but the social information carried by its various realizations.

It will now be seen why it is possible for a change to take a considerable time to reach completion without the rule that governs it being lost in the process. For clearly its *direction* will be maintained and its ultimate *regularity* guaranteed as long as the rule continues to exist, not so much in the performance of individual speakers but rather in their social evaluation of the speech of those around them. In other words, although an individual speaker does not 'know' the rule which governs the change in question, he is aware of the social significance of certain features of performance, or 'accents', indicative of an individual's status within the community. This awareness may be said to form part of his *communicative competence*.[1] The class of words to which a particular

[1] In fact a delicate issue is raised here regarding the scope of linguistic competence, namely the question whether this is reflected in a speaker's performance or in his intentions (that is, the target towards which he is aiming). Labov has amply demonstrated the fact that there may be a considerable discrepancy between performance and intention by showing that speakers may be found who make systematically phonetic distinctions of which they are totally unaware (1972b). The opposite is, however, the more common, namely that items 'known' to be different are pronounced in the same way.

change is applicable is held together by the distribution of the variation rule throughout the community as a whole no matter how incompletely it may be represented in the performance of any individual speaker. This is why the regularity principle does not make it necessary either for all speakers or for all eligible words to achieve the target of a change simultaneously.

It will be recalled that, in an earlier section of this book, we left open the question as to whether phonological change is gradual or instantaneous. The reason for this must now be obvious, for it is of course quite impossible to draw conclusions regarding the change *process* from a simple examination of rules set up in order to link successive grammars which are often separated from one another by centuries. The study of documented cases of change in progress has however helped us to obtain some insight into the way in which change actually appears to take place within a speech community and there is no reason why this process as currently observed need have been any different in the past. If indeed when dealing with past language states we find ourselves obliged to work with fictitiously uniform systems, this is not because we necessarily assume that there was no variation but simply because past variation is not recoverable, both because of the highly conventionalized nature of orthographies and because the methods of reconstruction, dependent on the regularity principle, are only able to recover completed changes.

All this unfortunately still tells us very little about how a change originates, apart from the fact that an innovation would appear to be associated initially with the speech of a particular subgroup of the community and to spread to adjacent groups given favourable socially determined conditions. We have seen that in the case of the *r*-glide the speech of the highest social class acted as the model for the classes situated immediately below it and that the change may be ultimately described as the spread of a prestige feature the origin of which lay outside New York itself.[1] The 'stigmatized' high vowel realizations of

[1] The change in progress in New York City affecting (r) raises an intriguing problem. Should the rule introducing an *r*-glide into preconsonantal and final position eventually reach completion, the resulting situation would in retrospect, and in the absence of detailed documentation of the currently observable intermediate stage, be interpreted diachronically as if no change had taken place at all, that is to say there would be no indication that New York speech had ever lost the glide allophone in these positions. In actual fact, however, it would have undergone first a partial merger and then a reversal of that merger, a situation which cannot be represented in a simple linear model of language change as described in the

(eh) and (oh) on the other hand represented the spread of a local feature up the social scale from a lower class origin, though this process is accompanied by hypercorrection. The aspirations and loyalties associated with the [ɪ:ᵊ] and [ʊ:ᵊ] values of these variables must clearly be very different from those associated with the *r*-glide. Labov attempted to capture the social values associated with them by eliciting in the evaluation tests the informant's estimate of the speaker's chances of winning a street fight and to assess his attitude to the speaker by asking him whether he would want him as a personal friend. However, even informants who answered positively in respect of these values still responded to [ɪ:ᵊ] and [ʊ:ᵊ] as stigmatized features in so far as job prospects were concerned.

All this suggests that linguistic heterogeneity is in itself a constant source of change and that, at the phonological level at least, a great deal of language change is likely to have a social motivation. Very much less work has been done outside the phonological level, although in principle the concept of the variable is of course equally applicable to all structural levels. In the case of lexical replacement it is certainly a well-attested fact that on the one hand dialect words which do not have a cognate in the standard language are likely to be lost and that on the other dialects do constitute a source of lexical innovation for standard languages. However, if one considers the interchange which results from a contact situation as a source of linguistic innovation, there is no reason why this should be limited to varieties of one and the same language. We shall return to this aspect in the following chapter. It should however be stressed that, in spite of its undoubted importance in this respect, language contact is by no means the *only* innovatory factor in language change, both analogy (p. 32ff.) and sound symbolism (p. 11f., 42) being internal forces which have considerable creative potential.

first part of this book. The presently observable change affecting (r) is only meaningful in terms of a model of language change which takes account of co-existing varieties of a language in a contact situation. This example shows how large a discrepancy there may be between a living sociolinguistic situation and the retrospective appraisal of data which have survived only in documentary form and which are interpreted in terms of a linear model based on the principle of descriptive economy.

6
Contact between languages

In this chapter we will consider the various ways in which different languages, as opposed to mere geographical or social varieties of the same language, may be affected by mutual contact. Although all transfer of language material across language boundaries may be said to be the result of some measure of bilingualism on the part of those who do the conveying, the precise nature and extent of the linguistic exchange will depend upon the detailed circumstances of the social and cultural relations between the communities concerned. In the following pages the notion of 'contact' will be interpreted in a very wide sense, so as to include not only close geographical proximity but also trade relations and other types of cultural encounter of varying degrees of sophistication. The most superficial kind of language contact is probably that which exists between the producers or conveyors of some commodity and their clients in other language areas, and it is a well-documented fact of recent language history that the names of such objects of international trade as *tea*, *coffee*, or *tobacco* readily travel with them and become part of the consumers' language. At the other end of the scale the most intensive kind of contact may be said to exist in fully bilingual communities, and here not merely lexical items but even phonological and grammatical rules may come to be shared by the languages in question.

Language contact therefore always presupposes some degree of cultural contact, however limited. And since, of all sectors of language, it is the lexicon which reflects the culture of its speakers most closely we shall in our consideration of the results of cultural contact on language turn first of all to the lexicon.

1 Lexical borrowing

1.1 *Loan-words*

For our first example of 'loaning', or 'borrowing',[1] we will take the transfer of lexical material which was to result from the encounter of the Germanic peoples with the worlds of Classical Antiquity and of the early Christian Church. The immense impact that these had upon the spiritual and material culture of the Germanic peoples may be inferred from the large number of lexical items which they borrowed from both Classical and Vulgar Latin. For some of these words Latin is not of course the ultimate source,[2] but what matters for our present purposes is that they all came in through Latin and in a Latin form. Table 1 gives a sample drawn from the five hundred or so words which entered the West Germanic languages from Latin during this earliest period of contact.

We are not here immediately concerned with the procedure whereby words are identified by the linguist as loans, but rather with the phenomena associated with the transfer of lexical material across language boundaries as known from the study of loan-words after these have been established as such. We may however briefly say at this point that these words are considered to be borrowed from Latin because they are innovations in both Old English and Old High German and show a systematic formal relationship with items of identical or closely associated meaning in Latin. Their identification as loans from Latin is also of course greatly facilitated by the fact that many are members of specific semantic fields referring to institutions, technical skills, etc. – the Church, book-learning, horticulture, building in stone – known to have been heavily influenced by Roman culture. We shall furthermore proceed in the following discussion as if our arguments were based solely upon an examination of the listed words. This is of course a considerable oversimplification of the reality, since we have at our disposal additional data and analyses which cannot be given here. As a result, what might on the face of it appear to be perfectly feasible alternative solutions have sometimes been ignored.

A number of observations can be made with regard to the *phonological*

[1] Although not altogether satisfactory (it has been remarked that the donor language never gets its 'loaned' or 'borrowed' words back) these are the established terms. *Loan-word* is a loan translation of German *Lehnwort*.

[2] *Discus*, *cista*, *monasterium* and *scola* come from Greek, *abbas* (via Biblical Greek) from Aramaic, *matta* from Punic (perhaps introduced by Saint Augustine), *piper* and *vinum* (through Greek) from other sources.

TABLE I

Latin	Old English	Old High German	Modern English	Modern German
abbās (acc. abbātem)	abbud	abbat	abbot	Abt
altāre	altare	altāri, altar	altar	Altar
cappa	cæppe	kappa	cap	Kappe
cāseus	cēse	kāsi	cheese	Käse
cella 'chamber'	cell	cella	cell	Zelle
cista	cist, cest	kista	chest	Kiste
coquīna, *cocīna	cycene	chuhhina	kitchen	Küche
cuppa	cuppe	kopf, chuph	cup	Kopf 'head'
discus 'quoit'	disc 'dish; table'	tisc 'dish; table'	dish	Tisch 'table'
matta	matte	matta	mat	Matte
menta	minte	minza	mint	Minze
mīlia (passuum) '1,000 (paces)'	mīl	mīla	mile	Meile
missa	mæsse	missa, messe	mass	Messe
monēta '(coined) money'	mynet	muniȝȝa	mint	Münze 'coin; mint'
monastērium, *monistērium	mynster	munistri	minster	Münster
palma	palm(a)	palma	palm	Palme
pāpa, *papes	pāpa	bābes	pope	Papst
pix (acc. picem)	pic	peh, beh	pitch	Pech
piper	pipor	pfeffar	pepper	Pfeffer
planta 'slip, cutting'	plante	pflanza	plant	Pflanze
pondo (abl.)	pund	pfunt	pound	Pfund
prūnum	plūme	pfrūma, pflūmo	plum	Pflaume
saccus 'bag'	sacc	sac	sack	Sack
sc(h)ōla	scōl	scuola	school	Schule
(via) strāta 'paved (road)'	strǣt	strāȝ(ȝ)a	street	Strasse
tēgula 'roof-tile'	tigele	ziagal	tile	Ziegel
templum	tempel	tempal	temple	Tempel
vallum 'rampart, wall'	weall	wal	wall	Wall 'rampart'
vīnum	wīn	wīn	wine	Wein

form of the words in Table 1. Let us first examine the reflexes in English and German of the Latin plosives. While Latin /p/ is uniformly represented in English by /p/, it may be represented in German by /p/, /pf/ or /f/. The latter two reflexes, however, are clearly the result of the High German Consonant Shift on an original */p/ and these sound correspondences taken together indicate that Latin /p/ was always identified with a /p/ phoneme in both English and German. In the case of German some of the words must have been borrowed early enough for their Latin /p/ to have been equated with the Germanic */p/ before it underwent the shift, whereas those which have a /p/ in Modern German must have been taken over after the shift had ceased to operate and the phonemic system of German had acquired a 'new' /p/.[1] The case of Latin /t/ is parallel to that of /p/; while English has /t/ throughout, German has /t/ in *Abt*, *Altar*, *Matte* and *Tempel*, but /ts/ or /s/ (both resulting regularly from the High German Consonant Shift) in *Ziegel*, *Pflanze*, *Strasse*, *Minze* and *Münze*.

Latin /k/ on the other hand, represented by the orthographic symbol *c*, has different reflexes not only in German (/k/ and /ts/) but also in English, where it appears either as /k/, /tʃ/ or /s/. German /k/ it will be seen corresponds to either /k/ or /tʃ/ in English, whereas German /ts/ regularly corresponds to English /s/. How are we to account for this distribution? It will be remembered that the reflexes in the Romance languages of Proto-Romance initial */k/ show that it was palatalized differently depending upon the nature of the following vowel (p. 28f.). Thus in French, for instance, while */ko/ has remained unpalatalized as /ko/, */ka/ has become /ʃa/ and */ke/ and */ki/ have become /se/ and /si/. If we now consider the reflexes in German of *cista* and *cella*, in both of which initial /k/ is followed by a front vowel, it would appear that *Kiste* must have been borrowed while the initial consonant was still a [k] whereas in the case of *Zelle* this must already have undergone some degree of palatalization – to [tʃ] (as it has remained in Italian) or perhaps already as far as [ts] (which would be an intermediate step on the way to French [s̩]). The reflexes /tʃ/ and /s/ in English could then be accounted for in the same way as being due to borrowing at different periods, [tʃ] being the reflex of /k/ before its palatalization and /s/ after its palatalization. We may thus assume that this palatalization process

1 This 'new' /p/ of the standard language largely represents the voiceless bilabial plosives of words imported from Latin and from those High German dialects which had devoiced the old Germanic */b/.

in Romance must, like the High German Consonant Shift, have fallen *within* the period of borrowing by late West Germanic from Romance that is reflected in our list of words.[1]

If we now turn to the reflexes /k/ and /tʃ/ in English, although this also is a relationship of non-palatalized to palatalized forms, the explanation for the different treatment must here be sought within the history of English itself. The situation regarding these two reflexes is neatly captured in the English word *kitchen*, from Latin *cocīna* (earlier *coquīna*). There are several arguments which suggest that the palatalization of its medial /k/ cannot be the result of the Romance palatalization but that its source word must have been borrowed before this took place. In the first place, the palatalization process in Romance was different, resulting in French for instance in a voiced fricative (*cuisine*, /kɥizin/). Secondly, assuming that the word entered English and German at approximately the same time, the German reflex *Küche* presupposes a source form [koki:na] and not for instance *[kotsi:na] since its medial [x] is the regular outcome of a pre-Shift intervocalic */k/. And finally, that palatalization of /k/ to /tʃ/ took place independently in English is demonstrated by such examples as English *chin*, when compared with its cognates (German *Kinn*, Swedish *kind* 'cheek', Greek *génys* 'jaw', etc.).

It will be noted that the initial /k/ of Modern English *kitchen* has not been palatalized in spite of the fact that it is followed by a high front vowel, and this is an important indicator of the chronology of certain vowel changes in English. For clearly at the time when palatalization was taking place this vowel cannot yet have had its present high front quality, which must therefore be the result of a subsequent change. As in the case of the first vowel of *minster* and *mint* (< *monēta*), this must be the result of umlaut on an earlier /u/. This can in fact easily be seen from the Old English spellings *cycene*, *mynster* and *mynet*, where the orthographic sign *y* represents the rounded front vowel /ü/ which regularly resulted from the umlaut of the back vowel */u/ and which was later to become unrounded and to merge with /i/. The /i/ in these words must then come from an earlier /u/. If we turn to their Latin forms, however, we do not find an /u/ but an /o/. The argument used in order to account for the development of the Old English forms of these words from their Latin sources runs therefore as follows. We have seen that Latin /o/ has been replaced by an /u/ and that this /u/ sub-

1 Consequently, as R.Lass has pointed out, Modern English *cell* cannot be the direct reflex of Old English *cell* but must be a reborrowing from French.

sequently underwent umlaut. But for this to have taken place it must have been followed by an /i(:)/ in the next syllable. The later forms of the words also show that this /i/ must have been short. We must therefore assume that the vowels of the second syllables of the Latin words all became /i/. This obviously poses no problem in the case of *monisterium*, which already has /i/ in this position, but in the cases of *cocīna* and *monēta* it requires the shortening of the /i:/ and the raising and shortening of the /e:/. These changes can be explained as due to the word stress having been shifted during the borrowing process so as to conform to the native Germanic system of the time, which demanded that stress fall on the initial syllable.[1] In the same way these words must have been adapted to the native phonotactic rules, which did not allow a sequence /–oCi–/ so that this was replaced by the nearest permissible sequence /–uCi–/. We are thus able to account for the fact that Latin /o/ was rendered by Germanic /u/ and not by /o/. We may therefore postulate for these loan-words an initial adaptation of the foreign form to the native phonological system and a subsequent evolution within the new system somewhat along the following lines: */ko'ki:na/ > */'kukina/ > /kütʃene/ > /kitʃən/; /moni'ste:rium/ > */'munister/ > /münster/ > /minstə/; /mo'ne:ta/ > */'munita/ > /münet/ > /mint/.

It will be seen from the above examples that where loan-words are concerned phonological correspondences may be set up by comparing the segments of a word in the donor language with the corresponding segments in the recipient language and that, *for any specific point in time*, these correspondences are quite as regular as are those between cognate words in related languages. In the case of loan-words in German and English from Vulgar Latin (or Early Romance) we have to establish four different correspondence sets, since each of the languages involved – the donor and both recipient languages – underwent phonological changes during the protracted borrowing period. Thus /k/ underwent palatalization independently in both Early Romance and English while in German it underwent either affrication or assibilation depending upon the environment. We can set up the following correspondence series between Vulgar Latin/Early Romance, Modern English and Standard German for the reflexes of Latin /k/ in initial position:

1 We see here an example of the important role played by prosodic factors in the further development of the forms in Germanic, with the dependence of segmental phonological structure on prosodic rules (see Allen 1973: 11 regarding the dominant role of prosodic features).

	Vulgar Latin/Early Romance	Modern English	Standard German	Example
(1a)	k	k	k	*kitchen, Küche; cup, Kopf*
(1b)	k	tʃ	k	*chest, Kiste*
(2)	k	k	k	*cap, Kappe*
(3)	ts	s	ts	*cell, Zelle*

Correspondence series (1) and (2) represent early borrowings which took place while the reflex of Latin /k/ was still a velar plosive [k], whereas series (3) represents later loans which were transmitted after it had become palatalized in certain environments. The difference between series (1a) and (1b) has a parallel origin, namely the fact that Old English /k/ became palatalized before the front vowels (the distinction between [k] before back vowels and [tʃ] before front vowels was initially only allophonic in Old English and the two correspondence series were thus in complementary distribution and, as far as the period of borrowing is concerned, count as a single series; subsequently, however, after umlaut and the unrounding of the resulting [ü] to [i], [k] and [tʃ] came to contrast in identical environments). We have seen that the Old High German Consonant Shift also fell within the period of borrowing, and we would therefore expect it to be reflected in a difference between series (1) for pre-Shift loans and series (2) for post-Shift loans. Unfortunately, as we have already seen, Standard German /k/ is ambiguous, representing both the shifted reflex of Germanic */k/ and a new post-Shift /k/.[1] As a consequence, in so far as /k/ is concerned, the two correspondence series are identical. If however we substitute /p/ for /k/, the distinction between them becomes visible, so that we can re-write series (1) and (2) as:

(1)	p	p	pf	*pepper, Pfeffer*
(2)	p	p	p	*palm, Palme*

The period at which a word was borrowed may thus be determined at least relatively by establishing in which changes known to have occurred in both the donor and the recipient languages it has and has not participated. Conversely if the period of borrowing is known, for

[1] There are Modern German dialects, for instance in Switzerland, which differentiate the two, and earlier forms belonging to such dialects are sometimes represented in the Old High German spellings (cf. *chuph*, *chuhhina*). The contrast equally shows up in medial position, as in pre-Shift *Küche* versus post-Shift *Dekan* ('dean'), from Latin *decānus*.

instance on the basis of external evidence such as dated documents or because of the nature of the referent, this may help in dating the linguistic changes in question. For once a loan-word has been integrated into a language, all subsequent changes undergone by that language and to which it qualifies as input will automatically affect it in exactly the same way as if it were a native word. (We will for the moment beg the question as to what precisely constitutes integration but will return to this point shortly.)

Apart from providing them with numerous loan-words as the result of prolonged contact, Latin is also *genealogically related* to English and German. Thus in cognate words Latin /p/ regularly corresponds to /f/, and /k/ to /h/, in both English and German while /t/ corresponds to /θ/ in English and to /d/ in German. Compare for example the initial consonants of the following words in the three languages:

Latin	English	German
pater	father	Vater /'fa:tər/
trēs	three	drei
caput	head	Haupt[1]

The differences between the Latin and the Germanic reflexes of these sounds are due to the fact that the Germanic languages underwent the First Consonant Shift whereas Latin has essentially retained the old Proto-Indo-European consonants. Thus, if related languages again come into a contact situation, the correspondence series established for cognates may be different from those for loan-words. This is not however, *necessarily* so, since the presence of formal differences between correspondence series presupposes changes in at least one of the languages after their separation and if this had taken place only a short time before the borrowing, no such changes may yet have occurred. Conflicting correspondence series, that is to say correspondence series in non-complementary distribution, therefore necessarily imply an extended relationship between the languages concerned, although this may be either one of contact at more than one point in time or of common origin followed at some later period by renewed contact.

[1] Old English *hēafod*, Old High German *houbet* (> *Haupt*) and cognates elsewhere in Germanic presuppose a protoform **haubuþ-* (< **/kauput-*), which does not fully correspond to Latin *caput* (< **/kaput-/*). The exact counterpart of the Latin form appears to be attested in Old English *hafud*, Old Norse *hǫfuð*. The existence of such variant or 'skewed' protoforms, although untidy, is not unusual.

English has of course borrowed not only directly from Latin but also over a period of many centuries from its descendant language French. Furthermore, it has again in recent times turned to Latin as a source of morphs and patterns of word-formation, these latter often pseudo-Latin, in order to meet the ever pressing demand for new scientific and technical terms (*carboniferous*, *insecticide*, *binoculars*, *supersonic*, etc.). In a case like that of English, therefore, questions of chronology are clearly of paramount importance and one of the most important keys to this is provided by differences in the correspondence series. Consider for instance the Latin word *caput* 'head' and the related English words, *head*, *chief*, *chef*, *chieftain*, *captain*, *chapter* and *capital*. Modern English *head* is the continuation of Old English *heafod* from Proto-Germanic **hauƀuþ-*, which itself is cognate with Latin *caput*. All the remaining words are loans going back ultimately to Latin *caput* or to one or other of its derivatives. Thus *chief* is from Medieval French *chef* 'head' and *chef* from Modern French *chef* (*de cuisine*) 'head cook'; *chieftain* and *captain* are from Medieval French *chevetain* and *capitaine*, both ultimately from Late Latin *capitān*(*e*)*us*; *chapter* is from Medieval French *chapitre*, ultimately from Latin *capitulum* 'title at the head of a section'; *capital* is a recent borrowing from French *capital*, which was itself borrowed from Latin (*capitālis* adj. 'of the head').

We have so far dealt with the question of phonological correspondences and relative chronology without however explicitly mentioning the phonetic and phonological interpretation of written forms. It has nevertheless become apparent from our comparisons that the way in which borrowed words are treated by a recipient language throws a great deal of light on the phonetic realization of specific phonemes in both the donor and the recipient languages at the time of borrowing. We have seen for instance that the Modern German form *Küche* presupposes a [k] in medial position when it was borrowed and thus indicates that Latin *c* must still have been pronounced as [k] at that period. The combined evidence of spelling and cross-language equations of sounds in loan-words is in fact one of the major sources for the establishment of the earlier phonetic values of orthographic signs (Allen 1965: vi; 1974: vii, 152).

Loan-words are innovations which cannot be accounted for in terms of inheritance and which can at the same time be systematically related to items in a donor language. We arrive at their form at the time of borrowing by reconstructing backwards, using the rules of the historical grammar of the recipient language, until we reach a form as close as possible to that of the source in the donor language. The comparison of the forms in donor and recipient languages then gives the correspondences between the two languages at the time of borrowing and their differences are to be ascribed to differences in the phonological systems of the languages concerned. This brings us to the question of the integration of loans into the recipient language. Discrepancies like that noted between the Latin source /mo'ne:ta/ and the earliest reconstructed Pre-English form */'munita/, or between /ko'ki:na/ and /'kukina/, are interpreted as the result of assimilation of 'foreign' forms to the phonological system of the recipient language. Unfortunately in the case of such ancient borrowings the assimilation process itself is no longer directly observable, although it can to a large extent be inferred from its results. In order to study the integration process itself we must therefore turn to present-day evidence. English words such as *restaurant* and *garage*, which have been borrowed only very recently from French, when pronounced ['rɛstrɔ̃] with final nasalized vowel and [gə'rɑ:ʒ] stressed on the second syllable and with [ʒ] in word-final position, are said to be unassimilated or only partially assimilated loans since they contain features which are 'foreign' to the native English system. Such features are typical of recently borrowed words and would appear to be felt as being in some way abnormal by native speakers since there is a general tendency for them to be eliminated by the language during the course of time, the normal outcome of this process being complete integration to the phonological rules of the recipient language. Thus when the above-mentioned loans from French are pronounced ['gæridʒ] and ['rɛstrənt] or ['rɛstrɔnt] they are said to be fully assimilated, the sounds they contain and the distribution of these being identical with those of native English words. Incompletely integrated forms, which may be preferred by speakers with some knowledge of the donor language, cause problems in any synchronic phonological description. If they are considered to have the same status in the language as any other word, certain general statements which could otherwise be made concerning the recipient language have to be abandoned, in the present case for example that in English there are no nasalized vowels and that [ʒ] never occurs in word-final position after vowel. Alternatively, words of this kind may be dealt with by setting up secondary or marginal phonological systems alongside the primary one (Fries and Pike 1949; Henderson 1951; Chomsky and Halle 1968: 373ff.). A decision as to which of these two solutions should be adopted is likely to be based on quantitative considerations. Thus if only a small number of words violate the 'native' rules, it may be more economical to simply mark them as exceptional in the lexicon and to keep the phonological system intact. If on the other hand their number is large it may be found preferable to modify the system so as to accommodate them. The situation is well illustrated by the change which took place in the status of the labial fricatives [f] and [v] in English. In Old English, prior to the influx of large numbers of loan-words from French, these can best be treated respectively as the initial-final and the medial allophones of a single phoneme. With the increasing number of loan-words from French having an initial *v-* (*village*, *veal*, *vine*, *very*, etc.) the balance was eventually altered in favour of an analysis which recognizes them as distinct phonemes. Whatever the solution adopted in any particular case, the problem will still remain of how in a synchronic description one should handle doublets, that is to say co-existing pronunciations of the same word *within a single grammar*, such competition between alternative forms being characteristic of recent borrowing.

Whether one adopts a strictly monosystemic approach or one which recognizes co-existent phonological systems, only some of the loan-words will be detectable on the basis of their incomplete accommodation to the synchronic phonology of the recipient language. In either case words which are in fact loans will go undetected, their phonological structure either matching that of the recipient language from the start or being so close to it that integration is more or less immediate. In cases on the other hand where there are substantial differences of phonological structure between the donor and the recipient languages, one might expect unintegrated forms to persist longer. In fact, however, there is no evidence that this is so, the speed and degree of integration of borrowed items apparently depending at least as much on socio-linguistic as on structural factors. Thus there are sociolinguistic contexts in which borrowing takes place not directly from the source language as spoken by native speakers, but rather through the intermediary of a local form of it which has already been to a very large extent adapted to the structures of the recipient language. In such cases the integration process may be carried very far indeed, so that the outcome may bear little resemblance structurally (and occasionally semantically) to its original source in the donor language. English loan-words in various Indian and Pakistani languages for instance have been transmitted through the medium of 'Indian English', which opposes dental and retroflex consonants. Thus English *three* /θri:/becomes [t̪ri:] and English *station*/steiʃn/becomes [s̪ṭe:ʃən], [s̪əṭe:ʃən] or [əs̪ṭeʃən]. Equally in the case of Swahili it is the section of the population bilingual in both Swahili and a local variety of English that has acted as the transmitter of loans so that we find such forms as /kip'lefiti/ 'traffic island' from *keep left*, /'taipuraita/ for *typewriter*, /'pakiti/ (and also/'pakti/) for *packet*, /'zipu/ for *zip*, /'kundu'rati/ for *contract*, /blekibodi/ for *blackboard*, etc. in which consonant clusters have been almost totally eliminated in conformity with Swahili phonotactic rules (Whiteley 1967a). The transmission of loans through the intermediary of *a local spoken variety of the donor language* is an easily observable phenomenon today, and we may safely assume that parallel situations existed in the past. The special features of such partially assimilated local varieties of languages are, however, rarely reflected in written records so that, although 'imperfect' second language learning is likely to be one of the ways in which the gap between a source form (such as /mo'ne:ta/) and the nearest reconstructed form in the recipient language (such as /'munita/) is bridged, there is unlikely to be concrete evidence of the process.

If we now turn to the *morphology* of loan-words it must be obvious that, since these have to be used like any other words in sentences of the recipient language, they must be subject to its syntactic rules. Thus in English borrowed nouns will have to inflect for plural while borrowed verbs will have to inflect for present (in the third person singular) and for past and will also have to distinguish a present and a past participle. With regard to the actual morphs representing these categories, in theory loan-words might either retain those of the donor language or adopt the appropriate English ones and we shall see that nouns and verbs do not behave identically in this respect. In the case of learned vocabulary in particular, borrowed nouns have sometimes brought their plural morphs with them from the donor language (*criteria*, *phenomena* from Greek, *cacti*, *indices*, *genera* from Latin). This means that certain of the unpredictable (or 'lexically conditioned') allomorphs of the English plural morpheme belong to loan-words whereas others (like those of *men*, *children*, *mice*, etc.) are native archaisms so that a borrowed noun cannot be identified simply on the basis of the morphological irregularity of its plural. The great majority of nouns have however been assimilated to the productive rules of English, so that one says *commas* (and not *commata*), *atlases* (and not *atlantes*), *cellos* (and not *celli*), *sputniks* (and not *sputniki*), *Volkswagens* (and not *Volkswagen*), etc. This may on the face of it appear to be a very 'natural' situation, but we shall see that the same process does not necessarily occur in all languages. Although a number of foreign inflectional morphs have been retained in the case of nouns, borrowed verbs today follow without exception the productive morphological rules of English (that is to say they suffix the appropriate sibilant for the third person singular present, the appropriate alveolar plosive for the past tense and past participle, and the suffix *-ing* for the present participle). And not only do they reject the use of all foreign inflectional suffixes but, with the solitary exception of the Old English verb *scrīfan* 'to write' from Latin *scrībere*, they do not inflect according to the 'irregular' strong conjugation.[1] The verb *scrīfan* has since been lost, but its German counterpart *schreiben*, which strikingly is also the only exception in that language, still survives. When we were dealing with analogical change we mentioned that analogical formations reflect the morphological patterns current at the time of the change and the same is of course true in the case of loan-words. If these are integrated the process will naturally follow the morphological rules productive at the time of integration and thus constitute evidence of what these were.

Although always totally integrated inflectionally, verbs of foreign origin in English raise a number of interesting problems in so far as their *derivational* morphology is concerned. Verbs like *to create*, *to contaminate*, *to ordinate*, *to incorporate*, *to terminate* were borrowed, for the most part in Middle English times, from Latin and it can easily be seen that their English form continues not the infinitive of the Latin verb (*creāre*, *contamināre*, etc.) but rather its past participle in *-ātus*. The inflectional morphology of Latin is of course very much more complex than that of English so that theoretically borrowed verbs might have entered in any one of a number of forms. Leaving aside the question of *why* these particular ones came in in the form of past participles, which is properly a matter of syntax, our concern here is *how* the termination *-ate* was interpreted morphologically in the recipient language. At first there was apparently some oscillation in its interpretation so that it was treated sometimes as an allomorph of the English past participle morpheme and sometimes as part of the verbal stem, to which the Eng-

1 The only other exceptions to this generalization are one or two members of a small group of what were originally weak verbs which went over to the strong inflection by analogy (see p. 35f.).

lish participial ending *-ed* was then added. We know that eventually it was the latter interpretation which was to prevail so that the ending *-ate* has now become no more than a 'semantically empty verb suffix' (Marchand 1960: 199f.). Its morphemic status in present-day English is in fact extremely marginal since, with few exceptions, segmentation leaves morphologically isolated forms (*cre-*, *contamin-* etc.) and its only possible function is that of marker of the verbal status of the lexeme in question (and perhaps to some slight degree its register). On the other hand the element *-ate* stands in very close derivational relationship to the nominal suffix *-ation* (*creation*, *contamination*, etc.) from Latin *-ātio*, *-ātiōnem*, and in certain registers of English it has become extremely productive as a means of creating new verbs from Latin lexical resources. Thus *to facilitate*, *to incapacitate*, *to paginate*, although based on Latin stems, are all purely English formations which lack any corresponding Latin verb in *-āre*. Scientific English, which has a 'Neo-Latin' basis, contains innumerable examples (*to chlorinate*, *to encapsulate*, *to dehydrate*, etc.) and it has also entered the everyday language in forms like *to orchestrate*, *to hyphenate*, *to cremate*.

The phenomenon of verbs borrowed from Latin appearing in English in the participial form is not restricted to those which end in *-ate*, for verbs like *to conduct*, *to dismiss*, *to convict*, *to act* also have a structure which matches most closely that of the Latin past participle. But there are also plenty of other verbs, sometimes even from the same Latin stems as verbs which have entered as participles (*to reduce*, *to remit*, *to convince*), which continue present tense forms of the source language so that by no means all the Latin verbs which were borrowed by English came in as participles. Nor does the mere fact that a present-day English verb resembles a Latin past participle necessarily imply that it was actually borrowed in that form. Thus the verb *to act* would appear to come not from *actus*, past participle of the Latin verb *agere*, but rather from the noun *actus* or *actum*.

English derivational morphology is rendered particularly complex by the existence of a large number of derivationally related word sets based on such suffix pairs as *-al* and *-ality*, *-ize* and *-ization*, *-ify* and *-ification*, *-ous* and *-osity*, *-able/-ible* and *-ability/-ibility*. In some of these sets both items have been borrowed from Latin or French, but in other cases only one is a loan and the other has been formed analogically in English, the patterns having become productive. For the historical linguist this raises in each individual case the delicate question of priority, that is to say what was the order of borrowing within the set, which forms are direct loans and which are analogical formations. However, although certain of these Romance derivational patterns have become productive in English, they are rarely extended to native Germanic lexical material. The only notable exceptions to this are the suffixes *-able* (*eatable*, *washable*, *drinkable*, etc.) and *-er* (*baker*, *driver*, *sleeper*, etc.).

At the syntactic level loan-words have to be integrated into the word-class system of the recipient language. In the case of borrowing from Latin into English the fit between word classes is sufficiently close for problems of assignment not to arise. The same is true in the case of English and German with the exception that the German noun class is subdivided into three genders whereas English nouns have no grammatical gender. Any noun borrowed by German from English must therefore be assigned to a gender class and this principle in fact applies to all borrowed nouns, even when taken from a language with a formally comparable gender system such as Latin or French, for nouns borrowed from these do not as might perhaps be expected necessarily bring their genders with them. As a general principle there would appear to be two criteria which determine the assignment of a borrowed noun to a gender class, namely its phonological form and the gender of synonyms and semantically related words in the recipient language. In so far as phonological form is concerned the great majority of morphologically simple native feminine nouns in German end in the weak vowel *-ə*, whereas masculine and neuter nouns tend to end in a consonant. On this basis the recently borrowed English word *Stress* might have been assigned either to masculine or to neuter gender. That it is masculine rather than neuter is probably due to the fact that other nouns within the same semantic field are masculine (cf. *Kampf* 'struggle', *Zwang* 'constraint', *Druck* 'pressure'). Presumably it is also on phonological grounds that German *Sport*, *Smoking*, *Jazz*, *Pop* and *Trip* are all masculine, whereas *Party*, *Bowle* 'punch' (from English *bowl*), *Mode* (from French *mode*, feminine), *Kravatte* 'tie' (from French *cravatte*, feminine), and *Violine* 'violin' (from Italian *violino*, masculine) are all feminine; *Bajonett* 'bayonet' (from French *baïonette*, feminine), *Konzert* 'concert' (from Italian *concerto*, masculine), and *Coca-Cola* on the other hand are neuter. Why the English loans *Bar*, *Whisky* and *Kricket* should be respectively feminine, masculine, and neuter is hard to say but it would seem that the gender of semantically close nouns rather than phonological criteria may have been responsible (cf. *Schenke* 'bar' feminine, *Schnaps* 'spiritous liquor' masculine, and *Fussballspiel*, *Tennisspiel* 'football, tennis game' neuter).

The role played by phonological form in the assignment of borrowed nouns to concord classes may be illustrated by the following examples from Swahili, a Bantu language in which nouns fall into a very much larger number of noun classes than the three genders of our European languages. English *mudguard* and *marching-order* have been treated in Swahili as plurals because their initial CV sequence resembles the plural marker of the *ma*-class and, since words of this class normally lack an overt marker in the singular, these words have ended up in Swahili as singular *digadi* and *ching'oda*, plural *madigadi* and *maching'oda*. English *keep left* on the other hand has been assigned to the *ki*-class, the prefix in this case marking the singular and corresponding to a plural prefix *vi*-, so that the final forms in Swahili are singular *kiplefiti*, plural *viplefiti* (Whiteley 1967b).

Finally, with regard to which lexical classes are most susceptible to borrowing, it is generally claimed that members of the 'open' classes (nouns, verbs, adjectives) are more readily borrowed than those of the 'closed' classes (pronouns, conjunctions, prepositions) and that nouns are the most frequently borrowed class everywhere (Haugen 1950). This distribution could however be to some extent simply a reflection of the overall sizes of the classes concerned and of the fact that the great majority of borrowed words are the names of new objects or materials. It is on the other hand to be expected that the class membership of borrowed items will also depend on the nature of the sociolinguistic context in which the borrowing takes place. Thus the borrowing of conjunctions and adverbs is well attested in bilingual communities (cf. Rayfield 1970, for Yiddish in America) but this would hardly seem likely in for instance the much more limited contact situation of trading. There is of course the well-known case of the borrowing by English of the pronouns *they* and *them* from Scandinavian in replacement of Old English *hī*(*e*) and *him*, although this probably took place in a context of considerable mutual intelligibility between Danes and Anglo-Saxons. It would at any rate seem likely that borrowing from closed classes will only be possible in situations of intense linguistic exchange since it presupposes the cross-linguistic equation of *syntactic* patterns, whereas mere lexical borrowing from open classes would require only a minimum of bilingual speakers in the transmission process. We shall return to this question in the section on grammatical borrowing.

From the *semantic* point of view loan-words may constitute mere additions to the lexicon of the recipient language (*tea*, *orang-outang*, *camera*), may replace native words (*fiancé(e)*, *mercy*), or may cause the semantic reinterpretation of specific lexical fields (*profound* versus *deep*, *mutton* versus *sheep*, *acid* versus *sour*). Some degree of semantic reinterpretation during the borrowing process is in fact extremely common, so that French *dancing* means 'dance hall', German and French *Smoking* means 'dinner jacket', German *Keks* /ke:ks/ (from English *cakes*) means 'biscuit' whereas German *Biskuit* refers to the light kind of cake-mixture used for sandwich cakes.

In this section we have considered the most direct kind of lexical borrowing, namely the adoption by and integration into a recipient language of both the form and meaning of a lexical item originating in another language. We shall now turn to certain other more subtle types of lexical borrowing.

1.2 *Loan translations (calques)*

Although the sample of Latin loan-words in English and German given in Table 1 contains a number of words relating to Christianity, it may have been noticed that many of the key concepts of the Christian faith are missing. And if we stop to consider the situation of the missionary faced with the task of introducing the concepts and institutions of an entirely new religion to a pagan people, the transfer from the source language of totally unfamiliar concepts together with the linguistic forms that represented them must clearly have appeared a less attractive solution than that offered by the alternative possibility, which was to adapt the language of his audience to meet the situation. This he could do by means of two types of indirect loaning, namely loan translation and semantic extension, and we shall consider each of these possibilities in turn.

In the first of these, the *loan translation* or *calque* (literally 'tracing, copy'), the form and meaning of a foreign word, instead of being carried over into the recipient language as a unit, is merely employed as a model for a native creation. For this to be possible it must be both morphologically complex and semantically transparent, and the process consists in substituting for each of its morphs the semantically closest morph in the recipient language and combining these according to its own native rules of word-formation. Thus, while the choice of constituent morphs and the overall meaning of the new construct will be modelled on the foreign source, the constituent elements themselves and the rules governing their combination will be native. As a result the newly created form will be fully motivated for the native speaker and in fact, if we compare the examples of Old English loan translations in Table 2 with their models in Latin, it will be seen that in spite of their novelty these words must have made the concepts they introduced very much more accessible to the Anglo-Saxon listener than the completely alien Latin forms.

TABLE 2

Latin	Old English	Modern English	Modern German
ascensio	ūpāstīgens	ascension	Himmelfahrt
	upstige		
euangelium	gōdspell	gospel	Evangelium
euangelista	gōdspellere	evangelist	Evangelist
humanitas	menniscnesse	humanity	Menschlichkeit
	manhōd		Menschheit
longanimis	longmōd	patient	langmütig
misericors	mildheort	merciful	barmherzig
	earmheort		
misericordia	mildheortnis	mercy	Barmherzigkeit
	earmheortnis		
omnipotens	ealwældend	almighty	allmächtig
	ealmihtig		
paganus	hēþen	heathen, pagan	Heide
paganismus	hēþendōm	heathendom	Heidentum
	hēþenhōd	paganism	
resurrectio	ǣrist	resurrection	Auferstehung
spiritus sanctus	hāliga gāst	the Holy Ghost	der Heilige Geist
trinitas	þrīness	trinity	Dreieinigkeit
	þrimnesse		
unanimis	ānmōd	unanimous	einmütig

It will also be seen that where Old English had a loan translation calqued on a Latin model, Middle English has often replaced this by borrowing the descendant of the Latin source item from Norman French. Perhaps by then the concepts conveyed by these words had become so well established that the initial value of the calque as a teaching aid had become redundant. The majority of the calques of the Old English period are based on a Latin model, and this in turn is often either borrowed from, or calqued on, Greek. An example of the former is Latin *evangelium*. In this case the Latin, being simply borrowed, is unanalysable whereas the English is directly calqued on the Greek ('good' + 'message') and is therefore analysable. The Latin *com-passio* 'compassion' on the other hand is calqued on Greek *sym-patheia* ('together' + 'suffering'), and has in turn acted as model for German *Mit-leid*, Dutch *mede-lijden*, Russian *so-stradanie*, etc. Similarly, Latin con-scientia 'conscience', which renders Greek *syn-eidesis* ('together' + 'knowledge'), is the model for German *Ge-wissen*, Dutch *ge-weten*, Swedish *sam-vete*, Russian *so-vest'*, etc. In cases like these it is extremely difficult to decide whether a particular form in Dutch, the Scandinavian or the Slavonic languages has been influenced by the German or whether it is an independent formation calqued directly on the Latin. More recent examples of loan translations are German *Fussball* 'football' (based on English *football*); French *chemin de fer*, German *Eisen-bahn*, Swedish *järn-väg*, Greek *sidero-dromos*, all meaning 'iron-way' although the direction of borrowing is not always clear; French *gratte-ciel*, Italian *gratta-cielo*, Russian *nebos-kr'op* and the closely parallel German *Wolken-kratzer* ('cloud-scraper'),[1] all from American–English *sky-scraper*. It may be noted that it is the relative arbitrariness of these images which makes it possible to identify them as loan translations with some degree of certainty. Where the image is a more 'natural' one however it becomes much more difficult to be sure that one is not dealing with parallel but independent formations.

Calques based on Greek, Latin and French models and coined at different periods in its history are very numerous in German. In the eighteenth century especially there was a deliberate movement to replace foreign words by native creations and the calque was the most convenient means of achieving this end. Many of these new words must at first have sounded rather contrived, but those that have survived are now in no way felt to be unnatural by the native speaker. In fact it is often extremely difficult to identify these loan translations with certainty if there is no record of their deliberate creation in the dictionaries of the

[1] The deviation in the case of the German construction is no doubt due to the fact that an exact rendering ***Himmelkratzer* would have combined the high register word meaning not only 'sky' but also 'Heaven' with the rather commonplace concept of 'scraping'.

time written with the express purpose of introducing 'germanizations' (*Eindeutschungen*). Because none of these new words violates the native rules of word-formation and they have no formal properties that would distinguish them from genuine native words it is sometimes impossible to say whether one is dealing with a calque or merely the semantic extension of a pre-existing word. For example German *entdecken* parallels English *discover* and French *découvrir* both in semantic structure ('un-' + 'cover') and in breadth of application. The word already existed however in Old High German with the meaning 'to remove the covering from' and its wider and more abstract meaning is

TABLE 3

English	German	Russian
circumstance	Umstand	
compassion	Mitleid	sostradanie
conscience	Gewissen	sovest'
convert	bekehren	
development	Entwicklung	razvitie
distracted	zerstreut	rassejannyj
enlightenment	Aufklärung	prosveščenie
enterprise	Unternehmen	
equilibrium	Gleichgewicht	
exception	Ausnahme	
exposition	Ausstellung	
expression	Ausdruck	
extraordinary	ausserordentlich	
impression	Eindruck	vpečatlenie
incorporate	einverleiben	
influence	Einfluss	vlijanie
omniscient	allwissend	vseznajuščij
orthography	Rechtschreibung	
prejudice	Vorurteil	
progress	Fortschritt	
respect	Rücksicht	
(responsibility)	{ Verantwortung Verantwortlichkeit	otvetstvennost'
(selfconfidence)	Selbstvertrauen	samonadežnost'
superficial	oberflächlich	
superhuman	übermenschlich	sverxčelovečnyj
subject	unterwerfen	

merely an extension of the earlier more literal one, although this might of course have taken place under the influence of a foreign model. Dutch, the Scandinavian and the Slavonic languages often have formations which directly parallel the German ones (Thomas 1975), but it is often extremely difficult to say whether these are calqued on the German or independently on a common model.

Table 3 gives a list of loan translations in German (with Russian parallels where available) based on Latin or French models. Since the corresponding English words are all directly borrowed from Latin or French, we have entered the English equivalents rather than the actual source items in column 1. This table brings out very clearly the fact that English has tended to borrow form as well as meaning from Romance where German or Russian have preferred to create a new form from their own native resources. It should however be borne in mind that this difference is, at least in the case of German, to a considerable extent the result of deliberate language policy. The analysis of a few of the examples will serve to illustrate the general principles involved. English *compassion* was borrowed from early French, the French term *compassion* being itself an adaptation of Late Latin *compassiōnem* (accusative of *compassio*). The German and Russian forms are not loans but native formations which exactly parallel the structure of the Latin word. This is an abstract noun built of the elements *com-*, an allomorph occurring before labial of the prefix *con-* 'with' which is related to the preposition *cum* 'with', the root *pat-* of the verb meaning 'to suffer', and a nominalizing suffix *-tiōn-* (a morphophonemic rule converting *-t-* + *-t-* to *-ss-*). Latin *con-* is rendered by German *mit-* and by Russian *so-*, each of these morphs being related to a corresponding preposition meaning 'with'. Latin *pat-* is rendered by the roots of the equivalent verbs meaning 'to suffer' in German and Russian, *leiden* and *stradat'*. And finally the nominal suffix *-tiōn-* corresponds to a zero morph in German (Middle High German had a suffix *-ung*) and to *-nie* in Russian having a parallel function. In the same way English *impression* came via French from Latin *impressio*, accusative *impressiōnem*, a noun which originally had a concrete meaning (referring for instance to the pressing of a seal into soft wax) but which was later extended to cover the abstract idea of impression of the mind. Again the German and Russian formations exactly parallel the Latin in structure, Latin *in-* (*im-* before labial) being rendered by German *ein-* and by Russian *v-*, etc. and all sharing the semantic extension of the verb from concrete to abstract. Again French *développement*, from a prefix *dé-* 'un-', an old verb of unknown origin *voloper* 'to wind' and the nominalizing suffix *-ment*, has gone into English direct as *development* but into German in the form of the calque *Entwicklung*, made up of *ent-* 'dis-', the verb base of *wickeln* 'to wind' and the nominal suffix *-ung*. The Russian is a parallel formation from *raz-* 'un-', *vit-* 'wind' and nominal suffix *-ie*. In the case of *responsibility*, the structural match between the Latin model and the German calque is somewhat looser. The English is again borrowed from the French which is itself derived from Latin *responsus*, past participle of the verb *rē-spondeō* 'to answer' (*responsible* 'who must answer for his acts'). The German form *Verantwortung* is derived from *antworten* 'to answer' by means of the perfective prefix *ver-* and the nominalizer *-ung*. The Russian is a direct calque on the German. *Incorporate* is from the complex Latin verb *in-corpor-āre* derived from *corpus*, genitive *corporis*, 'body'. The German equivalent *einverleiben* is built in a parallel way from *Leib* 'body' by means of the two prefixes *ein-* 'in-' and *ver-* (perfective). *Superficial* continues a Late Latin adjective *superficiālis* 'belonging to the surface' derived from *super-* 'above' and *faciēs* 'external form'; in exactly parallel fashion the German adjective derives from *ober-* 'above' and *Fläche* 'surface'. English *orthography*, borrowed through Latin from Greek (*orthó-* 'correct' plus *graphía* 'writing'), is exactly imitated in German by *recht* 'right' plus *Schreibung* 'writing'. English *to convert* is from Latin *con-* plus *vertō* 'to turn back' and is rendered in German by *be-* plus *kehren* which has the same analysis. It is known to be a very early calque.

1.3 *Semantic extension (semantic calques)*

If we return once more to the way in which the key terms of Christian doctrine were rendered in the Germanic languages, it will be noticed that a number of these (*God*, *Heaven*, *Hell*, *evil* for example) are neither loans nor loan translations but are in fact inherited words. Here then we find a third way in which a foreign concept may be taken into a language, namely by modifying the semantic range of an item of similar meaning in the native vocabulary or by expanding it so as to accommodate the new meaning alongside the original one. Here again in our particular case, as with loan translations, difficulties are likely to arise due to the fact that in Germanic there is often very little evidence as to the precise pre-Christian meanings of the words in question. The case of *Hell*, however, appears to be reasonably clear. In Old Norse, which often preserved heathen connotations that had been lost elsewhere, *Hel* was the name of the goddess who guarded the kingdom of the dead. She was not a terrifying deity nor was her underworld a place of punishment like the hell of Christianity but rather a pleasant abode where the dead led a peaceful collective existence. Although the exact details of the process may not be known, the old meaning evidently became modified under the influence of Christianity so as to meet the requirements of the new religion. In the same way in Greek, Romanian and a number of other languages the meaning of the word which originally referred only to the substance 'pitch' was extended so as to also include the concept of 'hell' (Sandfeld 1930: 36). Again, the important Christian symbol of the cross was rendered in Old English by *rōd* (Modern English *rood*), a word which originally simply referred to a wooden instrument for measuring land. *Heaven*, originally the Germanic word for 'sky', is now employed in English only for the religious concept and *sky* has been borrowed from Norse to cover the physical meaning; German *Himmel* on the other hand has retained both meanings. Perhaps the most difficult word of all is *God*, which is common to all the Germanic languages and translates Latin *deus*, Greek *theós*. It does not appear to have any direct cognates outside Germanic, although it may tentatively be traced to a Proto-Indo-European root meaning 'to invoke'. The most striking feature about it is that in the oldest records it has neuter gender and it has been suggested that this may be due to its originally having been an adjective meaning '(which is) invoked', its gender being determined by some noun such as 'being' that is understood. Others on the other hand have interpreted its neuter gender as evidence of an earlier reference to a non-personal god, so that the conversion of the word to masculine gender would have been the result of the conversion of its former meaning to a Christian one. It has, however, also been claimed that no missionary would think of employing a term with heathen connotations to refer to the God of Christianity, and it may therefore have had some totally different origin.

In this section on lexical borrowing we have seen some of the linguistic consequences of a shared cultural environment and we have attempted to isolate some of the linguistic devices effecting the transmission of cultural concepts from one language to another. In the case of the European languages, upon which we have drawn largely for our examples, these are also united by their common inheritance from Proto-Indo-European. In many ways, then, the European situation is especially complex since the effects of common inheritance and of cultural contact are very much interwoven. And, as we shall see in the following section on grammatical borrowing, these considerations are not limited to the lexicon but also apply at other levels.

1.4 *Structural effects of lexical borrowing*

In the case of English we have seen a number of instances in which lexical borrowing from Romance resulted in some kind of phonological reanalysis, in particular the phonologization of allophonic variants (/f/ and /v/, /ʃ/ and /ʒ/, for example). This is in fact a widely observed effect of lexical borrowing. But perhaps the deepest influence of Romance loan-words on English phonological structure was on stress placement (Chomsky and Halle 1968:70). At the morphological level the influx of new lexical items merely served to strengthen those inflectional processes which were productive at the time of borrowing, while the overall morphological structure was not affected. In the case of the derivational morphology on the other hand, a very large number of morphologically complex words have the morphological structure of Romance words. Diachronically speaking the majority of these are loans and only a small minority are in fact English creations. Nevertheless this intensive borrowing is responsible for the fact that English now possesses side by side two totally different derivational systems, one inherited and largely confined to the lexical resources of Germanic origin, the other the result of borrowing from Romance and largely confined to the Romance-derived sector of the lexicon.

2 **Grammatical borrowing**

2.1 *Bilingualism and interference between languages*

In the previous section on lexical borrowing the grammars of the donor and recipient languages were assumed to come into contact only through the intermediary of a small number of bilingual speakers who acted as vehicles in the transfer of lexical material. The great majority of speakers however remained monolingual, and the effect of the borrowing on the grammar of the recipient language was largely confined to the phonology and the morphology, the syntax remaining relatively untouched. We must now see what are the effects on the languages involved of widespread bilingualism within a community, that is to say of a situation in which a substantial proportion of the population employs two different languages, even though in such circumstances the use of these will normally be restricted to separate and well-defined social contexts. In such a situation we have to assume the presence within the linguistic competence of each bilingual speaker of two separate grammars, each with its own lexicon and system of rules.

If in such a bilingual situation the grammars of the two languages are compared a certain amount of overlapping of the systems will usually be found, and such overlap is likely to be the more pronounced the longer the languages have been in contact. This sharing of features by two languages as the result of their intimate contact within the competence of a single speaker is referred to as *interference* and it is a familiar phenomenon in second language learning. Thus for instance a native speaker of English will often transfer to his pronunciation of German the allophonic distinction which English makes between 'clear' and 'dark' *l* and, since German does not make this distinction but uses the same clear *l* in all positions, his pronunciation of, for example, a word like *Feld* 'field' as [fełt] rather than as [felt] will sound foreign to German ears. Conversely a native speaker of German or French is likely to use the English perfect tense in contexts in which it is not acceptable in English, saying for instance *I have been to the cinema yesterday*, since in German the formally parallel perfect tense is for most speakers in free variation with the simple past and in French this latter is no longer used except in written style. Of course such isolated instances of interference in the speech of individual second language learners normally have no effect whatsoever on the grammar of the native speakers of the target language. Prolonged bilingualism as a regular feature of the sociolinguistic situation of a community on the other hand is most likely to affect one or other or both of the languages concerned. Thus the varieties of English spoken in Wales and Ireland differ in quite specific ways from the variety spoken in England and these regional peculiarities correlate with corresponding features in the grammars of the Welsh and Irish languages (cf. Adams 1967), and in the same way Jewish communities in the United States often use varieties of English which show deviations from the norm ascribable to the interference of Yiddish (Rayfield 1970).

We shall first examine a contemporary case of languages in contact investigated by Gumperz (1971: 251–73). In the village of Kupwar, situated in southern India to the north of the Mysore border, the situation is one not so much of bilingualism as of multilingualism, for a total of four different languages are spoken by its population of 3,000. Two of these languages, Urdu and Marathi, belong to the Indo-Iranian branch of Indo-European while the other two, Kannada and Telugu, belong to the totally unrelated Dravidian language family. The community is divided into social groups by a rigorous caste system and, although family life is generally conducted in monolingual terms, almost all the men are at least bilingual and most frequently use Marathi for intergroup communication. On historical evidence it is known that Kannada and Marathi must have been in contact in the area for the past six hundred years and Urdu for about four hundred years. The present multilingual situation is therefore not a new one and, in view of the remarkable stability that it has so far shown, is likely to continue for as long as the present social system prevails.

Now the most striking thing about the Urdu, Marathi and Kannada spoken in Kupwar (we shall eliminate from further discussion the rather marginal case of Telugu) is the extraordinary ease of translation between them. This is clearly due to the fact that the local varieties of these languages have very largely identical constituent structures and grammatical categories, so that it would almost be true to say that a sentence in any one of them could be converted to one of the others by simply substituting the appropriate morphs in one-to-one fashion. Gumperz in fact found it possible to postulate a single surface structure for the syntax of all three languages, the only difference between them being one of lexical items and grammatical morphs. In addition he found the phonetic surface structures of all three languages to be largely held in common. Such remarkable convergence could only be the result of linguistic interference over a period of several centuries.

The convergence features exhibited by Urdu, Marathi and Kannada as spoken by the inhabitants of Kupwar can be isolated by comparing these local varieties with varieties of the same languages spoken outside the area, for instance with the standard forms of the three languages. The most striking differences between the local and the standard varieties are perhaps to be found in the case of Urdu. Thus, while Standard Urdu has a two-term system of grammatical gender comparable to, for instance, that of French (that is to say the masculine or feminine gender of a noun is normally grammatically determined but this is overruled by natural gender in the case of animates), in Kupwar Urdu gender has, as in all varieties of Kannada, a semantic basis, only female humans being feminine and all male humans and non-humans being masculine. It is to be noted however that, although there are three formally distinct genders in Kannada (nouns denoting male humans being masculine, those denoting female humans being feminine, and inanimates being neuter), Kupwar Urdu has not evolved a third marker of gender. It has merely reinterpreted its own formal resources following a Kannada model, putting all female humans into the same feminine class as Kannada but conflating this latter's masculine and neuter classes in its own unmarked masculine class.

There are however other cases in which it is Kupwar Kannada which has innovated following the pattern of Urdu or Marathi. For instance in constructions of the type 'NP *is* NP' and 'NP *exists*', Standard Urdu and Marathi have an overt marker of 'to be'. Standard Kannada has no copula in the former construction and a form of the verb 'to be' in the latter, but Kupwar Kannada uses the verb 'to be' in both. The lexical items representing 'to be' are, however, formally quite different in the Kupwar varieties of the three languages.

Again, Standard Urdu and Marathi form yes/no questions by means of an element which in other contexts is translatable as 'what' (Urdu *kya*, Marathi *kay*). This element is always sentence-final in Standard Marathi but can occur in any of several positions in Standard Urdu; in Kupwar Urdu, however, it can occur only in final position as in Marathi. Yes/no questions are formed in Standard Kannada by means of a verbal suffix *-a*. This does not occur in Kupwar Kannada which has instead the equivalent in that language of 'what' in sentence-final position. Thus 'Did you sell the horse?' would be represented in the different languages as follows (Gumperz 1971: 264):

Standard Urdu	*kya*	ghoṛii	dii
	'*what*	the horse	you sold'
Kupwar Urdu	ghoḍi	di ya	*kya*
Kupwar Marathi	ghoḍi	dil əs	*kay*
Kupwar Kannada	kudri	kwaṭṭ i	*yan*
	'the horse	you sold	*what*'

In the following case convergence has gone still further, there being not only isomorphism of construction in the local varieties of all three languages but the morph which acts as marker of the construction is also formally identical in all three. Indirect questions ('Tell me whether you . . .', as opposed to 'Did you . . .?') are introduced in Standard Urdu and Marathi by a subordination marker *ki* 'that' following the matrix sentence.

Standard Urdu	bol-o *ki*	kəhã	gəy-a	tha	kəl
	'tell *that*	where	you did go		yesterday'

('Tell (me) where you went yesterday')

This is exactly paralleled by Kupwar Kannada

heḷ ri *ki* yəlli hog idi ninni
'tell *that* where you did go yesterday'

although in Standard Kannada the two sentences would be in reverse order and the conjoining element (marking indirect speech) would be a form of the verb 'to say': 'where did you go yesterday? that (lit. saying) tell (me)'.

These last examples illustrate the two theoretical possibilities: either a construction current in one of the languages is imitated in the other so that although the syntactic pattern is borrowed it is realized by means of the latter's own native morphs, or both the construction and the relevant morphs are taken over by the borrowing language. That there will be transfer of lexical material under such circumstances is only to be expected, but here it is not simply the open classes of the lexicon which are affected but, as we have seen in the case of *ki* 'that', even those classes which have closed membership.

The present linguistic situation in Kupwar is to be interpreted in terms of convergent development resulting from several hundred years of contact in a multilingual setting. Although Marathi has for long been the dominant language in the area there has been exchange of material in all directions. After a careful study of the nature and the direction of the changes that led to the shared features, Gumperz came to the following conclusion: 'Almost all the changes can be interpreted as reductions or generalizations that simplify surface structure in relation to underlying categories and relationships. . . . While language distinctions are maintained, actual messages show word-for-word or morph-for-morph translatability and speakers can therefore switch from one code to another with a minimum of additional learning. . . . For many Kupwar residents, especially men, a model of linguistic competence must comprise a single semological, a single syntactic, and a single phonetic component, and *alternative* sets of rules for the relation of semantic categories to morphemic shapes' (1971: 270f.).

From the above it can be seen how convergent development resulting from the intimate contact of two languages in a bilingual situation may be investigated. For each grammatical rule which they share and which is an innovation in one of them the donor language and the recipient language must be determined. This is done by comparing the languages concerned with closely related languages outside the area of contact, and in each case those innovations which are peculiar to the local language and which have counterparts in the other languages spoken locally will be attributed to language contact. In this way the historical changes which were responsible for the current isomorphism of the local languages may be isolated.

Kupwar is an unusually favourable field for the investigation of convergence, since not only has the multilingual situation lasted for several centuries but it is still open to observation. Elsewhere, however, we can often only deduce past bilingualism from the presence in neighbouring languages, or in languages which we know or assume to have been in contact with each other in the past, of structural isomorphism. Isomorphism of structure under such circumstances is not of course necessarily diagnostic of convergence, for it is also a common feature of genealogically related languages whether these have become geographically separated or not. If then a group of languages which are either in contact or may have been in contact in the past share both formal (structural) and substantive (material) features, it may from a purely synchronic point of view be impossible to decide whether these are the result of convergence or of common inheritance. For such a decision must depend in the end not on the *nature* of the shared features but on their *relative chronology*, that is to say their position in the chain of innovatory changes that constitutes the historical grammar of each of the languages concerned. And, as we have already seen, this presupposes either well documented histories of the languages or the possibility of reconstructing these from comparison with related languages elsewhere. Since, however, we are not always in the fortunate position of having for each of the languages involved a closely related language outside the contact area, it may in extreme cases have to remain unresolved whether common structural features are the result of convergence or of common origin.

2.2 *Linguistic areas*

The term *linguistic area* is used to denote a group of geographically contiguous languages characterized by a number of specific structural isoglosses, these shared *areal features* having been acquired as the result of contact and not inherited. The linguistic area can therefore be seen as the natural counterpart of the language family, and this was certainly Trubetzkoy's intention when he first proposed the concept in 1928, coining the term *Sprachbund*, or 'language association', to describe it (Jakobson 1972b: 242f.). Thus, while languages may be grouped into language families on the basis of shared inheritance from a common ancestor, they may also be grouped areally on the basis of shared features which they have acquired as a result of mutual contact. But we have seen that in practice it may be extremely difficult or even impossible to assign a particular language group to one or other of these categories, the only sure means of deciding being the establishment of the relative ages of the features in question. Furthermore, while the membership of a language family is an all or nothing matter, the situation is much more fluid in the case of linguistic areas since some features may have a wider geographical extension than others. Equally, since the reality of the linguistic area as a living phenomenon may be verified from an examination of contiguous languages of the present, it is to be presumed that similar situations must also have existed in the past, and *former linguistic areas* have in fact been postulated on the basis of shared isoglosses for languages which are not now in contact (see Trubetzkoy (1939), for features shared by Indo-European and certain other language families[1]).

Linguistic areas have been postulated in various regions of the world and on the basis of a variety of criteria (Jakobson 1972b; Winter 1973; Trudgill 1974a: chapter 7). In South-East Asia, for instance, Chinese, Thai, Vietnamese and a number of other languages have in common the feature of tone and this has been attributed to contact (Henderson 1965). Again, the Indo-European languages of the Indian subcontinent share with their totally unrelated Dravidian and Munda neighbours, and in opposition to all other Indo-European languages, a series of retroflex consonants which contrast with the dental series (Emeneau 1956). In the area between the Black Sea and the Caspian, Eastern Armenian and Ossetic have a series of glottalized consonants, quite untypical of their Indo-European relatives elsewhere, which approximate their phonological systems to those of neighbouring Caucasian languages (Allen 1950). Certain Bantu languages of southern Africa share with the neighbouring Bush-Hottentot languages a set of click consonants otherwise confined to these latter (Guthrie 1967–71: ii, 106). And finally, various features have been claimed as characteristic of Europe as a geographical

[1] Although Trubetzkoy's attempt at a synchronic definition of Indo-European on a hybrid basis of historical and purely typological criteria has been rightly rejected, his further attempt to situate Indo-European within a wider linguistic area could be more useful.

area irrespective of the language families involved (Lewy 1964; Brosnahan 1961; Lakoff 1972b), and comparable divisions have been postulated for America (Boas 1940: 219–25; Swadesh 1951; Haas 1969: 78–97). In all these cases, groups of geographically contiguous languages are linked by specific shared structural isoglosses in spite of their belonging to different language families established on the basis of genealogical relationship.

2.2.1 The Balkan linguistic area

A well-studied example of a linguistic area defined by grammatical isoglosses exists in the Balkans. The area in question comprises the geographically contiguous languages Modern Greek, Albanian, Romanian, Bulgarian and, marginally, Serbo-Croat and Turkish. Although, with the exception of Turkish, all are Indo-European languages, they belong to different divisions of the family tree, Greek and Albanian being considered independent branches while Romanian belongs along with the other Romance languages to the Italic branch and Bulgarian and Serbo-Croat to the Slavonic branch. It has been suggested that the unifying force behind the area is the Byzantine civilization as represented by the Greek Church, and in many instances Greek can in fact be identified as the donor of, or model for, the shared phenomena (Sandfeld 1930: 213ff.; cf. Trudgill 1974a: 161ff.). Most of the isoglosses comprise features of surface grammatical structure, including the rules which combine single lexemes to form idiomatic expressions. As in the case of Kupwar, the situation has been described as four different languages with a single set of grammatical rules. Schleicher on the other hand saw the situation, in rather more negative terms, as 'a group of languages which have in common that they are the most corrupt members of their respective families' (Sandfeld 1930: 12).

The best known isogloss characterizing the area is probably the definite article suffixed to the noun, which unites Albanian, Bulgarian and Romanian, but excludes Greek (Albanian *mik-u* 'friend-the', *djal-i* 'boy-the'; Bulgarian *trup-at* 'body-the', *konj-at* 'horse-the'; Romanian *om-ul* 'man-the', *munte-le* 'mountain-the', these latter having the same morphs historically as the other Romance languages (cf. French *l'homme*, *le mont*) but in reverse order). The other Slavonic languages have no direct counterpart of the definite article. Greek does not participate in the construction, its definite article preceding the noun as a free form.

An example which concerns syntax is the use of a subordinate clause introduced by a conjunction and followed by the subjunctive in contexts in which most European languages, including Classical Greek, would have used an infinitive construction. For example 'Give me to drink' is rendered literally as 'Give me that I drink' (Romanian *da-mi sa beau*, Bulgarian *daj mi da pija*, Albanian *a-më të pi*, Greek *dòs mou nà piō̃*; note also the cognate forms for 'give', 'me' and 'drink'). The construction is already found in New Testament Greek. The infinitive of Classical Greek has not survived as a category, but formal traces of it are still to be found in derived nouns. The situation with regard to Bulgarian is similar to that of Greek. In Romanian, on the other hand, the spoken language follows the areal pattern while the written language still uses infinitives like the other Romance languages. In the case of Albanian, the northern dialects have the infinitive construction and the southern ones the subordinate clause construction except in set phrases. The passage from an infinitive to a dependent clause construction can be traced in Greek and would seem to have been internally motivated. After the Greek infinitive had lost the final *-n* of its ending *-ein* as a result of sound change the remaining sequence *-ei*, which had now become identical with the third person singular suffix, appears to have been reinterpreted as a finite form (Anttila 1972: 103). The new Greek construction would then seem to have been imitated not only in surrounding languages but even in New Testament Latin (cf. Mark 7: 26: *ērṓta autòn hina to daimónion ekbálēi* and *rogabat eium ut daemonium eiiceret* 'she implored him that he cast out the devil').

While Bulgarian generally appears to have been the receiver in matters of grammar, where phonology is concerned it has influenced the neighbouring Romanian in a number of features (Petrovici 1957). The most important of these is the 'prejotization', that is to say realization as [ye], of initial *e-* and the development of a series of palatalized ('soft') consonants, both well-known features of the Slavonic languages.

At the lexical level, a striking feature is the occurrence of numerous idiomatic expressions which have morph for morph equivalents in the various languages, for example *to eat oneself with somebody* for 'to quarrel', *to eat somebody's ears* for 'to make a frightful noise', *to remain without mouth* for 'to kill oneself', etc. There is in addition a rich fund of shared vocabulary, mainly loans from Greek and Turkish, distributed right across the area which completes the impression of unity suggested by the structural isoglosses.

The examination of the spatial extension of the shared features and of their order of acquisition by the individual languages led Sandfeld to the conclusion that in the great majority of cases the features had been developed within post-Classical Greek and had spread outwards from there at different periods (1930: 213). Of the various features involved it was the loan-words which he found to be of the greatest assistance in working out the historical relationships, since their spread through time and space could be traced with greater accuracy than was possible in the case of syntactic features. These shared lexical items, loan translations and semantic calques are perhaps best seen as the direct reflection of a cultural unity produced within the area by the influence of the Byzantine heritage in many ways comparable to that produced in the west by the influence of Rome.

2.2.2 Europe as a linguistic area

In the section dealing with syntactic change we saw that, in addition to their common inheritance, the Indo-European languages of western Europe share a number of grammatical innovations represented by isoglosses of varying geographical extension. Furthermore, since these shared features were not yet present in Classical Latin or in Proto-Germanic, we know that they must have developed within the past two thousand years after the break-up of Romance and Germanic into their constituent languages. Let us briefly consider some of the more important of these features which have developed in parallel fashion in the Romance and Germanic languages of western Europe.

Firstly, all these languages possess a definite and an indefinite article functioning as initial element in noun phrases. In all cases the definite article has developed from a demonstrative pronoun (French masc. *le* < Latin *illum*, fem. *la* < *illam*, plural *les* < *illos*, *illas*; German masc. *der*, fem. *die*, neuter *das*, English *the*, all from a Proto-Germanic demonstrative stem **de-/da-*), and the indefinite article from the numeral 'one' (French masc. *un*, fem. *une* < Latin *unum*, *una*; German *ein*, *eine* from *eins*, English *a*(*n*) from *one*). Thus it will be seen that in each of the Romance languages, not excluding Romanian in which the article is suffixed, the representative of the same Latin demonstrative pronoun lost some of its deictic content and its independent word stress and was reinterpreted as an article. Exactly parallel processes took place in the western Germanic languages and in Greek.

Secondly in both language groups the tense system developed periphrastic constructions in which a non-finite form of the verb (infinitive, present participle, past participle) is combined with one of a small set of auxiliary verbs. In Classical Latin the only construction of this type was the perfect passive (*amatus est* 'he has been loved') but in Vulgar Latin the number of periphrastically constructed tenses greatly increased. In both the Romance and Germanic languages the verbs 'to have' and 'to be' are used to form the so-called perfect tense, the original situation being that transitive verbs normally selected the former and intransitive verbs the latter (French *j'ai acheté*, German *ich habe gekauft* 'I have bought' but *je suis venu*, *ich bin gekommen* 'I have come'; English has generalized *to have*); the passive is formed by means of the verbs 'to be' and 'to become' (French *il est aimé*, English *he is loved*, German *er wird geliebt* using *werden* 'to become'); the future is formed by means of 'to have' in the Romance languages (Vulgar Latin **amare habeo* > Spanish *amaré*, French *j'aimerai* 'I shall love'), 'to become' in German (*er wird kommen*) and *shall/will* in English. Again, the lexical items are inherited but their grammatical function is new.

Thirdly the functions of the simple case forms of the older language states have been increasingly taken over by prepositional phrases (Latin *rosae* 'of the rose' but French *de la rose*), with concomitant loss of case endings.

And fourthly, an isogloss of more limited extension, the use of a subject pronoun is obligatory when the subject position is not occupied by a noun. This feature is restricted to a number of contiguous languages in the centre, namely all the modern Germanic languages, French and Rhaeto-Romansh; all the other Romance languages (and in fact all other Indo-European languages) behave like Latin in which an overt subject pronoun is used only as a marker of emphasis (Haiman 1974: 90). We have already seen that this feature is closely linked with the presence of impersonal pronouns and an 'it'-insertion rule.

One may attempt to explain these facts in a number of different ways. In the first place we have already seen that Late Latin, as the language of scholarship and of the Church, had a profound influence on the lexical stock of the western European languages. It might then seem reasonable to suppose that these grammatical isoglosses could have had a similar origin in a western European linguistic area reflecting the heritage of Rome in the same way that the eastern area continued to reflect that of Byzantium. There can be no doubt that both the dignitaries of the Church and educated people in general used Latin as the normal means of communication throughout the area from a very early period. Nor should it be forgotten that there must also have been a certain amount of bilingualism between the speakers of some of the early Romance and Germanic languages (Francs in Gaul, Goths in northern Italy, etc.). Bilingualism in certain influential sectors of the community, and in particular its written expression in the form of translation (notably of the Bible), might then have been responsible for the spread of these features.

It has on the other hand also been argued that, since the languages concerned all belong to the Indo-European language family, an explanation of their parallel development after separation should rather be sought in the joint inheritance of *intrinsic structural properties* and not in any subsequent outside influence. This claim would appear to receive support from the fact that all these developments may be described in terms of a single underlying principle, namely the passage from the internal marking of grammatical functions by morphological means to their external marking by means of free forms (prepositions, auxiliaries, articles). This passage from synthetic to analytic types of construction would be the result of what Sapir (1921: 150f.) calls *drift* and Lakoff describes as a 'metacondition on the way the grammar of a language *as a whole* will change' (1972b: 178). A further argument in favour of this hypothesis is the fact that somewhat parallel developments are also found in certain modern Indo-European languages outside the area in question, for instance Modern Persian, so that they need not be attributed to mutual influence. We shall return to this general typological aspect in the next chapter. The problem here is whether this principle is sufficient in itself to account for the uniformity of the replacements right across the area. For even if one were to admit the existence of a general drift towards analytic structures this would not explain why such very specific constructions have come into being in contiguous languages. In fact these two hypotheses are not as mutually exclusive as they might at first appear, for an inbuilt tendency towards analytic structures would not exclude the possibility of the innovations having developed in a contact situation.

In the case of phonetic and phonological isoglosses the situation is somewhat different. Here again quite specific features of articulation have been observed to extend in unbroken fashion over wide areas, apparently without regard to the boundaries of the individual languages concerned. The problem of their source is however complicated by the fact that, although the outcome may have been one of homogeneity, the origin of any particular feature would sometimes appear to have been different in the various languages. The situation is well illustrated by the case of the distribution of rounded front vowels in Europe. As can be seen from Map 4 (after Brosnahan 1961: 105), rounded front vowels

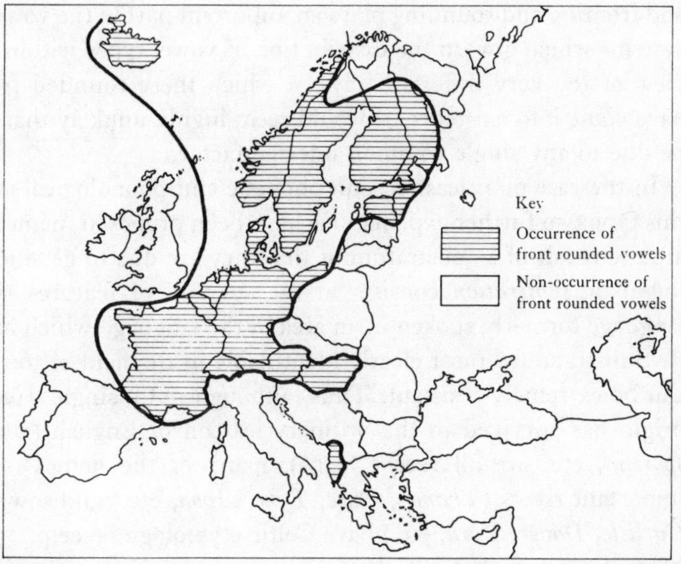

Map 4

(/ü/, /ö/, /ɔ̈/) form an integral part of the phonemic systems of speakers within a continuous zone which takes in the French, Dutch, German, Icelandic, Norwegian, Danish, Swedish, Finnish, Southern Lapp and Hungarian language areas; they are also found dialectally in north-western Italy, in Northumberland, in Scotland and in Albanian. The latter language is now separated from the main area by Greek but formerly this also had an /ü(:)/. One obviously hesitates to attribute such a strikingly homogeneous distribution to mere chance, yet as far as we know the origin of the segments in question was quite different in each of the language groups concerned. We have already seen that in the Germanic languages the rounded front vowels continue the allophones of back vowels which were fronted by an *i*-vowel in the following syllable (umlaut); in French on the contrary they result from the fronting of back vowels in closed syllables (Bichakjian 1974); and finally in Greek and Albanian the back vowel [u(:)] was fronted to [ü(:)] in all positions. All that is common then to the development of rounded front vowels in these Indo-European languages is that they all result from the fronting of back vowels. In the non-Indo-European languages on the other hand – Finnish, Lapp, Estonian, Hungarian, all members of the Finno-Ugrian language family – rounded front vowels are old, and fronting and rounding plays an important part in the vowel harmony systems which govern the distribution of vowel types within words.[1] In view of the very different ways in which these rounded front vowels have come into existence, it would seem highly unlikely that they could be due to any single common internal factor.

In the case of at least certain phonetic and phonological isoglosses of this type two further explanations have been proposed, namely that they are the result of a substratum or that they are due to genetic factors. A linguistic *substratum* consists in the survival of features typical of a language formerly spoken in an area in the language which has replaced it. Substrata are most clearly identifiable in the field of toponymy and can be extremely resistant. Thus, although not a single word of Celtic origin has survived in the ordinary lexicon of English (*whisky*, *plaid*, *sporran*, etc. are all recent loans), many of the names of the more important rivers (*Thames*, *Ouse*, *Tyne*, *Avon*, etc.) and towns (*London*, *Carlisle*, *Dover*, *York*, etc.) have Celtic etymologies (see p. 275f.). It has been suggested that a Celtic substratum may be responsible for the rounding of the French vowels, but there are a number of counter-arguments (Brosnahan 1961: 164f. with references) and, although the substratum is a very real and well-attested phenomenon with regard to certain aspects of language, recourse to it in order to account for the phonetic features in the present instance must be regarded as at least speculative.

[1] This means that in these languages both front and back, or rounded and unrounded, vowels may not co-occur within the same word, the vowel of the suffix being automatically determined in so far as these particular features are concerned by the vowel of the stem. As a result individual morphemes have a number of alternants depending on the vowels of the stems with which they can co-occur. Thus for example in Hungarian the morpheme 'to' has three allomorphs, *-hez* after stems with unrounded front vowel, *-höz* after stems with rounded front vowel, and *-hoz* after stems with a back vowel (Hajdu 1975: 75). According to Hajdu (1975: 94f.), however, only the alternation between front and back vowels is old, whereas that between rounded and unrounded vowels appears to be an innovation which occurred in a number of Finno-Ugrian languages.

The genetic hypothesis is based on an apparent correlation between the distribution in Europe of certain phonetic features and of blood-groups (Brosnahan 1961).[1] But even if one is to accept a certain measure of congruence between the distributions, the question remains as to whether such correlation represents a direct cause-and-effect relationship or whether it merely reflects the fact that the same historical events have often been responsible for both genetic and cultural distributions. For, while it might appear reasonable to associate sound types with purely physiological factors, a similar source in the case of shared grammatical and lexical features would hardly seem possible and an adequate theory would have to account for the distribution of *all* types of linguistic features.

2.3 *Restrictions on borrowing*

It has sometimes been claimed that not all areas of language are equally open to borrowing and in particular that the inflectional morphology, as the most 'central' part of the grammar, is least susceptible to outside influence. The examples of borrowing that we have so far examined have for reasons of convenience been drawn from European languages but, since these are genealogically related to one another and tend to have rather similar morphological systems, they do not perhaps form the best basis from which to assess this particular problem. If, however, we turn to languages which have no common inheritance the question of inherent compatibility of structure does not arise. There are in fact examples of the transfer of entire grammatical systems between languages which are totally unrelated, involving not only the exponents of categories but of the categories themselves. The most extreme example of the latter so far described is perhaps that of Mbugu (or Ma'a), a language spoken by a small population in and around Usambara in Tanzania. All the available evidence points to the conclusion that this language, although not itself a member of the Bantu language family,

[1] For instance the past and present distribution of dental fricatives is compared with the quantitative distribution of blood group O in the present population (maps in Brosnahan 1961: 56–7). However, although the two distributions appear to correlate reasonably well in Europe, W. S. Allen has pointed out that recent blood group distribution maps for the Caucasus show an equally impressive concentration of O-genes in the western part of that region yet there are no corresponding dental fricatives in the languages of the area (review of Brosnahan in the *Cambridge Review*, 1963).

has acquired the complex nominal and verbal morphology of the surrounding Bantu languages (Meinhof 1906; Whiteley 1960; Goodman 1971; Tucker and Bryan 1974). Thus Mbugu nouns are divided into nine concord classes each characterized by a pair of class prefixes, one marking singulars and the other plurals. Within a sentence various constituents must carry concord markers reflecting the class membership of the head noun and the verb also requires, in addition to exponents of tense, voice, mood and person, a marker of the class membership of the object noun.[1] However, in spite of these points of agreement with members of the Bantu language family, the great majority of nominal and verbal stems and all the personal, interrogative and demonstrative pronouns are quite unrelated to those of the Bantu languages and appear rather to be related to those of neighbouring Cushitic languages (generally classed as belonging to the Hamito-Semitic language family).

In spite of the absence of historical documents for any of the languages concerned, there are good reasons for believing that the morphological system of Mbugu is a fairly recent acquisition. Thus successive investigators have noted that the use of the prefixes is to some extent optional, this being particularly the case in the singular. Furthermore all speakers were observed to use concord prefixes more consistently in situations of formal exchange with strangers than when talking informally among

[1] The typical Bantu system may be seen from a comparison of the forms in the singular and the plural of two Swahili sentences (Gleason 1965: 39):

(1) sg. *mtu mzuri mmoja yule amenguka*
person good one that fell
'that one good person has fallen'
pl. *watu wazuri wawili wale wameanguka*
'those two good persons have fallen'

In this sentence the head noun has a prefix *m-* in the singular and *wa-* in the plural and it will be seen that concord markers reflecting this class membership occur with all the other elements of its noun phrase and with the verb.

(2) sg. *gari zuri moja lile limeanguka*
cart good one that fell
'that one good cart has fallen'
pl. *magari mazuri mawili yale yameanguka*
'those two good carts have fallen'

In this second sentence the singular has a zero prefix in the noun, which is reflected by zero markers in the dependent adjective and numeral but by a positive formally distinct marker in the demonstrative pronoun and the verb.

themselves, and younger people in particular used them more regularly than their elders. Such variation in the incidence of grammatical markers is quite unheard of in a true Bantu language. It does however fit in well with what we know about the socially determined variation of a prestige feature in a situation of change in progress (see chapter 5). Thus, although superficial inspection would undoubtedly have assigned Mbugu to the Bantu family of languages, in view of these arguments it is to be assumed that it is in fact a non-Bantu language, probably a member of the Cushitic group, which has acquired its Bantu morphology as a result of contact.

It is obvious that such replacement of the native Mbugu system by a foreign system presupposes some considerable degree of familiarity with the foreign model and therefore extensive bilingualism. What has no doubt made the learning, and consequently the transfer, of the system feasible in this case is the neat agglutinative structure of the model, that is to say the fact that as a rule each grammatical morpheme is represented by a single morph (– it is perhaps significant that in those areas of the Bantu grammar where this is not so, as for instance in the case of the pronouns, Mbugu has not adopted the Bantu rules). That such a neat one-to-one relationship between form and meaning greatly facilitates learning has for instance been shown in the case of language acquisition by children in a bilingual context.[1]

The case of Mbugu shows that the inflectional morphology of a language, the very part which it has been claimed is least susceptible to outside influence, may in fact be borrowed. This poses a problem with regard to the assignment of a language to one or other of two families when it shares grammatical features with both. For it is clear that preconceived ideas about the *relative stability* of various parts of a grammar may, in cases of intensive contact at least, result in a wrong assignment. Cases of incorrect assignment as a result of such assumptions are not in fact unknown. Thus for instance Thai (Siamese) was until recently considered to be related to Chinese, mainly on the basis of shared phonological features (lexical tone, monosyllabicity) and of a large shared vocabulary. It is now however considered more likely that these features are the result of borrowing from Chinese, and that Thai is in fact related to the Polynesian languages (Benedict 1972).

It would then seem that, given a certain intensity and duration of

[1] D. Slobin, reporting on Turkish and Iranian bilingual children (communication to the Third Child Language Symposium, London 1975).

language contact, there is nothing that may not be diffused across language boundaries. We have seen ample evidence of the fact that shared isoglosses, both structural and material, may be open to alternative historical interpretation. Neither isomorphism of structure nor shared lexical and grammatical morphs can as such tell us whether the languages which exhibit them are genealogically related or have acquired their common features as a result of contact or both. There simply does not seem to be any area of linguistic structure which is totally resistant to replacement, although it would seem likely that the sector least accessible to foreign influence is the basic vocabulary, however difficult to define this concept may be. The only other fairly general statement that can be made relates to non-productive rules governing the distribution of morpheme alternants, such as Latin *est* : *sunt* and German *ist* : *sind* 'is' : 'are' or English *good* : *be*(*t*)- (*better*, *best*) and German *gut* : *be*(*s*)- (*besser*, *beste*). It is clearly highly improbable that such complex constellations when attested in several languages should be the result of borrowing, and in practice they invariably appear to be the result of common origin.

3 Pidgin and creole languages

Pidgins and creoles could be described as the contact languages *par excellence*, for it is to contact that they are presumed to owe their very existence. The majority of those attested today would appear to have originated in a context of early maritime trade, their geographical distribution largely following the coastlines of Asia, Africa and the Caribbean (see map in Hancock 1971). Traditionally a pidgin or a creole used to be thought of as being no more than a debased form of whatever European language constituted the chief source of its lexicon, but today the tendency is to speak in rather more neutral terms of, for instance, a Portuguese (or French or English) *based* pidgin or creole.

Pidgins are in the first instance sociolinguistically defined as codes operating *between* the members of different language communities rather than within a single community. They are assumed to have originated in typically multilingual contexts such as may exist among seamen of mixed origin on board ship or in the course of contact between crews and local populations along the great sea routes. In such situations it may be assumed that numerous make-shift jargons, often short-lived and of fairly fluid structure, must have developed. Certain of these, having stood the test of time, have become stabilized in form and of more widespread distribution. Pidgins are to be considered marginal languages (Reinecke 1964) on several counts. Firstly their universe of discourse is restricted to particular areas of social interaction, notably sea-faring and trade, and in fact the very term 'pidgin' is believed to have its origin in the form taken in Chinese Pidgin English of the word *business*. Secondly, they differ from natural languages in that they are nobody's first code but are always acquired secondarily for the specific purpose of cross-cultural contact. And thirdly, they do not represent the vehicle of any particular culture but are used by members of totally different communities.

Occasionally what was originally a pidgin has developed into the normal everyday means of communication and expression within a new community formed from persons of diverse linguistic and cultural background. In such an event the children born to that community will be brought up to speak it as their mother-tongue so that it will eventually become the only language, or at least the first language, of the community. When this happens we no longer refer to it as a pidgin but as a *creole*. Creoles are in fact generally assumed to have developed from pidgins under the more stable sociolinguistic conditions which must have prevailed for instance on plantations, where speakers of different West African languages were thrown together as slaves under the often remote supervision of Europeans.

A pidgin may be treated for descriptive purposes as being derived by a process of *pidginization* from a 'target' language' (Hymes 1971: 84). The languages most readily identifiable as being the result of a process of pidginization are those whose target is constituted by some well-known European language. Where this consists in an obscure or relatively unknown language, however, the phenomenon is likely to be much less easily recognizable. The pidginization process may be understood as the reanalysis by adult speakers with a different linguistic background of the grammatical structures of the target language and may to some extent be characterized as a process of simplification leading to a reduction of the grammatical complexity of the target language, especially in the area of inflectional morphology. Generally the inflectional markers of gender, number, case and tense of the European target language are lost – perhaps, it has been suggested, through the intermediary of a tonal system of marking some of these oppositions – and their place is taken by new markers which often bring with them a new system of categories. The reduction of the morphological system of the target language is often attributed to 'imperfect learning' on the part of the non-European speakers, that is to say to their poor grasp of the grammatical system of the target language (Whinnom 1971); the reduction may on the other hand also to some extent reflect conventional notions on the part of native speakers of the target language regarding the way in which one's own language should be simplified when addressing foreigners ('foreigner talk': see Ferguson 1971). Whatever its precise motivation may be, however, there appears to be fairly general agreement among linguists that an essential element in the pidginization process consists in the simplification of the grammatical structure of the target language (Hymes 1971: 84).

Creolization on the other hand represents a process of expansion, for it is generally assumed that creoles derive from pidgins as a result of their adaptation to full language status by the enlargement of their grammar and lexicon. The model which underlies the creation of new grammatical categories and classes is not however the target language. We might reasonably expect the new grammatical structures to be calqued on those of the native languages of the speakers, and there is indeed some positive evidence to that effect, specific structures of Caribbean creoles (both English and French based) and even some of the actual morphs having been shown to derive from Ewe and other West African languages (Voorhoeve 1972; cf. Taylor 1956: 408; Hall 1958: 372). In other cases however it has often not been possible so far at least to identify native models. One of the difficulties, especially in the case of creoles of West African origin, is the large number of languages which must have been represented in the original immigrant population. It is at the same time true that West African languages show a degree of convergence of grammatical structure among themselves so that we can with some justification speak of a West African linguistic area, and it is therefore perhaps not so necessary to attempt to trace specific features to particular languages. The non-European structures of emerging creoles would also be likely to be reinforced by the limited availability of the target language, for both in the slave ships and subsequently on the plantations the new code would after all serve much more as a means of communication between Africans of different linguistic background than for communication with Europeans. In view of these considerations the lack of mutual intelligibility between creole and target language is hardly surprising.

In order to illustrate the process of creolization we will examine just one example of grammatical restructuring. The South East Asian creole known as Neo-Melanesian has a morph /fɛlə/ which, although formally derived from the English word *fellow*, has a completely different distribution. According to Hall (1965: 50ff.), who treats it as a single morphological unit, it is a marker of plural when combined with the personal pronouns of the first and second person (*mi* 'I', *mifɛlə* 'we', *ju* 'you', *jufɛlə* 'you (pl.)') and a marker of syntactic subordination to a head noun when combined with a word of a class which comprises the equivalents of English adjectives, numerals and demonstratives (*gudfɛlə mæn* '(a) good man', *smɔlfɛlə haws* '(a) little house', *wənfɛlə məŋki* 'one boy', *tu-*, *tri-fɛlə məŋki* 'two, three boys', *disfɛlə məŋki* 'this boy', *nədərfɛlə məŋki* 'another boy'). Thus, while the form can be readily related to an English model, the syntactic distribution follows altogether 'un-English' principles.

In spite of its foreign grammatical substratum and in spite of the absence of mutual intelligibility with the target language, we would be inclined to the opinion that an English-based creole should be classed as a variety of English, a French-based creole as a variety of French, etc., and this even when all the grammatical structure is alien to the target language. The strongest support for this viewpoint derives from the existence of what have been called *post-creole continua* consisting in series of language varieties ranging from at one extreme the broadest creole totally unintelligible to speakers of the target language, to at the other a local variety of the target language differing so slightly from its standard form that it could fairly be described in terms of a 'local accent'. Such continua are for instance found in Jamaica (DeCamp 1971), in Haiti (Valdman 1973), and in Hawaii (Carr 1972). Depending upon his social position, each speaker will control a specific portion of the continuum, so that the situation is in every way parallel to that of social or geographical variation or of the situation known as diglossia (Ferguson 1959) in traditional societies. In both situations there may be total absence of intelligibility between extreme varieties together with progressive levelling in the direction of a norm, represented by the target language in the case of a creole and by the standard language in the case of dialectal variation. This levelling process has in the case of creoles been termed *decreolization*. The very fact that decreolization is possible would seem to lend strong support to the argument that a creole should be classed as a variety of its target language.

This *polygenetic* model of the origin of pidgins and creoles, which assumes that these have come into existence independently at various points in time and space, does however face a number of difficulties. Attention for instance has been drawn to certain structural similarities which unite pidgins and creoles which come from quite different parts of the world and have different European languages as their targets. In certain cases, such as the English and French based creoles in the Caribbean area, some of these common features can be ascribed to a West African substratum (Hall 1958 versus Taylor 1956),[1] but in others their source has not been established. In addition there are structural features which are characteristic of pidgins and creoles as a whole, some fairly generalized such as the use of total or partial repetition in order to denote intensity or plurality or the use of free forms rather than affixes as markers of grammatical categories, others much more specific such as particular forms used as function words (for example *stay* as a marker of present progressive, *been* or *wen* of past or present perfect, *go* of future, all of which are found both in Hawaiian English and Cameroon Pidgin English: Carr 1972: 141f.) or specific lexical items (the most widespread probably being *sabir* or some similar form for 'to know': Voorhoeve 1972). These have been interpreted as suggesting a direct historical connection between the various pidgins and creoles throughout the world. Critics of the polygenetic hypothesis in fact hold that such features cannot be the result of chance nor of direct contact between individual pidgins and creoles. The most extreme hypothesis put forward in order to account for such widely distributed and yet highly specific features is that of the *monogenesis* or common origin of all pidgin and creole languages (Voorhoeve 1972). According to this model their ancestor would have been a proto-pidgin, probably Portuguese based and originally Mediterranean, from which all other pidgins and subsequently creoles would have developed through various *relexification* processes (that is to say through the substitution of essentially English or French vocabularies for the original Portuguese one). Words like *sabir* would then constitute relics of the earlier Portuguese lexicon. There is in fact positive evidence for the replacement of a number of Portuguese lexical items in particular creoles; thus a Portuguese lexicon has largely been replaced by a Spanish one in Philippino

[1] At least the *semantic* structure of West African creoles is to be considered 'West African' rather than English (D. Dalby). The same areal background is reflected in purely cultural isoglosses, for instance in the folk tales of the Caribbean which are clearly derived for the most part from West African sources.

Creole (Whinnom 1971: 107) and by an English one in Surinam (Voorhoeve 1972). There is however no reason why, in the absence of any positive evidence, a similar pattern of development should be postulated for *all* pidgins and creoles.

It would seem that neither an extreme polygenetic nor a monogenetic position can account satisfactorily for all the phenomena. A more realistic position would perhaps recognize three possible sources of shared grammatical and lexical features in the pidgins and creoles of the world and would consider the assignment of particular features to any one of these a matter for *empirical* investigation: (1) a common substratum (for example a West African substratum in both French based and English based creoles in the Caribbean); (2) common descent of a number of pidgins and creoles from a specific ancestor pidgin (for example all the English based creoles of the Caribbean from a single West African pidgin: Hancock 1971); (3) convergent developments among pidgins in various parts of the world due to direct contact, for example via the highly mobile sea-faring community. Much more detailed work will be needed however before specific isoglosses can be assigned with any degree of confidence to one or other of these sources.

7
Language and prehistory

1 Classification and language history

1.1 *Typology and language history*

We have so far dealt with two kinds of language classification, namely genealogical classification and areal classification. The first of these groups languages together into *language families* on the basis of shared features which have been retained during a process of divergence from a common ancestor, the second groups them into *linguistic areas* on the basis of shared features which have been acquired through a process of convergence resulting from spatial proximity. It will thus be seen that both the genealogical and the areal systems of language classification depend upon the interpretation of shared isoglosses as resulting in one way or another from the past history of the languages concerned. It is this diachronic aspect of both genealogical and areal classification which opposes them jointly to a third purely synchronic method of classifying languages. This is *typological classification*, which groups languages together into *language types* on the basis of isomorphism of structure without any regard to either their historical origin or their present or past geographical distribution (Greenberg 1957: 66–74; Robins 1973). Various structural characteristics have been proposed as a basis for typological classification but at the grammatical level there are essentially two systems, one based on morphological and the other on syntactic criteria.

The first of these, which is also the older, classes a language as being of isolating, agglutinative or inflectional (fusional) type according to the morphological structure of the word (Robins 1973: 13–17; Bazell 1958). Thus Vietnamese (in which the word is a fixed unanalysable unit) is classed as isolating, Turkish or Swahili (in which the word, at least ideally, is segmentable into a string of discrete morphs each representing a different morpheme) is said to be agglutinative, and Greek or Latin (in which the word is not neatly divisible into morphs, the relationship between morphological exponent and grammatical category being a complex one) is classed as inflectional.

The second and more recent system classes languages according to the order in which the basic constituents, subject (S), verb (V) and object (O), occur in simple declarative sentences (Greenberg 1966a). This results in an initial breakdown of all languages into three main types, SVO, VSO and SOV languages.[1] The most significant division would seem to be between SVO and VSO languages on the one hand, and SOV languages on the other, for it has been claimed that there is a large degree of correlation between the order of verb and object and certain other syntactic properties. Thus it would appear that if a language (such as Japanese) has basic OV order it can be predicted that it will also have postpositions and that its adjectival, genitival and relative clause modifiers will precede the noun. Typical VO languages (such as Thai), on the other hand, are said to place their possessives, adjectives, genitives and other modifiers after the noun and to have prepositions. If these claims are in fact justified, then this type of classification is clearly of considerable relevance to historical linguistics, for it should make possible certain generalizations with regard to syntactic change. Thus, if a language were to change its word order from OV to VO, the position of modifiers should also change and it should develop prepositions in place of postpositions. Precisely such a series of events is claimed to have taken place in a number of Indo-European languages, including English and French, so that the fact that all these languages also developed prepositions and auxiliaries preceding the main verb might be explainable on a purely internal basis as a corollary of the passage from OV to VO type. Change from an OV to a VO order has also been proposed as a possible explanation of why certain of the commonest adjectives in French may precede the noun (*grand* 'big, great', *vieux* 'old', *beau* 'fine, beautiful', etc.) whereas all other adjectives, and indeed all other modifiers, follow it. This anomaly it is argued would be a relic of an earlier OV order (Lehmann 1973). Again, the fact that early Indo-European languages like Greek and Sanskrit possess a very large number of compounds having the internal structure OV (Sanskrit *vīra-hán*, Greek *andró-phonos* 'man-killing' etc.) but hardly any of the type VO[2]

1 Although there could in theory be six possible types, not all of these are found in practice.

2 Proto-Indo-European compounds of VO structure, such as those reflected

has been interpreted as resulting from a syntactic order OV in the parent language (Lehmann 1969). All such explanations presuppose that the initial assignment of Proto-Indo-European to the OV type is sound and, in the latter case, that one accepts that the order of the elements in compounds necessarily reflects the syntactic order of the period in which these were coined. The evidence for classing Proto-Indo-European as an OV type language is, however, far from straightforward (Lehmann 1974 vs. Friedrich 1975), the main difficulty being that in the early Indo-European languages and in the protolanguage the syntactic functions of noun phrases were morphologically marked by case so that word order appears to have been fairly free and thus available to serve various other functions which are no longer readily recoverable (topicalization, emphasis, stylistic effect, etc.).

The mechanisms by means of which word order change is effected are also still very poorly understood, although quite a lot is known about specific word order changes in individual languages. In Chinese for instance certain OV structures can be shown to have resulted from the grammaticalization of the first of a series of verbs within a sentence (Li and Thompson 1974). Thus, in a sentence of the type SVOV(O) such as 'I've forgotten all their names'

wǒ	bǎ	tāmen-de míngzi	dōu	wàng	le
I (S)	CASE (orig. V 'take')	*their name* (O)	*all*	*forget* (V)	ASPECT,

the first verb lost its original verbal status and came to be interpreted functionally as a case marker with the result that the object now precedes the verb. Whether or not one is justified in going on from this to argue that Modern Chinese has become, or indeed is even in the process of becoming, an OV language (as is claimed by Li and Thompson) is another question. Parallel developments are claimed to have taken place in the Niger-Congo languages, the larger family grouping to which the Bantu languages are thought to belong (Givón 1975). There is, of course, no reason for supposing that this is the only way in which languages may change the order of their syntactic constituents.

Finally, given that the structure of a language can be usefully described in typological terms and that it can change its type during the course of time, there still remains the question of the sort of time-span

in Greek *Agé-laos* '(who) leads men', *Arché-laos* '(who) rules men' etc., are usually personal names and not common nouns. They are assumed to correspond to syntactically marked constructions with the object following the verb.

required for such a change to take place. Let us therefore consider the cases of two languages which have long historical records, namely Egyptian and Chinese. Recent work on the history of particular morphs and the constructions in which they figure over the 5,000 years or so which link Ancient Egyptian with Modern Coptic would appear to indicate that at various stages morphologically complex forms lost their analysability and that this led to their replacement by syntactic rather than morphological devices (Hodge 1970, 1975). Subsequently these analytic structures were in turn fused into morphologically complex forms, so that there was a development from a predominantly synthetic structure through a predominantly analytic structure back again to a predominantly synthetic structure. This would seem to lend some support to the hypothesis advanced in the nineteenth century that languages evolve through isolating, agglutinative and inflectional structures in recurrent cycles (Hodge 1970).

Although the documented history of Chinese spans only about three thousand years, the structural changes which occurred during that period are considerable. In terms of the traditional typology based on the morphological structure of the word, Chinese is usually considered to be an isolating language, its words being invariable and unanalysable. Strictly speaking, however, this characterization would appear to apply only to one particular phase of the language, that of Ancient Chinese. In the oldest recoverable stage, Archaic Chinese, there are still substantial traces of both an inflectional and a derivational morphology. Whether an initial plosive were voiced or voiceless, for instance, served to mark such diverse morphological oppositions as that between noun and verb, active and passive, intransitive and transitive, etc. (Karlgren 1949: 79ff.; Bodman 1951). Subsequently, however, the majority of these overt morphological distinctions were completely obliterated by sound change so that Ancient Chinese was characterized by invariable words having multiple membership of syntactic classes. This isolating structure of Ancient Chinese has in turn been superseded in Modern Chinese by new morphological processes showing a simple one-to-one relationship between form and function (Chao 1968). The history of the Chinese language thus comprises both a development towards and a development away from an isolating phase. According to Li and Thompson (1975), the syntax of the language would also appear to have undergone a parallel development away from and then back towards an OV structure, although the evidence for this is much less certain.

In conclusion, from the limited studies carried out to date it would appear that the structural type of a language is just as much subject to change as any other aspect of it. This means that there is no necessary correlation between language type and historical origin, so that shared typological features can neither be taken as excluding nor as indicating genealogical relationship.[1] Attempts to use isomorphism of structure either as a shortcut to genealogical classification (as has sometimes been done in the past, for instance in the fields of Bantu and American Indian linguistics) or as a way of penetrating further into the prehistory of a language than can be achieved by means of reconstruction are therefore quite without justification. However convenient such solutions might appear in theory, the historical linguist has to admit that for the time being at least the only proven means of reaching beyond attested language states remains systematic reconstruction.

Although we have been at pains to stress the absence of any necessary relationship between the type of a language and its genealogy, the possibility of there sometimes being a direct link between its structural type and the linguistic area in which it is or has previously been located would appear to be much more promising. For, although the extent to which areal pressures are instrumental in bringing about typological change is still poorly understood, there can be little doubt that particular structural types do tend to dominate specific geographical areas and that languages do appear to get attracted to them (see, for instance, the cluster of isolating languages in South-East Asia).

1.2 *Glottochronology* (*or lexicostatistics*)

The key to the prehistoric developments within a language family is the construction of a family tree. But, as we have already seen, a family tree situates reconstructed language states in relation to one another only in terms of relative time, and this relative chronology can be given an absolute value only in so far as it is possible to fit datable events into the tree model or relate them to it at specific points in its structure. If no points on the tree are datable on the basis of external

[1] In fact genealogical classification differs from both areal and typological classification in that members of a language family need not in principle have any common features at all, either formal or material. It is theoretically perfectly conceivable for genealogically related languages not to have retained a single inherited item or rule, although in practice by the time divergence has reached this level common origin will no longer be recoverable.

evidence the entire construct will then remain uninterpretable in terms of the real time in which historians are used to operating. It was in order to overcome this difficulty that a method was proposed in the forties which claimed to permit the dating of language splits in terms of real time on a purely internal basis. The intention of its originator, M. Swadesh, was clearly to provide for language prehistory a technique of absolute dating parallel to the methods of dendrochronology and Carbon-14 which were proving so successful in the field of prehistory. The basis of his argument was the general observation that the greater the time-depth which separates the members of a language family from their common ancestor the greater the degree of differentiation between them; if this could therefore be quantified in some way it might provide a means of determining the length of time during which divergent development had taken place. For the method to work, however, it would have to be applied to a sector of language within which change took place at a constant rate, corresponding to the growth rings of a tree which are added regularly at the rate of one per year throughout its life or the Carbon-14 contained in any organic substance which, from the moment that it is formed, breaks down at a constantly diminishing rate according to a precise mathematical curve. Swadesh decided that this area of language which universally undergoes change at a constant rate was its so-called *basic vocabulary*.

The basic vocabulary of a language is the sector of its lexicon which deals with those elements of universal human experience which exist irrespective of the speakers' culture and comprises such fundamental biological activities as eating, sleeping, giving birth, dying, such major divisions of the body as the eye, the mouth, the head, natural physical phenomena like fire, water, the sun, the moon, such general relational concepts as are represented by the personal pronouns, the demonstratives, negation, size, etc. From this body of universal meanings Swadesh chose a list of two hundred items, later reduced to one hundred (Swadesh 1971: 283), to be used in calculating time-depths according to his method, which is generally referred to either as glottochronology or as lexico-statistics.[1]

The process used to calculate the point in time at which two related or

[1] Although one might reasonably expect the term *lexicostatistics* to be used for any operation involving the counting of lexical items and *glottochronology* to be reserved for dating by means of the lexicon, a systematic distinction has not in fact always been made.

TABLE 1

1. I	26. root	51. breasts	76. rain
2. you	27. bark	52. heart	77. stone
3. we	28. skin	53. liver	78. sand
4. this	29. flesh	54. drink	79. earth
5. that	30. blood	55. eat	80. cloud
6. who	31. bone	56. bite	81. smoke
7. what	32. grease	57. see	82. fire
8. not	33. egg	58. hear	83. ash
9. all	34. horn	59. know	84. burn
10. many	35. tail	60. sleep	85. path
11. one	36. feather	61. die	86. mountain
12. two	37. hair	62. kill	87. red
13. big	38. head	63. swim	88. green
14. long	39. ear	64. fly	89. yellow
15. small	40. eye	65. walk	90. white
16. woman	41. nose	66. come	91. black
17. man	42. mouth	67. lie	92. night
18. person	43. tooth	68. sit	93. hot
19. fish	44. tongue	69. stand	94. cold
20. bird	45. claw	70. give	95. full
21. dog	46. foot	71. say	96. new
22. louse	47. knee	72. sun	97. good
23. tree	48. hand	73. moon	98. round
24. seed	49. belly	74. star	99. dry
25. leaf	50. neck	75. water	100. name

supposedly related languages separated is, in its broad outlines, as follows:[1] In each of the languages under consideration the non-complex lexical item which corresponds most closely to each meaning in the basic word list is selected. The forms of these items are then compared. Those pairs which, on the grounds of phonetic similarity or of phonological correspondence, appear or are known to be cognates are then counted as retentions from the common ancestor, whereas those which do not exhibit phonetic similarity or regular sound correspondence are considered to owe their dissimilarity to the loss of the reflex of the proto-item in one or both of the languages. The figure of common retention obtained for any language pair in this way is then converted into years of separate development by comparing it with a retention scale previ-

[1] For the theoretical considerations which underlie the calculations involved see Lees 1953; Chrétien 1962.

ously established from control cases. The series of test cases from which the standard retention rate was initially calculated included such ancestor and descendant pairs as Old English and Modern English, Plautine Latin and Early Modern French, Plautine Latin and Early Modern Spanish, Middle Egyptian and Coptic, Ancient Chinese and Modern Mandarin – thirteen pairs in all (Lees 1953). On this basis an average retention rate of 81 per cent per millennium was calculated, using a list of just over two hundred lexical items. Later, when the list was reduced to one hundred items, the rate was adjusted to 86 per cent. Using this standard retention rate as a yardstick, the date of split of any two languages could then be calculated on the assumption that over a period of a thousand years each of the languages would have retained 86 per cent of the basic vocabulary of the common protolanguage.[1] Relatedness would ideally be discernible up to the point where the level of chance similarity is reached. This is generally put at about 8 per cent which, according to the conversion of percentages into millennia, would correspond to a time depth of 11.72 millennia – far greater than the time-depth estimates for the parent language of any known language family.

Clearly the only way in which the validity of the method can be tested is to apply it to datable language states within established language families so that the results obtained can be compared with the known time-depths. However, even if the numerous practical problems associated with its application are disregarded (on what basis does one choose between synonyms, how is one to decide when two forms are sufficiently similar to be considered cognates, etc.) the results of such tests have not proved encouraging. The dates produced by the method in the Romance field are of particular interest, since the comparisons of forms taken from earlier and later language states within this family were among those used in the original calculation of the retention rate. The absolute dates at which individual Romance languages are found to have split by the application of the method are as follows: Spanish and Portuguese A.D. 1586, Italian and French 1586, Romanian and Italian 1130, French and Spanish 1045, Romanian and Spanish 874 (Rea 1958: 147). It can be seen that even the earliest of these dates, which may be taken as

[1] To give some idea of the correlation claimed to exist between retention rate and time-depth, 70 per cent retentions would correspond to a minimum length of separation of 1.18 millennia, 60 per cent to 1.69, 50 per cent to 2.29, 40 per cent to 3.03, 30 per cent to 3.99, and 20 per cent to 5.56 millennia (Swadesh 1971: 284).

representing the break-up of Proto-Romance, falls in fact within a period for which we possess written records of the individual languages showing them to be already well differentiated. According to accepted opinion the break-up of Proto-Romance must in fact have taken place almost a thousand years earlier, and the method thus has little validity even for the languages on which it is based (Rea 1973). Certain of the dates calculated for the divisions within Germanic might at first sight appear to be more in line with traditional views, such as the dating of the earliest split to 10 B.C. which does correspond sufficiently well to the estimated date for the break-up of Proto-Germanic. The fact that this earliest date represents the split of Gothic and Old Norse does not however correlate so well with traditional views, since many would consider these languages to be more closely related to each other than to the other Germanic languages. Some of the other dates appear even more absurd, such as English and Dutch having split in 860, English and German in 590, English and Swedish in 810, German and Dutch in 1575, German and Swedish in 750 (Arndt 1959: 185), for by the eighth century it can easily be demonstrated that the Germanic languages, at least those outside Scandinavia, were already well differentiated. The results for Slavonic (Fodor 1961), Semitic (Rabin 1975) and Indo-European in general (Tischler 1973) face similar objections. Thus Latin and Greek are calculated as having split in about 3000 B.C., Latin and Vedic Sanskrit in 3300, Latin and Old Irish as early as 3700, and earliest of all Hittite and Albanian in 4200 B.C., yet neither these absolute values nor the internal ordering of events which they imply correspond with traditional views.

In short, even if it were possible in practice to apply the method without having to make a disconcertingly large number of arbitrary decisions, the initial hypothesis of a constant retention rate has not been substantiated. Its use in the case of languages for which no historical documents are available, and where as a consequence there is no means of testing the results obtained against known facts (for instance Dyen 1964, 1965), would therefore appear difficult to justify.

While the value of the dating part of the method has come increasingly under suspicion, the possibilities inherent in the use of basic lexical correspondences as an indication of probable genealogical relationship would appear to be much more promising. That the sharing of lexical items may be the result of common origin is of course obvious, but by restricting his lexical comparisons to 'the basic vocabulary' Swadesh drew attention to the very much greater resistance to replacement of this sector of the lexicon and thus to its potential value as a diagnostic tool in assessing the likelihood of genealogical relationship between languages which have not yet been subjected to reconstruction. Such an instrument of initial diagnosis is particularly valuable as a means of deciding in which areas reconstruction is likely to prove fruitful – comparison after all cannot begin until the linguist has decided what he is going to compare. What is perhaps most needed now is a serious effort to define and delimit the concept of basicness in so far as it relates to items of lexicon together with the detailed study of the precise nature, content, and relationship to the other sectors of the lexicon of the basic vocabulary of specific languages.[1]

The use of basic vocabulary comparison not simply as a *preliminary* to reconstruction but as a *substitute* for it is more controversial. It has in fact been claimed that 'the arduous ritual of reconstruction by means of the comparative method' is quite unnecessary in order to establish genealogical relationship if the comparison is applied to the basic vocabularies not just of two but of *a number of languages simultaneously* (Greenberg 1966b). This comparison of several languages at the same time ('mass comparison') is claimed to constitute a valid test of genealogical relationship on the grounds that the likelihood of a number of languages simultaneously showing as the result of pure chance more than a minimal number of basic vocabulary agreements is so much more remote than in the case of a pair of languages that it may be discounted; and, since borrowing and sound symbolism are unlikely to occur in the basic lexicon, any such similarities can *only* be the result of common origin.

This claim has met with a certain amount of scepticism on the part of traditional historical linguists, who have not been slow in pointing out the inaccuracies which are bound to result from a reliance on mere similarity of form assessed intuitively and unsubstantiated by reconstruction. There can be no doubt that the method introduces an element of arbitrariness in that different investigators are likely to make different decisions with regard to the same data. It is also certain that, especially in the case of more remotely related languages, actual cognates will go

[1] An indication of the sort of lines along which such a process of definition might proceed may be obtained from Berlin and Kay's attempt to define the concept of 'basic' in relation to colour terms (B. Berlin and P. Kay, *Basic Color Terms: Their Universality and Evolution*, University of California Press, 1969, pp. 5–7).

unnoticed – would anyone, for instance, in the absence of additional information and merely on the grounds of phonetic similarity, suggest that French *chef* and English *head* were cognates? And conversely, would not such chance look-alikes as Latin *diēs* 'day' and English *day* be taken for cognates? Adherents of mass comparison would, however, argue that such cases are taken account of in the statistical calculations and would in any case tend to cancel one another out. Perhaps the most realistic view is to consider what useful purposes mass comparison may serve. It is clear that, as far as the historical linguist is concerned, it can in no way serve as a substitute for reconstruction, for to him the mere fact of relationship is of little interest in itself. What the historical linguist wishes to know is the internal history of the languages concerned, *how* they are related, what was the structure of their common ancestor, etc. The historian on the other hand may well consider that the simple knowledge that languages which now cover a wide geographical area or are separated from each other by a considerable distance in space once had a common origin provides him with valuable information about the speakers. For in areas with no written documentation of historical events, as is for instance the case for large parts of Africa, this in itself could constitute a vital clue to earlier migrations and contacts.

2 Linguistic reconstruction and prehistory

So far we have dealt almost exclusively with the history of languages in terms of their own internal structure, but it must also be evident that at all periods throughout its history a language has speakers and that these too have a history in political, social and cultural terms. What then can be learned from the reconstructed history of a language concerning the history of the people who spoke it?

We have already seen that the mere fact that two or more languages are genealogically related carries certain non-linguistic implications, for the loss of contact which is an essential prerequisite of language diversification can only be the result of the prior physical displacement of at least a portion of the speakers of the parent language. Such displacement may have taken the form of a general expansion outwards from the original centre or of the migratory movement of only a section of the community, it may have entailed the violent conquest of a preexisting population or the more peaceful colonization of what was previously a largely uninhabited territory. Thus we know that the present wide geographical distribution of the Indo-European languages is the result of all these processes, for much of it took place in the full light of history. Such expansions as the spread of certain Germanic languages to England and subsequently of English to North America and Australia, or of Latin to the Iberian Peninsula and subsequently of Spanish and Portuguese to South America, were the result of the large scale movement of migrant populations who formed new communities in the acquired areas, often absorbing in the process local populations who abandoned their indigenous languages in favour of that of the newcomers.

Documentation of the type which is available for the recent spread of the Indo-European languages is however not always at hand, and even when historical records exist evidence regarding the language or languages spoken by the populations who previously inhabited the occupied areas is often incomplete or totally lacking. In such cases the historical linguist may still recover a certain amount of information about the previous inhabitants from the evidence of a very specific type of borrowing usually referred to as a substratum (see p. 252f.). Language substrata are most obvious at the level of the lexicon, and within the lexicon the field that is most generally affected is that of toponyms. Thus a careful study of the names of the settlements, the rivers, the mountains etc. of a region can often tell a great deal about the geographical extension and the historical connections of its previous inhabitants. The second important source of evidence about the past history of a people is that which can be extracted from a careful study of their protolexicon, and of the origin and order of entry of the various loan-words which have come into the language from outside. This study of 'words and things' can often give some indications concerning the situation of the homeland of the speakers of the protolanguage, the character of their material and spiritual culture and the nature and extent of their subsequent relations with the speakers of other languages. We shall look first at the evidence of toponyms.

2.1 *The evidence of toponymy*

As we have said, place-names can be an important source of information regarding the people who have inhabited an area. This is the result of two main facts. The first of these is that the names attached to localities tend to be extremely persistent and to resist replacement even when the language spoken in the area is itself replaced. This resistance to replacement is particularly marked in the case of important topographical features such as large rivers and mountains, but is also characteristic of human settlements of all sizes. Thus both the *Thames* and *London* have carried their present names for at least the last two thousand years in spite of all intervening upheavals and the replacement on more than one occasion of the language spoken by the local population.[1] The second fact is that when a new name is given to a place it is naturally structured according to the synchronic rules of the language spoken by the persons who coined it. As a result, if a place-name is analysable in terms of the rules of a specific language state, this can be taken as a safe indication that persons speaking that language inhabited the region at the time when the rules were productive.[2] By therefore dividing up the total corpus of place-names of a region into groups and attributing each of these to a specific language state, the historical linguist can to a large extent reconstruct the history of the region in terms of the languages spoken by its inhabitants.

On the basis of such a linguistic analysis (see Ekwall 1966) six sources have been established for the place-names of England: English of all periods since Anglo-Saxon, Scandinavian, Norman French, Latin, Ancient Celtic and Pre-Celtic. Clearly the Norman French, Scandinavian, Anglo-Saxon and Latin names reflect the speech of populations entering Britain during historic times, whereas the Celtic and Pre-Celtic Indo-European names belong to a period preceding historical documentation.

The great majority of place-names in England are analysable by means of the grammar of Old English. Thus *Sewardstone* in Essex, attested in 1178 as *Siwardeston*, consists of the genitive in *-es* of the Old English personal name *Sigeweard* followed by the generic term *tūn* 'enclosed settlement' (whence Modern English *town*, cognate with German *Zaun* 'fence'); *Raynham*, attested in the Domesday Book (1086) as *Reineham*, consists of the genitive of the personal name *Regna* and the generic term *hām* 'village' (whence Modern English *home*, cognate with German *Heim* 'home' equally common as a second element in German place-names); *Reading*, attested in 872 in the dative plural form *Readingum*, consists of the Old English man's name *Rēad* to which is suffixed the morpheme *-ing* meaning 'the people of . . ., the followers of . . .'. Exactly the same formation is found in such German place-

1 The earliest attested forms are *Londinium* in Tacitus (Ekwall 1966 s.v.) and *Tamesis* in Caesar (Ekwall 1928 s.v.).

2 Allowance being made, of course, for colonists sometimes transferring no longer analysable place-names to which they are sentimentally attached from their land of origin to their new settlements.

names as *Hechingen*, *Sigmaringen*, 'the followers of (*-ingum*) the men named *Hacho*, *Sigimar*'. The same elements *tun* and *ham* preceded by descriptive adjectives have given such names as *Middleton*, *Newton*, *New(n)ham*. *Washington* is 'the enclosed settlement (*tūn*) of the people of (*-ing*) the man named *Wasa*', *Chillingham* 'the village (*ham*) of the people of *Cheul* (< **Ceofel*)', etc.

It can be seen that all these names readily fall into *types* characterized by one or more suffixed place-name elements (Mawer 1924). And, because of their analysability in terms of the grammar of Old English, the creation of these names can be attributed to the Anglo-Saxons, who are known to have arrived in Britain roughly during the course of the middle period of the first millennium A.D. If then these names are plotted on a map we can establish the area occupied by the Anglo-Saxon settlers during this period.

In areas of the country like Wales or parts of Scotland where the Celtic language still survives or in places like Cornwall where it was still spoken until fairly recently, one would naturally expect to find Celtic names. But Celtic names are also to be found elsewhere in Britain and the names of many of the more important rivers and towns of England have in fact a Celtic etymology. Thus *Avon*, *Ouse*, *Severn*, *Tees*, *Trent*, *Thames*, *Wye*, *Dee*, *Esk* are all Celtic (Ekwall 1928; Nicolaisen 1957) as are *London*, *Dover*, *Carlisle*, *York* and, combined with the Old English word *ceaster* 'fort' (< Latin *castra*), *Winchester*, *Manchester*, *Rochester*, *Gloucester*, *Dorchester*, or again, combined with Old English *burg*, *Salisbury*, etc. Often however the Celtic names have been replaced and it is only thanks to their attestation in historical sources that we know what they were. Thus the Celtic name for *Canterbury* (< Old English *Cantwaraburg* 'the town of the people of Kent')[1] was in Roman times *Durovernon* and that of *Colchester* (< *Colneceaster* 'the fort on the river Colne') was *Camulodunum*. This latter place-name belongs to a type which was well represented in Britain although, with the possible exceptions of *Branodunum* (mod. *Brancaster*) and *Sorviodunum* (mod. *Salisbury*), none of these has survived replacement (cf. *Margidunum*, mod. *Castle Hill*; *Segedunum*, mod. *Wallsend*; *Uxellodunum*, mod. *Castlesteads*, etc.). The second element of these names, which is rendered in Latinized form as *-dunum* and in Greek form as *-dunon*, is the Celtic cognate of Old English *tun* and must have meant

1 Although this is a formation of the Anglo-Saxon period based on the name of the county, *Kent*, this latter is itself of Celtic origin.

something like 'fortified settlement'. As can be seen from Map 5 (after Rix 1954: 103), *-dunum* names are not confined to Britain but have a wide distribution in Europe.

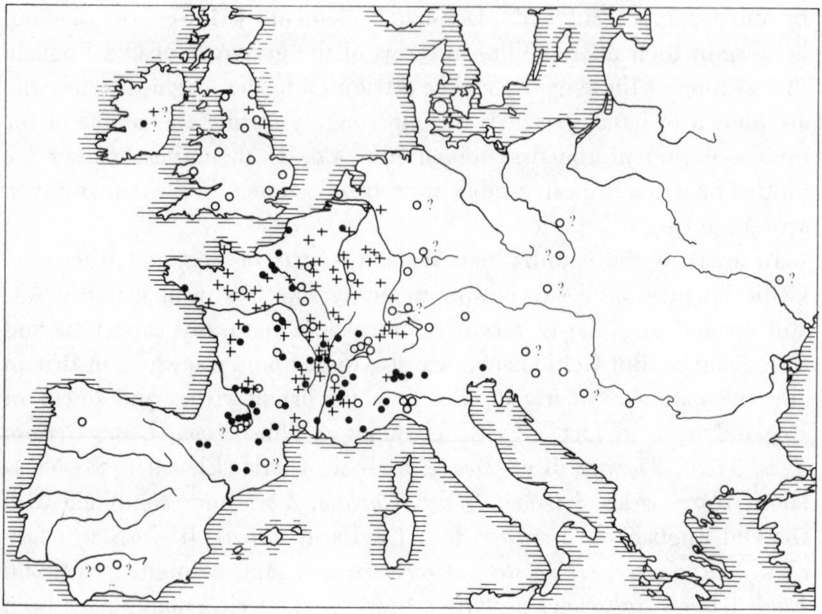

Map 5 Open circles represent *-dunum* names already attested in Antiquity, crosses those attested since the Middle Ages, and filled circles those attested only in the modern period; a question-mark indicates that the precise localization of the name is uncertain.

The first element in these names is as a rule the name of a person or of a river and, like the English names in *-ing* or *-ham*, they can be attributed to a specific period in the history of Celtic. They are in fact amply represented in Greek and Roman sources, and since some of them do not have a Celtic but rather a Latin first element the type must have continued to be productive well into the period of the Roman Empire. Thus *Autun*, the name of several towns in France, goes back to *Augustodunum*, with the name of the Roman emperor *Augustus* as first element.

Other typically Celtic name types in classical sources are those in

-briga ('hill fort', cognate with German *burg* 'castle', *Berg* 'mount', Modern English *-burgh* and *-bury*), in *-magus* 'field' (*Noviomagus*, mod. *Chichester*; *Caesaromagus*, mod. *Chelmsford*) and in *-lanum* 'plain' (*Mediolanum*, mod. *Whitchurch* in Shropshire), the geographical distributions of which differ in certain respects from those in *-dunum*. An overall map of the Celtic toponyms of Europe has not yet been drawn up, but these main types already give a fair indication of the geographical distribution of Celtic speakers at the period when they were formed. Thus, in spite of the fact that today Celtic is only spoken in a few regions of the British Isles and in Brittany, we know from the study of toponyms that at the time of the Roman Empire Celtic speakers occupied vast areas of Europe, reaching from Spain and Ireland in the west as far as the Balkans in the east.

In the preceding discussion we have described these place-names as 'Celtic' and this is of course also the name that we used when speaking of that branch of the Indo-European family tree which is today represented by Welsh, Irish, Breton, Scottish Gaelic, etc. But on what grounds are we justified in making this equation? For, although the linguist can easily demonstrate the common origin and the position within the Indo-European family tree of all these languages through systematic reconstruction, there is absolutely no tradition among their present-day speakers to the effect that their ancestors ever referred to themselves by means of the label 'Celts'. It is here that the evidence of place-names in linking the sources is crucial. For the classical authors not only gave the names of these peoples and described their habits and their distribution but, as we have already seen, they often recorded the names by means of which they knew their towns. And it is precisely on the purely linguistic grounds that we are able to interpret these place-names preserved in the classical sources in terms of the historical grammar of the language family of which Welsh, Scottish Gaelic, etc. are the living representatives that we are justified in linking this language family with the *Keltoi* of the Greeks and the *Galli* of the Romans.

Our knowledge of our more distant past is however no longer derived primarily from the written sources of the classical authors but is coming to depend more and more on the evidence produced by the techniques of *prehistoric archaeology*. Prehistory defines cultures in terms of associations of specific types of artefact, of habitation plan, of method of burial, etc. Here again the evidence of place-names forms the most reliable basis for any attempt to link particular cultures established in terms of the cultural isoglosses of prehistoric archaeology to language families established by means of the methods of linguistic reconstruction. Thus an important cultural complex of central and western Europe at the beginning of the fifth century B.C. was the Hallstatt Culture, which stretched from Austria in the east as far as northern Spain and Portugal in the west. And it is largely on the basis of the congruence between the distribution patterns of the urnfield burial grounds which are one of the principal characteristics of this culture and of certain place-name types which are linguistically Celtic that the bearers of this culture have been equated with the Celts (Powell 1963: 48–51).

2.2 *The evidence of the protolexicon*

While place-names can sometimes allow one to locate past language states in terms of geographical space, the lexicon of a protolanguage may provide information not only about the physical environment of its speakers (and hence indirectly about the geographical area in which they lived) but also about their material and spiritual culture. Thus the reconstructed lexicon of Proto-Indo-European indicates that its speakers were familiar with gold and silver, with the horse, the dog, the cow, the sheep, the pig and perhaps the goat but that they probably did not have the donkey or the domestic fowl; it also shows that they span and wove wool, that they used the yoke and the wheeled cart and perhaps had the plow and cultivated barley. They would also appear to have been members of a patriarchal society, to have had chiefs or 'kings' and to have worshipped deities associated with such natural phenomena as daylight, the sun, the dawn, the earth, etc. (Schrader 1911). It can readily be understood however that the reconstruction of the more abstract aspects of the protoculture raises much more serious problems of semantic interpretation than do the more material ones (see Benveniste (1973) for a detailed analysis).

As regards the area which they inhabited, the presence in the protolexicon of words for bear, beaver, otter, wolf, crane and snow suggests a northern temperate region. Arguments regarding the precise location of their homeland (*Urheimat*) are however mainly based on the names of plants of restricted habitat, especially trees, that can be reconstructed for the protolanguage. A key name in this respect is the word which is reflected in present-day English *beech* (Krahe 1954: 31f.; Krogmann 1955/6). This comes from Old English *bēce* (< **bōkya*-), and corresponds in the other Germanic languages to German *Buche*, Danish *bøg*, Dutch *beuk*, Old High German *buohha*, Old Norse *bōk*, all reflexes of a Proto-Germanic base **bōk-* 'beech'. The Germanic forms, Latin *fāgus* 'beech' and Greek (Attic) *phēgós*, (Dorian) *phāgós* 'a kind of oak', all derive from a common base **bhāg-*. Related forms, but with a different vowel, are found in Slavonic (Bulgarian *buz*, Russian *bozu* and *buziná*, all meaning 'elder'); apparent cognates in Iranian are now no longer accepted. All these suggest an original form **bhāug-/bhug-* for the protolanguage, the alternation in the stem vowel being interpretable as an indication of the great age of the lexeme. The difficulty however lies in assigning a precise *meaning* to the protoform. Those who postulate a primitive meaning 'beech' (*Fagus silvatica* L.) argue that Latin and Germanic have retained the original meaning whereas in the case of Greek and Slavonic it has been replaced because the speakers of these languages during the course of their migrations and in the regions in which they subsequently settled did not find beech-trees. We know from palaeobotany that *Fagus silvatica* L. has been a common tree in central and western Europe ever since the end of the last ice age but that it does not, and never did, grow east of a line which runs from eastern Prussia to the Black Sea. The argument is that if the Indo-Europeans were familiar with the beech they must have come from an area to the west of that line so that their homeland must have been situated somewhere in central or western Europe. Unfortunately however the meaning 'beech' is attested only in Germanic and Latin, languages which are known to have been in close contact since prehistoric times. This shared meaning may therefore not be a retention but rather an innovation stemming from the time when they reached an area in western Europe in which beeches were common. And, since the whole argument stands or falls on the original meaning of **bhāug-/bhug-*, unless more cogent reasons can be produced for its identification with the meaning 'beech' than those so far advanced[1] it can hardly be treated as anything more than conjecture. Parallel difficulties arise in the case of the other diagnostic terms which have so far been proposed (for instance the name of the salmon; see Thieme 1953; Krogmann 1960).

Of course various attempts have been made to correlate the diversification of the Indo-European language family from a protolanguage

[1] A Mysian form *musós* is well attested in classical sources with the meaning 'beech'. If this is in fact the regular reflex of **bhūgos* in this Thracian dialect, it can be considered to give added support to the theory that the original meaning was 'beech' (Krogmann 1955/6: 17).

situated in a fairly circumscribed centre with the spread of a prehistoric culture, bearer of the linguistic expansion. The most recent hypothesis in this respect suggests that the so-called Kurgan Culture should be equated with the original Indo-Europeans, which would imply that the parent language was spoken in an area situated to the north of the Black Sea at some time around 3000 B.C. (Gimbutas 1970). It is clear, however, that the identification of the Indo-Europeans with the bearers of the Kurgan Culture rests on infinitely weaker arguments than that of for instance the Celts with the Hallstatt Culture, where place-names and the records of the classical sources provide vital links in the identification. The location of the Indo-Europeans in time and space must remain, for the time being at least, an open question.

FURTHER READING

Textbooks

Aitchison 1981; Anttila 1972; Bloomfield 1933 (chs. 17–27); Boretzky 1977; Haas 1969; Goyvaerts 1975; Hoenigswald 1960; Jeffers and Lehiste 1979; King 1969a; Lehmann 1973.

Articles arranged by main topics within chapters

Introduction

Synchronic versus diachronic linguistics: Bailey 1980b, 1982; Coseriu 1974, 1975; Greenberg 1979; Lehmann 1968; Lieb 1968; Ramat 1982; de Saussure part 1 ch. 3.

Child language and linguistic change: Aitchison 1981 ch. 11; Andersen 1980; Baron 1977; Drachman 1978; Faust 1980; Major 1978; Slobin 1979

Introductions to Indo-European comparative and historical linguistics: Krahe 1970; Lockwood 1969, 1972; Meillet 1937 (especially ch. 1 on method); Palmer 1972; Szemerényi 1970

Chapter 1

Neogrammarian theory: Delbrück 1919; Hoenigswald 1978; Jankowski 1977; Osthoff and Brugmann 1878; Putschke 1969; Vennemann and Wilbur 1972

Sound change: Labov 1981; Melchert 1975; Schuchardt 1885; Wilbur 1972, 1976

Analogy: Anttila 1977; Best 1973; Davies 1978; Esper 1973 ch. 3; Kiparski 1974; Kuryłowicz 1966; Mańczak 1957–8, 1980a, b; Ross 1981; Winter 1969; Vincent 1974

Reconstruction, family tree, protolanguage: Allen 1953, 1978; Bailey 1980a; Chen 1976; Hall 1950; Hoenigswald 1950, 1966; Katičić 1966, 1970; Lass 1978; Michelena 1963; Pulgram 1959; Southworth 1964

Chapter 2

Structuralist method: Hoenigswald 1953; Kuryłowicz 1964

Phonological change: Anderson 1973 chs. 6, 7; Chen 1972; Dressler 1972, 1976; Fox 1976; Hockett 1965; Hombert et al. 1979; Jakobson 1972a;

Labov 1981; Martinet 1952, 1955; Sieberer 1958; Vincent 1974

Internal reconstruction: Chen 1976; Hoenigswald 1974; Lass 1975; Marchand 1956

Morphological, syntactic and semantic change: Anderson 1980; Benveniste 1968; Bybee 1980; Dressler 1969, 1971; Givón 1971; Hamp 1976; Harris 1978, 1979; Hooper 1979; Langacker 1977; Li (ed.) 1977; Timberlake 1977; Vincent 1980, 1982; Watkins 1964, 1976

Chapter 3

Theoretical position: Andersen 1973; Halle 1962; King 1969a

Phonological change: Anderson 1978; Anttila 1974, 1975, 1979; Chafe 1968; Chomsky and Halle 1968 ch. 6; Hogg 1979; Hooper 1976 ch. 6; Jeffers 1978; King 1973; Kiparsky 1971a, b; 1972, 1974, 1982; Klausenburger 1979; Newton 1971; Postal 1968 chs. 10, 11; Shibatani 1973; Vennemann 1972b; Wurzel 1975, 1980

Syntactic change: Aitchison 1980; Ard 1977a; Bennett 1979, 1980; Bever and Langendoen 1972; Haiman 1974; Hamp 1976; Klima 1964; Lightfoot 1976, 1977, 1979a (especially chs. 2, 3); 1979b; 1980a, b; Traugott 1969, 1972, 1974; Warner 1982

Chapter 4

Chen 1972, 1976; Chen and Wang 1975; Chambers and Trudgill 1980; Dauzat 1923; Pulgram 1953; Saporta 1972; Wang 1969; Weinreich 1950

Chapter 5

Bailey 1973; Bailey and Shuy (eds.) 1973; Bickerton 1973; Cedergren and Sankoff 1974; Labov 1963, 1972a; Labov et al. 1972; Romaine 1980, 1982; Trudgill 1974 ch. 2; Weinreich–Labov–Herzog 1968

Chapter 6

Principles: Weinreich 1953; Moravcsik 1978

Lexical borrowing: Any etymological dictionary; Carstensen 1980; Haugen 1950; Holden 1976; Thomas 1975

Grammatical borrowing: Nadkarni 1975; Szemerényi 1981; Ureland (ed.) 1979

Linguistic areas: Emeneau 1956, 1974; Göschel 1971; Jakobson 1972b; Masica 1976; Vogt 1954; Weinreich 1958; Winter 1973

Pidgins and creoles: Bickerton 1975; Bickerton and Givón 1976; Mühlhäusler 1974

Chapter 7

Language classification: Davies 1978; Greenberg 1957, 1966a, 1974; Robins 1973

Typology and language history: Aitchison 1979; Canale 1976; Gamkrelidze 1981; Greenberg 1966; Hawkins 1979, 1980; Holman 1980; Lehmann 1973b, 1975; Smith 1981; Tai 1976; Vennemann 1974, 1975

Language and prehistory: Cardona et al. 1970; Fronzaroli 1975; Krahe 1970: 54–68; Scherer 1968; Schrader 1911; *Journal of Indo-European Studies*

REFERENCES

Abbreviations used in references

IF	*Indogermanische Forschungen*
IJAL	*International Journal of American Linguistics*
JL	*Journal of Linguistics*
KZ	*(Kuhns) Zeitschrift für Vergleichende Sprachforschung*
TCLP	*Travaux du Cercle Linguistique de Prague*
TPS	*Transactions of the Philological Society*

Adams, G.B. (1967) 'Phonemic systems in collision in Ulster English' in Schmitt 1967, 1–6

Allen, W.S. (1950) 'Notes on the phonetics of an eastern Armenian speaker', *TPS* 1950, 180–206

– (1953) 'Relationship in comparative linguistics', *TPS* 1953, 52–108

– (1964a) 'On one-vowel systems', *Lingua* 13, 111–24

– (1964b) 'Transitivity and possession', *Language* 40, 337–43

– (1965) *Vox Latina*, Cambridge: Cambridge University Press

– (1973) *Accent and rhythm. Prosodic features of Latin and Greek: a study in theory and reconstruction*, Cambridge: Cambridge University Press

– (1974) *Vox Graeca*, second edition, Cambridge: Cambridge University Press

Anderson, J.M. (1973) *Structural aspects of language change*, London: Longman

Anderson, J.M. and C. Jones (eds) (1974) *Historical Linguistics: Proceedings of the First International Conference on Historical Linguistics, Edinburgh 2–7 September 1973*, 2 vols, Amsterdam: North-Holland

Anttila, R. (1972) *An introduction to historical and comparative linguistics*, New York: Macmillan

Ardener, E. (1971) 'Social anthropology and the historicity of historical linguistics' in Ardener (ed.), *Social anthropology and language*, London: Tavistock Publications, 209–41

Arndt, W. (1959) 'The performance of glottochronology in Germanic', *Language* 35, 180–92

Bach, E. and R.T. Harms (eds) (1968) *Universals in linguistic theory*, London and New York: Holt

Baugh, A.C. (1965) *A history of the English language*, second edition, London: Kegan Paul

Bazell, C.E. (1938) 'Analogical system', *TPS* 1938, 104–26

– (1958) *Linguistic typology*, London: School of Oriental and African Studies

– (1960) 'A question of syncretism and analogy', *TPS* 1960, 1–12

– (1974) 'Marginal'nye zvukovje zakony', *Voprusy Jazykoznaniya* 1974, 81–6
– (1975) Review of R.E. Diamond, 'Old English grammar and reader', *Linguistics* 143, 102–3
Behaghel, O. (1923–32) *Deutsche Syntax: eine geschichtliche Darstellung*, 4 vols, Heidelberg: Winter
Bender, M.L. (1974) 'Mutual intelligibility within Sidamo' in Caquot and Cohen 1974, 151–69
– (1975) 'Toward a lexicostatistic classification of Ethiopian languages' in Bynon 1975, 377–86
Benedict, P.K. (1972) *Sino-Tibetan: A conspectus*, Cambridge: Cambridge University Press
Bennett, P.R. (1967) 'Dahl's Law and Thagicu', *African Language Studies* 8, 127–59
Benveniste, E. (1966) *Problèmes de linguistique générale*, Paris: Gallimard
– (1973) *Indo-European language and society*, translated by E. Palmer, London: Faber (French original: *Le vocabulaire des institutions indo-européennes*, Paris 1969)
Best, K.H. (1973) *Probleme der Analogieforschung*, Munich: Hueber
Bever, T.G. and D.T. Langendoen (1972) 'The interaction of speech perception and grammatical structure in the evolution of language' in Stockwell and Macaulay, 32–95
Bichakjian, B.H. (1974) 'The evolution of French [y]: an integrated change' in Anderson and Jones, ii, 71–88
Bickerton, D. (1973) 'The structure of a creole continuum', *Language* 49, 640–69
Bierwisch, M. (1971) *Modern linguistics*, The Hague: Mouton
Bloomfield, L. (1933) *Language*, New York: Holt
Boas, F. (1940) *Race, language and culture*, New York: Macmillan
Bodman, N.C. (1951) Review of J. Chmielewski, 'The typological evolution of the Chinese language', *Language* 27, 204–6
Bopp, F. (1833–54) *Vergleichende Grammatik des Sanskrit, Zend, Armenischen, Griechischen, Lateinischen, Litauischen, Altslavischen, Gothischen und Deutschen*, 3 vols, Berlin
Brosnahan, L.F. (1961) *The sounds of language: An inquiry into the role of genetic factors in the development of sound systems*, Cambridge: Heffer
Bynon, J. (1970) 'The contribution of linguistics to history in the field of Berber studies', in D. Dalby (ed.), *Language and history in Africa*, London: Cass, 64–77
Bynon, J. and Th. (eds) (1975) *Hamito-Semitica*, The Hague: Mouton
Bynon, Th. (1970) 'Swabian Umgangssprache', *TPS* 1970, 25–61
Campbell, A. (1959) *Old English grammar*, Oxford: Clarendon Press
Caquot, A. and D. Cohen (eds) (1974) *Actes du Premier Congrès International de Linguistique Sémitique et Chamito-Sémitique, Paris 16–19 juillet 1969*, The Hague: Mouton
Cardona, G., H. M. Hoenigswald and A. Senn (eds) (1970) *Indo-European and Indo-Europeans*, Philadelphia: University of Pennsylvania Press
Carr, E.B. (1972) *Da kine talk: From pidgin to standard English in Hawaii*, Honolulu: University Press of Hawaii
Cassidy, F.G. (1971) 'Tracing the pidgin element in Jamaican Creole' in Hymes 1971, 203–21
Cedergren, H., D. Lightfoot and Y.C. Morim (eds) (1974) *Montreal working papers in linguistics*, McGill University
Chafe, W.L. (1968) 'The ordering of phonological rules', *IJAL* 34, 115–36

Chao, Y.R. (1968) *A grammar of spoken Chinese*, Los Angeles: University of California Press
Chen, M. (1973) 'On the formal expression of natural rules in phonology', *JL* 9, 223–49
– (1974) 'Metarules and universal constraints in phonological theory' in Heilmann 1974, 909–24
Chen, M. and H.I. Hsieh (1971) 'The time variable in phonological change', *JL* 7, 1–14
Chomsky, C. Schatz (1954) 'The role of context in the perception of stops', *Language* 30, 47–56
Chomsky, N. (1965) *Aspects of the theory of syntax*, Cambridge Mass.: MIT Press
Chomsky, N. and M. Halle (1968) *The sound pattern of English*, New York: Harper and Row
Chrétien, C.D. (1962) 'The mathematical models of glottochronology', *Language* 32, 11–37
Collinge, N.E. (1970) *Collectanea linguistica*, The Hague: Mouton
Cowan, W. (1971) *Workbook in comparative reconstruction*, New York: Holt
Dalby, D. (1975–6) 'The prehistorical implications of Guthrie's Comparative Bantu', *Journal of African History* 16, 481–501; 17, 1–27
Dauzat, A. (1922) *La géographie linguistique*, Paris: Ernest Flammarion
DeCamp, D. (1971) 'Toward a generative analysis of a post-creole continuum' in Hymes 1971, 349–70
Delbrück, B. (1919) *Einleitung in das Studium der indogermanischen Sprachen: ein Beitrag zur Geschichte und Methodik der vergleichenden Sprachforschung*, 6th edition, Leipzig: Breitkopf und Härtel. English translation (*Introduction to the study of language*), ed. by E.F.K. Koerner, Amsterdam: North-Holland
Deroy, L. (1956) *L'emprunt linguistique*, Paris: Les Belles Lettres
Düwel, K. (1968) *Runenkunde*, Stuttgart: Metzler
Dyen, I. (1964) 'On the validity of comparative lexicostatistics', *IXth International Congress of Linguists*, 238–52
– (1965) *A lexicostatistic classification of the Austronesian languages*, Indiana Publications in Anthropology and Linguistics, *IJAL* Memoir 19
Ekwall, E. (1928) *English river-names*, Oxford: Clarendon Press
– (1966) *The concise Oxford dictionary of English place-names*, 4th edition, Oxford: Clarendon Press
Ellis, J. (1966) *Towards a general comparative linguistics*, The Hague: Mouton
Emeneau, M.B. (1956) 'India as a linguistic area', *Language* 32, 3–16; also in Hymes 1964, 642–53
Esper, E.A. (1973) *Analogy and association in linguistics and psychology*, University of Georgia Press
Fairbanks, G.H. (1973) 'Sound change, analogy and generative phonology' in J. B. Kachru (ed.), *Issues in linguistics: Papers in honor of H. and R. Kahane*, University of Illinois Press, 199–209
Ferguson, C.A. (1959) 'Diglossia', *Word* 15, 325–40
– (1971) 'Absence of copula and the notion of simplicity: a study of normal speech, baby talk, foreigner talk and pidgins' in Hymes 1971, 141–50
Fillmore, C.J. (1968) 'The case for case' in Bach and Harms, 1–88
Fodor, I. (1961) 'The validity of glottochronology on the basis of the Slavonic languages', *Studia slavica* (Budapest) 7, 295–346
Friedrich, P. (1970) 'Proto-Indo-European trees' in Cardona et al., 11–34
– (1975) *Proto-Indo-European syntax: The order of meaningful elements*, *Journal of Indo-European Studies*, Monograph No. 1

Fries, C.C. and K.L. Pike (1949) 'Co-existing phonemic systems', *Language* 25, 29–50
Frings, Th. (1957) *Grundlegung einer Geschichte der deutschen Sprache* Halle: Niemeyer
Fronzaroli, P. (1975) 'On the common Semitic lexicon and its ecological and cultural background' in Bynon 1975, 43–53
Fudge, E.C. (1973) 'On the notion "universal phonetic framework" ' in Fudge (ed.), *Phonology*, London: Penguin
Gauchat, L. (1905) 'L'unité phonétique dans le patois d'une commune' in *Festschrift Henrich Morf*, Halle: Niemeyer
Gelb, I.J. (1969) *Sequential reconstruction of Proto-Akkadian*, University of Chicago Press
Gilbert, G.G. (ed.) (1971) *The German language in America*, University of Texas Press
Gilliéron, J. (1902–12) *Atlas linguistique de la France*, Paris
– (1912) *Etudes de géographie linguistique d'après l'Atlas linguistique de la France*, Paris: Champion
– (1919) *La faillite de l'étymologie phonétique*, Neuveville
– (1922) *Les étymologies des étymologistes et celles du peuple*, Paris
Gimbutas, M. (1970) 'Proto-Indo-European culture: the Kurgan culture during the fifth, fourth and third millennia B.C.' in Cardona et al., 155–97
Givón, T. (1971) 'Historical syntax and synchronic morphology: an archaeologist's field trip' *Papers from the 7th Regional Meeting of the Chicago Linguistic Society*, 394–415
– (1975) 'Serial verbs and syntactic change: Niger–Congo' in Li 1975, 47–112
Gleason, H.A. (1965) *Workbook in descriptive linguistics*, New York: Holt
Gneuss, H. (1955) *Lehnbildungen und Lehnbedeutungen im Altenglischen*, Berlin–Bielefeld: Erich Schmidt
Goodman, M. (1971) 'The strange case of Mbugu' in Hymes 1971, 243–53
Graham, A.C. (1969) 'The Archaic Chinese pronouns' *Asia Major* N.S. 15, 17–61
Greenberg, J.H. (1957) *Essays in linguistics*, University of Chicago Press
– (1960) 'A quantitative approach to the morphological typology of language', *IJAL* 26
– (1966a) 'Some universals of grammar with particular reference to the order of meaningful elements' in Greenberg (ed.), *Universals of language*, Cambridge Mass.: MIT Press; reprinted in Keiler 1972, 306–37
– (1966b) *Languages of Africa*, second edition, Indiana University Press
– (1974) *Language typology: A historical and analytic overview*, The Hague: Mouton
Gumperz, J.J. (1971) *Language in social groups*, ed. by A.S. Dil, Stanford University Press
Guthrie, M. (1967–71) *Comparative Bantu: An introduction to the comparative linguistics and prehistory of the Bantu languages*, Farnborough Hants.: Gregg Press
Haas, Mary (1969) *The prehistory of languages*, The Hague: Mouton
Haiman, J. (1974) *Targets and syntactic change*, The Hague: Mouton
Hajdu, P. (1975) *Finno-Ugrian languages and peoples*, London: Deutsch
Hale, K. (1973) 'Deep-surface canonical disparities in relation to analogy and change: an Australian example' in Sebeok 1973, 401–58
Hall, R.A. (1946) 'Bartoli's Neolinguistica', *Language* 22, 273–83
– (1950) 'The reconstruction of Proto-Romance', *Language* 26, 6–27; reprinted in Joos 1957, 303–14, and in Keiler 1972, 25–48
– (1958) 'Creolized languages and "genetic relationships" ', *Word* 14, 367–73

– (1965) *Pidgin and creole languages*, Ithaca, N.Y.: Cornell University Press
Halle, M. (1962) 'Phonology in generative grammar', *Word* 18, 54–72; reprinted in J.A. Fodor and J.J. Katz (eds), *The structure of language* (1964) 334–52
Halliday, M.A.K. (1964) 'The uses and users of language' in Halliday et al., *The linguistic sciences and language teaching*, London: Longman
Hancock, I.F. (1971) 'A provisional comparison of the English-derived Atlantic creoles' in Hymes 1971, 287–92; supplemented by a map and list of creole languages, 509–23
Haudricourt, A.G. and A.G. Juilland (1949) *Essai pour une histoire structurale du phonétisme français*, Paris: Klincksieck
Haugen, E. (1950) 'The analysis of linguistic borrowing', *Language* 26, 210–31
Hausmann, R.B. (1974) 'The origin and development of Modern English periphrastic *do*' in Anderson and Jones, 159–89
Heilmann, L. (ed.) (1974) *Proceedings of the XIth International Congress of Linguists* Bologna: Il Mulino
Henderson, E.J.A. (1951) 'The phonology of loan-words in some South-East Asian languages', *TPS* 1951, 131–58
– (1965) 'The topography of certain phonetic and morphological characteristics of South East Asian languages', *Lingua* 15, 400–34
Hermann, E. (1907) 'Über das Rekonstruieren', *KZ* 41, 1–64
– (1929) 'Lautveränderungen in den Individualsprachen einer Mundart', *Nachrichten der Gesellschaft der Wissenschaften zu Göttingen* phil-hist. Klasse, Berlin 1929, 195–214
Hirt, H. (1921) *Etymologie der neuhochdeutschen Sprache*, Munich: Beck
– (1939) *Die Hauptprobleme der indogermanischen Sprachwissenschaft*, ed. by H. Arntz, Halle: Niemeyer
Hockett, C.F. (1958) *A course in modern linguistics*, New York: Macmillan
– (1966) 'The quantification of functional load', *RAND Corporation Memo*. 1966, 300–20
Hodge, C.T. (1970) 'The linguistic cycle', *Language Sciences* 13, 1–17
– (1975) 'Egyptian and survival' in Bynon 1975, 171–91
Höfler, O. (1957) 'Die zweite Lautverschiebung bei Ostgermanen und Westgermanen', *Beiträge zur Geschichte der deutschen Sprache und Literatur* (Tübingen) 79, 161–350
Hoenigswald, H.M. (1946) 'Sound change and linguistic structure', *Language* 22, 138–43; reprinted in Joos 1957, 139–41
– (1950) 'The principal step in comparative grammar', *Language* 26, 357–64; reprinted in Joos 1957, 298–302
– (1960) *Language change and linguistic reconstruction*, University of Chicago Press
– (1964) 'Graduality, sporadicity, and the minor sound change processes', *Phonetica* 2, 202–15
– (1966) 'Criteria for the subgrouping of languages' in H. Birnbaum and J. Puhvel (eds), *Ancient Indo-European dialects*, University of California Press
– (1973) *Studies in formal historical linguistics*, Dordrecht: Reidel
– (1974) 'Relative chronology: notes on so-called intermediate stages' in Heilmann 1974, 369–73
Hogg, R.M. (1976) 'The status of rule reordering', *JL* 12, 103–23
Hyman, L. (1975) 'On the change from SOV to SVO: evidence from Niger-Congo' in Li 1975, 113–48
Hymes, D. (ed.) (1964) *Language in culture and society: A reader in linguistics and anthropology*, New York: Harper and Row

– (1971) *Pidginization and creolization of languages*, Cambridge: Cambridge University Press
– (1974) *Studies in the history of linguistics: Traditions and paradigms*, Indiana University Press
Jakobson, R. (1972a) 'Principles of historical phonology' in Keiler 1972, 121–38; German original *TCLP* 4, 1931; French version as appendix to Trubetzkoy, *Principes de phonologie* 1949
– (1972b) 'On the theory of phonological associations among languages' in Keiler 1972, 241–52; French original in *Proceedings of the IVth International Congress of Linguists*, Copenhagen 1938; also in Trubetzkoy, *Principes*
Jakobson, R. and M. Halle (1956) *Fundamentals of language*, The Hague: Mouton
Jankowski, K.R. (1972) *The neogrammarians: A reevaluation of their place in the development of linguistic science*, The Hague: Mouton
Joos, M. (ed.) (1957) *Readings in linguistics I*, University of Chicago Press
Käsmann, H. (1961) *Studien zum kirchlichen Wortschatz des Mittelenglischen 1100–1350: ein Beitrag zum Problem der Sprachmischung*, Tübingen: Niemeyer
Kaiser, R. (1961) *Medieval English: An Old English and Middle English anthology*, Berlin: Rolf Kaiser
Karlgren, B. (1949) *The Chinese language: An essay on its nature and history*, New York: Ronal Press
Katičić, R. (1966) 'Der Entsprechungsbegriff in der vergleichenden Laut- und Formenlehre', *IF* 71, 203–20
– (1970) *A contribution to the general theory of comparative linguistics*, The Hague: Mouton
Keiler, A.R. (1972) *A reader in historical and comparative linguistics*, New York: Holt
Keyser, S.J. (1974) 'A partial history of the relative clause in English' in J.B. Grimshaw ed., *Papers in the history and structure of English*, University of Massachussetts: Occasional Papers in Linguistics, No. 1
King, R.D. (1967) 'Functional load and sound change', *Language* 43, 831–52
– (1969a) *Historical linguistics and generative grammar*, Englewood Cliffs: Prentice-Hall
– (1969b) 'Push-chains and drag-chains', *Glossa* 3, 3–21
– (1973) 'Rule insertion', *Language* 49, 551–78
Kiparsky, P. (1968a) 'Linguistic universals and linguistic change' in Bach and Harms, 171–202; reprinted in Keiler 1972, 338–67
– (1968b) 'Tense and mood in Indo-European syntax', *Foundations of Language* 4, 30–57
– (1968c) *How abstract is phonology?*, Indiana University Linguistics Club
– (1971a) *Phonological change*, MIT Thesis 1965; Indiana University Linguistics Club
– (1971b) 'Historical linguistics' in W.O. Dingwall (ed.), *A survey of linguistic science*, University of Maryland 577–92
– (1972) 'Explanations in phonology' in S. Peters (ed.), *Goals of linguistic theory*, Englewood Cliffs: Prentice-Hall, 189–227
– (1974) 'From paleogrammarians to neogrammarians' in Hymes 1974, 331–45
Klima, E.S. (1964) 'Relatedness between grammatical systems', *Language* 40, 1–20
Kisseberth, C.W. (1970) 'On the functional unity of phonological rules', *Linguistic Inquiry* 1, 291–306; reprinted in E.C. Fudge (ed.) *Phonology*, Penguin 1973
Kluge, F. (1957) *Etymologisches Wörterbuch der deutschen Sprache*, 17th edition, Berlin: de Gruyter
Koutsoudas, A., G. Sanders and C. Noll (1974) 'The application of phonological rules', *Language* 50, 1–28

Krahe, H. (1949) *Ortsnamen als Geschichtsquelle*, Heidelberg: Winter

– (1954) *Sprache und Vorzeit*, Heidelberg: Quelle und Meyer

– (1964) *Unsere ältesten Flussnamen*, Wiesbaden: Harrassowitz

– (1970) *Einleitung in das vergleichende Sprachstudium*, ed. by W. Meid, Innsbruck: Innsbrucker Beiträge zur Sprachwissenschaft

Krogmann, W. (1955/6) 'Das Buchenargument', *KZ* 72, 1–29; 73, 1–25

– (1960) 'Das Lachsargument', *KZ* 76, 161–78

Kurath, H. (1941) *Linguistic atlas of New England*, Providence: American Council of Learned Societies

Kuryłowicz, J. (1964) *The inflectional categories of Indo-European*, Heidelberg: Winter

– (1966) 'La nature des procès dits analogiques' in E.P. Hamp, F.W. Householder and R. Austerlitz (eds), *Readings in linguistics II*, University of Chicago Press; first published 1949 in *Acta Linguistica* 5, 17–34

– (1974) 'Universaux linguistiques' in Heilmann 1974, 39–46

Labov, W. (1963) 'The social motivation of a sound change', *Word* 19, 273–309; reprinted in Labov 1972c, 1–42

– (1966) *The social stratification of English in New York City*, Washington D.C.: Center for Applied Linguistics

– (1972a) 'On the mechanism of linguistic change' in Keiler 1972, 267–88; first published in *16th Annual Round Table Meeting* Georgetown Monograph Series on Languages and Linguistics, 91–114; reprinted also in Labov 1972c, 160–82

– (1972b) 'On the use of the present to explain the past' in Heilmann 1974, ii, 825–51

– (1972c) *Sociolinguistic patterns*, Philadelphia: University of Pennsylvania Press

– (1972d) 'The internal evolution of linguistic rules' in Stockwell and Macaulay 1972, 101–71

– (1973) 'The social setting of linguistic change' in Sebeok 1973, 195–251; reprinted in Labov 1972c, 260–325

Lakoff, Robin (1968) *Abstract syntax and Latin complementation*, Cambridge, Mass.: MIT Press

– (1972a) 'Diachronic change in the complement system' in Keiler 1972, 217–34 (Lakoff 1968, ch. 5)

– (1972b) 'Another look at drift' in Stockwell and Macaulay 1972, 172–98

Lees, R.B. (1953) 'The basis of glottochronology', *Language* 29, 113–25

Lehmann, W.P. (1968) 'Saussure's dichotomy between descriptive and historical linguistics' in Lehmann and Malkiel 1968, 3–20

– (1969) 'Proto-Indo-European compounds in relation to other Proto-Indo-European syntactic patterns' *Acta Linguistica Hafnensia* 12, 1–20

– (1973a) *Historical linguistics. An introduction*, second edition, New York: Holt

– (1973b) 'A structural principle of language and its implications', *Language* 49, 47–66

– (1974) *Proto-Indo-European syntax*, University of Texas Press

Lehmann, W.P. and Y. Malkiel (eds) (1968) *Directions for historical linguistics*, Austin: University of Texas Press

Leskien, A. (1876) *Die Deklination im Slavisch-Litauischen und Germanischen*, Leipzig

Leumann, M. (1927) 'Zum Mechanismus des Bedeutungswandels', *IF* 45, 105–18

– (1963) *Lateinische Laut- und Formenlehre* (Handbuch der Altertumswissenschaft II.2.1), Munich: Beck

Lewy, E. (1964) *Der Bau der europäischen Sprachen*, Tübingen: Niemeyer

Li, C.N. (ed.) (1975) *Word order and word order change*, Austin: University of Texas Press

Li, C.N. and Sandra Thompson (1974) 'An explanation of word order change: SVO→SOV' *Foundations of Language* 12, 201–14
Lieb, H.H. (1968) 'Synchronic versus diachronic linguistics: a historical note', *Linguistics* 36, 18–28
Lightfoot, D. (1974) 'The diachronic analysis of English modals' in Anderson and Jones 1974, 219–49
Lockwood, W.B. (1968) *Historical German syntax*, Oxford: Clarendon Press
– (1969) *Indo-European philology: Historical and comparative*, London: Hutchinson
– (1972) *A panorama of Indo-European languages*, London: Hutchinson
Lyons, J. (1968) *Introduction to theoretical linguistics*, Cambridge: Cambridge University Press
Manczak, W. (1957–8) 'Tendences générales des changements analogiques' *Lingua* 7, 298–325; 387–420
Mann, M. (1973) 'Sound correspondences and sound shifts' *African Language Studies* 14, 26–35
Marchand, H. (1960) *The categories and types of present-day English word-formation: A synchronic–diachronic approach*, Wiesbaden: Harrassowitz
Marchand, J.W. (1956) 'Internal reconstruction of phonemic split', *Language* 32, 245–53; reprinted in Keiler 1972, 73–83
Martinet, A. (1952) 'Function, structure and sound change', *Word* 8, 1–32; reprinted in Keiler 1972, 139–74
– (1955) *Economie des changements phonétiques*, Berne: Francke
– (1964) *Elements of general linguistics*, translated from the French by E. Palmer, London: Faber
– (1975) *Evolution des langues et reconstruction*, Paris: Presses Universitaires de France
Matthews, P.H. (1974) *Morphology: An introduction to the theory of word-structure*, Cambridge: Cambridge University Press
Mawer, A. (1924) *The chief elements used in English place-names*, Cambridge: Cambridge University Press
McCawley, J.D. (1970) 'English as a VSO language', *Language* 46, 286–99
Meillet, A. (1921/36) *Linguistique historique et linguistique générale*, Paris: Société de Linguistique
– (1937) *Introduction à l'étude comparative des langues indo-européennes*, 8th edition, Paris: Hachette; reprinted by Alabama Press, 1964
Meinhof, C. (1906) 'Linguistische Studien in Ostafrika: X. Mbugu', *Mitteilungen des Seminars für Orientalische Sprachen* 9, 294–323
Melchert, H.C. (1975) ' "Exceptions" to exceptionless sound laws', *Lingua* 35, 135–54
Meyerstein, R.S. (1970) *Functional load: Descriptive limitations, alternatives of assessment and extension of application*, The Hague: Mouton
Miner, K.L. (1975) 'English inflectional endings and unordered rules', *Foundations of Language* 12, 339–65
Mossé, F. (1955/9) *Manuel de l'anglais du Moyen Age: I Vieil-Anglais, II Moyen-Anglais*, Paris: Montaigne
Moulton, W.G. (1962) 'Dialect geography and the concept of phonological space', *Word* 18, 23–32
– (1968) 'The mapping of phonemic systems' in Schmitt 1968
Nicolaisen, W. (1957) 'Die alteuropäischen Gewässernamen der britischen Hauptinsel', *Beiträge zur Namenforschung* 8, 209–68
Osthoff, K. (1878a) *Das physiologische und psychologische Moment in der sprachlichen Formenbildung*, Jena

– (1878b) *Das Verbum in der Nominalkomposition*, Jena
Osthoff, H. and K. Brugmann (1878) *Einleitung* to *Morphologische Untersuchungen*, 1; English translation in W.P. Lehmann, *A reader in nineteenth century historical Indo-European linguistics*, chapter 14
Palmer, F.R. (1958) 'Comparative statement and Ethiopian Semitic', *TPS* 1958, 119–43
Palmer, L.R. (1972) *Descriptive and comparative linguistics: A critical introduction*, London: Faber
Pattanayak, D.P. (1966) *A controlled historical reconstruction of Oriya, Assamese, Bengali and Hindi*, The Hague: Mouton
Paul, H. (1970) *Prinzipien der Sprachgeschichte*, reprint of the 5th edition of 1920, Tübingen: Niemeyer; English translation by H.A. Strong, London 1891
Pedersen, H. (1909) *Vergleichende Grammatik der keltischen Sprachen*, Göttingen
Petrovici, E. (1957) *Kann das Phonemsystem einer Sprache durch fremden Einfluss umgestaltet werden? Zum slawischen Einfluss auf das rumänische Lautsystem*, The Hague: Mouton
Pop, S. (1950) *La dialectologie: Aperçu historique et méthodes d'enquêtes linguistiques*, 2 vols, Louvain: Centre International de Dialectologie
Posner, Rebecca (1966) *The Romance languages: A linguistic introduction*, New York: Anchor
Postal, P.M. (1968) *Aspects of phonological theory*, New York: Harper and Row; chapters 10–11 reprinted in Keiler 1972, 175–97
Powell, T.G.E. (1963) *The Celts*, London: Thames and Hudson
Price, G. (1971) *The French language, present and past*, London: Arnold
Prokosch, E. (1938) *A comparative Germanic grammar*, Baltimore: Linguistic Society of America
Pulgram, E. (1953) 'Family tree, wave theory and dialectology', *Orbis* 2, 67–72; reprinted in Keiler 1972, 235–40
– (1959) 'Proto-Indo-European reality and reconstruction', *Language* 35, 421–6
Putschke, W. (1969) 'Zur forschungsgeschichtlichen Stellung der junggrammatischen Schule', *Zeitschrift für Dialektologie und Linguistik* 36, 19–48
Rabin, C. (1975) 'Lexicostatistics and the internal divisions of Semitic' in Bynon 1975, 85–99
Rayfield, J.R. (1970) *The languages of a bilingual community*, The Hague: Mouton
Rea, J.A. (1958) 'Concerning the validity of lexico-statistics', *IJAL* 24, 145–50
– (1973) 'The Romance data of the pilot studies for glottochronology' in Sebeok 1973, 355–68
Reinecke, J.E. (1964) 'Trade jargons and creole dialects as marginal languages' in Hymes 1964, 534–46
Rheighard, J. (1971) 'Some observations on syntactic change in verbs' *Papers from the Seventh Regional Meeting of the Chicago Linguistic Society*
Ringen, C. (1972) 'On arguments for rule ordering', *Foundations of Language* 8, 266–73
Rix, H. (1954) 'Zur Verbreitung und Chronologie einiger keltischer Ortsnamentypen', *Festschrift für Peter Goessler*, Stuttgart: Kohlhammer, 99–107
Robins, R.H. (1967) *A short history of linguistics*, London: Longman
– (1971) *General linguistics: An introduction*, 2nd edition, London: Longman
– (1973) 'The history of language classification' in Sebeok 1973, 3–41
Samuels, M.L. (1972) *Linguistic evolution*, Cambridge: Cambridge University Press
Sandfeld, K. (1930) *Linguistique balkanique: problèmes et résultats*, Paris: Société de Linguistique
Sankoff, D. (1970) 'On the rate of replacement of word-meaning relationship', *Language* 46, 564–9

– (1973) 'Mathematical developments in lexicostatistic theory' in Sebeok 1973, 93–114
Sapir, E. (1921) *Language*, New York: Harcourt
Saporta, S. (1972) 'Ordered rules, dialect differences and historical processes' in Keiler 1972, 289–98; first published in *Language* 41, 1965, 218–24
Saussure, F. de (1964) *Cours de linguistique générale*, reprint, Paris: Payot
Schaller, H.W. (1975) *Die Balkansprachen: eine Einführung in die Balkanphilologie*, Sprachwissenschaftliche Studienbücher
Schane, S.A. (1971) 'The phoneme revisited', *Language* 47, 503–21
– (1972) 'Natural rules in phonology' in Stockwell and Macaulay 1972, 199–229
– (1973) *Generative phonology*, Englewood Cliffs: Prentice-Hall
Scherer, A. (1968) *Die Urheimat der Indogermanen*, Darmstadt: Wissenschaftliche Buchgesellschaft
Schirmunski, V.M. (1962) *Deutsche Mundartkunde*, translated and revised by W. Fleischer, Berlin: Akademie-Verlag
Schleicher, A. (1869) *Die deutsche Sprache*, second edition, Stuttgart
Schmidt, J. (1872) *Die Verwandtschaftsverhältnisse der indogermanischen Sprachen*, Weimar: Böhlau
Schmitt, L.E. (ed.) (1967) *Verhandlungen des Zweiten Internationalen Dialektologenkongresses*, Zeitschrift für Mundartforschung, Beihefte N.F. 4 Wiesbaden: Steiner
Schneider, Gisela (1973) *Zum Begriff des Lautgesetzes in der Sprachwissenschaft seit den Junggrammatikern*, Tübinger Beiträge zur Linguistik
Schrader, O. (1911) *Die Indogermanen*, Leipzig: Quelle und Meyer
Schrodt, R. (1974) *Die germanische Lautverschiebung und ihre Stellung im Kreise der indogermanischen Sprachen*, Vienna: Halosar
Schuchardt, H. (1885) *Über die Lautgesetze; gegen die Junggrammatiker*, Berlin; reprinted with English translation in Vennemann and Wilbur 1972, 39–72 and 1–39
Schützeichel, R. (1956) 'Zur hochdeutschen Lautverschiebung am Mittelrhein' *Zeitschrift für Mundartforschung* 24, 119ff.
– (1961) *Die Grundlagen des westlichen Mitteldeutschen*, Düsseldorf
– (1973) 'Grenzen des Althochdeutschen', *Beiträge zur Geschichte der deutschen Sprache und Literatur* (Tübingen) 95, 23–38
Sebeok, T.S. (ed.) (1973) *Current trends in linguistics*, Volume 11: *Diachronic, areal and typological linguistics*, The Hague: Mouton
Shibatani, M. (1973) 'The role of surface phonetic constraints in generative phonology', *Language* 49, 87–106
Shorto, H.L. (ed.) (1963) *Linguistic comparison in South East Asia*, London: School of Oriental and African Studies
Sieberer, A. (1958) *Lautwandel und seine Triebkräfte*, Vienna
Simon, W. (1938) 'The reconstruction of Archaic Chinese', *Bulletin of the School of Oriental and African Studies* 9, 267–88
Snow, C. and C.A. Ferguson (eds) (1977) *Talking to children*, Cambridge: Cambridge University Press
Sommerfelt, A. (1960) 'External versus internal factors in the development of language', *Norsk Tijdskrift for Språkwedenscap* 19, 296–315
Sommerstein, H.A. (1974) 'On phonotactically motivated rules', *JL* 10, 71–110
Southworth, F.C. (1964) 'Family tree diagrams', *Language* 40, 557–65
Steinthal, H. (1857) 'Die aufsteigende Sprachentwicklung', *Zeitschrift der Deutschen Morgenländischen Gesellschaft* 11, 411–26
Stockwell, R.P. and R.K.S. Macaulay (eds) (1972) *Linguistic change and generative theory*, Bloomington: Indiana University Press

Sturtevant, E.H. (1917) *Linguistic change*, ed. by E.P. Hamp, University of Chicago Press 1962

Swadesh, M. (1951) 'Diffusional cumulation and archaic residue as historical explanations', *Southwestern Journal of Anthropology* 7, 1–21; reprinted in Hymes 1964, 624–37

– (1955) 'Towards greater accuracy in lexicostatistic dating', *IJAL* 21, 121–37

– (1971) *The origin and diversification of language*, ed. by J. Sherzer, Chicago: Aldine Atherton

Szemerényi, O. (1970) *Einführung in die Vergleichende Sprachwissenschaft*, Darmstadt: Wissenschaftliche Buchgesellschaft

Taylor, D. (1956) 'On the classification of creolized languages', *Word* 12, 407–14

Thieme, P. (1953) 'Die Heimat der indogermanischen Gemeinsprache', *Abhandlungen der Akademie der Wissenschaften und der Literatur*, Mainz, Geistes- und Sozialwiss. Klasse 1953, No. 11

Thomas, G. (1975) 'The calque – an international trend in the lexical development of the literary languages of 18th century Europe', *Germano-Slavica* 1975, 21–41, Canada: University of Waterloo

Tischler, J. (1973) *Glottochronologie und Lexikostatistik*, Innsbrucker Beiträge zur Sprachwissenschaft, 11

Traugott, Elizabeth Closs (1969) 'Towards a grammar of syntactic change', *Lingua* 23, 1–27

– (1972a) *A history of English syntax*, New York: Holt

– (1972b) 'Diachronic syntax and generative grammar' in Keiler 1972, 201–16

– (1974) 'On the notion of "restructuring" in historical syntax' in Heilmann 1974, 921–8

Trier, J. (1931) *Der deutsche Wortschatz im Sinnbezirk des Verstandes. Die Geschichte eines sprachlichen Feldes, I: Von den Anfängen bis zum Beginn des 13. Jahrhunderts*, Heidelberg: Winter

Trubetzkoy, N.S. (1939) 'Gedanken über das Indogermanenproblem', *Acta Linguistica* 1, 81–9

– (1967) *Grundzüge der Phonologie*, reprint, Göttingen: Vandenhoeck und Ruprecht; French translation by Cantineau, Paris 1949

Trudgill, P. (1974a) *Sociolinguistics: An introduction*, Pelican

– (1974b) *The social stratification of English in Norwich*, Cambridge: Cambridge University Press

Tsiapira, M. (ed.) (1971) *Generative studies in historical linguistics*, Edmonton: Linguistic Research, Inc.

Tucker, A.N. and M.A. Bryan (1974) 'The Mbugu anomaly', *Bulletin of the School of Oriental and African Studies* 37, 188–207

Twaddell, W.F. (1957) 'A note on Old High German umlaut' in Joos 1957, 85–7

Ullmann, S. (1962) *Semantics: An introduction to the science of meaning*, Oxford: Blackwell

– (1974) *Words and their meanings*, Canberra: Australian National University Press

Untermann, J. (1975) *Etymologie und Wortgeschichte*, Arbeitspapier No. 25, Universität Köln: Institut für Sprachwissenschaft

Vachek, J. (1968) 'On the interplay of external and internal factors in language development' in B. Malmberg (ed.), *Readings in modern linguistics* 209–23

Valdman, A. (1973) 'Some aspects of decreolization in creole French' in Sebeok 1973, 507–36

Van Coetsem, F. (1972) 'The Germanic consonant shift, compensatory processes in language', *Lingua* 30, 203–15

Vennemann, Th. (1972a) 'Sound change and markedness theory: on the history of the German consonant system' in Stockwell and Macaulay 1972, 230–74

– (1972b) 'Phonetic and conceptual analogy' in Vennemann and Wilbur 1972, 181–204
– (1974) 'Analogy in generative grammar: the origin of word order' in Heilmann 1974, 79–83
– (1975) 'An explanation of drift' in Li 1975, 269–305
Vennemann, Th. and T.H. Wilbur (1972) *Schuchardt, the neogrammarians and the transformational theory of phonological change*, Frankfurt: Athenäum
Vidos, B.E. (1968) *Handbuch der romanischen Sprachwissenschaft*, Munich: Hueber
Vogt, H. (1954) 'Contact of languages', *Word* 10, 365–74
Voorhoeve, J. (1972) 'Historical and linguistic evidence in favour of the relexification theory in the formation of creoles'. Mimeo.
Wagner, K. (1927) *Deutsche Sprachlandschaften*, Deutsche Dialektgeographie, 23 Marburg: Elwert
Wagner, K.H. (1969a) 'Analogical change reconsidered in the framework of generative phonology', *Folia Linguistica* 3, 228–41
– (1969b) *Generative studies in the Old English language*, Heidelberg: Winter
Wang, W.S.Y. (1969) 'Competing changes as a cause of residue' *Language* 45, 9–25
Wartburg, W. von (1962) *Einführung in Problematik und Methodik der Sprachwissenschaft*, second edition, Tübingen: Niemeyer
Watkins, C. (1962) *Indo-European origins of the Celtic verb, I: The sigmatic aorist*, Dublin University Press
– (1969) *Geschichte der indogermanischen Verbalflexion* (Indogermanische Grammatik III.1), Heidelberg: Winter
– (1970) 'Lachmann's Law in Latin', *Harvard Studies in Classical Philology* 74, 55–74
Weinreich, U. (1950) 'Is a structural dialectology possible?' *Word* 10, 388–400; reprinted in Keiler 1972, 253–66
– (1953) *Languages in contact*, New York; reprint 1964, The Hague: Mouton
Weinreich, U., W. Labov and M.I. Herzog (1968) 'Empirical foundations for a theory of language change', Lehmann and Malkiel 1968, 95–195
Weisgerber, L. (1963) *Die vier Stufen in der Erforschung der Sprachen*, Düsseldorf: Schwann
Whinnom, K. (1971) 'Linguistic hybridization and the "special case" of pidgins and creoles' in Hymes 1971, 91–115
Whiteley, W.H. (1960) 'Linguistic hybrids' *African Studies* 19, 95–7
– (1967a) 'Loan-words in linguistic description: a case study from Tanzania, East Africa' in I. Rauch and C.T. Scott (eds), *Approaches in linguistic methodology*, Madison: University of Wisconsin Press, 125–44
– (1967b) 'Swahili nominal classes and English loan-words: a preliminary survey' in *La classification nominale dans les langues négro-africaines*, Paris: Centre National de la Recherche Scientifique
Wilbur, T.H. (1972) 'Hugo Schuchardt and the neogrammarians' in Vennemann and Wilbur 1972, 73–114
Wilmanns, W. (1897) *Deutsche Grammatik, 1. Abteilung: Lautlehre*, Strasbourg: Trübner
Winter, W. (1969) 'Analogischer Sprachwandel und semantische Struktur', *Folia Linguistica* 3, 29–45
– (1973) 'Areal linguistics: some general considerations' in Sebeok 1973, 135–48
Wolfe, P.M. (1972) *Linguistic change and the Great Vowel Shift in English*, University of California Press
Wrede, F. (ed.) (1926ff.) *Deutscher Sprachatlas*, Marburg: Elwert
Wurzel, W.U. (1970) *Studien zur deutschen Lautstruktur* (Studia Grammatica, 8) Berlin: Akademie-Verlag

ADDITIONAL BIBLIOGRAPHY

Aitchison, Jean (1979) 'The order of word order change', *TPS* 1979, 43–65

– (1980) Review of Lightfoot 1979: *Linguistics* 18, 137–46

– (1981) *Language change: progress or decay?*, London: Fontana and Croom Helm

Allen, Cynthia L. (1977) *Topics in diachronic English syntax*, New York: Garland

Allen, W.S. (1978) 'The Proto-Indo-European velar series: neo-grammarian and other solutions in the light of attested parallels', *TPS* 1978, 87–110

Andersen, Henning (1973) 'Abductive and deductive change', *Language* 49, 765–93; reprinted in Baldi and Werth, 313–47

– (1980) 'Russian conjugation: acquisition and evolutive change' in Traugott et al., 285–301

Anderson, S.R. (1978) 'Historical change and rule reordering in phonology' in Fisiak 1978

– (1980) 'On the development of morphology from syntax' in Fisiak 1980, 51–69

Anttila, R. (1974) 'Formalization as degeneration in historical linguistics' in Anderson and Jones, vol. 1, 1–32; reprinted in Baldi and Werth, 348–76

– (1975) 'Was there a generative historical linguistics?' in Dahlstedt, 70–92

– (1977) *Analogy*, The Hague: Mouton

– (1979) 'Generative grammar and language change: irreconcilable concepts?' in Brogyany, vol. 1, 35–51

Ard, W.J. (1977a) *Raising and word order in diachronic syntax*, Indiana University Linguistics Club

– (1977b) *Methodological problems in the use of typologies in diachronic syntax*, Indiana University Linguistics Club

Árnason, Kristján (1980) *Quantity in historical phonology: Icelandic and related cases*, Cambridge: Cambridge University Press

Bailey, C.-J.N. (1972) 'The integration of linguistic theory: internal reconstruction and the comparative method in descriptive analysis' in Stockwell and Macaulay, 22–31

– (1973) *Variation and linguistic theory*, Arlington: Center for Applied Linguistics

– (1980a) 'Old and new views on language history and language relationships' in Lüdtke, 139–81

– (1980b) 'The role of language development in a theory of language', *Papiere zur Linguistik* 22, 33–46

– (1982) 'The garden path that historical linguistics went astray on', *Language and communication* 2, 151–60

Bailey, C.-J.N. and Shuy, R. (eds.) (1973) *New ways of analyzing variation in English*, Washington: Georgetown University Press

Baldi, P. and R.N. Werth (eds.) (1978) *Readings in historical phonology*, Pennsylvania State University Press

Baron, N.S. (1977) *Language acquisition and historical change*, Amsterdam: North-Holland
Baumgärtner, K. (1969) 'Diachronie und Synchronie der Sprachstruktur: Faktum oder Idealisierung?' in *Sprache, Gegenwart und Geschichte: Probleme der Synchronie und Diachronie* (Sprache der Gegenwart, 5), Düsseldorf, 52–64
Bennett, Paul A. (1979) 'Observations on the transparency principle', *Linguistics* 17, 843–61
– (1980) 'English passives: a study in syntactic change and relational grammar', *Lingua* 51, 101–14
Benveniste, E. (1968) 'Mutations of linguistic categories' in Lehmann and Malkiel, 85–94
Bickerton, D. (1973) 'Quantitative versus dynamic paradigms: the case of Montreal *que*' in Bailey and Shuy, 23–44
– (1975) *Dynamics of a creole system*, Cambridge: Cambridge University Press
Bickerton, D. and T. Givón (1976) 'Pidginization and syntactic change: from SXV and VSX to SVX', *Chicago Linguistic Society: Papers from the parasession on diachronic syntax*, 9–39
Birnbaum, H. (1970) *Problems of typological and genetic linguistics viewed in a generative framework*, The Hague: Mouton
Boretzky, N. (1977) *Einführung in die historische Linguistik*, Rowohlt
Brogyanyi, B. (ed.) (1979) *Studies in diachronic, synchronic, and typological linguistics: Festschrift for Oswald Szemerényi*, 2 vols., Amsterdam: Benjamins
Bruck, A. et al. (eds.) (1974) *Papers from the parasession on natural phonology*, Chicago Linguistic Society
Bybee, Joan Hooper (1980) 'Morphophonemic change from inside and outside the paradigm', *Lingua* 50, 45–60
Bybee, Joan Hooper and Mary A. Brewer (1980) 'Explanation in morphophonemics: changes in Provençal and Spanish preterite forms', *Lingua* 52, 201–42
Bynon, J. (1978) 'The internal reconstruction of Berber vowels and semivowels' in Fronzaroli 1978, 293–8
Bynon, T. (1978a) 'The Hamito-Semitic hypothesis and models of language relationship', in Fronzaroli 1978, 21–30
– (1978b) 'The neogrammarians and their successors', *TPS* 1978, 111–24
– (1980) 'From passive to active in Kurdish via the ergative construction' in Traugott et al., 151–63
Canale, M. (1976) 'Implicational hierarchies of word order relationship' in Christie, 39–70
Carstensen, S. (1980) 'The gender of English loanwords in German', *Studia Anglica Posnaniensia* 12, 3–25
Cedergren, H. and D. Sankoff (1974) 'Variable rules: performance as a statistical reflection of competence', *Language* 50, 333–55
Chambers, J.K. (1973) 'Canadian raising', *Journal of Canadian Linguistics* 18, 113–35
Chambers, J.K. and P. Trudgill (1980) *Dialectology*, Cambridge: Cambridge University Press
Chen, M.Y. (1974) 'Natural phonology from the diachronic vantage point', *Chicago Linguistic Society: Papers from the parasession on natural phonology*, 43–80
– (1972) 'The time dimension: contributions toward a theory of sound change', *Foundations of Language* 8, 457–98
– (1976) 'Relative chronology: three methods of reconstruction', *JL* 12, 209–58
Chen, M.Y. (1980) 'How Proto-Chinese was reconstructed' in Koerner, 311–22

Chen, M.Y. and W.S.-Y. Wang (1975) 'Sound change: actuation and implementation', *Language* 51, 255–81
Cherubim, D. (ed.) (1975) *Sprachwandel: Reader zur diachronischen Sprachwissenschaft*, Berlin: de Gruyter
Christie, W.M. (ed.) (1976) *Current progress in historical linguistics*, Amsterdam: North-Holland
Chung, Sandra (1977) 'On the gradual nature of syntactic change' in Li 1977, 3–55
Clements, G.N. (1975) 'Analogical reanalysis in syntax: the case of Ewe tree-grafting', *Linguistic Inquiry* 6, 3–52
Collinge, N.E. (1975) 'Lachmann's Law revisited', *Folia Linguistica* 8, 223–53
– (1978) 'Exceptions, their nature and place – and the neogrammarians', *TPS* 1978, 61–86
Coseriu, E. (1974) *Synchronie, Diachronie und Geschichte: das Problem des Sprachwandels*, Munich: Fink (German translation of *Sincronía, diacronía e historia. El problema del cambio lingüístico*, Montevideo 1958)
– (1975) 'Synchronie, Diachronie und Typologie' in Cherubim, 135–49
Dahlstedt, K.-H. (1975) *The Nordic languages and modern linguistics*, Stockholm: Almqvist and Wiksell
Davies, Anna Morpurgo (1975) 'Language classification in the nineteenth century' in Sebeok 1975 607–716
– (1978) 'Analogy, segmentation and the early neogrammarians', *TPS* 1978, 36–60
Dixon, R.M.W. (1981) 'Grammatical reanalysis: an example of linguistic change from Warrgamay (North Queensland)', *Journal of Australian Linguistics* 1, 91–112
Dorian, N.C. (1978) 'The fate of morphological complexity in language death', *Language* 54, 590–609
Drachman, G. (1978) 'Child language and language change: a conjecture and some refutations' in Fisiak 1978, 123–44
Dressler, W. (1969) 'Eine textsyntaktische Regel der indogermanischen Wortstellung', *KZ* 83, 1–25
– (1971) 'Über die Rekonstruktion der indogermanischen Syntax', *KZ* 85, 5–22
– (1972) 'Methodisches zu Allegroregeln' in Dressler and Mareš (eds.), *Phonologica*, Munich: Fink
– (1976) 'Können Morphemfugen die Domäne phonologischer Prozesse begrenzen?' in H.P. Pohl and N. Salnikov (eds.), *Opuscula slavica et linguistica: Festschrift A. Issatschenko*, Klagenfurt: Heyn 123–7
– (1977) 'Morphologization of phonological processes' in A. Juilland (ed.), *Linguistic studies presented to J.H. Greenberg*, Saratoga, Cal.: Anma Libri
Ebert, Peter Robert (1978) *Historische Syntax des Deutschen*, Stuttgart: Metzler
Emeneau, M.B. (1974) 'The Indian linguistic area revisited', *International Journal of Dravidian Linguistics* 3, 92–134
Emonds, J. (1972) 'A reformulation of Grimm's Law' in M. Brame (ed.), *Contributions to generative phonology*, Austin: University of Texas Press
Faust, M. (1980) 'Morphologische Regularisierung in Sprachwandel und Spracherwerb', *Folia Linguistica* 4, 387–411
Feagin, C. (1979) *Variation and change in Alabama English: a sociolinguistic study of the white community*, Washington: Georgetown University Press
Fischer, Susan (1975) 'Influences on word order change in American sign language' in Li 1975, 1–25
Fisiak, J. (ed.) (1978) *Recent developments in historical phonology*, The Hague: Mouton
– (1980) *Historical morphology*, The Hague: Mouton

Fox, A. (1976) 'Problems with phonological chains', *JL* 12, 289–310
Fries, C.C. (1940) 'On the development of the structural use of word-order in Modern English', *Language* 16, 199–208
Fritz, G. (1974) *Bedeutungswandel im Deutschen*, Tübingen: Niemeyer
Fronzaroli, P. (ed.) (1978) *Atti del secondo congresso internazionale di linguistica camito-semitica*, Università di Firenze
Galton, H. (1981) 'Woher stammt der Typus der Balkansprachen?', *Folia Linguistica Historica* 2, 251–64
Gamkrelidze, T.V. (1981) 'Language typology and language universals and their implications for the reconstruction of the Indo-European stop system' in Y.L. Arbeitman and A.R. Bomhard (eds.), *Bono homini donum: Essays in historical linguistics, in memory of J. Alexander Kerns*, Amsterdam: Benjamins, 573–609
Gerritsen, Marinel (1980) 'An analysis of the rise of SOV patterns in Dutch' in Traugott et al., 123–36
Givón, Talmy (1979) *On understanding grammar*, New York: Academic Press
Göschel, Joachim (1971) 'Artikulation und Distribution der sogen. Liquida *r* in den europäischen Sprachen', *IF* 76, 83–126
Goyvaerts, D. (1975) *Present-day historical and comparative linguistics: an introductory guide to theory and method*, Gent: Story-Scientia
– (1981) *Aspecten van semantische taalverandering*, Gent: Story-Scientia
Goyvaerts, D. and G.K. Pullum (eds.) (1975) *Essays on the sound pattern of English*, Gent: Story-Scientia
Greenberg, J.H. (1966) 'Synchronic and diachronic universals in phonology', *Language* 42, 508–17; reprinted in Baldi and Werth, 172–84
– (ed.) (1978) *Universals of human language*, 4 vols., Stanford University Press
– (1979) 'Rethinking linguistics diachronically', *Language* 55, 275–90
Greule, A. (ed.) (1982) *Valenztheorie und historische Sprachwissenschaft*, Tübingen: Niemeyer
Hamp, E.P. (1976) 'Why syntax needs phonology', *Chicago Linguistic Society: Papers from the parasession on diachronic syntax* 348–64
Harris, M.B. (ed.) (1976) *Romance syntax: synchronic and diachronic perspective*, University of Salford
– (1978) 'The interrelationship between phonological and grammatical change' in Fisiak 1978
– (1979) *The evolution of French syntax: a comparative approach*, London: Longman
Harris, Roy (1977) *On the possibility of linguistic change* (inaugural lecture), Oxford University Press
Hathaway, Luise (1979) *Der Mundartwandel in Imst in Tirol zwischen 1897 und 1973*, Wien: Braumüller
Hawkins, J.A. (1979) 'Implicational universals as predictors of word order change', *Language* 55, 618–48
– (1980) 'On implicational and distributional universals of word order', *JL* 16, 193–235
Hockett, C.F. (1965) 'Sound change', *Language* 41, 185–204
Hoenigswald, H.M. (1974) 'Internal reconstruction and context' in Anderson and Jones, vol. 2, 189–201
– (1978) 'The annus mirabilis 1876 and posterity', *TPS* 1978, 17–35
– (1980) 'Notes on reconstruction, word-order, and stress' in Ramat 1980, 69–87
Hogg, R.M. (1979) 'Analogy and phonology', *JL* 15, 55–85
– (1981) Review of Fisiak 1978: *JL* 17, 153–60

Holden, K. (1976) 'Assimilation rates of borrowing and phonological productivity', *Language* 52, 131–47
Holman, E. (1980) 'Typology as an instigator and regulator of linguistic change' in Traugott et al., 7–16
Hombert, J.-M., J.J. Ohala, and W.G. Ewan (1979) 'Phonetic explanations for the the development of tones', *Language* 55, 37–58
Hooper, Joan Bybee (1976) *An introduction to natural generative phonology*, New York: Academic Press
– (1979) 'Child morphology and morphophonemic change', *Linguistics* 17, 21–50
Hudson, G. (1979) Review of Bynon 1977: *Studies in Language* 3, 253–9
Hudson, R.A. (1980) *Sociolinguistics*, Cambridge: Cambridge University Press
Hyman, L.M. (1975) 'On the change from SOV to SVO: evidence from Niger-Congo' in Li 1975, 113–47
Jacobs, R.A. (1975) *Syntactic change: a Cupan (Uto-Aztekan) case study* (UCLA, PL 79), Berkeley: University of California Press
Janson, Tore (1979) *Mechanisms of language change in Latin*, Stockholm: Almqvist and Wiksell
Jeffers, R.J. (1976a) 'Typological shift and change in complex sentence structure' *Chicago Linguistic Society: Papers from the parasession on diachronic syntax* 136–49
(1976b) 'Syntactic change and syntactic reconstruction' in Christie 1976, 1–16
– (1978) 'Restructuring, relexicalization, and reversion in historical phonology' in Fisiak 1978, 213–20
Jeffers, R.J. and Ilse Lehiste (1979) *Principles and methods for historical linguistics*, Cambridge, Mass.: MIT Press
Joseph, Brian (1980) 'Linguistic universals and syntactic change', *Language* 56, 345–70
Kanngiesser, S. (1972) *Aspekte der synchronen und diachronen Linguistik*, Tübingen
Katz, Dovid (1980) 'The wavering Yiddish segolate: a problem of sociolinguistic reconstruction', *International Journal of the Sociology of Language* 24, 5–27
Kiparsky, P. (1974) 'Remarks on analogical change' in Anderson and Jones, vol. 2, 258ff.
– (1980) 'Concluding statement' in Traugott et al., 409–17
– (1982) *Explanation in phonology*, Dordrecht: Foris
Klausenburger, J. (1979) *Morphologization: studies in Latin and Romance morphophonemics*, Tübingen: Niemeyer
Koerner, K. (ed.) (1980) *Progress in linguistic historiography*, Amsterdam: Benjamins
Kovatcheva, Mira (1982) 'An aspect of the transition towards analytical sentence structure in English', *Folia Linguistica Historica* 3, 109–19
Krishnamurti, Bh. (1978) 'Areal and lexical diffusion of sound change: evidence from Dravidian', *Language* 54, 1–20
Kuryłowicz, J. (ed.) (in progress) *Indogermanische Grammatik*, Heidelberg: Winter
Labov, W. (1981) 'Resolving the neogrammarian controversy', *Language* 57, 267–308
Labov, W., M. Yaeger, and R. Steiner (1972) *A quantitative study of sound change in progress*, Philadelphia: US Regional Survey
Langacker, R.W. (1977) 'Syntactic reanalysis' in Li 1977, 57–139
Langdon, Margaret (1977) 'Syntactic change and SOV structure: the Yuman case' in Li 1977, 255–90
Lass, Roger (1975) 'How intrinsic is content? Markedness, sound change, and "family universals"' in Goyvaerts and Pullum, 475–504

– (1976a) ***English phonology and phonological theory: synchronic and diachronic studies***, Cambridge: Cambridge University Press

– (1976b) 'Variation studies and historical linguistics', ***Language in Society*** 5, 219–29

– (1978) 'Mapping constraints in phonological reconstruction: on climbing down trees without falling out of them' in Fisiak 1978, 245–86

– (1979) Review of Bynon 1977: *Belfast Working Papers in Language and Linguistics* September 1978, 115–23

– (1980a) 'Paradigm coherence and the conditioning of sound change' in Fisiak 1980

– (1980b) *On explaining language change*, Cambridge: Cambridge University Press

Lass, Roger and J.M. Anderson (1975) *Old English Phonology*, Cambridge: Cambridge University Press

Lehmann, W.P. (1972) 'The comparative method as applied to the syntactic comparison of languages', *Canadian Journal of Linguistics* 17, 167–74

– (1975) 'A discussion of compound and word order' in Li 1975, 149–62

– (1976a) 'A preface to diachronic syntactic investigation', *Chicago Linguistic Society: Papers from the parasession on diachronic syntax* 169–78

– (1976b) 'Diachronic semantics' in *Georgetown University: Round Table on Languages and Linguistics* 1976

– (1980) 'The reconstruction of non-simple sentences in Proto-Indo-European' in Ramat 1980, 113–54

Li, C.N. (ed.) (1977) *Mechanisms of syntactic change*, Austin: University of Texas Press

Li, C.N. and S.A. Thompson (1975) 'The semantic function of word order: a case study in Mandarin' in Li 1975, 163–96

Lightfoot, D.W. (1976) 'The base component as a locus of syntactic change' in Christie, 17–36

– (1977) 'Syntactic change and the autonomy thesis', *JL* 13, 191–216

– (1979a) *Principles of diachronic syntax*, Cambridge: Cambridge University Press

– (1979b) Review of Li 1977: *Language* 55, 381–95

– (1980) 'On reconstructing a protosyntax' in Ramat 1980, 27–45

– (1981) 'Explaining syntactic change' in N. Hornstein and D. Lightfoot (eds.), *Explanation in linguistics*, London: Longman

Lord, Carol (1976) 'Evidence for syntactic reanalysis: from verb to complementizer in Kwa', *Chicago Linguistic Society: Papers from the parasession on diachronic syntax* 179–91

Lüdtke, Helmut (ed.) (1980) *Kommunikationstheoretische Grundlagen des Sprachwandels*, Berlin: de Gruyter

McCalla, K.I. (1980) 'Phonological and morphological forces in syntagmatic change', *Lingua* 51, 1–16

Maher, J.P. (1969) 'The paradox of creation and tradition in grammar: sound pattern of a palimpsest', *Language Sciences* 7, 15–24

Major, R.C. (1978) 'Does sound change originate in children?', *Wiener Linguistische Gazette* 17, 3–15

Malkiel, Y. (1979) 'Problems in the diachronic differentiation of near-homophones', *Language* 55, 1–36

Mańczak, W. (1980a) 'Frequenz und Sprachwandel' in Lüdtke, 37–79

– (1980b) 'Laws of analogy' in Fisiak 1980

Masica, C. (1976) *Defining a linguistic area: South Asia*, Chicago University Press

Michelena, L. (1963) *Lenguas y protolenguas*, Universidad de Salamanca

– (1971) 'Gramática generativa y lingüistica histórica' *Revista Espanola de Lingüistica* 1, 211–33

Milroy, J. (1978) 'Lexical alternation and diffusion in vernacular speech', *Belfast Working Papers in Language and Linguistics* 3, 100–15
Moravcsik, Edith A. (1978) 'Universals of language contact' in Greenberg 1978, vol. 1, 93–122
Mühlhäusler, P. (1974) *Pidginization and simplification of language* (Pacific Linguistics Series B, No. 26) Canberra
Nadkarni, M.V. (1975) 'Bilingualism and syntactic change in Konkani', *Language* 51, 672–83
Naro, A.J. (1978) 'A study on the origins of pidginization', *Language* 54, 314–47
– (1981) 'The social and structural dimensions of a syntactic change', *Language* 57, 63–98
Newton, B. (1971) 'Ordering paradoxes in phonology', *JL* 7, 31–53
Poplack, S., A. Pousada and D. Sankoff (1982) 'Competing influences on gender assignment: variable process, stable outcome', *Lingua* 57, 1–28
Posner, Rebecca (1974) 'Ordering of historical phonological rules in Romance', *TPS* 1974, 98–127
Ramat, Paolo (1977) 'Linguistic reconstruction and typology', *Journal of Indo-European Studies* 4, 189–206
– (1980) (ed.) *Linguistic reconstruction and Indo-European syntax*, Amsterdam: Benjamins
– (1982) 'Historische und synchrone Sprachwissenschaft', *Folia Linguistica Historica* 3, 3–24
Reighard, J. (1971) 'Some observations on syntactic change in verbs', *Chicago Linguistic Society: Papers from the Seventh Regional Meeting*
Robins, R.H. (1978) 'The neogrammarians and their nineteenth-century predecessors', *TPS* 1978, 1–16
Romaine, Suzanne (1980) 'The relative clause marker in Scots English: diffusion, complexity, and style as dimensions of syntactic change', *Language in Society* 9, 221–47
– (1982) *Socio-historical linguistics*, Cambridge: Cambridge University Press
Ross, J.F. (1981) *Portraying analogy*, Cambridge: Cambridge University Press
Sankoff, G. (1973) 'Above and beyond phonology in variable rules' in Bailey and Shuy, 44–61
Schmidt, K.H. (1980) 'Typologie und Sprachwandel' in Lüdtke, 20–36
Schmitt, R. (ed.) *Etymologie*, 2 vols., Darmstadt: Wissenschaftliche Buchgesellschaft
Scollon, R. and S.B.K. (1979) *Linguistic convergence: an ethnography of speaking at Fort Chipewyan, Alberta*, New York: Academic Press
Sebeok, T. (ed.) (1975) *Current trends in linguistics*, vol. 13: *Historiography of linguistics*, The Hague: Mouton
Seebold, Elmar (1981) *Etymologie: eine Einführung am Beispiel der deutschen Sprache*, Munich: Beck
Seiler, H. (1979) 'Etymology as an operational principle' in Brogyanyi, vol. 2, 829–35
Skousen, R. (1975) *Substantive evidence in phonology*, The Hague: Mouton
Slobin, D.I. (1977) 'Language change in childhood and in history' in J. Macnamara (ed.), *Language learning and thought*, New York: Academic Press
Smith, Neil V. (1981) 'Consistency, markedness and language change: on the notion "consistent language"', *JL* 17, 39–54
Solta, G.R. (1980) *Einführung in die Balkanlinguistik mit besonderer*

Berücksichtigung des Substrats und des Balkanlateins, Darmstadt: Wissenschaftliche Buchgesellschaft

Sommerfelt, A. (1962) *Diachronic and synchronic aspects of language*, The Hague: Mouton

Stampe, David (1979) *A dissertation on natural phonology*, New York: Garland

Steele, Susan (1975) 'On some factors that affect and effect word order' in Li 1975, 197–268

– (1976) 'A law of order: word order change in Classical Aztek', *IJAL* 42

Steever, S.B. et al. (eds.) (1976) *Papers from the parasession on diachronic syntax*, Chicago Linguistic Society

Stockwell, R.P. (1978) 'Perseverance in the English vowel shift' in Fisiak 1978, 337–48

Strunk, K. (1976) *Lachmanns Regel für das Lateinische* (KZ, Ergänzungsheft 26)

Szemerényi, O. (1981) 'Sprachverfall und Sprachtod, besonders im Lichte indogermanischer Sprachen' in Y.L. Arbeitman and A.R. Bomhard (eds.), *Boni homini donum: Essays in historical linguistics, in memory of J. Alexander Kerns*, Amsterdam: Benjamins, 281–310

Tai, J.H.-Y. (1976) 'On the change from SVO to SOV in Chinese', *Chicago Linguistic Society: Papers from the parasession on diachronic syntax* 291–304

Timberlake, A. (1977) 'Reanalysis and actualization in syntactic change' in Li 1977, 141–77

Traugott, Elizabeth Closs, et al. (eds.) (1980) *Papers from the Fourth International Conference on Historical Linguistics*, Amsterdam: Benjamins

Trudgill, P. and J.K. Chambers (1980) *Dialectology*, Cambridge: Cambridge University Press

T'sou, B. (1972) 'Reordering in diachronic syntax', *Chicago Linguistic Society: Papers from the Eighth Regional Meeting* 591–606

Ureland, P.S. (ed.) (1979) *Sprachvariation und Sprachwandel* (. . . Akten des 3. Symposiums über Sprachkontakt in Europa), Mannheim

Van Coetsem, F., Hendricks, R. and S. McCormick (1981) 'Accent typology and sound change', *Lingua* 53, 295–315

Vennemann, T. (1972) 'Rule inversion', *Lingua* 29, 209–42

– (1974) 'Topics, subjects and word order: from SXV to SVX via TVX' in Anderson and Jones 1974

– (1975) 'An explanation of drift' in Li 1975, 269–305

Vincent, N. (1974) 'Analogy reconsidered' in Anderson and Jones 1974

– (1976) 'Perceptual factors and word-order change in Latin' in Harris 1976

– (1978) 'Is sound change teleological?' in Fisiak 1978, 409–30

– (1980) 'Iconic and symbolic aspects of syntax: prospects for reconstruction' in Ramat, 47–68

– (1982) 'The development of the auxiliaries *habere* and *esse* in Romance' in Vincent and Harris

Vincent, N. and M. Harris (eds.) (1982) *Studies in the Romance verb*, London: Croom Helm

Voyles, J.B. (1973) 'Accounting for semantic change', *Lingua* 31, 95–124

Wachowicz, Krystyna (1977) 'The synchronic description and historical change' in Paul H. Hopper (ed.), *Studies in descriptive and historical linguistics*, Amsterdam: Benjamins

Wade, T.L.B. (1980) 'Indirect loans in German and Russian', *The Incorporated Linguist* 19, 43–48

Warburton, I.P. and N.S. Prabhu (1975) 'Diachronic processes and synchronic grammars', *Glossa* 9, 202–17

Warner, A. (1982) *Complementation in Middle English and the methodology of historical syntax*, London: Croom Helm

Washabough, W. (1975) 'On the development of complementizers in creolization', *Stanford Working Papers in Linguistics* 17, 109–40

Watkins, C. (1964) 'Preliminaries to a reconstruction of Indo-European sentence structure', *Ninth International Congress of Linguists*, Mouton, 1035–42; reprinted in F.W. Householder (ed.), *Syntactic theory* 1, Harmondsworth: Penguin

– (1976) 'Towards Proto-Indo-European syntax: problems and pseudoproblems', *Chicago Linguistic Society: Papers from the parasession on diachronic syntax*, 305–26

Weijnen, A. et al., *Atlas linguarum europae:* (1975) *Introduction*; (1976) *First questionnaire*; (1979) *Second questionnaire*, Assen: Van Gorcum

Weinreich, U. (1958) 'On the compatibility of genetic relationship and convergent development', *Word* 14, 374–9

Wilbur, T.H. (1976) *The Lautgesetz controversy*, Amsterdam: Benjamins

Woolford, E. (1979) 'The developing complementizer system of Tok Pisin: syntactic change in progress' in K.C. Hill (ed.), *The genesis of language*, Ann Arbor: Karoma

Wurzel, H.U. (1975) 'Morphologische Regeln in historischer Sicht' in Dahlstedt

– (1980) 'Ways of morphologizing phonological rules' in Fisiak 1980

INDEX

Abaza 80
ablaut (vowel gradation) 97
Adams, G.B. 240
adaptation of loans *see* integration
age 204ff
agglutinative languages 255, 262
analogical change 20, 34–9, 122–40
  creation 34, 40–3
  extension 37f, 123, 130ff
  levelling 37, 39, 125ff
analogy 20, 24, 32ff, 42, 129
  versus sound change 43ff
Anglo-Saxon *see* English, Old
Albanian 68, 246f, 251f, 270
Alemannic 182, 193
Allen, W.S. 79n, 80f, 92, 105ff, 118ff, 224, 245, 253n
American English *see* English, American
American Indian 135, 266
Anatolian 68
Anderson, J.M. 82
Anttila, R. 247
Arabic 197
arbitrariness of linguistic sign 11f, 22
Ardener, E. 71n
Armenian 68, 245
Arndt, W. 270
Arntz, H. 74
article, definite 246f, 248f
  indefinite 248f
Aramaic 217 n2
aspect 159
Assamese 68
assimilation, phonological 29, 94f, 118f; assimilation of loans *see* integration
atomism 76, 190
auxiliary 159–64
Avestan 68

Balkan linguistic area 246ff
Balochi 68
Baltic 59, 69
Bantu 121, 231, 245, 254f, 264ff
Bartoli, M. 191
basic vocabulary 43, 256, 267–72
Baugh, A.C. 32n, 35
Bazell, C.E. 32n, 262
beech tree 278f
Behaghel, O. 41
Bender, M.L. 196
Benedict, P.K. 255
Bengali 68
Bennett, P.R. 121
Benveniste, E. 12n, 278
Berlin, B. 271n
Best, K.H. 43 n2
Bever, T.G. 158
Bichakjian, B.H. 251
bilingualism 172 *and passim*, 239ff
bleeding order 127ff, 153
Bloomfield, L. 42, 179
Bloomfieldians 76
Boas, F. 246
Bodman, N.C. 265
Bopp, F. 70
borrowing 26, 70, 194, 217ff; *see also under* loan-
Breton 69, 277
British English *see* English, British
Brosnahan, L.F. 246, 251ff
Brugmann, K. 24n, 25, 34n, 45n, 46
Bryan, M.A. 254
Bulgarian 23, 69, 246f, 279
Bush-Hottentot 245

calque *see* loan translation
  semantic *see* semantic extension
Campbell, A. 18n, 79n
Carr, E.B. 259f
case 59f, 102ff, 148–54
Catalan 23, 69
Caucasian 80, 245
Celtic 69, 252, 274ff
Chao, Y.R. 265

Chafe, W.L. 121
change in progress 204ff
channel of transmission 10, 45
Charmey 208n
Chen, M. 112
Chinese 58f, 245, 255ff, 264f, 269
Chomsky, C. 87, 89
Chomsky, N. 3, 75n, 79n, 82, 108, 112, 117, 163, 225
chronology of phonological changes 220; *see also* relative chronology
of language splits 266f
Chrétien, C.D. 268n
class, social 199ff
classification of languages: areal, genealogical, typological 262ff
communicative competence, 172, 213
comparative method, the *see* reconstruction, phonological
competence/performance 3, 138f, 145, 158ff, 213
complement 61, 167ff
conjunction reduction 163–7
Consonant Shift, First (or Germanic) 83ff, 116f
Second (or High German) 174–83, 220ff
context-free rule *see* phonological change, unconditioned
context-sensitive rule *see* phonological change, conditioned
continuity of language through time 2, 67
convergence 193, 241ff
Coptic, Modern 265, 269
core area 191
Cornish 69
correspondence (set, series) 14, 46ff, 51ff, 106ff, 174, 221ff
creole 256ff
creolization 258ff
Cushitic 254f
Czech 23, 69

Dahl's Law 121
Dalby, D. 260n
Danish 23, 69, 251, 278
dating of changes 223f
Dauzat, A. 179, 183, 187ff, 197
DeCamp, D. 259
decreolization 259f
Delbrück, B. 24 n1, 2; 34n
diachronic/synchronic 1ff, 140ff, 171, 204ff
dialect borrowing 185
boundaries 190
levelling 193
deep structure/surface structure 136ff, 145, 155, 169
dephonologization 77
derivational morphology *see* morphology
diffusion 193
diglossia 197, 259f
divergence 193, 267ff
drag-chain 82–8
Dravidian 240ff, 245
drift 150, 250
dual articulation 24, 76f, 108f
Düwel, K. 72
Dutch 23, 69, 174, 234ff, 251, 270, 278
Dyen, I. 270

économie (linguistic economy) 89
Edmont, E. 184
Egyptian, Ancient 265, 269
Ekwall, E. 274f
Ellis, J. 106f
Emeneau, M.B. 245
English, Modern 23, 69, 87f, 165
Early Modern 100, 157, 160
Middle 8, 11, 20, 32f, 40, 99, 117, 124f, 228, 233
Old: loan-words and loan translations 217–37; morphology 102f, 148ff; phonology 30–8, 55f, 124f, 133; place-names 274f; syntax 155ff, 160ff
American 35, 137, 199–215, 234
British 37
Canadian 130f
Indian 226f
Martha's Vineyard 208ff
New York City 199–215
Norwich 204
scientific 224, 229
Scottish 251

analogical changes 5, 32–7
analogical creations 40–3
and German: cognates, correspondences 21f, 46–52, 106f, 174f, 256
-based pidgins/creoles 256ff
Celtic substratum 252
family tree 65ff, 69
glottochronological datings 270
Great Vowel Shift 82ff
internal reconstruction 93–6
loan-words, from and into 217–37
Lord's Prayer 7ff
morphological changes 20, 36f, 99f, 104
names 274ff

English (*cont.*)
phonological changes 30f, 46–53, 124f
phonology 117, 120, 135
socially motivated change 199–215
syntactic changes 149–64
syntax 61, 147ff, 166f
Western European features 248f
Ervin-Tripp, S. 43n
Estonian 252
etymology 62
evaluation test 203, 206, 214f
Ewe 258
exception (to sound laws) *see* phonological change, regularity
explanation 15, 18, 46, 70, 75, 132, 184

family tree 63ff, 193, 266ff
features, phonological 80ff, 108ff
semantic 63
feeding order 127, 130ff
Ferguson, C.A. 197, 258f
Fillmore, C.J. 148n
Finnish 11, 25, 252
Finno-Ugric 11, 252
Fodor, I. 270
Frankish 182, 193
French 11, 23, 28ff, 40, 69, 81ff, 87, 104, 147ff, 181–90, 195, 197, 219ff, 224ff, 229–52, 256, 263, 269, 272
Norman 233f, 274
Old 99, 224
Swiss 208n
Friedrich, P. 264
Fries, C.C. 225
Frisian 23
Frings, Th. 176, 179
functional load (yield, burden) 87f
fusional *see* inflected

Gaelic 69, 277
Gauchat, L. 208n
Gelb, I.J. 97
gender 103f, 148ff, 230, 241f
genealogical relationship 10f, 21f, 63ff, 223, 267–72
genetic *see* genealogical
German, Modern Standard 23, 31, 41, 43 n3, 65, 69, 87, 96, 104, 110, 115, 125, 129, 135, 142ff, 174ff, 194, 221f
Early Modern 37
Middle High 26ff, 53ff, 91, 103, 115, 142, 218, 236
Old High 8, 26ff, 39, 47ff, 57, 65ff, 72, 78ff, 91, 102, 174ff, 217, 223n, 235, 279
High *versus* Low 174–82, 193ff
Middle 177–81, 193
Swiss 44n, 127ff, 144, 197, 222n
Texas 193

analogical changes 37–45
and English: correspondences 21f, 46–52, 106f, 256; shared innovations 64f; syntactic rules 149–67
dialects 142, 178
diphthongization 192, 238
final devoicing 90ff, 115, 140
gender 99, 230f
loan-words from Latin 218–32
loan translations 233–7
Lord's Prayer 8ff
number 147
phonological changes 26–31, 53ff, 77ff; *see also under* umlaut
place-names 274ff
s-stems 102f
syntactic changes 61, 155f
Western European isoglosses 240, 248–52
Germanic 23, 26, 36, 46, 50, 60ff, 65, 69, 72, 83ff, 95, 100ff, 116, 195, 217, 221ff, 237ff, 248ff, 270, 273, 278f
Proto- 57, 65f, 72, 83, 224, 248, 270, 279
West 174, 217, 220
Gilbert, G.G. 193
Gilliéron, J. 184–90
Gimbutas, M. 280
Givón, T. 264
Gleason, H.A. 254n
glottochronology 266–72
Goodman, M. 254
Gothic 27, 50f, 69, 72, 84, 100, 195, 270
Graham, A.C. 59
grammatical categories 58ff, 99ff, 147ff, 154, 159ff, 227ff, 260ff
Grassmann's Law 121
Greek, Ancient 12ff, 20, 23, 42, 44, 55ff, 65f, 68, 72ff, 81ff, 102, 113, 121, 137, 159ff, 217 n2, 227, 234ff, 247f, 262ff, 270, 275f
dialects 66, 81f, 279
Homeric 68, 164
Koinē 68, 247f
Modern 197, 246f
Mycenaean 23, 68, 72
Greenberg, J.H. 262f, 271
Grimm's Law *see* Consonant Shift, First
Gujarati 23, 68
Gumperz, J.J. 240ff

Guthrie, M. 245

Haas, M. 246
Haiman, J. 155–62, 249
Hajdu, P. 252n
Hale, K. 138f
Hall, R.A. 71, 179, 191, 258ff
Halle, M. 5, 75n, 79n, 81f, 108–18, 225
Hallstatt Culture 278, 280
Hamito-Semitic 254
Hancock, I.F. 256, 261
Haudricourt, A.G. 30, 81
Haugen, E. 231
Hausmann, R.B. 161
Henderson, E.J.A. 225, 245
Hermann, E. 208n
Herzog, M.I. 80, 208n, 212
heterogeneity 2ff, 172, 215
Hindi 23, 68
Hirt, H. 74
Hittite, 23, 68, 73, 104, 270
Hockett, C.F. 3, 87, 178
Hodge, C.T. 265
Höfler, O. 181n
Hoenigswald, H.M. 10, 30, 77f, 90n
Hogg, R.M. 120n, 130, 133
homonymic clash 186ff
Hungarian 7, 9, 11, 251f
Hymes, D. 257f
hypercorrection 185, 206f

Icelandic 23, 69, 251
idealization 2ff, 198; *see also* heterogeneity
incidence 36, 77ff, 255
incommensurability 106
Indic 23, 68
Indo-Aryan 66ff, 71
Indo-Iranian 23, 65f, 68, 240
Indo-European 11, 20, 23, 41, 45, 57ff, 67, 70, 73, 83, 92, 100ff, 148f, 159, 164ff, 240, 245, 248ff, 263ff, 270ff, 279
  Proto- 55, 57, 62, 64ff, 72ff, 81, 84, 92, 97, 99ff, 119, 166, 194f, 223, 238, 264, 278
inflected languages 262
inflectional morphology *see* morphology
innovation 27, 42, 49, 64ff, 114–21, 143, 173–83, 192, 214, 217, 224, 244, 248f
integration of loans: phonological 225ff, morphological 227ff, lexical 230ff
interference 239f
internal reconstruction 89–98
Iranian 23, 66ff, 225n, 279
Irish 69, 240, 270, 277
isogloss 173ff, 246ff, 278
isolating languages 58, 262
isomorphism 107, 242ff, 262ff
Italian 23, 69, 81, 230, 234, 251, 269
Italic 69, 119, 195, 246

Jakobson, R. 1n, 30, 77, 81, 245
Jankowski, K.R. 24 n2
Japanese 263
Joos, M. 131
Juilland, A.G. 30, 81

Kesswil 127–30
Kaiser, R. 7
Kannada 240ff
Karlgren, B. 58f, 265
Kay, P. 271n
Khotanese 68
King, R.D. 43n, 78ff, 85n, 87, 108, 114–45 *passim*, 174, 179
Kiparsky, P. 104, 116–67 *passim*
Kisseberth, C.W. 135, 137
Klima, E.S. 151f
Krahe, H. 43 n2, 195, 278
Krogmann, W. 278f
Kupwar 240–4, 246
Kurath, H. 208
Kurdish 23, 68, 279
Kurgan Culture 280
Kurylowicz, J. 38, 101, 104

Labov, W. 80, 138, 199–215 *passim*
Lachmann's Law 118ff
Lakoff, R. 168, 246, 250
language family 245ff, 255ff; *see also* genealogical relationship
langue (*versus* parole) 3, 186
Langendoen, D.T. 158
Lapp 251f
Latin, Classical 12ff, 28f, 44, 55ff, 60, 63, 69, 71ff, 92f, 102, 104, 118ff, 134, 137, 148f, 167ff, 184–90, 195, 218–25, 227ff, 232–8, 248ff, 269f, 272–9
  Late 187, 224, 236, 249
  Neo- 229
  Vulgar 28ff, 61, 81, 167, 207, 221f, 247ff
Latvian 69
Lees, R.B. 268f
Lehmann, W.P. 263f
Leipzig 23
Leumann, M. 61
lexical replacement 183–90

lexicon 133f, 167ff, 186, 216ff, 231ff, 247ff, 273ff
lexicostatistics *see* glottochronology
Lewy, E. 246
Li, C.N. 264f
Lightfoot, D. 159, 160
linguistic area 244–56, 266; Balkan 246–8, West African 260, Western European 248–53
Linguistic Atlas, of France 184ff, of Germany 173ff, 184
Lithuanian 69
Lockwood, W.B. 7, 61
loan translation 232–7
loan-words 181, 196, 217–32; phonological form 217–27, morphological form 227–31; lexical structure 230ff
Lord's Prayer 7ff
Luwian 68
Lyons, J. 147

Ma'a 253ff
Maori 138f, 158
Marathi 23, 240ff
Marchand, H. 11, 40, 229
market word 181
Martha's Vineyard 208ff
Martinet, A. 24, 80–9 *passim*
mass comparison 271f
matched guise test 203
Mawer, A. 275
Matthews, P.H. 91
Mbugu 253ff
McCawley, J.D. 156
mechanism of change 171, 198, 213
Meillet, A. 71n
Meinhof, C. 254
merger of phonemes 31f, 77, 185; reconstruction of 47ff, 78, 87f
Meyerstein, R.S. 87
Miner, K.L. 94
modal verbs 159ff
models of language development 17, 76, 108
monogenesis of pidgins/creoles 260f
mood 159, 164–7
morphology, inflectional/derivational 38, 40, 103, 134, 228ff, 253ff
Mossé, F. 32n, 79n
Moulton, W.G. 44n, 80, 129
multilingualism 240ff, 256ff
Munda 245
mutual intelligibility 196, 259ff
Mysian 279n

names 273ff
neogrammarian manifesto 24, 46, 173
neogrammarians 23f, 185
neolinguistics 191
Neo-Melanesian 259
New York 199–208, 212–15
Nicolaisen, W. 275
Niger–Congo 264
Norse, Old 69, 72, 165, 223n, 237f, 270, 279
Northumbrian 251
Norwegian 23, 69, 251
number 33f, 100ff, 147ff

Old Church Slavonic 69
onomatopoeia 11f
orthography *see* spelling
Oscan 69
Ossetic 68, 245
Osthoff, H. 24 n2, 25, 27, 34n, 45n, 46

Pahlevi 68, 70
Palaic 68
palatalization 29, 56, 219ff
Pali 68
Palmer, F.R. 106
Panjabi 23, 68
parent language *see* protolanguage
Pashto 23, 68
Pattanayak, D.P. 71
Paul, H. 18/19n, 24 n2, 42ff, 139, 187
perceptual strategy 158f
performance *see* competence
periphrastic tenses 249
permanent rule *see* rule, permanent
Persian 23, 66, 68ff, 100ff, 250
person 148ff
Petrovici, E. 247
phonological change 24–32, 77–89, 108–40
  'blindness' of 27
  conditioned 29, 84, 90ff
  minimal step 81, 86
  phonological *versus* morphological conditioning 43ff, 113, 122, 125, 128, 132, 135f, 140ff, 187
  rate of 6, 266ff
  regularity of 25ff, 183
  spread of 183
  sociolinguistic factors 204ff, 213ff
  unconditioned 30f, 84, 89
phonological space 80ff, 212f
phonologization 30, 77
phonotactic rule/constraint 135ff, 221f
pidgin 256ff
pidginization 257f
Pike, K.L. 225

place-names 182, 273ff
Polish 23, 69, 100f
polygenesis of pidgins/creoles 259f
Polynesian 138, 255
Portuguese 23, 69, 256, 260, 269, 273
Postal, P.M. 113
post-creole continuum 259
Powell, T.G.E. 278
Prague School 76
Prakrit 68
Pre-Celtic 274
prehistory 272ff, 277ff
productive (*versus* non-productive) rules, patterns 17ff, 28, 34, 62, 116, 120, 139, 238f, 256f
Prokosch, E. 83
Proto- *for names of protolanguages see under respective language*
protolanguage 11, 46ff, 70–5, 278ff
Provençal 23
Prussian, Old 69
Punic 217 n2
push-chain 82–8

questionnaire 175, 184

Rabin, C. 270
Rayfield, J.R. 231, 240
reconstruction 14, 105ff
  lexical 61ff, 272ff
  morphological 57ff
  phonological 45–58; of merger 47ff; of split 49ff
  syntactic 61ff, 163ff, 263ff
régression *see* hypercorrection
regularity (*versus* irregularity), synchronic 17–21, 101f, 129, 136, 160, 213ff, 227
  of phonological change 25ff
related languages *see* genealogical relationship
relative chronology *see* rule order
Rea, J.A. 269f
Reinecke, J.E. 257
relexification 260ff
relic forms 126, 144
restructuring 33, 46, 100ff, 114ff, 122–40, 143, 157
retention rate 269ff
Rhaeto-Romance/Romansh 23, 69, 249
Rhenish Fan 176 map, 179
Rix, H. 276
Robins, R.H. 12n, 34n, 76, 262
Romance 23, 31, 61, 71, 190, 195, 219ff, 230, 236, 239, 248ff, 269
  Proto- 28n, 71, 181, 184, 219, 270
Romanian 23, 69, 238, 246ff, 269
rounded front vowels 251ff
rule addition 114–21, 146, 181, 213
  conspiracy 135ff, 157f
  form 55ff, 108ff, 123ff
  innovatory *versus* permanent 92, 95, 120f
  insertion 118ff
  loss 123
  order 53ff, 65f, 86f, 194, 224ff
  reordering 126, 146, 151ff, 162ff
  simplification 123–6, 146
Russian 23, 69, 111, 194, 234ff, 279

Sandfeld, K. 238, 246ff
Sanskrit 12ff, 44, 55ff, 66f, 71ff, 97f, 102, 121, 159, 164, 263
  Vedic 23, 59, 68, 164, 270
Sapir, E. 150, 250
Sardinian 23
Saussure, F. de 1n, 12n, 76
Scandinavian 231, 234, 236, 274
Schaffhausen 127–30
Schane, S.A. 110f, 131
Schirmunski, V.M. 178–83 *passim*, 190
Schleicher, A. 24 n2, 45n, 74, 246
Schmidt, Joh. 192
Schrader, O. 278
Schuchardt, H. 26n, 140
Schützeichel, R. 180
semantic calque *see* semantic extension
semantic change, 30, 61ff, 105ff, 278ff
semantic extension 237–9
Semitic 270; Proto-Semitic 97n
Serbo-Croatian 23, 69, 246
Sherwood, P.A. 7
Shibatani, M. 136
Siamese *see* Thai
Sieberer, A. 89
simplification 114, 122, 150ff, 256ff
  of structural analysis part of rule 123ff
  of structural change part of rule 125ff
Sindhi 68
Sinhalese 23, 68
Slavic *see* Slavonic
Slavonic 23, 59, 69, 195, 234, 236, 246f, 270, 279
Slobin, D.I. 255n
social evaluation 181, 213
Sogdian 68
sound change *see* phonological change
sound shift 82
sound symbolism 11f, 42
South East Asian languages 266
Spanish 23, 69, 168f, 187f, 249, 260, 269, 273

speech community 171ff, 197ff
spelling 79, 82, 183, 224
split, phonemic 30, 49ff, 78
split(ting up) of language 64, 267ff
Sprachbund *see* linguistic area
Steinthal, H. 45n
style 202
subject pronoun, obligatory 156f, 249
substratum 252f, 259ff, 273ff
Swabian 63
Swadesh, M. 246, 267ff
Swahili 227, 231, 254n, 262
Swedish 23, 69, 234, 251, 270

target language 258f
Taylor, D. 258, 260
Telugu 240ff
tense 159, 164ff
Thai 245, 255, 263
Thieme, P. 279
Thomas, G. 236
Thompson, S. 264f
Thracian 279n
time-depth 10, 267ff
Tischler, J. 270
Tocharian 68
toponymy *see* place-names
transition area 191
Traugott, E.C. 149, 155, 161
Trier, J. 105
Trubetzkoy, N.S. 1n, 80f, 244f
Trudgill, P. 204n, 245f
Tucker, A.N. 254
Turkish 167, 246f, 255, 262
typological change 264ff
typological classification: morphological, syntactic 262
Twaddell, W.F. 27, 78f

Ukrainian 23
Ullmann, S. 105
Umbrian 69
umlaut 26ff, 30, 38ff, 78ff, 89, 95, 117, 123f, 140ff, 221
uniformitarian principle 45
universals 24, 63, 108ff, 146, 262ff, 267ff
Urdu 23, 68, 240ff
Urheimat 278

Valdman, A. 259
Van Coetsem, F. 83
variable 198ff, 213ff
variation 3f, 198ff, 259ff
Vennemann, Th. 26n, 112, 125n, 136, 140, 154, 174
Verner's Law 83ff, 144
Vidos, B.E. 191
Vietnamese 245, 262
Voorhoeve, J. 258, 260f

Wagner, K. 180, 192
Wagner, K.H. 139, 155
Wartburg, W. von 182
Watkins, C. 101, 120
wave theory 67, 192–5
Weinreich, U. 80, 125, 208n, 212
Weisgerber, L. 42
Welsh 7ff, 69, 240, 277
Wenker, G. 174ff, 184
Whinnom, K. 258, 261
Whiteley, W.H. 227, 231, 254
Wilbur, T.H. 26n
Winter, W. 42, 245
word order 150ff, 157, 263ff
Wrede, F. 175n
Wurzel, W.U. 141ff

Yawelmani 135
Yiddish 125ff, 144, 231, 240

HOW TO STUDY A RENAISSANCE PLAY: Marlowe, Webster, Jonson

Chris Coles

M
MACMILLAN

First published 1988

Published by
Higher and Further Education Division
MACMILLAN PUBLISHERS LTD
Houndmills, Basingstoke, Hampshire RG21 2XS
and London
Companies and representatives
throughout the world

Typeset by Wessex Typesetters
(Division of The Eastern Press Ltd)
Frome, Somerset

Printed in Hong Kong

British Library Cataloguing in Publication Data
Coles, Chris
How to study a Renaissance play : Marlowe, Webster, Jonson.—(How to study literature)
1. English drama—Early modern and Elizabethan, 1500–1600—History and criticism 2. English drama—17th century—History and criticism
I. Title II. Series
822'.3'09 PR651
ISBN 0-333-39922-6

Contents

General editors' preface		vi
Acknowledgements		vii
1	**Getting started**	1
2	**Christopher Marlowe**	9
	Doctor Faustus	9
	Edward II	30
3	**John Webster**	40
	The Duchess of Malfi	42
	The White Devil	64
4	**Ben Jonson**	76
	Volpone	79
	The Alchemist	97
5	**Writing an essay**	108
	The question	108
	The answer	114
Further reading		131

General editors' preface

EVERYBODY who studies literature, either for an examination or simply for pleasure, experiences the same problem: how to understand and respond to the text. As every student of literature knows, it is perfectly possible to read a book over and over again and yet still feel baffled and at a loss as to what to say about it. One answer to this problem, of course, is to accept someone else's view of the text, but how much more rewarding it would be if you could work out your own critical response to any book you choose or are required to study.

The aim of this series is to help you develop your critical skills by offering practical advice about how to read, understand and analyse literature. Each volume provides you with a clear method of study so that you can see how to set about tackling texts on your own. While the authors of each volume approach the problem in a different way, every book in the series attempts to provide you with some broad ideas about the kind of texts you are likely to be studying and some broad ideas about how to think about literature; each volume then shows you how to apply these ideas in a way which should help you construct your own analysis and interpretation. Unlike most critical books, therefore, the books in this series do not simply convey someone else's thinking about a text, but encourage you and show you how to think about a text for yourself.

Each book is written with an awareness that you are likely to be preparing for an examination, and therefore practical advice is given not only on how to understand and analyse literature, but also on how to organise a written response. Our hope is that although these books are intended to serve a practical purpose, they may also enrich your enjoyment of literature by making you a more confident reader, alert to the interest and pleasure to be derived from literary texts.

John Peck
Martin Coyle

Acknowledgements

My first debt must be to the general editors of the *How to Study Literature* series, Martin Coyle and John Peck, for inviting me to contribute this book. Like the good teachers they are, they have been tolerant of my shortcomings and full of encouragement and advice, and the very appearance of this book is a tribute to their hard work. I must also thank my two painstaking typists, Colin Coles and Mollie Brittan, for their help and concern. Apologies are probably in order to my students, past and present, who have found themselves on the receiving end of many of my ideas – at least they can now go out and buy the book. Finally my thanks must go to Ron, for sitting on the manuscript, and to Madeline, for everything.

C. C.

To Madeline

1

Getting started

THE dramatists discussed in this book are Marlowe, Webster and Jonson. Together with Shakespeare they are the principal English Renaissance playwrights, and as such their works are still frequently performed, widely available in print and quite accessible. In addition, all three are enjoyable and rewarding writers to study. Their plays are strong and interesting but not too obscure, not too difficult. Admittedly they can look daunting at first sight, and as you start to study one of their plays your initial impression may well be that Renaissance drama is very difficult indeed.

Reading the play

The first problem you are likely to encounter is the difficulty of reading the play. If you are lucky enough to see the play performed you will start with a marvellous advantage, for on the stage the whole play has a force and impact that makes it easier to follow. In plays written so long ago the language can be difficult to understand, but in the theatre you can respond to what you see as well as to what you hear. You should, therefore, come away from a performance with some understanding of what the play is about. A performance will help you grasp the personalities of the main characters, how they embody good and evil impulses and how they come up against good and evil in others. Studying the play will involve a lot more, but the stage performance will at least have given you some sense of the human issues at the heart of the work.

It is not, however, always possible to see the play in the theatre or on video. Most studies start with a reading, which is a less direct and immediate experience. It can even be rather bewildering. Most modern editions of Renaissance plays have long introductions as well as lots of footnotes to explain points, and these can come to seem more important than the text itself. You might wonder whether you are supposed to get on with reading the play or whether you have got to consult all the explanations in case you miss something. The answer is, get on with reading the play; you can return to the footnotes later.

This is easy advice to give, of course, but following it might not be so simple. You won't be alone if you find reading a Renaissance play hard work. I'll go further than that: you may feel lost before you've got half way down the first page. The reason for this is the dense and difficult language in which these plays are written. Studying a play is going to involve coming to terms with its language – indeed your focus as a student of the play should eventually be on the language – but at the outset don't worry about struggling to understand every word and every line. If you come across a baffling passage, slide over it: concentrate on following the story, seeing what happens next and who does what. The stage directions of the play will often be helpful in doing this. Try to get hold of the situations presented and the personalities of the characters involved. It helps if you try to visualise a performance in your mind's eye; try to imagine the characters on stage, the nature of the events they are involved in, and how they respond and react to each other.

If you follow this advice you might feel that you have achieved a clear sense of what is happening, but still be worried by the fact that you have little idea of the significance of it all. It is at this point – where you begin to wonder what the play amounts to and what it is saying – that you have moved on from your first reading and started to think about shaping a critical response. This is where the real difficulties begin. Every student who perseveres will find that he or she can read the play, but many students never really sort out a critical response. So let's confront this problem now.

Shaping a critical response

Having read the play, what do you do next? Many students, unfortunately, decide to do the wrong thing, and get so bogged down in the details of the text that they can't see the wood for the trees. I have come across many examination candidates who know a lot about the characters in a play and who can quote at length, but who have no real sense of the play as a whole. Often their hard work is wasted and it would have been better if they had channelled their energies into thinking about the whole effect of the play instead of making lots of notes with no particular aim in mind. Certainly thinking is now of vital importance: once you have read the play, start thinking about what it all amounts to.

'What exactly am I supposed to be thinking about?' you may ask. Well, you need to start considering the overall shape of the play, and a few simple ideas about Renaissance drama in general might help here. The most important idea to grasp is that most Renaissance plays are built upon a fairly simple pattern, and we can see the same pattern underlying nearly all plays in the period. The shape of this pattern can be seen at its clearest in plays written near the beginning of the Renaissance period, that is to say about 1500, and I shall consider one of these plays in a moment. Before we look at the pattern of Renaissance plays, however, some basic points of information may be useful.

First, the term *Renaissance drama*: we use this to cover all plays written between about 1500 and 1642. The first date can only be approximate; the second is exact because in 1642 the theatres in England were closed down by order of the Puritan government. The three dramatists considered in this book were all born in the middle of this period. Marlowe (1564–93), who was killed at the age of twenty-nine, did all his writing during the reign of Elizabeth I (1558–1603), while the most famous work of Webster (1580–1625) and Jonson (1572–1637) was done during the reign of James I (1603–25). The fact that three major playwrights were all writing their best work within the short space of twenty years or so would be remarkable enough were it not for the fact that the greatest playwright of all, Shakespeare (1564–1616), was also active at the same time. This is why Renaissance drama is so important in the history of English literature.

But what does the word 'Renaissance' actually mean? It means 'rebirth', and is the word used to describe the widespread cultural developments which happened all over Europe during the sixteenth century. These changes occurred as a rather static medieval world yielded to a more dynamic, energetic modern world built around business, commerce and exploration. Old values were giving way to new, and the arts found different ways of expressing these changes and responding to them. Certainly the greatest glory of the English Renaissance was the unprecedented growth of professional stage drama. Around 1500 most plays had a simple moral message and were performed by amateurs on religious holidays, but by 1600 vastly more sophisticated plays were being performed by professional actors in purpose-built theatres. As much as things changed, however, it is clear that later writers such as Marlowe, Webster, Jonson, and indeed Shakespeare, drew on the dramatic tradition of earlier plays. It is to one of these plays, *Youth*, that we turn now. What we are looking for is the shape or the pattern that underlies *Youth* and which will continue to influence the pattern of plays written throughout the Renaissance period.

The pattern of Renaissance plays

Like most early sixteenth-century plays *Youth* is a short play with a straightforward plot. At the start a character called Charity comes on stage and tells the audience that only those who obey God's laws will be saved and go to heaven. No sooner has Charity finished speaking than Youth, the impetuous young hero of the play, comes on: he has got plenty of money and announces that he's going to have a good time eating, drinking and womanising. Rejecting Charity's advice, he calls for Riot, Pride and Lechery to join him in his pursuit of pleasure. Much of the action of the play is taken up with their silly tricks and unruly behaviour, but at the end Youth begins to regret that he has been so impulsive and turns to Charity to help him save his soul from eternal punishment in hell. He then repents and is able to find salvation.

Your first response to a play like *Youth* might be to dismiss it as being too intent on preaching a religious lesson, and it is true that the play begins and ends with very direct advice to the audience on how they should conduct their lives. Yet there is more to the play than this, and what really brings the play to life is the unruly behaviour of Youth himself. What the play thus offers us, if we take account of both its religious message and its entertainment value, is a sense of the gap between how people ought to behave and the way they do behave, the way they follow their own unruly impulses and desires. It is the tension between these two things that gives the play its dramatic shape and force.

If you can see this, then really you have got hold of the basic pattern of all Renaissance plays. Time and time again what we find in Renaissance drama is the same broad contrast in which an idea of order is set against the reality of disorder. In the case of *Youth* we can see that an idea of order is set out in Charity's speech at the beginning of the play, and that in particular it is an idea of God's order. Set against this in the rest of the play is a dramatisation of the way people refuse to be tied down by rules, even by God's rules. It is this broad theme, this tension between an idea of traditional order and the reality of the disorder created by people, that playwrights return to time and again throughout the Renaissance period. This is not to say that they all write in the same way; indeed, we might more often be struck by the different rather than the similarities between various Renaissance plays. Yet this underlying pattern is always there if we look for it.

This is extremely useful for us as students of Renaissance drama, because an awareness of this pattern makes it relatively easy to grasp the broad significance of any play from the period. For example, the first reading of a Jonson play might leave you overwhelmed and fairly lost as to what it is all about. If you stand back from the details, however, and think of the play in terms of a broad contrast between an idea of order and an idea of disorder, the play should start to make some sense. In the case of a Jonson play you will soon realise that many of the characters are behaving in a foolish or outrageous way as they pursue their desires; the play will also manage to suggest that such characters are deviating from an ideal standard of reasonable and responsible behaviour. And what is true of a Jonson play is true generally. Different dramatists will develop their material in their own distinctive ways, but the easiest approach to any Renaissance play is to assume that it is bringing to life this theme of the contrast between how life ought to be and the messy reality of life as it is actually lived.

Looking at a play in the light of this opposition is productive in various ways. First, as already suggested, it will help you see some shape and significance in the play as a whole, but it should also help you to come to terms with individual scenes and speeches. You might, for example, have encountered a speech that you find virtually incomprehensible. What you can assume is that the character speaking will somehow be wrestling with the desire of not wanting to conform to the rules laid down by God or society, and that there will be a tension present between expected standards of behaviour and the character's unruly desires or impulses. A sense of this opposition will help you to grasp the significance of a play as a whole and of the individual scenes within a play. From this basis your whole critical analysis can be shaped. What criticism eventually tries to get at is the distinctive qualities of any play, so it is very important to compare and contrast the ways different plays work. A sense of what a play has in common with other plays can begin to sharpen your ideas about the distinctive way a dramatist has shaped his material.

A sense of the unique qualities of any play will, however, only develop slowly as you study the play in detail, and there might still seem a vast gap between your sense of the general pattern of Renaissance drama and detailed analysis of an individual play. What this book tells you is how to bridge that gap. It shows you how to move forward from a sense of the standard shape of Renaissance drama, and explains how, in a series of steps, you can develop your own detailed critical response. The method asks you to concentrate on just a few scenes from the work. You might feel that an approach which neglects the majority of scenes cannot hope to do justice to a play, but as this book goes on I hope it becomes apparent that such selective focusing on a few scenes is likely to be far more productive than any attempt to discuss too much of the action at one time. I shall now dwell on the method here, as each chapter is meant to illustrate the approach. What I do hope you will see is that I am not going to interpret the plays for you, since it is not the purpose of this book to give you my idea of what the plays mean. I am primarily concerned to illustrate a method which, if you try it for yourself, should enable you to shape and articulate your own distinctive response. Before turning to the individual plays, I want to suggest some ways in which later Renaissance dramatists began to complicate the basic pattern we found in morality plays.

The changing nature of Renaissance drama

The main characters in *Youth* all have abstract names: 'Youth', 'Riot', 'Humility', 'Pride', 'Charity'. They are not so much individual characters as personifications of abstract ideas: they stand for a particular type of behaviour or course of action. Youth himself, for example, is meant to stand for all young people, and we are meant to see that he represents the way in which young people are supposed to be short-sighted and self-indulgent. As Renaissance drama developed through the sixteenth century, however, it became more realistic. The most obvious indication of this is that the characters have proper names and come across as flesh-and-blood individuals.

What also changes is the kind of world the plays reflect. *Youth* is about an essentially medieval world where the main relationship is between God and man. Later Renaissance plays reflect and reveal a more modern view of the world as social behaviour, moral behaviour and religious behaviour all become more complex. These later plays do tackle the question of religious values, but political and social considerations now weigh heavily as well. Often there is a conflict because characters are not sure whether to obey God's laws or to follow their own desires, and this conflict troubles them profoundly. In *Youth* the main character is easily seduced by the temptations of the world, but in an instant can rediscover the need to obey God. In later Renaissance plays the alternatives are not so clear-cut, and the quick reversal of fortune experienced by Youth is not so easy to obtain in a more complex world.

This is apparent if we consider Shapespeare's *Hamlet*. You might not have read this play, but nearly everybody has heard of its hero, a young man dressed in black who seems uncertain how to act when he learns of his father's murder: everyone knows that he makes a famous speech beginning 'To be or not to be . . .'. That speech alone gives us a clue as to the kind of complexity to be found in *Hamlet* and in Renaissance drama generally. Hamlet is debating with himself whether to live or die, questioning whether it is worth going on. He is grossly offended by the nature of the world and by what he has seen of human behaviour, but what he discovers is that there are no easy solutions, no easy answers to the problems he faces. These problems include both the evil that he finds in others and the fact that he himself is torn between good and bad impulses; even worse, he doesn't know whether a course of action would make things better or worse. Whereas Youth could turn to Charity for advice and readily repent of his evil ways, Hamlet seems trapped in the problems of his Renaissance world where God's order is no longer simple or self-evident.

As we turn to the plays of Marlowe, Webster and Jonson we can expect to see the same kind of thing happening; the problems of mankind will be complex and difficult to resolve. The directions, though, that these writers take will vary from play to play, for, like Shakespeare, they are all trying to explore difficult issues in different ways. In order to do justice to their plays you will need to be fairly flexible, and there is certainly a lot of scope for you to pursue your own ideas as a critic. But, however much you become concerned with chasing the distinctive qualities of these dramatists as individual writers, you should try to remember that at the heart of Renaissance drama there is a broad tension between order and disorder. It is this central idea which will always provide you with a way of getting hold of what matters from any play of the period.

In the discussion of the plays that follow I shall be using the Penguin editions for all my references: line references therefore refer to either Christopher Marlowe, *The Complete Plays*; John Webster, *Three Plays*; or Ben Jonson, *Three Comedies*. These are readily available, but if you are using another edition of the text you may find that the line references do not exactly correspond.

2

Christopher Marlowe

Christopher Marlowe (1564–93) was the first great playwright of the Elizabethan and Jacobean stage. Indeed, apart from the works of Shakespeare, Marlowe's play *Doctor Faustus* is the best known of Renaissance dramas. You might occasionally come across the suggestion that Marlowe is important as a dramatist only because he was a forerunner of Shakespeare, and that his plays merely paved the way for Shakespeare's works. This is emphatically not the case; Marlowe is a great dramatist, in particular a writer of great tragedies, whose plays still make a very powerful impression on stage. To appreciate just how his plays make such a strong impact we have to look closely at what he wrote; we have to see how his plays work and what kind of view of life they convey. The whole purpose of this book is to show you how to achieve this for yourself. In the following discussion of *Doctor Faustus*, therefore, do bear in mind that my interpretation is not an infallible guide to the play; my aim is to show you how to build your own critical analysis stage by stage. Such an analysis always has to start with reading the play and getting some broad ideas about what is going on. We can make this our first step.

Doctor Faustus

1 *Read the play, then think about its overall effect and what sort of broad pattern you can see in the plot*

A very brief summary of *Doctor Faustus* should provide enough information to get us started. The story, quite simply, is of a man called John Faustus who sells his soul to the devil in order to gain knowledge and power. Irritated by the restrictions placed on him by conventional learning and wisdom, Faustus turns to black magic, entering into a pact with the devil. The pact gives him twenty-four years of unlimited powers, and such knowledge as his devil servant, Mephostophilis, will provide. In return for these powers Faustus agrees to surrender his soul to Lucifer at the end of that period of time. Most of the play is taken up with Faustus exercising his powers in a variety of ways, but at the very end Lucifer claims his part of the bargain and the desperate Faustus is dragged off to hell.

One thing that might strike you is that Marlowe's play has a lot in common with the morality play I mentioned in Chapter 1, except that *Doctor Faustus* has an unhappy ending. Like *Youth*, *Doctor Faustus* has a central character who thinks he knows best and so rejects conventional morality to pursue his own desires. The real difference is that for Faustus, unlike Youth, there is no quick, easy reversal of fortune leading to redemption, and he is made to pay the full price for the error of his ways. This is what makes the play a tragedy. From the minute Faustus makes the decision to sell his soul, we know that the action will inexorably lead to a moment of reckoning where he has to pay his debt.

Yet it is not only in Renaissance drama that we find this sort of pattern of sin and retribution. Take, for example, the familiar and much-filmed story *Frankenstein*. True to the genre of the horrow movie, as soon as the single-minded Dr Frankenstein begins to rob graves for bits of body we know that he has gone beyond the pale. He has put aside all human and moral considerations to create his beloved monster, and we recognise that he will get his come-uppance as a result of his obsession.

Once we realise that plots such as those of *Doctor Faustus* and *Frankenstein* work on the same principle – both employ a central character who is blind to the evil of what he is doing – then it is not too difficult to spot other similarities in their dramatic patterns. Thus both plots highlight the folly of the main characters by providing a vivid contrast between what they aspire to and what really happens. Dr Frankenstein has a vision of life created from death, a perfectly constructed human being which turns out to be a hideous travesty of life, a real monster. Similarly, Faustus has a vision of 'a world of profit and delight, of power, of honour of, omnipotence' (I.i.52–3), but ends up playing the fool, cuffing the Pope around the ears and leaving the village idiot stranded in a pool of water. It is all a mockery of his original high ideals. I do not want to take these parallels between *Frankenstein* and *Doctor Faustus* too far, but, just as they share similar concerns about the foolish pride of man, so both works have similar dramatic patterns woven into them in order to spotlight those concerns.

The first move in making sense of a play is to try and see this sort of broad pattern in the text and to grasp the larger concerns of the play. In the case of *Doctor Faustus* we have already established that it is about an ambitious man who, in pursuit of his ambitions, forgets all moral considerations. The rewards he gains, however, are disappointing, and the ultimate outcome is tragic, for he has to pay for his mistakes with death and damnation. We can say that here we have identified the essential theme of the play, the way in which people's desires can be tragically destructive. We could also say that we have seen the kind of moral warning the play offers, the way it warms us of the dangers of ambitious pride. However, to concentrate on the moral message in *Doctor Faustus*, as with any Renaissance play, would be a reductive step. After all, what we want to get at in our criticism is the complexity of Marlowe's achievement, not the simplest moral message we can extract from the text. The rest of our analysis, therefore, must concentrate on how Marlowe brings his theme to life. To lead us into this we can begin with one or two more comments about the basic shape of the plot.

An important point is that, in common with a lot of plays that seek to reveal the folly of man's desires, the plot of *Doctor Faustus* falls into three main stages. First, there is the introduction to the situation and to the aspirations of the main character. During this first stage we see a confident Faustus giving voice to his ambitions and his plans for the future. In the second stage these plans are put into practice, and we see the contrast between what Faustus said he would do and what he actually achieves. Finally, there is the moment of reckoning when Faustus has to recognise his folly and pay the price for his previous errors. So far, so good. There is probably something of Faustus in all of us: we all dream of how we should like to behave if freed from moral, social or religious rules. Like Faustus, we sometimes make hasty decisions that look foolish with the benefit of hindsight. This is why the theme of *Doctor Faustus* interests us, but what really gives the play impact is the skill with which Marlowe brings Faustus's experiences to life on stage. The best way to show this at work, and certainly the best way to build your analysis, is to examine single scenes from different parts of the play. Close examination of a scene has the advantage of narrowing down what we have to do so that we do not have to consider the entire play at once and so we avoid trying to discuss too many details simultaneously.

Even dealing with a small episode from a play such as *Doctor Faustus*, however, may seem a daunting prospect. What do I say? How do I know if what I am saying is worthwhile or not? How do I know if I am interpreting a particular passage correctly? These questions are bound to cross the mind of even the most capable student, but one of the secrets of criticism is to build your analysis slowly, gradually exploring the text and extending your ideas at your own pace. Provided you base everything you say on the text, your ideas will be worthwhile. It is now time, then, that we begin to contruct such an analysis.

2 *Look at the opening scenes and try to achieve a sense of what is happening and what the play is about*

Even this straightforward instruction can prove unnerving for someone unfamiliar with Elizabethan language, especially given the complicated opening of *Doctor Faustus*: as well as a Prologue there are lots of long speeches and difficult references. However, we need not be concerned with all these complications at this stage; all we want is a very basic idea of what is going on. We might produce something like this: after the Prologue Faustus gives a long, complicated speech in which he denounces all the learning he has had so far as worthless. He then resolves to dabble in black magic in order to get what he wants. A Good Angel tries to restrain him but an Evil Angel urges him on, and at the end of the scene Faustus tells his friends Cornelius and Valdes that he wants their help in practising black magic.

The problem that now confronts us is trying to find something to say about this. We have a basic idea of the action, but in itself this is not enough. We need to try and make some sense of it, to comment on its significance, and this is where many students begin to feel unsure of themselves. However, if we look back to the points we made in the last section we do have a means of coming to terms with what is going on. The play is about human choices and the misguided decision of a man who thinks he knows best. What we are giving in this scene are the dreams of Faustus, and in a very vivid way the character himself gives us a vision of what life will be like once he has the power he wants. Yet Faustus faces a dilemma: in order to get this power he has to make a choice, and the presence of the angels remind us of all the arguments for and against Faustus selling his soul. We might notice that the Good Angel gets short shrift, and that Faustus seems to have made up his mind already, urged on by his desires.

In this scene, then, we see a very positive Faustus, full of himself and his own ideas, with nothing as yet to trouble his hopes for an exciting and rewarding life. At this same time we are aware of how Faustus has stored up problems for himself in the future by turning his back on God.

In order to see how these issues are developed we obviously have to look at more scenes in the play. Before we do so, there is one point I ought to mention. The edition of *Doctor Faustus* I am using is divided into acts and scenes, but yours may simply be divided into scenes. The scene number according to this alternative scheme is given below in italics every time there is a change in the scene discussed. However, texts of *Doctor Faustus* vary a great deal and you may find that some of the lines I quote are slightly different in your text. If you are studying *Doctor Faustus* as a set text and a particular edition is recommended, make sure the references you give in essays correspond to your particular edition.

3 *Choose a scene from Act II and try to clarify your impression of what the play is about and how it is developing*

Something that might have surprised you is the brevity of my discussion of the first scene. In fact the discussion could have been much longer. I could have explored the scene thoroughly, finding all sorts of images and ideas in it that would recur throughout the play. Yet what I want to stress is how it is possible to build a logical and systematic response to a play by moving forward carefully and sensibly. At this point I am still establishing the foundations of my analysis; I am confirming that the first scene bears out my initial ideas about the play as a whole, and so deliberately holding back from making my analysis too detailed. Now, as I turn to a scene from the second act, I can begin to extend and expand my analysis, building on the impressions put together so far. We know that Faustus is a man dissatisfied with conventional life, wisdom and learning, and is willing to devote himself to black magic in order to get himself greater power. We also know that he is very confident and enthusiastic, and is convinced that his decision is the right one.

In Act II we can expect this to begin to change in some way as complications or problems arise to disrupt Faustus's plans. In particular we can expect a gap to open up between Faustus's dreams and what actually happens. This may seem vague, but at the moment you must remember that we are dealing with the broad development of a whole act. We now need to focus on one scene in order to make more specific comments. But which scene? The opening scene from each act is often a useful one to consider, but any scene where you feel the play's plot moves forward in a significant way will provide interesting material for analysis. As with the scene we looked at in the first act, the method is first to say what is happening and then to try to comment on its significance.

Act II then (*or scene vi*, depending on your edition), opens with Faustus once again in his study, but this time he is cursing Mephostophilis for denying him the joys of heaven. He announces that it is his intention to 'renounce this magic and repent' (II.i.11; *or scene vi*); in this he is encouraged by the Good Angel, who assures Faustus that God will pity him. The Evil Angel, however, maintains with some force and conviction that 'Faustus never shall repent' (II.i.17). Faustus himself seems to acknowledge that his choice has been made and that there is no turning back, and begins to question Mephostophilis again. They begin to talk about astronomy and the heavens, but Faustus then puts a question to Mephostophilis which the latter refuses to answer. After a slight argument between the two, Mephostophilis leaves, and the Good and Evil Angels once more take the stage to argue their various cases. Just as Faustus appears to have been persuaded by the Good Angel, Lucifer and Beelzebub appear and make Faustus renew his pledge to them. Then they show him a parade of the Seven Deadly Sins, and, with a final promise to show Faustus hell at a later date, they all go their separate ways.

This is what happens in the scene; we now need to discuss its significance. Perhaps the first thing we can notice is how this scene provides a dramatic contrast to the opening of Act I. There we saw a confident Faustus outline his plans for the future, perfectly prepared to make a deal with the devil in order to get what he wanted. Faustus is a much more uncertain figure now, and much of the action in this scene serves to highlight the issue of that decision: was it wise or not? We are beginning to see a character torn two ways, and the Good and Evil Angels seem to take on more significance. We could say that they represent the way in which human beings have to confront conflicting impulses when making difficult decisions. Faustus himself seems twice to be on the point of repenting and pulling out of the whole thing; once he stops himself from doing so, but on the other occasion he has to be reminded of his obligations by Lucifer and Beelzebub, who also provide the show of Seven Deadly Sins to help take Faustus's mind off things. We seem to have arrived at a point in the play where problems are arising, where doubts about the wisdom of his action are creeping in for Faustus, and where the overwhelming optimism of the first scene seems to have dissipated.

We have now identified what is going on and made some broad comments about the action in terms of what we know so far. Our next step is to look in the text for some indication of the way the play not only recognises Faustus's dilemma, but also presents it forcefully and makes it interesting to watch. As before, the best way to appreciate this is to narrow our focus and concentrate on a short section or extract from within the scene. We should be able to see how just a few lines can reflect some of the major issues we have already encountered. Let's take, for example, the opening lines of the scene where Faustus is beginning to realise that he can never hope to get to heaven and blames Mephostophilis for his unhappy state:

FAUSTUS. When I behold the heavens then I repent,
And curse thee, wicked Mephostophilis,
Because thou hast deprived me of those joys.
MEPHOSTOPHILIS. 'Twas thine own seeking, Faustus, thank thyself.

(II.i.1–4)

It is not too difficult to see that in these lines Faustus is expressing regret about his decision. Having gained some knowledge of heaven, he now appreciates the joys. Ironically, however, the very bargain which gave him his knowledge denies him access to heaven for all eternity. Frustrated by this seemingly vicious circle Faustus turns to Mephostophilis and begins to take it out on him. Yet Mephostophilis, with some irony and even more perception, points to the fact that Faustus made the choice of his own free will, and therefore has no one else to blame but himself. Faustus's vision of unlimited knowledge has backfired on him: the one thing he has gained knowledge of is that he will be denied access to the one place he wants to be.

The extract, then, provides a good example of the growing tension between Faustus's original view of what he was doing and the rather uncomfortable reality of what is happening. But what it also conveys is Faustus's awareness of what has happened. He has chosen evil, but his use of religious words such as 'repent', and his awareness of divine 'joys', together with his recognition that Mephostophilis is 'wicked', all serve to emphasise that he knows he has made the wrong choice. The extract thus shows the painful plight of a man who recognises the difference between good and evil, but who is also aware that he has damned himself. In other words, the speech vividly points out why Faustus begins to waver between repentance and despair when he realises what he has done.

There are many other bits of the text that I could have chosen to discuss here, and you will undoubtedly find examples of your own as you read through the play. The thing to remember is that the basic approach and principles for discussing any such extract will remain the same. Good criticism consists of nothing more than having clear ideas about the play which you can illustrate and support with evidence from the text. As you look at an extract, however, you should find yourself managing to convey a vivid sense of how the dramatist brings his ideas to life. Here, for example, we can see that Faustus has made a mistake and begins to realise it. Nevertheless he still continues with his course of action and is easily distracted from a full consideration of the issues by the display of Deadly Sins at the end of the scene. In this way we get an idea of the abstract theme being dramatised, but we also have the sense of a particular man facing an individual dilemma, which, as the play progresses, will become increasingly painful.

4 *Choose a scene from Act III and begin to look more closely at the principal characters in the play*

As I have said before, *Doctor Faustus* is a play which can be divided into three stages. The first part deals with the setting up of Faustus's contract and the hopes and expectations that he has from his bargain. The second, and by far the largest part, deals with a wide variety of episodes which show Faustus actually living out his time of power and fantasy. The final and most dramatic part of the play deals with the moment of reckoning when Faustus has to confront the enormity of what he has done. There is almost a fairy-tale structure to the plot, with Faustus given his time of freedom rather like a demonic Cinderella, yet with the stroke of midnight Faustus does not merely change back into his old clothes – he is dragged to hell screaming.

Many of the most puzzling and confusing aspects of the play belong to the middle section, which is the part of the play we are dealing with here. The first and last parts concentrate on Faustus and it is fairly easy to see their relevance. But what are we to make of the numerous odd scenes and sketches that make up the middle part of the play? How are we going to say anything about the large number of characters who pop in and out of the action, and what relevance do they have to the play as a whole?

The best thing to do when confronted with problems of this kind is to go back to basics. We need to remind ourselves that all the details in a play are going to be connected with major issues that we have already identified. We need to be aware of the contrast between what Faustus thought he would gain from making his pact with the devil and what we actually see him achieving on stage, for this is a section of the play where Faustus is putting his powers into practice, where he is getting the rewards for his unholy bargain. If we look closely at a particular episode we ought to be able to see these ideas in action.

The climax of Act III involves a weird and wonderful confrontation between Faustus and the Pope. It will be useful to describe the action that takes place here quite fully before we try to comment on its significance. In Act III, scene ii (*or scene viii*), Mephostophilis brings Faustus to the Pope's palace, where a rather bizarre ritual is going on. Bruno the Saxon is being humiliated by being forced to act as a footstool for the Pope. The Pope is asking his cardinals to sit in judgement over Bruno and the Emperor who elected him, in order to declare them heretics. The trick that Faustus plays on the Pope is to make the synod of cardinals fall asleep over the case they are supposed to be judging. Faustus then pretends to be the representative of the synod and tells the Pope that Bruno and the Emperor should be declared heretics, and that Bruno himself should be burnt to death. He then magically spirits Bruno back to Germany, and, when the cardinals awake and go back to give their verdict (in III.iii, *or scene ix*), the Pope says he has received it already. Confusion naturally ensues. Moreover, when the assembled company try to sit down to dinner, Faustus gets Mephostophilis to make him invisible so that he can dash among them unseen, taking food from their hands, stealing their drink, clipping the Pope round the ear and generally making a nuisance of himself. Finally the Pope is forced to call for a bell, book and candle and perform a ceremony of exorcism to try and get rid of Faustus.

Our method of analysis involves working with a few, simple controlling ideas and interpreting the action in the light of these ideas. We can certainly comment on what is going on here in terms of what we have come across so far. Faustus has made a decision to sell his soul in return for power, but has he struck a worthwhile bargain? When we consider that this is the part of the play where Faustus is at the height of his powers, we may once more begin to question his wisdom in making that decision. Certainly the farcical realities of this episode are in stark contrast to the high-minded ideas that Faustus saw for himself in Act I – the action may be very funny to watch, but Faustus is going to pay for his practical jokes by spending an eternity in hell. This discrepancy between Faustus's impressive declarations and the futile uses to which he puts his power serves to remind us how Faustus has betrayed himself by being satisfied with trivialities: he has compromised his learning and his intellect for a series of momentary gratifications.

What we have done so far with this episode is to identify how it fits into the overall pattern of the play. This is an essential response to every new scene, for we need to see how it confirms our general impression of the play. However, we should also be seeking to extend our appreciation of the distinctive qualities of the text. We began to do this in discussing Act II as we focused on the dilemma of Faustus as expressed and crystallised in a few words. But now, as we discuss Act III, we should think about taking this sort of close analysis further. The easiest way to do this is simply to look more closely at the presentation of one or more of the characters.

The obvious character to choose, of course, is Faustus himself. What we need to do is to look at how Faustus is behaving at this stage of the play. Is he, for example, too busy enjoying himself to think about his future, or is he at all concerned about the terrible fate that awaits him? The only way to answer such questions is to select a few lines of his speeches and to think carefully about what he says:

Sweet Mephostophilis, thou pleasest me.
Whilst I am here on earth let me be cloyed
With all things that delight the heart of man.
My four and twenty years of liberty
I'll spend in pleasure and in dalliance,
That Faustus' name, whilst this bright frame doth stand,
May be admired through the furthest land.

(III.ii.58–64; *or scene viii*)

Faustus is talking to Mephostophilis about his plans, and on the surface he seems to be totally absorbed in earthly pleasures and distractions: he speaks of being 'cloyed'; of being filled with 'delight' and 'dalliance'. Our impression of Faustus here, then, may well be of a man concerned with excessive enjoyment and fame. Are there, however, any bitter or more painful notes in any of his words? Is there not a hint of something worrying in what he says? My own view is that there is something desperate about Faustus's repeated reference to pleasure in the words 'sweet', 'pleasest', 'cloyed', 'delight', 'admired', as if he wants to shut out any darker or more unpleasant thoughts. Again, I feel that the reference to 'four and twenty years of liberty' not only reminds us of the grim cost of Faustus's pleasure but of his delusion that he is free. Similarly, his talk of being admired 'whilst this bright frame doth stand' indicates that there might be a time when he cannot speak so confidently, when he might be brought down.

What I am suggesting here is that in looking at a character's speech in a play you should be trying to achieve a sense of the playwright's skill in dramatising his themes. Many of the scenes in *Doctor Faustus* might seem no more than knockabout farce, but if you look closely at what is said there is a very good chance that you will find the central issues of the play coming to life in them. Don't be put off if you have to search around for a speech to work on, as I did with Faustus's speech above. Indeed, in Act III of *Doctor Faustus* you might find it difficult to say much about Faustus at all. There is, however, no reason why you should not look at another character to help you build your analysis. As much of the third act is taken up with Faustus's tricks on the Pope, he might be a good character to look at here. Why is the Pope brought into the play at this stage? Why does he behave in the way he does? Mephostophilis makes it clear that what he and Faustus intend to do on visiting the Pope's palace is 'to cross the Pope, / Or dash the pride of this solemnity'

(III.ii.81–2). Yet when they arrive they witness a humiliating scene: the Pope, as a sign of his superiority, is using Bruno the Saxon as a human footstool. Even this, however, is not enough for him. He decrees that the Emperor, who supports Bruno, also 'grows too proud in his authority' and should be deposed from government. When Bruno protests that the authority of the Emperor should be recognised, the Pope overrules him:

> BRUNO. Pope Adrian, let me have some right of law:
> I was elected by the Emperor.
> . . .
> Pope Julius swore to princely Sigismond,
> For him and the succeeding popes of Rome,
> To hold the emperors their lawful lords.
> POPE. Pope Julius did abuse the Church's rites,
> . . .
> And therefore though we would we cannot err.
> (III.ii.127–8, 148–51, 154 or *scene viii*)

On reading this passage you may be able to understand what is happening, and to see that the Pope is not a pleasant character. But what else is there to say about him? Even more important, how do we relate what we say to the major concerns of the play? The way to proceed is to go back to what we do know about the play and try to see some links between what has already happened and what is happening here. The Pope, in belittling his opponent and treading on his neck, is clearly not acting in the way a Pope should. In condemning someone else for growing too proud he is feeding his own sense of pride and haughtiness, and the humiliation of Bruno is an arrogant display of dominance designed to show off his power. In short, we have a character abusing his position in order to satisfy his own pride and ambition.

The interesting thing, of course, is that in acting like this the Pope resembles Faustus. Faustus could be said to have displayed many of these characteristics in the first act: he was a scholar and a man of learning, but he was not satisfied with what he had. To make himself greater and obtain more knowledge he abused the learning he had and made a pact with the devil to satisfy his own pride. Here, in Act III, we see Faustus using his power to make the Pope look foolish in much the same way as the Pope uses his power to humiliate Bruno. Both Faustus and the Pope are using their positions not to act wisely but to indulge their ambitious pride. With both characters we have a sense of improper behaviour resulting from the greedy desire for power. That there are other figures in the play who exhibit the same weaknesses helps to explain why Faustus is so interesting as a character: it is not that he is a peculiar, eccentric individual, but that he is simply a man who takes real human desires to a logical conclusion.

5 *Choose a scene from Act IV to analyse and begin to look more closely at the language of the play*

Act IV seems even more hectic and madcap than Act III. Faustus puts on a theatrical show for the Emperor Charles, fixes horns on people's heads, sells a magical horse, pretends to lose his head and leg, and ends the act by striking everyone dumb. Most of the action is designed to ridicule and embarrass people who have very similar human weaknesses but who are not clever enough to outwit the powerful Faustus. Thus, for example, when Faustus humiliates Benvolio by putting a pair of horns on his head, the latter, aided by his friends, plots a vicious ambush of Faustus by way of revenge. Faustus, not to be outdone by anybody's trickery, comes prepared with a false head, which is duly chopped off. As his attackers stand gloating over the 'dead' body, Faustus rises up, and to their amazement, delivers the following speech:

I call your hearts to recompense this deed.
Know you not, traitors, I was limited
To four and twenty years to breathe on earth?
And had you cut my body with your swords,
Or hewed this flesh and bones as small as sand,
Yet in a minute had my spirit returned,
And I had breathed a man made free from harm.

(IV.iii.72–8; *or scene xiii*)

At some stage of your analysis of a play it is important that you should try to look more closely at the language. Most students know this but are never quite sure why it is important. It may be helpful, therefore, if I explain why. *Doctor Faustus* could be acted out as a mime with no words at all; we could see a man positioned between a Good and Evil Angel and choosing to move towards the Evil Angel. The moment Faustus speaks, however, this adds immeasurably to our sense of a man caught in a dilemma because it reinforces our sense of the issues at stake in the play. This is why we need to look at a play's language, but we need to find a way of tackling it. If we take Faustus's speech above, it is far from clear what we can say about it. We know Faustus is a man who has chosen evil and who, despite chances to repent, has continued on his course; we know that he has gained power which he is not using in a very wise way, and we know that in the long run death will overtake him. This gives us a start for looking at the speech, but that is all. What I suggest, therefore, is that we follow some very basic steps. In order to come to grips with the speech we need to sort out

(i) what Faustus says,
(ii) what the speech tells us about him, and then
(iii) the significance of the actual words and how they raise important issues.

In the speech Faustus tells Benvolio and his followers to repent for their attack. He points out the futility of their actions; because he has been guaranteed twenty-four years of life they cannot harm him. This seems to deal with the first point about what Faustus is saying. We now need to think about (ii) – what the speech reveals about Faustus. My feeling is that the speech reveals a very confident Faustus who thinks that he is immune to death and 'free' from any injury. It is a Faustus who has contempt for human effort, who stands above his fellow creatures judging and ridiculing them. There is also, though, another level to the speech. Faustus is berating Benvolio for his evil actions and threatening him with punishment. Yet the audience is aware of how applicable these issues are to Faustus himself, and this allows us to view what is said in a slightly different, ironic way. Dramatic irony can be briefly described as a situation in which the audience is aware of more significance in what is said than the characters themselves. Faustus's call on Benvolio and his gang to repent is ironic because of his own refusal to take the advice of the Good Angel earlier in the play. Because the audience has knowledge of his previous episode, a different perspective is given on what Faustus is saying here.

We could, then, take Faustus's speech as an example of the way his moral blindness is revealed by dramatic irony. It is always useful when looking at a speech in a play to think of it in terms of irony; it will help you see how major issues are dramatised and how particular situations can add to a play's effect. Here, for example, Faustus sees himself as a 'man made free from harm', but we are aware that his freedom is an illusion, that he has sold his soul and will have to pay the price for his action. The word 'free' is thus charged with ironic significance, and we can see that its use adds to the dramatic richness of the language. It is talking about (iii) – the significance of the actual words used and how they raise important issues – which often seems difficult to students, but it is really quite a simple step to take.

Let us start with the significance of the words used. If you look at Faustus's speech you'll see how he calls Benvolio and his friends 'traitors' and calls on them to 'recompense' this deed. The actual words he uses reminds us of what the play is about, that it is concerned with repentence and sin and evil. The speech, however, goes beyond this, and by its particular use of language it makes us aware of broader issues. In a few lines we see how the text, by using such words as 'hearts', 'traitors', 'breathe', 'body', 'flesh', 'spirit', 'free', 'harm', can reach out ambitiously to cover all the tensions and worries that beset mankind. What I am saying here is that if we look closely at the language of the text we should begin to see the sheer range of the play's exploration of issues. Not only does it give us the particular experience of Faustus as a character, but it also makes us think about the nature of experience, about the issues of life, death, morality and religion which constitute the problems of being human. The play does not do this in a vague or undirected way: it is the individual speeches, such as the speech we have just considered, which directly raise all the big questions about life and how it is lived.

Rather than over-burden you with examples I'd like to suggest that you try discussing the play in this way for yourself. Pick out a speech by Faustus in this act and ask yourself what he is talking about. Try to see how the language of his speech confronts us with a whole range of issues, a whole range of questions about moral choice, religious duty and individual responsibility.

6 *Choose a scene from Act V which shows how the play's issues are resolved and try to draw together the threads of your analysis*

The final scenes of the play give, in powerful detail, the inevitable moments when time catches up with Faustus, when the debt becomes due and he has to pay it. In many ways it is a very moral and conventional ending to a play, with someone who has acted wrongly being punished for his evil-doing. Yet there is obviously something much more than this, for we see and hear Faustus's agony as he confronts the consequences of his decision to abandon God and bargain with the devil. All the hopes of knowledge and glory have now disappeared; even the passing pleasures which Faustus enjoyed have evaporated, and he is left to contemplate his fate.

There is another factor that makes *Doctor Faustus* both more complicated and more powerful than earlier dramas. We see Faustus as a doomed man struggle with the inevitable consequences of his own human weaknesses, and this in turn gives us some marvellously dramatic moments. For example, as time runs out and Faustus is due to pay his forfeit, we get a vivid insight into the thoughts of a condemned man, knowing what is to come but still hoping for the impossible. He hopes that time will stand still, or that the remaining hour stretch itself out so that he might have time to repent. He then expresses a desire that he might be hidden by the mountains and the hills so that he can escape the wrath of God. He wants to be drawn upwards to the stars so that he can escape to heaven. He wants God to have mercy on his soul, or at least to put some limit on his time in hell so that he might attain redemption at last, even if he has to wait a hundred thousand years for it. He even fantasises that his soul might pass into an animal and then find release on the animal's death. As the final moments draw near, Faustus gets ever more desperate, asking for his body to be turned to air and his soul to water to prevent him from being taken off.

Here we see a terrifying enactment of the problem that Faustus has had to confront throughout the play. His desires have always been at odds with reality, and even at the last he is voicing futile wishes about changing the inevitable.

Marlowe, we see, reminds us of the consequences of evil actions, but he also allows us to feel the suffering of Faustus, just as at the start of the play he allows us to share the attractiveness of Faustus's desires. This double process by which we can see faults in characters and yet still sympathise with them is a chracteristic that is common to the best tragedies, and explains in some measure their power over us.

7 *Pursuing aspects of the play*

By this stage you should be able to see how to build your own views of *Doctor Faustus*. I have not dealt with everything, of course, but you can add to your account of the play by choosing any scene and adapting the same basic approach: take a few lines from the scene and extend your understanding of the play by looking closely at the text. If you have to write about the play, however, you may be asked to concentrate on aspects which we have touched on, but not dealt with fully so far, such as character or themes or language or staging. Everything you want to say about these can be an extension of what we have discovered already. In other words, looking at an aspect of a play does not involve a search for new ideas. It does mean, though, that you have to channel your ideas in a particular direction. Again, what you need to remember is that the way to work effectively is to pay close attention to the text. It is the way in which you illustrate how the text brings your ideas to life that will develop your skill as a critic and help you tackle course essays and examinations. I shall, however, deal with the particular problems of essay-writing and tackling examination questions in the final chapter, and simply concentrate here on aspects of *Doctor Faustus*.

(a) *Character*. The main character you will want to consider is, of course, Faustus himself. We have already said quite a lot about him, so let me just reiterate here the importance of focusing on specific incidents in the text. In an essay you might want to say that Faustus is an ambitious man. Saying that on its own, however, would gain you little credit. You need to be able to point to a specific action or speech in the play that enables you to claim that he is ambitious. Similarly, it is not enough to say he suffers in the end. You need to look closely at his suffering, pondering and discussing the evidence from the text that shows how he suffers. When it comes to an examination, the candidates who will do well will be those who can make the effective use of the text to support their view. A problem with a play such as *Doctor Faustus*, however, is that often students don't look beyond the main character. Because Faustus is such an interesting and dominant individual, there is a tendency to concentrate on him and to dismiss most of the other characters as incidental. You need to appreciate that other characters do serve a function, and, as with everything else in the play, they are closely linked to the major issues that make up the drama.

We have already seen how the character of the Pope is introduced in Act III. He is a victim of Faustus, but he is also similar to Faustus in that he exhibits the same human weaknesses by abusing a position of power and acting in a way he shouldn't. You should be able to see, on looking through the play, the way in which many minor and seemingly unimportant characters demonstrate the same tendencies. All characters who make wrong decisions or who act in inadvisable ways mirror the actions of Faustus himself, so keeping the central issues of the play constantly in front of the audience. For instance, in Act IV Faustus sells a horse to a lowly Horse-courser, giving him strict instructions that under no circumstances is he to ride the horse into water. This, however, only fuels his curiosity, and so,

> thinking my horse had had some rare quality that he would not have had me known of, I, like a venturous youth, rid him into the deep pond at the town's end. I was no sooner in the middle of the pond but my horse vanished away, and I sat upon a bottle of hay, never so near drowning in my life.
>
> (IV.v.52–7; *or scene xvi*)

What we need to realise here is the way the actions of the Horse-courser remind us of the central concerns of the play. He thinks that there is some hidden secret about the horse that is being kept from him, and so he does the very thing he has been forbidden to do in order to try and gain access to this 'rare quality'. This pattern of action is very reminiscent of Faustus, who, dissatisfied with the limitations placed on him by conventional learning, does something in order to find out hidden secrets. Both Faustus and the Horse-courser are victims of greed, desiring things which have been denied to them and suffering as a consequence of their folly. This sort of parallel is present throughout the play, but it does not happen by accident. The play is itself about the way human nature can be corrupted by ambition and desire, and it is quite easy to see how many of the characters exhibit this pattern of behaviour. The aim of your analysis, therefore, should be to show how the actions of individual characters show human weaknesses. When you look at Faustus himself, however, your analysis will also have to show why he is so important and so interesting. The obvious answer is that he is a more complicated figure because he is torn between what he ought to do and what his ambitions tell him to do. This conflict of interests gives his character added dimension, and also gives his speeches their dramatic force. But, as I have said, to consider Faustus fully you need to work from specific incidents to show how the details of the text reveal the changes, shifts and tensions in his character as he moves towards his inevitable death.

(b) *Themes*. A theme is an issue that a play deals with. Very often examination questions will ask you to discuss certain themes in an essay. For example, you might be confronted with a question which says, 'Discuss the themes of free will and repentance in *Doctor Faustus*'. This might seem a very abstract question, but if we use our basic idea of what the play is about we should be able to tackle the essay quite easily. The question goes back to the fact that Faustus refuses to be confined by conventional behaviour and tries to gain forbidden powers for himself. He makes the choice of entering into a pact with the devil in the hope of making his dreams come true. This choice is made of his own free will in the anticipation of a particular reward. However, even though he believes he is gaining a new-found freedom, under the terms of the contract he has sold his soul to the devil, and from that moment on all his achievements are made 'on loan', for we know that when the time is up the devil will claim what is due to him, whether Faustus wants it or not. In his search for freedom Faustus is captured, and his idea of freedom turns out to be an enslavement.

What I hope you can see here is the way in which even a seemingly complicated topic can be tackled by breaking it down into simple terms which you already know about. The theme of free will is only another way of talking about the decision that Faustus takes and its consequences, but with a particular emphasis on the gap between the freedom Faustus anticipated and the captivity that actually ensued. In the same way, when the question asks you to discuss the theme of repentence it only wants you to discuss one particular aspect of Faustus's ambitious behaviour: his continual refusal to repent and conform to orthodox religious rules. Once again, what you need to do is to look at particular incidents where these issues seem to come to a head, where Faustus is on the point of repenting but then chooses to continue with his course of action.

The scenes with the Good and Evil Angels are obvious places to start your examination.

It is important to realise that you can always use your basic analysis of a play to give you an interpretative framework for discussing any new theme you might come across. Most Renaissance plays deal with a complex web of themes; for example, 'pride', 'magic', 'damnation', 'knowledge', 'despair' could join 'free will' and 'repentance' as major themes of *Doctor Faustus*. Obviously you cannot pursue all of these in your initial work on the play, but can you see that each of these themes is only another way of focusing a discussion on the central issues of the text? Very often in writing about, say, the theme of magic in *Doctor Faustus*, students describe all the magic tricks Faustus performs, but never relate these to the central part of the play; they don't say that Faustus's magic is part of his desire for power and his refusal to conform, and so is a gift which brings temporary gratification but cannot save his soul. In other words, they don't see that the theme of magic leads them to a discussion of the main issues of the play; they should not just give a plodding account of Faustus's magic tricks. If you can see that all the themes in a play lead back into the central concerns you have spotted, then you will have no difficulty in tackling and making sense of any thematic question.

(c) *Language*. The only way to get to grips with the language of a play is to look closely at individual speeches and to see how they express the main issues of the play. A method for discussing Faustus's speeches is given in the discussion of Act IV (see pp. 21–3), but the same method can be applied to all the speeches in the play. One point worth remembering is that in Renaissance drama as a whole we can expect the language to be built on contrasting images. For example, words and images of heaven and light and harmony will be set against words and images of hell and darkness and discord. The use of such contrasts emphasises the way Renaissance drama returns again and again to the sense of mankind caught between opposites, with human life seen as a conflict between duty and desire, heaven and hell. Each play, however, will also have its own particular images which help define its originality. Thus, for example, *Doctor Faustus* is rich in blood- and body-imagery, in time-images, and in images of wealth and power. All of these help to reinforce the central issues of the play and to raise broader questions about the way life should be lived.

In addition to looking at the broader significance of the play's language, however, you will find it rewarding to think about the sort of dramatic effect individual speeches can produce. For example, at the opening of the play there is Faustus's vivid description of his own desires:

> I'll have them fly to India for gold,
> Ransack the ocean for orient pearl,
> And search all corners of the new-found world
> For pleasant fruits and princely delicates.
> (I.i.82–5; *or scene i*)

Ask yourself whether Faustus's vision sounds attractive or unattractive, noble or foolish, whether his words suggest something of real value or just an expression of man's over-ambitious pride. My own response is that we must feel the attractiveness of Faustus's desires for the play to make sense, so the vision we get sounds grand and impressive. Yet you may feel that this speech also registered how shallow Faustus's desires really are, that he just requires ostentatious wealth and gourmet food.

In order to get a fuller idea of the way that language can affect the mood of the play, you might find it helpful to set one of Faustus's early speeches against one of his later ones, such as the final speech in Act v, scene ii (*or scene xix*), with its gentle opening, increasing desperation and terrible final cries. In fact, all Faustus's long speeches are worth looking at from the point of view of language, for by paying close attention to the actual words you will gain a rich, complex sense both of Faustus's own experience and of the major issues of the play. Of course, it is not just Faustus's language that conveys the play's themes, and it is important to see how all the things we have been discussing are interrelated: character, themes and language all combine together to make the drama work. For the purpose of criticism, however, it is useful to bring one area at a time into sharper focus. This also applies to the final category.

(d) *Staging*. It is essential to remember that the text you are studying is intended to be performed, and that much of the effectiveness of a play depends on its visual impact. As you read the play, then, try to keep the idea of a performance on stage in your mind's eye. Very often the words of the text will help you do this.

For example, at the end of *Doctor Faustus* the entrance to hell opens and the Evil Angel peers down to describe the horrors inside. A few minutes later the devils appear and drag Faustus towards that very same opening. We already know of the torment there, so seeing Faustus literally disappearing into hell before our eyes is not just a startling visual effect: it makes everything that Faustus has been dreading suddenly very real, both for him and for us. It is a spectacular moment which is calculated to disturb the audience.

There are many great dramatic moments in *Doctor Faustus* and looking at these will give you an insight into its central concerns. You might, for example, look at those set pieces in the play where Faustus is pictured between figures who stand for opposing values. This happens in the last scene, where we see him between the beautiful Helen of Troy and the anonymous Old Man, who pleads with him to repent. Think about how such powerful moments on stage help to reinforce the play's themes: Faustus is poised between wisdom and repentance as offered by the Old Man, and sensual pleasure as offered by Helen. Helen is visually the more attractive figure, but the Helen who appears is only a spirit conjured up by Mephostophilis, and is thus only a momentary, insubstantial gratification.

If you are asked to think about the staging of a play, it is worth trying to give such carefully constructed tableaux their proper weight in your study, as well as dealing with more obviously theatrical elements such as the use of fireworks or the food-throwing farce in the Pope scenes.

Staging on its own, however, is only one of the ingredients that make up a play. As I hope I have shown, in talking about one aspect, whether it be character, theme, language or staging, you will inevitably be making valid observations about the others. The way in which all these aspects work together should again be clear if we turn now to consider another of Marlowe's plays, *Edward II*.

Edward II

1 *Read the play, then think about its overall effect and what sort of broad pattern you can see in the plot*

In all Marlowe produced seven plays. These were *Tamburlaine the Great Part One*, *Tamburlaine the Great Part Two*, *The Jew of Malta*,

Edward II, *Doctor Faustus*, *The Massacre at Paris* and *Dido, Queen of Carthage*. They were written in the last six years of his brief life (he was killed in a tavern brawl). *Doctor Faustus* is the most famous, but *Edward II* is often set as a text to study on literature courses. It is a historical play, based on real events and real people. The central action involves the overthrow of Edward II by a group of rebellious nobles. What interests us, however, are not the historical facts behind the play but the dramatic use Marlowe makes of his material. The analysis of the play that follows is deliberately brief. As is the case throughout this book, I don't want to interpret the play for you. My aim, rather, is to show you the moves that you can make to construct your own analysis. This has to start with thinking about the pattern of the play as a whole.

Edward II, like *Doctor Faustus*, is a play where the central character wants something which he cannot get without destroying himself. In this case Edward wants the constant companionship of his favourite, Piers Gaveston, despite the fact that his presence at court antagonises the nobles and causes dissension in the kingdom. On his accession to the throne Edward recalls Gaveston, and the nobles, led by Mortimer, revolt. The country is thrown into a state of civil war and Gaveston is captured and executed. Much of the action of the play consists of the changing fortunes of the King and his enemies, with first one side and then the other appearing to get the upper hand before Edward is finally captured, forced to abdicate, and murdered. Order is only restored at the end when Edward's son takes over the throne and has Mortimer executed.

Try to see the broad pattern that shapes the action of the play. Edward's decision to have Gaveston at court immediately sets up a conflict between his desires as a man and his duty as a King. We can see that Edward, like all tragic figures, is caught between conflicting impulses, and that the play, like *Doctor Faustus*, seems to be dealing with the destructive nature of man's desires. Like Faustus, too, Edward suffers terribly: he is degraded, tortured, and eventually horribly murdered with a red-hot poker inserted into his anus. It is this terrifying fate that establishes Edward, like Faustus, as a suffering hero.

There are, then, similarities between *Edward II* and *Doctor Faustus*, especially regarding the central characters. In both plays we see a man who is torn between indulging his own desires and conforming to society's rules; both plays deal with the way people's individuality brings them into conflict with the world around them.

Nevertheless, there is a limit to the common ground we can find between them. Indeed, a sense of their differences should give us a sharper sense of what features characterise both works. The most obvious point would seem to be that, whereas Faustus is struggling with God and the devil, Edward is at odds with his fellow men. *Doctor Faustus* is therefore nearer to the old-fashioned type of play dealing with the traditional theme of the struggle for a man's soul. *Edward II*, by contrast, is a political play dealing with tensions and conflicts in society. Edward himself is not pulled between abstract forces of good and evil, but is caught between his social and political commitments as king and a temperament that craves indulgence and escape from the cares of high office. This, combined with the fact that the individual characters alongside the King are more fully realised than the subsidiary characters in *Doctor Faustus*, gives the play its political dimension. Clearly, if we are to do the play justice we have to pay attention both to its tragic force and also to its political slant.

2 *Look at the opening scenes and try to achieve a sense of what is happening and what the play is about*

The method to adopt here, as before, is to describe what happens and then move on to try and comment on its significance. The play opens with the exiled Gaveston being called back to court by the newly crowned Edward. Gaveston speaks of his wish to live a life of ease and luxury under the patronage of Edward, whom he describes as a 'pliant king' (I.i.54). Clearly Gaveston is out to enjoy himself at the expense of others, but it might seem hard to know what to say about his speeches beyond this. The key to interpreting Gaveston's words (and indeed the speeches of all the characters) is to remind yourself that *Edward II* is a political play, and, like all political plays, it is concerned with the contrast between the way things ought to be in society and the way things really are. In an ideal society there would be peace and order, but in reality there are always people whose desires create conflict. If you look at Gaveston's speeches and ask whether his actions are going to lead to harmony or disorder, it ought to be fairly clear that his presence is not going to lead to wise and sensible government by the King. Again, his disregard for the common men in the first scene is not a good sign: Gaveston is too concerned with his own selfish wishes to pay attention to the good of society as a whole.

The issue is highlighted by the arrival of the King and his nobles. Mortimer and Lancaster consider that Edward's desire to have Gaveston at court is a recipe for disaster, and they threaten to withdraw allegiance to the King unless Gaveston is dismissed. Once again, the way to interpret this is to ask whether the actions of the nobles are going to lead to harmony or conflict. The answer is obviously the latter: the nobles see that the presence of Gaveston at court will lead to a disordered state, but the only sanction they have is to withdraw allegiance to the King, an act which in itself will throw the country into turmoil. A central concern of the play, then, is the way in which society is thrown into disarray by the conflicting interests of two sets of people, and this is brought out in the opening scenes by the constant clashes of the rival sides. What is less evident from the opening scenes, however, is why we should consider *Edward II* to be a powerful tragedy. None of the characters so far seems to gain our sympathy, and there is not the same sense of heroic greatness that marks the opening of *Doctor Faustus*. Clearly part of our analysis will have to try and come to terms with the sort of tragedy *Edward II* is and what sort of vision it offers.

3 *Choose a scene from Act II and try to clarify your impression of what the play is about and how it is developing*

There is obvious unrest in Act II, and any scene you choose to discuss will show antagonism between the various factions. In Act II, scene ii, for example, Gaveston returns from exile after being banished at the end of Act I. In order to get back into favour with King Edward, Queen Isabella has persuaded the nobles to allow Gaveston to return to the country, and the scene is supposed to be one of reconciliation. On Gaveston's arrival, however, a violent quarrel breaks out. Young Mortimer wounds Gaveston, and this provokes the King into making preparations for civil war.

Look for ways in which the action here picks up and develops the ideas that are established in Act I. Order in society is impossible as long as there are characters with opposed and irreconcilable wishes: the King is emotionally dependent on Gaveston and will not rule the country without him; the nobles refuse to be loyal to a king who is so dependent on such a fickle upstart as Gaveston. Both sides thus wish for something that they cannot possibly have: the King wants a life of pleasure with Gaveston uninterrupted by the censure of the barons, while the barons themselves want

Edward to give up Gaveston and rule the kingdom in accordance with their wishes. You should be able to see how the confrontations in the play centre around these two points of view; both factions constantly accuse the other of creating unrest and disorder, and the result of such accusations is bound to be unrest and disorder itself.

These tensions are evident both in the main actions of this scene and in nearly every individual speech. Look at this speech by Gaveston, for example, where he is reunited with Edward:

> Sweet lord and king, your speech preventeth* mine, *anticipates
> Yet have I words left to express my joy.
> The shepherd, nipt with biting winter's rage,
> Frolics not more to see the painted spring
> Than I do to behold your majesty.
> (II.ii.59–63)

Can you see how Gaveston's words centre on the issues we have been discussing? One set of words in the speech – words such as 'joy', 'frolics', 'spring' – concentrates on an idea of luxurious indulgence in pleasure, while another set of words – 'lord', 'king', 'majesty' – suggests the order in the state that is being disrupted. Part of the problem that faces Edward is that he cannot or will not recognise the political consequences of his relationship with Gaveston, and, as is suggested here, he hopes it may be possible to escape into an artificial world of joy free from duty and responsibility. In order to explore this more fully, look at other speeches in the play, and see how they are built on the idea of an opposition between an ideal world of pleasure and a real world of problems.

4 *Choose a scene from Act III and begin to look more closely at the principal characters in the play*

Act III begins with the seizing of Gaveston by Warwick, and we soon learn that he has been taken off and executed. Meanwhile Edward sends his wife away to settle affairs in France. News is brought to him of the death of Gaveston, and Edward determines to take revenge; the nobles in turn continue to demand that the King remove all other undesirable influences from court. In the battle that follows the King defeats the barons, imprisons the chief rebel, Young Mortimer, and banishes his own brother, the Earl of Kent.

So far, as with our analysis of *Doctor Faustus*, we have established some ideas about the play and then seen how actions and speeches from specific scenes reflect those ideas. At this stage, therefore, having established the foundations of our analysis, we need to move towards a sense of how Marlowe brings his themes to life. Here there are always three main things to look at: how the writer creates a vivid sense of characters caught in certain dilemmas; how the language of the play presents and explores those themes; and how the action we see on stage brings the issues to life in a particularly forceful way. To some extent it is possible to consider all these issues at once, but the most practical approach is to begin by concentrating on some of the principal characters. The most obvious choice is Edward. Here he is talking about the necessity of taking action against the barons:

> Now 'tis time
> To be aveng'd on you for all your braves,
> And for the murder of my dearest friend,
> To whom right well you knew our soul was knit,
> Good Pierce of Gaveston, my sweet favourite.
> Ah, rebels, recreants, you made him away!
> (III.iii.40–5)

The first way to get hold of a speech such as this is to look for an opposition between images which suggest harmony and images which suggest disorder. Gaveston is looked upon as 'my dearest friend', a 'sweet favourite' to whom Edward was linked in spiritual harmony: 'To whom you knew right well our soul was linked'. By contrast the nobles are seen as 'rebels' and 'recreants' (cowards) who have committed the sin of 'murder', and Edward's call for vengeance is based on a response to the disruption that the nobles have caused in his life as a man and as a king. We can see, therefore, that the central tension of the play is again in evidence here. By being aware of this tension we can understand what Edward is talking about, but we should also be trying to understand Edward as a character. What comes across here is his affection for Gaveston. There is a genuine tone of anguished mourning over the loss of someone he loved, and that gives us a strong clue to his character. Whereas Faustus might have been motivated by conceited intellectual ambition, Edward comes across as a much more emotional and vulnerable man. He prefers the ease of a private life to the demands of public office, and thus seems unsuited to the high-ranking life he has to live; we see him as a weak rather than a wicked man. You should also be able to see, however, that Edward's desire for revenge on the killers of his favourite provokes a mixed response. On a personal level we can view his desire for revenge on the murderers of his beloved Gaveston with some sympathy. On another level we can see that his determination to plunge the country into civil war makes him a bad king. It is this mixture of responses to Edward that makes him such an interesting character; we cannot totally condemn or endorse what he is doing, but we can understand his grief and anger and appreciate his violent response to the problems he faces. In turn this helps us to think about Edward as a tragic hero: it is not simply the horrible suffering he endures at the end of the play that makes him a tragic figure, but rather our sense of a man struggling against the consequences of his own ill-fated actions.

5 *Choose a scene from Act IV to analyse and begin to look more closely at the language of the play*

Act IV begins with the escape of Young Mortimer, the leader of the rebels, who forms an alliance with the disillusioned Queen Isabella. Edward is defeated in battle and at the end of the act we see the King taken prisoner. As this brief summary indicates, Act IV sees the country in the turmoil of civil war. Any scene you look at, then, should provide evidence of characters caught up in the messy reality of politics. People are acting from a variety of impulses, both good and bad, but are only managing to create a state of chaos. In order to strengthen your impression of what is happening in the act, focus on one particular character; for example, you might concentrate on Edward's brother, Kent. In Act IV, scene i, he deserts Edward and denounces him as an 'unnatural King' (IV.i.8), only to reconsider his decision after the King's defeat, when he appeals to God to punish the 'unnatural revolt' of the rebels (IV.v.18).

What we see in Kent's behaviour is the way in which questions of loyalty and allegiance can seem a terrible dilemma in a world in which order has collapsed and in which both sides appear corrupt. Nor is Kent free from this corruption, as he himself recognises:

Vile wretch, and why hast thou, of all unkind,
Borne arms against thy brother and thy king?
Rain showers of vengeance on my cursed head,
Thou God, to whom in justice it belongs
To punish this unnatural revolt!

(IV.v.14–18)

In his anguish here Kent sees that he has broken the harmonious ties that ought to bind brother to brother and subject to sovereign. He thus considers himself 'cursed' and calls upon God to punish him for his rebellion.

If you look at Kent's speech in detail you should be able to see how it sets ideas of order (in the words 'brother', 'king', 'God', 'justice') against images of disorder (in the words 'borne arms', 'vengeance', 'revolt'), You should thus be able to see how the speech touches on the central political issues of the play concerning rebellion and disorder in the state. What you might also spot, though, is how Kent's speech contains a further dimension, how it starts to raise larger questions about life as a whole. In particular, you might consider how Kent is asking questions about whether there is any controlling force to establish order in the world, or whether people are just subject to the vagaries of their own base appetites and desires. It is this larger significance of Kent's language which we need to grasp if we are to make sense of *Edward II* as a tragedy as well as a political play. The most obvious scenes in which to consider this issue, however, occur during Edward's humiliation and death in Act V.

6 *Choose a scene from Act V which shows how the play's issues are resolved and try to draw together the threads of your analysis*

The final act begins with Edward being deposed as King and imprisoned by Mortimer. Mortimer then hires Lightborn to kill Edward, and in Act V, scene V, we see him carrying out the dreadful, sadistic murder of the King. The play ends, though, with Edward III, Edward's son, taking over the throne, punishing Mortimer with death and arresting his mother for her part in the conspiracy. We could therefore say that a sense of order and equilibrium has been achieved at the close of the action, but what we have to weigh against this is the terrifying cruelty of Edward's treatment in prison in Act V, scene iii, and of his death in Act V, scene v. These are the most disturbing scenes in the play, and you are likely to find yourself sympathising with Edward as he confronts a situation which is far removed from the pleasant life he wanted with Gaveston.

The best way of coming to terms with these scenes is, as ever, to focus on a small section of the text so that you can concentrate in some detail on how Marlowe uses his characters, language and staging to bring his themes to life.

Thus, for example, you could consider the way Edward is degraded by his captors in Act v, scene iii, as '*They wash him with puddle-water, and shave his beard away.*' The stage direction points to the savage cruelty of this scene: Edward is humiliated by being washed in filthy water and is brutally abused by his tormentors. Yet worse is to come, and in Act v, scene v, we again find another moment of horrific spectacle when Lightborn orders his accomplices to pin Edward down beneath a table so he can be murdered with a red-hot spit. There seems little relationship between an idea of justice in the world and this horrific murder, and we are perhaps left to wonder whether life on earth is being shown as a sort of living hell. Certainly many details about the staging point this way: there is the darkness of Edward's cell, the red-hot spit, and the agonised death-cries of Edward.

I have deliberately drawn attention to the stage directions in these scenes, for they provide one way we can trace the tragic impact of the play and so see how the audience is made to feel both fear and pity at the plight of the tragic hero caught in a vicious world. Besides staging, however, you ought to look at the language of the prison scenes so that you can round off your analysis and draw together various threads. In keeping with some of the comments on the staging, you may well find that Marlowe's language is filled with powerful images of hell and torture and pain and fear.

I have moved quite quickly through *Edward II*, but you should now be able to identify and tackle some of its complications. Edward's desire to live the life he wishes in congenial company may seem innocuous, but it prevents him from acting efficiently as a king. Mortimer's frustration as he sees his country declining is also understandable, but his own arrogance and methods of achieving his ends make him an unpleasant character. Unlike the earlier morality plays, however, *Edward II* does not present the audience with a simple idea of good versus evil. Instead it shows both good and evil as part of a complicated reality.

You may feel that your act-by-act analysis has only just begun to see how these issues are dramatically presented in the play, but if you have come this far you have a coherent view of *Edward II*, and you can build up your ideas by looking at other scenes and speeches in the same way. Indeed, that seems an appropriate not on which to round off this chapter. I have deliberately avoided going into every aspect of Marlowe's plays. I haven't tried to explain everything, and I've often held back when I wanted to say more. This should leave you with room to develop your own ideas. Start, as I have done, with a few clear thoughts about the play as a whole, and then, by focusing on particular scenes in terms of their characters, language and staging, build your analysis of the play. The whole time you will be adding to your understanding of the themes at the heart of the work. But the real point to grasp is that this is a systematic, logical approach. There's no point in sitting around hoping for inspiration to strike: you actually have to work on the text, adding to, building and refining your analysis as you go along.

3

John Webster

CHRISTOPHER Marlowe is usually regarded as one of Shakespeare's forerunners, even though his plays were written around the same time that Shakespeare was beginning to write – that is, in the late 1580s. In the same way, John Webster (*c.* 1578–*c.* 1632) is often regarded as belonging to the generation of dramatists after Shakespeare, despite the fact that his two great plays, *The White Devil* and *The Duchess of Malfi*, were written about the same time that Shakespeare completed his last major play, *The Tempest* (1611). This, in turn, suggests something of the sheer concentration of great drama produced during a thirty-year period at the turn of the seventeenth century. One extraordinary thing about many of these plays is that they seem to speak to us far more directly than many plays written in later times. A great deal of eighteenth-century drama, for example, seems light and inconsequential, while the Victorian age, before the revival of drama in the latter years of the nineteenth century, seems only to have produced rather trivial melodramas. Most Renaissance plays, by contrast, seem forcefully to consider universal human problems.

Indeed, the simplest way of describing nearly all of these plays is to say that they present people confronting problems in their lives. Time and time again we see the harmony of life disrupted by problems. Faustus, for instance, unsettles his life as a scholar by his desire for forbidden knowledge and power, while *Edward II* provokes unrest by his irresponsible doting upon Gaveston. In both cases the main protagonists are not common people, but the fact that an extreme case is presented adds another dimension to the universal relevance of the play. We see this again in Webster's plays. While his characters and their circumstances are far from commonplace, his plays, nevertheless, seem to deal directly with issues and problems that affect us all.

Part of the extreme nature of Webster's plays results from the fact that he writes tragedies. I touched on the nature of tragedy in the previous chapter, but this seems a good point to deal rather more fully with the subject. We know that people in plays confront problems, and the first thing that we can say about tragedies is that they present people in difficult or extreme situations. In the course of a tragedy, we see life getting out of control, and things cannot return to normal until a price has been paid. That price is, without exception, death. What we are confronted with in a tragedy, therefore, is a grim and disturbing vision of a world close to chaos. There is, it is true, always a tragic hero or heroine for us to identify with, but this identification further concentrates our attention on the problem. This is because tragic heroes or heroines always have a tragic flaw or weakness in their personalities, some irrational strain in their make-up that creates problems. It is this weakness that renders the character unable to cope, and pushes him or her into extreme and vexing situations, so that a vision comes across of a world where things have got out of control.

All this can be applied to the Marlowe plays we discussed in the previous chapter. Both Faustus and Edward II are largely responsible for creating their own problems by yielding to the irrational, irresponsible strains in their personalities. But we need to be careful here. So far the emphasis of this chapter might lead you to think that a tragedy is an entirely negative play, or that we must morally condemn the main characters for their stupidity. This is certainly not the case: the central character in a tragedy exhibits an unusual kind of heroism in facing up to and trying to understand the worst of experience. It is this heroic struggle between the protagonists and their circumstances that often provides the most memorable features of the play. We could go further and say that these struggles are actually a positive force in the play. Certainly, if we were discussing *Doctor Faustus* or *Edward II* as tragedies, it would be essential to draw attention to a certain growth in wisdom and understanding displayed by Faustus and Edward II in the latter stages of the plays.

One question that might occur to you is why there should have been such a wealth of great tragedy written during the Renaissance. I have already touched on why this might be in Chapter 2, where I talked about the shift from the medieval to the modern world. In the medieval vision of the religious morality plays there is an order God imposes upon the world, and that order is clear and uncomplicated. In the more secular world of Renaissance drama God's order seems less self-evident. Instead the emphasis falls on mankind's capacity for creating disorder, both in the life of the individual and in society as a whole. It is as if the old order has collapsed and in its place there is a shocking new awareness of the nature of life. A radical change in society produces a radically new kind of play, characterised by its questions about man's nature and role in the universe, and in particular showing individuals trying to cope with the disruption that their desires cause.

The plays that I discuss in this chapter, *The White Devil* (written sometime between 1604 and 1612) and *The Duchess of Malfi* (1613), are both tragedies that directly reflect the pressures and strains of the period. There is no doubt that they are complicated plays in terms of the language they use and the subjects they deal with, and indeed they might strike you as both more elaborate and disturbing than those of Marlowe. Yet, even given this complexity, we should be able to begin our analysis by picking out a fairly simple, fairly conventional pattern. Let's start by seeing how this is the case in *The Duchess of Malfi*.

The Duchess of Malfi

1 *Read the play, then think about its overall effect and what sort of broad pattern you can see in the plot*

The Duchess of Malfi is a widow. She has fallen in love with Antonio, one of her courtiers, but is expressly forbidden to remarry by her jealous, dominating brothers. Nevertheless, the Duchess and Antonio secretly marry. All goes well until Bosola, one of the Duchess's servants (who is working as a spy for her brothers) discovers that she is pregnant.

The Duchess and Antonio flee the city, but they are hunted down and the Duchess is captured. She has to suffer terrible tortures before she and her children are strangled. However, her two brothers, Ferdinand and the Cardinal, eventually pay the price for their cruelty; Ferdinand goes mad, and the Cardinal is killed by the remorseful Bosola, who is also fatally wounded. By error, Bosola has already killed Antonio, mistaking him for the Cardinal, and he rounds off the carnage by also killing Ferdinand. The play ends with the stage strewn with corpses as Antonio's eldest son is newly established in power.

The most striking thing you might notice about this play is its preoccupation with cruelty, horror and death. You are also likely to find yourself interested in characters such as the Duchess and Bosola. Beyond that, however, you might not know where to turn. Indeed, if your response resembles that of the majority of students reading the play for the first time, then you probably feel fairly confused. As always with Renaissance drama, there are going to be some scenes that do not seem immediately relevant to the plot, and you may find these puzzling, particularly if the language used in them is also difficult. But, rather than losing yourself in all the complications, or even giving up, try to find the most basic pattern. You might remember that when we looked at *Youth* in Chapter 1 I talked about a pattern in plays where characters lose sight of their duties and moral responsibilities and indulge their desires. This was true of *Youth*, and was also the case with Marlowe's *Doctor Faustus* and *Edward II*. Can you see that the same basic pattern is in evidence here? An unwise love affair ends in death due to the cruel obsessions of the Duchess's brothers. There is a basic division between 'good' characters such as the Duchess and Antonio and the 'evil' characters such as Ferdinand and the Cardinal, but they all get embroiled in the disruption that results from the breakdown of moral and religious restraints.

That is the basic pattern of the play, but clearly the pattern of the plot is a lot more complicated than in *Youth*. It is, after all, the good characters who start the whole sequence off by their unwise decision to marry. In addition, the evil characters, even though they act in an unacceptable and extreme way, do act out of a sense of outraged righteousness. There is also the strange case of Bosola, who starts off as an evil character, but repents after he has helped to kill the Duchess and tries to make amends. The conclusion we might draw, therefore, is that *The Duchess of Malfi* is concerned with a world where good and evil exist, but that the relationship between them is a complicated one.

2 *Look at the opening scenes and try to achieve a sense of what is happening and what the play is about*

The Duchess of Malfi begins with a number of characters moving on and off stage, and it is difficult to hold on to the gist of any conversation for very long. You may be able to discern on first reading that some characters spend time discussing other characters, but feel unable to work out what they are saying or why. Do not be put off by this. Simply take note of the fact that the opening exchanges are difficult to understand and move on to a stage in the play where you can identify what is happening more clearly. It is worth remembering, however, that puzzling scenes can be used by the dramatist to create an impression of a world that is complicated and perplexing. (The text I refer to here is the Penguin edition of the play, where the first act is divided into two scenes. In some editions you will find that the first act is just one long scene. Don't be put off by this: the action falls naturally into smaller sections or movements that can be easily identified and worked on.)

Most people will probably begin to form some idea of the plot of the play during the conversation between the Cardinal, Ferdinand and the Duchess in I.ii (ll. 216–71). The exchanges here are easier to follow and we begin to get some idea of what is going on. The Cardinal and Ferdinand are about to leave the court, and as they depart they give a warning to the Duchess that she must now use her own discretion in looking after matters. In particular, they warn her not to succumb to any temptations to remarry during their absence. The Duchess comments that their speeches seem very practised and rehearsed, and, as soon as they have gone, she asserts that in affairs of the heart she will be guided by her own desires, and will certainly not be put off by warnings from her brothers.

The way to make sense of any scene (as I suggested earlier) is to begin by identifying what is going on, and then to try and make a general comment about the significance of what is happening. We know that plays are concerned with human problems, and in particular the problems that arise from conflicting desires. In this scene we see a conflict of interests between what the Duchess would like to do and what her brothers want her to do. There is obviously a potential clash between her desires and the restraints imposed by her brothers, who threaten her and warn her that she will regret the consequences if she tries to remarry. This gives us a sense of the play's issues, of the way personal desires are often set against social and political restrictions. We see this again at the end of the scene, where the Duchess proposes to Antonio, the man she loves. Antonio is a steward, and therefore socially inferior to the Duchess. This is alluded to by the Duchess as a central part of her dilemma (part of her 'misery', she says at I.ii.361–2, is that those who are born great 'are forc'd to woo, because none dare woo us'). She is forced, against convention, to take the initiative in wooing Antonio, and even then she cannot speak directly, but has to go through an elaborate charade to indicate to Antonio that she loves him. So here is another problem. The Duchess's desire for love has broken the restrictions placed on her by her brothers, but it has also broken social convention as well. We thus have a central character who is not only rebelling against a court that seems oppressive, but is also at odds with a society that stands against women following their own instincts in love.

This is as much detail as is required in a preliminary look at the opening scenes. There is always material that can be re-examined later, but your first task should be to identify one or two major issues rather than get bogged down in a mass of confusing details. The way in which the Duchess finds herself at odds with the world around her is the simple issue on which a constructive analysis can be based and this provides a solid foundation on which we can build our discussion of everything else.

3 *Choose a scene from Act II and try to clarify your impression of what the play is about and how it is developing*

The basic method I am illustrating involves looking at what is happening and then commenting on its significance. Any scene will do, but the first scene in each act, where the action and issues have moved on, often provides good material, and the opening scene of Act II is the one I shall be considering here.

Act II begins with a puzzling conversation between Bosola and a character called Castruchio. This is then followed by an equally odd exchange between Bosola and an Old Lady. Remember that our task here is still to try and identify broad central issues, and anything that seems strange or incidental to the main part of the plot can be left for consideration later. That's the case here: we can leave these puzzling opening speeches until we have gained a firm grasp of the play's central issues. You will only succeed in bringing yourself to confusion and despair if you try to work out the significance of each and every detail before you have identified the main issues of the play.

After Castruchio and the Old Lady go out, the scene moves on to pick up the story of the Duchess and Antonio, and this is where things become easier to follow. The Duchess has married Antonio and is now pregant, although she has managed to keep these facts secret from anyone who may wish to harm her. Antonio is talking to Bosola about how fortune is treating them when they are interrupted by the arrival of the Duchess. The Duchess asks Antonio to support her and then tries to persuade him to wear his hat in her presence, in the manner of the French courtiers. Bosola, acting as a spy for Ferdinand and the Cardinal, suspects that the Duchess is pregnant and gives her a dish of apricots, with the result that she immediately goes into labour. Fearing that the truth may be discovered, Antonio and his friends hurry to think up a story to account for the Duchess's incapacity. Delio suggests that a rumour be put out that Bosola has poisoned the Duchess. Antonio points out that this will only draw medical attention to her, but Delio has an answer to this as well; he suggests that they pretend the Duchess is using her own antidote and will not let the doctors near her for fear they might repoison her.

This is a brief outline of what happens in the scene. Any of its details could be picked on for comment, but obviously it makes sense to focus on the Duchess at this stage; she is the central character, and her actions are easy to follow. We know that there is a tension in the play between the Duchess's desires and the social restrictions that have been placed upon her, and what we want to find are some details that reveal this tension. Take, for example, the moment when the Duchess wants Antonio to wear his hat in her presence. What we can say about this is that it shows the Duchess adopting an unconventional approach to courtly behaviour. In her desire to treat Antonio as her equal she is prepared to challenge the restrictions of conventional courtly manners. This is a small incident, but even so we can see the Duchess struggling to assert her freedom: she wishes to act in a way that seems natural as opposed to the artificial rules that society has imposed upon her.

While the Duchess is struggling to assert her wishes, the overwhelming atmosphere is one of deception and corruption. Much of this has to do with Bosola, who is a spy working for the Duchess's brothers. He presents her with a dish of apricots as a gift, but really this is a trick to confirm his suspicions about her pregnancy. It is important to recognise Webster's use of dramatic irony here, and, indeed, throughout the play as a whole. Dramatic irony occurs when the audience is fully aware of what is happening while some of the characters on stage are ignorant of the real situation. The effect of such irony is to distance the audience so that they can see the full significance of events. In this scene, for example, Bosola has taken great care to explain his suspicions to the audience, so we know exactly what is going to happen when he presents the dish of apricots to the unsuspecting Duchess. The audience is in on the conspiracy, so to speak, and can view the situation with considerably more knowledge about what is happening than the Duchess; we see her as the victim of Bosola's evil deceit.

What we also see, however, is the way the Duchess is becoming entangled in the play's complications and ambiguities. After she eats the apricots the Duchess falls into premature labour. Her brothers' threats make it impossible to reveal the truth and so Antonio and Delio have to pretend that she is poisoned in order to get her away from the public gaze. The pressure of events thus forces the Duchess to comply with deception, and she has to go along with this plan in order to save herself and Antonio. This, though, does not necessarily mean the Duchess is evil. You might come across the suggestion that, far from rebelling against the court, the Duchess represents its very corruption and deceit. Certainly the Duchess has to adopt a number of different roles, as with her wooing of Antonio in Act I, but one of the issues the play is dealing with is the complex relationship between good and evil. In particular, it seems to be concerned with those ambiguous situations where goodness sometimes has to act less than honestly in order to preserve itself in an evil world.

To sum up: what we have done in looking at this scene is to analyse the way in which the Duchess has become caught up in a complex situation. The contrast between her desire to act according to her feelings and the restraints that have been imposed upon her leads to a series of deceptions. Because of the nature of the threats made against her, the Duchess's involvement in these deceptions makes her world a more uncertain and dangerous place in which to live. From the evidence we have looked at so far it seems that Webster, in focusing on the problems of human behaviour, is concerned with dramatising this issue. He is concentrating on what happens when people are forced to live in a world where they cannot act freely or honestly, and in which appearances are deceptive.

4 *Choose a scene from Act III and begin to look more closely at the principal characters in the play*

The Duchess of Malfi is a complex play, and certainly the sequence of actions we have examined so far is extremely complicated, yet at the same time there is also something very simple about the impression Webster is creating. We can best understand this if we talk about the difference between an ideal and the real world. In an ideal world there would be no problems; people in society would get on with each other; families would be happy and united; and when people fell in love it would be a joyful and uncomplicated business. Look, however, at the reality as Webster presents it: it's a world of families divided, of plotting, spying, deception, of endless problems for would-be lovers. The actions we see on stage may often be extreme or bizarre, but they effectively create an impression of the complex nature of real life. We can see that Webster has created a powerful picture of world where people find it impossible to be open and honest, and where intrigue and villainy are the norm.

You may have developed a different impression from your reading of the first two acts, but that is not problem. I am not at all interested in winning you over to my view of the play. All I want to do is to demonstrate a method of interpreting the text. The best basis on which to start is the approach I have followed here of trying to get a coherent impression of the simple issues or themes at the heart of the play. Now that we have got to the third act, however, we can begin to fill out this basic picture. It would be possible to look at a range of different aspects, but the easiest thing to consider is the behaviour of one or more of the principal characters. The reason for this is simple: by now we are in the middle of the play's complications and a whole range of pressures will be building up on the central characters.

Before turning to study a character, however, we need to select a scene for analysis and relate it briefly to the ideas about the play that we have put together so far. As is often the case, the opening scene of the act presents itself as a very suitable extract for discussion. What happens in the opening scene of Act III is that Antonio tells Delio that the Duchess has had two more children. We also learn that gossip is spreading about Antonio and the Duchess. The common people are accusing the Duchess of being a strumpet, while others suspect that Antonio is making himself rich at the Duchess's expense. Ferdinand joins the action, and offers the Duchess a potential suitor, the Count Malateste. The Duchess says he is totally unsuitable. Then, perhaps to test Ferdinand's reaction, she claims that some scandalous rumours have been spread about her. Ferdinand falsely reassures her, saying that, even if the rumours were true, his love for her would outweigh any sins she may have committed. As soon as the Duchess has gone, however, he reveals his true state of mind, telling Bosola that the blame for her promiscuity lies solely within herself. Moreover, he says he intends to wring a confession from her that very night. The scene ends with Ferdinand taking the key to the Duchess's bedchamber that Bosola has procured for him, but refusing to reveal what he intends to do.

This thread of the plot is continued later in Act III, scene ii, when Ferdinand goes to the Duchess and accuses her of ruining her good name. After Ferdinand has left, the Duchess, realising that Antonio is in danger, pretends to banish him for theft as a pretext for getting him out of the country. The wily Bosola, seizing his opportunity, pretends to be upset at the news of Antonio's 'crime' and speaks well of him to the Duchess. The Duchess is taken in by this response and lets Bosola in on the secret of the pretended exile. He suggests that she go on a feigned pilgrimage so that she can meet up with Antonio at Ancona. Even away from Malfi, however, the lovers are not safe, and, when Bosola delivers an ambigious message from Ferdinand saying that he wants Antonio's 'head in a business' (III.v.27), the Duchess acts on her suspicions and sends Antonio away once more. She, however, does not escape, and an armed guard, led by Bosola in disguise, takes her back to Ferdinand.

You may be able to see from this brief summary just how complicated things are becoming and just how much the play's action turns on the idea of deception. The effect of this, as I have said before, is to give a sense of how the antagonism between desire and restraint is dragging everyone into a world of plot and counter-plot. We have, though, spent long enough establishing the general picture of the play's action and now need to look closely at the characters involved in these events. The obvious choice for investigation is the Duchess herself. I am, however, going to delay looking at her for a fairly obvious reason. *The Duchess of Malfi* is a tragedy, and the Duchess is the tragic heroine. The crucial part of the play for her, therefore, comes in the next act, where we see her heroically facing up to the worst life has to offer. It might be better to consider her in more detail later, when we want something more positive to set against the bizarre, disturbing vision that Webster's play offers. (Of course, if I were preparing for an examination, I should need to look closely at the character of the Duchess at the beginning and in the middle of the play, as well as during her torture and death in Act IV; I deal with this sort of analysis in the final chapter.)

Having decided not to look at the Duchess at this stage, it seems to make sense to look directly at one of the embodiments of evil in the play, the character of Ferdinand. There are two ways we can approach a character such as Ferdinand: we can either look at the things he says and base an analysis on that, or we can see what other people say about him and how this reflects on his character. As a general rule, the first course is more direct and therefore more profitable, but it is often possible to note some interesting comparisons between what other people say about a character and what that character says for himself or herself. This happens in Act III, scene iii, with Ferdinand. As Delio and Antonio are discussing whether news of the Duchess's children has reached her brothers, the conversation turns to the nature of Ferdinand's character:

DELIO. Pray sir tell me,
Hath not this news arriv'd yet to the ear
Of the Lord Cardinal?
ANTONIO. I fear it hath;
The Lord Ferdinand, that's newly come to court,
Doth bear himself right dangerously.
DELIO. Pray why?
ANTONIO. He is so quiet, that he seems to sleep
The tempest out, as dormice do in winter;
Those houses, that are haunted, are most still,
Till the devil be up.

(III.i.16–23)

Antonio here draws attention to a worrying facet of Ferdinand's character: his appearance is not to be trusted. Paradoxically, the quieter he seems, the more menacing he is, while his outward appearance serves to disguise his true feelings, not reveal them. If we go back to the issues we have identified in the play so far, we can see how well this fits in with our idea of a world in which openness has disappeared and deceit is rife. Ferdinand is one of those disruptive characters who make life complicated by seeming to be what he is not.

A striking example of this occurs when Ferdinand himself talks to the Duchess later in the same scene. He seems to be reassuring her that all is well, but in reality is setting her up for a more terrible revenge later. Here he is dismissing the rumours that have been flying around the court and protesting that his love for her will excuse any errors she might have committed:

FERDINAND. Yet, say that it were true,
I pour it in your bosom, my fix'd love
Would strongly excuse, extenuate, nay deny
Faults were they apparent in you. Go, be safe
In your own innocency.
DUCHESS. O bless'd comfort,
This deadly air is purg'd.
(III.i.51–6)

By eloquently protesting the strength of his love, Ferdinand lulls the Duchess into a false sense of security. However, we have just been warned by Delio and Antonio about the deceptive appearance of Ferdinand; he pretends that his love is strong enough to overcome, even obliterate, all faults in her, but we know that this is only a mask and that Ferdinand is putting on the guise of the devoted brother in order to conceal his biting jealousy. Ferdinand has something unpleasant in store for the Duchess at a later date, and deceit is once more being used to disguise evil. By using the language of forgiveness – Ferdinand talks about 'fix'd love', and says he could 'excuse', 'extenuate', 'deny / Faults' in her and that she is 'safe' in her 'innocency' – he seems to adopt the role of absolving the Duchess from her sins. This is reinforced by the Duchess's own reference to 'bless'd comfort' and to the 'deadly air' being 'purg'd'.

An analysis of Ferdinand, therefore, shows him to be more than just a simple embodiment of evil. He is violently opposed to the relationship between the Duchess and Antonio because he sees love only in terms of lust. Having failed to restrict the natural instincts of the Duchess, he is now intent on taking vengeance on his 'guilty' sister. Yet his attitude is far from straightforward. He uses deception as an integral part of that revenge, appearing to be kind and forgiving in order to maximise the effect of his cruelty. Ferdinand considers what the Duchess is doing to be unnatural, but, by looking closely at what is going on in the text, and in particular at his language, we can see that it is his twisted and perverse character which is to blame.

The method used for looking at Ferdinand's character is one that can be applied to all the main figures. It involves looking at what other characters say about him and then looking at his actions and speeches and assessing them. In this way it is possible to build up a sense of a character as being more than just a simple type or stock figure, and to see how the dramatist creates a complex impression of people. At the same time, though, we have not lost sight of the main issues of the play. Many students tend to look at characters simply as individual personalities, as 'real life' figures, and ignore their dramatic function: in other words, the way they bring the themes of the play to life. In the case of Ferdinand, for example, it would be possible to construct a very elaborate psychological analysis, hypothesising about the reasons for his behaviour and his relationship to the Duchess. In the end, however, such an analysis would not be very profitable if it were not related back to the main issues of the play and to its vision of life disintegrating into chaos.

5 *Choose a scene from Act IV to analyse and begin to look more closely at the langauge of the play*

What we have been talking about in terms of theme and the behaviour of characters is also very evident in what we see on stage in a performance of *The Duchess of Malfi*. Many of the events take place at night, and this alone gives an impression of dark, furtive action. Again, we frequently see two characters on stage engaged in secret or whispered conversation, creating a sense of plotting and secrecy that adds to our impression of a dark world. This is reinforced by the very shape that Webster gives his scenes. Take, for example, the last scene we looked at, III.i. There we focused on Ferdinand's character, but it would be just as legitimate and rewarding to focus on the staging and movement of the action. It begins with Antonio and Delio discussing Ferdinand; then Ferdinand, Bosola and the Duchess enter, and there is a short episode with five characters on stage; then Ferdinand and Bosola are left alone to discuss the Duchess at the end of the scene. Both the beginning and the end of the scene, therefore, have two characters secretively discussing the situation; in the middle of the scene, by contrast, there is the courtly entrance of brother and sister. So we are made aware of the falseness of the polished image of courtly harmony and grandeur. Through the dramatic contrast of the staging we can see the corruption that lies beneath the surface.

The effects of staging in *The Duchess of Malfi*, then, help create and convey an impression of a world of subterfuge and deceit. In a play, however, staging always works together with theme, character and language to give the play its overall impact. It is particularly important that we recognise the central importance of language in Renaissance drama, for it is the quality of language above all that gives Renaissance plays such power. As we saw with Marlowe's plays, there is a force to the writing that enables the dramatist to suggest that he is undertaking a more profound exploration of experience than that conveyed in earlier morality plays. As we turn to Act IV it is worth making a special effort to focus on the language of the play, simply to ensure that we do not overlook the most striking element in the drama of the period. First, though, as usual, we need to get a grip on what is happening and what fresh complications have been introduced to the plot.

Act III ends with the arrest of the Duchess and her children. Act IV is devoted to the terrifying portrayal of the Duchess's torture and eventual death. At the start of the act we see Bosola telling the Duchess that Ferdinand wishes to be reconciled to her. Because he has sworn never to see her again, however, he wants the meeting to take place in the dark. Ferdinand enters and the Duchess asks his pardon, which he grants, giving her a hand to kiss. She takes the hand but is horrified to find it is the hand of a dead man. Ferdinand tells her it is, in fact, Antonio's hand, and then shows her wax figures of Antonio and her children, looking as if they are dead. Questioned by Bosola about his motives, Ferdinand says he has acted in this way in order to bring the Duchess to despair. Rejecting all pleas for compassion, Ferdinand, determined to cause her yet further torment, orders some madmen to perform a masque or dance before her. This takes place in Act IV, scene ii, and the scene creates a vivid sense of a nightmare world ungoverned by any reason, compassion or human feeling. The Duchess's coffin is then brought in, and Bosola, disguised as an old man, oversees her murder. After the Duchess has been strangled, Ferdinand enters and we see a curious change in Bosola. Previously he has been instrumental in inflicting cruel torments on the Duchess. Now, however, he questions Ferdinand's motives for her death, and, when Ferdinand refuses to pay him, we see Bosola resolving to carry out the Duchess's final wishes concerning the disposal of her body.

It is relatively easy to see how the action here fits in with the overall pattern of deceit and evil that we have been tracing in the play. It is also very apparent how much the scenes focus on cruelty and suffering. This, we can say, is the negative side of Webster's vision; he creates a disturbing picture of human cruelty. Yet the effect of these scenes is far from being simply negative. Set against the picture of man's cruelty is the positive figure of the Duchess herself, powerful and self-controlled even though she is a prisoner. Look, for example, at the calm and dignified way she orders her murderers to 'pull, and pull strongly' (IV.ii.230) when the moment of her death arrives. It is important in looking at these scenes that you do try to see the play as more than a series of bizarre incidents. You need to see how Webster makes use of this particular material to focus on the main issues that we have discussed so far. As ever, the best way to do this is to turn to the text and concentrate on a particular moment. But in addition I suggest that, in looking at the text here, you try to focus your attention on two things: one is the presentation of the Duchess as a tragic heroine; the other is Webster's use of language. Before we can do this, however, we need to choose a part of the text to analyse. One of the most horrific moments comes when the Duchess is confronted with the mock figures of her husband and children, looking as though they are dead. When the Duchess sees the figures she is appalled, and her immediate reaction is to wish herself dead as well:

BOSOLA. Come, you must live.
DUCHESS. That's the greatest torture souls feel in hell,
In hell: that they must live, and cannot die.
Portia, I'll new kindle thy coals again,
And revise the rare and almost dead example
Of a loving wife.
BOSOLA. O fie! despair? remember
You are a Christian.
DUCHESS. The Church enjoins fasting:
I'll starve myself to death.
BOSOLA. Leave this vain sorrow;
Things being at the worst, begin to mend:
The bee when he hath shot his sting into your hand
May then play with your eyelid.
DUCHESS. Good comfortable fellow
Persuade a wretch that's broke upon the wheel

> To have all his bones new set: entreat him live,
> To be executed again. Who must dispatch me?
> I account this world a tedious theatre,
> For I do play a part in't 'gainst my will
>
> (IV.i.69–84)

The first point you might want to make about the Duchess here is her courage in the face of suffering and cruelty. That might seem too obvious a point to make, but it is a crucial one if we are to talk about her as a tragic heroine. Very often students give the impression that the only tragic element in a tragedy is the death of the central character, or even, indeed, that the only thing of consequence that the tragic hero or heroine does is to die. This is not the case, and here we have a vivid example of the way the Duchess not only endures the worst life has to offer but also defies her tormentors. There is obviously something noble about her actions here, but the effect of the scene goes beyond this. It does so because of what the Duchess says; how she welcomes death because life has become a series of endless tortures, a cruel play in which she is forced to act against her will. The point to grasp here is the way the Duchess's speech offers us an insight into the nature of existence when evil takes over. Normal values are lost entirely, and life itself becomes a 'tedious theatre', a stale play where everything is artificial and false. Such speeches help convey a sense not just of the Duchess's nobility in suffering, but also of how she has gained knowledge of the ways of the world.

This complex impression of both the Duchess and of the play's tragic vision has, of course, much to do with Webster's language. Your analysis of the tragic hero or heroine in a play is only really going to stand up if you can say something about the words they use. There are three main points to grasp about language. The first, and most obvious, is what the language reveals about the speaker; the way it tells us something about character, mood, attitude and values. This is what we've been talking about so far in the Duchess's speeches. The second point to grasp about language has to do with theme. The language used in a play always reflects its central issues: here, for example, we are intensely aware of the disturbing gap between how things ought to be and the awful reality of how they are in this chaotic, senseless world. This is brought out in the stark contrast between words such as 'loving wife', 'Christian' and 'Church', all implying an ordered state that no longer applies, and 'torture', 'hell', 'tedious theatre', all suggesting how far ordinary life has sunk into a dark abyss. But the final point to grasp about the language of this scene is the way in which the fullness and depth of the language ensures that the Duchess's particular plight takes on a much larger significance. Look at how crowded these lines are with images and references to hell, torture, death, the breaking of bodies and execution, all suggesting that the fate of mankind is one of terrible, even meaningless suffering in a dark world.

Let me hasten to add that you may see the Duchess's speeches very differently from me. At the centre of your analysis, however, almost certainly will be the idea of an individual confronting a terrifying universe, together with the contrast in these scenes between nobility and cruelty, the best and worst in humankind. The really important thing to grasp is that by focusing closely on the language of the play you can add immeasurably to your analysis, exploring the richness of the text and developing your own response.

6 *Choose a scene from Act V which shows how the play's issues are resolved and try to draw together the threads of your analysis*

Usually a tragedy ends with the death of the main character, but this is not so in *The Duchess of Malfi*. As a result you might feel that the last act of the play is something of an anti-climax, consisting only of a sequence of skilfully plotted murders which bring the play to a close but which do not merit close consideration. This, however, is not a very constructive approach, and it is much better to look carefully at the end of the play in the light of what your analysis has revealed so far. Our starting-point for thinking about the last act can be the fact that even though the Duchess has been killed, her death has not put an end to the dark intrigues that make up the plot of the play. This continued scheming is evident in the death of Julia in Act v, scene ii.

Julia is the Cardinal's mistress, and Bosola gets her to question the Cardinal about the part he played in the murder of the Duchess and her children. The Cardinal tells her what has happened, but makes her swear to secrecy by kissing a Bible. The Bible, however, is poisoned, and Julia's lips are sealed, not by her vow, but by death. On stage this is a powerful piece of action full of ironies, but what we need to do now is to see how it ties in with the issues we have found in the play so far. We know the play is concerned with the way the darker side of human nature upsets the order of things by secrecy and deception. Here, for example, we see the Cardinal taking a Bible, the symbol of truth and goodness, and turning it into an instrument of murder. His corrupt nature taints everything it touches, and once again, as in the Duchess's death, we see how far moral values have been perverted and twisted.

Another death which makes a great dramatic impact is that of the Cardinal himself in Act v, scene v. Looking for a way to dipose of the body of Julia, he forbids anyone to enter his lodgings that night, even if he should cry out or seem to be in danger. Once again there is dramatic irony at work here, and the audience can see how the Cardinal sets a trap for himself: when Bosola threatens him, the Cardinal calls for help, but none of the courtiers who might save him dare to enter. The Cardinal is thus a victim of his own deceitful and corrupt power, for he has surrounded himself with such a cloak of secrecy that genuine cries for help cannot be recognised. Like Ferdinand, and indeed like all the characters, he is caught in the labyrinth of dark deceit he has created, and his death, like that of Julia, raises the question of whether there is, after all, a sort of justice operating in the play. Indeed, one way of looking at this last act is to see how contrasts are drawn between the dignified, noble death of the Duchess and the grim, ironic deaths of the other characters.

I feel that we have come a long way in our analysis of *The Duchess of Malfi*. We started with some simple ideas about the standard patterns in drama, and building steadily on those ideas we do seem to have gained a coherent impression of this play, but a coherent impression which is also quite complex and detailed. Once you have reached this stage in analysing a play, however, you need to take stock and reflect on what you have managed to prove. Let's think about where we have got to with *The Duchess of Malfi*: we know that Webster has focused on the idea that human beings are capable of reducing the world to a disordered and dangerous state. Yet we also know that by the end of the play those responsible for the chaos lie dead upon the stage. The final speech made by Delia tells us that the deeds of those 'wretched eminent things' are like footprints in the snow, forgotten 'as soon as the sun shines' (v.v.114–16). This is a common pattern at the end of a tragedy and shows the world returning to a state of relatively ordered calm. From a wider perspective we might say that many characters have paid the price for their faults, and there has even been a certain amount of natural justice. The Cardinal, after all, falls victim to his own deceit; Bosola, who served the interests of Ferdinand but was rejected by him, gets revenge from the poor repayment of his service, but is in turn killed by the man who employed him to do the evil deeds. There is thus a moral element at work here, ensuring that, even though chaos may reign for a while, things will finally be put to rights.

Although you may thus feel that many characters get what they deserve, you may also feel that there is a great deal of injustice in the play. The Duchess, for example, although reckless in her passion for Antonio, clearly doesn't deserve the torments that are visited upon her. Antonio also seems to be another victim of the uneven justice in the play, while the corpses of the Duchess's children serve as a grisly reminder that the innocent suffer as well as the guilty. What we are given, in short, is a tension between two different views of the world. One is the rather old-fashioned, medieval view, which sees good and evil as simple opposites and which believes God's justice and order are evident in the world. The other is a more modern and more pessimistic view, which sees life as a mess and the world as a place without any sense of order where all sorts of things can happen for no apparent reason. Webster, in a complex and vivid way, is presenting these tensions in *The Duchess of Malfi*, and that is why we find conflicting ideas at work when we come to sum up the play.

7 *Pursuing aspects of the play*

Much of the general advice about tackling an aspect of a play that I offered on *Doctor Faustus* (*see* pp. 9–30) also holds good for *The Duchess of Malfi*. The main aspects of any play to look at are the ones that have surfaced repeatedly in overall analysis: character, themes, language and staging, but it might be helpful if I reinforce what I said before by looking at these considerations in *The Duchess of Malfi*.

(a) *Character*. It is very easy to talk vaguely about characters, saying what you like or dislike about them without ever getting to grips with their part in the play at all. The main point to grasp about the central characters is that they all embody the main issues of the play. They present concrete and interesting examples of the play's theme, and this is their main dramatic function.

Consider Bosola, for example. He is a complex character in that he appears in a number of guises throughout the play. He is disillusioned with the ways of the world, and is prepared to do anything as long as it leads to personal advancement. To this end he serves Ferdinand and the Cardinal and is prepared to undertake any number of unpleasant tasks. After the Duchess has been killed, however, and Ferdinand refuses to recognise the value of his help, Bosola changes. In the final act he joins forces with Antonio to try and avenge the Duchess's death. This ultimately leads to his death at the hands of the Cardinal in the series of fights which close the play. Because he reflects so many aspects of the play and so many of its themes, Bosola is an awkward character to deal with, but our basic distinction between an ordered and just world and a world of chaotic injustice will help us comment on his actions. What you should be able to see is that Bosola is caught in the same dilemma as the other characters: how to survive in a corrupt world. He is a man who experiences both extremes. He starts off as a discontented cynic; the only way he can see to get on in a corrupt world is to steep himself in the values of corruption. In the first three acts he serves as an agent of chaos, and comes across as cruel and unfeeling. However, with the death of the Duchess, Bosola's growing disillusionment with his way of life is increased by his pity for and admiration of her; he is no better off because of his excesses, and he seems to have realised the horror of what he has done. From then on he adopts the opposite view. There is, or ought to be, some controlling influence or sense of justice in the world, and Bosola tries to act in a way that will prove this to be so. Yet this, too, brings only sorrow and death, and Bosola is left in his final speeches to lament the 'gloomy world' where mankind is forced to live in 'a shadow, or deep pit of darkness' (v.v.100–1). You might thus feel that there is, in the end, something tragic about Bosola which adds both to his stature and to that of the play as a whole. The only way to prove this, however, is to cite the evidence of the text and lend your case weight by showing how Bosola's words support your view. This is the most important point to make about any of the characters in the play. Whatever you choose to say about any character has to be based on the evidence of the text, and in turn your textual analysis will give you a more complex sense of the character's function and personality.

(b) *Themes.* A theme is an important subject or issue in a play. As we saw with Marlowe's *Doctor Faustus*, most Renaissance plays deal with several overlapping themes at once. This helps us to grasp a full sense of the complexity of the problems that the characters face. Because of this complexity, however, it is sometimes difficult to know how to tackle a particular theme or to see how it fits in to the play's overall significance. Take, for example, the theme of 'justice' in *The Duchess of Malfi*. It would be easy to go through the play and merely list the scenes or episodes which raise the idea of justice without actually getting hold of the theme itself. Yet the broad contrast between order and disorder that we have noticed so many times will help you to grasp the significance of any theme in the play and give you a framework to discuss it. In tackling the theme of 'justice', you need to bear in mind the way the idea of an ordered, harmonious society where people get their just deserts is set against a cruel, repressive society, where corruption is rife and the law is used to persecute the innocent. More simply, by keeping in mind a contrast between how things ought to be and how the play shows us they actually are, you will have a way of structuring your thinking about any theme. You might have noticed that there is a lot of talk about cruelty, or death, or revenge, or corruption in the play, and so decide to tackle one of these as a theme. Let's take the theme of cruelty as an example. Obviously, your first move is to gather some material together, to look at some scenes and speeches and actions where the characters are caught up in a series of cruel and violent deeds. As with the theme of justice, the danger at this point is that you will just end up with a list of actions in the play which prove that many of the characters are nasty. However, if you set the idea of cruel, violent behaviour designed to destroy relationships against kind, ordered behaviour designed to promote harmony, you will have established a framework on which to build your analysis and develop your ideas.

(c) *Language.* Webster's language is especially rich in images and repays a good deal of attention. In particular, *The Duchess of Malfi* is packed with images from nature, with body-images, images of sickness, of prison, of heaven, of darkness. In order to explore the way these images work in the play it is essential to focus on small extracts from the text and to work on them methodically, asking yourself some simple questions. How does the language work here? How does it reflect the main issues of the play? How does it broaden the significance of the action to make a general statement about human life? Or you might simply want to ask, how does the language here help create a certain impression of the speaker, of his or her feelings or state of mind? Remember that language can serve several functions at once and produce several effects.

A good place to start your analysis of the language of *The Duchess of Malfi* is with the Duchess's own speeches. Take, for example, this speech near the start of the play:

The misery of us, that are born great,
We are forc'd to woo, because none dare woo us:
And as a tyrant doubles with his words,
And fearfully equivocates: so we
Are forc'd to express our violent passions
In riddles, and in dreams, and leave the path
Of simple virtue, which was never made
To seem the thing it is not.

(I.ii.360–7)

You should be able to see how this speech reveals the Duchess's dilemma, how her position is at odds with her desires. You might also see how the speech sets the idea of 'simple virtue' against words such as 'tyrant' or 'equivocates', which suggest corruption or something less than ideal. So far, then, the speech appears to be working on two levels: it reveals the Duchess's feelings, but it also incorporates the idea of how virtuous actions seem impossible in a corrupt world. To these two levels we can add a third level: Webster's use of language extends the significance of this speech beyond a simple expression of the Duchess's feelings. In a wider context, the images of tyranny, dreams, riddles and morality used in the speech seem to touch on the whole plight of humankind in a hostile universe.

The advantage of looking closely at speeches like this is that it enables you to expand your grasp of the play's ideas very rapidly. You can also build your analysis by looking at other speeches later in the play and making comparisons or contrasts. This is simply a question of adopting the same method that we have followed for our analysis of the play as a whole. Here, for example, is Bosola, in the guise of an old man (symbolising age or perhaps death?) seeking to bring the Duchess to despair just before her death in Act IV:

DUCHESS. Am I not thy Duchess?

BOSOLA. Thou art some great woman, sure; for riot begins to sit on thy forehead (clad in grey hairs) twenty years sooner than on a merry milkmaid's. Thou sleep'st worse, than if a mouse should be forc'd to take up her lodging in a cat's ear: a little infant, that breeds its teeth, should it lie with thee, would cry out, as if thou wert the more unquiet bedfellow.

DUCHESS. I am Duchess of Malfi still.

(IV.ii.133–41)

Bosola is accusing the Duchess of being disturbed, unable to sleep and looking old before her time. He is trying to get her to accept an image of herself as corrupt, absurd, fearful, restless; to see herself as the very antithesis of a noble and dignified figure. Her magnificent rejoinder – 'I am Duchess of Malfi still' – is an assertion that she is untouched by his accusations. I have chosen this example because it offers such a stark contrast between the plain, simple words of the Duchess and the twisted complexity of Bosola's imagery. However, I have also chosen it because it reveals how the Duchess's own language has changed in the play. She no longer speaks in the 'dreams and riddles' that she was forced to adopt earlier in the play. Facing death, she can now assert her identity and greatness in simple statements. In this way the language contributes to the tragic grandeur of the Duchess as a character. Just by looking at these two examples, then, we are in a better position to talk, not just about the play's language, but about its tragic impact and how this is achieved.

(d) *Staging*. The staging of a play ought to be an important element in your analysis, but it can be difficult to know what to focus on. Some obvious places to start your analysis are the stage directions of scenes and the stage directions implied by the characters' words. For example, in Act IV, scene ii, the repeated references to darkness make it plain that the Duchess is in a darkened chamber. These references also remind us just how much meaning and weight the staging can carry: we might realise that darkness in this scene is not just a matter of there being no light, but an expression of Ferdinand's perverse evil, of the way he views the Duchess as a creature of darkness and of the way he operates in the murky world of suspicions. In addition to stage directions, however, a great deal is always implied by what the characters say.

For example, in the previously quoted extract (IV.ii.133–41) where the Duchess talks to Bosola, we gain a sense from her words of how she should appear on stage – unbent, proud, calm and dignified – and how her appearance forms a striking contrast with the grotesque impersonation of Bosola, or with the frantic gestures of the madmen that have just appeared. Indeed, we might see the whole bearing of the Duchess as a contrast to the nightmare world that surrounds her.

Webster is famous for gruesome set pieces such as the spectacle of the bodies of the Duchess's husband and children in Act IV, scene i. This could just be viewed as gratuitously morbid, but it is more constructive to try and think of how Webster is using spectacular stage effects to create and convey the meaning of the play. It is not too difficult here in Act IV, scene i, to see how the waxwork bodies are being used to terrify the Duchess and entrap her in a grim world of artifice and illusion. In turn we might say that Ferdinand, too, is unable to cope with the complexities of the real world; part of his evil is to manipulate people artificially to fit his own needs, just as he has always wanted the Duchess to be reduced to an unthinking, obedient sister. In other words, the spectacle here reflects the contrast in the play between the Duchess's natural love for her husband and children and the warped, perverse nature of Ferdinand's relationship with his sister.

The waxworks scene is clearly an elaborate piece of staging, but smaller scenes can also provide material for comment. For example, there is a short scene (III.ii) where Ferdinand enters the Duchess's bedroom as she prepares for bed. Here we can see very clearly the subtle but important effects staging can have. These lie in the contrast of mood between the joy and playfulness of the Duchess and Antonio and the dark, menacing entrance of Ferdinand. The contrast not only brings out the clash between the characters' personalities, but also the way Ferdinand exercises his grim, destructive power against this small family group with all its naturalness, love and warmth.

I have only touched briefly here on the range of staging-effects in the play, and there are obviously many other scenes you may wish to look at – for example, you could examine how the groups of characters in the opening scene manage to give the immediate effect of a sense of conflict; or you could look at the 'echo scene' in Act V, scene iii, where Webster manages to convey the idea that the world without the Duchess is a lesser place. The main point to remember in looking at staging, however, is always to show how the details you choose dramatise the main issues of the play.

The White Devil

1 *Read the play, then think about its overall effect and what sort of broad pattern you can see in the plot*

Most people encountering Webster for the first time are surprised by the viciousness of the world he presents. Given that Renaissance drama reflects the kinds of social changes that were taking place at the time, you may wonder whether there was a distinct shift towards a more bitter and jaundiced view of life and humankind's capacity for destructiveness as we move from the Elizabethan to the Jacobean period. Certainly there is evidence that this was the case; remember that the English Civil War occurred in 1642, less than a decade after Webster's death. With the Civil War we have moved a long way from the medieval structure of a society held together by shared values and beliefs. Instead of a world dominated by religious belief, Renaissance plays introduce elements of a sceptical, secular world influenced by the court, politics and money. Webster's plays are part of this movement, and certainly the vision of life we find in the next play we are going to consider, *The White Devil*, is just as dark and disturbing as that in *The Duchess of Malfi.*

Before we start, however, let me point out that I am not going to deal with this play in great detail. All I want to do is to emphasise the moves you can make in constructing your own critical analysis; this is, after all, the purpose of this book. The first thing to tackle, of course, is the basic plot. *The White Devil* deals with the adultery between Brachiano and Vittoria Corombona. So that they can marry, Brachiano arranges for both his wife, Isabella, and Vittoria's husband, Camillo, to be murdered. Although technically innocent of carrying out the murders, Vittoria is arrested with her two brothers and brought to trial in front of Cardinal Monticelso. She is committed to a house for reformed prostitutes, but is later rescued by Brachiano and escapes. Cardinal Monticelso, having become Pope, excommunicates Brachiano and Vittoria, while Francisco, Isabella's brother, appoints a self-confessed villain called Lodovico to carry out his revenge on the adulterous pair.

Lodovico poisons Brachiano, torments him as he lies dying, and eventually strangles him. After Brachiano's death, Flamineo, Vittoria's brother, who was instrumental in first bringing the lovers together, demands a share of Brachiano's legacy from Vittoria. She refuses, and Flamineo is just about to kill her and her maid when Lodovico and his confederates burst in and kill all three. Finally Giovanni, Brachiano's son, arrives; Lodovico is killed and all the guilty parties remaining alive are arrested.

As this brief summary suggests, the plot of *The White Devil* is extremely complicated, and it may take you some time to work out all the relationships between the characters. As ever, though, the way to come to grips with such a perplexing work is to begin with one or two very simple ideas, and then to use those ideas to help you build a more detailed reading of the text. Thus you should be able to see that, like *Youth*, which we looked at in Chapter 1, *The White Devil* takes as its basic pattern the actions of people who have unwise desires, and who have to face the consequences of their choices. The love affair between Brachiano and Vittoria leads them to act in an evil way, and both have to pay for their immoral conduct. On this level we might say that *The White Devil*, like so many Renaissance plays, has an underlying morality-play pattern in which good battles against evil. As the outline of the play suggests, however, things are not that straightforward. Vittoria, for example, is guilty of adultery but is not guilty of murder, and this means there are different degrees of guilt to be considered even between the two lovers. Again, those seeking to punish the errant lovers do not do so from the best of motives or conduct themselves in an exemplary fashion. As in *The Duchess of Malfi*, then, we can say that in *The White Devil* Webster dramatises a complicated, corrupt world in which people pursue their own desires through plotting and intrigue. Like earlier plays, it is concerned with the issues of good and evil, desire and restraint, order and disorder, but at the same time it is aware that these issues do not exist as simple opposites in the world.

It will help in thinking about the action of *The White Devil* if you keep in mind the idea of *revenge tragedy*. A revenge tragedy is a play that shows characters taking things into their own hands rather than trusting in God's justice to punish crime. However, this direct action does not usually have the effect of restoring order: the desire for revenge, like the desire for lust or money, is a disruptive impulse that leads to things becoming more chaotic and brutal. We can see this most clearly at the end of *The White Devil*, where revenge, betrayal and death all coalesce into a bloody climax to the play, with no individual in control of the action. As you look at *The White Devil*, then, you can expect to find a constant tension between the idea of a just, ordered world and the creation of a disordered world running out of control. This tension will give you a framework for your comments on the play's actions and help you to organise your own response to the text.

2 *Look at the opening scenes and try to achieve a sense of what is happening and what the play is about*

The first scene of *The White Devil* begins with a minor character, Lodovico, on stage. It turns out that he has been banished from court for 'certain murders here in Rome' (I.i.31), having previously squandered his fortune and ruined his earldom. He is, however, unrepentant; pointing to the corruption that is rife within the court, he threatens retribution on Brachiano and Vittoria for his banishment. The scene doesn't seem to advance the plot very much, so you may wish to move on and leave it for later consideration.

In the second scene Flamineo, Vittoria's brother, arranges a meeting between his sister and Brachiano, her lover. Brachiano is unsure whether Vittoria wants him, but Flamineo assures him that her shyness is only a coy device. He then clears the path for an assignation between Vittoria and Brachiano by persuading Vittoria's husband, Camillo, that the best way to keep his wife faithful is to increase her desire by separating himself from her. When Brachiano joins Vittoria she tells him of a dream she has had in which the branch of a yew tree fell and killed her husband and Brachiano's wife. Flamineo interprets this dream as a hint to Brachiano to carry out the murders. Vittoria's mother, Cornelia, who has overheard all this, now steps forward and denounces their wickedness. In turn she is scorned by Flamineo, who wishes that 'the common'st courtezan in Rome / Had been my mother rather than thyself' (I.ii.332–3).

The way to interpret the events of this scene is to go back to the play's basic issues and look at how Webster shows the world being thrown into disarray by people selfishly pursuing their own desires. For example, in this second scene we watch Flamineo duping Camillo, telling him to stay away from Vittoria. He pretends this is the way to increase her love for him, but really his plan is aimed at removing Camillo from the scene so that Vittoria and Brachiano can commit adultery. You should be able to see that by saying one thing and doing the opposite Flamineo demonstrates a complete disregard for morality and so is at odds with the creation of an honest, orderly society.

Once you have begun to gain a sense of how the details in the scene reflect the tension between the honest creation of order and the dishonest creation of disorder, you can begin to broaden your analysis. The character of Cornelia, for example, seems to stand for values which are opposed to those of Flamineo. She chastises him for being a pander to his own sister and says that people in high positions should always be aware of the example they set, for they have the power of affecting the workings of the world around them. Cornelia is expressing a forlorn hope for a well-governed, moral society, a plea which is rejected outright by Flamineo, who replies that the world is not a perfect place in which to live, that virtue is not its own reward, and that, instead of meekly submitting to fortune, a man must be prepared to take his chances in order to make his way in the world, even if it means following the path of deception and immorality. Not only is this a clash between two opposing views of the world; it is also a clash on stage between mother and son, a heated argument which leads to fierce denunciations on both sides. What we see in this scene, then, is the way in which disruptive behaviour undermines different aspects of life, from the whole ordered running of the state to individual marriages and family relationships.

The moves I have made here are very simple: they involve summing up the events of the scene and then interpreting those events in terms of a tension between order and disruption. Any details in the play should fall into place if you tackle them in this way. We can put this to the test by looking back to Lodovico in the opening scene. Like Flamineo, he considers that 'Fortune's a right whore' (I.i.4) and that because the world lacks natural justice it is perfectly reasonable to indulge in crime or to take one's own revenge. Lodovico's violent disposition and disregard for moral restraints clearly make him a dangerous influence. As a member of the nobility he ought to be an example of order and good government, but he has rejected these standards in order to indulge his desire for debauchery and mayhem. To this extent he seems to be a very symbol of courtly competition and the lack of any moral order in the world, something which should become increasingly evident as we move into the second act of the play.

3 *Choose a scene from Act II and try to clarify your impression of what the play is about and how it is developing*

What you should be looking for in Act II are details of the characters' actions and speeches which will help you develop your impressions of the main concerns of the play. As you look at the play, however, remind yourself that the characters in Renaissance dramas are not the simple stereotypes or representatives of a particular virtue or vice that appeared in the earlier medieval dramas. They are more complicated characters living in a more complicated world, and an awareness of the tensions that exist between order and disorder can help us analyse these complexities.

Act II, for example, opens with Cardinal Monticelso upbraiding Brachiano in a very high-minded way for abusing the privilege of his birth and neglecting the duties of a ruler in order to enjoy the pleasures of adultery with Vittoria. Clearly Monticelso is on the side of propriety and order as he seeks to correct Brachiano's behaviour and to bring moderation and good government to the state. Yet later in the same scene Monticelso deceives Camillo by giving him a fruitless commission to go and rid the coast of pirates. This is part of his plan with Francisco to catch Brachiano and Vittoria in adultery so that they can take full revenge on the pair. This piece of double-dealing has clear parallels with what Flamineo did in Act I, and we are certainly aware of a gap between the ideals Monticelso preaches and the duplicity of his actions. As with Lodovico and Flamineo, then, we see that Monticelso gives way to his own baser instincts. Throughout the play we are being shown people who should exemplify order and morality acting badly, thus building up our sense of a corrupt society.

Your analysis of the play will develop rapidly if you bear in mind the way Webster uses dramatic irony to bring these issues to our attention. Here, for example, the audience is made aware of the high moral line adopted by Monticelso so that his later actions form an ironic contrast to the ideals he professes. Similarly, his appearance in the robes of a cardinal provides a visual reminder of the gap between the base reality of his behaviour and the values that he should represent. It is by dramatic touches such as these that Webster brings the idea of courtly corruption to life on stage in a vivid, powerful way. You will often find that thinking about staging in these terms will help you clarify your impressions about the play's concerns and will give weight to your analysis.

4 *Choose a scene from Act III and begin to look more closely at the principal characters in the play*

Having seen that there are two sides to Monticelso's character, it becomes possible to spot further ironies at work in subsequent episodes. His motivation is a desire for personal revenge, yet while secretly plotting his retribution he is perfectly prepared to pontificate on the shortcomings of others. Such hypocrisy not only makes him an unattractive character, but also undermines any claims he might have to be a representative of justice and Christian morality. This is important to bear in mind when trying to come to terms with crucial episodes such as the trial of Vittoria in Act III, scene i.

Flamineo has killed Vittoria's husband, Camillo, while Brachiano has had his wife, Isabella, poisoned; seizing their opportunity, Francisco and Monticelso arrest Vittoria and put her on trial for her part in the death of Camillo. Monticelso has gathered various ambassadors for the trial so that they might spread the news of Vittoria's 'black lust' and thus make her 'infamous to all our neighbouring kingdoms' (III.i.7–8). The trial begins with speeches by a verbose and long-winded lawyer who soon tries everybody's patience. The lawyer is dismissed by Francisco, and Monticelso takes on the prosecution himself. He attempts to discredit and abuse Vittoria, but she answers him with calmness and dignity. At the end of the trial, however, Vittoria is committed to a home for reformed prostitutes, while her brothers, Flamineo and Marcello, are released on bail.

At this stage you should be looking at the main characters in the play: Vittoria and Monticelso obviously stand out as the chief protagonists here. Vittoria, we know, is guilty of adultery, yet in the trial she emerges as a more worthy character than her accusers. Indeed, you are likely to come away from this scene thinking how brave and defiant she appears to be in such a corrupt world, while Monticelso seems, by his language and attitude, to be the real villain. This not only emphasises how far Webster departs from the simple idea of setting good against evil, but it also points to the central contradiction contained in the play's title. We see that there might indeed be something innocent and tragic about the 'devilish'

Vittoria, while Monticelso, who appears to represent law and order, is actually vile and corrupt.

To explore these ideas further, we need to take one or two small sections of the text and analyse them in more detail. Here, for example, Monticelso is replying to Vittoria's claim that it is improper for a cardinal to act as a lawyer:

O your trade instructs your language!
You see my lords what goodly fruit she seems,
Yet like those apples travellers report
To grow where Sodom and Gomorrah stood
I will but touch her and you straight shall see
She'll fall to soot and ashes.

(III.ii.62–7)

Monticelso is trying to persuade the court that Vittoria is not the virtuous lady she seems. An innocent damsel, he suggests, would not have the command of language to argue so forcefully, and her outward appearance of goodness is merely a guise to hide the rotten corruption underneath. Notice, however, how Monticelso, the supposed representative of order and correctness, dwells on unpleasant details in his obsessive desire to blacken Vittoria's name. He likens her to corrupt and rotten fruit, and there is something menacing about the way he offers to touch her to reduce her to 'soot and ashes'.

Contrast Monticelso's twisted, excited lines with the tone of Vittoria's speech when she is charged with being impudent and cunning by the Cardinal (who is acting as both prosecutor and judge):

You shame your wit and judgement
To call it so. What, is my just defence
By him that is my judge call'd impudence?
Let me appeal then from this Christian court
To the uncivil Tartar.

(III.ii.124–8)

Vittoria is claiming that the whole trial is a mockery, that her honesty is being perversely interpreted as a defect of her character, and that those people who are supposed to be giving her a just and civilised Christian trial are giving her less of a fair hearing than a group of lawless barbarians would. Her words not only arouse our sympathy and admiration, but also suggest why she is at the heart of a play called *The White Devil*. Though guilty of adultery, there is clearly something very positive about Vittoria as she stands up to the bullying, brutal tactics of the corrupt court. Indeed, we might argue that it is only because Vittoria is guilty that Webster can present her as a tragic heroine. If she were totally pure, this scene would simply show us how justice in a corrupt society destroys the innocent, and we should be left with a neat but uncomplicated moral message. As it is, however, the scene offers us the more ambiguous picture of a guilty woman defending her right to just and civilised treatment in the face of a vicious attack by the corrupt upholders of law and order. Here, perhaps, we can see some of the complex issues that are incorporated into Webster's tragedy. The play starts to raise crucial questions about human behaviour; about whether society is merely a veneer that covers over more barbaric impulses. It begins, too, to raise questions about whether any order exists in the world at all. We can see this in Vittoria's speech, with its references to the 'uncivil Tartar', and indeed throughout the scene, especially in its use of religious imagery, for this brings into question the idea of divine justice as well as human justice. The specific effect of language, however, is something we can look at next.

5 *Choose a scene from Act IV to analyse and begin to look more closely at the langauge of the play*

In Act IV Francisco writes a bogus love letter to Vittoria, detailing a planned escape and elopement. He sends the letter to the house of convertites (repentant prostitutes) where Vittoria is being kept, knowing full well that Brachiano will intercept the letter. Brachiano does so, and charges Vittoria with infidelity to him. Eventually they are reconciled, and Brachiano arranges her escape, using the same plan as outlined in Francisco's letter. Francisco, hearing of the escape, feigns annoyance, but is secretly pleased at the success of his scheme to discredit Vittoria once again. He gets Monticelso, who has now been elected pope, to excommunicate Vittoria and Brachiano and to banish their followers from court. Francisco also plans more direct action against the lovers by reminding Lodovico of his vow to kill Brachiano. Monticelso is suspicious of Francisco's association with Lodovico, and presses Lodovico for information.

In his confession to the new pope, Lodovico admits that he loved Isabella and has sworn to Francisco to avenge her murder. Monticelso orders him to abandon the plan on pain of damnation, and Lodovico is just about to give up his murderous ideas when Francisco sends him a thousand ducats, saying they are from Monticelso. Lodovico immediately changes his mind about the murder, believing that Monticelso wants him to carry out the plan.

Having looked at Vittoria and Monticelso in the last act, you will probably want to consider the role of Francisco in this part of the play. Together with his co-conspirator, Monticelso, he has been involved in the attempt to revenge the murder of his sister, Isabella. When the act opens, however, he seems to be taking a very moral stance, saying that his princely regard for the interests of his subjects must outweigh any thoughts of going to war to avenge his sister. When Monticelso tries to persuade him that there are more devious ways of getting revenge, Francisco adopts a holier-than-thou attitude, piously exclaiming that those who practise treason only end up entangled in their own webs of deceit. His moral attitude, however, is only an appearance, and he reveals something of his real intentions by asking Monticelso for his black book of criminals' names, showing particular interest in the murderers' page. While Monticelso fetches the book Francisco reveals in a soliloquy that he does not trust his companion, and that his pretence is just a way of keeping all his plots and schemes to himself. What we see here, therefore, is Francisco adopting a moral stance to cover up his plans for revenge. It is this which gives many of his speeches an ironic twist. Here, for example, he is explaining to Monticelso why he considers revenge to be an unwise action:

> Free me my innocence, from treacherous acts:
> I know there's thunder yonder: and I'll stand,
> Like a safe valley, which low bends the knee
> To some aspiring mountain: since I know
> Treason, like spiders weaving nets for flies,
> By her foul work is found, and in it dies.
>
> (IV.i.22–7)

Francisco is saying that it is best to keep a low profile and not to get involved in teacherous acts because traitors often end up constructing their own death traps. The image is particularly ironic if we remember that Francisco is simultaneously plotting his 'foul' revenge against Brachiano and Vittoria, but in addition it also serves to draw attention to the link between retribution and death that runs through the play. This is what we might expect of Webster's language; that it works on several levels at once, so that it reinforces our sense of character and theme as well as touching on larger issues and questions that trouble humankind. Here, in particular, Francisco's reference to 'thunder yonder' seems to suggest the idea of a retributive justice in nature which overtakes evil-doers and sees to it that evil destroys itself. The problem of evil is one that haunts Renaissance drama, since it brings into question the whole workings and order of the universe. Besides having an ironic bearing on the character himself, therefore, Francisco's words, with their emphasis on morality and the natural order of things, reinforce the importance of these questions for the audience as the play moves to its retributive and bloody climax.

6 *Choose a scene from Act V which shows how the play's issues are resolved and try to draw together the threads of your analysis*

The last act of *The White Devil* is very long and your initial impression may well be one of a series of violent, almost absurdly contrived deaths. Certainly Webster's plays are often thought of as being loosely constructed around macabre, spectacular scenes in this fashion, but this is not very helpful when it comes to assessing the significance of what is happening in the final act. What you need to do is to focus on one or two episodes or particular dramatic moments which will allow you to draw your ideas together. One promising episode is the death of Brachiano in Act v, scene iii.

To celebrate his marriage to Vittoria, Brachiano holds a tournament. During the tournament Lodovico 'sprinkles' Brachiano's helmet with poison, and at the beginning of Act v, scene iii, we see Brachiano staggering about inside the poisoned helmet, raging in pain. Lodovico and Gasparo enter disguised as Capuchin monks and take Brachiano away under the pretence of giving him the last rites. Under the influence of poison, Brachiano has some strange, terrifying hallucinations, and the 'monks' try to calm him with prayers. Saying they must be left in private with Brachiano, Lodovico and Gasparo then order everyone from the room. Once alone, however, they throw off their disguises and reveal themselves to Brachiano, tormenting and insulting the dying man until he calls out for his wife. She enters, only to be told to avoid the chamber 'For Christian charity' (v.iii.175). The two conspirators strangle Brachiano and then go off to announce his death.

What you are looking for are ways in which the action here reflects the play's concern with the workings of a chaotic world. Lodovico and Gasparo appear to be monks bringing a dying man to a state of grace, and therefore part of an ordered, harmonious and forgiving universe. In reality, however, they are sadistic murderers operating in a world of retribution who condemn the unclean soul of Brachiano to hell. The gap between illusion and reality is brought home on stage by the sudden contrast between the quiet ministrations of the monks and the vicious verbal and physical attacks of the murderers. As in the trial of Vittoria we are thus aware of the amoral barbarism hiding beneath the surface appearance of civilised Christianity, and, indeed, Vittoria's comment 'O me! this place is hell' (v.iii.18) sums up the horror perfectly.

At the same time, though, we may also be aware of the grim appropriateness of Brachiano's death. It is a fitting end, after committing adultery and being party to murder, to face a vision of hellish torments. His death could suggest that there is a sort of justice operating in the play by which the wicked are punished for their sins and the schemers are eventually caught in their own web of deceit. This is one way of interpreting the last act and its deaths. Yet you may find, because of the way Brachiano's death is handled on stage, that you have some sympathy for him in his suffering, despite his guilt. This is where you need to bear in mind that Webster is not writing a simple morality play in which good triumphs over evil. Part of the fascination of a tragedy such as *The White Devil* comes from the fact that even the evil characters may provoke terror and pity by their sufferings in a world that seems to be horribly out of control.

They may also, however, as in the case of Vittoria, gain our admiration. Vittoria dies in Act v, scene vi (the last scene), killed by Lodovico and Gasparo in their bout of revenge murders. Before they kill her Vittoria ironically mocks their bravery, but this is mixed in with a recognition of her own guilt:

O my greatest sin lay in my blood.
Now my blood pays for't.

(v.vi.237–8)

She faces her death heroically, yet at the same time her last words identify her as a victim who has been inextricably caught up with events over which she has no control:

> O, happy they that never saw the court,
> Nor ever knew great man but by report.
> (v.vi.259–60)

Vittoria's words give a complex impression of someone who is caught in a confusing, disordered world but still refuses to submit meekly to its injustices or to hide from her own guilt. Perhaps it is this that marks her out as the tragic heroine of the play.

That, however, is for you to think about and decide. All I have tried to do here is to show you how to steer a course through the play, slowly building up your analysis and ideas so that you achieve a firm sense of the text and understand your own response to it. Obviously there are many aspects of the play I have left out – you would need to examine the part played by Flamineo in a fuller account and also to look at the staging in a lot more detail – but the principles and the method outlined here should help you to tackle any aspect you wish to pursue, and lead you towards your own distinctive interpretation of the play.

4

Ben Jonson

IN the opening chapter of this book we looked at a play called *Youth*. There we saw the central character, Youth himself, pursuing his own selfish desires and rebelling against the established moral and social order. Since then we have seen that the plays of Marlowe and Webster have a similar structure, with both writers presenting characters whose individual desires bring them into conflict with the world around them. The plays of Ben Jonson follow this same broad pattern and deal with the same broad issues. This may seem surprising because most of Jonson's plays are comedies, whereas the other plays we have looked at are tragedies. Yet if we look at what makes a comedy and what makes a tragedy we should be able to see that, while comedy and tragedy differ in tone and effect, they are essentially concerned with the same issues, the same questions of human behaviour.

In a tragedy we see how the desires of the individual characters create chaos in their own lives and in the lives of those around them. At the centre of a tragedy is the tragic hero or heroine, who is forced to confront base and irrational instincts in humankind. Tragedy shows how these desires can be destructive and lead to pain, anguish and death. Comedy is also concerned with the desires of individual characters, but this time it shows how silly these desires are and how they create a muddled world in which everybody makes fools of themselves; comedies, in other words, are packed with characters who cannot prevent themselves from acting irrationally. If tragedy shows how destructive human desires are, then comedy shows how human desires lead to folly and stupidity. So close, indeed, are the connections between tragedy and comedy that the same basic story could, with different endings, be presented as either a tragedy or a comedy. Shakespeare's *Othello*, for example, is the well-known tragedy of a jealous husband who suspects his wife of infidelity, but the jealous, over-possessive husband can be equally well presented in literature as a comic figure, as, for example, in Chaucer's *Merchant's Tale*. If you have studied Marlowe's *Doctor Faustus*, which was considered in Chapter 2 of this book, you will know that the play presents the tragedy of a man who sells his soul to the devil in return for power. This theme of the search for power is also dealt with in the sub-plot involving Faustus's servants and other minor characters, but here the idea is dealt with comically, and the various characters are made to look very foolish indeed.

Not only are many stories capable of being developed as either tragedies or comedies, but the formal patterns of tragedy and comedy are very similar. Both kinds of drama share a basic dramatic shape made up of three parts. These are usually referred to as *exposition*, *complication* and *resolution*. In the exposition the basic situation of the play is set up, the characters introduced and their desires made clear. In the complication stage, as you might expect, the actions of the characters create complex situations as order or harmony is overthrown. In this part of the play tragedies emphasise the darker side of human nature while comedies focus on humankind's silly behaviour. Finally we have the resolution stage, the ending. The real difference between comedy and tragedy is most noticeable at the end of a play. Tragedies are only resolved after a great deal of suffering and the death of one or more of the major characters. Things become so serious in tragedies that the only way order can be restored is by violence and death. In comedies, however, there is a much gentler way out, with characters acknowledging their own weaknesses and promising to lead a better life in the future.

It is because comedy presents a situation that we know will be resolved without real violence that we can afford to laugh at the predicaments of the characters. They have desires which are disruptive, but we see those desires as silly rather than dangerous. In the type of comedies that Ben Jonson wrote, called *satiric comedies*, we are shown characters who are grotesque in their attitudes and ambitions and at whom we are invited to laugh as they get tangled up through their own idiocy. Indeed, the first impression you are likely to have of a Jonson play is one of characters being held up to ridicule. The other thing you are likely to notice from a first encounter is a sense of excess, a feeling that the whole thing is a mad complex whirl of silliness and indulgence. This, as we shall see later on, is very important. For the moment, however, let me deal with a reservation you might have about comedies in general. You might be tempted to feel that, by comparison with tragedy, comedy is a very slight form of drama. Certainly, tragedies strike us as profound: they are serious plays in which the dramatist asks the most fundamental questions about life. In addition, even though the impression of life that tragedies present is often disturbing, the tragic hero or heroine often provides us with an inspiring sense of the potential dignity and heroism of humankind. By contrast, the comic writer might seem only to present us with a ridiculous vision of life. His plays might not seem very substantial at all, and the characterisation might seem thin, with the real, complex nature of people being left unexplored. Indeed, it could be argued that the comic playwright merely presents a jaundiced and glib view of people as greedy fools.

The fact that these kind of doubts about comedy are fairly common is, I think, reflected in examination answers on Jonson, where it often appears to the examiner that the candidates cannot think of very much to say. Questions on tragedies seem to spark off candidates, but answers on Jonson's comedies are often rather thin and basic. Most candidates catch on to the fact that satire is a form of writing that hopes to improve human behaviour by exposing folly, and so they state that Jonson's satiric comedies present a vision of unacceptable behaviour to warn people against acting in such a way. Jonson, the argument goes, presents a vision of people dominated by sexual lust and greed for money in order to criticise such behaviour. The result, as expressed in examination answers, is that Jonson has a serious moral purpose behind his comic writing to show immoral behaviour in a bad light. There is nothing actually wrong with this view of Jonson. The criticism I would make of it, though, is that it reduces extremely lively and interesting plays to simple moral messages, and therefore misses the comic complexity that is present in Jonson's plays. However, rather than state in advance what kind of complexity we can expect to find, and rather than defend comedy in an abstract way, I hope that sufficient evidence will emerge in the following discussion of *Volpone*. I have suggested that examination candidates are often at a loss for something to say about Jonson; the method presented here will, I hope, help you find something interesting to say about him. In addition, I hope you will gain a sense of the originality of his vision, for Jonson is a very disturbing and thought-provoking writer. The edition of Jonson's play I am using is the Penguin *Three Comedies*. This edition divides the play scenes up according to the entrances and exits of the characters. Not all editions follow this format, and if you are using another edition you will find that scene and line references do not correspond. The acts are divided in the same way in all editions, however, and it should not be too difficult to locate a given speech in the play.

I have decided to start with *Volpone* (1605) because it provides a clear illustration of the nature of Jonson's approach and characteristic concerns as a playwright. It also shows the degree of originality he can bring to the comic format. The first step, as always, is to consider the play as a whole.

Volpone

1 *Read the play, then think about its overall effect and what sort of broad pattern you can see in the plot*

Volpone is a rich man, intent on making himself richer. He pretends that he is dying and then watches with amusement as three potential heirs to his fortune, Voltore, Corbaccio and Corvino, all make fools of themselves. Mosca, Volpone's helper, persuades them to make lavish gifts to his dying master in the hope that they will be made sole heirs to Volpone's fortune. Their own greed and the cleverness of Mosca and Volpone make them easy victims. The middle part of the play is taken up with the complications arising out of Volpone's lust for Corvino's wife, Celia. With Mosca's help, Volpone dupes Corvino into bringing the unwilling Celia to his bed. She is, however, saved from rape by the timely intervention of Bonario, Corbaccio's son. Charges are brought against Volpone, but the subsequent trial is a travesty of justice and ironically Bonario and Celia are declared guilty of adultery. Delighted with his victory and restless for further knavery, Volpone gives out news that he is dead. Everyone gathers round for the spoils, only to find that Volpone has left everything to Mosca in his will. Mosca then turns the tables on his master by insisting that he really is dead, aware that Volpone cannot contradict him without revealing everything. Forced into a desperate situation. Volpone confesses, and all the guilty parties receive a just punishment for their misdeeds.

This is, I think you will agree, a fairly simple plot to follow. There is obviously a degree of complexity in it, apparent in

Volpone's scheming and double-dealing, but the basic outline is quite straightforward. All the characters, apart from Celia and Bonario, are motivated by greed and a desire for personal gain: this is true of Voltore, Corbaccio and Corvino, and equally true of Volpone and Mosca. As we might expect in a comedy, the desires of the central characters lead to a series of bizarre situations, and as the play goes on many characters are exposed as foolishly obsessive. At the centre of the play is a sequence of actions and events where things are in disarray: this is apparent in the continual manipulation of the three suitors by Mosca, in Volpone's attempt to get Corvino's wife into bed, in the false news of Volpone's death, and in the trick played by Mosca on Volpone. Then, at the end of the play, there is a return to a less chaotic state of affairs as the true situation is revealed. Good order is restored as soon as Volpone is forced to confess in front of the court, and punishment is then meted out.

The pattern of this play, and indeed of all Jonson's comedies, is basically simple: greedy, inflexible characters create a state of chaos until the truth appears and order is restored at the end. Indeed, it is because this pattern is so simple that examination candidates often find themselves at a loss for something to write about. In a similar way, the characters are rather one-dimensional if they are compared with, say, Shakespeare's great tragic heroes, but we must remember that Jonson's whole method depends on people being motivated by simple desires, and this seems to preclude complex development in characterisation. So, as we turn to specific scenes from the play we should be trying to see how Jonson brings this basic pattern to life, how he makes his plays more than simple moral comedies where we disapprove of the silly behaviour of bad people. If we can see the way he fills out the idea of characters creating chaos, we can begin to appreciate the overall complexity of his vision within an individual play.

2 *Look at the opening scenes and try to achieve a sense of what is happening and what the play is about*

In the first scene Volpone wakes up and looks adoringly at the piles of gold he has accumulated. He goes on to say that his satisfaction lies not merely in the possession of wealth, but in the acquisition of it; he is proud of the ingenious way he persuades people to part with their money. Mosca takes up this theme and expands on it. He points out how different Volpone is from the run-of-the-mill money-grabbers who make the innocent suffer, or the secretive misers who jealously covet their wealth. Pleased by Mosca's fine-sounding words, Volpone rewards him with gold. Then, left alone on stage, he outlines his scheme to the audience. Because he has no family he is able to prey on the greed of those who hope to inherit his wealth. By pretending that his death is imminent, he manages to get the various 'suitors' to bring him expensive gifts and compete with each other to become his sole heirs.

Jonson, it is clear, does not waste any time at all in declaring what the play is about: from the moment the action starts we know that the drama hinges on Volpone's love of gold. Moreover, everything else in the scene backs up the impression that Jonson's central concern is with the way people are motivated by greed for money. Volpone is obviously the dominant character, but during Act I we also see Voltore, Corbaccio and Corvino, all of whom are intent on trying to gain possession of Volpone's fortune. That, then, is the simple meaning and moral message of the action, but we can begin to fill out more details if we pay attention to how Jonson actually presents the ideas along the way. This isn't a difficult procedure – you aren't searching for hidden meanings or concealed clues. All it involves is concentrating on small sections of a scene and finding your own words to describe the effect of the passage in question.

I should like to consider the effect of the very opening of the play as an example. We can say that this shows Volpone's love of gold, but we could also go further by saying that he seems to have turned his store of gold into a shrine or a place of worship. What should strike you about this is the way Volpone's values are distorted to the point of blasphemy; the love of God has been replaced by the love of money. As the scene develops we see the devious Volpone outlining plots and schemes to increase his wealth. It is not enough, though, to just note what happens, for our analysis must come to grips with the significance of the action. The things to say are the obvious ones: standards of openness and honesty are brushed aside in favour of the underhand, devious plots which Volpone is hatching. Can you see that even a simple statement such as this takes us a considerable way towards characterising what is distinctive about Jonson's art? We have immediately moved beyond just saying that he deals with people's greedy desires, and begun to discuss how such desires can turn characters like Volpone into twisted, devious and blasphemous villains. He is more than just a rascal; there is something rather sinister and disturbing in his ritual worship of gold and his delight in the ingenuity of his own schemes for accumulating more wealth.

All we have done so far is to work with our broad ideas about the pattern in the play and then tried to combine this with a look at specific details. By this method we have begun to define what is distinctive about the play's dramatic presentation. The kind of things to look for, as I have explained here, are fairly simple, obvious points. Rather less obvious, or at least, less easy to describe, is Jonson's use of dramatic irony. One of the most noticeable things about the opening of the play is that the 'plot' intended to fool the three suitors is carefully explained to the audience. This means that, when the action involving these suitors starts, the audience knows more than the characters involved and can fully appreciate the ways in which they are making fools of themselves. This contributes to the moral effect of the play, in that we can see ourselves as much wiser and morally superior to Volpone's victims. But also, and perhaps just as importantly, it adds to the comedy of the plays: we can relish the experience of watching characters blindly wandering into a situation we already know about. This whole question of dramatic irony, however, is so central to Jonson's method that we shall have to return to it again and again in discussing *Volpone*.

3 *Choose a scene from Act II and try to clarify your impression of what the play is about and how it is developing*

Act II begins by introducing a new character, Sir Politic Would-Be, and shows him making a fool of himself. I did not mention this character in my overall summary of the play as he isn't really central: he is, in fact, part of the sub-plot (a storyline which can run through a play but which only touches tangentially on the main events being presented). Don't ignore the sub-plot in your overall thinking about the play. A sub-plot echoes the themes of the main plot and it is always worth considering for the way it provides you with another perspective on the themes at the centre of the play. In the case of Sir Politic Would-Be, for example, we are given another character who is blinded by his own folly, and in introducing him Jonson is touching on that absurd self-confidence or pretence of being in the know that self-important people like to adopt, and this pride proves to be his weakness. The sub-plot, therefore, is dealing with the themes we have already mentioned, yet it is also broadening the issues, showing the pervasiveness of all types of foolishness in humankind. What I have said here, however, might well go beyond anything that you could find to say about Sir Politic at this stage of your analysis. When your view of the play as a whole is worked out you may well want to come back to look at the sub-plot, but for the moment it is a good idea to stick to the main line of action in the play and the events concerning the main characters.

The rest of the act, then, concerns Volpone's infatuation with Corvino's wife, Celia. Volpone disguises himself as a street-seller of medicines called Scoto Mantuano. He starts to peddle his wares outside Corvino's house in order to catch sight of Celia at the window, but he is driven away by Corvino before he can progress further. Corvino, obsessively jealous, turns on Celia and threatens her with violence should she shame him further with her forward behaviour (Celia has thrown down her handkerchief to Volpone). Mosca, however, has devised a scheme to get Volpone his heart's desire. He visits Corvino and claims that Volpone has staged a remarkable recovery through taking Scoto Mantuano's oil, which was procured for him by Corbaccio and Voltore, the other two suitors. As part of the restorative medicine, Mosca tells Corvino, Volpone must also have 'some young woman . . . Lusty, and full of juice, to sleep by him' (II.vi.34–5). Hearing that someone else has already offered their daughter to the cause, and fearing the advancement of others at his expense, Corvino immediately offers Celia as the young woman to sleep with Volpone.

As always, the next move is to comment on the significance of the action that is taking place here, picking up and working from the most striking details. We know that the play is concerned with disruptive impulses, and certainly Volpone's actions here seem to fit in with this idea. His lust for Celia is yet further evidence of his excessive desires, this time threatening to undermine the ordered relationship of marriage. Lust for money and sexual lust are both now part of the play's concerns, though Volpone is not the only character who acts badly, and we need to look at other ways in which Jonson presents us with excessive, disruptive actions. In any play there will be a tension between reasonable, rational behaviour which leads to order and harmony in society and obsessive, irrational actions which disrupt things. In order to see how *Volpone* reflects this we can focus on one or two details from this part of the play.

One thing that is likely to attract your attention is the behaviour of Corvino in Act II, scene vi. As he drags Celia across the room and attacks her for her supposed wantonness, we can see his jealousy manifesting itself in an unpleasant and shocking form. After a series of crude innuendoes about her behaviour he resolves to lock her away to keep temptation at a safe distance. If we look at this action in terms of the tension between rational and irrational behaviour, it is clear how his excessive possessiveness has destroyed any sense of a rational, loving relationship between man and woman; driven by his jealous desire to keep her away from other men, Corvino treats Celia as a possession rather than as a person. His behaviour, however, is made to look even more ridiculous and unacceptable by what happens later in the scene. An audience which has seen him so unpleasantly possessive about his wife then sees him prepared to give her away in order to please Volpone, as the extreme passion of jealousy is replaced by the even more dominant obsession of greed. By making the audience well aware of this ironic contrast, Jonson is able to let us judge Corvino's actions for ourselves. There is no question of our having any sympathy for him as he is duped by Mosca, but neither is there any explicit moralising by Jonson the playwright. What he does is to leave us to draw our own conclusions about the relationships between Corvino's folly, greed and viciousness. Indeed, the final thing that may strike you about this phase of the play is its cruelty. *Volpone* is meant to be a comedy, so why do things become so nasty between Corvino and Celia?

In thinking about why the play develops in this way it is useful to remind yourself that tragedy and comedy are two sides of the same coin, and that the breakdown of harmony can lead to violence or to silly behaviour, according to the tone of the play. Sometimes, as in *Volpone*, the two become amalgamated in an interesting way, and it is worth noting that there is a darker side to Jonson's portrayal of human folly. Indeed, that darker side may well capture our attention as we continue our analysis of the play. So far we have spotted Jonson's theme and seen how he presents villainous rogues intent on the pursuit and indulgence of their own desires. Just on the basis of looking at a few details – essentially, so far, our initial impression of Volpone and the behaviour of Corvino – we have seen the way the play presents bad behaviour.

The action is, of course, comic, for there is something absurd about people putting so much energy into the futile pursuit of wealth and being blind to their own folly as they do so. There is also a fairly simple moral message we can extract from this: it is unwise and unproductive to be obsessed, and if we act foolishly because of these obsessions we make ourselves seem grotesque and less than human. Yet there is also something more than just a moral message at work here. The desires (Volpone's desire for gold, or Corvino's jealous desire to restrict Celia) are so absolute and all-consuming, and the violence that runs through the play so powerful, that we might well begin to feel that there is another way of looking at Jonson. Rather than being merely a writer of satiric comedies intent on improving human behaviour, we might suspect that he views chaos as an inevitable outcome of such extreme and outrageous desires. This makes his overall viewpoint rather more pessimistic; indeed, he might well feel that there is no hope for any improvement in people's behaviour. This kind of vision of the world as governed by irrational instincts certainly seems in keeping with the bizarre sense of disorder that appears to prevail in the play. Possibly, then, the way to find more to say about Jonson is not to concentrate so much on the constructive, reforming impulse behind his plays, but to focus on the dark and disturbing side of the comic chaos in society that he presents. This is something we can bear in mind as we move to the next act.

4 *Choose a scene from Act III and begin to look more closely at the principal characters in the play*

So far we have focused on how the obsessive desires of characters disrupt ordered values and make the world a crazy place to live in. Act III extends the scope of the play's complications even further by bringing in other plots and counter-plots. Yet in our first consideration of the play we just want to stick to the main plot involving Volpone, Corvino and Celia, and this is what I shall look at next.

In Act III, scene iii, Celia is brought by Corvino to Volpone's house in order to sleep with him. She entreats her husband not to degrade or dishonour her, but Corvino threatens her with violence should she disobey and hands her over to Volpone. As soon as they are alone, Volpone jumps up from his sick-bed, discards his feigned illness and reveals his real amorous intentions. Celia refuses to have anything to do with him, despite his persuasive entreaties. Losing patience, Volpone is just about to force himself upon her when Corbaccio's son, Bonario, bursts in. Bonario has been brought to Volpone's house by Mosca to witness his father's treachery in making a new will in Volpone's favour, and has been eavesdropping on the attempted seduction. Luckily for Celia, he prevents Volpone's assault, and, pausing only to wound Mosca, effects her rescue.

The simple question to ask yourself about this scene is whether the attempted rape is funny. My own response to this is ambiguous. Celia is definitely portrayed as a victim who is placed in a very perilous situation, and it is the combined immorality of Volpone and Corvino that puts her at risk. From this point of view Jonson presents behaviour which is sick, diseased and so lacking in moral substance that it can only disturb us. Yet, at the same time, this scene is perversely funny, with the grotesque figure of the 'dying' Volpone suddenly galvanised into action, putting so much effort into trying to impress Celia, and then being finally thwarted. This is my own response to the play, and you might well disagree with my view. What I do hope, however, is that the logic behind this whole method of analysis is again apparent in this section. We can talk at an abstract level about the concerns and technique of Jonson, but it is only when we point to a specific scene in the text and analyse how that scene brings to life all these issues that our analysis has any real substance or merit.

It is partly the details of the action that bring the issues of the play to life, but it is also the words spoken, and Volpone, like most comic rogues in literature, is given some superb speeches. Such characters might be saying immoral things, but they entertain us with lively and exaggerated speeches which show a complete disregard for honesty and truthfulness. In this scene, for example, Volpone, having revealed that he is far from infirm, outlines a sumptuous and decadent scene for their love-making, relating to Celia how they will play the parts of classical lovers from antiquity. He continues,

Then will I have thee in more modern forms,
Attirèd like some sprightly dame of France,
Brave Tuscan lady, or proud Spanish beauty;
Sometimes unto the Persian Sophy's wife,
Or the Grand Signior's mistress; and, for change,
To one of our most artful courtesans,

Or some quick Negro, or cold Russian;
And I will meet thee in as many shapes;
Where we may so transfuse our wand'ring souls
Out at our lips and score up sums of pleasures . . .
(III.vii.226–35)

Volpone here catalogues the variety of guises that he wishes Celia to adopt in order to add spice to their love-life. The speech itself is fairly easy to follow, and it's not hard to see how it shows Volpone as prone to excessive fantasising. However, what might puzzle you is how to link the speech with the wider concerns of the play discussed so far. This is where our distinction between reasonable, rational behaviour and obsessive, irrational actions becomes so useful; not only does it enable us to grasp the thematic connection between Volpone's love of money and sexual lust, but it also lets us see how far Jonson extends his idea of human irrationality. Here, for example, it is clear that Volpone wants his already bizarre relationship with Celia to enter the realm of make-believe. He thus becomes the very embodiment of irrational sexual obsession as his desire moves him farther and farther away from reality, presenting us with a character who is both absurd and menacing. What you might also spot in this extract is the way the excessive language of irrational desire is set against the idea of social and moral order. We might say that, whereas order is usually implied by a stable and unchanging relationship, Volpone's fantasy involves overturning such order by offering Celia an ever-changing series of roles from 'dame', 'lady', 'beauty' and 'wife' to 'mistress' and 'courtesan'. Such roles, however, deny her any real identity or stability as a person, and in the end we see that Celia is only the cipher for Volpone's desires – the blank sheet on which he works out his 'sums of pleasures'.

What I have said about the language of this speech applies to the language throughout *Volpone*, and, indeed, the rest of Jonson's plays. Often you will find a cluster of ideas, words and images that suggest control, discipline and good order. But these will be far outweighed by ideas, words and images that suggest excess, disorder and rampant extremes. Such words coming together, as in the speech above, vividly suggest a world that is characterised by instability, dangerous fantasy and the pursuit of excessive desire. When you are watching a Jonson play, of course, it is primarily the action on stage that brings the themes to life, but the point I am making here is that both character and theme are inextricably bound up with the language of the play. This is why it is so profitable to analyse speeches closely: you immediately get hold of the actions and the characters, but in addition you can build up your ideas about the issues the play is dealing with.

5 *Choose a scene from Act IV to analyse and begin to look more closely at the language of the play*

In Act IV, Volpone is to be tried for attempted rape, but ironically it is the innocent Celia and Bonario who are arrested and accused of adultery. The most striking feature of this part of the play is the trial in Act IV, scene V. All Volpone's suitors testify at the trial, and, primed by Mosca, each of them gives false evidence against Celia and Bonario to protect their own interests. Volpone says that Celia and Bonario have been carrying on for a long time, and that Bonario's apparent virtue is only a front adopted to disguise his wicked vices. Corbaccio then confirms that his own son intended to kill him, and Corvino testifies to the sinful lewdness of Celia, an opinion that is seconded by Lady Would-Be, who ludicrously identifies Celia as a courtesan who was supposed to have seduced Sir Politic.

At this stage in the play things have got out of hand, and the contrast between order and chaos is apparent everywhere as all proper values are disregarded. The trial, which should be a means to establish the truth, turns into a parody of justice, a sort of absurd lie-telling contest. The two innocent characters in the play are on trial for villainy, while the real villains sit in the witness box, fabricating stories. It is the very absence of ordered values in such a topsy-turvy situation that brings comedy so close to potential tragedy. If things were not to be put right at the end of the play we would have to view the sufferings of Celia and Bonario in a very different light. As it is, we know this is only a temporary state of affairs, and we can see through the absurd pretentions of the witnesses and recognise how justice is being perverted by self-interest.

So much for the general thematic significance of the trial scene. What we now need to do is to look at the sort of writing Jonson uses in the scene and see if we can comment on the way in which the langauge works. In this extract, for example, Corbaccio denounces Bonario and then Corvino steps forward to give evidence against Celia:

CORBACCIO. . . .
He is an utter stranger to my loins.
BONARIO. Have they made you to this?
CORBACCIO. I will not hear thee,
Monster of men, swine, goat, wolf, parricide!
Speak not, thou viper.
BONARIO. Sir, I will sit down,
And rather wish my innocence should suffer,
Than I resist the authority of a father.
VOLTORE. Signor Corvino!
SECOND AVOCATORE. This is strange.
FIRST AVOCATORE. Who's this?
NOTARIO. The husband.
FOURTH AVOCATORE. Is he sworn?
NOTARIO. He is.
THIRD AVOCATORE. Speak, then.
CORVINO. This woman, please your fatherhoods, is a whore
Of most hot exercise, more than a partridge,
Upon recòrd –
FIRST AVOCATORE. No more.
CORVINO. Neighs like a jennet.
NOTARIO. Preserve the honour of the court.
(IV.v.109–18)

What we want to comment on here is the effect of Jonson's language and the ideas it conveys. Our contrast between rational and irrational behaviour will again come in useful, but we can start simply enough by summing up what is being said. Corbaccio accuses his son of acting unnaturally and emphasises his monstrous quality by using animal images, accusing him of being everything from a swine to a viper. Corvino uses a similar technique, comparing his wife to a partridge and a jennet (horse) to convey her sexual excesses. Both are seeking to stress the wanton and intemperate characters of Bonario and Celia by contrasting their uncontrolled animal-like behaviour with that of the rational, moderate attitude expected of human beings.

Having summed up the speeches in this way, our next move is to see how the language works on the level of character, theme or larger significance. Let's start with character. It is fairly easy to see that the characters who are acting in an irrational way here are Corbaccio and Corvino. Jonson's irony lets us view them critically: we see them lying, but we also know that those lies stem from an uncontrollable desire to get Volpone's wealth. What really gives them away, however, is their language: look how excessive and immoderate it is, particularly compared with the quiet restraint of Bonario, whose respect for order is such that he would rather be found guilty than challenge his father's authority. It is Corbaccio and Corvino who are clearly acting unnaturally by denouncing their own son and wife, and their use of animal imagery allows us to see how perverse their actions are. From the start of the play their names have been associated with animals, 'Corbaccio' being Italian for 'raven', and 'Corvino' for 'crow'. Now, through their continual reiteration of animal images, we are ironically reminded of the baseness of their characters.

The animal imagery, however, also serves to highlight the darker side of Jonson's theme, stressing the way people can be governed by uncontrollable, animal-like lusts and desires which turn them into vicious monsters. This is why it is always so important to look at imagery in a play. Not only does it serve to reveal character and draw out the characters' feelings and preoccupations, but the language used also serves to emphasise the play's themes and ideas. It is not too difficult here to spot a tension between words such as 'innocence', 'honour' and 'fatherhood', suggesting rational, civilised behaviour, and words such as 'monster', 'parricide', 'whore' and 'hot exercise', suggesting base, irrational behaviour. We must bear in mind, too, that Jonson is using imagery in an ironic, topsy-turvy way, and this gives the dramatic situation a sharp, penetrating quality; those accused of being animals are, in fact, the only civilised and rational characters in the whole play, while the figures of authority who are accusing them have been turned into monstrous parodies of human beings by their greed. The dominance of the unpleasant characters in this scene make goodness and innocence seem slightly unreal qualities in a world where people give way so readily to their bestial appetities.

What might puzzle you about the vision of the world that this play offers is how it differs from, say, the picture that Webster offers in *The Duchess of Malfi*; in other words, what is it that makes this play a comedy while Webster's play is a tragedy? Well, on one level it does not differ at all. Indeed, if you took the previous extract and set it against an extract from Act IV of *The Duchess of Malfi* you would probably find that the two passages share similar language, and that they both refer to the replacement of concepts such as honour and innocence by those of suffering and degradation. The difference between tragedy and comedy lies in the way we are asked to look at what is presented. In tragedy we are given, through the identity of the tragic hero or heroine, an impression of human beings desperately trying to make sense of a chaotic world or heroically confronting its excesses. In comedy we are forced to recognise that there is something absurd about trying to hold on to order in the face of humankind's propensity for creating chaos. Because of the emphasis on characters who upset the order of things, we get the impression that it is essentially silly to pretend that we can 'preserve the honour of the court' or any moral or social order, given our irrational, foolish natures. One reason (and it is only one) why Jonson is a comic dramatist rather than just a moral satirist is the extent to which he both delights and disturbs us by concentrating on our faults, making the irrationality of human behaviour amusing yet worrying.

6 *Choose a scene from Act V which shows how the play's issues are resolved and try to draw together the threads of your analysis*

As I mentioned at the beginning of this chapter, the part of a play where comedy is most easily distinguishable from tragedy is the end. In both types of play the difficulties of the action are brought to rest, but in comedy things are restored to a balanced state without violence and death.

In the final act Volpone attempts to have one last laugh at his suitors by faking his death and then leaving everything to Mosca. However, his plot backfires when Mosca refuses to play the game. Volpone, now in disguise but supposedly dead, is locked out of his own house and cannot reclaim what is his without revealing himself to be a fraud. Still disguised, he goes to court and tries to arrange a deal with Mosca, but Mosca has become ambitious and asks that this stranger in court be taken off and beaten. Realising that everything is lost, Volpone takes off his disguise and confesses. Bonario and Celia are then declared innocent; Mosca is sent to the galleys; Volpone is sent to prison and his money given to a hospital for incurables; Voltore is disbarred as a lawyer and banished;

Corbaccio is to be placed under house arrest in a monastery and his estate given to Bonario; Corvino is to be rowed round and round Venice with a cap of ass's ears; and Celia is to be allowed home to her father with her dowry repaid threefold for the wrongs done to her. Order is thus restored at the end of the play, and, as in the earlier morality plays, we see characters who have done wrong getting fitting punishments. If we are to do real justice to Jonson, however, we want to try and identify differences as well as similarities between him and earlier playwrights.

We can notice first of all that the emphasis of the last few scenes is, in fact, on the discomfort of Volpone as the tables are finally turned on him. Indeed, even though order is restored at the end, it all happens quickly and arbitrarily, and the greater part of Act v is taken up with the breakdown of the devious scheming that has dominated the play rather than with the positive assertion of justice. *Volpone*, then, is not really concerned with the redemption of mankind, or even with ways to correct bad behaviour. Instead, it gives us a chance to laugh at the ridiculous situations which the excesses of human nature can contrive and at characters who are unaware of the traps they are setting for themselves. Volpone, for example, is so wrapped up with the deceits he is practising on other people that he fails to see he is vulnerable himself. This inability to recognise one's own weaknesses characterises the behaviour of everyone in the play. By following their particular desires to excess the characters lose sight of any stabilising values and end up being completely disorientated.

The resolution of *Volpone* is very straightforward, but you may feel that the actual ending is at odds with the rest of the play and that there is a tension between the simple, comic ending and the complexity that has been built up previously. This is not something to be ignored, and by looking at a single episode in more detail we might see this tension at work. Act v, scene x, provides an interesting episode to examine here, for it seems that the truth is going to be revealed prematurely in this scene. Voltore stands up in court, and, suffering from pangs of conscience, begins to confess everything. He acknowledges the innocence of Celia and Bonario and reveals that Mosca was instrumental in persuading the suitors to give false evidence at the trial. At this stage in the play Voltore is the only person who is prepared to speak the truth. What happens to him, however, makes it clear why Jonson's drama is so significantly different from plays written a hundred years previously

It is no longer enough for the truth to be uttered for it to stand out as the self-evident order of things; the truth can get caught up in falsehoods and deceits as well. Corvino, for example, fearing the consequences of what is being said, declares that Voltore is mad, then claims that he is acting out of envy because Mosca has been made sole heir, and finally pronounces that he is possessed by the devil. Part of the corruption of humankind is this ability to explain away truth as part of another devious scheme, a fact that is reinforced later when Voltore tries to explain away his confession by feigning madness. Jonson is taking great pains to point out that in human affairs there is no longer any simple distinction between the true and the false, between the natural and the unnatural, or between the right and the wrong; humankind takes each of these elements and bends them to suit a wide variety of selfish ends.

This is why your conclusions about the play may seem ambiguous. *Volpone* has a conventional comic ending in which poetic justice is done, but set against this simple resolution is the idea of a shifting set of values that makes the world complicated and difficult to live in. What makes Jonson's comedies so interesting is the way he allows the real problems of life to come up against the artificial form of his comic plays, and your analysis should take you some way towards seeing how and why this happens; towards seeing, that is, why Jonson's plays are simultaneously funny and disturbing.

7 *Pursuing aspects of the play*

Four main aspects to think about further are character, themes, language and staging. Of course, as I have said before, it is impossible to consider these as totally separate, and in practice they all combine to constitute the overall impact of the play. Nevertheless, they are worth thinking about as individual categories, and I want to begin this section by looking at the idea of staging.

(a) *Staging*. Many episodes in the play will start to fall into place if you think about how they might be staged. For example, in Act III, scene vii, there is the attempted rape of Celia by Volpone. The effect of this scene depends in part on the fact that Bonario is also on stage at the time, but hidden from the view of the other two characters. To ignore Bonario's presence on stage here would be to miss much of Jonson's dramatic irony, for Bonario has been hidden by Mosca as part of the machinations concerning the will. Volpone is thus caught in his own trap, or rather in Mosca's plans, just as he is at the end of the play. Again, Bonario's presence might also lead us to consider Volpone's behaviour as an absurd revelation of his own vices rather than as a real threat to Celia, and so we are once more invited to take an ironic view of Volpone's speeches. I mentioned earlier the importance of irony in *Volpone*, and certainly it is worth including a discussion of staging if you wish to consider how Jonson's dramatic irony works.

As a further help in thinking about the staging of *Volpone* you should bear in mind the actual setting of the play in Venice. In the seventeenth century Venice was seen both as the epitome of modern civilisation and as a rather decadent place. The staging of *Volpone*, including its costumes and props, should perhaps try to reflect these two aspects, giving an idea of extravagant richness and moral decline. So, for example, you might think of Volpone's bed (around which so much of the action takes place) in these terms. The bed can be seen as a symbol and as a prop, as a sign of sickness but also, with its hangings and drapes, as a sign of wealth. However you choose to interpret such details, the important thing in any discussion of the play is to show that you have thought about staging and performance in relation to the play's major issues and themes.

(b) *Character*. Jonson's characters are caricatures in that they follow a fixed pattern of behaviour. Yet, even though we might recognise certain character types, their impact on the play is still quite complex and it is this which sometimes makes them difficult to discuss. I noted earlier that often it seems as though there is not much to say about them, and many students can identify a character-type but are unable to go much further. You may notice a difference between, say, Shakespeare's characters and those of Jonson. Shakespeare's characters seem rather more accessible; they reveal much more about themselves and their personalities, whereas with Jonson's characters we are often left to deduce and infer about them. So, for example, we have to work out for ourselves what it is that appeals to Volpone about the trickery he has set up. His way with words certainly conveys wit and intelligence, and from the ambitious excesses of his language we might deduce a delight in his own virtuoso acting and a pride in the mental agility necessary to maintain his absurd pretences. Such qualities are necessary to his schemes and seem attractive. Altogether less attractive, however, is his lack of moral values and the excesses he is carried to by his lust for Celia. We might say that there is also an unattractive foolishness about the Volpone who fails to see himself being duped by Mosca and who finally has to confess because he has lost control of events.

What I am suggesting here is a mixed response to Volpone which itself reflects some of the complexities of his character type. In turn that complexity is evidence of the way Jonson uses Volpone to sound out all the implications of his theme. We can see this if we think about Volpone's household, consisting of Nano, a dwarf, Castrone, a eunuch, and Androgyno, a hermaphrodite. Taken together they express the perverted abnormality of Volpone's desires, suggestive of the way his love of wealth has bred a new sort of impotent, monstrous family and created a new sort of twisted human nature. As with the staging of the play, it is possible for the characters to take on a symbolic value, but, as ever, the best way to explore this, and character generally, is to focus on a small extract for analysis. So, for example, at the end of Act I, scene ii, we see Volpone getting ready to dupe his first suitor, Voltore, by putting on a guise of illness:

> Now, my feigned cough, my phthisic, and my gout,
> My apoplexy, palsy, and catarrhs,
> Help, with your forcèd functions, this my posture,
> Wherein, this three year, I have milked their hopes.
> He comes, I hear him – uh! uh! uh! uh! O!
> (I.ii.124–8)

Here we have Volpone the actor, the fraud and the cheat getting himself into the right frame of mind for a performance. But what Jonson also manages to suggest is the way that Volpone's greed and love of wealth is itself an all-consuming sickness which has turned into a way of life. The chief way that this is achieved, of course, is through Volpone's language, and this is what I want to consider next.

(c) *Language*. Whatever aspect of the play you are looking at, you are bound to take language into consideration. The language of the play is always there, involved in staging, character and theme. With Jonson's language, in particular, there is a richness and a vitality that deserves comment. Look, for example, at Volpone's lines above, at how the list of diseases crowds one illness upon another, and at how Volpone's invocation almost makes it seem as though they have a life of their own. Look too, at the weight of meaning contained in a single word such as 'milked', which manages not only to suggest that Volpone has duped his suitors, but also that he gains sustenance from doing so; that his counterfeit illnesses are a life-giving force to him.

This concentration on unpleasantness is typical of Jonson, and helps build up a picture of human beings as subject to disease, illness and decay, often little more than amoral pieces of rotting flesh. This is brought out forcefully in Volpone's performance as a quack doctor in Act II, scene ii:

> For, when a humid flux, or catarrh, by the mutability of air falls from your head into an arm or shoulder, or any other part, take you a ducat, or your chequin of gold, and apply to the place affected: see, what good effect it can work. No, no, 'tis this blessed *unguento*, this rare extraction, that hath only power to disperse all malignant humours . . . . To fortify the most indigest and crude stomach, ay, were it of one that through extreme weakness vomited blood, applying only a warm napkin to the place, after the unction and fricace; . . . . (II.ii.87–98)

The emphasis on disease and the image of vomiting blood is calculated to create a sense of revulsion and disgust, yet at the same time we get a grotesque comic enjoyment from Volpone's performance as he bluffs his way through his act. Paradoxically, however, Volpone's patter also gives us an ironic insight into the wider issues of the play. He asks what good wealth is when people are faced with illness, and words such as 'mutability', 'blessed', 'malignant', 'fortify' and 'crude' all help to remind us of the wider implications of humankind's mortality; at the same time, of course, Volpone is highlighting the fruitlessness of a life devoted to the acquisition of wealth, and this ironic insight gives an added dimension to this speech.

Throughout *Volpone*, in fact, there are many images dealing with disease or sickness and money or wealth, so that we are never allowed to forget Jonson's central concerns. This is something students sometimes ignore when they are discussing the language of *Volpone*, and they fail to show how Jonson's imagery reinforces our sense of his complex treatment of the major themes, and how he creates, through language, character and staging, a full impression of the issues he is presenting. The point to grasp here, though, is that Jonson's use of language gives his plays a dramatic force and an intellectual impact that we should miss if we just considered him as a moralist. Rather than press this any further, however, it may be more helpful if we turn to look at another of Jonson's plays. There are a number we could discuss, but the one I have chosen is *The Alchemist*. Before we turn to it, though, I should like to make one more point. You may wonder why I've not discussed 'themes' in *Volpone*: the answer is that, really, I have! Whenever we look at staging, or character, or language in a play we inevitably end up discussing the themes of the play as well. I hope the truth of this will again be apparent as we consider *The Alchemist*.

The Alchemist

1 *Read the play, then think about its overall effect and what sort of broad pattern you can see in the plot*

The Alchemist deals with the confidence trickery of three rogues. One of them, Face, is the butler of Mr Lovewit. Terrified by the plague, Lovewit has left London, and Face, together with Subtle, an alchemist, and Dol Common, a prostitute, operates a profitable racket from Lovewit's empty house, deluding people with daydreams of wealth. In exchange for money or goods the tricksters offer their victims a variety of alchemical 'secrets', ranging from good-luck charms to the production of gold from base metals. The three are so skilled, and their victims are so willing to be led, that business is soon flourishing.

Much of the middle part of the play deals with the frantic attempts of the three rogues to keep the deception going. As they take on a larger and larger clientele, life becomes a giddy whirl of plots, close escapes and quick changes. Matters really come to a head, however, when Lovewit returns unexpectedly. Face is forced to admit that a deception has been practised and tries to bribe his way back into Lovewit's good books by offering to get him a beautiful young wife, Dame Pliant. Meanwhile, the other two conspirators, Subtle and Dol, have planned to run off together, taking Face's share of the profits with them. Face is aware of this, and waits until they are counting out the spoils before he tells them that he has confessed to Lovewit. They curse him and flee empty-handed, while Lovewit takes possession of all the goods they have accumulated. Various victims then arrive and try to lay claim to the booty, but the newly married Lovewit sees them off. The victims depart poorer but wiser, and Face returns to his old job as the humble butler, Jeremy.

In this first step all we want to establish are some basic points. We might start, for example, by thinking about the shape of the play. We know that the action of all plays is divided into three parts: exposition or set-up, complication and resolution. What we need to do is to see how the pattern works in this play. As in *Volpone* we can see that Jonson is looking at the way people's desires lead them to act foolishly. The exposition is the con-trick that the three conspirators set up to play on people's greed. The more convincing the conspirators sound, the greater the riches the victims believe they are going to get and the more willing they are to part with their money in anticipation.

In considering the complications that arise, we need to think about the conspirators themselves. The increasingly complex, frenetic pace of the play is a direct result of their greedy desires. They take on client after client, each one of whom has been individually duped, but as their pretences become more elaborate their ingenuity becomes stretched to the limit in trying to avoid discovery. The eventual resolution, however, does restore some order to this frenzy. Two of the villains are forced to flee with nothing, whilst the third has to return to his old job. The foolish victims also exit empty-handed, and the newly married Lovewit seems to be the only real beneficiary. What you might immediately notice about this ending is that it is not nearly as clear-cut as that of *Youth*, the morality play we discussed in Chapter 1. Nor does the play have a formal ending like *Volpone*, where judicial punishment is handed out to wrongdoers once the truth is known. The more open and less conclusive ending of *The Alchemist* is something we shall have to return to.

For the moment, however, we ought to try and sum up our initial impressions. We can see that in *The Alchemist*, as in most plays, we are presented with a picture of individual desires disrupting society. We know that in some plays the dramatist might develop such a theme in a tragic direction, but this is obviously a comedy, with Jonson making us laugh at the folly of mankind. There is a moral dimension to such drama, and Jonson exposes the folly of yielding to excessive sexual or mercenary desires. But merely to stress the moral purpose of Jonson's play seems somehow to miss out on the real experience of what *The Alchemist* is like. There is the ending, for example: in a traditional morality play order would be restored and the wrongdoers would be punished. In *The Alchemist*, however, as we have already discovered, the ending is more ambiguous. But it is not only the ending that signals that this is going to be more than just a moral comedy: the pace of the action is so frenetic that you might well feel that Jonson, rather than condemning such folly, almost revels in the wildness of it all. Indeed, far from hoping to correct the folly of mankind, Jonson seems to view it as inevitable, and the frantic pace of the play helps convey the sense of a madcap world created by the giddy vagaries of human nature. If that is not very clear yet, a closer look at the evidence of the text should help things fall into place.

Before we move on, though, let me make one more point. *The Alchemist* has quite a lot in common with *Volpone* in terms of form and content, so my analysis will be very similar in some aspects. Jonson, however, was a prolific writer and clearly not all his plays can be discussed in exactly the same way. You can, though, apply exactly the same *method* of analysis to all Jonson's plays, for all critical analysis has the same aim. You need to remember that in looking at any play you are really seeking to assess how each particular play is unique. You are trying to define your sense of the impression a play makes on you. As I have tried to stress throughout this book, the process of working closely with the text will provide you with all the evidence you need to define those impressions and build your own analysis. You may find the particular critical comments I make useful, but remember that I am seeking to show how to analyse the text and how to draw conclusions from the evidence examined. My own conclusions, therefore, are not the only valid ones. *The Alchemist*, like all Renaissance plays, is a complex work, capable of supporting a great many interpretations and responses. The way to develop confidence in putting forward your own ideas about these plays is always to remember that your interpretation will stand up to examination if you base it firmly on the text.

2 *Look at the opening scenes and try to achieve a sense of what is happening and what the play is about*

The chaotic, giddy quality of *The Alchemist* is evident from the start of the play, and in the first scene there is a whirlwind argument between Face and Subtle which is only settled when Dol intervenes. The substance of the argument seems entirely lost in the flurry of words that fly across the stage, and to begin with you might find it hard to work out what is going on. Do not, however, spend a long time poring over the details of the argument and so lose sight of the main action. Think instead of our basic distinction between orderly and disorderly behaviour, which will immediately help you to comment on the significance of the action; an argument clearly suggests unruly behaviour, frayed tempers and disorder, so that from the very start the play is striking a discordant note.

In the second scene it is possible to pick up a better idea of how the tricksters operate, for their first victim is brought in. The previous evening Face has met Dapper, a lawyer's clerk, who now arrives to see if the alchemist can give him a familiar spirit to help in his gambling. Face, disguised as a captain, offers Subtle money on Dapper's behalf. Subtle refuses. Face, in turn, pretends to be angry and threatens to leave unless Subtle takes on their case immediately. Subtle picks up the initiative and asks why Face is being so helpful towards someone who will win all the money in town and leave him with nothing. Encouraged by this conversation, Dapper changes his initial modest request and asks for a more powerful spirit. As Dapper parts with more and more money, so Face and Subtle build up his hopes, culminating in the revelation that he is specially favoured by his 'aunt', the Queen of Faery. Before he can meet her, however, Dapper must go home and ritually cleanse and prepare himself.

If we think about the action here, we should be able to clarify our sense of the play's themes, of what it is about. Obviously Dapper wants to be wealthy, and in his greed he is easily taken in by the deceptions of Subtle and Face. Their way of working, as with confidence tricksters everywhere, is to appear the opposite of what they are, to seem to be helping the people they are fleecing. In reality they are deceiving Dapper, but their little performance makes it appear as though Subtle is doing him a great favour by accepting the commission. They even contrive to make him part with more money than he intended simply by feeding his desire for wealth, and the audience, because they know the truth, are invited to laugh at the ridiculous behaviour of Dapper as he contributes to his own downfall. In short, we are given a portrayal of the folly of human desire and its willingness to exchange fantasy for reality.

That, in a rather abstract way, says what the scene is about, but as you read the play, or even more if you see it on the stage, you will probably be struck by the effrontery, the sheer nerve and style with which the tricksters carry out their deception. They create a world of dreams and fantasies for their victims, and the words flow from them as they cheekily manipulate affairs to their advantage. Jonson, it could be argued, staggers us with the sheer brilliance of the con-man's style, a style that conceals the reality of gross self-interest. Yet even with the tricksters themselves you might feel that greed is secondary, for it seems as if they revel in deception for its own sake, loving a way of life that involves intrigue, pretence and false appearances. So this gives us a clue about the special qualities of Jonson's comedy, for we can see that it is giving us much more than simple moral messages about human behaviour; we could say, in fact, that the play seems to celebrate disorder. Quite how and why this happens is something we can think about as our analysis progresses.

3 *Choose a scene from Act II and try to clarify your impression of what the play is about and how it is developing*

So far we have established that *The Alchemist* is about a group of villains who take advantage of people by substituting appearances for reality. The play seems to be offering us a picture of a topsy-turvy world of greed and folly in which people are duped because of their own foolish and selfish desires. The list of victims grows rapidly. After Dapper comes Drugger, and then, in Acts II and III we get Sir Epicure Mammon, Tribulation Wholesome and Ananias. The plots come thick and fast and this contributes to our sense of a play cracking along at a furious pace.

The most sensible way of dealing with Act II is to select just one of these plots and use it to build your ideas up further. The obvious choice is Sir Epicure Mammon, the play's main victim. Sir Epicure is already convinced that alchemy is his way to a better life, and we first see him trying to convert the sceptical Surly while they are waiting to see Subtle. Wrongly believing Subtle to be a very pious man, Sir Epicure assures him that if he is given the philosopher's stone (the alchemical substance supposed to change base metal into gold) he will only use it for the general benefit of society and not for personal gain. Subtle and Face, however, have other plans for Sir Epicure and arouse his curiosity by giving him a glimpse of

Dol disguised as the mad sister of a nobleman. Never one to resist fleshly pursuits, Sir Epicure's carnal appetites are stimulated by this sighting. In his keenness to get to know Dol, however, Sir Epicure makes a complete fool of himself by pretending to be an acquaintance of her non-existent brother, much to the amusement of everyone in the know.

In common with all the other foolish people who are conned by Subtle and his associates, Sir Epicure clearly falls victim to his own desires; his vice is the search for idle pleasures, his folly is the greed for excessive riches. There is, though, more to Sir Epicure than this, as we see when he pretends to want to employ Subtle's alchemy for 'pious uses' (II.iii.49) such as the setting up of schools, hospitals and churches. Because the audience knows what Sir Epicure is really like, there is an amusing irony when this gross character, the very embodiment of selfish pleasure, takes on the role of social benefactor. As a result, we are immediately aware, not only of a gap between appearance and reality, but also of the way Sir Epicure's desires prompt him into being deceitful. This connection between desire and deceit is a significant one in the play, but it is important to recognise that Jonson is not merely making a moral point here. Sir Epicure is a funny character and the whole scene (Act II, scene iii) of his interview with Subtle is comic. Sir Epicure is funny because he makes a fool of himself, but what we can also identify is the way he tries to assume the attitude of a respectable, moral person. We all know of cases where behind a front of respectability people hide baser, more corrupt desires. Indeed, there may be a case for saying that corrupt and self-interested people are very often the most 'correct' in their public image. As with Dapper, then, the audience is well aware of the real nature of Sir Epicure and can readily identify his greed as the case of his ridiculous posturing. Yet through him we also recognise very clearly one of the central issues of the play, the close link between desire and deceit, and it is this that we can bear in mind as we proceed.

4 *Choose a scene from Act III and begin to look more closely at the principal characters in the play*

We have been looking at how the ideas of desire and deceit play a significant part in *The Alchemist* and how characters such as Dapper and Sir Epicure fit into the scheme of things. Nevertheless, because it is such a fast-moving play you may still feel unsure about your grasp of the central issues. What might help clarify things is a look at the personality of the central character, Subtle, and Act III, scene ii, is a good place to analyse him in action.

Here Subtle starts off by giving his line of patter to two Puritans, Ananias and Tribulation Wholesome. As he goes through his routine he is constantly interrupted by the annoying Ananias. Provoked by this nuisance, Subtle rounds on the Puritans and attacks them, denouncing their hypocritical piety and their holy humbug. Far from stirring up indignation, the attack simply makes Tribulation Wholesome more ingratiating in his attempts to placate Subtle and to persuade him to turn all their metal pots and pans into gold and silver.

It is not difficult to spot that the two Puritans here are yet another embodiment of the play's central theme of greed. They provide us with a very clear example of the difference between a public mask of decency and devotion and the greedy self-interest that can lie behind outward appearance. As ever, the point to remember is that all the characters reflect and reveal the concerns and complications of the play. Here, for example, although we know that Subtle is a con-man, we can see that the Puritans are even worse because of their hypocrisy. Your view of these two characters may be slightly different, but I feel that their own moral blindness makes them more unpleasant. They not only pretend to others that they are respectable, God-fearing men, but practise this deception on themselves (though Tribulation is all too ready to agree with Subtle's attack on Ananias). Subtle, by contrast, revels in deception and trickery, and knows perfectly well the game he is playing. There is a kind of straightforwardness about his dishonesty which is particularly apparent to the audience when he upbraids the Puritans, though it is also true that the real reason Subtle can abuse these people is because he holds power over them. Because their desire for money dominates all their other feelings, Subtle is at liberty to say what he likes. It is his chance to do some plain speaking, and what he says about the Puritans rings true; as the two wriggle about and try to justify their greed, the audience sees what hypocrites they are.

Subtle, then, even though he is a con-man, here speaks out on behalf of a proper moral order against hypocritical religious fanaticism. What makes things complicated is that the revelation of the truth does not change anything. Subtle and the Puritans are playing the same game of greed and deception, and truth as well as falsehood are part of that game. The reason for these complications lies in the sort of vision of the world Jonson is presenting. He is not out to give us a simple picture of a world in which people are either innocent or guilty, but instead is attempting to provide an idea of how, in the complex real world, moral values get as mixed up as everything else.

What you should be able to see by now is why it will not do to describe *The Alchemist* just as a moral play, for that would suggest that Jonson provides a clear moral standard that people can be recalled to. Rather than pointing us towards absolute and incontrovertible values. *The Alchemist* seems designed more to unsettle or shake up moral certainties and convictions. It does this by making us feel that villains might be more attractive characters than victims and by letting us admire the energy and wit with which the deceptions are executed. Jonson acknowledges that the motivating power behind human nature is an unalterable and very basic greed or desire, yet he does not constantly moan about this or crusade to put things right. On the contrary, given that the play is a comedy, we are likely to feel that wickedness is funny rather than shocking and that Jonson actually enjoys using wickedness as a subject for his comedies.

5 *Choose a scene from Act IV to analyse and begin to look more closely at the language of the play*

In our analysis of Subtle in Act III we have seen how Jonson presents us with a complicated, comic world rather than a simple, moral picture. What we now need to look at are the ways in which the language of the play also creates this impression. In Act IV, scene i, we see Sir Epicure trying to woo Dol Common, whom he believes to be the sister of a nobleman. He is trying to persuade her that she is wasting her time cloistered up in Subtle's house learning about alchemy; her beauty and position fit her for a much more luxurious life, and this is exactly what he offers her:

> We'll therefore go with all, my girl, and live
> In a free state, where we will eat our mullets,
> Soused in high-country wines, sup pheasants' eggs,
> And have our cockles boiled in silver shells;
> Our shrimps to swim again, as when they lived,
> In a rare butter made of dolphins' milk,

Whose cream does look like opals; and with these
Delicate meats set ourselves high for pleasure,
And take us down again, and then renew
Our youth and strength with drinking the elixir,
And so enjoy a perpetuity
Of life and lust! And thou shalt ha' thy wardrobe
Richer than Nature's, still to change thyself,
And vary oft'ner for thy pride than she,
Or Art, her wise and almost-equal servant.
(IV.i.155–69)

Mammon wants to take Dol away from her mundane existence to particiapte in a perpetual orgy of eating and love-making. He promises her a life of sexual extravagance, an indulgent existence in which they will be able constantly to renew their sexual appetite with fine food. By any standards it is a marvellous speech, and Sir Epicure's preoccupation with bodily pleasure clearly comes through, but what you should also be able to see is the way the language of the speech reflects the play's comic vision of humankind's obsessive greed. This is apparent in individual details; for example, the 'rare butter made of dolphin's milk' has cream 'like opals', which suggest both rarity and a coveted value. Indeed, throughout the speech runs the notion of a richer, more sensuous world than that which nature can provide. Sir Epicure's vision is of a state free from all mundane rules and limits, a world where the lovers remain every young and strong to enjoy their 'perpetuity / Of life and lust'.

Sir Epicure's vision, then, is a sort of heavenly daydream, and certainly if you wished you could stress Jonson's irony here, how he presents us with characters whose only desire is to transform the world to suit their own fantasies, casting aside all moral and social responsibilities as they do so. This interpretation is reinforced by Jonson's use of dramatic irony, for the audience is aware that the 'lady' Sir Epicure addresses is only Dol Common, a prostitute, and that in reality he has been completely deceived. So there is a moral element here, and we can disapprove of Sir Epicure, but to say that this is the only function of the speech would be to underestimate its comic force. In many ways the sheer excesses of the speech give it an imaginative life of its own, and this makes it hugely entertaining. Indeed, it is precisely because the imagery is excessive yet attractive that the speech, like *The Alchemist* as a whole, seems to celebrate rather than castigate the desire of people to change their base, ordinary lives and selves into something richer and more attractive. There might also be a case for saying that such speeches make it difficult for an audience to preserve a prim, detached moral outlook, for they are actually drawn into an enjoyment of excess by the sheer scope and imagination of Sir Epicure's fantasies.

6 *Choose a scene from Act V which shows how the play's issues are resolved and try to draw together the threads of your analysis*

All the way through, *The Alchemist* has been a play of extravagant excesses which have taken place at a furious pace. It has also been a play which has entertained us with the inventiveness and intelligence of its villains, so we might not expect it to end in quite such a clear-cut and moral way as *Volpone*. This turns out to be the case. Lovewit, the owner of the house, returns unexpectedly. Face tries to bluff his way through but all is eventually revealed, and the only way he can save himself is by offering Lovewit a young and wealthy wife. Subtle and Dol try to run off with Face's share of the profits, but he thwarts them by admitting that he has told Lovewit, and they leave empty-handed. The clients who have unwisely given things to the alchemist come back to try and lay claims to their goods, but Lovewit, now married to Dame Pliant, sees them off.

There is no question here of justice being done. While the three villains of the play are not rewarded for their efforts, they are not exactly punished either; Dol and Subtle escape, and Face returns to his original position as Lovewit's butler. Again, many of the victims who are taken in by the trio are made to pay the price of their folly by losing their valuables, and yet some, such as Kastril and Dame Pliant, actually come out of the situation rather well. Lovewit, the most straightforward figure in the play, puts an end to the wheeling and dealing, but compromises himself by accepting Face's offer and playing a part in the deception by disguising himself as a Spaniard.

Events, then, are not easy to categorise at the end of the play. All the characters seem flawed in some way and this adds to our sense of things not fitting neatly into a rigid pattern. In a more straightforward play we might expect Act v, scene iii, where Face confesses to Lovewit, to be the end of all the confusion. The truth has emerged and an ordered resolution might be possible. Yet such an ending would seem artificial in such a crazy world, and so Face tempts Lovewit into one more deal, one more chance to complicate life by disguising the true state of affairs. So, although this ending is in keeping with the overall tone of the play, it does differ from the neat tidying-up of conventional comedies. Jonson is straining against the convention of the comic ending because it seems at odds with his vision of a muddled, complicated life in which ordered values are out of place.

One of the things that I hope has emerged in this brief discussion of *The Alchemist* is the way in which it is a similar play to *Volpone*, yet at the same time it has a distinctive character of its own. This is what your discussion of a play should ultimately aim at: you are looking for ways in which this play is special, the particular features that contribute to its overall effect. I hope it is clear by now that the method I have followed helps you to do this. Starting with broad ideas about drama, you can begin to build up a detailed picture by repeatedly focusing on manageable chunks of the text. By looking closely at specific sections of the text, you will be able to move from general ideas to your own distinctive, detailed sense of the play. It is a method that helps you come to terms with the complexity of a play, and, as the next chapter should show, it also helps when it comes to expressing your ideas on paper.

5
Writing an essay

An essay is a piece of writing in which you are required to put forward an argument about a particular idea or issue in a play. It should be the place where all your ideas about the play you are studying come to fruition, but for a variety of reasons students do not always succeed in achieving this. Many students, for example, simply hope that detailed knowledge of the play will automatically mean a good essay. This is far from being the case, and the skills necessary for good essay writing can and should be learnt. The skills themselves are very simple; all you need is a clear idea of what you are trying to do and a technique which allows you to present your argument in a convincing way. An obvious way to begin this task is by looking closely at the essay question.

The question

Answer the question set

The first rule of all essay-writing is **answer the question set**. This applies to both class and examination essays (this chapter deliberately concentrates on exams, but the advice should help you with all your written work). Questions always direct you towards particulars aspects of the play you are studying, and it is your job to deal sensibly with what you are asked to discuss. Many students, however, try to ignore the question that is set. They have their own ideas of what they want to write about and plough on regardless, perhaps adding a desperate last paragraph to try and prove what they have written has some relevance to the question. Irrelevance is the most common fault in examination essays: candidates are faced with a question they didn't expect and simply write about the question they would like to have had. For example, a candidate might be expecting a question on the character of Doctor Faustus, but instead finds a question asking about the themes of repentance and retribution in the play. He/she starts off the essay by writing, 'Dr Faustus is a character who experiences a lot of repentance and retribution throughout the play . . .' and then continues with the essay he or she intended to write about Faustus's character, leaving the real question – the themes of repentance and retribution – unconsidered. This may be an extreme example, but it is surprising how common this sort of approach is. The real pity is that quite a lot of the candidate's material on the character of Faustus would have been relevant to the themes of repentance and retribution if only he/she had stopped to think about the best way of applying his/her knowledge to the question set.

Remember, in an exam it is unlikely that you will be asked a question that conforms exactly to what you would like to write about. The aim of the examiner is to see if you know the play sufficiently well to be able to focus on and answer a question that you have not considered previously. Your aim should be to show the examiner that you are thinking about the question that has been set and that you are using the material you know to deal with what is being asked.

Understanding the question

Exam questions are not set to confuse you or to throw you into a state of panic. Examiners do not want to humiliate you by forcing you to show your ignorance: they frame their questions with the genuine aim of allowing you to display knowledge about the play. The questions themselves are never too obscure, and they always give you a chance to discuss a topic you will be familiar with if you have studied the play in enough detail. Sometimes the phrasing of a question may cause you problems – it may contain a long quotation, or it may seem to contain ideas that you haven't come across in relation to the play. Almost invariably, though, there is a simple idea lying just beneath the surface of an awkwardly phrased question.

The most common kinds of essay questions are about the characters in a play, or about the themes of a play, or about the dramatic technique used by the author. In every case you will be asked to discuss a specific topic or question or statement. The essential thing to realise is that in each case you are being asked to present an argument. This is a vital aspect of essay-writing that students tend to ignore. Faced with a question about a character in a play, they will slavishly detail the story of that character's involvement in the plot. This, however, is description rather than argument, and, no matter how well you remember the story, you will get little credit for this sort of answer. **An essay answer must always argue a case.** If you like, the function of an essay-writer is rather like that of a lawyer in court. A lawyer must say what happened, produce evidence, and then comment on the significance of that evidence. In a similar way, the essay-writer tells you what a particular issue is about, refers to a specific scene where we can see the process in action, and then provides a comment on the significance of the scene in order to prove the point. If you don't comment on the significance of the scene you are not presenting an argument, and, like the lawyer who produces a piece of evidence but neglects to say whether it proves innocence or guilt, you are not doing your job properly.

All this will become clearer if we look at the type of questions set. The most straightforward types of question, but also the easiest to miscalculate, are *questions about characters*. Here, you may be asked to discuss one of the main characters, showing how he/she is presented and discussing the significance of his/her actions. Very often, character questions are linked to a discussion of the dramatic role of the characters, saying what purpose they serve in the play or contrasting their behaviour with other characters. The questions are often phrased in one of the following ways:

> How appropriate is the characterisation of Volpone to Jonson's moral purpose in *Volpone*?
>
> 'The Duchess is a colourless character who is interesting only in that she provides a contrast to the others.' Discuss this comment on *The Duchess of Malfi*.
>
> 'Doctor Faustus dominates the action: there is no other developed character in the play.' How far do you agree with this stagement about *Doctor Faustus*?

In each case, you are asked to move beyond saying what happens to the characters in the play and show the way they help us to understand what the play is about. This is a crucial part of any discussion of character: not only do you have to focus on the individual mentioned in the question, but you must also respond to a sense of the broader issues at work in the play.

Questions about themes, on the other hand, always ask you to construct an argument about the way a particular topic or issue is presented in the play. As with questions about character, you must be prepared to move beyond detailing what happens where, so that your answer is informed by an awareness of what is going on in the play as a whole. If, for example, you were confronted by a question which asked you to discuss the theme of 'justice' in *The White Devil*, you could get bogged down in a detailed account of who got revenge on whom, and whether you think all of the characters finally received their just desserts. Your essay could turn into a listing of isolated events unless you see how the idea of justice is linked to the broader issue of order and disorder in the play; how, in a perfect world, justice and order would enable people to live harmoniously with one another, but how, in this play, injustice and disorder are created by characters wanting their own way. Can you see how recognising this broad framework to the question actually gives you a lot more to write about? Any theme which occurs in a play can always be traced back to tensions which are central to the working of the play. All plays deal with problems and conflicts, so when you begin to consider a theme you need to be aware of how it dramatises these larger tensions. From this point of view it is often helpful to think about themes in relation to the central concepts of order and disorder that we have seen at the heart of Renaissance drama.

Any theme is likely to relate to how things should be in a perfect, ideal world, or to how things are in the imperfect and unsatisfactory existence that mankind creates. However, this does not mean that you can simply write about 'order' and 'disorder' in a play and automatically assume relevance to the theme you were meant to be considering. Even though you are using your larger sense of the play to give you ideas and to help you think about the question, you must concentrate on the specific topic which the question asks you to discuss. This means finding scenes where your particular theme is in evidence, looking at the details, and commenting on their significance in relation to the tensions you have found. In this way you will be arguing your case very cleverly, using your own original examples to show how important the chosen theme is to the play as a whole.

Questions about technique can vary a great deal in the scope of what they ask you to do. They can focus on a partiuclar act or scene, asking you what effect it has on the way you view the rest of the play, or they can ask you to discuss a much larger idea, such as whether a play is a tragedy or not. An example of the first type of question might be 'Do you consider the conclusion of *Volpone* to be in keeping with the comic tone of the play?', whereas the more general type of question might be phrased, 'Do you think that the world of *Volpone* is realistic or unrealistic?' Such questions are quite straightforward and easy to understand.

You might be asked, however, to consider the way a play combines various elements, such as humour and seriousness, or whether a play successfully mixed different dramatic aspects, such as realistic characters with an improbable plot. You can see from the following examples that these questions are more complex: 'Does the spirit of fun prevent *The Alchemist* from being taken seriously?' and 'Do you consider that the horror of *The White Devil* detracts from its tragic impact?' Such questions seem more difficult because they are more abstract. They do not appear as straightforward as talking about characters or themes, and so students naturally tend to be put off answering them because they think they need some sort of specialised knowledge to tackle more abstract ideas.

Exactly the same sort of approach is required for questions about technique, however, as for questions about character or themes. You are being asked to look at a certain aspect of the play, or to consider the way certain elements combine, but nevertheless the broader conflicts and tensions at the heart of the play will help you shape your response. Thus, for instance, if you were going to consider whether the spirit of fun prevents *The Alchemist* from being taken seriously, you could begin by thinking about the tension between the way characters ought to act and the way they do act. Their desires force them to deviate from ideal behaviour, and when those desires become obsessive they act in a way that brings ridicule upon themselves and highlights their folly. This is obviously funny. But, on the other hand, the desires of human beings make the world a complicated and sometimes dangerous place, and this is a serious consideration. Can you see how this helps us provide a logical answer to the question based securely on what we already know about the play? By having a clear idea of the play's broader significance we can focus on the particular tension that is under discussion and go on to find examples of where we think this tension is most evident in the play. The same principle applies to any question, whether you are dealing with character, themes or technique. You need a larger sense of the play as a whole to inform and organise your comments on the specific issue raised by the question. Essay-writing is simply a question of combining the broad view with the narrow view. You need to be able to find and discuss individual examples, incidents or details, but your discussion will lack direction unless it is related to a more general idea of what the play is about. I shall go on later to discuss how to achieve this combination, but first I want to discuss one further aspect of examination questions.

What the examiner wants to see

The examiner wants to see a clear, well set-out answer which refers frequently to the text. When examiners are reading examination essays they like to be able to follow a clear central argument which is carefully illustrated by reference to relevant scenes or speeches in the play. (It is not necessary to learn the act and scene number of every incident in the play you are studying: a general reference to 'the scene where Bosola discovers the Duchess is pregnant' is a precise-enough reference for Act II, scene ii, of *The Duchess of Malfi.*) Examiners are not looking for a single, right answer, and are perfectly prepared to give you a chance to prove your case, whatever approach you take. Candidates often worry about whether they are writing the sort of things that please examiners. To do this, however, is to misunderstand what the process of essay-writing is about. Examiners are not interested in whether you take one view of the text or another. What they are interested in is how effectively you organise, present and argue the case you are offering. To use our legal analogy again: a good lawyer will always present an effective case for a client, but his or her skill depends on the presentation of the evidence, not on whether the client is innocent or guilty. In the same way, any essay question can be tackled from any point of view. You do not always have to agree with statements that are given in essay questions, particularly if you find that they are at odds with the way you have considered the play. What you do have to do is to prevent a convincing argument for what you are saying: this involves being able to see the issues in the play, being able to discuss the text in detail, and being able to develop a broader argument along the lines of your own point of view.

The answer

So far it may seem that the advice I have given could be difficult to put into practice and that you are supposed to achieve a very difficult balance between an awareness of the play as a whole, attention to specific details and developing an argument. I am not going to pretend this is always an easy balance to achieve, but it does become a lot easier once you realise that you can use your essay format to help you produce a coherent piece of work. The main secret of essay-writing is to keep the overall structure simple. This doesn't mean that what you have to say has to be naïve or uncomplicated, but it does mean that the shape of your argument will be easy to follow, and that, as I have indicated earlier, is one of the main things an examiner is looking for. Before we look at how to structure an essay, however, I would like to consider, very briefly, two things that can go wrong with an essay.

One problem that can arise is an over-eager tendency to display all you know about a play. You may well have a mass of knowledge which you have accumulated through study and revision, but it is a great mistake to try and write down everything you know. Material must be carefully selected for its relevance to the question, and you must be prepared to sacrifice a good deal in the interests of a coherent, well-structured essay. However, don't think that all your hard work has been wasted: your detailed study of the text will have given you a clear idea of what the play is about, and it is this which will help you to analyse the significance of the material you do write about. The second mistake that can occur is in choice of material. Some people think certain scenes are bound to come up or are bound to be relevant, so they confine their knowledge of the play to one or two key scenes that they know almost by heart. While there is little doubt that some scenes do have a very important dramatic impact, it is equally important to realise that you are being asked to show knowledge of the play as a whole, and not just selected highlights. As ever, the first principle must be to choose your material to fit the question, not to bend the question to fit your material.

We are now at the stage where you are ready to start answering your essay question. You have selected the question you want to answer and thought about what it means. You are aware that the answer you have to give must be more than just a piece of descriptive story-telling: in your essay you need to consider a problem referred to in the question. Without this awareness your essay will be without an issue to discuss, and you won't be able to shape your material into a coherent argument. It may be that you already know what your response to the problem is going to be. If you do, fine: you will have a sense of where your essay is going. If you are not sure of your response to the problem, don't worry: as you consider the issues and build an argument a conclusion will inevitably suggest itself. The important thing at this stage is to recognise the problem being raised in the question.

You can help to define the problem as you write your **first paragraph**. Indeed, the best thing to do with the opening paragraph of an essay is to identify the nature of the problem you are being asked to consider. The opening paragraph need not be very long, perhaps ten to twelve lines, but it does need to focus on the issue at the heart of the question. There's no point, however, in wading straight in and saying what your conclusion is going to be: after all, you are meant to be arguing a case, supplying evidence to support that argument and then reaching a conclusion. It is much more logical and convincing to provide an answer at the end of a process of consideration than to anticipate all you are going to say at the outset. The aim of your first paragraph, then, should be to say something like 'Here is a problem, but as yet I don't know the answer. The question seems to be asking me to consider these issues, and as I turn to examining the text, an answer should begin to become clear.'

In the **second paragraph** you can begin to build your answer. The only way to do this is to go to the text for the evidence you require, so begin by finding a particular scene or speech in the play to discuss. It must, of course, be a scene or speech which is relevant to the question, but this shouldn't be too difficult to find if you know the play well enough. For example, if you are answering a question on a character, a good place to begin would be that character's first appearance on stage, or that character's first long speech. Similarly, if you are answering a question on a theme, use a scene or speech where the language associated with that theme seems much in evidence. Having chosen your extract, how do you work out what to say? Well the secret here is to limit yourself to one or two obvious or outstanding details. If you try to give a line-by-line account of a whole scene or speech you will get so bogged down that your essay will lose its drive and direction. Concentrate on one or two details and really work on these instead of trying to cover everything. If you have followed the method outlined in the previous chapters for constructing your own reading of the play you should have a good idea of the technique to adopt. This technique also has the advantage of enabling you to draw larger ideas from the evidence of the text. Follow the same pattern of briefly summarising the incident or speech you have chosen, discuss its dramatic significance and analyse its language; that way you will build your case in a very solid fashion. However, don't leave the examiner to draw his or her own conclusions about the connection between your evidence and the essay title. Your paragraph should end with a very definite conclusion which establishes what you have discovered about the problem you are looking at, and which shows how the evidence you have produced advances your argument.

Can you see how a format like this is not only simple, but also guarantees that you do all the things you should be doing in an essay? It starts in paragraph 1 by identifying a problem, so it immediately develops some ideas about the larger significance of the play; it then focuses (in paragraph 2) on the details of the play and argues a case based on concrete evidence. Finally, by drawing together the threads of your argument at the end of every paragraph it ensures that you are both answering the question and developing your argument as you go along.

As you reach the end of the second paragraph you will have established the first step in your argument and answer. It is essential that you make proper use of paragraphs in essay-writing. Each paragraph is an additional step in your argument. At the end of each paragraph the evidence you have produced and the analysis you have carried out should have advanced your argument one stage further. If you do not write in paragraphs, or if your paragraphs are too long, the logic of your argument is liable to get muddled. This can happen even if you are analysing textual evidence, for the essay can soon turn into a series of quotes and comments. If, however, your essay is divided into similar-length paragraphs (about half to three-quarters of a side is a reasonable guide), then it is easier to build a solid argument.

By the time you start the **third paragraph** your essay has begun to use the text in order to build an answer. Your second paragraph establishes the presence of the problem you are discussing, and now you want to develop your ideas further. The way to do this is to turn to another scene or speech in the play, discuss and analyse it, and again end the paragraph with a clear conclusion. Do make sure, however, that the evidence you choose advances your argument. It is little use analysing a speech in paragraph 3 which just leads you to say the same things as you said in paragraph 2. If you are aware of the shape of the play you should be able to avoid this. For example, we have seen how matters tend to get increasingly complicated during the middle acts of Renaissance plays. If you are answering a question on characters, therefore, and your second paragraph deals with their first appearance, your third paragraph ought to be analysing their behaviour in a later, more complex or uncertain situation. By doing this you will be showing an awareness of both the shape of the play and the development of the characters.

The main thing to remember about this technique of building an essay is that you must work directly from the play, proving your argument with the help of specific examples from the text. **Subsequent paragraphs** can follow the same format, each one looking at further evidence from the text and advancing your argument by analysing the passage chosen. You may consider that the format sounds too mechanical, but it is much better to have a systematically structured answer than a rambling and illogical series of observations. Again, you may feel that this approach precludes the chance of writing an inspired, original essay. This is certainly not true, and in fact a simple framework such as this can support a very complex and sophisticated answer. After all, the originality will lie in the way you perceive the text and illustrate your argument; the advice I have given you simply enables you to put across your ideas in an effective way.

What I am suggesting, then, is that you try using this format of an opening paragraph that defines the problem, followed by another six to eight paragraphs, each of which turns to the text, examines an incident or speech in the light of the problem, and arrives at a running conclusion. You have to be aware of how each paragraph must advance your argument, and your running conclusions will help you here, for as you round off each paragraph you will be able to see how you are answering the question and whether the specific incidents you discuss have led you to examine the larger issues of the play. Six or eight paragraphs is only a guideline, of course. You may find you have more material than you want to discuss and so need to add more detail in the shape of extra paragraphs. However, you are unlikely to give an adequate answer with less than six paragraphs. If your essay is too short, then the evidence you give is likely to be skimpy; no matter now reasonable your argument, your case is likely to be asserted rather than proved, and you will lose marks as a result. Six central paragraphs should be enough to allow you to go into the problem thoroughly and to establish a closer answer. At the end you will need a **concluding paragraph** which sums up the argument and gives your final thoughts, but really this is only a concise version of the conclusions which have been built into the course of your argument.

Everything I have said so far is intended to help you with your essay-writing. There are other methods which can be used with equal facility and you may find that you are more at home with these. I am not claiming the exclusive secret to perfect essay-writing. On the other hand, you will have to take into account the necessity for a clear, logical answer soundly based on the text, and whether you follow this method or adapt it to your own needs you should always bear this aim in mind. One advantage of the method I have discussed, however, is that it does help with the process of **essay-planning**. This is particularly important when it comes to examination writing. Most students are advised to plan their essays, but all too often they are so impatient to get on with the actual writing that their plans are little more than a couple of hastily scribbled ideas together with a quotation or two.

Essay-planning is important because it gives you a direction to follow and allows you to concentrate on your writing. You may start off with a clear idea in your mind of what you want to include in your first paragraph, but then have to stop to decide where you are going next. This problem can be avoided by planning your essay in full before you start. Some people go to the other extreme, of course, and end up writing so much at the planning stage that they have little time left to write the actual essay. Certainly your planning-time should not extend to more than a quarter of the time allotted for answering the question. This is where the method of thinking about your material in paragraphs can pay dividends. If you are aiming at, say, an essay which consists of an opening paragraph, six other paragraphs to develop the argument and a concluding paragraph, then you can begin by writing down the numbers 1–8. Against number 1 you can quickly write the central problem that the essay title seems to be raising. Alongside numbers 2–7 you can jot down the names of the particular scenes or speeches you want to consider, together with a brief comment about what you think each example will illustrate. Number 8 will depend on how you see the shape of the essay. As I have mentioned before, you may have a very clear idea of your final conclusion, in which case you can just pencil in your ideas. On the other hand, you may wish to leave your conclusion free until you have examined the evidence in detail.

The advantage of a planning-system such as this is that it allows you to be flexible in your approach. As you write down the episodes you may see, for example, a connection between the scene you chose for paragraph 2, and the speech you chose for paragraph 5. From the point of view of advancing the logic of your argument you may want to adjust the sequence: paragraph 5 should become paragraph 3 for a more coherent structure of ideas. This kind of shuffling is easy to achieve at the planning-stage, but it is impossible to carry out once the writing has begun.

One further aspect of essay-writing of which you need to be aware is the use of quotations. Quotations are important, but you must use them properly. Writing out large chunks of the text because you have learnt them by heart will not get you very far. From a practical point of view, I would suggest that it is much better to learn a number of small quotations (of up to, say, six lines in length) than to learn one or two large speeches. The reason for this is very simple. If you know a variety of small quotations you are much more likely to be able to adapt your material to suit the question you are answering. If, on the other hand, you have taken the trouble to learn an entire set speech, you are likely to twist your answer in order to write about it, even though it may not be immediately relevant.

Even more important is the way in which you use the quotations you learn. If you quote you must always discuss the quotation; that is, you must discuss what the quotation says, suggests and reveals. You have got to move from the quotation to the ideas that you extract from it, for this is the real point of supplying textual evidence. One of the most common faults is assuming that a quotation is self-explanatory. Students often introduce their quotation with the words 'This is illustrated by the following:' and then simply leave the lines of the play to speak for themselves. The quotation may well be relevant, but unless you supply a discussion of what is said, and its significance, you will not be able to show the way the specific words add to your argument. I hope to be able to illustrate the way this process works later, when I go on to discuss types of questions and the method of approaching them. First, however, I shall summarise the main points about essay-writing.

(i) The main rule of essay-writing is to keep the overall structure of your essay simple.
(ii) The sequence in which you present your material should be planned in advance.
(iii) Remember that you are always examining a problem and your answer must therefore develop an argument.
(iv) The first paragraph should define the problem you are going to examine.
(v) Subsequent paragraphs need to look closely at the evidence of the text, establishing an answer from specific incidents and details in the play.
(vi) An essay needs to develop an argument, and each paragraph should be thought of as a step in an argument, advancing the case beyond the point reached at the end of the previous paragraph.
(vii) Each step in the argument must develop from the actual evidence of the text.

To conclude this chapter I am going to work through three essay titles, so you can see the method in action. I shall deal in turn with the three types of essay: an essay about character, an essay about theme, and an essay about dramatic technique. I shall use examples from three of the plays considered in this book. Do not be put off, however, if I am considering a play you have not studied or read: my main concern is to illustrate the essay method described above, and you should be able to see how the technique will work with your own essays.

1 *An essay on character: '"He that loves pleasure must for pleasure fall." Is this a fitting epitaph for Doctor Faustus?'*

The first thing I need to do when faced by an essay title is to identify the problem it raises. The question seems to me to point to the central contrast in the play between the benefits that Faustus believes he is going to get out of his pact with the devil and the reality of eternal damnation that he has to face. This is the particular problem that the question is asking me to consider, but behind it lies the wider issue of the gap between how people ought to behave and the way they pursue their own desires. It is this wider issue which should help me see the full implications of the question. However, I am not going to anticipate anything further about my answer until I have looked at the evidence.

In the second paragraph I want to begin to examine the first part of the problem: what did Faustus expect to get out of his pact with the devil? To do this I need to turn to a scene or speech at the beginning of the play and analyse it. The obvious place to start is with Faustus's opening speech. In this speech he rejects conventional learning as something which he has mastered but still found lacking. What I now want to do is to find a few lines that seem to sum up his attitude towards black magic and examine them in terms of the essay question. When talking about the study of necromancy, or the black arts, Faustus says,

O, what a world of profit and delight,
Of power, of honour of, omnipotence,
Is promised to the studious artizan!
. . .
A sound magician is a demi-god.
Here, tire my brains to get a deity.
(I.i.52–4, 61–2; *or scene i*)

What I need to do is to relate these lines to the essay question. The question itself considers the idea of 'he that loves pleasure'. Faustus does mention 'delight', but he mentions a lot of other things as well, such as 'profit', 'power', 'omnipotence' and becoming a 'demi-god'. So my conclusion at the end of the second paragraph may want to take issue with the question. Faustus's expectations of what he will gain does include an idea of pleasure, but there is much else besides; his aim is at something much more grandiose and impressive than simply taking his pleasure.

My third paragraph can develop this argument further. I have identified that the problem contained in the question involves the contrast between the benefits that Faustus believes he is going to get with the reality of his eventual damnation. This split seems t me to be dramatised by the appearance of the Good and Evi Angels, so the next episode to consider is Faustus's reaction to thei materialisation on stage. The Good Angel advises Faustus to pu aside his books of black magic and read the scriptures, while th Evil Angel encourages him to carry on by promising Faustus tha he will 'Be . . . on earth as Jove is in the sky, / Lord an commander of these elements' (I.i.75–6). In my view the Evil Ange is appealing to that desire for power or omnipotence that Faustu was talking about in the first extract I analysed. This is wha Faustus says:

> How am I glutted with conceit of this!
> Shall I make spirits fetch me what I please
> . . .?
> I'll have them fly to India for gold,
> Ransack the ocean for orient pearl,
> And search all corners of the new-found world
> For pleasant fruits and princely delicates.
> (I.i.77–8, 82–5; or *scene i*)

What I find interesting here is the way that Faustus's respons concentrates on his own personal enjoyment rather than on an more abstract benefits. I would want to point out how the languag of the passage gives me this idea: the way he uses the wor 'glutted', or talks about making spirits 'fetch me what I please'. H also seems to want personal wealth and adornment, evidenced b his desire for 'gold' and 'orient pearl'; and finally he seeks t indulge his sensual appetites by obtaining 'pleasant fruits' an 'princely delicates'. The evidence I have found here is differen from that which I used in the second paragraph, and is more i accord with the idea of 'pleasure' that the essay question pu forward. My conclusion here, therefore, might be that, althoug Faustus starts with high ideals, the idea of indulging his ow personal pleasures soon takes over.

My next three or four paragraphs will work on the sam principle. I will want to focus on a particular episode or extrac from the text, and by considering the ideas and language in it, tr to supply evidence to support and extend my argument. Throughou the essay, however, I want to keep in mind the dramatic contras between Faustus's indulging of his desires and the reality of his los soul. I could, for example, look at the scene involving the appearance of the Seven Deadly Sins (Act II, scene ii; *or scene vi*), and concentrate on the way Faustus is just about to repent and realise the enormity of what he has done when he is diverted by the appearance of Lucifer and his side-show. Alternatively, I could look at the episode later on in the play (Act V, scene i; *or scene xviii*), where the Old Man reminds Faustus that repentance and grace are still within his power, but Faustus immediately turns to Mephostophilis and asks him to gratify his physical desire for the beautiful Helen of Troy. Can you see how each of my examples not only gives me material to discuss, but also allows me to examine the central problem raised by the essay question? A paragraph drawing material from the end of the play could round off my argument: in Act V, scene ii (*or scene xix*), for example, the Good Angel talks about the real pleasures Faustus could have had if he had lived a good life, while the Evil Angel shows him the horrific reality of the hell he is about to enter and the eternity of pain he is about to suffer. This seems to me to dramatise the reversal of values that Faustus has chosen. His idea of pleasure is false and transitory, but he does not realise this and it costs him dear.

My concluding paragraph would be a summary of my whole argument, indicating that although Faustus starts with high ideals he is soon deceived and misled by pleasurable indulgence, and because these pleasures prevent him from fully recognising the folly of his decision it could, indeed, be said that 'He that loves pleasure must for pleasure fall'. At the same time I might well want to add a comment about the way the scenes I have considered dramatise this particular issue.

The structure of my essay has allowed me to examine the question in the light of specific incidents from the play. It could be argued that I have left a good deal out, and I am prepared to accept this, for in any essay the writer must be selective in the material he/she discusses. You might have chosen different incidents to discuss, and indeed reached a completely different conclusion from mine. That would be fine. As I said previously, there is no single correct answer: what matters is the use you make of your material to construct a clear, logical essay which offers the reader your own response to the play and to the question.

2 *An essay on theme: 'Write an essay on the theme of just reward and punishment in "The Duchess of Malfi".'*

I must begin by identifying the problem contained in the question. The idea of just reward and punishment seems to me to belong to an ideal world, a world where everyone would get his/her just desserts according to the way he/she has acted. We know, however, that Renaissance drama seeks to contrast the real with the ideal, emphasising the fact that reality is complex and unbalanced. So this is the problem I want to consider in my essay: how the ideal of just reward and punishment is at odds with what actually happens during the course of the play. I may already have an idea that some characters are treated more unfairly than others, but I shall resist drawing any conclusion until I have examined my evidence.

In my second paragraph, I want to begin looking at extracts from the play and to see whether I can relate what I have found about my chosen theme to the larger problem suggested by the question. The logical thing to do seems to be to find the first mention of reward or punishment in the play and to proceed from there. I do not have to look far. The very first scene has Bosola complaining to the Cardinal about the way he has been treated: 'I have done better service than to be slighted thus. Miserable age, where only the reward of doing well, is the doing of it!' (I.i.31–3).

Almost immediately the play has begun, then, we see somebody complaining that he is not getting the just reward for the services he has performed. This seems to be a source of discontent, for Bosola talks of being 'slighted' and of the 'miserable age' in which he is forced to live. Relating this idea back to the central problem I identified in the question, I could say that, where a gap appears between what should happen in an ideal world and what does happen in reality, unhappiness is likely to result. I could confirm this by quickly looking at the speech that ends the scene. Antonio is talking to Delio about Bosola, and he says,

'Tis great pity
He should be thus neglected, I have heard
He's very valiant. This foul melancholy
will poison all his goodness, . . .
(I.i.73–6)

In this speech Antonio picks up the idea of Bosola not being rewarded and relates it to the idea of corruption. He seems to be arguing that there is a link between injustice and evil: in an ideal world, service would be rewarded and goodness would flourish as a result, but, in a world where good qualities go unrewarded, corruption can set in. The images that Antonio uses in his speech brings this idea of corruption to life – he talks of 'goodness' being 'poisoned' by Bosola's state of 'foul melancholy', as if Bosola presents a threat to the well-being of society because of his discontent. The conclusion I might reach at the end of the second paragraph, therefore, is that the theme of just reward seems to be bound up with the way the world at large is ordered. More specifically, the absence of just reward seems to lead to evil and corruption.

In my third paragraph I wish to find more evidence and to develop my argument further. Having looked at the idea of just reward in paragraph 2, I feel I ought to move on to consider punishment here. It is a common fault of essays to concentrate on just one aspect of a two-part question, so you must give detailed consideration to both themes in such questions. The passage I have found comes a little later in the play. Against the specific instruction of the Cardinal and Ferdinand, the Duchess has married Antonio, her lover, and is now pregnant. Bosola, however, acting as a spy for the brothers, has discovered the pregnancy, and sends back word of her disobedience. The brothers, and Ferdinand in particular, are incensed by what has happened, and immediately begin to think of how the Duchess should be punished for her actions. Here is the Cardinal questioning Ferdinand about the violence of his reaction:

CARDINAL. Why do you make yourself
So wild a tempest?
FERDINAND. Would I could be one,
That I might toss her palace 'bout her ears,
Root up her goodly forests, blast her meads,
And lay her general territory as waste,
As she hath done her honour's.
(II.v.16–21)

What we see here is Ferdinand searching for a fitting way to punish the Duchess's dishonourable actions. But if we look more closely at the language he uses we can relate these lines to the larger issues of the play. Ferdinand wishes that he might be a tempest, so that he might reduce the Duchess's whole world to a wasteland. Notice the way he talks about destroying all the order and natural abundance in the Duchess's life: he wants to 'toss her palace 'bout her ears', 'Root up her goodly forests' and 'blast her meads [meadows]'. So the idea of punishment here seems to be linked to an idea of total chaos. My conclusion to this, my third paragraph, therefore, would point out that the evidence I have examined about both 'just reward' and 'punishment' suggests the imminent collapse of the play's world into a dark chaos which has little to do with true justice or proper reward.

My next three or four paragraphs will look at other scenes in the same way and look to develop my argument further. I could, for example, look at the punishment that the Duchess actually suffers. I could say that the 'ordeal by madmen' that she undergoes is a terrible and unjust reward for her actions, and that the inversion of the values of sanity and madness represents the chaotic state brought about by the disruptive obsessions of her brothers. On the other hand I could write a paragraph about the death of the Cardinal, saying that it is particularly ironic that he should forbid anyone to enter his room no matter what they heard, so that, when Bosola attacks him and he cries out, no one comes to his aid. I could conclude this paragraph by saying that, with the death of the Cardinal, there is a hint of a return to an ordered state, where the evil characters are justly punished for their sins. I could also devote another paragraph to examining the actions of Bosola, weighing up the evidence as to whether his death is a fitting punishment because of the terrible acts he has performed previously, or whether it is an ironic reward for his repentance and his attempts to compensate for the bad things he has done.

My final paragraph would want to draw together the threads of my argument, and I would want to say that through his twin themes of just reward and punishment Webster examines the problem of a world which seems torn between a belief in a natural God-given moral order and the immoral, irrational chaos which seems to be created by humankind. The point I would want to make about the original problem identified in the question is that there are no easy answers, and Webster uses the themes of just reward and punishment to examine problems rather than to supply answers.

3 *An essay on technique: 'Do you consider the conclusion of "Volpone" to be in keeping with the comic tone of the play?'*

As with questions on character and theme, I need to begin by identifying the nature of the problem I am being asked to consider. The question seems to be suggesting that most of the play is comic while the ending is serious, and that this is dramatically incongruous. What I am being asked to do, then, is to weigh up the dramatic effects of the comic and the serious in the play, and to examine the relationship between them. I can do this if I think about the larger issues involved in the play. If I turn once more to the contrast in Renaissance plays between an ideal, ordered existence and messy reality, I can see the potential for both comedy and seriousness. When ordered values break down it can be amusing or threatening, according to the tone of the play, and it is the dramatic relationship between these two aspects that I must keep in mind.

My second paragraph could consider the last scenes of the play and begin by identifying their tone and effect. However, I feel I want to establish what the rest of the play is about first, and perhaps to examine exactly what constitutes the 'comic tone' to which the question refers. It seems logical to begin with the opening scene, and to examine what sort of 'tone' that sets for the rest of the play. In his opening speech Volpone wakes up and immediately turns to examining his beloved pile of gold. He begins the play with these words:

Good morning to the day; and next, my gold!
Open the shrine, that I may see my saint.
[MOSCA *draws a curtain, revealing piles of gold*]
Hail the world's soul, and mine!
(I.i.1–3)

As an opening to the play the speech seems fairly straightforward, and allows the audience an unambiguous view of a character who suffers from an obsession: a love of gold. A man waking up in bed and immediately turning to look at his wealth may seem an amusing eccentricity, but if I look more closely at the langauge Volpone is using I may see something else. He uses words such as 'shrine', 'saint' and 'soul', and turns the store where his gold is kept into a place of worship. This suggests something unpleasant and blasphemous: he has taken his obsession with gold to the point where it has replaced God as the object of worship. The conclusion to my second paragraph, therefore, could point to some reservations I have about regarding the opening of the play as purely comic, because of some of the language used by Volpone and its more serious implications.

In my third paragraph I want to find more evidence to extend and advance my argument. I could do this by looking at the rest of the opening scene and examining the way Jonson builds up our comic expectations. He does this by letting Volpone outline his plan for obtaining more money: Volpone allows people to think that he is dying, and then waits for the valuable gifts to arrive as various suitors try to insinuate themselves as sole heirs to his fortune. This immediately sets up an amusing situation for the audience, who see the various suitors come in and try to ingratiate themselves with Volpone. The audience is 'in' on the plot and can therefore laugh at the stupid behaviour of characters who mistakenly think they are going to make a fortune. This dramatic device works simply and effectively, but Volpone's 'confession' to the audience in the first scene also allows us to see what a deceitful and disruptive character he is. He is responsible for making the world of the play underhand and devious, and we might see that, besides opening up the possibility of comedy, Volpone is exhibiting a warped and twisted sense of values. The conclusion to my third paragraph, then, could pick up the idea I discussed at the end of the second paragraph, that there is an ambivalence in the way the comic expectations of the audience are set up in the play. While we are let in on the secret of Volpone's deception so that we can laugh at the stupid behaviour of other characters, we are also made aware of Volpone as a devious and rather unpleasant man.

My next few paragraphs could pick on specific incidents where we see the comic action developing, and by close reference to what is happening in the text I could examine whether this tension between the comic and the serious continues to build up in the play. For example, if I examined the episode in Act II where Corvino is fooled into offering his own wife, Celia, as a sexual gift for Volpone, I could say that the trick played on Corvino is very amusing, especially as he is so jealously protective of his wife and yet ends up by almost begging to give her away. I could also point out that there is a darker side to this episode, especially when we witness Corvino's violent and sadistic behaviour towards the innocent Celia. Alternatively, I could choose to look at the trial scene in Act IV and see how everybody tells outrageous lies to try and protect their own interests, but then point out how the superior knowledge of the audience allows us to ridicule the falsity of these absurd witnesses. Yet there is also another sinister aspect to the trial scene, because Celia and Bonario, the innocent victims, are reviled, denounced and eventually imprisoned – they have no chance of defending themselves in such a travesty of justice.

In each of my paragraphs, then, I can follow a similar method to examine the relationship between the serious and the comic in the play. This is the problem that I found in the question, and the conclusions I have reached in the examination of the evidence have allowed me to reflect on larger issues. I have found a number of incidents in which there is a curious tension between the comic and the serious, and so could say that throughout the play there is an examination of both aspects of human behaviour. The desires and folly of human beings can lead to a breakdown of pretentions that is amusing to watch, yet at the same time the potential is there for the breakdown of all civilised values, and this moral anarchy is worrying. If I have established this as the overall tone of the play, I can now turn to the last act and see whether any contrasts or comparisons can be made between what happens here and what has occurred previously.

My penultimate paragraph, then, would look at what happens at the end of the play. The truth is revealed and the real villains are punished: Volpone is sent to prison; Mosca, his helper, is sent to the galleys; and the three suitors are respectively banished, placed under house arrest in a monastery and rowed around Venice wearing a cap of ass's ears. This might seem to be a sombre ending, but when we realise that we have finally seen an end to the deception and lying, and the innocent Celia and Bonario are justifiably released, then we can also view the ending with some relief: the disruptive influences in the play have received their just desserts. My conclusion to this paragraph, therefore, would view the ending as a settling of some of the tensions that have been present in the rest of the play. Here the conclusion seems to adopt a serious moral tone to chastise the wrongdoers, but at the same time there is an end to disruption and a re-establishment of harmony that provides the happy ending of a comic drama.

My final paragraph would draw together the threads of my examination. In answer to the question I would claim that I have not found the 'tone' of the play as clear-cut as it assumes. I have noticed an ambivalence about the relationship between the serious and the comic throughout the play, and, although the ending may seem to differ in tone, that ambivalence is still present. I would also want to point out that the tension between the comic and serious is a result of the way Jonson examines human behaviour; he sees in the desires of humankind a potential for disruption that can be both ludicrous and disturbing.

I hope that these three examples have given you a clear idea of how to build an essay and how to use your essay structure to explore the text in your answer. What will also help your essay-writing, however, is if you let your reader see that you have enjoyed reading or watching the play you are discussing, and that you have thought about your own response to it carefully. That, of course, is what this book as a whole has been about, and it will have served its purpose well if it does encourage you to have confidence in your own views and your own interpretation of Renaissance drama.

Further reading

THE whole aim of this book has been to encourage you to develop your own responses to Renaissance drama. To this end I have deliberately avoided mentioning any critical books on the three playwrights we have considered; the most important thing is for you to being your studies by thinking for yourself. After reading and thinking about a play you will be in a better position to make intelligent use of criticism. I want to stress that it is a great mistake to turn to critics before you have read the text carefully and thoroughly. If you do so you will find yourself swallowing someone else's views and be unable to formulate your own original ideas and opinions; indeed, you will never be in a position to convey your own impressions of a text or responses to a dramatic performance. This is something that students all too often forget; they make the mistake of thinking the critic must be right and passively adopt the critic's views without realising the bad effect this has on their essay-writing. Instead of writing from a position of confidence and authority, with a sense of the enjoyment of the text, they end up writing bland, rather abstract essays which have no life or force. Do be cautious, therefore. However, critics can be of help to you if you use them in a reasonable way. Remember, a critic is someone who also enjoys literature a lot, who thinks hard about the details of a text, and who seeks to write a persuasive, illuminating discussion on an aspect of the text that interests him or her.

This is the sense you should gain from reading, for example, the essays on Marlowe or Webster or Jonson to be found in the Macmillan *Casebook* series. These are perhaps the most useful collections of essays for students, as they do give a range of views on the plays. It is always much better to read two critics than just one because in that way you will remind yourself that there is no single correct interpretation of a text. Reading two critics will also encourage you to judge what you read and assess its real value; has the critic conveyed a clear impression of the work's interest and complexity? Has the case been proved or is it just a series of assertions? In this way you can sharpen your own idea of what critical practice should involve.

Besides the *Casebook* volumes you might find it useful to read a study of an individual play. The best series in this respect is *Studies in English Literature*, published by Edward Arnold. There are separate books on Marlowe's *Doctor Faustus*, Webster's *The Duchess of Malfi* and Webster's *The White Devil*. A very good book on Jonson is Anne Barton's *Ben Jonson Dramatist* (Cambridge University Press, 1984). In addition to studies of individual plays and authors, you may also find it illuminating to read more wide-ranging books about the drama of the time. For example, there are a number of very interesting books on the relationship between plays and their original actors and audiences. Two I would particularly recommend are Peter Thomson's *Shakespeare's Theatre* (Routledge and Kegan Paul, 1983) and Michael Hattaways' *Elizabethan Popular Theatre* (Routledge and Kegan Paul, 1982). Finally, another series you may find it helpful to consult is Macmillan's *Text and Performance* series. Even if the particular play you are studying is not specifically covered in any of the books in this series, it is worth looking at a related book in order to get some idea of how a play actually looks, feels and works on the stage.

This brief list of books could be extended many times over, but I am not seeking to provide an exhaustive book list. What I have tried to suggest here is that you can make intelligent use of criticism if you approach it in the right way. It is best to use critics sparingly, and to try to read the argument they put forward critically, trying to see how they construct and present their views. It may be appropriate, however, if I end by saying that by far the best criticism I have read on Renaissance drama, the freshest and liveliest writing, has come from students with a genuine interest in literature. If you read the text, think about its details, and then build your ideas into a well-organised essay, I am sure you will find satisfaction in the criticism you produce.